D1712697

social psychology

Prentice-Hall, Inc.
Englewood Cliffs, New Jersey 07632

Jonathan L. Freedman
Columbia University

David O. Sears
University of California, Los Angeles

J. Merrill Carlsmith
Stanford University

third edition

social psychology

Library of Congress Cataloging in Publication Data

FREEDMAN, JONATHAN L
Social psychology.

Bibliography: p.
Includes index.
1. Social psychology. I. Sears, David O., joint
author. II. Carlsmith, J. Merrill, joint
author. III. Title
HM251.F68 1978 301.1 77-17624
ISBN 0-13-817809-7

THIRD EDITION
social psychology
FREEDMAN • SEARS • CARLSMITH

COVER ILLUSTRATION: *The Group* by Ruth B. Rieber

Printed in the United States of America

10 9 8 7 6 5 4 3

PRENTICE-HALL INTERNATIONAL, INC., *London*
PRENTICE-HALL OF AUSTRALIA PTY. LIMITED, *Sydney*
PRENTICE-HALL OF CANADA, LTD., *Toronto*
PRENTICE-HALL OF INDIA PRIVATE LIMITED, *New Delhi*
PRENTICE-HALL OF JAPAN, INC., *Tokyo*
PRENTICE-HALL OF SOUTHEAST ASIA PTE. LTD., *Singapore*
WHITEHALL BOOKS LIMITED, *Wellington, New Zealand*

contents

3 social perception 68

attribution theory 100

liking and attraction 148

aggression 202

environmental and urban psychology 536

preface

In the years since the last edition of this book was written, there have been some substantial changes in the field. Most of these changes are the result of typical cycles in a science in which certain topics capture the attention of people while other topics become temporarily of less interest to those working in the field. In social psychology it seems fair to say that some of the traditional areas such as group dynamics, leadership, affiliation and attitude change, though still of great importance, have received relatively little attention recently. In contrast, other traditional areas such as liking and attraction, aggression, and social perception have shown a resurgence. At the same time, interest has continued high in altruism and compliance and has grown enormously in attribution theory and environmental psychology. None of these shifts of interest mean that a particular topic is less important than it used to be, nor that some new topic is suddenly more important than it was. But there is no denying that in any given period of years, there is more research and progress on certain issues than on others.

Naturally, this text to some extent reflects these changes by giving attention to those issues of current interest. Thus, there is now a whole chapter on attribution theory whereas in the previous edition it was given only part of a chapter. The chapter on environmental psychology is greatly expanded and not only covers the topics in more detail but also deals with more topics in this new and growing field. In addition, liking, aggression, altruism, and prosocial behavior are given more space than before because there is a great deal of new research to discuss.

However, just because issues are not receiving a lot of attention right now does not seem to us to be a good reason for reducing coverage substantially. The classic work on attitudes and group dynamics in particular is still enormously valuable. There is no question that it is part of that body of knowledge to which all students in social psychology should be exposed. Therefore, while expanding coverage of the new areas in response to trends in the field, we have not short-changed the traditional areas. In some instances we have compressed the material somewhat, but generally we have maintained full coverage.

A revision of a textbook consists in part of bringing it up to date by including research that has been conducted since the previous edition. Of course we have done this, and there are a great many references to very recent work. On the other hand, we have not dropped classic references just because new ones were available, nor added new ones just so we could boast about the number of recent citations. This text is not an encyclopedia of studies in social psychology, nor is it a list of the table of contents of recent journals. The point of the text is to present what we know in the field as clearly and comprehensively as possible, to discuss unresolved issues where appropriate, and to explain the findings using the best theories that are available. Through all of this, however, we have tried to keep in mind that this is a book for introductory students in social psychology. They do not want and do not benefit from long lists of references, from descriptions of ten studies to make a single point when one or two would suffice, nor from a presentation of every possible explanation of the same finding. We have tried to make the information in social psychology easy and accessible while at the same time making it interesting and relevant to the students' lives.

As before, we have tried to simplify without oversimplifying. The concepts and knowledge of social psychology should be within the reach of all college students and we have tried to accomplish this. On the other hand, this is by no means a simple text in the sense of being "low-level." In our opinion, it contains the material that students at any level, any kind of school should know about the field; and it presents the material in such a way that any student should be able to understand it while the best students should still be challenged by it. This is the material we teach in our classes at Columbia, UCLA, and Stanford and also the material we would teach anywhere else. Indeed, we recommend the book to graduate students for a thorough review of the field. Thus, it is comprehensive and rigorous but, we hope, easy to read and interesting.

The material for this book is drawn from a wide variety of sources. Rather than limiting ourselves to laboratory experiments conducted by social psychologists, we included many different kinds of research done by people in many different disciplines. Indeed, we tried to use any source that seemed appropriate and scientifically rigorous. In addition to laboratory experiments, we relied on findings from field experiments, correlational field experiments, surveys, observational work, and archive data. This research was conducted by social psychologists, of course, but also other psychologists, sociologists, anthropologists, ethologists, political scientists, and biologists. It is all grist for the mill, all knowledge about social behavior as long as the work itself is done. But in all cases, it is rigorous, scientific work.

In writing this edition we received help from many people. Our colleagues and friends offered suggestions, read parts of the manuscript, told us about studies we overlooked, criticized, and encouraged us. At Prentice-Hall, Neale Sweet, the psychology editor, got reviews of the work, discussed in great detail our ideas for revision, criticized, cajoled, and generally supervised the revision. Tom Pendleton, production editor, took charge of all the details of turning the manuscript into a finished book, and did this painstaking, difficult job with great skill and managed to keep his humor and maintain ours throughout. And Lorraine Mullaney was responsible for the neat, elegant design of the finished book. We thank them all—they were a great help.

Finally, let us note that in recent years the field of social psychology has experienced substantial upheaval. Some people in the field have expressed increasing concern about what they think is a lack of progress as well as a lack of relevance to real world problems. They have argued that the concept of research in social psychology is outdated or inappropriate; that basic research should be replaced by more action oriented or applied work; and that traditional methods are not applicable. These kinds of complaints are by no means new (we remember making them many years ago in graduate school) nor limited to social psychology (practically every field of scientific endeavor goes through periods of intense internal questioning). However, they have been especially widespread in the last four or five years and we think the field has, to some extent, responded to them. There is more applied research today than five years ago, considerably more field research, and probably more searching for important issues. All this is to the good.

But we disagree strongly with the notion of abandoning research in social psychology or giving up the traditional methods entirely. Yes, the progress is sometimes slow; and yes, we have not yet solved society's most pressing problems; but social psychology continues to hold great promise and progress has been substantial. Just because there are limitations and difficulties is no reason to throw out the whole enterprise. This book is written in part to support that position—to show that the field has a great deal to offer, has made strides, and will continue to do so as long as serious, talented people work on problems they consider both interesting and important.

1

introduction and methods

Social psychology is the systematic study of social behavior. It deals with how we perceive other people, how we respond to them and they to us, and how we are affected by being in social situations. The field covers all areas of interaction between people, as well as various behaviors directly related to social phenomena that occur even when others are not present. The specific topics on which social psychology has focused include most of the important kinds of interpersonal behaviors and feelings—liking, love, aggression, conformity, affiliation, communication, and influence. There has been considerable work on the effect of groups—how being in a group affects an individual's behavior. More recently, the relatively new field of environmental psychology has begun to study how we respond to the world around us, especially to noise, housing, space, and crowding. In a sense, any question you can ask about how people affect one another is included in the field of social psychology. Of course, not all of them have been answered fully, but the job of the social psychologist is to ask the important questions and then to try to find the answers.

One of the fascinating and at the same time troublesome aspects of social psychology is that everyone knows so much about it from their own experience. The topics of social psychology are the behaviors of everyday life with which we are all familiar. We spend our lives surrounded by other people. We observe them and ourselves, and naturally we learn a great deal about social behavior. Thus, we all start with a considerable amount of knowledge of the field. Other scientific disciplines are quite different. Nuclear physics deals with the composition of matter. Although we are, of course, surrounded by atoms and even composed of them, we cannot observe them directly and so we know nothing about them from firsthand experience. Therefore, the whole field of nuclear physics is new to us—we bring little or no knowledge to it. In contrast, psychology, and in particular social psychology, deals with subject matter that we do experience and observe directly. This means that much of social psychology will sound familiar. It will fit in with what you already know, will coincide with your own experience, and will accordingly be relatively easy to relate to and to learn.

On the other hand, this familiarity with the field has its problems. Often you will feel that you already know much of the material. You may wonder why you are studying the field and why people are doing all this research when the facts are obvious. You may also sometimes feel that a particular finding is wrong because it is not consistent with your own experience. The difficulty is that our personal experiences are not always good indicators of how people generally behave. In addition, our observations of what happens are usually quite casual. We are not systematic, we do not write down each incident, describing it in an objective, unbiased way. Thus, we form impressions of how people behave that are sometimes correct and sometimes incorrect. For example, consider the following statements:

> When we are anxious, we like to be with other people.
>
> Advertisements that try to make people afraid backfire and are less effective than ads that do not arouse fear.
>
> If it is in their own self-interest, people in groups will cooperate rather than compete, and raising the stakes increases the amount of cooperation.
>
> The more you pay someone to make a speech against his own beliefs the more he will change his mind to agree with the speech he makes.
>
> In choosing friends and lovers, the most important principle is that opposites attract.

You may not agree with some of these statements, but it is fair to say that they all sound plausible. At least some people would agree with each of them. Yet, research has demonstrated that all of them are either false or oversimplifications.

We need systematic research because often we cannot trust our own impressions or those of others. This may be because we perceived incorrectly, because we were biased and misinterpreted what happened, because we saw correctly but remember it wrong, or because we saw a very unusual group of people or situations. In sciences such as chemistry or physics, you would not trust your casual observations of the operation of weights levers and gravity—you would not even want to trust Newton's. If all he had done was notice an apple falling down rather than up and he had then decided that there was a force called gravity, you would not be impressed. It is the careful research supporting his idea that makes us believe in Newtonian mechanics. And, of course, even more careful work demonstrated that there were errors in this theory, and modern physics has corrected them. Casual observations, even by very careful people, cannot replace systematic research in any field.

If someone says he has decided that men are smarter than women because almost every man he has met has been smarter than almost every woman, you would certainly question his conclusion and his data. How many men and women has he met, where did he meet them, are they representative, and how did he decide how smart they were? It would not be enough for him to say that he has met thousands of people and that he is very good at telling how smart they are, you would want some proof, some hard facts. Show me the numbers! That is exactly what systematic psychology does. It collects data in such a way as to rule out any sources of bias, to make sure the people are representative, and to keep track of the "numbers" so we do not rely on memory or general impressions. In fact, research indicates that men and women do not differ in intelligence—but it has taken a great deal of careful investigation to demonstrate this. In social psychology we deal with very complex questions that are difficult to answer. The only possible way to get the answers is with systematic research. Systematic research in turn means following certain methods of investigation.

the beginning of the research—the question

All research begins with a question we would like to answer. What makes people like each other? How does fear affect affiliation? How can we reduce prejudice? In what ways do people in groups behave differently from people alone? We then design a study that can provide information which helps us answer the question as directly as possible. Of course, this is not always easy. In fact, the main difficulty of research is taking a problem that may be extremely complex and finding some way to get an answer. As we shall see, this often involves great ingenuity and patience, and even then any one study or series of studies may not give us a firm conclusion. That is why psychologists do many studies on the same problem, each designed to answer one part of the question or to narrow down the possible answers.

theoretical research

Before discussing how one goes about designing a study, it is important to know what kind of question one has. There are two basic kinds of questions: those that are directly related to a theory and those that are not. Theoretically related research starts with a deduction from a theory. We have a theory and want to know if it is correct. To do this, we focus on some prediction that the theory makes and then see if the prediction comes true. For example, Einstein's theory of relativity predicts that light will be bent by a large body. To test this, the light from a star was observed at a time when it passed very close to the sun. Sure enough, the deviation was exactly as had been predicted. In the same way, though less dramatically, social psychologists test predictions from theories that relate to social behavior. Social learning theory predicts that a child will be more aggressive after watching someone being rewarded for being violent. So children are shown films in which people behave violently and are rewarded, and then the children are given an opportunity to be aggressive themselves. As predicted, these children are more aggressive than others who do not watch violent films or who see people being punished for acting violently. Social comparison theory, which we discuss in the next chapter, predicts that people will want to be together when they are unsure of their emotional reactions. So, people are made afraid, given an opportunity to affiliate, and we see that they affiliate more when they are afraid than when they are not.

In each case, the research began with a specific derivation (prediction) from a theory. The major goal of the research is to evaluate the theory. If the prediction comes true, the theory is supported; if the prediction is incorrect, the theory is either totally wrong or at least wrong in some detail. We would then go back and discard the theory or alter it to make it consistent with the new finding.

empirical research

Research that is not directly related to a theory is usually called empirical research. Instead of testing a specific prediction, the experimenter is interested in a variable, such as fear, or a particular phenomenon, such as persuasibility. He usually has no clear hypothesis as to the effect of the variable or the specific factors that affect the phenomenon. Empirical research, therefore, is not designed to see if a specific hypothesis is correct, but rather to gather information about the variable or phenomenon in question. The major difference between empirical and hypothesis-testing research is that empirical work tends to deal with many variables at once and to have many dependent measures in order to collect more data on the general problem. For example, an experiment designed to study the factors that affect altruism would have the subjects take a comprehensive personality test; would obtain information on demographic characteristics such as age, sex, and birth order; and might also vary the number of people present and the sex of the communicator. Then, the experimenter would examine all the data to see if any relationships appeared. Of course, the variables are not selected entirely at random. The experimenter has some ideas about what might be important—for example, he could assume that age, sex, and self-esteem were more likely to be related to altruism than blood type or the number of vowels in a subject's last name. He would study some variables and not others, but he would try to collect as much information as he could.

differences between the two

A major difference between theoretical and empirical research is the likelihood of finding positive results, that is, a relationship between the variables or an effect of the experimental conditions. A study testing a deduction from a theory is relatively likely to produce such results. All theories are explanations of an organized body of data. This means that predictions from a theory are based in part on previous findings. Of course, the better established the theory, the more probable it is that its predictions will be supported. Nontheoretical research varies in the extent to which it is based on other research, but it tends to be less so than theoretical research. It is based not on a theory, but on someone's hunch or intuition and is therefore less likely to produce positive results. On the other hand, when it does, there is a big payoff—unexpected new relationships that open up important new areas of study may be discovered.

Another difference between the types of research is the significance of negative results (the lack of difference between conditions or lack of relationship between variables). In theoretical research, negative results (e.g., fear level has no effect on affiliation) are very important. Since the theory predicts a difference, the lack of one constitutes nonsupport for the theory. In empirical research, negative results have relatively little meaning. They do not tell us anything about an existing body of facts. The study was based on someone's hunch, so all that negative results tell us is that one person was wrong or that a particular variable is not related to some other variable in this particular situation. Thus, theoretical research has a high likelihood of payoff. Positive results are prob-

H. Armstrong Roberts

able, negative ones are useful, and the payoff is primarily in terms of supporting or not supporting an existing theory. In contrast, empirical research has a relatively low chance of payoff, because positive results are less likely and negative ones have little meaning; but when there is a payoff, it is often a big one because it may constitute a discovery.

In general, hypothesis testing is most effective when a body of information is already available on a subject, and the empirical approach is most effective when the area is one about which very little is known. Testing hypotheses is a systematic way of adding to the available knowledge and validating the theories that tie it together; empirical research is a way of collecting a lot of information quickly but in a relatively unsystematic way that does not lend itself to efficient theory building. Both approaches have their place in social psychology, although there seems to be a feeling in the field (not shared by the present authors) that empirical research is somehow less worthy than hypothesis testing.

basic and applied research

Another major difference between types of research is the extent to which the experimenter is interested in a particular concrete situation. Both theoretical and empirical research may or may not be focused on a situation that actually exists in the real world. For example, the effect of fear arousal on attitude change can be investigated from a theoretical point of view (e.g., learning theory) or without any theory. Regardless of the theoretical position or lack of it, the research can deal with a specific issue or can be concerned only with the general question. Experimenters in this field may concentrate on the question of whether high fear increases the effect of antismoking campaigns. They are interested in the effects of fear on attitude change, but they focus on attitudes toward smoking. Perhaps arousing fear will have different effects on other kinds of attitudes, or perhaps the levels of fear aroused will work differently with other issues. For the moment, they want to find out how to change attitudes toward smoking. The research may have applications to the general question of how fear affects attitude change, but that is not the primary concern.

In contrast, investigators may not be interested in any particular attitude, but only in the general question of how fear affects attitude change. With this starting point, they will use many different issues and situations in order to make the findings as general as possible. The results may not be especially applicable to attitudes toward smoking except in the broadest sense. That is, the most general findings will of course apply to all attitudes, but they will probably not be able to specify the exact levels of fear that will produce the most change in attitudes toward smoking.

Work that focuses on a particular situation has usually been referred to as *applied* research, while the other has been called *basic* research. Unfortunately, "applied" research has acquired somewhat negative connotations in the United States. For many years, most of the prestige and status went to those who conducted basic research and were, by and large, uninterested in specific problems. This was not only unfair, but also tended to make an unrealistic distinction between the two approaches. Actually, basic research usually grows out of a concern with existing problems and must necessarily deal with particular issues. Thus, the fear arousal literature has tended to focus on issues related to health, even though at least some of the experimenters chose these for convenience rather than because they were interested in these particular questions.

Since some kind of issue must be chosen, it seems reasonable to expect an experimenter to choose issues of general concern whenever possible. When studying the effects of fear arousal, it would be desirable for the experimenter to pick an issue with which society is concerned—smoking or cancer or safe driving—rather than issues of little importance, such as whether teeth should be brushed up and down or sideways. Naturally, basic researchers will want to pick issues that fit the research design as well as possible, but with that one restriction, they should try to pick issues that are important in their own right. Similarly, those who are going to focus on a particular issue, such as smoking, can try to design their experiments so that the findings will have as general an application as possible. They should try to relate the research to previous work, and whenever possible design the study so that it will test propositions that have been suggested by other results. In this way, basic and applied psychologists can complement each other, working back and forth between specific issues and more general propositions and progress in the field can be accelerated.

research methods

Regardless of how research begins, the next step is to decide what method is to be used. There are two basic varieties—correlational and experimental. Each has advantages and disadvantages. As we shall see, which type is preferable depends largely on the problem being studied and the goals of the experimenter.

correlational research

Correlational research consists of observing the relationship between two or more variables. It asks the question, when variable A is high, is B also high (a positive correlation), is B low (a negative correlation), or is B's value unrelated (no correlation)? For example, in studying fear and affiliation, one could look at some people who are afraid and some who are not afraid and see how much each group affiliates. One might compare people in wartime with people in peacetime, or Londoners during a bombing raid and afterward. One might observe people during an air raid and compare those who show a lot of fear with those who show very little. If it turned out that the people experiencing a lot of fear tended to affiliate more than those showing less fear, one could report that high fear was correlated with affiliation.

ADVANTAGES A correlational study is an efficient way of collecting a large amount of data about a problem area. For example, we could collect thirty personality variables about a large number of people and twenty different measures of behavior. Then we could see which personality factors correlate with which behaviors. In this way, we can discover a large number of relationships and interrelationships in a relatively short time. In contrast, it would take many experimental studies to investigate the effect of each personality factor on each behavior. For this reason, correlational studies are often used in empirical research; they make possible the efficient collection of large amounts of data.

Correlational techniques also sometimes enable us to study problems to which experimental methods may not be applicable. For example, much of the research on the effects of crowding on people has involved correlations. It is impossible experimentally to place individuals in high-density situations for very long periods of time. Since being in a crowded situation for ten years might produce very different effects from being in it for only four hours or even twenty days, the experimental work, although useful, is limited. Therefore, investigators turned to statistics collected in actual situations. Data on the population density of various cities and parts of cities were available, as were data on crime and mental illness in those areas. By correlating measures of density with measures of crime and mental illness, it was possible to get some indication of the relationship between density and pathology. Naturally, this had all the difficulties of correlational studies, particularly the problem of making causative statements and ruling out other variables such as income; but it had the great advantage of providing some evidence on the effects of density over much longer periods of time than would have been possible in an experimental design.

DISADVANTAGES The major weakness of correlational studies is that they leave the cause and effect relationship ambiguous. If a study indicates that people who are more afraid affiliate more than those who are less afraid, this does not necessarily mean that high fear leads to greater affiliation. It may be that affiliating increases fear rather than the other way around. Those who affiliate tend to get frightened; those who do not affiliate become less frightened. Therefore, we find a relationship between affiliation and fear. In other words, the direction of causality (does fear lead to affiliation or does affiliation lead to fear) is unknown.

This is not always a serious drawback in a correlational study. In many cases we can be fairly certain of the direction of causation. The science of astronomy is based on correlations, and yet there is little doubt about most of the directions of causality. When the moon is in particular positions, there are high tides on earth. We assume that the moon is causing the high tides, rather than the high tides causing the moon to be in that position. First-born children who are anxious affiliate more than later borns. Obviously, if there is any causal relationship between these two factors, it must be birth order causing greater affiliation—not the other way around. No matter how much you affiliate as an adult, it cannot affect the order of your birth.

A more serious ambiguity than the direction of causality is the possibility, in all correlational studies, that neither variable is directly affecting the other. Rather, some other unspecified factor may be affecting both of them. When we find that people who are very frightened affiliate more than those who are less frightened, there is always the chance that these two groups of people differ in more ways than their amount of fear. People who frighten easily may be weaker, more dependent, younger, less intelligent, or more other-directed than those who frighten less easily. If frightened people are generally weaker than those less frightened, this weakness could explain their greater affiliation. They are weak, need protection more, and therefore affiliate more in order to get protection.

Any of the other factors could also cause the greater affiliation in a high-fear subject, and we can never be certain. We have divided the subjects in terms of the amount of fear that they felt and then looked at their affiliation. We would like to say that the greater fear is producing the greater affiliation. Even if we are certain that the direction of causality is correct, however, we cannot be certain that it is the fear that is producing the effect. It might be weakness or some other factor that goes along with fear, rather than the fear itself. All that we have discovered is that fear and affiliation are related, that they go together, but we do not know if it is the fear that is important or some entirely different factor that is correlated with both fear and affiliation.

This problem of attributing causation is even more obvious in the research on the relationship between crowding and crime in the cities. As we shall see, the finding is that there is a substantial correlation between the two—higher densities are associated with higher crime rates. But what does this mean? One possibility, of course, is that crowding causes crime. Another possibility—the opposite—is that crime causes high density. Choosing between these is not too difficult in this case. *If* one causes the other, it is more plausible that living under high-density conditions makes people commit crimes than it is that people move into areas because there is a lot of crime there.

However, it is even more likely that neither relationship is correct and that some other factor is producing the correlation. Crowding is strongly associated with income level—poor people tend to live under more crowded conditions than do rich people. Crime is also strongly associated with income level; poor people commit more crimes. Now we can see that the relationship between crowding and crime may be due entirely to the fact that both of them are associated with income level. Poor people live in high-density areas and commit more crimes. Therefore despite the correlation between density and crime, density itself may have no effect on crime rate.

experimental research

In the experimental method, conditions having different levels of a factor (the independent variable) are produced by the investigator or some external force, subjects are randomly assigned to the conditions, and some dependent variable is measured. If we are interested in factors that affect affiliation, we select one such factor and deliberately vary it in an experiment. Suppose we want to know whether fear increases affiliation. To study this, we want to have two groups of subjects who are identical in every respect except their amount of fear. If they differ in any other way, we cannot be certain the degree of affiliation is due to the different levels of fear—it might be due to other differences. As explained above, if one group is more afraid and also weaker, there is no way to be certain which factor is causing the increased affiliation. On the other hand, if the groups do not differ in anything except their level of fear, any difference must be attributed to greater fear.

RANDOM ASSIGNMENT A crucial problem, then, is to be sure that the subjects differ only in terms of the variable being studied. They must, as far as possible, be identical when they enter the experiment. This is accomplished by *randomly* assigning the subjects to experimental conditions, by deciding entirely by chance which experimental condition to put them in. Random assignment can be achieved by flipping a coin, by cutting a deck of cards, or ideally, by using a random number table, which guarantees that the choice is entirely by chance.

The basic idea behind random assignment is that nothing the subject brings with him to the experimental situation should determine which group he is in. This determination is made by the experimenter, and he makes it purely on a chance basis. If the subjects were assigned to conditions on any basis other than this, the groups might differ in some way unrelated to the experimental procedures. For example, we might ask subjects to choose between high- and low-shock conditions and perhaps pay enough extra for the high-shock condition so that some would choose it. If we did this, however, it is likely that subjects who chose high shock would be different from those who chose low shock. The former subjects would probably be less afraid of shocks, perhaps more concerned about money or whatever incentive was offered, and so on. They might also be more suggestible, since they were more willing to do what the experimenter wanted them to do. Any of these factors could, by itself, produce a difference in affiliation. Although no experimenter would use this assignment procedure, this kind of selection often occurs in natural situations and introduces ambiguity into correlational research. People who sky dive experience more fear than people whose favorite sport is tennis. We might observe how much these two groups affiliate in order to study the effect of fear on affiliation. But obviously people who choose to sky dive, who have selected a risky, frightening sport, are different from those who choose tennis. Thus, a correlational study comparing sky divers and tennis players in their amount of affiliation would have the disadvantage that the groups probably differ in ways other than fear. The experimental method avoids this through random assignment.

Similar problems occur if subjects are assigned to conditions on the basis of something they do or some attribute they have, even if they do not choose the condition themselves. We would not assign subjects who arrive early to one condition and those who arrive late to another, or even subjects who sign up on weekdays to one and weekend subjects to another. We do not know how these groups differ, but the possibility exists that they do—and any experimental results might be due to that difference.

It would also be incorrect to put subjects who understand the instructions in one condition and those who do not understand them in another. This is a tempting method of assignment, because often one condition is more complicated than another and we would like to be certain that everyone understands the instructions. But obviously, the groups would then differ in intelligence or interest in the proceedings, and such differences might affect the results. It can also happen that subjects are randomly assigned, but some subjects do not understand the instructions and must be eliminated from the study. If the instructions in one condition are more difficult and more subjects in that condition do not understand them and are therefore eliminated, there is no longer random assignment. There has been some self-selection. The less bright subjects in the difficult condition have decided (not intentionally, perhaps, but just as surely) not to participate. Thus, the other condition, in which even the less bright had no difficulty with the instructions, has on the average less bright subjects. Any time something a subject does or an attribute of his determines his condition in a study, random assignment has been lost.

One way of conceptualizing random assignment is this: Before an experiment begins, no one can specify any characteristic on which the subjects in one condition differ from those in another. They are, as far as anyone can tell, identical, except that some have been put in one condition and some in another. When assignment has been random, we can be certain within the confidence limits established by statistical tests that the two groups do not differ in any systematic way. Any differences between the two, say, in intelligence, would be due entirely to chance. There is a possibility that one group would be more intelligent on the average than another group. But the likelihood of this happening has been well established by statisticians, and the statistical tests we conduct on the results obtained are based on the likelihood of differences occurring by chance. If, for example, we find that a high-fear group affiliates more than a low-fear group, we ask the question: What is the likelihood that this would have happened by chance? This means, what is the likelihood that we assigned more affiliative people to one group than another?

We apply a statistical test to the difference so that we state exactly what that chance is. We might find that only one time in a hundred would the two groups have differed that much simply by chance. This makes us believe that the results are probably due to our experimental manipulation. Thus, as long as we are certain that the subjects have been randomly assigned to conditions and that the experimental manipulation differed only in the way we intended (e.g., one produced high fear and the other produced low fear), we can be confident that the differences that appear are due to the manipulation and not some unknown factor. This ability to specify the particular aspect of the situation that produced an effect is the major advantage of the experimental method.

DISADVANTAGES The major limitations of experimental research derive from difficulties involving the independent variable. Experiments tend to involve a restricted range of a variable, because it is difficult to produce strong emotions or to expose subjects to extreme conditions. Some subjects can be made more afraid than others, but none of them will be terrified. We shall discuss the difficulties involved in the manipulation of the independent variable in more detail below. For the moment, the point is that we are restricted in the kinds of procedures we can use and, therefore, in the strength of a variable we can produce.

The experimental method is generally not applicable to a study of the effects of natural occurrences. Air raids, floods, surgery do not strike people entirely randomly, and therefore subjects are not assigned randomly to conditions. Sometimes there appears to be a high degree of chance in whom such occurrences affect and randomness might be approximated, but it is never perfect. Thus, any findings are correlational rather than experimental.

Finally, experiments are relatively inefficient for collecting large amounts of data on many variables. Since each factor must be produced by the experimenter, he is usually limited to one or two factors at a time. He could certainly not vary twenty factors at once as is often done in correlational studies.

experimental and correlational: a comparison

Correlational and experimental work complement each other. There are many cases in which both methods are useful. In general, correlational studies are particularly effective in the collection of large amounts of data; they provide us with ideas and hypotheses, which can then be studied in more detail experimentally.

Since the experimental method allows us to conclude that a particular variable is the cause of a particular effect, it enables us to test a hypothesis about how one variable affects another. It is therefore useful primarily in testing such hypotheses, in pinning down and specifying in detail relationships between variables, and in providing us with explanations of such relationships. For example, during wartime, people tend to cluster together more than during peace. This might suggest that fear leads to affiliation. But the greater affiliation might be due to other factors. Note that the greatest clustering occurs in air raid shelters, which are naturally small and which people occupy, not to be together, but to be safe from bombs. The bombs make the people afraid, so they go to bomb shelters—which are invariably crowded. Perhaps they would prefer to be alone and safe rather than with others and safe, but since the shelters are crowded, they have no choice. The suggestion that fear leads to affiliation must accordingly be tested in more controlled situations—in an experiment in which two or more levels of fear are produced and affiliation measured. In other words, correlational work can produce data on which a hypothesis is founded, and experimental work can test the hypothesis.

field and laboratory research

The next step in the research is to decide where it should be done. Although most research in social psychology during the last ten or fifteen years has been conducted in the laboratory, some has always been conducted in the field and the amount of field research now seems to be increasing. Both experimental and correlational research can be done in either the laboratory or the field, and each setting has advantages and disadvantages.

field research

ADVANTAGES Research in the field tends to deal with real people in real situations, as opposed to experimental subjects in relatively unreal situations in the laboratory. Accordingly, field research tends to minimize suspicion, so the subjects' responses are more spontaneous and less susceptible to the kinds of bias that suspicion produces.

The researcher in the field can often collect data from types of

Sybil Shelton/Monkmeyer

people who cannot be attracted to an experimental laboratory. It has often been said that American social psychology is based on college sophomores, because they are the ones who are most available for experiments in laboratories. Field research can collect data from a wider variety of subjects and thus adds to the generality of the findings.

Another advantage of work in the field is that we are sometimes able to deal with extremely powerful variables and situations that could not be studied in the laboratory. This is particularly true of correlational work, because experimental field work is limited by the same kinds of factors that limit it in the laboratory. With correlational work, we can, as mentioned previously, observe people in extreme situations—when they are waiting to be operated on in a hospital or huddled together in an air raid shelter. This advantage sometimes applies to field experiments when the manipulation is done not by the experimenter but by some natural event that just happens to affect people randomly and therefore fits the criterion of an experiment.

DISADVANTAGES The major disadvantages of field research stem from the lack of control over the situation. It is generally extremely difficult to assign subjects to conditions randomly, to be certain that they are all experiencing the same thing, to get accurate measures on the dependent variable, and so on. A great many random events and conditions enter into a field study and often obscure the effects of the variables in which we are interested.

In particular, it is difficult to find pure manipulations of the independent variable and pure measures of the dependent variable. The experimenter must find or arrange circumstances that produce specific differences—and no others—between conditions. Even if one could find a situation that would, for example, produce two levels of fear, it is exceedingly difficult to be certain that the two conditions do not differ in other ways. In the laboratory one could design a pure procedure that would accomplish this; in the field it is much more difficult. If subjects have been randomly assigned to conditions, the experimenter can conclude that any difference in their behavior is due to the experimental manipulation. But if that manipulation is not pure (e.g., not just differences in fear), the interpretation of the effect is ambiguous. Yes, it is due to the manipulation, but does that mean it is due to fear or to some other variable? Similarly, measurement of the dependent variable is often elusive in the field. The experimenter must not only produce differences in fear, but must also obtain a measure of affiliation in the same setting. If there is an ideal independent manipulation, it is highly unlikely that it would be accompanied by a convenient method of assessing its effect.

With sufficient ingenuity and hard work, it is sometimes possible to find or arrange appropriate situations, but they are few and far between. The world is generally not set up to facilitate the study of a specific problem that happens to occur to a psychologist. He may therefore find that field research does not lend itself to the problem in which he is interested.

laboratory research

ADVANTAGES The advantages and disadvantages of laboratory research are mirror images of those of field research. The major advantage of work in the laboratory is the control over the situation that it affords. Experimenters can be quite certain what is happening to each subject; if they are doing experimental work, they can randomly assign the subjects; subject them to the exact experiences necessary to study the problem; minimize extraneous factors; and go a long way toward eliminating random variations in the procedure. Even when variations do occur, they can at least be reasonably certain that they know exactly what happened. Similarly, they have great control over the dependent variable and can measure it in considerably more detail and in a more uniform manner than in the field. Therefore, the laboratory is the ideal place in which to set up a situation designed to study a specific problem.

DISADVANTAGES The problems with laboratory work center around two aspects of the situation—the fact that subjects know they are being studied and the limitations on the kinds of manipulations that can be used. Whenever someone knows he is a subject in an experiment, there is always the possibility that he is not behaving naturally or spontaneously, that he is trying to please or displease the experimenter, that he is behaving in the way he thinks he should, that he is not accepting the experimental manipulation because he is distrustful, and so on. Any of these effects could produce bias in the results or obscure relationships and effects that actually exist. Although there are ways of minimizing these problems, as we shall discuss in detail below, they always exist to some extent.

Limitations on the kinds of manipulations that can be used mean that laboratory research usually deals with low or moderate levels of variables. Subjects cannot be terrified; they cannot be made terribly sad; they cannot be made hysterical with laughter. In most cases this simply means that the effects are less strong than they would be if the variables were more extreme, but that the basic relationships are the same. However, it is a serious weakness when there is reason to believe that high levels of a variable would produce different effects from intermediate ones. In the work on the relationship between fear and attitude change, for example, it has been suggested that very high levels of fear would interfere with attitude change, whereas lower levels increase change. Since laboratory work never deals with extremely high levels of fear, this possibility has never been adequately tested. In most cases, however, the main problem created by this limitation is that it makes it more difficult to find the effect of a variable even though the effect exists.

A relatively minor disadvantage, mentioned previously, is that laboratory work tends to deal with a limited population of subjects. The vast majority of laboratory studies involve college students or perhaps students at a university nursery school. This problem is not inherent in the laboratory method. With sufficient ingenuity and a little hard work, it should be possible to attract a wide range of subjects to experimental laboratories, particularly if the laboratories are not located on college campuses. Perhaps anyone who agrees to take part in a psychological study is unrepresentative of the population. But psychologists can, at least, try to employ a wide variety of subjects.

field and laboratory: a comparison

It is true that field and laboratory research tend to differ in the ways we have described, but to a large extent these differences have been exaggerated in discussions of the relative advantages of the two techniques. It is possible to obtain considerable control of variables outside the laboratory and it is possible to make laboratory situations extremely realistic. The study on the foot-in-the-door technique discussed in Chapter 12 demonstrates that under appropriate circumstances, field situations allow as much control as laboratory studies. In that study housewives were randomly assigned to conditions, an experimenter went from door to door manipulating the independent variable, and a second experimenter obtained a dependent measure. There was tight control over the manipulation, no haphazardness in the random assignment, and an unambiguous dependent measure. From the point of view of control, the study was as good as most studies conducted in the laboratory. It would probably have been set up differently in a laboratory, but that would not have provided any additional controls over either the independent or dependent variables.

Similarly, laboratory settings can often be exceedingly realistic. In a study by Carlsmith and Gross (see page 272), some subjects delivered electric shocks to their partners and were then asked to work for the Save-the-Redwoods campaign. This was a realistic situation as far as they were concerned. True, they were in an experiment during the shock part of the study, but nevertheless they were delivering electric shocks and presumably feeling guilty because of it. Then, after the experiment was over (in their view), they were asked to do a favor for the person whom they had shocked. This request and the subsequent compliance were as realistic as anything that could take place in the field.

The basic issue is not where the experiment takes place but how realistic it is. If the subjects know they are in an experiment and think the request is part of the experiment, there tends to be a loss of realism. They would probably wonder why the request was being made and worry about its significance. If, on the other hand, the request is made outside the experimental situation (whether in the field or in the laboratory), the subjects should not be suspicious, the situation should be realistic for them, and the data obtained should not suffer from lack of naturalness on their part. Field studies tend to be more realistic and easier to make realistic than laboratory studies, but the distinction is one of degree. The important distinction is between realistic and nonrealistic studies, and realism can be produced either in the field or in the laboratory.

research techniques

archive and cross-cultural studies

Two other kinds of research are in a sense special cases of the field and laboratory types. The first is the so-called archive study, in which the investigator does not collect the data himself but uses data that are already available in published records. In most cases this is actually a kind of field study, with the main difference being that someone else has done the hard work. An example of the use of archives is the study described in Chapter 6 on the relationship between cotton prices and lynchings in the South. The investigators started with the hypothesis that frustration leads to aggression and then argued that a drop in cotton prices would produce frustrations, which would, in turn, produce an increase in aggression in the form of lynchings. The data on cotton prices and on the number of lynchings were readily available in statistics collected by the United States government and others, and the investigators simply looked up these data and ran correlations between the two variables. Similarly, the studies of the relationship between population density and crime relied entirely on data that were already available.

Since there is rarely any random assignment of subjects to experimental conditions, archive work is almost always correlational—but it can be very informative. The major problem with using archives is the difficulty of finding data with which to test the hypothesis we are interested in. However, there is a vast amount of data collected for other purposes that can be fruitfully used to study a variety of problems. Included in this is all the work done by psychologists both within and outside the laboratory; the accumulated data are generally available to other psychologists. Thus, reanalysis of previous work is one way of conducting research.

Cross-cultural work can be done in the field, in laboratories, or even by the use of archives. The only requirement is that data be collected in more than one culture. This type of research has two purposes. First, it allows for greater generality of findings if they hold in more than one culture. There is always the suspicion that a particular relationship between, say, fear and affiliation may hold in the United States but not in Japan. If we want to consider this relationship a basic process in human social interaction, we naturally want it to hold for all kinds of populations. Cross-cultural work is one way of testing the limitations and generality of any particular finding.

Another, more sophisticated use of cross-cultural work is in studying the importance of variables that differ in two societies. One of the basic hypotheses we discuss in this book is the relationship between frustration and aggression. This relationship could be tested by observing whether societies that are high in frustration exhibit more aggression than those low in frustration. Of course, observing only two societies would not be particularly useful, because they would differ on many variables beside frustration. Just as correlational studies on individuals need fairly large numbers to produce meaningful results, so do cross-cultural studies. The research must assess frustration and aggression in a large number of societies and see whether high levels of frustration generally tend to be associated with high levels of aggression. In this way, the extraneous, incidental factors present in each society become less important, and the relationship between frustration and aggression emerges.

Naturally, cross-cultural work can also tell us how societies differ. Any time different results are found in different cultures, we have discovered something about each culture. We have, for example, found that Norwegians conform more than the French in a particular situation. We may not know why they do, we may not know whether or not it is due to the particular situation, but we know that in the limited set of circumstances, there is more conformity in Norway than in France.

observational research

A research technique that is being used more and more is direct observation of behavior. Social psychologists typically rely heavily on asking subjects how they are feeling, obtaining measures of behavior such as how much someone contributes to charity, or giving specific measures such as having subjects vote for the leader of a group or play a game. All of these are legitimate, useful procedures. However, it is also possible simply to watch what people are doing either in a natural setting or in the laboratory. For example, in studying group behavior, you can observe the interactions and note what everyone says, how often they talk, how often they look at or touch one another, and so on. With children, you might observe the number of fights, sharing, talking, and playing with toys. The psychologist need not introduce any specific measure; instead, the natural behavior of the subjects is recorded. It is the same technique ethologists (people who study animals in their natural habitat) use to discover the behavior of animals. They obviously cannot ask a lion how often he fights or a chimp whether he uses tools. So, of necessity, ethologists have always merely observed what the animals do. In the early days of social psychology, this was a common technique for studying human interactions. Then there was a long period in which observations of this kind were not used much. Now they are coming back, and that is a very favorable trend.

Observational research is usually quite difficult and tedious. Researchers must first construct a rating scale on which to record the behaviors. In doing this they must face the fact that they cannot record everything. There are an almost unlimited number of individual behaviors and pieces of behavior in any group interaction. For example, even talking is enormously complex. It is easy to record how often someone talks and what that person says, but each act of speaking also involves the pitch, amplitude, and speed of the utterance; the tone used; the number of pauses between words; and so on. People who study speech can spend hours analyzing a two-minute speech. Moreover, when talking, an individual uses very complicated facial and bodily gestures. Thus, unless you are going to focus entirely on speech, you must decide what aspects of communication you are most interested in.

Similarly, even a simple interaction can be described briefly, as A hit B on the head, or in pages that include the bodily stance, strength of the blow, gestures, the preceding and following actions, and so on. In other words, the first task of the observer is to decide what actions to record. Next, a simple method of recording them must be devised so that various observers will agree on what happened. For example, a category called "acted friendly" would not be useful because it is often difficult to decide whether or not an act is friendly. Instead, observers use more specific categories, such as "smiled at other person," "offered to share toy," "helped up from ground," and so on. Then it can be decided later that all of these are indications of friendliness. Much of the difficulty with observation in research and in the real world is that we disagree on what a particular behavior means. A well-designed rating scale minimizes disagreements.

The importance of observational research is that it allows us to describe in some detail how people act in relatively natural settings. We record their actual behavior and do not have to rely on complex measurement methods that might make the situation less natural. When children fight in a schoolyard, we can conclude with some certainty that aggression is being expressed. When someone in the laboratory gives an electric shock to another subject after the experimenter has told him that is his job, it is less clear that true aggression is involved. We need the controlled laboratory research, but the observations are more true-to-life and help us relate the laboratory work to the real world.

research ethics

After an investigator has decided what kind of study to do and where to do it, he faces the most difficult decision—how to do it. In designing any research, and particularly any that involves humans, ethical considerations must be taken into account. The social psychologist wants to discover how people behave in social situations. To do so, he must expose subjects to certain conditions and observe how they respond. But he must be concerned about their privacy and about the conditions to which he exposes them.

privacy

An individual's right to privacy must be respected and cherished. As the president's panel on privacy and behavior research stated, every individual must be allowed to "decide for himself how much he will share with others his thoughts, his feelings, and the facts of his personal life." The social psychologist must guard the individual's privacy and at the same time pursue his research. Although this is a complex, personal matter, certain guidelines should be observed. The president's panel has listed several that are particularly important.

"Participation by subjects should be voluntary and based on informed consent to the extent that it is consistent with the objectives of the research." Ordinarily, individuals should not be subjected to experimentation unless they have agreed to it, and, whenever possible, this agreement should be given after they have heard exactly what is going to take place during the course of the study. The experimenter has an obligation to tell a potential subject as much as possible about the study before asking him to participate.

Often, however, it is not possible to tell a subject everything about the study. This is typical of research in social psychology. Studies of impression formation, in which subjects are given a list of adjectives and asked to form an impression of the person, can be conducted with subjects who know all about the purposes and procedures of the work. But virtually all the other studies described in this book require concealment of certain aspects of the investigation. In some experiments, such as the similarity and liking work, only the purpose and specific hypotheses need be concealed. In others, such as the Asch conformity study, both purpose and details of procedure must be concealed. The experimenter must give as much information as he can, but the president's panel did not feel, nor do we, that research that requires concealment must cease. Instead, the panel added: "In the absence of full information, consent [should] be based on trust in the qualified investigator and the integrity of his institution." In other words, the individual may volunteer for a study without knowing everything about it because he trusts the investigator and the institution responsible. In essence, he is putting himself into their hands, because he believes they will do nothing to which he would object if he could be told. This is a legitimate and meaningful form of consent, but it places a particularly heavy burden on the investigator to be worthy of that trust.

"In some research, however, soliciting consent at all . . . destroys experimental purpose." An example of this type is the work on the foot-in-the-door effect (Chapter 12), in which housewives were asked to post signs and were never told they were in a study. Sometimes this is the only feasible way of investigating a problem, and with appropriate safeguards it is allowable. It should be used only when it is the sole way of conducting the research, when the work is important enough to warrant an invasion of privacy (no matter how slight that invasion is), and particularly when there is minimal possibility that the invasion of privacy will produce unpleasant consequences for the subject.

A distinction should be made between personal, private information about an individual and public information. Information about an individual's finances, sexual behavior, or even preferences for movies is personal. An individual's behavior when he is angry or frustrated is also quite personal. Research designed to obtain such information must carefully observe the guidelines on privacy. In contrast, whether someone crosses the street when the light is red, is willing to post a sign for safe driving, or smokes cigarettes is relatively public information. Almost anyone can obtain this information merely by watching the individual's behavior in public. Although an investigator should always be careful about the right to privacy, collecting public information of this sort need not be done under such strict guidelines.

In summary, the guidelines for the protection of privacy are to obtain informed consent if possible, to obtain consent based on trust if some concealment of purpose is necessary, and to conduct research without consent only when there is no other way to do it and there is minimal danger of causing distress.

experimental conditions

Another ethical consideration perhaps even more complicated than that of privacy concerns the conditions to which the subject is to be exposed. The determination of what should be done rests largely with the individual investigator. This is as it should be, because ultimately it is his responsibility. However, all universities now have a special committee to provide some supervision for the experimenter. Certain guidelines apply to all research in social psychology.

It is obvious that nothing should be done to a subject that has any likelihood of causing lasting harm. It may seem somewhat foolish to mention this, but unfortunately, it is sometimes lost sight of. Medical research, for example, has often exposed willing or unwilling humans to drugs, viruses, and other agents that could conceivably cause great harm. There have been lawsuits over such practices, and they are better controlled today. But the researcher is in conflict; his goals are noteworthy—he wants to save lives, discover a cure for cancer, in social research perhaps discover how to prevent war—so he may think some risk of harm to a subject is justified. We feel that, at least in social psychology, this is not so. A subject, even with his permission, should not be exposed to potentially harmful conditions.

After this criterion is satisfied, the problem becomes subtle and more difficult. Is it allowable to cause subjects some pain or distress if it is not lasting or extreme? We feel that it is, but only if stringent criteria are met. The experimenter must consider all the ways of studying the problem that do not cause distress. Often the same problem can be studied without aversive conditions, and if so, they must be used. If this is not possible (e.g., the study involves reactions to pain or frustration), the experimenter must decide whether the importance of the problem warrants the use of procedures that will cause distress. Although we are talking about procedures that will not cause lasting pain or distress, there must be ample justification for exposing someone to an unpleasant experience. It is, of course, difficult to decide how important a problem is, but an attempt should be made to do so. Thus, a replication of earlier work, a small point in a larger problem, or a slight extension of a previous finding would be less justification than a test of an important theory, a possibility of discovering a new relationship, or a major extension of previous work. The greater the distress the procedure will cause, the more justification, in terms of the importance of the work, is needed to use it.

Assuming that no other procedure is possible and the problem seems important enough, the experimenter must next give careful attention to the procedure to be used and the setting in which it will be used. Two issues are involved: first, conditions produced in the laboratory that are similar to those the person is likely to encounter in normal life are always preferable to unique conditions. Being threatened with an injection may be frightening, but it is a usual occurrence in the world—we all get injections. In contrast, being threatened with total isolation for five hours is also frightening, but it is not a usual occurrence—most people never face this threat. The advantage of the natural situation is that it is more likely to produce valid results that are comparable to behavior in the real world. More important from an ethical point of view, it is less likely to cause distress that individuals cannot handle or that will produce a lasting impression on them. The ruling considerations should be that the experiment not change the subjects' lives in any meaningful way (except insofar as it teaches them something, which is always a possibility). If the experiment exposes them to a natural situation, it will probably not be an important event in their lives; if the situation is unnatural, it is more likely to become an important and perhaps harmful event. Thus, whenever possible, the conditions should be similar to ones that occur naturally. The details need not be similar, but the emotion they arouse and the general feelings should be.

Second, the subjects should have volunteered to be in the study. As stated above, they need not necessarily be told everything that will happen, but they should know that they are in an experiment and should have freely given their permission. In other words, only someone who has given informed consent or consent based on trust should be exposed to distressing conditions. Subjects who have not given consent should be exposed only to conditions that have a minimal chance of causing distress.

Finally, in all experiments great care should be taken to guarantee, as much as possible, that subjects leave feeling no more distress than when they arrived. This can be accomplished by extended explanations of the study, its purpose, significance, methods, etc., and by reassuring subjects in whatever way is appropriate. This so-called debriefing is an essential part of all research and is particularly important when the experimental procedures are likely to cause the subjects distress.

These ethical considerations impose considerable restrictions on the social scientist, but they need not prevent him from doing legitimate research. With sufficient ingenuity and care, he can study virtually any problem and still safeguard the privacy and well-being of his subjects.

However, ethical considerations usually do prevent him from conducting experiments on the effect of very strong aversive conditions; this is one of the limitations of the experimental method in social psychology.

role-playing technique

Concern about the ethical problems of research and also the difficulty of doing experimental research, has caused some people in the field to suggest what they consider an alternative to the experimental method. This consists of substituting what are called "role-playing" studies for actual experiments. In the typical role-playing study, the investigator describes a situation to the subject, and asks the subject what he or some other person would do under those circumstances. For example, a subject reads a description of the Festinger and Carlsmith (1959) experiment that we discuss in Chapter 12. He is told that a subject performed a task which is described in detail, that he was then asked to tell the next subject that the task was very enjoyable and that he was offered money for doing this. He is then asked how much he thinks someone in that situation would say that he liked the task. Or he is asked how much he thinks he would say he would have liked the task in that situation. In this role-playing study, some subjects would be told that the individual was paid one dollar and some would be told he was paid twenty dollars, thus repeating the conditions of the original experiment. The data then are simply what the subject says he or the other person would do under these circumstances.

Obviously this way of doing research is extremely efficient and avoids many of the problems inherent in the experimental method. There are no ethical problems because the subject is not himself involved in any experimental situation nor in any deception. There is no great skill necessary in presenting the instructions to the subjects or designing the specific procedure, because everything can be written down on a piece of paper and there is no reason for the subject to feel any suspicion. The whole procedure can be very quick and can even be done in large groups. The temptations of using this method are evident.

Unfortunately, the data obtained from this kind of procedure are not very useful for psychologists. What a subject says he or another subject would do in a given situation may or may not be what the subject actually would do in that situation. You are asking the subject to guess what he would do if he found himself in those circumstances, and people are not very good at making those guesses. Typically, role-playing subjects will give the correct answers only when the results are obvious beforehand. In any situation where we are not certain what the behavior will be—that is, in almost all interesting situations—we could not count on the subjects' responses. There is no more reason to trust the subjects' guesses than there is to trust your own. If the subject can guess what he would have done, presumably the experimenter could guess just as well—perhaps better if he is experienced. Therefore, there is little advantage to running a role-playing study over simply recording the experimenter's hunches. But the whole business of doing research is to test the experimenter's hunches, not to assume they are correct. We would not automatically accept an experimenter's hunches, and there is no more reason to accept the guesses of a large number of subjects. No matter how many subjects are asked, what they say is only guessing—not real behavior. In order to find out how subjects will behave in a real situation, it is necessary to put them in it.

In fact, the whole basis of psychology and social psychology as a science is that we do not trust anyone's intuitions about how people behave. This is the difference between the scientific and the nonscientific approach to the study of human behavior. As soon as we start trusting people's guesses as to how they or others would behave, we are no longer treating psychology as a science. No matter how realistic the role-playing situation is made, as long as subjects are playing the roles and not actually experiencing the situation, their responses will be only guesses and as such are not scientific data. They are, of course, interesting as indications of people's perceptions of themselves and of others. If this is what you are interested in, the role-playing technique could be very useful. But it must always be understood that subjects' responses tell us something about how they perceive and how they guess, not how they would behave in that situation.

designing the study

With these ethical considerations in mind, the investigator must design and conduct a study. As an example of this process, we shall now discuss in detail the design and execution of a laboratory experiment.

The investigator has a problem he wants to study. He must set up a situation in which one or more variables (the independent variables) are experimentally manipulated and in which subjects are randomly assigned to groups in such a way that the groups differ only in terms of these independent variables. Everything about the situation must be identical for the groups except the one variable in which he is interested. Then the experimenter must measure one or more responses (the dependent variables) in order to see what effect the independent variable has. He must take his measurements in such a way as to minimize the subject's suspicion. Only then can he elicit responses that reflect, as much as possible, the way the subject would respond if he were in a similar situation that occurred naturally rather than in one produced by the experimenter.

the independent variable

The first step in the process generally is to decide on the specific way to manipulate the independent variable. The psychologist starts with a variable that is defined on a conceptual level. For example, he hypothesizes that high fear leads to an increase in affiliation. He may or may not have a detailed definition of *fear* in his mind, but he must have a fairly clear picture of the variable. Let us say he defines *fear* as the internal feeling produced by the anticipation of pain or harm from a known source. This conceptual definition may sound impressive, but it is very general. The experimenter's big problem is deciding on the particular way in which he is going to arouse fear. According to the definition, he must set up a situation in which the subject is anticipating harm from a known source, but the definition says nothing about the specific conditions under which this should be done.

CHOOSING A MANIPULATION There are several criteria for a good manipulation of this sort. Ideally, it should work on all subjects. The more uniformly the method works, the stronger is its effect and the more likely it is to produce significant and meaningful results. Therefore, the psychologist wants to use something that everyone or almost everyone is afraid of.

A second point is that social psychologists typically deal with several levels of a particular variable rather than simply its presence or absence. An affiliation study would probably involve high- and low-fear conditions rather than high- and no-fear conditions. There are two reasons for this.

First, and more important, is the necessity of making the conditions as similar as possible in all respects except the one that differentiates them in terms of fear. This is difficult to do unless we use almost identical terms when describing the situation to both groups of subjects. For example, if we told one group of subjects that they were going to be given electric shocks and did not mention this to the other, the two groups would differ in many ways. They might differ in terms of fear (the variable we are interested in), but they would also differ in feelings about the experiment and the experimenter, in how much they wondered what the study concerned, and so on. Also, we have talked longer to one group of subjects than to the other, and although we cannot be sure what effect this would have, it is potentially important. In contrast, we could tell both groups that they are going to be shocked but make it more frightening for one than the other by varying the description of the shocks. We could tell one group that the shocks will be severe and painful and the other group that they will be mild and not painful. This would make the conditions virtually identical except for the few words necessary to produce the difference in fear. Then, any differences in the behavior of the two groups would be attributable to fear level and not to extraneous variables.

The second reason for dealing with two levels of a variable rather than its presence and absence is that it is generally not possible to be certain that a particular internal state is entirely absent. Even if the external conditions would not ordinarily arouse fear, many subjects may be afraid simply because they are in an experiment or because they are people who are always somewhat frightened. Similarly, even someone who has just eaten may be slightly hungry, even someone who has just slept twelve hours may be tired, and so on. Thus, from a conceptual and practical point of view, it makes little sense to think in terms of the total absence of a variable—instead, we talk in terms of less and more.

Other considerations in choosing the experimental procedure revolve around its practicality, morality, legality, and so on. Obviously we want to choose something we are able and willing to do to a subject. Under most circumstances, we could not take him up in an airplane and suddenly tell him the engine has failed. Although this probably would make him afraid, most of us would feel it was highly unethical. Also we would not have the resources at our disposal to carry it out. Thus, we must choose a method that is feasible from a practical point of view and that will not harm the subject or do anything else we would consider unethical.

In choosing a manipulation, we must also take into account the necessity of collecting dependent measures. The manipulation of the independent variable that is chosen must be compatible with some acceptable dependent measures. Closely related to this is the necessity of finding a manipulation that is plausible, that would not arouse too much suspicion, and that, accordingly, would enable us to set up a situation in which the subject would respond as spontaneously as possible.

ETHICAL AND PRACTICAL PROBLEMS With all these considerations in mind, the experimenter eventually chooses a manipulation. He might decide to tell the subjects that they are going to be handling snakes. Many people are afraid of snakes and some snakes are dangerous, so this should arouse a considerable amount of fear. The problem with this manipulation is that many subjects are, in fact, not afraid of snakes as long as the snakes are not dangerous. Thus many subjects would not be at all afraid and the manipulation would not be successful. We could, of course, say they are poisonous snakes or perhaps giant anacondas. The few subjects who believed it might be terrified, but it would probably raise considerable skepticism among most subjects and they would feel no fear.

Another possibility might be to lock subjects in a room and simulate a fire that, presumably, would be threatening to engulf the building. If this were done convincingly, the subjects would probably be exceedingly frightened. However, in addition to obvious ethical problems, there are several difficulties with this technique. First, many subjects probably would not believe there was a fire. To make the fire believable would require elaborate apparatus, shouting people, firemen breaking down doors, etc. But most important is the virtual impossibility of finding a comparable situation for the low-fear or control group. A small fire might be thought to arouse less fear than a large one, but if the fire is dangerous, the subjects will be afraid; and they will probably be just as afraid of burning to death in a small fire as in a large one. If there is no fire, the conditions are so different that it might be hard to compare them. Certainly any difference between the high-fear (fire) subjects and the low-fear (no fire) subjects would be difficult to attribute entirely to the amount of fear they felt.

Finally, this manipulation would make it extremely difficult to maintain good control over the situation and collect reliable measures of the dependent variable. In a study that used essentially this manipulation (French, 1944), uncontrollable events occurred. A group of subjects were put in a room at the top of an old building at Harvard, ostensibly to discuss a problem. Soon after the experimenter left, smoke began coming under a door in the room. The subjects soon discovered that all the doors were locked, and at this point they presumably should have been very frightened. Unfortunately (or perhaps fortunately), human beings do not usually take this kind of situation lying down. Several groups included varsity football players, and they broke down the door, terminating the experiment. Other groups managed to break into the closet from which the smoke was pouring and discovered the smoke machine. Still others convinced themselves that it was an experiment and calmly went about discussing the problem, ignoring the smoke that was beginning to fill the room. If the investigators had been studying responses to crisis situations, these would be interesting results. However, they were attempting to study a specific dependent variable (organization). When this is the aim of an experiment, crisis situations often make it difficult to exert sufficient control so that dependent measures can be collected.

ELECTRIC SHOCK One manipulation that has been widely used in social psychology experiments has been found to arouse fear in most subjects, enables the experimenter to produce several levels of fear conveniently, and also minimizes the amount of suspicion the subjects might feel. This is the anticipation of electric shocks. For most subjects, electric shocks are particularly frightening, partly because they rarely experience them and partly because they know that electric shocks can be extremely painful. Thus almost all subjects are frightened by the threat of receiving them. Yet electric shocks are not so strange and unfamiliar that the subject is being exposed to a situation likely to harm him.

Moreover, it is extremely easy to manipulate the amount of fear shocks arouse by describing them in different terms for different conditions. All the subjects would presumably be somewhat afraid, but the more painful they expected the shocks to be, the more afraid they would be. In this way all the subjects could be given almost identical instructions, and yet the intensity of the fear could be manipulated conveniently by changing a few words in the description of the shocks. The high-fear group could be told: "These shocks will hurt, they will be painful. . . . It is necessary that our shocks be intense. . . . These shocks will be quite painful, but of course, they will do no permanent damage." A low-fear group could be told: ". . . very mild electric shocks. . . . What you will feel will not in any way be painful. They will resemble more a tickle or tingle than anything unpleasant." If the instructions are delivered convincingly, they should arouse relatively little suspicion, because even sophisticated subjects know that psychologists often use electric shocks. Also the experiment can be described as, say, a study on responses to intense stimuli.

CHECKING VALIDITY There are obviously many other ways of arousing fear that could be adapted for this type of study. It is desirable to vary the independent variable in more than one way in different studies so that we can be more certain that we are dealing with fear and not some other emotion. If the findings on fear and affiliation, for example, are based entirely on the anticipation of electric shocks, someone might argue that they were not the result of fear but something specific to electric shocks. By manipulating fear in many ways, all of which are consistent with our original conceptual definition of fear (see p. 29), and finding the same results, we increase confidence in our interpretation of the findings in terms of fear rather than in terms of the specific manipulation. Sarnoff and Zimbardo (1961), for example, demonstrated a difference between fear and anxiety by using different procedures for arousing the emotions (see the chapter on affiliation, pp. 42–67). This reinforced our belief that fear leads to affiliation and also made the definition of fear more specific.

Another way of increasing confidence in the interpretation of the independent variable is to provide some sort of independent check on the manipulation. On the face of it, telling subjects they are about to be shocked should arouse fear. The more severe the description, the more fear it should arouse. The possibility always exists, however, that the manipulation did not arouse fear, that for some reason the subjects were not worried about electric shocks, or perhaps that the two groups did not differ in the amount of fear they felt. If we know that there is some response or behavior that is highly correlated with fear, by measuring it we can provide an independent verification of the presence of fear. For example, we could take measures of the subjects' blood pressure and pulse rate. Although physiological measures are generally poor indicators of the presence of fear, they do tend to be correlated with it. The greater the fear, the higher should be the blood pressure and pulse rate.

If we find that the subjects in the high-fear condition actually do have higher pulse rates and blood pressure than those in the low-fear condition, our confidence in the effectiveness of the manipulation is increased. We are not absolutely certain that it is fear we are producing, but we do know that we have aroused some internal state differentially in the two conditions and that fear is one of the likely possibilities. Another kind of check on the manipulation is a self-report from the subjects. We can ask the subjects how frightened they feel, how nervous, whether or not they are nauseated, and so on. If the high-fear subjects report that they are more afraid than the low-fear subjects, and particularly if the two groups do not differ on irrelevant feelings such as nausea, it becomes highly probable that the manipulation really was affecting fear levels.

Thus there are two ways of pinning down the meaning of the experimental manipulation. One is to use many different kinds of fear manipulations, all derived from our conceptual definition of it. If the different manipulations produce the same effect on the dependent measure (for example, if in all cases the high-fear group affiliates more than the low-fear group), we can be quite confident that it is fear that is producing the effect. The other way is to provide a direct check on the manipulation, either by the use of self-reports or by some other variable that we know from previous research to be highly correlated with fear. Unfortunately, neither of these approaches is particularly easy in most instances. A great deal of care is required to be certain of our interpretation of the manipulation, and much of the controversy in social psychology revolves around different interpretations of the same experimental manipulation.

the dependent variable

The original problem was to study the effects of fear on affiliation. We have decided how to manipulate fear; we must now decide how to measure affiliation. We want to do it in such a way that there is a minimum of ambiguity in the meaning of the dependent measure because we would like to be absolutely certain that it is affiliation we are studying. Also we must minimize the possibility of biasing the subjects' responses. We do not want subjects to respond in a perticular way because they think it is "correct" or because they think the experimenter wants them to respond that way or for any other extraneous reason. We want them to respond spontaneously, with the responses being due to the experimental situation and the independent variable.

In the case of affiliation, our first criterion for a good dependent measure is not particularly difficult to meet. There are relatively few possibilities for measuring affiliation. They all are variations of allowing the subjects a choice of affiliating or not affiliating and observing which they choose. The particular way in which the choice is presented would depend in large part on making it fit in with the experimental manipulation of the independent variable and the whole setting of the study. But there is no great difficulty in assessing the desire to affiliate.

Dependent variables other than affiliation, however, are often more difficult to measure. In studying the effect of modeling on aggression, for example, the experimenter is faced with a considerable problem in finding a good dependent measure of aggression. He can observe whether the subject punches someone, draws a knife and stabs him, or performs other violent acts. These are clearly aggressive behaviors and would be excellent, unambiguous indications of aggressiveness. Fortunately for our society, but perhaps unfortunately for the experimenter, the likelihood of any subject committing a violent act such as these is virtually zero. Therefore, the investigator must depend on subtler indications of aggressiveness. He could ask a subject to make comments about another person and then code these comments in terms of their aggressive content. But many people would not consider it aggressive behavior to make negative comments about somebody else when asked to do so by an experimenter. Even delivering an electric shock to another person might not be considered aggressive if the experimenter has told them that this is part of the study. In other words, it is quite difficult to find a dependent measure that fits the conceptual definition of aggression, is feasible, and is unequivocal. Considerable ingenuity is necessary to design such a measure. The same is true of many other variables that are important to social psychologists.

Often we cannot find a perfect measure of the variable we are interested in. For practical or ethical reasons, we are forced to resort to somewhat equivocal measures. Other interpretations of the measure are possible, and therefore the experimenters cannot be certain their results reflect the variable they are investigating. One solution to this problem is to use many different measures of the same variable. If the measures all produce the same results and are all designed to tap the same variable, they can have increased confidence in the meaning of the findings. Any one measure of aggression might be interpreted in a variety of ways, but ten different measures of aggression that produce the same results, even if each of them separately could be interpreted in several ways, make it more likely that the variable measured is aggression.

Having many measures also reduces the possibility that the results are due to some characteristic peculiar to a given measure. For example, delivering electric shocks carries with it a variety of meanings and connotations, not all of which the experimenter can know. Therefore, results based only on giving electric shocks are to some extent confused with characteristics of that particular behavior. If, on the other hand, the same results are obtained from delivering electric shocks, making negative statements, taking money from another person, slapping someone across the face, and drawing nasty pictures of someone, it begins to appear that they are not due to any specific characteristics of any one measure. The results appear regardless of the measure of aggression, so we have considerably more confidence in them.

This does not mean that we always use more than one measure in an experiment or even that it is essential to have experiments that use different measures. Occasionally we find a measure that is very compelling, that has few alternative interpretations, and that just about everybody will accept as an adequate measure of a particular variable. But most of the time it is helpful to have a variety of measures of the same variable, if not in the same experiment, at least in different experiments. In this way we can increase both the generality of the results and our confidence that they are due to the variable in which we are interested.

This, then, is the basic procedure for conducting an experiment in social psychology. A hypothesis is formed, an independent variable is chosen, the manipulation is constructed, the experimental situation is designed, and a dependent measure is selected. Generally, a considerable amount of pretesting is necessary to work out the exact method of manipulating the independent variable, smooth out the procedure, and make as certain as possible that the dependent measure is appropriate to the situation. When the pretesting has been completed and the type of subjects selected, the experiment is ready to be run.

bias

Up to now we have been talking about aspects of the experimental method that are more or less general to all kinds of research. The choice of setting (laboratory or field) is not unique to social psychology, although it is more important in this area than in most others. The difficulty of manipulating the independent variable and of choosing a dependent measure is common to virtually all fields of science. In addition, there is one problem that, although not unique to social psychology, is particularly relevant and troublesome in this field—bias due to the experimenter or the subject.

experimenter bias

As we discuss in Chapter 11, subjects in a study are extremely susceptible to influence by the experimenter. They do virtually anything he asks. This is true even if he does not make any direct request. If he implies, consciously or otherwise, that he would like the subjects to respond in a certain way, there is a tendency for them to respond in that way. If, for example, the experimenter would like the subjects in one condition to be more aggressive and those in another condition to be less aggressive, subjects in the two conditions may differ in the way he expects simply because explicitly or implicitly he communicates his wishes. Moreover, the experimenter may not have made any deliberate attempt to influence the results. On the contrary, experimenters are aware of this problem and try to be as neutral and consistent as possible. But subtle cues tend to be picked up by the subjects and influence their behavior.

Many studies (e.g., Rosenthal, 1966) have shown powerful effects produced by the experimenter's expectations and desires. In school settings, students a teacher thinks are bright do better than students the teacher thinks are less bright—even though the students do not actually differ in intelligence. This is even true of rats in a simple learning situation with identical rats: if an experimenter is told the rats are smart, they do better than if he is told they are dumb. Perhaps experimenters tend to handle the "smart" rats somewhat more gently and to encourage them somewhat more than they do the "dumb" rats. If an experimenter's expectations can have an important effect on such fairly simple, noninteractive behavior as learning in rats, obviously they can have an even more dramatic effect on complex social processes.

There are two solutions to the problem of bias. One is to keep the experimenter ignorant as to the experimental condition of the subject. This is usually referred to as keeping the experimenter "blind." If he does not know which experimental condition he is dealing with, there is no way for him to affect the conditions differentially. Although he may behave differently from one experimental session to another and these differences may affect the way the subjects respond, he cannot systematically behave one way for one condition and another way for another. This guarantees that randomness still prevails, because the experimenter cannot make the variations in his procedure anything other than random. He can, of course, try to guess what condition a subject is in, and if he wants or expects one condition to produce more aggression than the other, he may behave in differential ways to subjects he thinks are in the two conditions. But since he does not know who is in what condition, his differential behavior cannot produce systematic differences. In other words, as long as the experimenter is totally blind (i.e., ignorant) as to the condition subjects are in, any differences in the way they are treated are randomly distributed between the various conditions. These differences may affect the way subjects behave and may increase the variance in their behavior, but they cannot produce overall differences between conditions.

In many experiments, however, it is impossible to keep the experimenter blind as to the subjects' condition. Typically, the experimenter himself must deliver the experimental manipulation in one way or another. He tells the subject to expect severe or mild shock, he brings the subject a Coke, he knows how many confederates are present in a conformity situation, and so on. The experimenter is the main source of instructions and manipulations, and his skill is generally necessary to make certain that the manipulation is effective. Even in these cases, however, some degree of blindness can be introduced into the experiment. For example, two experimenters can be used, with one of them delivering the experimental manipulation and the other collecting the dependent measure, thus keeping the person who collects the dependent measure blind to the experimental condition. This relatively simple procedure was generally used in the altruism studies described in Chapter 7. One experimenter produced guilt and another made the request. It is not quite as good as having an experimenter who is totally blind, because the first experimenter might communicate in some way what he wanted the subject to do later or might affect in some way the later behavior, but the procedure should substantially reduce bias.

A second solution to the problem of experimenter bias is to standardize the situation in every way possible. If everything is standardized and there are no differences between conditions other than those that are deliberate, there can be no bias. This is usually not easy to accomplish, but various procedures can maximize the amount of standardization between conditions. In the extreme case, a subject might appear for an experiment, find a written instruction on the door telling him to enter, have all instructions presented on tape, and complete the experiment before he meets a live experimenter. In this way, every factor in the situation would be absolutely standardized, and experimenter bias would be eliminated.

This degree of standardization is rarely feasible. Most manipulations require the presence of at least one live person. The experiments concerning guilt all depend on another person being hurt in some way, and that person's presence should make the arousal of guilt stronger. Tape recordings do not allow any procedural variations, which might be necessitated by variations among subjects. A live experimenter can repeat instructions if they have not been understood, emphasize aspects to which the subject seems to be responding, and increase the strength of the manipulation by these variations. In addition, most manipulations are more forceful when delivered by a live experimenter, simply because people respond to other people more strongly than they respond to impersonal tape recordings. This is not always true. Being told by a tape recording that he is going to be given severe electric shocks might be very frightening for a subject—even more so than hearing the same thing from a live experimenter. But this is a special instance. Generally, a live experimenter has more effect than a recorded or written message.

Another problem with taped instructions is that the situation becomes somewhat unreal. As we have already discussed, many experiments suffer from a lack of realism, and the careful experimenter exerts considerable effort to make the setting more realistic. Written or taped instructions tend to make the situation more unusual and magnify this already serious problem. The subject tends to be more suspicious and less spontaneous, and the results become less valid.

These drawbacks do not mean that written or taped instructions are impossible—on the contrary, they are often useful—but at least part of the manipulation usually has to be conducted by a live experimenter. Nevertheless, the more standardization that can be introduced, the more likely it is that experimental bias will be eliminated.

In actual practice, the solution to the problem of bias is usually a combination of the two procedures we have described. As much as possible, the experimenter is kept blind as to the subjects' experimental conditions; also as much as possible, instructions are standardized by the use of tapes or written materials. It is often impossible to eliminate completely the possibility that some bias has crept into a study, but experimenters must take this into account and do whatever they can to minimize the likelihood that there is any.

subject bias

An even subtler source of bias in a social psychology experiment is the subject's desire to give the "correct" response in the situation. When people know they are subjects in a psychological experiment, there is some pressure on them to think about what they are doing. Under these circumstances, most subjects want to give the socially acceptable response, in part because they want to please or impress the experimenter. They feel that if they give the "correct" response, the experimenter will be more favorably impressed than if they give an inappropriate response. This feeling could be minimized somewhat by having the subject respond anonymously so that the experimenter would not know how he behaved in the situation. Unfortunately, this does not solve the problem entirely. Most subjects want to impress not only the experimenter but also themselves. They want to think of themselves as good people and therefore do what they can to behave in the right way. As long as a subject is thinking about these considerations, it is virtually impossible to eliminate this kind of bias.

For example, if an experimenter were interested in the effects of frustration on aggression toward whites and blacks, he might frustrate a subject and then give him an opportunity to aggress against either a white or a black. If this were done in a straightforward manner, most subjects would be aware that the experimenter was interested at least in part in differential aggression toward whites and blacks. At this point, every subject would have some feelings about the appropriate or most acceptable behavior. Most white college students would probably think that it is wrong to be prejudiced and, in particular, that it is bad to aggress more against a black than against a white. These subjects live in a social environment in which bigotry, discrimination, and prejudice are considered wrong by most people. Clearly the socially acceptable and desirable response would be to treat the white and the black equally or even to bend over backward and aggress more against the former than against the latter. The problem is that if they acted this way the subjects might be responding the way they think they should respond, not necessarily the way they would respond in a natural situation. The responses would be influenced not by the subjects' natural tendencies, but primarily by their assumptions about the correct way of responding. In fact, many white subjects may feel considerable prejudice against blacks and may have a tendency to aggress more against them than against other whites, but their knowledge about what is socially acceptable behavior interferes with this spontaneous behavior and causes them to respond differently.

This kind of bias is almost impossible to eliminate entirely but can be minimized in a variety of ways. The goal is to produce a situation in which the subjects respond spontaneously without worrying about the correctness of the response. The basic tactic is to disguise the dependent measure or to distract subjects from its importance. One way of doing this is by not telling subjects that they are being observed. In field research, within the ethical limits described above, people sometimes are not told that they are subjects in an experiment. They are approached and their behavior may be measured, but nothing is said about a psychological study. For example, we could observe how white salespeople in a store treat black and white customers on a particularly busy, hard day compared to an easy day. If frustration leads to aggression, the salespeople should be nastier on the hard day, and even more so to blacks than to whites if that aggression is directed at people differentially.

In the laboratory, disguising the measure and distracting the subject are somewhat more difficult. As we discussed previously, experiments can be set up so that the crucial measure is taken after the subject thinks the experiment is over. In the Carlsmith and Gross study, for example, the manipulation of guilt occurred during what the subject thought was the experiment, but the measure of compliance was obtained afterward. Another tactic is to make the subject think that he is an experimenter rather than a subject. The subject is told that he is to act as an observer or to assist the experimenter, but in the description of his role not much emphasis is placed on observing his behavior. This distracts him from the main emphasis of the experiment and tends to make him behave more spontaneously. A third tactic is using unobtrusive or so-called nonreactive measures, in which the subject does not know that a measure is being taken. We could count how many cigarettes he smokes or how often he blinks as measures of stress, or observe whether he chooses a task that requires sitting with other people as an indication of desire to affiliate. All these techniques reduce the possibility that the dependent measure is affected by the subject's view of what is socially desirable rather than by the subject's natural inclinations in the situation.

As a final note, we should emphasize that social psychology is, in general, a probabilistic science. Its findings and predictions are stated in probabilistic terms. We will see that high fear leads to greater affiliation than low fear. This does not mean that all people who are feeling high fear affiliate more than all people who are feeling low fear. It does not even mean that all people affiliate more when they are afraid than when they are not afraid. In other words, it does not apply to every person nor to all situations. It does mean that greater fear *tends* to cause people to affiliate more than low fear. More of the people who are feeling high fear affiliate than do those who are feeling low fear. There is a greater probability that a particular individual who is afraid affiliates than that a particular individual who is not afraid does so. Similarly, a communication from a high-prestige communicator *tends* to produce more attitude change than one from a low-prestige communicator, but not everyone who reads the high-prestige communication changes more than everyone who reads the low-prestige communication. In addition, some people may actually change more as a result of a particular low-prestige communication than a high-prestige communication. For a variety of reasons, any given individual might be more influenced by a communication from a nursing student than by one from a Nobel Prize winner. But *most* people are influenced more by the high-prestige communication. If all we know is that one person received a high-prestige communication and another received a low-prestige communication, our best prediction is that the former is influenced more. This is, however, a probabilistic prediction and may not hold true in any given case.

A great deal of the variation in most situations has not been fully explained by social psychology. We have found that some percentage of the variance in affiliation is due to the amount of fear the individual is feeling. Many other factors, such as birth order and some we do not know about yet, also affect the amount of affiliation. Therefore, we can now say that high fear *tends* to produce an increase in affiliation. In discussing liking (Chapter 5) we say that proximity, similarity, and rewardingness explain a considerable amount of the variance. Someone who is close by, who is very similar to us, and who is rewarding *tends* to be liked more than someone who does not have these qualities. But someone who fits all these criteria is not necessarily going to be a friend. He tends to be and is more likely to be than someone who does not have them, but the correspondence is not perfect. A group of high-fear subjects affiliate more, on the average, than a group of low-fear subjects, but any given member of the high-fear group may affiliate less than a particular member of the low-fear group.

This does not mean that the findings of social psychology are false or imprecise. It means that we have not yet specified all the factors that affect any given behavior and that the factors we have discovered do not affect all individuals equally in all conditions. However, these factors do affect behavior in the ways we have described, so we are able to understand and predict behavior better because of the research.

SUMMARY

1. Social psychology is the systematic study of social behavior. Although we all know a great deal about social behavior from our daily observations and experience, some of our impressions are incorrect. Systematic research is necessary to be certain which of our intuitions are right and which are wrong, and also to make discoveries about how we behave in social situations.

2. There are two types of questions with which to begin research. One kind is directly related to an existing theory. Theoretical research is designed to test the theory, to compare two theories, or to assess the limits and exceptions to a theory. The other kind of research is empirical—it starts with a general question that is not directly related to a theory and tries to discover new relationships or to test a hunch or intuition.

3. A second distinction among types of research is between basic and applied. Basic research deals with fundamental questions, general principles, or theories. Applied research is directed toward answering a question related to a specific problem in the world—how to reduce prejudice, sell toothpaste, or design housing.

4. There are two basic types of methods in social psychology—experimental and correlational. Correlational research asks the questions: are two or more variables related? If one variable is high, is the other also high; or is the other consistently low? Correlational research can deal with a great many variables at once, and can investigate factors that cannot usually be manipulated in the laboratory, such as very high fear, poverty, or social class. But correlational research does not allow us to make causal inferences—we do not know if A caused B, B caused A, or some third, unknown variable caused both. Experimental research consists of comparing two situations that differ in only one deliberately varied way. If there is any difference in behavior, it is due to that one variable. This provides great control over the situation and allows causal statements.

5. Research can be done in the laboratory or in natural or field settings. The former provides more control, the latter is closer to the real world and often permits a greater range of intensity in the variables studied.

6. Archive research uses existing data; cross-cultural studies compare more than one culture; and observational research involves careful, systematic observations of behavior.

7. Social psychologists face many ethical problems in doing their research. They must be careful to guard the safety of the subject, to respect their privacy, and to have no harmful effects on anyone involved in the research.

8. In designing a study, the key questions are how to manipulate the independent variable and to measure the dependent variable. Moreover, great care must be taken to avoid the effects of experimenter and subject bias—ways in which the experimenter unintentionally can affect the results or the subject can give results that he thinks are "correct" but are not what he would have done spontaneously.

SUGGESTIONS FOR ADDITIONAL READING

ARONSON, E. *The Social Animal, 2nd Edition.* San Francisco: W. H. Freeman, 1976. A brief, well-written, light introduction to the field.

CARLSMITH, J. M., ELLSWORTH, P. C., & ARONSON, E. *Methods of Research in Social Psychology.* Reading, Mass.: Addison-Wesley, 1976. Excellent discussion of this area from three psychologists who should know.

DEUTSCH, M. & KRAUSS, R. M. *Theories in Social Psychology.* New York: Basic Books, 1965. Still the best coverage of theories, though it is somewhat out of date.

2

affiliation

human beings are gregarious animals. Almost all people spend their lives in close contact with other people. Moreover, this contact is not limited to close family members. It is rare for someone to live with his or her family away from all other members of the species. On the contrary, most of the world's human population lives in large groups, surrounded by hundreds, thousands, or millions of other people. Some other animal species also live in very large groups—herds of gnus, zebras, and gazelles; schools of sardines and shrimp; and, of course, vast colonies of ants and bees. But none of these social groupings can compare in complexity and few in size to ours. Certainly the enormous progress we have achieved and the changes we have caused on earth are both due in large part to the fact that we seek out other people and interact with very large numbers of them in extraordinarily complicated ways. This tendency to spend time with other people, to affiliate, is the beginning and the cause of social psychology and is therefore an appropriate place to begin discussing social phenomena.

It is hardly a new idea that we are a gregarious species. The bible tells us that "It is not good that man should be alone." (Genesis 2:18); and "Woe to him that is alone when he falleth, for he hath not another to help him up" (Ecclesiastes 14:10). And various authors have described the advantages or disadvantages of societies and tried to explain why people form them. "Man seeketh in society comfort, use and protection" (Bacon, *The Advancement of Learning*); "We do not by nature seek society for its own sake, but that we may receive some honor or profit from it. . . ." (Hobbes, *Philosophical Rudiments Concerning Government and Society*). Though not all agree on the virtues of societies. "Society is always diseased, and the best is the most so" (Thoreau, *Excursions*); "Though the world contains many things which are thoroughly bad, the worst thing in it is society" (Schopenhauer, *Our Relations to Ourselves*).

Regardless of their point of view, these statements are primarily theoretical or philosophical. With a few exceptions, they are not so much concerned with why people affiliate as in outlining the good and bad aspects of existing societies. Social psychologists, in contrast, ask why. We want to know why people affiliate. Instead of attacking the phenomenon from a philosophical point of view, social psychologists want to discover causes. There are two levels of answers to the question. First, there are fairly general basic explanations of the affiliative tendency in humans. Second, there are particular factors that increase or decrease this tendency.

basic explanations

instinct

Early social psychologists such as McDougall believed that gregariousness is one of man's instincts. Just as ants collect in ant colonies by instinct, and baboons build elaborate social structures, so people live together in groups. We do this not because we think it is good or right or even useful; we do it without thinking, just as a baby sucks on a nipple or is afraid of heights.

Humans are born with many genetically determined characteristics, and it is conceivable that among them is a tendency to seek out and to congregate with other human beings. If this were true, a child who had been raised in total isolation with a minimum of stimulation would be expected to affiliate with other people as soon as she was given the chance. It would not be necessary for a child to have any experiences after she was born in order for her to be an affiliative creature; she would affiliate even if she received no rewards or comfort from others.

Although there may be considerable truth in this idea, it is almost impossible to test. One way to do so would be to raise a child in isolation and study her later behavior. Obviously we cannot and would not do this kind of experiment; and even if we could, it would not be a perfect test. Total isolation is not a normal environment for a human baby and would probably have harmful effects that would obscure any natural tendency to affiliate.

Although we cannot test the idea directly, we can easily conceive of reasons why humans might have developed an affiliative instinct. Because of natural selection, any characteristic that increases the chance of the animal surviving (that has high survival value) should over many generations become dominant. Assuming that the characteristic is genetically determined in the first place, those animals that have it will survive and breed more and their offspring will tend to have that quality. Since there will be more of their offspring than of those without the quality, eventually all or most animals of that species will have the quality. Under most circumstances, people who are gregarious will have a better chance of surviving and breeding than those who are solitary. This must have been true many thousands of years ago when our forebears were fighting a primitive world. There was strength in numbers. The group provided some protection and an increased opportunity to get food by hunting in groups, and so on. Moreover, once young were born, they needed protection that could not be provided by a solitary woman or even a small family. Thus, it is highly plausible that people who congregated in large groups managed to live longer and to produce more children who lived. If this tendency to affiliate is determined in any way by genes, it is likely that people who are alive today have inherited some genetic tendency to affiliate.

Keep in mind that this does not prove affiliation is genetically controlled. It may simply not be genetic in nature at all. The point of this argument is mainly to demonstrate that an explanation in terms of genetics is possible and even plausible. But, as we shall see, whether or not affiliation is instinctive, there are many other reasons why people want to be together.

innate determinants

Closely related to the idea that affiliation is instinctive is the obvious fact that we are gregarious because our other innate characteristics make it absolutely essential for our survival. We cannot survive alone; therefore, most of us spend time together.

This dependence on others is most evident when we are very young. Unlike most other animals, a human baby is virtually helpless for a long period of time. His early dependence on his parents for food and protection makes it necessary that he live with others for many years. Whereas most animals, even mammals, nurse for only a short time and can then forage for food on their own, the human baby is unable to feed itself for several years. It is conceivable that in a mild, protected, rich environment a child could stay alive after he was one or two years old, but under normal circumstances this would not be possible. He needs food, he needs protection from predators, he needs some kind of shelter, and so on. Similarly, a mother is extremely dependent on other humans for protection, particularly while she is taking care of her baby. Although it is possible for a solitary woman to survive even while nursing her child, under most circumstances she is dependent on at least one other human for protection and food.

Thus people are gregarious, by necessity, for the early years of their lives. If the parent and child did not stay together, the child would die. In this sense our innate characteristics, particularly our early helplessness, do cause us to affiliate. At a certain stage in life, however, we cease to be absolutely dependent on others. We no longer need them to give us food or protection. We could, in terms of our innate needs, become solitary. In our modern society a person could live in a penthouse apartment, have food delivered, watch television, read newspapers that were delivered with the food, and lead a safe, secure, comfortable, solitary life for many years. Or he could live on an isolated farm and accomplish the same thing without any help from others.

Occasionally someone does. There are cases of people becoming hermits, living alone, and, as far as we can tell, surviving perfectly well. But these are unusual, deviant cases. There are very few voluntary hermits, and those that do exist are generally considered somewhat crazy, certainly eccentric, and objects of curiosity. They are rebelling against perhaps the most universal characteristic of man, the tendency to be gregarious. Solitary confinement is almost always considered a severe punishment. Although it seems that our gregariousness is to some extent innately or instinctively determined, we are still left with the question of why people affiliate when they no longer need to.

learning

One answer is that people learn to affiliate just as they learn anything else. The child depends on others for essentials such as food, warmth, and protection, and each time one of these basic needs is satisfied by someone else, the child learns something. By the simple process of association, other people become connected with rewards and the child learns to consider people positive aspects of his environment. In addition, because the child is rewarded when he is with other people, the act of associating with people is reinforced. He learns that when he needs something, seeking out other people usually leads to satisfaction. Thus, he has learned to affiliate with others; it has become a customary part of his daily life.

This learning affects an individual's behavior throughout life. As an adult, he no longer requires other people in order to survive, but still associates with them because he has learned to. Thus, as children learn all sorts of habits that shape their lives, so they learn affiliation. And because all children in all cultures to some extent must learn to affiliate, it becomes a characteristic of all people.

satisfaction of needs

It is also true that we have needs other than those that are necessary for personal survival—needs that only other people can satisfy. For example, although the solitary life leaves an individual with some means of sexual satisfaction, it denies us the outlet of sexual intercourse with other humans. In addition, the needs for achievement, love, appreciation, comfort, respect, and power, although not innate, are sought by most people, and these needs are extremely difficult to satisfy in isolation. Thus, although someone could stay alive in isolation, most people have acquired through early social learning many needs that can be satisfied only by others.

specific causes

Instinct, innate characteristics, learning, and the satisfaction of needs are all explanations of why people affiliate. They are, however, general answers that do not allow us to specify much about the forces that control affiliation. If we say that animals eat because they have a need to eat or because they have learned to eat, we are correct but we do not learn very much about eating. On the other hand, if we say that animals eat when they have been deprived of food for four hours or when their blood-sugar level is low, we have specific knowledge about hunger and eating and can control the amount an animal will eat.

This distinction between general and specific explanations is also applicable to affiliation. Social psychologists have tried to determine the factors that increase or decrease the tendency to affiliate. We want to discover specific conditions that produce more affiliation and those that produce less in order to gain a more detailed understanding of the nature and causes of affiliation. We begin with the premise that almost all people have a tendency to associate with others. But we know there are times when this need is felt strongly, times when it is weak, and even times when people prefer to be alone. The question is: What factors increase and decrease affiliation?

British Airways

fear and affiliation

A report of the most systematic attempt to study the causes of affiliation was published in 1959 by Stanley Schachter. In order to gain insight into factors that might increase affiliation, he began observing what happens when people are not allowed to affiliate. If affiliation is satisfying a need, this need should become very important when a person is denied the source of its satisfaction.

A study of case histories of people in total isolation—members of some religious orders, people who had been shipwrecked, volunteers for isolation experiments—did show some similarities. Almost all accounts of long-term isolation included descriptions of sudden fearfulness and feelings resembling anxiety attacks. Within limits, longer isolation produced greater fear and anxiety. Although it is impossible to conclude anything definitive from this observed relationship because many other explanations are also plausible, it does suggest that fear and affiliation are closely linked. If isolation produces fear, affiliation may reduce fear. Thus, Schachter was led to the specific hypothesis that persons with high fear would affiliate more than those with low fear.

To test this hypothesis, we must examine individuals who differ in their amount of fear. One method of investigation would be to study individuals who differ in the amount of fear they are experiencing in life situations. However, such people almost certainly differ on dimensions other than degree of fear. For example, although airplane pilots who are about to make their first solo flight are probably more afraid than pilots who have flown for years, they also differ in length of experience, probably in age, and certainly in attitude toward flying. Any differences found in affiliative tendencies might be due to factors other than the amount of fear they are experiencing. By using controlled situations, we can select people who are similar and experimentally manipulate their degree of fear, making some more afraid than others. Then, when the subjects are given an opportunity to affiliate, the amount of affiliation they exhibit can be compared and any differences attributed to the degree of fear that had been aroused in them. This is what Schachter did, and his experiment has served as a model for almost all the subsequent work in this area.

When a subject arrived for Schachter's experiment, she found an experimenter in a white laboratory coat, surrounded by electrical equipment of various sorts. The experimenter introduced himself as Dr. Gregor Zilstein of the department of neurology and psychiatry and explained that the experiment concerned the effects of electric shock. In order to make some subjects more afraid than others, the experimenter used two different descriptions of the electric shock.

Instructions designed to arouse a considerable amount of fear (high-fear condition) described the shocks in ominous terms. Subjects were told, "These shocks will hurt. . . . In research of this sort, if we're to learn anything at all that will really help humanity, it is necessary that our shocks be intense. . . . These shocks will be quite painful but, of course, they will do no *permanent* damage" (italics added). By continuing at some length in this vein, the experimenter communicated the notion that the subject was in for a very frightening and painful experience.

In the low-fear condition, by contrast, every attempt was made to make the subject feel relaxed and at ease, while minimizing the severity of the shocks. For example, the subjects were told, "I assure you that what you will feel [i.e., electric shock] will not in any way be painful. It will resemble a tickle or a tingle more than anything unpleasant." Thus, although both groups of subjects were told the experiment would concern electric shock, one group expected a painful and frightening experience, whereas the other group expected a mild and unthreatening experience. As shown by questioning the subjects, the result was that the former group was more afraid than the latter.

Following the arousal and measurement of fear, the experimenter told the subjects there would be a ten-minute delay while he prepared the equipment. He explained that there were a number of other rooms in which the subjects might wait—comfortable rooms with armchairs, magazines, and so on. The experimenter continued that it had occurred to him that perhaps some of the people would prefer to wait with other subjects in the experiment and for these there was a classroom available. Each subject was asked to indicate whether she preferred to wait with others, alone, or had no preference. She was also asked to indicate the strength of her choice. In this and most subsequent experiments on this topic, the choice and rating of the intensity of subjects' desire to affiliate were the basic measures of the tendency.

The results of Schachter's study are shown in Table 2–1. The answer to the question of whether highly fearful subjects want to affiliate more than subjects with low fear is yes. The greater the fear, the greater the tendency to affiliate.

TABLE 2–1
effect of fear on affiliation

	PERCENTAGE CHOOSING			
Condition	Together	Don't Care	Alone	Strength of Affiliation[a]
High fear	62.5	28.1	9.4	.88
Low fear	33.0	60.0	7.0	.35

[a]Figures are ratings on a scale from −2 to +2.
Source: Adapted from Schachter (1959).

Now that we have found a relationship between fear and affiliation, the next step is to explain it. Why do fearful people affiliate more? There seem to be at least two explanations—fear reduction and social comparison.

fear reduction

We have seen that isolation appears to increase fear, which in turn leads to an increase in affiliation. One probable explanation of this increase in affiliation is that people affiliate in order to reduce their fear. Schachter's first experiment did not test this explanation directly, but some support for it was provided in a subsequent study (Schachter, 1959). Subjects were told that if they chose to wait with others they could either not talk at all or talk only about things unrelated to the experiment. The purpose of this restriction was to make it more difficult for subjects to reduce fear by reassuring one another. To the extent that high-fear subjects were affiliating in order to reduce fear, there would be less preference for waiting together than there had been when talking about the experiment was allowed. That is just what happened. Restricting discussion reduced the desire to affiliate. The result supports the idea that fear reduction is one reason why people want to be with others.

birth order

Even when high fear is aroused, some people have stronger needs to affiliate than others. Is there any systematic reason for this? An important, although supplementary, finding in Schachter's study of affiliation is that birth order is an important determinant of a person's desire to affiliate. First-born children and only children when afraid have a stronger tendency to affiliate than do later-born children. In fact, the tendency decreases progressively for the later-born children; those born second show a greater tendency to affiliate than do those born third, who, in turn, show a greater affiliative tendency than those born fourth, etc. As shown in Figure 2–1, this progression is maintained regardless of the size of the family. The affiliative tendency of someone born second in a family of six is about the same strength as that of someone born second in a family of two. In other words, the order of birth, not the size of the family, is the determinant. Why should birth order have this effect on affiliation?

Theoretically, the effect might be caused by some innate difference between first and later borns, but there is no evidence of such genetic differences. Most psychologists feel that the way children are brought up is crucial. One possible analysis is as follows. Parents are more concerned about their first child than about later children. When a first-born child falls, her mother runs to comfort her. Therefore, the first-born child soon learns that when she is uncomfortable, her mother is a marvelous source of comfort. Eventually the child learns that people in general provide comfort. With later children, parents become less concerned about the trials and tribulations of growing up. They learn that children are surprisingly resilient and their misery mostly transient. Moreover, the parents are a little tired of oohing and aahing over every scraped knee, and

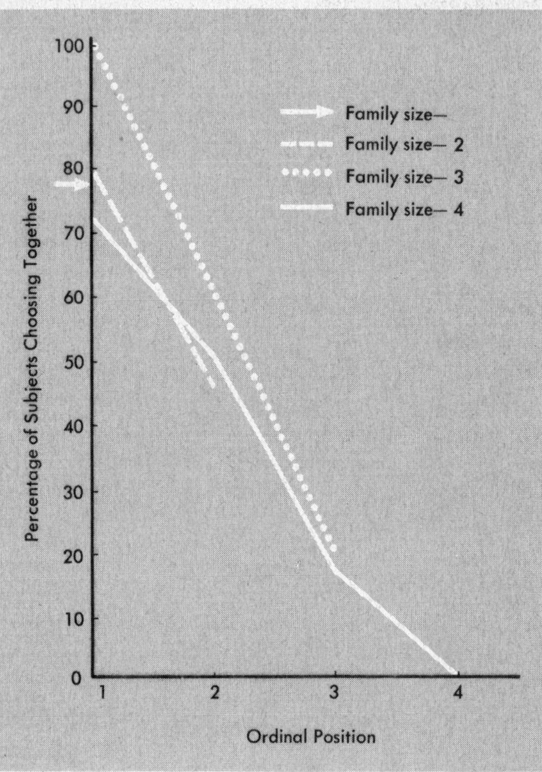

FIGURE 2–1
First borns, when afraid, affiliate more than second borns, who, in turn, affiliate more than third borns, and so on. This holds regardless of the size of family—order of birth, not number of siblings—determines affiliation. (Reprinted from The Psychology of Affiliation by Stanley Schachter with the permission of the publishers, Stanford University Press. © 1959 by the Board of Trustees of the Leland Stanford Junior University.)

they now have two children to care for and not so much time for each. Therefore, the affiliative tendency of the second child is reinforced less than that of the first child. The second child learns less that other people are a source of comfort and thus he learns to depend less on other people. By the time the third child is born, the parents are quite calm about raising children. They have even less time for a third child, so she learns even less, and so on. Thus, the earlier a child is in the birth order, the more she learns to depend on other people as sources of comfort when she is afraid.

This difference between first and later borns seems to affect many aspects of their lives. For example, first borns tend to seek psychotherapy (another person) more than later borns, while many more later borns are alcoholics (nonpersonal "solution"). Also fighter pilots, who must face danger alone, are very likely to be later borns.

To summarize: When people are afraid, they vary greatly in the extent to which they seek other people as a means of reducing their fear. One factor that affects this is birth order. First borns seek others when they are worried, and the tendency decreases progressively for the later born.

This finding on the effect of birth order provides additional support for the conclusion that one cause of affiliation is the desire to reduce fear.

Although the birth-order effect could be interpreted in other ways, it seems that first and later borns differ in their dependence on others in reducing fear. The first borns are more dependent and show the effect of fear on affiliation more strongly.

fear versus anxiety

The situation is complicated somewhat by the distinction between *fear* and *anxiety*. Although people generally use the two terms more or less interchangeably, psychologists use them to refer to quite different feelings. Freud suggested that being afraid of a realistic object or source of injury is different from being afraid when there is no real danger. He called the former *realistic anxiety* or *object anxiety*, and we shall call it *fear*. He called the latter *neurotic anxiety;* today, it is generally called *anxiety* to distinguish it from fear.

Someone being charged by a lion, advancing under enemy gunfire, or balancing on a narrow precipice while mountain climbing feels fear. He is in real danger and experiences the normal reaction to it. A person may be worried by a tiny mouse, upset at meeting new people, or nervous about standing on a wide ledge with a high protective fence. And there are times when he feels a sense of dread and becomes nervous and afraid but cannot connect the emotion to any specific object or situation. In all these instances there is no danger, he cannot be harmed, and yet he may experience a reaction similar to fear. This is anxiety.

According to Freud, anxiety is aroused by unconscious desires—sexual, aggressive, or otherwise—that people have but consider unacceptable. For example, men may unconsciously wish to be submissive, to act like children and be babied and taken care of by their mothers. But modern society puts pressure on men to be assertive, dominant, independent. Most men assume the role society dictates and deny to themselves and others that they have the childish feelings. Then, when they are exposed to a situation that arouses these desires, men have a tendency to feel uncomfortable. However, because they are denying their needs, they do not know what is bothering them. Another example is the latent homosexual who feels uncomfortable in a communal shower. He is unaware of his homosexual feelings, but the situation arouses sexual feelings that he denies. He is, in a sense, afraid of his feelings, and it is this fear that we call anxiety. Stimuli that arouse hidden and/or unacceptable feelings produce anxiety.

Accepting this conceptual distinction, it is clear that Schachter's study of affiliation involved fear rather than anxiety. Almost everyone recognizes that electric shocks can cause pain and harm and it is realistic to be frightened of them. Thus, we have been careful to state the original finding as high *fear* produces greater affiliation than low *fear*. This distinction is important because the reaction to anxiety is different.

Most people have learned that being with others usually reduces fear of something realistic. Other people reassure them, they realize that the others are going to experience the danger also, and there is strength in numbers. When our worry is unrealistic, however, associating with others is less likely to help and may even make things worse. The others presumably are not feeling anxious, because there is nothing real to worry about; therefore, we cannot talk freely about our worries. The others would be surprised, we might be embarrassed, and the interaction might increase rather than decrease anxiety. Even if we could talk to others, it would be more difficult for them to reassure us because they would not understand the real cause of our discomfort. Because associating might increase anxiety by producing embarrassment, a high-anxious subject would try to conceal rather than reveal his feelings. Accordingly, he should want to be alone more than a low-anxious subject.

To test this hypothesis, Sarnoff and Zimbardo (1961) conducted a study similar to Schacter's, with one important difference—both fear and anxiety were tested. One group of subjects was told, as in Schachter's experiment, that they were going to receive electric shocks; some members of this group were told the shocks would be quite severe (high fear), whereas others were told the shocks would be mild (low fear). Another group was put in a situation designed to arouse anxiety. They were told they would have to suck on a variety of objects. Some in this group were told they would have to suck on breast shields, rubber nipples, and other emotionally laden objects. The subjects were undergraduate men who felt reasonably mature and adult. On the premise that being asked to suck on infantile, ludicrous objects would arouse oral anxiety and would make them feel uncomfortable and foolish, these subjects were considered high anxious. Other subjects were told they would have to blow on relatively acceptable, innocuous objects such as whistles. This was expected to produce little or no discomfort, so these subjects were considered low anxious. The point was that neither anxiety group had anything realistic to be afraid of. Then the four groups—high and low fear, high and low anxiety—were given the measure of affiliation described previously. They had to indicate their preference for being alone or with others while waiting to go through the expected procedure.

The results are shown in Figure 2–2. As before, those anticipating severe shocks (high fear) wanted to wait together more than did those expecting mild shocks (low fear). However, as predicted, anxiety produced the opposite effect. The high-anxious subjects wanted to wait alone more than did the low-anxious subjects. The higher the anxiety, the *less* the desire for affiliation.

This complex finding was repeated by Teichman (1973) using a somewhat different manipulation of fear. Instead of directly threatening subjects with electric shock, the experimenter produced different levels of fear by varying how ominous and frightening the general situation appeared. In the high-fear condition, people wore white lab coats, acted impersonally, were surrounded by impressive recording equipment, and

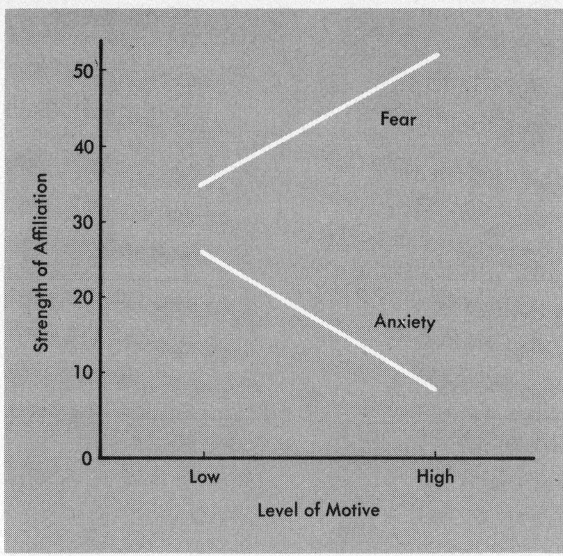

FIGURE 2–2
The desire to affiliate depends on the particular emotion that is aroused. High fear produces more affiliation than low fear; but high anxiety produces less affiliation than low anxiety. Note that the overall level of affiliation is higher under conditions involving fear than under those involving anxiety.

the subjects were told that various physiological responses would be measured. In the low-fear condition, everything was less formal, warmer, and less frightening. High and low anxiety were varied using the same procedure as Sarnoff and Zimbardo employed. As before, there was more affiliation with high than with low fear, and with low than with high anxiety.

We thus have two distinct findings: Fear leads to increased affiliation. Anxiety leads to decreased affiliation. In social psychology, making this kind of distinction aids in understanding a social phenomenon—in this case, affiliation. We can now make a more precise explanation of the relationships involved. Other people are a source of both comfort and embarrassment. When we expect them to provide comfort, we seek them out; when we expect embarrassment, we avoid them. Associating with others seems generally to decrease fear, so when fear is heightened, people seek others as a means of reducing it. But being around other people can increase anxiety, so when anxiety is heightened, people avoid affiliating.

social comparison

The analysis of affiliation in terms of fear reduction is only a partial answer. Schachter's original finding can also be explained in terms of Leon Festinger's theory of social comparison (1954). This important and influential theory contains two basic ideas: People have a drive to evaluate themselves; and in the absence of objective, nonsocial criteria, they will evaluate themselves by comparison with other people.

Everyone wants to know how good they are at whatever they do.

Is she a good tennis player, a fast runner, a talented writer, a graceful dancer? We want to know if we are smarter, less smart or similar to most other people; whether we are attractive compared to others and so on. Sometimes there is a fairly obvious objective criterion for evaluation. For example, if you get a perfect score on an exam or as a marksman, you know that you are doing very well. But most of the time, there is no such convenient criterion. How does a runner know if he is fast? Is a five-minute mile good? How about a mile in four minutes ten seconds? Twenty years ago, the four-ten mile would have been superb; today, because others are running faster, it is less outstanding. Is a man 5 feet, 10 inches in height short or tall? In the United States, he is about average; in Japan, he would be tall; among the Watusi in Africa, he would be short. Only by comparison with those around us, can we evaluate ourselves.

An example of self-evaluation by comparison with others can be seen in the experiences of high school students who enter college. In high school they were the brightest ones around and they and everyone else considered them quite exceptional. But in college many of the freshman class had been outstanding high school students. Each must now

Nancy Hays/Monkmeyer

compare himself to an essentially all-star high school group. Most discover that they are not so outstanding after all, that in this new group they are just average. Their own intelligence has not changed—the comparison group by which they evaluate their intelligence has. They feel that they adequately evaluate their abilities only by comparing themselves to the people around them. When these people change, their evaluations of themselves change.

This is especially true when feelings and emotions are involved. Because there are rarely objective criteria to indicate if one's feelings are appropriate to a situation, other people are the only source of information. In fact, to a large extent individuals define an appropriate reaction as the one most people have. Should one be afraid of a huge but harmless snake? By any realistic standard, the answer is no. But most people probably are somewhat frightened of a five-foot snake, regardless of its potential danger. Because the typical reaction is fear, most people would consider feeling fear to be more appropriate than not feeling fear. In fact, someone who was not frightened by such a snake would generally be considered rather odd. Thus, the so-called normative response is considered correct; anything else is, in a sense, wrong.

The appropriateness of any emotional reaction, therefore, can be ascertained only by seeing what others are feeling. This can apply to the type of emotion and also to the strength of the emotion. People clarify and evaluate their reactions by comparing them with others' reactions. Therefore, when we are uncertain about our feelings, we try to clarify them. When other people are the only useful source of information, we compare ourselves to them. Thus the desire for social comparison is another possible reason for affiliating. And, the more uncertain an individual is about his feelings, the more he will want to affiliate with others in order to reduce the uncertainty. How does this explain the greater affiliation with high fear?

When subjects are told they are going to be given a severe electric shock, they naturally become frightened; we have seen that this leads to greater affiliation than if they were less afraid. One reason for this heightened affiliation is the subject's desire to reduce his fear and his expectation that being with other subjects will accomplish this. However, though they know it is appropriate to be afraid, they are not sure how afraid they should be. Should they be terrified, moderately scared, or only slightly worried? They are in a state of some uncertainty as to what the appropriate emotional reaction is. In contrast, mild shocks arouse only a slight reaction in the first place and subjects are pretty sure this is about right. Therefore, according to the theory of social comparison, high-fear and uncertain subjects should have strong needs to affiliate in order to find out what others are feeling and thereby to evaluate and clarify their own reactions. Low-fear subjects experience little uncertainty and little need to affiliate.

hunger

This explanation in terms of social comparison is supported by the finding that the arousal of needs other than fear reduction can also increase affiliation. Whenever someone has a strong need, he tends to be uncertain about how he should be feeling. This uncertainty leads to a desire for social comparison and thus to affiliation. For example, Schachter (1959) demonstrated that a high degree of hunger causes people to want to affiliate more than a low degree of hunger. Subjects were called the night before they were to take part in the experiment and told that it would involve the effects of particular kinds of food deprivation on sensations. One group of subjects (classified as high hunger) was asked to fast for approximately twenty hours by omitting breakfast and lunch on the following day, and one group (medium hunger) was asked to fast for six hours by omitting lunch. A third group was also asked to omit breakfast and lunch, but when these people arrived for the experiment, they were presented with an array of foods and told to eat as much as they wished. The subjects in this group, who were then not at all hungry, were classified as low hunger.

All the subjects were put in individual rooms. The experimenter explained that the study actually involved four different tests. They were called binocular redundancy, visual diplacity, auditory peripherality, and aural angular displacement, all meaningless terms made up just for this study. The key points were that each subject would take part in only one test and two of the tests, the first and third, would be taken with another subject while the second and fourth would be taken alone. In addition, before each test there would be an adaptation period during which the subjects would be waiting either with the other subject, if they chose the first or third test, or alone. The subjects then ranked the tests in the order in which they would like to take them. Thus, if they wanted to wait with another subject, they could choose test one or three; if they wanted to wait alone, they could choose test two or four.

The results, shown in Table 2–2, indicate that high hunger increased the preference for being with another subject. Of the subjects in the high-hunger condition, 67 percent chose a test in which they would

TABLE 2–2
effect of hunger on affiliation

	PERCENTAGE OF SUBJECTS CHOOSING	
CONDITION	TOGETHER	ALONE
High hunger	67	33
Medium hunger	35	65
Low hunger	30	70

Source: Adapted from Schachter (1959).

wait with another subject; only 35 percent in the medium-hunger condition and 30 percent in the low-hunger condition chose one of those tests. Because moderate hunger is not a particularly unusual experience, it did not produce great uncertainty and did not lead to strong pressures toward affiliation for social comparison. By contrast, twenty hours of hunger, being unusual for these subjects, led to considerable uncertainty about feelings and therefore produced strong pressures toward affiliation for the purpose of social comparison.

affiliation with whom?

A more direct effect of the drive for social comparison can be seen when we examine whom the subjects want to affiliate with. One of the basic hypotheses of the theory is that people wish to compare themselves with others similar to them. The more similar they are, the stronger the drive for social comparison. For example, if a student is worried about a test and feels the need to find out how worried it is appropriate to be, does he want to talk to another student or the teacher? In most cases, another student. It would not help at all to find out that the teacher is not worried,

Fujihira/Monkmeyer

because the teacher does not have to take the test. Moreover, the student wants to compare himself to others who are similar in ability. A better student may not be worried, but that would tell the poorer student very little about what is appropriate for himself. In comparing, he prefers someone as close as possible to himself in ability, diligence, concern for grades, and so on. Such a student would give him the best information about how he should be feeling.

This leads to a clear prediction in terms of affiliation. To the extent that people affiliate for reasons of social comparison, they should have a stronger desire to affiliate with people who are similar to them than with people who are dissimilar. When they are concerned about evaluating their own emotions, they should particularly desire to affiliate with someone who is in their own situation.

Several studies have tested this prediction. Schachter (1959) used his standard procedure in which subjects were threatened with severe shock and then asked whether they would like to wait alone or with others. But for this experiment, the people with whom the subjects could wait were either other subjects who were waiting to take part in the study or students who had nothing to do with the experiment but who were waiting to talk to their advisers. In other words, one group of subjects was given a choice of waiting alone or with people who were similar to them; the other group was given a choice of waiting alone or with subjects who were quite different from them.

The results strongly supported the prediction from the theory of social comparison. Under high fear, subjects showed a strong preference for waiting with other subjects who were similar to them but did not want to wait with subjects who were different from them. However, in some sense the choice the subjects were given was not really fair. After all, there could have been considerable reluctance to walk into a room of students who were waiting to talk to their advisers, who may have known one another, and who certainly knew nothing about what the subject was doing.

A better test of the hypothesis was provided in a study by Zimbardo and Formica (1963), in which subjects were given the choice of waiting either with people who, like themselves, were about to take part in the study or with others who had just completed the study. The results of this test are more convincing because the people with whom the subject could wait were identical in both conditions, except that those who were about to take part in the study were presumably in the same emotional state as the subject making the choice whereas the others were in a different emotional state. Once again, the results supported the social-comparison hypothesis. Subjects showed a greater preference for waiting with those who were about to take part in the study than they did for waiting with those who had already been through the procedure. The more similar the others, the stronger was the drive to affiliate. Schachter has summarized these results: "Misery doesn't love just any company, it loves only miserable company."

Drawing by Charles Schulz; © 1965 United Feature Syndicate, Inc.

However, fear and anxiety appear to affect somewhat differently whom people affiliate with. One study (Firestone et al., 1973) replicated the Schachter and the Zimbardo and Formica results for fear but got exactly the opposite with anxiety. Using the standard techniques, they aroused either high fear or high anxiety. Then, as in Schachter's study, subjects were told they could spend some time either alone or with other people. For half of the subjects, the other people were subjects in the same study; for half, they were people waiting in a room for some entirely different purpose. The results are shown in Table 2–3. You can see that frightened subjects wanted to wait with people like themselves and avoided being with others who were different, but anxious subjects did the reverse—they sought out dissimilar people.

TABLE 2–3
fear, anxiety, and type of companionship

TYPE OF COMPANIONSHIP	AROUSED EMOTION	
Others	Fear	Anxiety
Similar	67%	37%
Dissimilar	45%	66%

Note: Percent choosing to wait with others rather than alone. Based on Firestone et al, 1973.

This finding makes sense if we take into account both motives—social comparison and the reduction of negative feelings. The fearful subjects seek out others to compare their levels of fear and perhaps also to reduce that fear; the anxious subjects avoid similar others because they think that will embarrass them and make them even more anxious since the others will know what they have just done. On the other hand, perhaps they feel that being with irrelevant people will reduce their anxiety, the notion being that sitting with these other, normal people, will provide a contrast with the weird activities they have just been engaged in. Whatever the exact explanation of these findings, this experiment does suggest that the characteristics of the group are very important. We still are uncertain what the effect would be if the members of the group were close friends rather than strangers. It might be that any negative or even strong feeling would cause most people to seek out their friends rather than be alone. For the moment, we do not know.

the role of uncertainty

The central assumption of the social comparison analysis is that uncertainty produces a need for comparing oneself to others. The more uncertain people feel about their reactions, the stronger should be this need for social comparison. Because the need for comparison leads to affiliation, the implication is that increasing uncertainty increases the desire to affiliate. A series of studies by Harold Gerard investigated this relationship between uncertainty and affiliation.

Gerard argued that merely arousing fear, as Schachter did, is not a very powerful way to make people want to compare themselves with others. The subjects in Schachter's experiment may not have been sure how frightened they should be, but they must have been sure that what they were feeling was appropriate (assuming they were frightened). In terms of the theory, the important factor influencing the strength of the desire for social comparison and consequently the drive toward affiliation should be the degree of uncertainty as to the appropriateness of one's feelings. When a person is extremely uncertain as to how he should be feeling, the drive for social comparison should be very high; the more certain he is that what he is feeling is appropriate, the weaker should be the drive for social comparison and the less the tendency to affiliate.

One critical factor affecting the degree of uncertainty is how much the person knows about his own feelings and the feelings of others. Thus, the more information he has about these feelings, the less the need for social comparison and, accordingly, the less the desire to affiliate. Gerard and Rabbie (1961) tested this hypothesis. The basic design of their experiment was similar to Schachter's. However, before the subjects made the choice of waiting either alone or with others, some of them were given information about their reactions and those of the other subjects and some were not. In this way, the subjects' degree of uncertainty was manipulated directly, so that its effect could be clearly observed.

The procedure for informing the subjects of their reactions was quite ingenious. Each subject was seated in a separate cubicle, and electrodes were attached to his ring finger and forehead. The experimenter explained that these measuring devices gave an accurate picture of the subject's "emotionality," that is, recorded how afraid he was. Subjects in one condition were shown four dials, supposedly corresponding to the subject being tested and three others. The subject saw that he registered 82 on a 100-point scale and that the other subjects were registering 79, 80, and 81, respectively. Thus, he learned what he and the others were feeling and that they were all feeling about the same amount of fear. In another condition, the subjects were shown only their own rating, and in a third condition, they were given no information. Then all the subjects were asked to state their preference for waiting alone or with others.

The analysis of uncertainty in terms of social comparison implies that the desire to affiliate should be affected by the degree of uncertainty people feel about the appropriateness of their own reactions. Because they are concerned about how they compare with others, when they know their own and others' reactions and also that they all are experiencing about the same amount of fear, there should be little uncertainty. When they have either no information or information about only their own reaction, there should be considerable uncertainty. As shown in Table 2–4 the results agreed with these expectations. The subjects who had been given information about themselves and others showed the least preference for waiting together, whereas the other groups did not differ appreciably in their desire to affiliate. In other words, removing uncertainty—and therefore the need for social comparison—reduced the tendency to affiliate. This finding strongly supports the theory that one reason for affiliating is social comparison.

Uncertainty is also affected by the ambiguity of the information the

TABLE 2–4
information, fear, and strength of desire to affiliate

	STRENGTH OF DESIRE TO AFFILIATE	
Condition	High Fear	Low Fear
No information	66.80	54.53
Information about self	70.50	64.12
Information about self and others	55.09	47.67

Note: Figures are ratings on a scale from 0 to 100.
Source: Adapted from Gerard and Rabbie (1961).

person has about his own feelings and those of others. We have seen that the amount of information is an important determinant of affiliation. In addition, the more difficult it is to understand the information,the more uncertain the person should be and the greater should be his tendency to affiliate in order to reduce this uncertainty. In another study by Gerard (1963), subjects were shown dials that either wavered wildly or remained steady. Thus they had either clear or ambiguous information about fear levels. If one knows how afraid he is and how afraid others are, there is little to be gained by social comparison and therefore little need to affiliate. If the information is vague (and a rapidly oscillating needle on a meter is vague), there is good reason to affiliate—to find out what this vague information means. The study showed that with steady dials, subjects who knew their own and others' scores had little desire to affiliate; with wavering dials, however, even subjects who knew their own and others' scores had a strong need to affiliate.

The effect of uncertainty on affiliation was demonstrated in a particularly elegant way in a recent study by Mills and Mintz (1972). The idea was to produce a physiological arousal by the use of a drug and to tell some subjects what had caused the arousal and not to tell others. Presumably those who knew that they had been aroused by the drug would feel little or no uncertainty about their emotional state, but those who did not know would feel uncertain as to what they were feeling and why. Therefore, those who knew that the drug had caused the arousal should feel little uncertainty and should not have a strong tendency to affiliate. Those who were aroused and did not know why should be quite uncertain and should have strong tendencies to affiliate. As you can see in Table 2–5, this is exactly what was found, once more supporting the notion that uncertainty is a major cause of the desire to affiliate.

TABLE 2–5
desire to affiliate related to arousal and knowledge about the arousal

CONDITION	STRENGTH OF AFFILIATIVE TENDENCY
Placebo—no arousal	4.7
Caffeine—informed (Aroused and told what produced it)	4.5
Caffeine—misinformed (Aroused but not told what produced it)	5.4

Source: Adapted from Mills and Mintz (1972).

All this evidence indicates that the need for social comparison is one reason why people affiliate. The major factor affecting the strength of this need seems to be the individual's degree of uncertainty about his feelings. The more uncertain he is, the more he can gain by comparing himself to others and, consequently, the greater the desire to affiliate.

the effect of affiliating

We have explained the effect of fear on affiliation in terms of two quite different mechanisms: the frightened person wants to affiliate in order to reduce his fear; he also wants to affiliate in order to compare his feelings with those of other people to discover if his feelings are appropriate. A somewhat separate but obviously related question is whether or not these two processes actually occur when affiliation is permitted. That is, does the individual become less afraid and does he compare his emotions?

If fear reduction is a rational reason for affiliating, waiting with other people should reduce fear even if the others are also afraid. If social comparison is a strong motive for affiliating, we would expect subjects to notice what others are feeling and to be concerned about the appropriateness of their own feelings. To the extent that their own feelings are different from those of the others (i.e., are inappropriate), subjects should tend to modify their feelings to make them less different. If everyone in the group does this, the feelings of the various members of the group should become more similar.

An experiment designed to test these two hypotheses was conducted by Wrightsman (1960). People who were very frightened were allowed to wait together or were forced to wait alone, and measures of fear level were taken before and after the waiting period. It was found that waiting in a group reduced fear more than waiting alone, with this apply-

Michael D. Sullivan

ing particularly to first-born subjects. The group also showed a strong tendency toward uniformity of feeling.

McDonald (1970) also demonstrated the fear-reducing effect of waiting with others. However, this occurred primarily for first-born subjects and surprisingly was most strong for those first-borns who said that they would prefer to wait alone but were forced to wait with others. Despite these somewhat perplexing findings, this study does provide more evidence that, in general, highly fearful subjects who wait in groups become less fearful. Thus both fear reduction and social comparison apparently do operate when people affiliate under conditions of high fear.

To summarize, people affiliate for many reasons. The desire may be partly instinctive; it is certainly the result of innate characteristics that make humans dependent on others during their early years. In part because of this forced association in childhood, we learn that affiliation is a way of satisfying needs, and it becomes a learned behavior that continues into adulthood. Throughout life, other people are the only or primary means of satisfying certain needs, and we therefore affiliate in order to obtain this satisfaction.

Within this general framework, there are a number of more specific factors that increase or decrease the desire to associate in a particular situation. Fear, anxiety, uncertainty, similarity of other people, possibility of verbal communication all affect the amount of affiliation. Explanations of these effects in terms of fear reduction and social comparison provide us with more detailed understanding of the phenomenon of affiliation.

SUMMARY

1. Affiliation may be instinctive, but there is no evidence to support this idea. On the other hand, our innate characteristics, especially the infant's long dependence on others for survival, forces us to affiliate.

2. Learning and the satisfaction of specific needs must also play a role in producing affiliation.

3. When people are afraid, they affiliate more. One reason for this is that people expect affiliation to reduce their fear. This is especially true of first-borns who rely on others for relieving their fear more than do later borns.

4. Fear increases affiliation, but anxiety reduces it.

5. Another explanation of the effect of fear is that people are uncertain how they should be feeling, and they affiliate in order to compare their reactions with those of others. This tendency to evaluate ourselves by comparison with others is an important psychological principle called social comparison. A high degree of hunger also causes affiliation for purposes of social comparison.

6. According to the theory of social comparison, people should prefer to compare themselves to others who are similar to them. The research supports this prediction.

7. The more uncertain people are of what they are feeling and whether their feeling is appropriate, the stronger the need for social comparison and the greater the affiliation.

8. When frightened people affiliate they become less afraid and more similar in their feelings.

SUGGESTIONS FOR ADDITIONAL READING

HARLOW, H. F. The nature of love. *American Psychologist,* 1958, 13, 673–85. Presents Harlow's work with monkeys. Though not directly relevant to affiliation, it gives a different approach to the question of why animals like to be together.

SARNOFF, I. & ZIMBARDO, P. G. Anxiety, fear and social affiliation. *Journal of Abnormal and Social Psychology,* 1961, 62, 356–63. The experiment discussed in detail in this chapter.

SCHACHTER, S. *The Psychology of Affiliation.* Stanford, Calif.: Stanford University Press, 1959. The most important work in this field. A nice example of systematic research on a particular problem.

3

social perception

affiliation is determined to some extent by one's expectations about interactions with other people and by one's knowledge of them. As we have seen, high anxiety reduces affiliation because one expects the interaction to be embarrassing and high fear increases affiliation only if the other people are in a similar emotional state. Since our knowledge of and expectations about others are determined in part by impressions we form of them, it is appropriate now to consider the phenomenon of person perception. A glance at someone's portrait or at someone passing on the street gives us some ideas about the kind of person he is; even hearing a name tends to conjure up pictures of what its owner is like. And when two people meet, if only for an instant, they form impressions of each other. With more contact, they form fuller and richer impressions that pervade their entire relationship. These impressions determine how they behave toward each other, how much they like each other, whether the two associate often, and so on. First impressions are not only the beginning of social interaction, they are one of its major determinants. Consider the following situations.

A murder trial hinges on the testimony of one witness. The jury's belief in this witness, which will determine their decision, depends almost entirely on the impression they form of him in his brief time on the witness stand. They examine his face, his features, his clothes, the quality of his voice, and his answers and try to decide what kind of person he is.

Two freshmen who are destined to be roommates arrive at college and meet for the first time. Each one's personality – how easy he is to get along with, how nice he is – will have an enormous effect on the other's life. In the first few minutes of their meeting, they try to form an impression of each other, because they know they will be spending a great deal of time together during the year. They try to find out as much about each other as they can so they can behave accordingly.

People use whatever information is available to form impressions of others—to make judgments about their personalities, to adopt hypotheses about the kind of persons they are. This chapter deals with this process of social perception—with the kinds of information on which it is based, with the factors that affect it, and with the question of whether or not it is accurate.

forming impressions

One important and apparently universal tendency is that people form extensive impressions of others on the basis of very limited information. Having seen someone or even his picture for only a few minutes, people tend to make judgments about a large number of his characteristics. Although ordinarily individuals are not overly confident of opinions formed in this way, they are generally willing to estimate the other's intelligence, age, background, race, religion, educational level, honesty, warmth, and so on. They would also tell us how much they thought they would like the other person if they could get to know him better and how much they like him at the moment. We shall discuss the accuracy of these impressions below; for the present, it is important merely to note that people form impressions quickly on the basis of very little information.

consistency

Moreover, given a few pieces of information, people tend to form consistent characterizations of others. In this respect, person perception is different from other kinds of perception. When people look at a house, a car, or any other complex object, they usually get a mixed impression. A house is large, is attractive, needs painting, has a nice dining room, is cold and unfriendly, and so on. In viewing a house, they do not force themselves to conclude that the whole house is warm or attractive. Objects do not have to be consistent. But when another person is the object of this kind of judgment, there is a tendency to view him as consistent, especially in an evaluative sense. A person is not seen as both good and bad, honest and dishonest, warm and frightening, considerate and sadistic. Even when there is contradictory information about someone, he usually will be perceived as consistent. The perceivers distort or rearrange the information to minimize or eliminate the inconsistency. This may also happen to some extent when people perceive objects, but it is particularly strong in person perception.

Naturally, people do not always form consistent impressions of another's personality. There are times when two pieces of information about an individual are so contradictory that most people are unable to fit them into a consistent pattern. In such a situation, some may succeed in forming a pattern. Others, unable to resolve the inconsistencies between the contradictory qualities, end up with a relatively unintegrated impression. However, there are strong tendencies toward forming a unified impression of another person, even though the attempt to do so is not always successful.

the centrality of evaluation

The evaluative dimension is the most important of a small number of basic dimensions that organize these unified impressions. This was shown in work by Osgood, Suci, and Tannenbaum (1957) on the so-called semantic differential. Subjects were given a list of pairs of words denoting opposite ends of various dimensions and were asked to indicate where on these dimensions they felt particular concepts, persons, objects, and ideas fell. The list consisted of such dimensions as happy-sad, hot-cold, and red-blue, and the items the subjects had to place consisted of all sorts of things from mother to boulder.

When the subjects' responses were collected, Osgood and his associates analyzed them to see if any clusters of adjectives emerged that could be considered basic dimensions on which all things had been described. They found that three dimensions accounted for a large percentage of the variation in all descriptions. By determining where subjects had placed a particular item on the dimensions of *evaluation* (good-bad), *potency* (strong-weak), and *activity* (active-passive), the experimenters needed little additional information in order to describe that item fully. To a large extent, all other dimensions (e.g., brave-scared, polite-blunt)

Monkmeyer/Mimi Forsyth

were aspects of these major dimensions rather than separate attributes. This phenomenon is most dramatic when applied to the perception of people. Impressions of people can also be described in terms of the three basic dimensions, but one dimension—evaluation—accounts for most of the variance in them and appears to be the main distinction made. Once we place someone on this dimension, much of the rest of our perception of him falls into place. A favorable or unfavorable impression in one context, at one meeting, extends to all other situations and to other seemingly unrelated characteristics.

Later research has used much more sophisticated mathematical techniques, and it has mainly served to emphasize these early results: evaluation is by far the most important underlying dimension of person perception. But it has also led to the identification of two distinct dimensions of evaluation in common use. Rosenberg, Nelson, and Vivekananthan (1968), using a procedure called multidimensional scaling, found people evaluated others in terms of their *social* and their *intellectual* qualities. Some of the traits which were most common are shown in Table 3–1. In a later study, Hamilton and Fallot (1974) found that presenting subjects with these more social attributes tended to affect judgments of a stimulus person's *likability*, whereas presenting them with some of the more intellectual attributes affected *respect* for the stimulus person.

TABLE 3–1
social and intellectual traits used in evaluation of people

EVALUATION	SOCIAL	INTELLECTUAL
Favorable	Helpful	Scientific
	Sincere	Determined
	Tolerant	Skillful
	Sociable	Intelligent
	Humorous	Persistent
Unfavorable	Unhappy	Foolish
	Vain	Frivolous
	Irritable	Wavering
	Boring	Unreliable
	Unpopular	Clumsy

Source: Rosenberg, Nelson, and Vivekananthan, 1968, p. 290.

These results suggest that people do evaluate others in a slightly more complex fashion than implied above. At least they sometimes think in terms of separate interpersonal and task-related qualities. It is important to keep in mind, however, that this distinction does not alter the basic point we are making here: people think primarily in terms of liking and disliking when they preceive other people. That is, evaluation is the main dimension in person perception.

One interesting implication of the centrality of evaluation is that certain traits imply more about an individual than others. For example, the pair of traits warm-cold appears to be associated with a great number of other characteristics, whereas the pair polite-blunt, under most circumstances, is associated with fewer. Traits that are highly associated with many other characteristics have been called *central* traits. In a classic demonstration of their importance, Asch (1946) gave subjects a description of an individual that contained seven traits—intelligent, skillful, industrious, warm, determined, practical, and cautious. Other subjects were given exactly the same list except the *cold* was substituted for *warm*. Both groups of subjects were then asked to describe the individual and also to indicate which of various pairs of traits he would most likely possess. The portraits elicited from the two groups were extremely different; substituting *cold* for *warm* made a substantial change in the subjects' impression of the other person. In another condition, instead of the warm-cold pair, Asch used polite-blunt. He found that substituting *polite* for *blunt* made considerably less difference in the overall picture formed by the subjects.

A later study by Kelley (1950) replicated this result in a more realistic setting. Students in psychology courses were given descriptions of a guest lecturer before he spoke. The descriptions included seven adjectives similar to those Asch used: half the students received a description containing the word *warm*, and the other half were told the speaker was *cold;* in all other respects their lists were identical. The lecturer then came into the class and led a discussion for about twenty minutes, after which the students were asked to give their impressions of him. The results are shown in Table 3–2. As in the Asch study, there were great differences between the impressions formed by students who were told he was warm and those who were told he was cold. In addition, those students who expected the speaker to be warm tended to interact with

TABLE 3–2
effect of "warm" and "cold" descriptions on ratings of other qualities

	INSTRUCTIONS[a]	
Quality	Warm	Cold
Self-centered	6.3	9.6
Unsociable	5.6	10.4
Unpopular	4.0	7.4
Formal	6.3	9.6
Irritable	9.4	12.0
Humorless	8.3	11.7
Ruthless	8.6	11.0

[a]The higher the rating, the more the person was perceived as having the quality.

Source: Adapted from Kelley (1950).

him more freely and to initiate more conversations with him. Thus, the different descriptions affected not only the students' impressions of the other person, but also their behavior toward him.

Since Kelley's study, there have been various criticisms of the notion of central traits. Careful work has shown that the centrality of a particular trait depends to some extent on the context in which it is used. When someone is described as obedient, weak, shallow, unambitious, and vain, it does not matter much whether he is warm or cold—warmth does not affect these other characteristics. Similarly, *polite* or *blunt* can have a considerable effect on the significance of certain other qualities even though generally it is not important. The significance of a particular dimension also depends to some extent on the characteristics the judges are supposed to determine. If they were asked to decide how sociable or popular an individual is from a list of other traits, the dimension of warmth would be important because warmth is highly related to sociability and popularity. But warmth has relatively little effect on other qualities and would be less central if the judges were asked to rate the individual on these.

This work gives us more detailed knowledge of the factors that determine the centrality of a particular characteristic. The dimension warm-cold is still considered central, but we now understand that centrality depends on the context and the responses required. When a dimension is called central, we mean it has a considerable effect in a large number of contexts and on a large number of responses.

averaging versus adding

How do people form an impression of someone when they have many pieces of information about him? One basic issue is whether they tend to add or average the facts they know. As we shall discuss in more detail in Chapter five, traits can be rated in terms of how positive they are. For example, sincerity is generally considered an extremely favorable quality and, accordingly, people might usually assign it the maximum value (+3); determination only moderately favorable (+1); and dishonesty very unfavorable (−3). The question is how traits are combined to form an overall evaluation. If an individual is known to have one highly positive trait and one slightly positive trait, how positively is he rated? The averaging model suggests that someone who is rated sincere (+3) and also determined (+1) would receive an evaluation that was approximately an average of the two traits, that is, he would be considered moderately positive (+2). Thus, learning of a slightly positive trait in someone whom we already know has a highly positive trait reduces the overall evaluation, even though both pieces of information are positive. In contrast, an additive model suggests that the two pieces of information would be summed and the final evaluation would be higher (+4) than an evaluation based on either one alone.

Some sample predictions of the two models are shown in Table 3–3. The first trait set includes three highly positive traits. The second adds three moderately positive ones. According to the averaging model, this should reduce the overall evaluation; according to the additive model, it should increase it. The evidence indicates that in such situations most people average. The third set adds three highly positive traits to the original three. Averaging would result in the same evaluation as that with the original set; adding would result in a higher evaluation.

TABLE 3–3
averaging versus adding in impression formation

	PREDICTIONS OF RELATIVE LIKING	
Trait Sets	Averaging Model	Adding Model
Sincere (+3), intelligent (+3), warm (+3)	+3	+3
Sincere (+3), intelligent (+3), warm (+3), persistent (+1), cautious (+1), perfectionist (+1)	+2	+4
Sincere (+3), intelligent (+3), warm (+3), friendly (+3), humorous (+3), loyal (+3)	+3	+6

Note: All predictions are in relative rather than absolute terms. Thus, to make the models comparable, the adding model's prediction for the first situation is +3 rather than +9; for the second situation, +4 rather than +12; and so on. The important point is that the averaging model predicts, for example, that the first and third situations would produce equal evaluations, whereas the adding model predicts that the third situation would produce an evaluation twice as positive as the first.

Although there has been a considerable amount of research on this problem, a final answer is not yet available. Norman Anderson, in a series of careful and precise experiments (1959, 1965, etc.), produced strong evidence to support the averaging model. He found that when a piece of information that is only moderately favorable is combined with a previous evaluation that had been based on very favorable information, the overall evaluation did not increase and could even decrease. Similarly, two strongly negative traits produced a more negative evaluation than two strongly negative plus two moderately negative traits. On the other hand, there is some evidence (Fishbein and Hunter, 1964) that one's knowing five strongly positive characteristics about another individual makes him somewhat more positive than knowing only two positive characteristics about him. Anderson (1968, etc.) has proposed a resolution of this contradictory evidence in terms of a weighted averaging model. He presented data showing that people form an overall impression by averaging all traits but giving more weight to polarized (highly positive or highly negative) traits. This model appears to explain most situations, although under some circumstances adding does occur. It also seems to account for activity judgments, but neither works particularly well for potency (Hamilton and Huffman, 1971). Thus, one's overall impression seems to be determined by a combination of adding and averaging, with averaging explaining most situations.

CONTEXT The averaging principle has some important exceptions, however. For one thing, the context also affects judgments. The contribution of any given attribute to our overall impression of a stimulus person will depend on the rest of the information we have about him. Knowing that someone is "intelligent," generally quite a good attribute, will not have as favorable an impact on our impression of a "cold, ruthless" person as it will on our impression of a "warm, caring" person. The context is different, and so is the impact of the trait. These context effects are closely related to the tendency to form consistent impressions. Good traits go together. Someone who is warm is also seen as positive in other respects, thus producing a consistent picture. They cause a person's traits to be distorted to produce consistency within an impression (Kaplan, 1971). This does not mean we only perceive people as good or as bad. But it does mean that we distort incoming information in that direction.

The mechanism producing such context effects is a matter of some debate. Asch (1946), working out of the *gestalt* tradition, suggested that we form a different overall concept of the person every time part of it is altered. The whole, he suggested, is different from the sum of its parts. The implication is that the *meaning* of any given trait changes, depending upon its context. "Intelligence" in a cold, ruthless person could be threatening, potentially hostile, and destructive. In a warm, caring person, "intelligence" might be expected to contribute to empathy, to insight, and to the ability to give to another person.

Anderson (1966), more of a learning theorist, suggested that the context simply provided a *generalized halo effect*. The value of the attribute would be a weighted average of the intrinsic, absolute value of it, and the value of the context. In this example, if "intelligent" is a +2, its value in this context would be an average of 2 times the value of cold-ruthless, or of +2 times the value of warm-caring.

A good bit of research has been done on these two quite different ideas. One way to approach the controversy is to determine whether in fact the attribute has different interpretations in different contexts (Ostrom, 1967). Hamilton and Zanna (1974) tested this directly by checking whether the connotations of a particular trait changed when placed in different contexts. They found evidence for just such shifts in meaning with context. For example, in a positive context the word "proud" bore the connotation of "confident." In a negative context, it connoted "conceited." Similarly, Wyer (1974) found that context determined which other attributes were implied by a given trait. His study went one step further, and showed additionally that these implied attributes themselves bore evaluations highly related to the context. To use the example above, the quality ("conceited") of the original trait ("proud") implied by a negative context itself bore a negative evaluation.

Such studies show that contextual effects are partly determined by a *shift-of-meaning* phenomenon. Nevertheless, this body of research as a whole is very convincing in leading us to think that the major principle accounting for impression formation is the weighted average. Researchers in this area share a broad consensus that an averaging principle is the dominant, though probably not the only principle at work in impression formation.

THE NEGATIVITY EFFECT Another exception is that positive and negative traits are not treated exactly alike. Although people seem to average the traits they hear about to arrive at a complete impression, they weight negative information more heavily than they do positive information. That is, a negative trait affects an impression more than does a positive trait, everything else being equal. It follows that a positive impression is easier to change than a negative one (Hodges, 1974; Warr, 1974). Subjects are more confident of evaluations based on negative traits than of those based on positive traits (Hamilton & Zanna, 1972). And it also follows that the averaging principle does not hold for negative traits quite as well as it does for positive traits. This difference is particularly noticeable with the more extreme negative traits. Instead of simply being averaged in, the way moderately negative (or any positive) traits are, they seem to have a "blackball" effect: one extremely negative trait produces an extremely negative impression, no matter what other traits the person possesses (Anderson, 1965). When we are told that a prominent public leader is "a crook," our evaluation of him becomes quite

Monkmeyer/David Strickler

negative, regardless of what else we know about him. But if we are told he is "impatient," we will just average that mildly negative quality in with whatever else we know about him.

There are two main explanations, at the moment, for this negativity effect. As we will see below, positive evaluations of other people are much more common than negative evaluations. Negative traits, being more unusual, are therefore more distinctive. In a simple perceptual sense, then, a negative trait stands out, the way an unusual deformity or bright clothing or unusual size stands out. People may then simply attend more to those negative qualities, and thus give them more weight in arriving at an overall impression. The other possibility is based on an idea in attribution theory, which we will discuss in the next chapter. Jones and Davis (1965) suggested that behaviors low in social desirability (that is, unconventional, bad behaviors) are normally taken by other people to be more indicative of one's true personality than are more conventional, ordinary behaviors. Someone who robs a bank is regarded as expressing his true personality. He would be regarded as truly a criminal. However, writing a check in the bank is something that anyone could do, no matter what his personality. Such deeds would not inform us about his personality.By this explanation, negative traits like "dishonest" might generally be regarded as "truer" indicators of the person's personality than positive traits such as "friendly." Either way, the negativity effect seems to be a fairly reliable one, and dependent at least in part on the more uncommon nature of negative traits and evaluations.

accuracy of judgments

Most people assume they can determine other people's emotions and know what their personalities are like. But how accurate is person perception? One argument is that people must be reasonably accurate in their perception of others in order for society to function as smoothly as it does. After all, we interact with other people hundreds of times every day and most of these interactions seem to require accurate judgments of others. Since the interactions proceed without serious conflict or mistake, person perception must be fairly accurate.

It is generally no more difficult to judge the height of a man than it is to judge the height of a bookcase, a car, or a camel. The same is true of weight, color, and even attractiveness. We make these kinds of judgments of all objects and we make them fairly accurately. The characteristic that distinguishes person perception from all other kinds is that we infer that individuals have internal states—feelings, emotions, and personalities. The bookcase obviously has none of these; the car has them only in advertisements and fantasies; perhaps the camel has them, but we usually do not worry about camels. However, we do attempt to make judgments of the internal states of human beings. We look at people and perceive them as being angry, happy, sad, or frightened. We form an impression of another person and think of him as warm, honest, and sincere. We also make judgments about such internal characteristics as a person's attitudes toward various issues. We guess whether he is a Republican or a Democrat, religious or nonreligious, promiscuous or not promiscuous.

As long as the appropriate cues are provided, it is fairly easy to make judgments about somebody's role. We recognize that the woman standing behind a counter in a clothing store is a salesperson and we ask her how much a particular item costs. The man in the blue suit with the gun strapped to his side is a policeman and we treat him accordingly. The man rushing down a platform toward a train is obviously in a hurry and we get out of his way to make it easier for him to catch the train. The contexts in which we see the people enable us to make accurate assumptions about their roles and sometimes even their emotions and feelings.

But under most circumstances, judgments of internal states are extremely difficult. The internal state cannot be observed directly—it must be inferred from whatever cues are available. Therefore, we must restate our aim in studying the accuracy of judgments and the cues on which they are based. We are interested primarily in determining the kinds of judgments individuals can make of internal states and the cues on which these judgments of emotion, personality, and attitude are based.

How a person is feeling—whether he is happy or afraid, horrified or disgusted—is a type of judgment we often make. Therefore, much of the work on the accuracy of person perception has focused on the recognition of emotions. It began in 1872 when Darwin asserted, on the basis of his evolutionary theory, that facial expressions universally conveyed the same emotional states. Since then, experimenters have been studying how accurately people can make inferences about emotional states. The basic procedure is to present a subject with a stimulus representing another person and ask the subject to identify the other's emotion. For some studies, trained actors portrayed a number of different emotions and pictures were taken of their expressions. One picture was chosen for each emotion. These were then shown to subjects, who were asked to indicate what emotion was depicted. Some of these pictures are shown in Figure 3–1.

Other studies used different kinds of stimuli. In some (e.g., Boring and Titchener, 1923), subjects were simply shown drawings of a person's face, each of which was supposed to represent an emotion. Other experiments have employed motion pictures (Cline, 1964) and, occasionally, real people (Sherman, 1927). Subjects have also been presented with disembodied voices (Davitz, 1964) and voices from which the content has been removed and the emotion supposedly left in (Starkweather, 1956).

In addition, the emotions the stimuli were supposed to portray

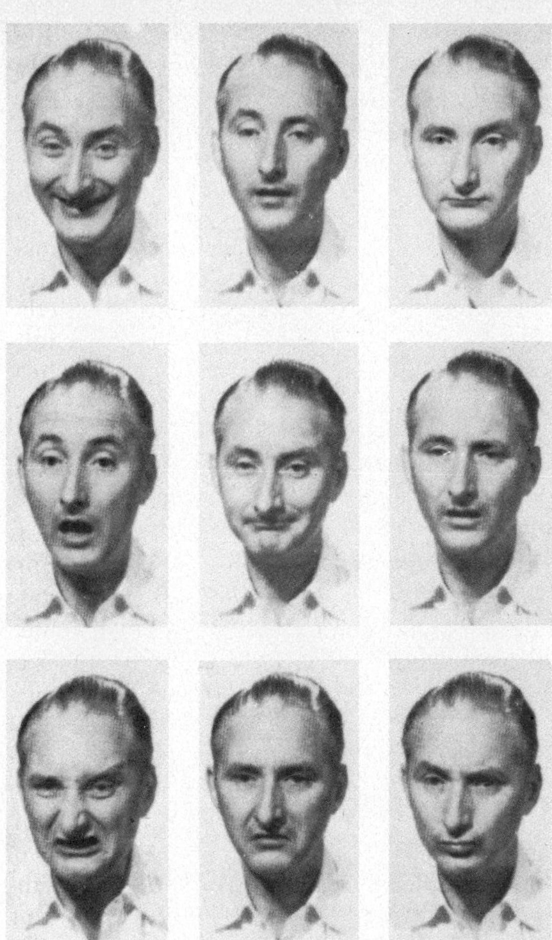

FIGURE 3–1
Examples of stimuli used in the study of the perception of emotions. The photographs illustrate expressions posed to portray the emotions listed. (You might try to identify them before looking at the key below.)

Top (left to right): Glee, passive adoration, complacency. Middle: amazement, optimistic determination, dismay. Bottom: rage, mild repugnance, puzzlement. (From Hastorf et al., 1966.)

were produced in a variety of ways. In one study (Langfeld, 1918), they were drawn by an artist who was trying to represent faces showing particular emotions. In other studies, actors expressed emotions (Ruckmick, 1921), emotions were produced in the laboratory by exposing people to situations designed to arouse them (Sherman, 1927), or emotions were produced in actual situations (Munn, 1940).

Given this wide range of techniques, it is perhaps not surprising that the results have also been varied. A number of studies (e.g., Guilford, 1929; Sherman, 1927) indicated that people cannot judge emotions any better than they would by chance. But other studies (Langfeld, 1918; Munn, 1940; Thompson and Meltzer, 1964) have shown that subjects label emotions consistently and accurately.

Which emotions people are asked to determine is an important variable; some are extremely difficult, whereas others are relatively easy. Although individuals may not be able to discriminate perfectly among all emotions, they can discriminate among groups of emotions. Woodworth (1938) suggested that emotions can be arranged on a six-point continuum, with confusion between any two emotions being inversely related to the distance they are from each other. The six groups of emotions are

1. love, happiness, mirth
2. surprise
3. fear, suffering
4. anger, determination
5. disgust
6. contempt

Apparently people are quite adept at distinguishing emotions in categories that are three, four, or five points apart—they rarely confuse happiness with disgust or contempt with surprise. But they are much poorer at discriminating emotions that are closer on the continuum and find it almost impossible to discriminate emotions in the same category or only one group away. There is also some evidence, collected by Thompson and Meltzer (1964), that even on this continuum some emotions are more consistently identified than others. Happiness, love, fear, and determination tend to be relatively easy to discriminate, whereas disgust, contempt, and suffering are much more difficult.

The lack of consistency in the results of work on the accuracy of person perception is due in part to the methodology used in the research and in part to confusion about the issue. The central issue is whether there is a particular facial expression or body posture for each emotion. Does everyone who is feeling a particular emotion have the same facial expression or are there great variations among people in how they manifest emotions? Is it possible, for example, that one person's expression of disgust is another person's expression of contentment? (See Figure 3–2.)

The more general question concerns the determination of a correct identification. When an artist tries to draw someone experiencing disgust

FIGURE 3–2
The people pictured here have very different expressions on their faces and appear to be experiencing different emotions. Yet they were all in the same photograph, which was taken while they were witnessing a rally. They may, in fact, be feeling different emotions. On the other hand, they may simply be expressing the same emotion in different ways.

or an actor tries to portray disgust, is it appropriate to say that disgust is the correct identification? Perhaps the artist or the actor did not do a good job. Or perhaps their impression of what disgust looks like is different from other people's. In a study by Langfeld (1918), subjects were shown an artist's drawings of various emotions and only 32 percent of the subjects agreed with the artist's labels. However, other subjects were shown what the artist had called the picture; when they were asked whether they agreed or disagreed, 75 percent accepted the artist's labels. Thus, the artist's picture could represent, say, disgust, but it could also represent other emotions. When subjects were told it was supposed to represent disgust, most of them agreed that it could; however, when they were asked for their own label, most chose other emotions.

Nevertheless, it appears that Darwin was approximately correct after all: A given facial expression appears to convey approximately the same emotion throughout the world. Ekman, Sorenson, and Friesen (1969) found that college-educated subjects in Brazil, the United States, Argentina, Chile, and Japan labeled the same faces with the same emotion words. However, all these subjects might have simply been exposed to a common set of television portrayals of facial expression from which they might all have learned a common set of Hollywood conventions for how best to communicate emotions through facial expressions.

Ekman and Friesen (1971) repeated the study with natives of New Guinea who had seen no movies, understood neither English nor Pidgin, had not lived in any of the Western settlement or government towns, and had never worked for a Caucasian. Presumably these subjects had had no visual contact with conventional Western facial expression of emotions. Each of these subjects was given a brief story depicting an emotion, such as, for "sadness," "His child has died, and he feels very sad." Then he was given one photograph supposedly depicting that emotion, and two pictures depicting other emotions. On the average, adults chose the correct picture more than 80 percent of the time. Children were only asked to choose between one correct and one incorrect picture, and they averaged 90 percent correct. This does not prove there are no cultural differences in the facial expression of emotion, but it does provide evidence of universals that transcend cultural boundaries.

factors affecting judgments

Although there has been a great deal of work on the judgment of personality and emotions, it has not provided a definitive answer to the question of whether people can make accurate judgments of others. Instead, this research has demonstrated forcefully that in making these judgments people are influenced by a wide variety of factors relating to themselves, the person being judged, and the situation in which the judgment is made.

the state of the judges

A series of studies has demonstrated that how judges are feeling and their current life situation influence their judgment of others to some extent. As early as 1932, Bartlett showed that men who were liable to be drafted into the military rated pictures of military officers as more threatening and indicating greater command ability than did men who were not draftable. Murray (1933) had girls judge photographs of faces after some had played a frightening game. Those who had played the game judged the photographs to be more menacing than those who had not played the game. And in 1957, Feshbach and Singer found that subjects who were frightened because they were expecting electric shocks perceived other people as more fearful than did subjects who were not frightened. Thus, as might be expected, a judge's needs and feelings greatly influence his perception of other people – he tends to project his own feelings onto others and to be more sensitive to particular characteristics because of his own emotional state.

perceptual biases

HALO EFFECT Several biases seem to influence impression formation for most people most of the time. As we said earlier, most judgments of other people are made primarily in terms of good and bad. Then all their other qualities are deduced from this decision. This is called the *halo effect* because one who is labeled *good* is surrounded with a positive aura and all good qualities are attributed to him. The converse (what should be called a "negative halo" or "forked-tail" effect) is that one who is labeled *bad* is seen as having all bad qualities.

A good illustration of these effects is provided in a study by Dion, Berscheid, and Walster (1972). Subjects were given pictures of people who were either physically attractive, unattractive, or average. They then rated each of the people on a number of characteristics that have nothing to do with attractiveness. As you can see in Table 3–4, the attractive person was rated highest and the unattractive person lowest on almost all characteristics. Just because they looked good and therefore had one positive trait, they were perceived as having other positive traits (conversely, those who looked bad were perceived as having other bad traits).

LOGICAL ERROR There is a strong tendency for people to infer from the presence of one trait in an individual that he has various other traits. Knowing someone is intelligent causes most people to expect him also to be imaginative, clever, active, conscientious, deliberate, and reliable. Knowing someone is inconsiderate leads most people to expect him also to be irritable, boastful, cold, hypocritical, etc. As Bruner, Shapiro, and

TABLE 3–4
the "halo" and "forked-tail" effects illustrated by ratings of attractive, unattractive, and average persons

TRAIT ASCRIPTION[a]	UNATTRACTIVE STIMULUS PERSON	AVERAGE STIMULUS PERSON	ATTRACTIVE STIMULUS PERSON
Social desirability of the stimulus person's personality	56.31	62.42	65.39
Occupational status of the stimulus person	1.70	2.02	2.25
Marital competence of the stimulus person	.37	.71	1.70
Parental competence of the stimulus person	3.91	4.55	3.54
Social and professional happiness of the stimulus person	5.28	6.34	6.37
Total happiness of the stimulus person	8.83	11.60	11.60
Likelihood of marriage	1.52	1.82	2.17

[a]The higher the number, the more socially desirable, the more prestigious an occupation, etc., the stimulus person is expected to possess.

Source: Dion et al., "What Is Beautiful Is Good," *Journal of Personality and Social Psychology*, 1972, *24*, 285–90. Reprinted by permission of the publisher.

Tagiuri (1958), who collected these data, point out, these inferences are not derived logically from the given trait; they are based on the individual's assumptions about personality. Intelligence does not necessarily denote activity, nor does inconsiderateness denote irritability. The tendency to make these assumptions is sometimes called the *logical error*, because people see certain traits as going together and assume that someone who has one of them also has the others.

This tendency has been explained in terms of implicit personality theories. We all categorize people into a limited number of types, and when we meet anyone we do not know, we try to fit him into one of these molds. If we discover that he has some of the traits supposedly characteristic of a particular type, we assign him to that type. Once he is so stereotyped, of course, he is assumed to have all the other traits belonging to that type. In this way, our implicit theories about personality influence our perceptions of others. As will be indicated later, sometimes these "theories" are quite common, and sometimes quite unique to the specific perceiver. Our point here is to emphasize the common, consensual aspect of them.

POSITIVITY BIAS Finally, there is a general tendency to express positive evaluations of people more often than negative evaluations. This has been called the *leniency effect* or sometimes the *positivity bias* (Bruner and Tagiuri, 1954; Sears and Whitney, 1973). Ratings of stimulus persons in laboratory studies are consistently positive, on the average, whether the subject knows the person or not. Similarly, public opinion polls show that political leaders are consistently rated positively more often than they are evaluated negatively. In the Gallup polls done in the United States over the period 1935 to 1975, 76 percent of the 535 persons and groups asked about were evaluated favorably. Similarly, in surveys done during the 1960s and 1970s throughout the United States by the University of Michigan Survey Research Center, 76 percent of the 50 politicians asked about were evaluated favorably. And in California during the same period, the California poll found that 84 percent of the 263 politicians asked about were evaluated favorably (Sears, 1976). Positive evaluations of other people are rated as more pleasant, are learned more readily, are expected in the absence of any specific information about them, and are expected to result from any changes in interpersonal relationships. When change in an impression does occur, it generally occurs toward more positive evaluations, everything else being equal.

One hypothesis about the origins of the positivity bias is that it reflects a particular leniency we have in evaluating our fellow human beings. If the positivity bias has specifically to do with the evaluations of people, then it should not show up when impersonal objects are being evaluated. That is, there should be a positivity bias in person perception, but not in object perception. The problem with testing this idea is that usually the stimuli themselves are so different it is hard to compare them. You could compare the evaluations of a rock with evaluations of one's mother, but they differ in so many other ways that it would be difficult to attribute any difference in evaluation just to the fact that one is an impersonal object and the other a person.

To try to make this object versus person comparison in a fair way, Sears (1976) turned to evaluations of professors. UCLA uses a standard form for evaluating instruction, which has comparable items for the evaluation of the instructor (a personal stimulus) and for the evaluation of the course (an impersonal object): "What is your overall rating of the instructor" and "What is your overall rating of the course?" Presumably, both sets of ratings concern approximately the same experience—a specific course the student took. But in one case, mostly the impersonal aspects of it were being rated; i.e., the books, exams, class meetings, as well as the instructor. In the other case, only the personal aspect of it was rated in the person of the instructor.

Confirming the positivity bias, 96 percent of a one-sixth sample of professors in the 1974–75 school year (n = 218) were rated positively (i.e., above "average"). And the personal stimulus, the instructor, was rated higher than the impersonal object, the course, in 74 percent of the cases (in 7 percent they were equal, and 19 percent of the time the course was rated higher). There was additional evidence that the positivity bias is like a "bonus" positive rating that is awarded when a specific individual is being evaluated, and is not awarded to impersonal objects.

These forms also had items dealing with a variety of specific aspects of the course, such as the exams, breadth or organization of the course, freedom to ask questions and interact, and so on. The rating of the course as a whole was approximately at the average of these other items, suggesting (as Anderson would expect) that students essentially averaged their evaluations of the course's many separate attributes to arrive at an overall impression. But the instructor rating was higher than the average of these other items in 84 percent of the cases. This suggests that people add some positive bonus when they are evaluating some specific person to the average of the impersonal information they are given. Perhaps simply being a specific, concrete human being, with whom we can identify and empathize, makes us give a person a little break when we evaluate him.

ASSUMED SIMILARITY There is a strong tendency for people to assume that others are similar to them. This is particularly true when they are known to be similar in demographic features such as age, race, national origin, and socioeconomic status, but also occurs when they differ considerably on these characteristics. If one likes large parties, he tends to assume that other people like large parties; if he is aggressive, he assumes other people are also aggressive; and so on. In Freud's terminology, this would be called *projection*—individuals attribute their own characteristics to others.

Monkmeyer/Mimi Forsyth

There are two related results of this phenomenon. First, the individual rates another more similar to himself than he actually is; he distorts the other's personality to make it more like his own. For example, Schiffenbauer (1974) found some evidence that varying the subject's own emotion, by playing either a comic or a disgusting tape, would affect the subject's judgment of others' facial expressions in photographs; the subject would tend to interpret others' faces as expressing the emotion he himself was experiencing. Second, this distortion usually is so great that his rating of the other person corresponds more to his own personality (as he sees it) than to the other's personality (as the other sees it). As we shall discuss in more detail below, this means that perception of another person is often influenced more by what the rater is like than by what the person being rated is like.

Another result of this tendency to project is that people are more accurate in rating others who are similar to them, not because they are more perceptive with such people, but because they always rate people similar to themselves, so when they finally find one who is, they are naturally correct. Paradoxically, perhaps the most interesting implication of this phenomenon is that one's rating of others may be as good a measure of his own personality as it is of the other person's—or even a better one. It may actually be a better measure of his personality than is his own self-rating, because he is less likely to be concerned about concealing faults or exaggerating strengths. Therefore, if we want to find out what someone is like, the best procedure may be to ask him to rate other people.

knowledge of the other

A factor that increases the accuracy of judgments of personality and behavior but seems to have little to do with person perception is one's knowledge of the group or subculture to which the person to be judged belongs. Members of subcultures (e.g., jazz musicians, baseball players, college students) share, to some extent, certain characteristics, values, and behaviors. If one knows the characteristics shared by a group, he is better able to make an accurate guess as to a member's responses. A rating of a person in terms of the stereotype for his group will be accurate insofar as the stereotype is accurate and the person judged conforms to that stereotype. Thus, knowledge of a person's group increases accuracy, but this increase may have nothing to do with person perception.

To demonstrate this phenomenon, Gage (1952) had subjects rate people whom they had never seen but who were identified as college students. Then he let the subjects see the students and rate them again. He found that the ratings made before the subjects saw the students were more accurate than those made afterward. Evidently, the subjects' stereotype of college students provided a better estimate of the students than did their visual impressions.

prejudice and accuracy of perception

For some time, a controversy raged as to whether or not some people were better than others at identifying ethnic groups. In particular, some anti-Semites claimed to have an unerring eye for a Jewish face. And an American pilot in Vietnam thought he could tell a Vietcong from a loyal South Vietnamese from 5,000 feet in the air. The same kind of confidence seems to imbue people having other prejudices—they all feel they are specially adept at identifying members of the group toward which they are prejudiced. Recent research indicates that prejudiced people, while not much better at picking out members of the group in question, have a great deal more *confidence* in their judgments than do nonprejudiced persons (Dorfman, Keeve, and Saslow, 1971).

In terms of our discussion, their confidence is not entirely misplaced. We have seen that to the extent a stereotype is accurate and the person to be judged is characteristic of his group, knowledge of the stereotype does increase accuracy of judgment. It is theoretically possible for this to work in reverse. If one is familiar with the stereotype of a particular ethnic group and if the stereotype is accurate, one's accuracy in identifying members of the group should increase. Thus, anti-Semites,

"You are trustworthy, loyal, helpful, friendly, courteous, kind, obedient, cheerful, thrifty, brave, clean, reverent."

Drawing by Chas. Addams; © 1936, 1964 The New Yorker Magazine, Inc.

who presumably are concerned about Jews and have strong stereotypes about them, could be better at identifying them. However, it would seem that members of the ethnic group would be even more familiar with the group characteristics (if any existed) and therefore would be even better at this kind of identification.

But accuracy does not depend primarily on knowledge of a stereotype—the critical factor is the validity of the stereotype. Since most stereotypes tend to be somewhat inaccurate, they are usually of doubtful help in identifying members of particular groups. If one believes that most Swedes have blonde hair, it will probably help him identify Swedes because this is a fairly accurate picture. Although not all Swedes are blonde, a high percentage are. But, believing that all Jews wear glasses will be little help because Jews and non-Jews do not differ appreciably in this respect. Obviously, knowing anything correct about someone or some group tends to make our perceptions more accurate, but having false information or misconceptions does not.

Although this distinction between accurate and false stereotypes may seem evident, it is often obscured. Many people feel that all stereotypes are bad, that they automatically indicate prejudice and produce inaccuracies. Of course, it is true that people should not be treated in accordance with a stereotype just because they belong to a particular group; as much as possible we should treat people as individuals. However, if we have no knowledge about a person, knowledge of the groups he belongs to often helps us perceive him more accurately. If we know that someone is a twenty-year-old male college student, we are probably correct in assuming that he would prefer a football game to a horticultural exhibit and rock and roll to revival music. We might be wrong in these assumptions because not all twenty-year-old male college students have these tastes, but we are more likely to be right because most of them do. Often we must interact with someone before getting to know him, and these interactions can be smoother if we rely to some extent on what we know about the groups to which he belongs. The danger with such reliance is that the individual may be atypical, the stereotype may be wrong in general, and we may never bother to find out what the person is like as an individual simply because our superficial knowledge enables us to interact with him reasonably well.

the perceiver and the perceived

Although, as we have said, the three basic dimensions of the semantic differential explain a great deal of the variance in person perception (with the evaluative dimension accounting for most of the variance), there are obviously more than three dimensions. We also care about specific qualities of individuals, such as whether they have a good sense of humor, whether they are good athletes, and whether they are beautiful.

In order to give a complete description of anyone, we would want to use many such dimensions.

One of the interesting aspects of person perception is that different people organize their perceptions of others along different dimensions. For example, one person might always describe others in terms of their sense of humor, their physical attractiveness, their warmth, their honesty, and their intelligence. Someone else might consider these characteristics to be relatively unimportant and instead would emphasize the individual's diligence, aggressiveness, religiosity, and athletic prowess. This was illustrated in a study by Dornbusch et al. (1965), in which each child at a camp was asked to describe, in his own words, every other child. The children were provided with no scales or specific questions but were simply asked to give free descriptions of the others. These descriptions were then analyzed in two ways—in terms of the characteristics on which each child was described and in terms of the characteristics each child used in making his own descriptions. The experimenters could then examine the characteristics in terms of those used in each perception or in terms of those used by each perceiver.

When the data were examined in this way, a clear pattern emerged. It might have been thought that some children would have a particularly outstanding characteristic, such as a sense of humor or aggressiveness, and that everyone would describe them in these terms. This was not the case. There was no agreement among the descriptions on which dimensions were important for a particular child. Many different characteristics were used to describe each child, and those used to describe one did not differ from those used to describe everyone else. But the situation was entirely different for the children writing the descriptions. Here great consistency emerged. Each child tended to use the same characteristics no matter whom he was describing. The children differed among themselves as to which characteristics they used, but each of them had his favorites or those he considered important and used them for virtually all his descriptions. So it was found that the dimensions used depended much more on who was perceiving than on who was being perceived.

This is a further indication that each person has his own view of personality and of the qualities that are important in other people. This has been called *implicit personality theory* (Schneider, 1973), to underline the fact that each of us carries around some theory of personality that helps us form coherent impressions of other people. Some research shows, indeed, that these implicit assumptions about how different traits go together can have a profound biasing effect upon our observations of other people. Berman and Kenny (1976) have termed this the *correlational bias;* we each have certain assumptions about which traits normally go together (i.e., are correlated with each other) in people. So when we see one trait in a person, we assume the other is there too—whether or not it really is. Berman and Kenny have shown that this phenomenon produces biased observations of other people's personalities, even when their personalities are actually described in quite detailed terms. We just automatically impose our own implicit personality theory on the stimulus person, whether it fits them or not.

Sometimes this "theory" is rather commonly shared, as for instance the "theory" that a warm person is probably also generous. But it may also be quite unique to the specific perceiver, as in the Dornbusch study of children cited above.

So each of us tends to organize the world and, in particular, other humans in our own terms and to use these terms for all our perceptions. Whenever we meet someone, we form an impression of him in terms of the characteristics we consider important. Regardless of what the other person is really like, our impression tends to be organized along the same dimensions of personality.

One implication of this is that it is difficult to get accurate or meaningful descriptions of someone unless we allow the person giving the description to provide his own terminology. Although it is always more convenient to provide subjects with a series of scales on which to make ratings, the subjects may do poorly because they are not accustomed to using the chosen scales. Or perhaps the scales are similar to those used by one subject but not by another. The first subject would be able to use them comfortably and well, whereas the second one would be handicapped. Letting subjects use their own scales avoids this problem but, unfortunately, makes their judgments virtually impossible to evaluate and compare.

A more profound implication of this phenomenon is that people do not see the world in the same way; they emphasize different aspects of other people, notice and focus on different qualities. Sometimes this is merely the result of using different terminology for essentially the same characteristic. When one person talks about another's warmth and sense of humor and someone else talks about his kindness and good-naturedness, the only disagreement may be one of semantics. On the other hand, people do differ on the personality qualities they consider important, and their impressions of others are based on their own standards.

nonverbal communication

In making judgments of other people, we must obviously rely on many kinds of information. We use our knowledge of the others' behavior and of the general context in which it occurs. Language, what the person says, is an important source of information. And, as we saw earlier in this chapter, facial expressions are used in judging emotions and feelings. Facial expressions are one example of so-called *nonverbal communication*, ways in which we transmit information without using language. Other nonverbal means of communication are the use of personal space (which will be discussed in chapter 15), and paralanguage (nonverbal aspects of language), gestures and eye contact which we will cover in this section.

paralanguage

Variations in speech other than the actual words and syntax carry a great deal of meaning. Pitch of the voice, loudness, rhythm, inflections, and hesitations, also convey information. Parents can often tell whether their baby is hungry, angry, or just mildly cranky by how it cries. Dogs bark in different ways and each means something different to someone familiar with the animal. And, of course, the significance and meaning of adult speech depend in part on these paralinguistic factors. A simple statement such as "You want to go to medical school," can mean entirely different things depending on emphasis and inflection. Say it aloud as a flat statement with no emphasis, with an inflection (rising voice) at the end (becomes a question) and then as a question, but with added emphasis on the first word (questioning whether the person addressed is qualified). These variations are often crucial in conveying emotions.

The short phrase "I like you" may indicate almost anything from mild feeling to intense passion depending on paralinguistic characteristics of how it is said. In fact, these variations are so important that they often must be added to written language. Using our earlier example, to show that someone thought medical school was an unlikely choice the sentence might read " 'you want to go to medical school' he said sarcastically (or disbelievingly)," or " 'I like you' she murmured passionately." Without these clues, the statements are difficult to interpret unless you know what is intended from the whole context.

A particularly fascinating finding from work on paralanguage is that it may be possible to tell when someone is lying by noting the pitch of their voice. Several studies (Ekman et al, 1976; Krauss et al, 1976) indicate that the average (or more technically, fundamental) pitch of the voice is higher when someone is lying than when the truth is being told. The difference is small and you probably cannot tell just by listening. However, analysis of the voice by electronic equipment may reveal lying with considerable accuracy. Conversely, if you want to be believed it is a good idea to speak deeply—it sounds sincere.

One of the difficulties in studying paralanguage (and most other kinds of nonverbal behavior) is that most variations are ambiguous. To a large extent, we all agree on the meaning of words. We all know what "medical school" refers to, and with some variations we know that when someone says he "likes" you, he is making a statement of positive feelings. But people differ considerably in the meanings they attach to paralinguistic variations. For some people a pause may be for emphasis, for others it may mean uncertainty; higher pitch may mean excitement or lying; loudness can be anger, emphasis, or excitement. The particular meaning depends on the context (if the speaker talks louder and makes a fist at you, it is anger), and also on individual habits and characteristics of the person. Thus, the problem of interpreting paralinguistic cues is enormous. We cannot conceive of a dictionary of such cues because they do not have specific, fixed meanings. Rather they depend on all the other factors we have mentioned.

Nevertheless, it is clear that paralanguage is an important source of information. We can tell quite a bit from these nonverbal aspects of speech even without the actual words, and words themselves change in emphasis and meaning as a result of the paralinguistic variations. As anyone who has watched or participated in a play knows, it is simple to read a line, but only a real actor can say it with the right paralinguistic characteristics so as to convey the precise meaning.

gestures

In recent years there have been many popular books dealing with gestures, or body language as it is sometimes called. These books have suggested that you can tell exactly what someone is thinking or perfectly interpret what they say by merely observing their bodily movements and posture. An open palm is an invitation, crossed legs are defensive and so on. Unfortunately, these books are generally not based on scientific research and should be read with healthy skepticism (if at all). No one has constructed a reliable dictionary of gestures. Even more than with paralanguage, the meaning of gestures depends on the context, the person doing the action, the culture, and probably other factors also. An open palm is not always an invitation, as would be obvious to anyone who thought of the familiar gesture of putting up your hand palm out to mean "stop" not "go," or the reverse gesture with the palm in and the fingers moving toward the body to mean "come" or "enter." We do not know in detail what most gestures mean with the possible exception of standard ones such as those just described. And any book that offers to provide a gestural vocabulary will be unable to fulfill its promise.

However, this is by no means meant to deny that bodily gestures and posture carry information; clearly they do. They range from straightforward, direct gestures to very subtle ones. There are many bodily movements that are generally accepted and which convey specific information or directions. The gestures for "stop" and "come" are examples, as are pointing and gestures for "sit down," "yes," "no," "go away," "goodby," and various obscene gestures that have well-known meanings. In a sense all of these gestures are sign-language for words.

There are also gestures that are usually used unintentionally and are not meant to take the place of speech. It has been suggested that these gestures are a truer indication of what someone is feeling than what is said. In Ekman's terms (Ekman and Friesen, 1974) there is *nonverbal leakage* with true emotions "leaking out" even if the person tries to conceal his emotions. For example, someone may say she is not nervous about a test, but will lick her lips and blink more than usual. These actions often indicate nervousness. Or someone waiting for a job interview will attempt to appear calm and casual, but will cross and uncross his legs continually, straighten his tie, touch his face, play with his hair and generally look like a nervous wreck despite his attempts to seem calm.

On the other hand, gestures can also serve to conceal your feelings. Indeed, that is why the man waiting for the interview tries not to do the various things we mentioned. If he can manage to sit without moving much and without "nervous" gestures, we would be impressed by his calmness even though he might be terribly nervous. Robert Krauss (Krauss et al, 1976) demonstrated that subjects were *less* able to detect lying when they both saw and heard someone than when they had only the voice to go on. Apparently, the nonverbal gestural clues concealed rather than revealed the lie.

Thus, we must not think that gestures reveal trust while words are unreliable. Both forms of communication carry either accurate or inaccurate information. Moreover, interpreting gestures accurately depends on a thorough knowledge of the context and the particular individual, and even then many gestures will be ambiguous or even meaningless. The main point is that bodily movements can convey information and that under some circumstances they are an important form of communication.

eye contact

Eye contact is an especially interesting form of nonverbal communication. As with other forms of nonverbal communication, the meaning of eye contact varies greatly and depends on the context; but in nearly all social interactions eye contact does communicate information.

To begin with, eye contact is used to regulate conversations. Typically, a speaker looks away as he starts talking and looks up just before finishing. Looking away seems to prevent the listener from responding or interrupting while looking up signals the end of a thought and allows the other to talk (Kendon, 1967).

Eye contact also indicates interest or the lack of it. Hollywood movies often have a couple staring into each other's eyes to portray love, affection, or great concern. Certainly we are all familiar with eye contact held for a long time, as a means of demonstrating attraction for someone. An otherwise casual conversation can become an expression of romantic interest if one of the speakers maintains eye contact. Conversely, avoiding or breaking the contact is usually a sign that the person is not interested. Indeed, when someone does not make eye contact during a conversation, we tend to interpret this as an indication that he or she is not really involved in what is going on. No matter how attentively someone answers questions, nods at appropriate times, and carries on the conversation, lack of eye contact typically means he is not interested in what we are saying (Weisbrod, 1967).

However, there are obvious exceptions to this general principle. Lack of eye contact can sometimes mean that the person is shy or frightened. In addition, somone who is conveying bad news or saying something painful may avoid eye contact. And avoiding eye contact can be a way of respecting someone's privacy when discussing an intimate subject. Thus, the interpretation depends on several factors.

Moreover, eye contact can be used to threaten. In several studies, experimenters stared at or did not stare at people who were walking past a street corner. Those who were stared at walked across the street faster than those in the no-stare condition. Similarly, when the experimenters stared at people in cars, they drove through the intersection more quickly (Ellsworth et al, 1972). In another experiment, someone stared at a subject who was in a position to act aggressively toward the starer. Subjects who were stared at were less aggressive than when there was no staring (Ellsworth & Carlsmith, 1975). Apparently prolonged eye contact can be interpreted as a threat and causes people to escape or act in a conciliatory manner.

It is perhaps not surprising that eye contact can have two seemingly contradictory meanings—friendship or threat. In both cases, eye contact indicates greater involvement and higher emotional content. Whether

De Wys

the emotion is positive or negative depends on the context. Once again, the nonverbal communication has no fixed meaning and therefore must be interpreted using knowledge about the situation and the other person.

objective self-awareness

Just as we notice what other people are doing, we are aware of our own behavior and feelings. However, the degree of awareness of ourselves varies greatly. Sometimes we pay careful attention to what we are doing while other times we act more or less automatically without thinking much about our actions. A series of studies on this phenomenon demonstrates that self-awareness can have dramatic effects on our behavior.

Robert Wicklund and Shelley Duval (1971) proposed a theory of objective self-awareness which states that sometimes people look at themselves as if they were objects. That is, under some conditions we look at ourselves the way we look at other people. We "stand back" and observe our own behavior, taking the point of view of an outside observer. When we do this, we tend to become more self-conscious, more aware of how we look and what we are doing, and especially, more concerned about doing the "right" thing.

For example, it has been demonstrated that heightened self-awareness of this sort can either increase or decrease aggressive behavior depending on what the subject thinks is appropriate behavior. Under most circumstances, males in our society think that it is wrong to hurt females. When males were asked to deliver electric shock to women in a presumed learning experiment, the males gave fewer shocks under conditions of high self-awareness (Scheier et al, 1974). On the other hand, another study showed that females who were self-aware gave more shocks to males when the experimenter made a point of saying that giving shocks was the expected behavior in the situation (Carver, 1974). The point is that objective self-awareness makes a person want to "look good" in terms of society's standards or the standards of whomever happens to be important in the situation.

Perhaps the most fascinating aspect of this research is the method of producing objective self–awareness. In theory, anything that calls your attention to yourself should work, but how can this be done? The most obvious technique is to make the person feel that he is being watched. For example, if you are calmly sitting in a room and someone takes out a camera, all of a sudden most people begin to feel self-conscious and to worry about their appearance. This is even more powerful if it is a television camera and you are going to be on videotape or, even worse, watched by a television audience. Under these circumstances you begin to wonder how others are responding to you and to imagine how you might look to them.

The simplest and surely the most surprising way of increasing objective self-awareness is to sit in front of a mirror. Of course, the mirror provides an actual image of the self and you can actually see how you look and what you are doing. There is no need to imagine how you appear to someone else, because in a sense you can be the other person and watch your own image. It may be difficult to believe that a mirror, a common everyday object, can have such a powerful effect, but a great deal of research shows that it does. Try it for yourself and you will probably find that having a mirror in front of you does make you more self-conscious.

SUMMARY

1. People tend to form highly consistent impressions of others, even with very little information.

2. The evaluative dimension is the most important organizing principle behind first impressions. People seem to decide first how much they like or dislike another person, then ascribe characteristics to them that fit this pleasant or unpleasant portrait.

3. There are two rival points of view about how people process information about other people: the learning approach, which has people essentially averaging (or adding) information in a quite mechanical manner; and the *gestalt* approach, which has people thinking anew about a person after every fresh piece of information, and forming a coherent, meaningful impression that incorporates everything they know about the stimulus person.

4. Our judgments of other people are not very accurate. In particular we have a hard time judging their emotions from their facial expressions. We can tell fairly easily if their emotion is a positive or a negative one, but we have difficulty telling *which* positive or negative emotion is being experienced.

5. There are various identifiable perceptual biases that distort our judgments of others: the halo effect (we tend to think a person we like is good on every dimension), the positivity bias (we tend to like most people, even some who are not so likable), and assumed similarity (we expect others to be like us).

6. Each of us has an implicit personality theory. That is, we have some organizing principles for how people behave. This helps us organize the various different pieces of information we have about another person.

7. We use nonverbal cues like voice inflection, gestures, body language, and eye contact to communicate with others. These are fairly reliable ways of communicating.

SUGGESTIONS FOR ADDITIONAL READING

ANDERSON, N. H. Application of a linear-serial model to a personality-impression task using special presentation. *Journal of Personality and Social Psychology*, 1968, *10*, 354–362. This gives the flavor of the averaging-adding research using trait adjectives about hypothetical stimulus persons.

ASCH, S. E. Forming impressions of personality. *Journal of Abnormal and Social Psychology*, 1946, *41*, 258–290. This is the classic statement of the *gestalt* approach to impression formation, and indeed to social perception in general.

EKMAN, P., FRIESEN, W., & ELLSWORTH, P. *Emotion in the human face.* New York: Pergamon Press, 1972.

HALL, EDWARD T. *The hidden dimension.* New York: Doubleday, 1966. An original statement by one of the pioneers in the study of nonverbal communication.

HASTORF, A. H., SCHNEIDER, D., & POLEFKA, J. *Person perception.* Reading, Mass.: Addison-Wesley, 1970. A relatively short paperback (113 pp.) that pursues the material we have discussed in this chapter in more detail.

TAJFEL, H. Social and cultural factors in perception. In G. LINDZEY & E. ARONSON (EDS.), *Handbook of social psychology, Rev. Ed.* (Vol. 3). Reading, Mass.: Addison-Wesley, 1969. A relatively complete account of psychological theory and research dealing with the effects of cultural and social factors on perception.

WEITZ, S. (ED.) *Nonverbal communication.* New York: Oxford, 1974. An excellent collection of experimental and observational studies of nonverbal communication.

4

attribution theory

In the previous chapter we saw that our perception of another person's traits is central to all our perceptions of him. If we see another person as "warm," a whole series of connected perceptions fall into line. Moreover, as will be seen in later chapters, these first impressions have a great deal to do with how we like and behave toward that person. But this does not answer the question of how we perceive the traits of another person. How do we know that that person is a "warm" person? Indeed, how do we come to judgments about a whole series of other dispositions in another person? How do we decide that the person is intelligent, or a good curve-ball hitter, or an anti-Semite? And how do we come to conclusions about other, more transient mental states, such as intentions or moods?

The perception of people differs from the perception of inanimate objects in just this way. It often involves inferences about internal states. When we are thinking about a person, we are concerned about motives, personality, emotions, and attitudes. We must make such inferences on the basis of limited information, because we only have access to such external cues as facial expressions, gestures, what the person says about his internal state, what we remember about his behavior in the past, and so forth. We do not have direct information about his internal state; we have only the indirect information given by external cues.

theoretical approaches

The study of these inferences has become one of the most active areas of social psychological research. It has been organized under several theoretical approaches, which have been called *attribution theory*. An *attribution* is the inference an observer makes about the internal state of an actor or of himself on the basis of overt behavior.

Heider's naive psychology

Theorizing about attributions began with Heider (1958), whose concern was with phenomenal causality. That is, he was interested in how people in everyday life figure out what causes what. He postulated two strong motives in all human beings: the need to form a coherent understanding of the world around us, and the need to control our environment. One of the essentials for satisfying each motive is the ability to predict how people are going to behave. If we cannot predict how they will behave, our view is likely to be of a random, surprising, incoherent, staccato world around us. Without the ability to predict others' behavior, we would not know whether to expect reward or punishment for our work performance, whether to expect a kiss or a punch in the jaw from our friend, or whether to expect our darling daughter to eat her pancakes or throw up all over the dining room table. Making some prediction about other people's behavior, even if it is only a probability rather than a sure thing, is essential to a stable, coherent view of things around us.

Similarly, there is no way we can have a satisfactory level of control of our environment without being able to predict others' behavior. We need to be able to count on a salesperson's giving us a pair of slacks, rather than calling the police if we give her the proper price for them. We need to be able to count on that big truck not suddenly doing a U turn into our front bumper as we inch along Fifth Avenue. We need to be able to count on getting veal scallopini not pigs feet when we order in a restaurant. So a key factor in controlling our environment is being able to predict how others are going to behave in it. To be able to do this, we need to have some elemental theory of human behavior. So Heider proposed that everyone, not just psychologists, invests considerable energy in searching for causal explanations for other people's behavior. And he suggested that the result was a *naive psychology;* that is, a general theory of human behavior held by each ordinary person.

The key element in such a naive psychology is the ability to identify what others' stable, underlying dispositions are. To predict how they will behave, we need to be able to form a judgment (even if it is only a snap judgment), of their personalities, motives, emotions, and attitudes. If our daughter looks unhappy, we need to know whether she is hungry and peeved because her mom and dad spent a little too long (from *her* point of view!) in bed, or because her stomach is upset and she is about to lose all those cookies she was gobbling in the meantime. Is old Mr. Hodgkinson anti-Semitic and will not take our $97,000 or even our $99,500, for the house he has listed at $99,500; or does he just want to bargain? Is that blonde we cannot get our mind off just playing a little hard to get, so we should continue to chase her; or is she really uninterested, so we should just give up? In order to predict and control our environment, we need to make all kinds of judgments about others' internal dispositions.

EXTERNAL vs. INTERNAL CAUSES It turns out that the central issue in most perceptions of causality is whether to attribute a given act or event to internal states or to external forces. A person is generally perceived as acting either because of some internal state or because of some external force. The blonde wants to know whether we are motivated primarily by an overwhelming and undiscriminating internal sexuality (we will go out with any female), or by the uniqueness of her, an external object. A student who is failing a course wants to know whether it is because he is not smart enough or doesn't work hard enough (internal causality), or because the professor's lectures are ambiguous, the text is set at a level too difficult for the class's background, or the tests are unfair (external causality). Debates rage in school board meetings, academic conventions, courtrooms, and legislative halls about whether black children do less well in school than white children because of inferior native endowment and low motivation (internal causality) or because of racial discrimination, insensitive middle-class white teachers, inferior facilities, and unstimulating peer groups (external causality).

So the major question is whether to make an external attribution or an internal attribution. External attributions would ascribe causality to anything external to the actor, such as the general environment around him, the specific person he is interacting with, the role constraints he is operating under, the proffered rewards or threatened punishments for his actions, luck, the specific nature of the task he is working on, and so on. Internal causes include personality traits, motives, emotions, moods, attitudes, abilities, effort, or anything else the person carries around with him. So the assumption made by Heider is that we are constantly asking ourselves why another person behaves the way he does, and trying to answer that question in terms of ascribing a cause internal to the individual or a cause external to him.

STABILITY OF CAUSE A second important, but subsidiary issue in perceptions of causality is whether the cause is *stable* or *unstable*. That is, we need to know whether or not the cause is a relatively permanent feature of that external object or of the internal dispositions of the actor. Some external causes are quite stable, such as rules and laws (the prohibition against running a red light, or against breaking the throwing arm of an overly successful opposing quarterback), occupational roles (professors are called upon to give lectures year in and year out), or the difficulty level of certain tasks (it is always hard to hit a curveball, and always easy to get our daughter to laugh by tickling her). But some external causes are quite unstable: in competitive sports it is hard to judge how much of an obstacle the opposing player or team is because they are not always playing at exactly the same level of proficiency. Nolan Ryan could be brilliant one day, and the next he might not be able to get a ball over the plate. So his performance would not be a stable external cause of the performance of the batters against him. Similarly, certain jobs vary a good bit in the external demands they place on the jobholder. Being a general places quite different external forces upon a person in wartime than in peacetime, and even quite different demands depending on the particular sector of combat one is involved in.

An illustration is Weiner's typology for simple achievement tasks, shown in Table 4–1. One usually does attribute a student's success or failure at a particular task to one or more of four possible causes: ability, effort, luck, or task difficulty. And these causes fall quite neatly into the internal-external, stable-unstable categories, as the table shows.

TABLE 4–1
classification scheme for the perceived determinants of achievement behavior

	LOCUS OF CONTROL	
STABILITY	Internal	External
Stable	Ability	Task difficulty
Unstable	Effort	Luck

Source: Weiner, 1974, p. 6.

Finally, the importance of the stable-unstable distinction relates back to the original motivation that people have for causal attributions. If an outcome is attributed to a stable cause, it will be given more weight in determining predictions for the future. Valle and Frieze (1976) had subjects judge a hypothetical applicant for a position as a life insurance salesperson. They asked the subject to explain why he had sold so much insurance in the past and to estimate his prospects for the future. When the subjects attributed past performance to stable factors, such as ability or personality, these attributions were more highly associated with their projections for the future than was the case when the explanations for past success had to do with unstable factors, such as luck, unstable effort, or the particular season in which the sales took place.

It is not really possible to list all the possible causes that people attribute other people's behavior to. There are many too many, as these examples indicate. And they differ a good bit, depending upon the particular sector of life we are talking about. But they do generally fit rather neatly into the four categories generated by the intersection of these two dimensions: internal-external, stable-unstable.

PRINCIPLE OF INVARIANCE How do we arrive at such causal attributions? There are two simple principles we can start with. First, Heider suggests we generally use the *principle of invariance.* We normally all assume that any given behavior is determined by multiple causes. But what we do, according to the principle of invariance, is look for the association between a particular effect and a particular cause, across a number of different conditions. If a given cause is associated with a particular effect in many different situations, and if the effect does not occur in the absence of that cause, then we attribute the effect to that cause. Suppose our boss tells us she likes our work whenever she has just returned from a vacation, and she criticizes us all the rest of the time; we attribute her behavior to whether she has recently had a vacation. Suppose our department chairman hires beautiful women for secretaries but always opposes any qualified woman for a faculty position; we attribute his behavior to his chauvinistic attitudes. Suppose the local NBA team always loses to the Boston Celtics and always beats the Atlanta Hawks; we attribute its performance to its ability level (moderate), and the ability level of the opposition (high and low, respectively).

This principle of invariance is, of course, exactly the same as the scientific method that scientists use. A scientist also arrives at a judgment of casuality by seeing that a particular factor is associated with a particular effect across a number of different conditions. If a scientist finds, for example, that objects invariably fall from higher elevations to lower elevations, no matter whether they are feathers or cannonballs, no matter whether they dropped from the top of a building or waist height, he comes to the conclusion that there is a general causal factor, namely, gravity. Similarly, as naive psychologists we observe the behavior of others and look for regular, invariant effects that follow a particular stimulus. In that way we arrive at an attribution of the critical cause.

THE DISCOUNTING PRINCIPLE The other main principle is what Kelley (see below) has called the *discounting principle:* "the role of a given cause in producing a given effect is discounted if other plausible causes are also present" (1972, p. 8). That is, we make less confident attributions, and are less likely to attribute the effect to any particular cause, if more than one cause is likely. An insurance salesperson is very nice to us and invites us to dinner, but we may not be able to make a confident attribution about why he is so friendly. We could take him at his word and attribute his behavior to his real liking for us. More likely, we may discount his behavior and attribute it partly to liking and partly to his wanting our business. Of course, if we have no money to buy insurance, we may not have to bother about such discounting.

Two studies by Thibaut and Riecken (1955) provide a clear demonstration of the discounting principle. In the first experiment, the subject induced both a high status and a low status person to comply with his request. Then he was asked why they had complied. The idea here is that a low status person should be perceived as responding primarily to external pressure (a request has been made by a more powerful person), whereas the high status person would be seen as responding to some combination of external pressure (a request has been made of him, but it is not very compelling because it has been made by a less powerful person) and internal preferences (the request could be ignored if the high status person did not want to comply). And indeed the actual results came out just this way. When the subjects were asked to indicate why the other people were influenced, in almost all cases they reported that the high-status person "had wanted to anyway." Yielding by the low-status person was more often attributed to the pressure put on him. Thus the locus of causality was more internal for the high-status than for the low-status person. This is what the discounting principle would lead us to expect. When the behavior is perceived as being caused by a mixture of internal and external forces (as was the case with the high status complier), then we tend to divide up our attributions accordingly.

Perhaps the most common dilemma we are faced with is whether to attribute some behavior purely to an internal cause, or discount it and make an attribution to some combination of internal and external causes. In a second study, for example, Thibaut and Riecken showed that a strong person who performs a helpful act is perceived as nicer and as a better person than a weak person who performs the same act. Being helpful when strong portrays more internal causality; being helpful when weak is probably some combination of internal (being a nice person) and external causality (being forced to be helpful or suffer the consequences).

Kelley's cube theory

So far the processes we have described are fairly simple. The perceiver is trying to determine whether the cause is internal or external to the actor, and tends to allocate causality to more than one cause if plausible multiple causes exist. But in this form attribution theory is neither very systematic nor sufficiently specific to account in detail for people's judgments. Kelley (1967) has generated the most comprehensive theory accounting for attributions when people have multiple situations available to them. His general principle is a principle of *covariation:* People look for the simultaneous occurrence of (or covariation between) the causes and effects across three different dimensions: (1) stimulus object (entities), (2) actors (persons), and (3) context or situations (time and modality).

Because people are assumed to check across these three independent dimensions, this can be called a cube theory. The principle of covariation is essentially like Heider's principle of invariance; what the person does is to look for regularities amidst all this information. If the person sees that a particular event occurs invariably with a certain set of conditions, he knows what cause to attribute the event to. So what the person is looking for, in Heider's terms, is that invariable effect given a certain set of conditions or, in Kelley's terms, the regular covariation of conditions that determines whether or not the effect occurs.

Irene Bayer/Monkmeyer

This sounds complicated, but it is really a simple idea. It is easiest to grasp with a simple example. Take the dilemma of whether or not to believe a friend Bill's report that he has seen the new local movie four times, that it is terrific, and that we should go see it ourselves. What caused that report? In particular, was the report caused by a truly terrific movie (the stimulus object, or entity)? According to this model, our automatic response would be to ask ourselves: (1) Does he always say *any* movie is good, or is this report unique to this movie? (2) Have we heard the same report from others, or is it just something peculiar to him and his weird taste in movies? (3) Did he like the movie consistently over the four times he saw it, or did he like it some times and not other times? Was it just that he had eaten well, or got in free? Or did he like it no matter whom he went with, when he went, or where he sat?

Kelley's theory then leads to three different kinds of information that people use in trying to arrive at a causal attribution: (1) *Distinctiveness* information: this person acts in this manner only in regard to this entity (that is, this stimulus or object), and not in regard to other entities. To return to our example, does Bill only like this movie and not many other movies? That is, is his reaction distinctive to this particular entity, as far as he is concerned? (2) *Consensus* information. Do other people act in the same way in this situation? Did other people like this movie as well? (3) *Consistency* information, treating consistency over time and situations. Does this person react the same way at other times or in other situations? Or is this a consistent reaction that this person has to this entity in any situation? If Bill sometimes likes this movie and other times doesn't, then maybe there is something about this particular occasion, or his particular mood; his reaction cannot be attributed just to the movie. This, then, is the process Kelley hypothesizes to occur, however, implicitly and automatically, as we attempt to attribute a given effect to a given cause. We quickly review our store of information along these three dimensions.

For an external attribution to be made, that is, for the movie to be the cause of his enjoyment, all three tests have to be passed in the appropriate manner: high-distinctiveness, high consensus, and high consistency. That is, Bill's reaction has to be distinctive to this movie and not to others; other people have to like the movie; and he has to consistently like the movie in this and other situations.

McArthur (1972) has made the most systematic study of predictions from Kelley's "cube." She gave subjects a very simple hypothetical event, varied the kind of consensus, distinctiveness, and consistency information available to them, and then measured their attributions. The three main predictions, and the results, are shown in Table 4–2, with the example of trying to explain why Mary laughed so uproariously at the nightclub comedian last night. The first case is regarded as the clearest kind of information promoting an attribution to the entity itself, since it passes all three tests. Everyone was laughing, she didn't laugh at any of the other performers, but she always laughs at this one. So he must be a funny comedian. Mostly, the subjects saw it that way too; 61 percent attributed her reaction to the comedian. The second example leads the observer to make a person attribution: Mary laughs at any comedian and always laughs at this one—but hardly anyone else did. Mary must be a laugher (86 percent). The third case leads us to think there is something special about the situation: she didn't laugh at anyone else, she has almost never laughed at him before, and hardly anyone else laughed. Something unique must have happened.

TABLE 4–2
why did Mary laugh?

	AVAILABLE INFORMATION			ATTRIBUTION
CONDITION	Consensus	Distinctiveness	Consistency	
1	High—Everyone else laughed too.	High—She didn't laugh at anyone else.	High—She always laughs at him	Stimulus: The comedian (61%)
2	Low—Hardly anyone else laughed.	Low—She always laughs at comedians.	High—She always laughs at him.	Person: Mary (86%)
3	Low—Hardly anyone else laughed.	High—She didn't laugh at anyone else.	Low—She has almost never laughed at him.	Situation/circumstances (72%)

Source: Adapted from McArthur, 1972.

attributions about others

How do we make these judgments about causality? In particular, when do we think a person's act reflects his dispositions? That is, under what conditions do we infer that actions reflect traits, attitudes, moods, or other internal states? Sometimes clearly they do not. A prisoner of war often may say things contrary to his real attitudes. Or a boy may try to act cheerful and happy in school the morning after his girlfriend jilted him. On the other hand, sometimes a POW expresses real, heartfelt criticism of his own nation's war effort, with which he may disagree. This certainly happened in the Vietnam war with some American soldiers and airmen. And the boy may have some genuine sense of relief, if his affair had been depressing him for a long time. So how can we tell when to infer an internal state that corresponds to the act, and when to infer some other cause?

Heider suggests that we typically observe the person's act and then subtract out the environmental force. We use our own past experience to determine how this environment normally affects normal people. For example, we assume that hostages under armed guard are not making honest statements about their own attitudes; rather, we assume they are acting under coercion, and any statement they make is caused by these strong environmental forces.

trait attribution

Once we have established that the environmental forces are insufficiently strong to determine the act and that the cause is internal, how do we arrive at an attribution to a trait? Jones and Davis (1965) define this problem as one of predicting to *correspondent inferences*. They ask under what conditions an observer perceives a person's actions as reflecting his unique stable internal attributes (his motives, traits, attitudes, ability, and so on). That is, when do we infer that a person's actions correspond to real dispositions? The main condition is that the act is low in *social desirability*. It is something generally frowned upon, is deviant, noncomformist, and inappropriate to our social role. For example, when we ask a friend "How are you?" and she says "I'm fine," how are we to understand that? It is possible that the person really is fine, but on the other hand, it's equally possible that the person is just being polite, and expressing the conventional, expected, normative response. So the person's response is not informative about her genuine internal state. However, if she says "I'm lousy," there is only one explanation possible: she must in fact feel lousy.

Remember that in making attributions, the person is always trying first to weigh the strength of environmental or external forces, and then will arrive at an internal attribution only if the external forces are weak.

With socially desirable acts, there are strong external forces: the person could be committing them to maintain the approval of others. But with socially undesirable acts, he must be flying in the face of fairly strong environmental forces, so the critical cause must be internal.

attitude attribution

The major application of this theory has been to the attribution of another person's attitudes. How do we know when a person is expressing his real attitude, as opposed to expressing one that is not? That is, how do we know when to attribute his statement of opinion to his real attitude (an internal attribution), rather than to external forces operating on him? Social psychologists certainly know that people often give false opinion statements to others, succumbing to conformity pressures to avoid social disapproval. We discuss this in detail in Chapter 11. And apparently ordinary people take this into account when they make attributions.

What has generally been found is that when external forces are strong, a person's stated opinion is not necessarily perceived as an accurate reflection of his true underlying attitude. On the other hand, when external forces are weak, the expressed opinion tends to be trusted as reflecting the internal attitude. Jones and Harris (1967), for example, presented subjects with essays written by other students, in several conditions: the essays either supported Fidel Castro or opposed him (at a time when most college students and other Americans opposed Castro), and were supposedly written in some cases on an assigned side, and in other cases with free choice of position. With free choice, of course, the observers readily inferred that the writer's expressed opinion was the same as his true underlying attitude. This can be seen in Table 4–3. With free choice, the pro-Castro and anti-Castro speeches are seen as reflecting pro- and anti-Castro underlying attitudes, respectively. Even when the writer was described as having no choice of position (strong external forces), the observers still generally felt the written position reflected the underlying attitude. However, they were much less confident this was so, especially when the assigned position deviated sharply from that expected from most college students (i.e., when the writer had been assigned to write a pro-Castro essay). This too can be seen in Table 4–3. As long as the writer took the position expected of most college students (anti-Castro), whether it was done under choice or not did not matter much. The best guess was that the writer held the opinion most students held. In either case, the essay was taken as reflecting a real underlying anti-Castro position. But when it took the unexpected pro-Castro position and the writer had no choice, the subject was not as confident about the writer's real position. The writer might or might not hold a deviant pro-Castro position, but the subject was not as sure, because of the strong external forces operating.

TABLE 4–3
attitude attributed to writer

CONDITION	SPEECH DIRECTION	
	Pro-Castro	Anti-Castro
Experiment 1		
Choice	59.6	17.4
No choice	44.1	22.9
Experiment 2		
Choice	57.7	22.9
No choice	41.3	23.7

Source: Jones and Harris, 1967, pp. 6, 10. A high score indicates a pro-Castro position attributed to the writer.

In a later experiment, Jones et al. (1971) dealt with expectation more directly. In this case, the essay writer again either had or had not free choice about the position taken on the subject of legalization of marijuana. But this time the subject had direct information about the writer's normal attitudes, in the form of a prior attitude questionnaire with items on various freedom and civil liberties issues. So again the subjects were confronted with essays that had been written under either choice or no-choice conditions, and that took positions either expected or unexpected on the basis of the writer's usual political and social attitudes. Again, free choice led to perceiving the overt position as being the writer's true position, whereas observers were not so confident with no choice. But the other interesting finding was that when the position was expected from the writer's normal attitudes, a correspondent inference was made whether or not choice was present. This is shown in Figure 4–1. Put another way, the subjects made a correspondent inference when the writer

FIGURE 4–1
Attribution of attitude as a function of expectancy, choice and essay direction (strong essays only). (Jones et. al. 1971)

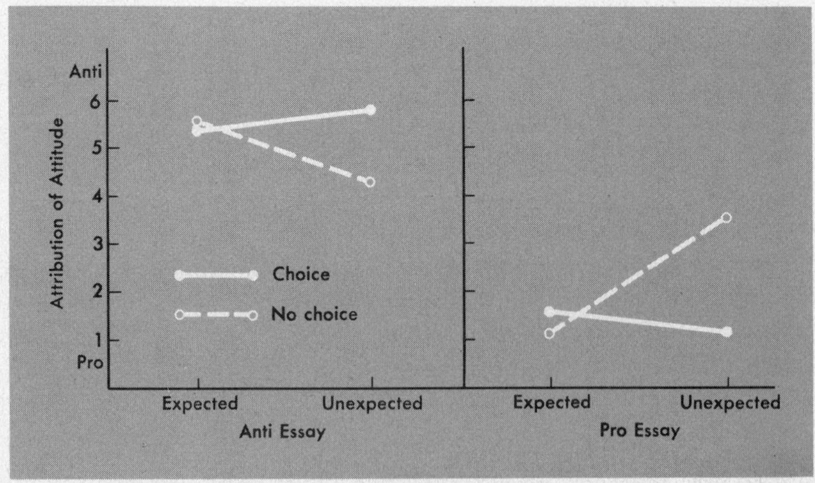

had free choice and when there was no choice but the position was consistent with the writer's overall sociopolitical attitudes. Only when the position was inconsistent with the writer's normal attitudes *and* the writer had no choice about position was no confident internal attribution made.

The general point is that when a person is seen as *not* being under the control of environmental circumstances, his statements are perceived as more sincere and trustworthy reflections of his true internal attitudes. The important further implication is that he has more persuasive impact under such conditions. This can be seen in two ways. When a speaker advocates a position contrary to his own self-interest, or to that of his audience, he is regarded as more sincere. Generally it appears that people are in doubt about a persuasive appeal when it can be interpreted as self-serving, ingratiatory, or made in response to strong external demands. To illustrate that point, Walster, Aronson, and Abrahams (1966) found that a criminal advocating a position counter to his own interest, namely that the courts do not have enough power, was regarded as more credible than a higher-status communicator (a prosecutor) advocating the same position. Advocating a position contrary to his own interest gave the criminal much more credibility. Mills and Jellison (1967) extended this point. They showed that a speaker is regarded as more trustworthy when his speech contradicts the environmental pressures coming from his audience's self-interest. They presented subjects with communications allegedly given by political candidates who had given a speech supporting radical increases in license fees for truckers. In one condition, the speech had allegedly been given to a local union of long-haul truck drivers; in the other condition, to a meeting of a local union of railwaymen, whose interest presumably would be supporting increased license fees for truckers. They found that agreement with the communicator was lower when his position coincided with the interest of his audience than when his position opposed the interests of his audience. Presumably the reason is that he was regarded as less sincere, less honest, less impartial, and more cynical when his position coincided with the interest of his audience. He was rated as more opportunistic, more obliging, and more tactful, as well. All these studies, then, show that attitude expression under strong external constraint, or environmental forces in general, yields a lack of certainty about what real internal attitude to attribute to the communicator. This in turn makes the perceiver more suspicious about other internal states of the speaker, such as honesty, hidden motives, and so on.

self-perception

One of the most provocative hypotheses in attribution theory is that people arrive at perceptions of their own internal states in the same way that they arrive at perceptions of others' states. This work proceeds from the general assumption that our own emotions, attitudes, traits, and abilities are often unclear and ambiguous to us. So we have to infer them from our overt behavior and from our perception of the environmental forces surrounding us. In other words, we try to attribute causality for our acts using substantially the same data, and the same attributional processes, as we use in attributing causality for other's acts. This work has been especially active with respect to emotions and attitudes.

emotions

The major theorist concerned with the self-perception of emotions is Stanley Schachter. He and his co-workers have proceeded from the assumption common to all attribution theorists that people are strongly motivated to understand themselves and their world. In this context, the assumption is that people are motivated to get a clear assessment of their own subjective experience. It is further assumed that the physiological cues yielded by different emotions are essentially ambiguous and undifferentiated.

Traditional theorists of emotion proposed that we recognize what we feel by considering our physiological state, our mental state, and the external stumulus causing these states. But recent evidence indicates that many, if not all, emotional reactions are biochemically similar—perhaps identical. That is, their internal physiological characteristics are indistinguishable, and we need cognitive labels to explain our emotions. So Schachter suggests that emotional experience is a function of two factors: (1) physiological arousal (which is more or less undifferentiated) and (2) an appropriate cognitive label. The experience of any given emotion therefore increases with generalized arousal and with attribution to some appropriate emotion-arousing stimulus. This emphasizes the importance of external cues concerning both our own behavior and the environment. To arrive at an appropriate cognitive label for our ambiguous feelings of arousal, we check the situation and/or how we are behaving, and from that we infer what our emotion must be.

The simplest form of the attribution hypotheses is this: When a person believes his internal physiological arousal is due to a clear and present external stimulus, he will (1) make an external attribution (i.e., infer that he feels strongly about the stimulus), (2) display appropriate overt emotion toward it, and (3) label his emotion accordingly. If, on the other hand, he believes his arousal is due to circumstances irrelevant to the stimulus, he will not make an external attribution, nor will he be likely to become emotional in relation to it. With this as a starting point, Schachter conducted a series of studies on the interrelationship between physiological and social factors in emotion. These experiments varied the availability of an internal attribution for physiological arousal, hypothesizing that when no internal attribution was available, arousal would be attributed to emotion-arousing properties of the external situation.

In the first, Schachter and Singer (1962) varied (1) whether or not subjects were given an arousing drug (epinephrine), and (2) the availability of cognitive labels pointing either to an attribution to the drug, or to the subject's own emotion producing a state of physiological arousal. The drug epinephrine, in appropriate quantities, produces the kind of physiological arousal that is generally associated with emotions but that does not resemble any particular emotion. Some of these subjects were told that the drug would produce a noticeable physiological arousal—such as more rapid heartbeats—and others were not. Thus, some of the aroused people could attribute their internal state to the drug, whereas others were unable to. A final group of subjects was not given epinephrine and so was less aroused physiologically. Both the aroused and unaroused subjects were then placed in a situation in which a confederate of the experimenter pretended to be experiencing a particular emotion. Half the subjects were exposed to someone behaving in a euphoric, elated way; half were exposed to someone acting very angry. The euphoric confederate made paper planes and flew them around; started a small game of basketball using crumpled papers and an old wastebasket; sang, danced, hopped around, and in general presented a zany, light-headed attitude. The angry confederate made nasty remarks, had an unplasant expression on his face, muttered to himself, and generally presented a disgruntled, annoyed picture. The question was, how did the subjects react to these two conditions?

Those who had been aroused by the drug and not informed of this (the "external attribution condition") became more euphoric in the euphoria condition and more angry in the anger condition than the other groups. When there was arousal and no irrelevant cause to which to attribute it, the subjects presumably interpreted their arousal as being caused by an emotion-arousing situation—the same situation causing the other person's behavior. When he was happy, they became happy; when he was angry, so were they. But when aroused subjects could attribute their arousal to the drug (in the "drug attribution" condition), they were relatively unaffected by the other person's behavior. They knew that their physiological state was due to the drug and therefore did not interpret it as emotional arousal. The procedure and results of this experiment are shown in Table 4–4.

TABLE 4–4
the schachter-singer experiment

SEQUENCE CONDITION	STEP 1 GIVEN AROUSING DRUG	STEP 2 TOLD IT WOULD BE AROUSING	STEP 3 CONFEDERATE'S BEHAVIOR	STEP 4 PRESUMED ATTRIBUTION (UNMEASURED)	STEP 5 BEHAVIOR (MEASURED)
Drug attribution	Yes	Yes	Euphoric or angry in all cases	Drug	Calm
External attribution	Yes	No		Situationally-induced emotion	Euphoric or angry
No arousal	No	No		None	Calm

Source: Schachter and Singer, 1962.

The key element here is that when the person was both aroused and placed in a situation with no other attribution, he "caught" the salient emotion from the external situation. That is, in the absence of any alternative, he attributed his arousal externally to the situation's capacity for producing either euphoria or anger. Consequently, he acted in a more euphoric or angry way. In the other condition, where arousal was attributed to the drug, no such emotion was aroused. In short, what was important for the experience of emotion was first of all the *arousal*, and second the *cognitive label* or the attribution made for the arousal. When the label attributed the arousal to the drug, the subjects acted as if they experienced no particular emotion. On the other hand, when they did not know that the drug was responsible for their arousal, they took their cues about their emotions from the external environment.

MISATTRIBUTION OF AROUSAL This led to a series of what have been called *misattribution* studies. The idea was to give the subject a neutral pill (or some other neutral stimulus), and then get him to misattribute some normal everyday emotion to the pill and thus reduce his experienced emotionality. The model for such misattributions was the "drug attribution" condition in Table 4–4. When a person attributes his experienced emotionality to a drug, he does not attribute it to environmental events (as in the Schachter-Singer experiment) or to his own real emotions (as in the experiments to be described next). And as a result he does not perceive himself as "really" emotional; he thinks his subjectively experienced arousal is just caused by the drug.

In one such experiment, Nisbett and Schachter (1966) gave all subjects an ordinary sugar pill. Experimental subjects were told the pill would produce physiological symptoms, such as hand tremors and palpitations; control subjects were told it would produce only nonphysiological symptoms. Finally, all subjects were administered painful electric shock. The hypothesis was that the experimental subjects would attribute their physiological reactions after the shock not to the shock itself, but to the pill and would think the shock hurt less. The control subjects, having no basis for an attribution to the pill, would blame their reactions on the shock itself. And indeed it was found that these control subjects found the shock more painful than did the experimental subjects.

If normal emotions could be so easily reduced by misattributing them to a sugar pill, then perhaps harmful emotions could be reduced in the same way. It could be a useful kind of therapy if disruptive and maladaptive emotions could be dispensed with through a "reattribution" treatment. Storms and Nisbett (1970) tried this with insomniac patients. The patients were given placebos (harmless sugar pills) before going to bed. In the arousal condition, they were told the pills would cause physiological arousal; in the sedation condition, they were told it would actually reduce arousal. As expected, arousal subjects got to sleep more quickly, because they attributed their jumpiness and restlessness to the pills rather than to any emotional preoccupations. On the other hand, the sedation subjects actually got to sleep later than usual, because they were still jumpy and restless after taking a supposedly relaxing pill. They could only infer that their emotional problems and worries were even worse than usual. Once again the point is that reattributing one's normal emotional arousal (insomnia anxiety) to something external to the emotion itself (in this case the drug) reduces the emotional experience, with the beneficial behavorial consequence of reducing insomnia.

On the other hand, a study by Kellogg and Baron (1975) not only failed to replicate these findings, but actually found the opposite—subjects given a pill that was supposedly arousing had more trouble sleeping. Since this was a very careful study, it raises the possibility that the original result is not correct, or that this particular misattribution effect occurs only in certain, limited circumstances that we are not yet able to specify. In other words, although the Storms and Nisbett study produced fascinating results, we should be very careful about accepting them until they have been repeated by other experimenters. However, we should also keep in mind that the effect we are talking about here—actually reducing insomnia—is very large and dramatic compared to most effects in social psychology. Thus, it is perhaps not surprising that the effect is difficult to demonstrate and may occur only under restricted conditions.

Another demonstration of the misattribution effect (Dienstbier and Munter, 1971), involved giving all subjects a placebo and telling some to expect arousal and others not to. Then all subjects were given an opportunity to cheat on a vocabulary test. Subjects who expected arousal from the pill cheated more, presumably because they interpreted their feelings as caused by the pill rather than from fear of guilt associated with cheating. Subjects who expected no effects from the pill associated their emotionality with guilt about the temptation to cheat, and thus refrained from cheating. In another study, Valins and Ray (1967) recruited subjects who were afraid of snakes. Then they showed these subjects slides of various snakes. Interspersed among the slides were other slides imprinted with the word "Shock." Throughout these presentations, the subjects were exposed to something they thought was their own heart rate. But this of course was a prerecorded tape that made it sound as if their heart rate was increasing when the "shock" slides were flashed and not increasing when the snake slides were flashed. The idea was that the subjects would attribute their increased heart rate to the shock slides and not to the snake slides. After the slides they were asked to approach a thirty-inch boa constrictor. Subjects whose fake heart rate had been attributed to the shock slides were able to approach the snake more closely than subjects who had not had the procedure reattributing their arousal to the shock.

FALSE FEEDBACK ABOUT AROUSAL These misattribution studies hold arousal constant and vary the attribution (or cognitive label) applied to the arousal as a way to change behavior. Schachter's general theory can also be tested, however, by manipulating the person's perception of his own arousal, holding constant the attribution, and then seeing if behavior changes. Suppose you go to see *Butch Cassidy and the Sundance Kid.* You get heart palpitations every time Paul Newman comes on screen, but you don't feel anything for Robert Redford. You are likely to attribute the heightened arousal to Butch and not to the Kid. You may say you are attracted to Paul Newman but not to Robert Redford.

But of course Paul Newman may really, objectively, be more attractive than Robert Redford. To test this idea fairly clearly requires giving random false feedback to subjects about their own arousal. So Valins presented male subjects with slides of nude females, and after each slide provided faked feedback to the subject about rate of heartbeat. Each subject was wired to fake electrodes and told that his own heartbeat was played into his earphones. After each slide, some subjects heard increased heartbeats, which they thought were their own, and others heard what they thought were irrelevant sounds. Valins found that subjects rated nudes as more attractive when they had been accompanied by their own supposedly increased heartbeat. Also, after the experiment was over, subjects were allowed to take some slides home. They mostly took slides that had been associated with increased heartbeat. This was evidence that people infer their own internal subjective states (in this case sexual attraction to a particular woman) on the basis of what their body tells them, and not necessarily on their perceptions of the external stimulus itself.

One possibility is that this was simply a transitory relabeling of the attractiveness of the women, rather than a genuine, lasting, thoroughgoing reevaluation of them. The subject might not be really perceiving the women in a new way, seeing good things about this one and bad things about that one. He might just say one is attractive and the other is not. Valins, in a later study (1974) tried to show that in fact, in an effort to account for his own apparent arousal, the subject would reinterpret his reaction to the woman. If that were correct Valins argued, then debriefing the subject (telling him that the physiological feedback is in fact false) would not alter his feelings about the relative attractiveness of the different women. And this indeed was the case. Thus, the reattribution process in this case is interpreted as being one in which the subject actually reevaluates the stimulus, on the assumption that it has aroused him, and subsequently perceives the stimulus in a way that would justify his becoming aroused to it. This hypothesis was also supported in a study by Barefoot and Straub (1971). If the subjects simply relabeled each slide as more or less attractive, they could do it quite quickly. If they were to reinterpret the attractiveness of each woman, that would presumably take much longer. In their study, they varied the amount of time each subject was able to spend initially with the slide from 10 to 25 seconds. They found that with 25 seconds, the false feedback about their physiological arousal affected rated attractiveness; given only 10 seconds, no such reevaluation occurred. The long search time was therefore essential to changing the subject's feeling toward the slides (Nisbett and Valins, 1972, p. 73).

All these studies make the general point that any given arousal can be attributed, misattributed, or reattributed to stimuli other than those to which it is normally attached. Given this reattribution, our emotional arousal can be increased and understood as caused by the stimulus (as in Valins' studies of *Playboy* nudes) or it can be reattributed to the neutral stimulus, and the originally arousing stimulus can elicit only emotional indifference (as with the snake phobias or insomniacs). The theoretical analysis is exactly the same as that Schachter applied to affiliation, as covered in Chapter 2. Given physiological arousal, under situations in which there is a great deal of ambiguity and uncertainty about the origins of the arousal, the subject attempts to arrive at an explanation for it. In these experiments, the subject normally is given an explanation, which he then adopts and which controls his experience of emotional arousal. Similarly, in the Gregor Zilstein affiliation experiments, the subjects seek an explanation for their own emotions from the companions with whom they wish to affiliate. The important point added in these studies is that the magnitude of emotional experience is affected by this attribution process, as is the nature of it. We can feel highly aroused or unaroused depending on what cognitive explanation we have for the arousal; and we can experience different kinds of emotions, depending on how we explain it.

When these studies were first done, they gave some promise of providing a new therapeutic tool for dealing with disruptive anxieties, fears, depressions, low self-esteem, and other seemingly neurotic emotions. A variety of other studies have tried to apply reattribution therapies to public speaking anxiety, test anxiety, depression, and other unwanted emotions. Some have been successful and others have not (Berkevec, Wall, and Stone, 1974; Koenig, 1973; Nisbett et al, 1976), and perhaps it is too early to judge the approach as a whole (Harvey and Smith, 1977).

attitudes

Conventionally, psychologists have assumed that people determine their own attitudes by reviewing the various cognitions and affects in their consciousness, then expressing the result. But Bem (1965) has made the same argument about attitudes that Schachter made about emotions:

people infer their own attitudes by reviewing their own external behavior rather than by inspecting their insides. In other words, people come to know their own attitudes in the same way that they infer other people's attitudes: by inspecting whatever external cues are available, and then making the appropriate attribution. He assumed that we receive only minimal and ambiguous cues to our attitudes from inside, just as we have no direct access to internal cues in others. So we must infer our own attitudes by self-observation rather than introspection. Bem does not hold that people never use internal evidence, but his work does suggest that to a surprising degree people rely upon the external evidence of their overt behavior, and the conditions under which it occurs, to infer their own true attitudes.

The direct evidence for this theory involved studies that manipulate the individual's overt behavior, and then measure his report of his internal dispositions. If the self-perception process is working, he will report different dispositions depending on his overt behavior. For example, Salancik and Conway (1975) subtly manipulated subjects' reports of their own religious behavior. Some subjects were induced to report a lot of religious behavior, whereas others were induced to report very little, even though both groups actually engaged in about the same amount. Then the subjects were asked how religious they were, and those who had reported engaging in a lot of religious behavior said they were more religious. The way experimenters induced such differences in reports of behavior was by manipulating whether the subject said he or she did the behavior "occasionally" or "frequently." For example, to induce the subject to report a high level of proreligious behavior, he was asked if he "occasionally" subscribed to a religious newspaper or magazine, attended a church or synagogue, and consulted a minister about personal problems. To induce the subject to report a low level of proreligious behavior, he was asked if he "frequently" did each of these things. Since most college students, even those who are rather religious, do these things at most "occasionally," they tended to agree when asked if they did them "occasionally," but to disagree when asked if they did them "frequently." So one group of subjects kept saying they engaged in religious behaviors, while the other group kept denying it. And sure enough, when later asked "how religious are you?", the group that had been describing themselves as engaging in religious behaviors said they were more religious.

We shall discuss most of the research related to this idea in the chapter on cognitive dissonance. For the moment, the important point is that even attitudes, which are usually considered to be internally determined, may to some extent be affected by attributions based on overt behavior. Generally, though, we do not find this a plausible view of the situation. We believe that people do have attitudes that endure from one moment to another and are not based entirely on current behavior. We do not believe that a subject decides whether or not he likes spinach on the basis of whether or not he has recently eaten spinach. We think he has real feelings toward spinach and it is these feelings that determine his responses. Israelis have certain attitudes about Nazis, and bigots have certain attitudes about minorities, which they are quite clear about regardless of their most recent behavior.

Most likely this self-perception effect holds only when the attitude issues involved are unimportant and inconsequential. To test this idea, Shelley Taylor (1975) ran an experiment that involved presenting female college students with pictures of full-face color photographs of clothed male graduate students. She first had each of the women rate these pictures for attractiveness. Then she set up a situation in which the subject was given false feedback about her physiological reactions to one of the slides. The subject was allowed to overhear a confederate saying that she (the subject) had reacted noticeably and more strongly to that slide than to any other slide. Half the time this false feedback of high arousal was given concerning a slide the subject had already rated as highly attractive, and the rest of the time it concerned a slide of a man the subject had rated as only medium in attractiveness. So according to the self-perception idea, this false high arousal feedback ought to boost the subject's ratings of the attractiveness of both slides, though it should have more impact on the subject's rating of the initially only moderately attractive stimulus person.

But the critical variable was how important the attitude was, to test Taylor's notion that self-perception works only with relatively inconsequential attitudes. In the high importance case, the subject was told she would be meeting some of the men whose pictures she had seen. In the low importance condition, no such future meeting was mentioned.

When the subject expected to meet the man, she gave quite similar ratings both before and after the false arousal feedback. As shown in Table 4–5, one SP became slightly less attractive, and the other slightly more so. False feedback changed initial attitudes mostly when there was no future consequence of the ratings.

Although there has not been much additional research on this

TABLE 4–5
effects of false high arousal feedback on attractiveness ratings

CONDITION	INITIALLY HIGH ATTRACTIVE SP	INITIALLY MEDIUM ATTRACTIVE SP
Future meeting	−0.59	+1.17
No future meeting	+1.09	+2.75

Source: Adapted from Taylor, 1975, p. 130. A positive score means an increase in attraction.

point, it seems fairly evident that Bem's theory is primarily relevant to cases in which the subjects have few internal cues to their own attitudes and dispositions. When they have strong attitudes or strong preferences to start with, it seems unlikely that the Bem self-perception process is very important.

attributional biases

Attribution theory, particularly in the version emphasized by Kelley, describes an essentially rational, logical process. In fact, Kelley draws an analogy between the naive psychologist, the person in the street, trying to arrive at causal attributions for everyday events, and a systematic scientist, who applies the scientific method to achieve causal explanations for natural events. In that form, attribution theory presumes that people process information in a rational way, that they are fairly objective in assessing information and in combining it to produce a conclusion. But we know that people are not always logical and rational. Indeed, most of this book, and most of psychology, is devoted to studying the irrationalities in human behavior. So in some ways, the more interesting questions come when people behave in an unscientific, irrational, illogical fashion. For that reason, we now turn to the several biases in the attribution process that have been identified in empirical research.

There are essentially two categories of biases: motivational and nonmotivational. For example, it turns out that people frequently attribute their own successes internally and their failures externally, even when in formal terms the available information is the same. They take personal credit for their success and blame their failures on other people or the situation. Presumably the reason is to preserve or enhance their own self-esteem. That is an example of a motivationally based bias. On the other hand, there seem to be a number of biases that simply represent errors in information processing. We do not pay as much attention to consensus information as we ought to, from a logical standpoint. That is, we overgeneralize from a single case that we know about. We seem to take too seriously information about internal, dispositional causes, and to ignore more than we should information about environmental causes. Neither of these biases seems to serve any special ego needs or satisfy any special motive; rather, they just seem to be systemic mistakes in our information processing. Let us start with these, and see where they might come from.

non-motivational biases

The German perceptual psychologists of the 1920s and 1930s came to be known as Gestalt psychologists because they emphasized the human tendency to form a "good Gestalt," that is, a coherent pattern or form or organized perceptual field. People would take an ambiguous set of stim-

GROUPING BY:

Proximity	Common fate	Similarity
•• •• ••		• • × × • • • • × × • •
Common boundary	**Good form**	**Past experience**
	| □ □	Boy and Girl

FIGURE 4–2
Examples of Perceptual Grouping. Proximity leads to the perception of three pairs of dots. Grouping is by common fate when some dots move in one way and others in another, or by similarity when dots that look alike are grouped together. Perceptible boundaries may decide which dots are grouped together. In the fifth figure, the five vertical lines are separated into groups by the fact that two pairs of them contribute to good forms, i.e., to squares. In the last example, the ten letters divide at once into three words if the past experience of the perceiver has been with the English language. (Deutsch and Krauss, 1965, p. 21.)

uli and perceive a coherent "good form." Their early work dealt with basic perceptions, and it was easy to show that people tended to group stimuli, in a simple, perceptual sense, according to principles of proximity, similarity, common boundaries, and simplicity. Some examples are given in Figure 4–2. The main idea is that simple aspects of the perceptual situation, like proximity or good form, lead us to particular kinds of structuring our experience.

One application of this thinking to social perception has already been covered in Asch's view of impression formation (see Chapter 3). He, you will remember, argued that people formed coherent and meaningful impressions, seeing the parts in interrelation, as forming a complete impression even when the person has only minimal information, and as promoting a structured impression. Unlike Anderson's averaging and additive models, he did not view impressions as formed in an arbitrary, mechanical, or impersonal way. Heider and Simmel (1944) made a similar demonstration of how naturally and readily we perceive causality in simple perceptual relationships. They showed subjects a film that involved the movements of two triangles and a circle. These are shown in Figure 4–3. During the course of the film, these shapes moved around

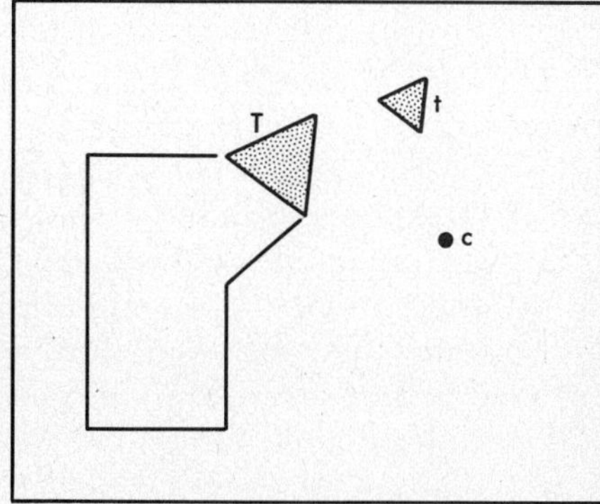

FIGURE 4–3
Geometrical figures used in the study of phenomenal causality. (Adapted from Heider and Simmel, 1944.) (Shaver, 1975, p. 37.)

in various ways. For example, the large triangle moved toward the small one and contacted it vigorously. The subjects described the movements as if they were the movements of animate beings, whether they were instructed to do so or just asked generally to interpret the film. They mentioned such relationships as "chasing" and "fighting," and dispositions such as "shy" or "bully." The point of the demonstration was that people quickly arrive at causal judgments when they see even simple perceptual forms moving, and they attribute the movements to internal dispositions of the stimuli and to characteristics of the surrounding environment.

Bassili (1976) extended this research using computer-generated films depicting movement of abstract figures across a stimulus field. These figures moved closer or farther from each other (spatial contingency) and did so either moving right after one another or separated by more time (temporal contingency). Then he asked subjects to describe what they had seen. He too found that people talked about the intentions of the circles, but the most important point was that he showed temporal contingency was crucial for the perception of an interaction between the figures. That is, one figure had to move immediately after the other for a causal relationship to be perceived. Spatial contingency was critical for determining the nature of that relationship. When they came closer together, relationships like chasing, following, and hitting were ascribed. When they did not move in concert with one another, such relationships were not perceived. These two studies indicate how spontaneously we perceive causality even when the stimuli we are dealing with are simple abstract forms moving in simple spatial relationships. More important, they suggest that we arrive at causal attributions on the basis of rather simple perceptual Gestalts—that an attribution is made on the basis of what makes a simple, coherent explanation. This implies that biases and distortions are likely to intrude when they can promote simplicity, and occur on the basis of simple perceptual relations like movement, precedence, contact, propinquity, or proximity in general.

overattributing to dispositions

Perhaps the most important attributional bias is that we overestimate the importance of dispositional factors in other peoples' behavior. Kelley (1971) puts it this way: "Too little account is taken of external causes (contextual factors) in judgments of other persons' behavior." We have already seen one example of this in the Jones and Harris (1967) study of attributions about the true attitudes of people writing essays on Fidel Castro. In this study, even when the essay writer was given no choice about the position taken in the essay, observers perceived his position as indicating his true attitude. People forced to write a pro-Castro essay were perceived as actually more pro-Castro than people forced to write an anti-Castro essay. That is, the perceivers disregarded the evidence of external force (lack of choice) and attributed the behavior to an internal disposition (real attitude about Castro). This can be seen back in Table 4–3. The explanation for this underattribution to external forces has been suggested by Heider: "It seems that behavior . . . has such salient properties that it tends to engulf the field rather than be confined to its proper position as a local stimulus whose interpretation requires the additional data of a surrounding field—the situation in social perception" (1958, p. 54). Another way to put the same explanation is that the *behavior* becomes *figure,* and therefore stands out against the surrounding *ground* of the *situation.*

Quite a number of studies have been done to determine whether the Jones and Harris result is typical. It is a very important one, because it is a key illustration of the principle that behavior engulfs the field. In its original form, it made quite a strong statement: Even when subjects knew that the writer had no choice about the position to be advocated, they still perceived the position he advocated as his true position. Much of the later work took up the possibility that observers might correctly have been attributing the essay to the writer's true position because the essay was in fact rather strong and persuasive (having been prepared for the occasion by the investigators). Perhaps essays that were genuinely forced would be weaker and less convincing, so no internal attribution would be made. Snyder and Jones (1974) did five experiments, this time using essays actually written by students assigned to advocate a particular position. But again, the subjects perceived the position advocated as the true position of the communicators, even under no-choice conditions.

It was thought that perhaps with a drab, unenthusiastic, unforceful presentation, subjects would observe that the behavior was being forced and would attribute the essay position to the situation and not to the communicator's true position. Schneider and Miller (1975) conducted two experiments with speakers in which they varied enthusiasm. The enthusiastic speaker spoke from notes, sat erect, maximized eye contact with the audience, and used hand gestures for emphasis. The unenthusiastic speaker simply read a transcribed version of the talk, spoke in a monotone, and used no gestures. However, the same finding held. Even in the absence of choice, the observer subjects took the speaker's position at face value, and felt that it represented his true opinion. They also varied the presence or absence of forcefulness in the presentation, in terms of what they called "certainty phrases," such as "I firmly believe," "the situation is certainly not going to change," and so on. That too made no difference. Whether or not the presentation was actually authored by the captive, no-choice speaker, whether or not he was enthusiastic, and whether or not he sounded very certain of himself, the effect was always the same as in the Jones and Harris experiment. Even under no choice, a speaker's or writer's overtly expressed position was perceived as reflecting his true position.

Finally, the intrinsic strength of arguments has also been varied. Again the hypothesis was that with patently weak arguments, observers might no longer take the writer's overt position as his true one. Jones et al. (1971) presented subjects with either strong or weak essays, ostensibly written under no choice. The issue was legalization of marijuana. In the strong essay, the writer made four points on his own side; for example, that legalizing marijuana would reduce organized crime, that it was a safe and effective tension reducer, that it could increase creativity, and that it was neither harmful nor addictive. In the weak essay, the writer presented two arguments from each side, and then simply concluded that his side was right. With the strong essays, the Jones and Harris effect occurred: the apparent position was taken as the true position. But with the weak essay and no choice that was no longer true. In fact, the opposite side was taken as the true position. This is shown in Figure 4–4.

Other studies have tried to explore the ramifications of not having any choice, to see if they could find sufficiently clear cases of no choice to yield an external attribution. Miller (1976), for example, presented subjects with speakers reading essays that someone else wrote. Still the speaker's position was taken to be his true position. In one final experiment, Snyder and Jones told the subjects that the speaker had no choice about the position he took and that the speech was constructed of specific arguments given by the experimenters, but that the speaker had made up the speech itself. In this case the effect disappeared. The position taken by the speaker was not taken as his true position.

All in all, it appears that the tendency to take a speaker's position

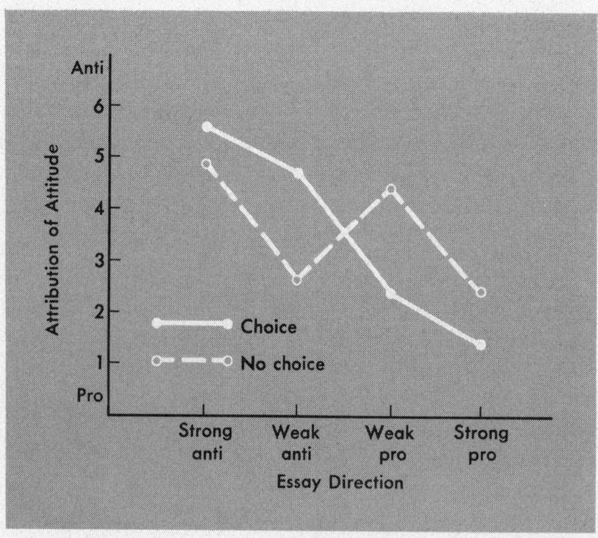

FIGURE 4–4
Determinants of attitude attribution. With choice, the expressed position is seen as the true attitude. With no choice, this is true for strong essays but reverses for very weak ones. (Jones et al., 1971, p. 69.)

as his true attitude seems amazingly resilient, even in conditions when he has no choice, is unenthusiastic, gives weak arguments, and is simply reading somebody else's speech. Only under the most extreme conditions of situational constraints, and with very weak arguments, does the "behavior engulfing the field" phenomenon disappear, and observers finally are driven to accept the preeminent causal role of external forces.

actors vs. observers

One of the most provocative elaborations on this fundamental attributional bias that observers have is that it is not, apparently, shared by actors perceiving their own behavior. They instead seem to overemphasize the role of external factors. Or at least so Jones and Nisbett (1971) contend. Observers, they claim, overestimate dispositional causes, while actors overestimate situational ones. A wife who gets angry at her husband for spending too long in the corner of a cocktail party talking to that blonde is likely to attribute it to him: to his lack of caring for her, his wife; to his infidelity, his selfishness, his immaturity; and other such dispositions. He, on the other hand, is likely to attribute it to some characteristics of the blonde, to her fascinating conversation or stimulating personality. So the observing wife makes internal attributions, while the offending husband actor makes external attributions.

This has proved to be one of the most interesting and widely researched of the various attributional biases. In one of its earliest demonstrations, Nisbett et al. (1973) asked male student subjects to write a paragraph on why they liked the woman they dated most, and why they had chosen their major. Then they were asked to write similar paragraphs for their best friend. These responses were scored for the extent to which the behavior was attributed to the person's disposition (e.g., I need someone I can relax with, or I want to make a lot of money) or to the stimulus entity (e.g., a relaxing person, or chemistry is a high-paying field). As can be seen in Table 4–6, external reasons are given for one's own

TABLE 4–6
number of entity and dispositional reasons given by subjects as explanations of their own and best friend's choices of girlfriend and college major

	REASONS FOR LIKING GIRLFRIEND		REASONS FOR CHOOSING MAJOR	
Explanation	Entity	Dispositional	Entity	Dispositional
Own behavior	4.61	2.04	1.52	1.83
Friend's behavior	2.70	2.57	.43	1.70

Source: Nisbett et al. 1973, p. 159.

behavior much more than for another person's behavior. And there is some tendency, though it is not as strong, to give internal reasons for a friend's behavior.

In another study, West, Gunn, and Chernicky (1975) presented subjects with an elaborate plan for burglarizing a local advertising firm. Under some conditions they were told that the burglary was to be committed for a government agency (the Internal Revenue Service) for government purposes and the burglars would be given immunity from prosecution. Under other conditions other rationales were given. The subjects, the actors, were then asked whether they would agree or refuse to participate in the burglary and their reasons for their decisions. Parenthetically, it might be noted that 45 percent of the subjects agreed to participate in the burglary, given that the burglary was sponsored by the government and immunity from prosecution was part of the deal. That is why the study was called "Ubiquitous Watergate." But in this context the critical comparison is with some other subjects, the observers, who were given an extensive mimeographed booklet describing in detail one of these experimental conditions. They were then told that a hypothetical undergraduate had agreed or refused to participate and asked to explain his decision. Environmental factors were given more often by the actors than by the observers.

Finally, two other actor-observer comparisons were done in a teacher/learner situation. In one, Gurwitz and Panciera (1975) assigned the subjects to the roles of teacher or learner. At the end of the session, each was asked how free the teachers were to give reward and punishment as they saw fit. The learners invariably attributed more freedom to the teachers than the teachers did to themselves. That is, the learners, as observers, felt that the teachers were free to act on their own internal dispositions, and were relatively unconstrained by external forces. Similarly, Miller (1975) had observers watch learners through one-way windows. They concluded that these actors (learners) were behaving in a way typical of the way they would behave on other tasks. In contrast, the learners generally did not feel their performances were representative of what they would be on other tasks. Again, the observers felt that behavior was a function of some kind of internal disposition, whereas the actors felt it was determined by external forces, such as the unique nature of that task.

DIFFERENT PERSPECTIVES Jones and Nisbett offer two explanations for this actor-observer difference in attributions. One is that they have access to *different information,* and therefore naturally come to different conclusions. The actor knows more about his past behavior and present experiences than does the observer. Hence the actor can more clearly see the distinctiveness of his behavior in any particular situation. He is more likely to attribute it to the unique characteristics of that particular situation, and less likely to attribute it to some chronic disposition of his. The other explanation, and the one now favored by most researchers, is that the difference is due mainly to *different perspectives*, or perceptual orientations, at the moment. The actor is naturally focused on the situation around him, while the observer is naturally focused on the actor. The argument follows from Koffka's (1936) observation that stimuli which stand out, perceptually, from the background, attract the most attention. This is the fundamental principle of Gestalt perceptual psychology: the *figure* attracts more attention than the *ground*. As Nisbett et al. (1973) say:

> The actor's attention at the moment of action is focused on the situational cues—the environmental attractions, repulsions, and contraints—with which his behavior is coordinated. It therefore appears to the actor that his behavior is a response to these cues, that is, caused by them. For the observer, however, it is not the situational cues that are salient but the behavior of the actor. In Gestalt terms, action is figural against the ground of the situation (p. 154).

For the observer, the actor's behavior engulfs the field, being figural, and so it then attracts causal explanations. For the actor, on the other hand, the environment rather than behavior is figural, and *it* attracts causal explanations. So the general notion is that whatever is figural attracts attention, and whatever attracts attention also becomes perceived as the causal force in the situation, just as Heider and Simmel had suggested in their early studies of abstract forms. There have been some ingenious tests of these ideas. Taylor and Fiske (1975) tested the simple idea that whatever is perceptually salient will attract dominant causal explanation. They had two confederates serve as "actors." They engaged in a conversation, facing each other. The ordinary subjects were "observers" sitting either behind the confederates or next to them. Each actor thus had observers both sitting behind him and facing him. Clearly, the actor and his behavior would be more salient for those who faced him than for those who sat behind him. But both actors ought to be equally salient for the observers sitting to the side, equidistant from the two actors. This arrangement is illustrated in Figure 4–5. The confederates then held a standardized five-minute conversation, chatting as if they had just met. They exchanged information about majors, common job plans, home towns, family, extracurricular activities, and the like. The conversation was carefully monitored to make sure that roughly the same conversation occurred in all experimental groups.

Then the subjects were asked for their causal perceptions: How much had each confederate set the tone of the conversation, determined the kind of information exchanged, and caused the other actor to behave as he did? The results are shown in Table 4–7. It shows that the more perceptually salient actor (the confederate the subject faced) was given the dominant causal role, that the less salient actor (the one the confed-

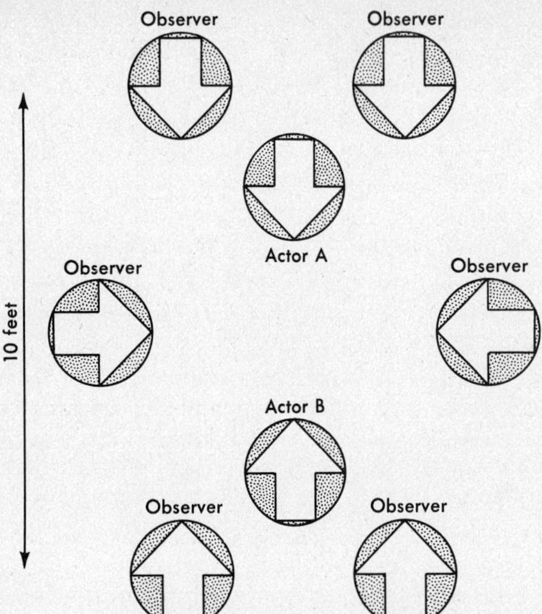

FIGURE 4–5
Seating arrangement for actors and observers, with arrows indicating visual orientation. (Adapted from Taylor and Fiske, 1975, p. 441.)

erate sat behind) was given the less causal role. When one sat equidistant from both confederates, they were seen as about equally potent. This study was later replicated by the same authors, using videotaped rather than face-to-face interactions. The results were the same. This study, then, is a simple demonstration that perceptual salience induces stronger perceptions of causal role among observers.

TABLE 4–7
mean ratings of causal role attributed by observers to each actor as a function of the observer's seating position

OBSERVER'S POSITION	ACTOR	
	A	B
Facing Actor A	20.25	15.54
Center	17.51	16.75
Facing Actor B	12.00	20.75

Source: Taylor and Fiske, 1975, p. 441

Storms (1973) showed that this difference in perspective could explain the actor-observer difference in locus of perceived causality. He reasoned that the actor is watching the environment and consequently attributes causality to it; the observer, on the other hand, is watching the actor and consequently naturally ascribes the causality to the actor. The situation could be reversed, he thought, by reversing point of view. If the actor's own behavior was videotaped and played back to him, he ought to perceive himself as the figural object in the field and ascribe causality to his own dispositions. Similarly, if the observers see more of the situation to which the actor is responding, rather than just focusing on the actor, they ought to ascribe more causality to the situation rather than simply seeing the actor's dispositions as the major cause.

To test this hypothesis, Storms also set up a situation in which two strangers (actors) meet to get acquainted. Sitting at the other end of the table from them were two observers watching their conversation, each instructed to watch a specific one of the two actors. Both actors were videotaped. But on playback, one actor's behavior was shown and the other's was not (the experimenter said that one camera had not worked). Thus one actor saw himself, which should have increased dispositional attributions; the other actor saw just the same thing that he had seen during the conversation, namely, the other actor, this time on videotape. Similarly, one observer saw a videotape of the actor to whom *his* actor has been responding, and therefore should have been more attuned to the situational forces operating on his actor. The other observer saw simply a repeat of the same thing he had seen earlier.

The standard actor-observer effect came out when the subjects saw no videotape replay, or when they saw a videotape repeating what they had already seen. That is, the observers made more dispositional attributions than did actors. But the crucial condition was the one reversing the actors' and observers' perspectives. Here the effect reversed, as expected. When actors saw their own behavior played back and observers saw a playback of the person to whom their actor had been responding, the actors became more dispositionally oriented and the observers more situationally oriented. This is shown in the third column of Table 4–8. The finding was repeated by Arkin and Duval (1975).

This experiment confirms the basic actor-observer prediction of Jones and Nisbett, that under normal circumstances actors make more

TABLE 4–8
tendency to give dispositional, rather than situational attributions

ATTRIBUTION	SAME ORIENTATION	NO VIDEOTAPE	NEW ORIENTATION
Actors' attributions of own behavior	.15[a]	2.25	6.80
Observers' attributions of matched actor's behavior	4.90	4.80	1.60

[a]Higher the number, the more dispositional relative to situational attributions.
Source: Adopted from Storms, 1973, p. 169.

situational attributions and observers make more dispositional attributions. But they suggest that this difference occurs because of their different perceptual orientations or points of view. That is, they are receiving different current information engulfing their respective perceptual fields. And when this perceptual orientation is reversed, so too are the causal attributions. Regan and Totten (1975) added yet another wrinkle to this same idea. They reasoned that if the observer adopted a more empathetic attitude and tried to think or see things the same way the actor did, then the observer ought to see the world the same way the actor does. That is, if the observer adopted the perceptual orientation of the actor, through empathy, the observer ought to make more situational attributions. This is a somewhat surprising prediction in that we might expect empathy on the part of the observer to increase even further his understanding of the personality and mental working of the actor, and consequently ascribe even more causality to the particular individual characteristics of the actor. But if the different point of view explanation is correct, more empathy and understanding among observers should make them more sensitive to the strength of external forces.

Again, the experiment was done in the "get acquainted" pattern. The subjects were shown a videotape of two women students chatting for about 7 minutes about their home towns, intellectual interests, and travel. In one case the subjects were given instructions such as the following: "Please try to empathize with the girl on the left side of the screen. Imagine how Margaret feels as she engages in the conversation. While you are watching the tape, picture to yourself just how she feels in

H. Armstrong Roberts

the situation. You are to concentrate on the way she feels while talking. Think about her reaction to information that she is receiving from the conversation. In your mind's eye you are to visualize how it feels for Margaret to be in this conversation" (pp. 852–53). At the end of the conversation the subjects were again asked to describe the target's behavior, and then to assess how important personal characteristics as opposed to situational characteristics were in determining the target's behavior. Personal characteristics included personality traits, character, mood; characteristics of the situation included factors such as being in an experiment, conversation topics, the way the other student behaves. They found that the empathetic view reversed the usual actor-observer finding. That is, when the observers had the normal observer set, they were inclined to give more dispositional than situational attributions. However, under instructions to empathize with the actor, this reversed slightly, and the situational attributions became more prominent, presumably just as they would have been for the actor herself.

These studies give good evidence that the actor-observer effect is due to the different points of view that actors and observers have. Observers are most oriented to the behavior of the actor, and that behavior engulfs their perceptual fields, so they ascribe causality to it. Actors, on the other hand, are most impressed by the situation, because that is what is perceptually salient to them.

underusing consensus information

Kelley's model of attribution assumes that consensus, distinctiveness, and consistency information will all be used about equally. None of these is regarded as inherently more informative than any other. Yet experiments comparing them have found that subjects do not use consensus information as much as they should. For example, in trying to explain why Mary laughed at the comedian, it makes little difference to most observers whether other people were laughing at him or not. In trying to explain why Ralph tripped over Joan's feet at the dance, most observers feel it is irrelevant whether or not other men have tripped over her feet in the past. Or, in trying to explain why Susy is afraid of the dog, it doesn't seem to matter whether all the other children are afraid of the dog or not (McArthur, 1972, 1976; Nisbett and Borgida, 1975; Ruble and Feldman, 1976).

In fact, in one recent study (Wells and Harvey, 1977) subjects seemed so dedicated to making dispositional rather than situational attributions for others' behavior that they completely ignored information of extremely high consensus (e.g. that 73% of the people in that situation had done exactly the same thing). Rather, they came to the conclusion that those people were an unrepresentative group of people. In other words, instead of interpreting such common behavior as reflecting a very compelling situation, the subjects concluded the behavior was caused by something internal to the actors—the fact that so many people did the same thing was interpreted as reflecting that they were weird people!

A number of writers have noted the parallel between such indifference to consensus information and a comparable lack of regard for what is called *baserate information* (Kahneman and Tversky, 1973). That is, people seem to disregard the probabilities and easily get distracted by concrete details. For example, suppose you are told that Jack is forty-five, married, with four children, conservative, careful, and ambitious. Most of his free time is spent on his hobbies, which include carpentry and mathematical puzzles, and he is completely uninterested in politics. Then you are asked to judge the likelihood that Jack is an engineer or a lawyer, knowing that he is a member of a population that includes either (1) 70 lawyers and 30 engineers, or (2) 30 lawyers and 70 engineers. The laws of probability would of course dictate that he would be much more likely to be an engineer in the latter case. But in fact this variation in baserate information makes little difference. Subjects are pretty convinced that Jack is an engineer, no matter which population they are told he comes from, because his personal characteristics make him sound more like an engineer.

Nisbett et al. (1976) have speculated that such indifference to consensus and baserate information derived from their abstractness. Possibly people simply take more seriously concrete, vivid, singular instances, and tend to ignore the more abstract, bland, statistical kinds of information. To test this, they offered psychology students two different kinds of information about upper-division psychology courses: the consensus, baserate subjects got the average course evaluations based on the scales filled out by the students in each course the previous term. The concrete-information subjects got comments face to face from two or three students who had been in the courses. It turned out that the face-to-face comments had much more impact on the subjects' desires to take the courses in question. Later they repeated the study by adding to the consensus baserate information the verbatim, transcribed comments of the two or three students who had been in the courses. The face-to-face comments were still more influential than the consensus baserate information, even with these concrete written comments added.

Consensus information may influence attributions only in the absence of direct, more valid, more concrete information. Feldman et al. (1976) showed subjects videotapes of five persons, one of whom (the actor) was depicted choosing one of several pictured items. Immediately after his choice, the other four visible within camera range were asked whether or not they liked that one best too. Either they all responded positively that they did (high consensus) or negatively (low consensus). Then the subject was asked whether the actor's choice told you more about the actor or about the pictured item. From Kelley's theory, high consensus should lead to a stimulus (entity) attribution: if everyone likes it, it must be wonderful. Low consensus should lead to a person attribution: if only the actor liked it, it must be some special kinky taste of his. The other variation was access to direct information about the concrete objects the actor was choosing among. The subjects either were shown the same pictures the actor was or not. The results are shown in Figure 4–6. Consensus information has little or no effect when the subjects were exposed to direct information about the object in question.

Exactly why people ignore more statistical, abstract information like consensus or baserate information is not known. It does seem to be an important biasing factor in forming attributions. It could be that direct information about an object is so much more vivid and emotionally evocative, compared to dry statistics, that it simply attracts more attention. The individual case becomes figural, in a way that a bland statistical analysis cannot, so the specific case becomes of overriding importance. The same thing happened in another study, by Hansen and Donoghue (1977), who varied whether or not the subject himself had personally engaged in the relevant behavior. Consensus information affected attributions only when the subject had had no personal experience with the act. Apparently, with personal experience, one's own behavior becomes figural, and consensus information is relegated to a much less influential ground.

Or it could be that people find direct information more credible than indirect information. The Nisbett et al. subjects may have really believed the face-to-face testimony of former students and have been more skeptical about the reported statistical analysis given of course evaluations. Whatever the reason, it appears that people disregard consensus information more than they should, and overutilize and overgeneralize from specific, concrete, vivid experiences.

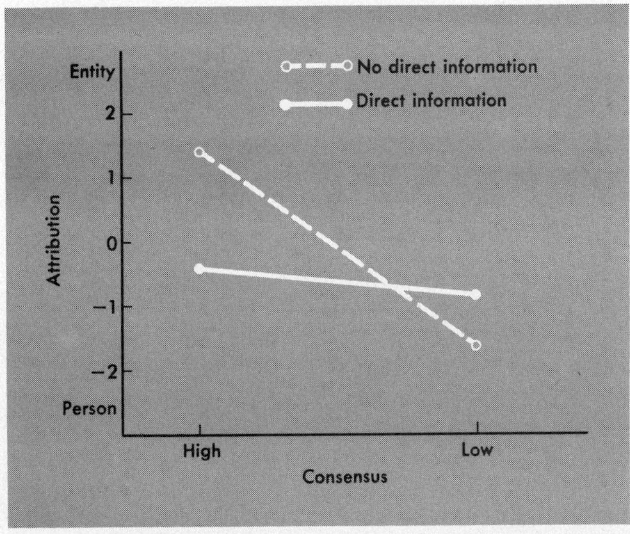

FIGURE 4–6
Attributions from consensus information. (Adapted from Feldman et al., 1976, p. 696.)

defensive attribution

One of the irrational biases in the attribution process has been called *defensive attribution.* This describes attributions that enhance the ego or defend self-esteem. These are the self-serving biases. Perhaps the simplest example and most common case is the taking of credit for success and the externalizing of blame for failure. We attribute our successes to internal causes such as our own ability, hard work, or general wonderfulness. We blame our failures on external factors like bad luck, an oppressive political structure, a nagging wife or chauvinistic husband, obstacles too great for anyone to surmount, bad weather, and so on. A homey example of this process comes from interviews by Kingdon (1967) with the winning and losing candidate in each of thirty-three races in Wisconsin for U.S. senator, U.S. congressman, state senator, state assemblyman, and five statewide offices. They were asked a series of questions about why they thought they had won or lost. The winners thought the most important factor was the characteristics of the candidates! The losers downplayed that factor and blamed the outcome on party label (the voters just voted a party line against my side), and on the voters' ignorance. The results are shown in Table 4–9. In addition, seventy percent of the losers said the voters were "not informed," compared to 32 percent of the winners, while only 3 percent of the losers said the voters were "very informed," compared to 26 percent of the winners.

TABLE 4–9
comparison of winners and losers on the rank which they assign to party label, issues, and candidates' characteristics

VARIABLE	MOST IMPORTANT		LEAST IMPORTANT	
	Winners	Losers	Winners	Losers
Party Label	21%	59%	47%	17%
Election Issues	17	7	50	55
Characteristics of the Candidates	62	35	3	28
	100%	101%[a]	100%	100%
N	29	29	30	29

[a]Rounding error.

Even more impressive were the results from an open-ended question, "Could you summarize the major factors that have contributed to your wins and defeats over the years?" For the "wins," 75 percent of the respondents emphasized matters within their control: "their hard work, personal service to constituents, matters of campaign strategy, building a reputation, and publicizing themselves" (p. 141). For the "defeats," 90 percent of the respondents emphasized matters beyond their control, "the party makeup of the district, the familiar name or other unbeatable characteristics of the opponent, national and state trends, lack of money, or other uncontrollable circumstances" (p. 141). Only a few (10 percent) attributed their losses to internal factors such as laziness or mistakes in strategy.

The same self-serving discrepancy in causal explanations for success and failure was shown in an experiment by Cialdini, Braver, and Lewis (1974). They instructed subjects to try to persuade another person (actually a confederate) of something. The position to be advocated was assigned to the persuader, who read a standard, prepared statement on it. Other subjects watched this procedure as observers. The confederate was instructed to act either as easily persuaded, or as not convinced. Then both persuaders and observers rated the confederate in intelligence. The persuaders rated the successfully persuaded confederate as more intelligent than did the neutral observers. But the persuaders rated their failures, the unconvinced confederates, as less intelligent than did the observers. So it is apparent that the persuaders were biasing their perceptions of the situation to enhance their own self-esteem. In Kingdon's terms, they were congratulating the persuaded confederate on his great insight. But the stubborn confederate got blamed as being stupid and insensitive.

This kind of effect has been tested in a wide variety of experimental studies. Some involve a teacher-learner situation, in which a subject tries to teach a student something, with the student's success or failure being manipulated. Others focus on the subject's own personal achievement. In these cases, the subject is given a success or a failure experience, and then asked to evaluate the reasons for his success or failure. Either way, if self-serving biases are important, we should find more internal attributions for success, and more external attributions for failure. And these differences should be magnified with ego involvement. As an issue becomes more important to the individual, he should be more motivated to bias his attributions to salve his bruised ego.

EVALUATION What does this research show? In the first place, it seems clear that when the subject has a success experience, internal attributions such as ability or effort give the subject a more positive feeling than do external attributions such as task ease or chance (Riemer, 1975). So we can be assured that it is to the subject's advantage, in terms of self-esteem, to claim the credit for success internally rather than sharing it externally. A wide variety of studies do in fact find that our own failure produces external attributions such as to bad luck or difficult tasks, while our own success produces internal attributions such as to effort or ability (see Stevens and Jones, 1976; Luginbuhl et al., 1975; Nicholls,

1975). Similarly, Johnson et al. (1964) found that teachers accepted responsibility for a student's improved performance, but blamed continued low performance on the student (though later studies using this teacher-learner pattern got somewhat more mixed results, see Beckman, 1970, Ross et al., 1974).

This externalizing blame for failure and taking credit for success increases with greater ego involvement, as shown in a study by Miller (1975). To create high-involvement, he told subjects the test was a well-established social perceptiveness test used by many agencies and businesses in client and employee decisions, and that high scores were probably indicative of desirable characteristics such as intelligence, marital happiness, and so on. In the low-involvement condition, the experimenter told the subject that it was a recently developed test and had not been tried out very thoroughly. The results showed that high ego involvement exaggerated defensive attribution; that is, it produced even more external blame for failure, and more credit for success.

This defensive attribution process ought also to be more marked for actors than for observers. In terms of ego enhancement, the actor has everything to gain and the observer nothing to gain by making defensive attributions. A number of studies have been done that show precisely this finding. One example is by Snyder, Stephen, and Rosenfield (1976). In this case, subjects were run in a game against each other. They were randomly assigned to win and lose conditions. And the subjects were asked to attribute the causes for their own winning and losing, as well as for their opponents' outcomes. The data are shown in Table 4–10. It can be seen very clearly that actors attribute their wins to internal factors such as skill and effort, whereas opponents are more likely to attribute the actor's wins to easy tasks and to luck. On the other hand, losses are blamed by the actor far more on external factors like luck, whereas observers are likely to give some credit to lack of skill and lack of effort. Taylor and Koivumaki (1976) show the same thing. When asked to account for one's own deeds, subjects were more likely to give dispositional explanations for good deeds and situational attributions for bad deeds. On the other hand, when asked to explain an acquaintance's be-

TABLE 4–10
attributions of actors and observers for winning and losing

ATTRIBUTION	ACTOR		OBSERVER	
	Actor Wins	Actor Loses	Actor Wins	Actor Loses
Internal (skill, effort)	8.13	0.56	3.54	3.00
External (luck, task difficulty)	4.25	4.74	6.00	3.38
Internal-external	+3.88	−4.18	−2.46	-0.38

Source: Adapted from Snyder et al., 1976, p. 438.

havior, and therefore be in an observer role, it did not matter as much whether the deeds were good or bad.

In another experiment, Stephan (1975) had a confederate try to get the subject (actor) to help her find a lost contact lens. Meanwhile, an observer watched. Half the subjects were told that they had helped more than most subjects, and the other half that they had helped less. Then both the actor and the observer were asked to explain the actor's behavior. The observer paired with the "unhelpful" actor was more likely than the actor to make a dispositional attribution. In contrast, the observer paired with the very helpful actor was more likely to make a situational attribution than was the actor herself. A final example is a study by Fontaine (1975). He found that defensive attribution was much more likely to occur when the subject was actually confronted with his own success and failure than it was when a simulation experiment was done in which the subject only had to imagine the possibilities given a hypothetical stimulus person.

NONMOTIVATIONAL INTERPRETATIONS There are some reasonable questions about the interpretation of these findings. Some authors (e.g. Miller and Ross, 1975; Ross, 1977) suggest that there might be informational rather than motivational reasons for these findings. We have been emphasizing the role of ego enhancement. But these critics argue that most subjects in these experiments are much more used to success than to failure experiences (e.g., few Fs are given in high school or college), and so failure is much more unexpected than success. In Kelley's terms, a failure would be low in consistency, whereas a success would be consistent with past experience. And as we saw earlier, high consistency provokes a personal attribution, whereas low consistency produces an attribution to circumstances. If I always perform this way, then it is me. If my performance varies a lot depending on the test, then it must be the test, or luck, or something about the situation. So people might show a defensive attribution pattern simply for cognitive, attributional reasons, without ego enhancement being a factor at all.

There are several problems with this argument. One is that most people do not have universally successful experiences. Their judgment of their success is normally determined by some subjective level of aspiration rather than by some absolute standard. For example, most college students do not regard getting a C or D as a success experience, even though it is a passing grade. If I call up five women for dates and three agree to go but two say they think I am a creep and I should get lost, I feel like a failure. Only one team wins the Super Bowl or the World Series or the NBA championships. A UCLA basketball team can win all but three or four games, but if it fails to make the NCAA final championship round, its season is a failure. So the question of our histories of success and failure is much more complicated that these critics suggest. We have probably experienced many failures as well as successes so it is doubtful that our past history leads most of us to expect to be successful (by our own standards) most of the time.

Secondly, even violations of expectation get interpreted in an ego-defensive way. Stevens and Jones (1976) conducted an experiment using a series of sensory discrimination tasks in which they manipulated success or failure. They also varied Kelley's attributional dimensions of distinctiveness (inconsistent performance across different tasks), consistency (of performance on the same task), and consensus (others' performance on these tasks). The logical attribution processes seemed to make relatively little difference. For example, inconsistency over the same task should increase attributions to unstable characteristics such as luck or effort. However, this did not happen. Inconsistent performances led to explanations in terms of task differences, even though the tasks were in fact very similar. Low distinctiveness (consistent performance over different tasks), ought to have been attributed to stable factors in an effort to account for the fact that performance remained constant while the tasks changed. However, consistent failure over different tasks led to unstable, external attributions, especially to luck. Consistent success, however, led to a stable internal attribution to ability. So if people consistently failed over different tasks, they simply wrote it off to luck. If they consistently succeeded over different tasks, they claimed to have great ability at all of these tasks. In perhaps the most devastating condition, the subject was made to fail all the tasks (some new and some repeated), while everyone else supposedly succeeded. Although this high consistency, low distinctiveness, and low consensus ought to have produced internal attribution—to a complete lack of ability—it did not. Only 18 percent said ability was reflected. Rather, luck was emphasized (by 40 percent). The authors quite reasonably conclude that defensive attribution processes, safeguarding the subjects' self-esteem, account for the data better than do more cognitive, informational interpretations.

Finally, the fact that defensive attribution seems to increase with greater ego involvement, and to be greater for actors than observers, is consistent with the notion that it is based on motivational needs rather than cognitive mechanisms. In short, there seems to be quite a strong tendency for attributions to be biased by self-esteem needs, especially to take credit for good events and to avoid blame for bad ones.

POSITIVITY BIASES These ego-enhancing biases are of course mainly devoted to enhancing the subject's own ego. But from our discussion of positivity biases in the last chapter, it should be clear that people also have a generous streak when it comes to other people. The positivity bias, it will be recalled, is the tendency to evaluate other people more positively than negatively, to give a "bonus" of positive evaluation to other people, everything else being equal. Applying it to the question of defensive attribution leads us to expect that perhaps people will extend some of the same generous rationalizations to others that they apply to themselves. That is, if people really do like other people as much as we claimed they did, then we should see some defensive attribution on behalf of other people. We should be inclined to give them credit for their good deeds with internal attributions and write off their bad deeds as a result of uncontrollable external forces. This does not mean we will be *more* generous to others than we are to ourselves, but that we will give the other person a break also.

There is considerable evidence that people do extend this defensive attribution generosity to others. Taylor and Koivumaki (1976) asked subjects to explain three positive behaviors (paying a compliment to someone, talking cheerfully to another person, and having fun) and three negative behaviors (having a heated argument with someone, being rude to someone, and forgetting to do something) on the part of various persons: oneself, one's spouse, a friend, and an acquaintance. In all cases they found dispositional causality attributed much more often for positive acts than for negative acts. The data are shown in Table 4–11. In another study they asked the extent to which a wide variety of different adjectives applied to a liked or a disliked acquaintance, to the spouse, and to the self. They found that subjects in general said the highly favorable adjectives applied to all these stimulus persons, whereas adjectives of medium or low favorability did not apply. So not only do subjects use dispositions or traits to explain the good behavior of others and rationalize others' bad behavior in terms of the crummy situations they are in, but they attribute good traits to other people and say bad traits do not apply. This is true even for disliked acquaintances. Similar results are found in a study by Regan and Totten (1975) in which bystanders seem to give a "sympathy vote" in evaluating the performance of actors.

TABLE 4–11
mean ratings of dispositional causality

STIMULUS PERSON	POSITIVE ACT	NEGATIVE ACT
Acquaintance	6.41	4.74
Friend	7.41	3.92
Spouse	7.66	3.36
Self	7.57	3.31

Source: Adapted from Taylor and Koivumaki, 1976, p. 405.

In simple learning situations, in which observers are asked to explain children's or adults' performances, there seems to be a tendency to ascribe success to effort and ability, and failure to difficult tasks. The data

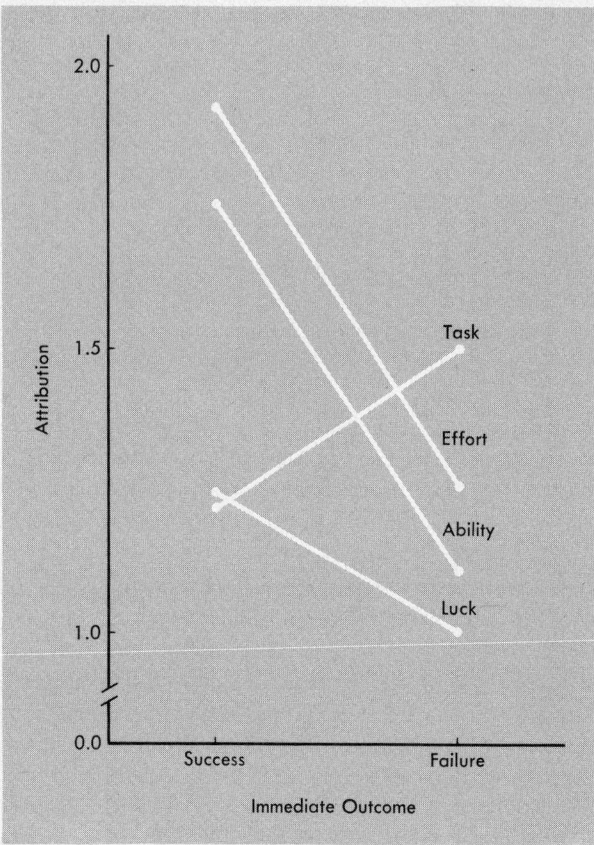

FIGURE 4–7
Attributions to ability, effort, task difficulty, and luck as a function of the immediate outcome (success or failure).

from one study are shown in Figure 4–7. Weiner and his colleagues presented subjects with a hypothetical person who had just either succeeded or failed at a particular task. Then the subjects were asked to indicate why this had occurred. In this case, failure was externally attributed to a difficult task, while success tended to be attributed primarily internally to effort and ability (Frieze and Weiner, 1973). Fontaine (1975) obtained similar results. It would appear that in these experiments the subjects were giving rather generous explanations for the stimulus person's actions. One wonders if they would be so generous with a member of a social group against which they were prejudiced.

In a more realistic study, Ross et al. (1974) had real teachers actually teaching spelling problems to an eleven-year-old boy (a confederate), who either succeeded or failed. In this case the teachers tended to blame themselves when the boy failed, rather than laying the blame on him. The fact that they were being videotaped for later viewing may have made them reluctant to blame the child (see Stephan, 1975), or they may simply have been being generous to a young boy they scarcely knew. Finally, Karaz and Perlman (1975) found a positivity bias in explanations for race horse's performances like those in these studies of people. Subjects were shown videotaped horse races, in which the horse in question won or lost. Subjects attributed wins to the horse, and losses to a highly competitive field of other horses or to the circumstances of the race. So even a horse gets personal credit for his good performance, and does not get blamed for his poor performance.

"a just world"

A phenomenon that some people have noticed is a tendency to "blame the victim" for events. If a person gets into a traffic accident, he must have been driving carelessly. A woman who is raped must have been acting in a provocative manner and brought it on herself. Minorities who are discriminated against are too pushy, or too unmotivated, or alienate people with their demands, or are too passive, so they deserve their fates. Earthquake, tornado, hurricane, and flood victims showed insufficient preparedness. People get what they deserve, and deserve what they get.

To explain such observations, Lerner (1965) has offered the notion that we believe in a "just world": good people get good outcomes, and bad things happen to bad people. The key point is that observers make moral attributions to others' dispositions based on the events that happen to them. I attribute to you the characteristic of being a lousy driver because someone ran a red light and hit you at an intersection on the way to school. To test this notion, Lerner ran several experiments showing that subjects tended to derogate completely innocent victims picked at random to be given electric shock. Lerner suggests that we need to feel that we can control events. Therefore, to protect this sense of control, we blame people for the bad things that happen to them. If people in general are responsible for any disaster that befalls them, presumably we ourselves can avoid disaster by acting properly. This kind of defensive attribution symbolically protects us from feeling vulnerable to the "slings and arrows of outrageous fortune." Chance horrors won't happen to *us*, because they only happen to bad people.

A variant on this theme has been developed by Shaver (1970) and others, bringing it closer to what we have described as defensive attribution; that is, attributions primarily motivated by the need to protect or enhance our own egos. He suggested that responsibility for accidents is allocated partly in terms of the aversive implications of the outcome for the observer. Most important, when we feel quite similar to the perpetrator, we defend *ourselves* best by assigning lower responsibility to him, because our own behavior might some day have the same effect, and we would not want to be blamed for it. Chaiken and Darley (1973) set up an experiment to test the notion that people use attributions to avoid future blame. They placed subjects in a worker-supervisor experiment in which one subject was to take the role of worker, and the other, that of supervisor. Working together, they were to arrange blocks in a certain pattern. The worker was to be paid partly on the basis of work completed. Before starting, the subjects were shown a videotape of what was supposedly a previous session. At the end of it, as the supervisor was getting up to leave, he accidently bumped the table and knocked all the blocks off into a big mess. In one condition this reduced the worker's pay somewhat (mild consequences); in another, it ruled out any pay at all for his work (severe consequences). How was this accident interpreted by the new pair of subjects, who would soon take their positions as worker and supervisor? As shown in Table 4–12, the future supervisors were not nearly as likely to blame their predecessors for the accident, presumably hoping to avoid being blamed themselves, if the same thing should happen. Supervisors instead blamed the accident on chance, or on equipment failure.

TABLE 4–12
attributions of responsibility

	CONSEQUENCES	Future Worker	Future Supervisor
ATTRIBUTIONS TO THE SUPERVISOR	Mild	9.00	7.70
	Severe	8.90	4.90
ATTRIBUTIONS TO CHANCE OR EQUIPMENT FAILURE	Mild	4.30	5.40
	Severe	3.65	6.65

Source: Adapted from Chaiken and Darley, 1973, p. 271.

These seem to be two additional distortions in attributional processes. Completely innocent victims tend to be seen as responsible for their fates, and we avoid attributing responsibility for accidents when we feel similar to the perpetrators. Clearly this places perceived similarity to the person in the accident in a very central role, and we will explore that in some detail in the next chapter. Also, it should be apparent how easy it is for this set of biases to encourage our tolerating degrading social conditions on the grounds that their victims deserve what they are getting. It may be that such misperceptions are yet another instance of the general error of overattributing dispositional or internal control over events, as discussed earlier. But Lerner's reasoning suggests an ego-defensive basis for that general bias.

SUMMARY

1. Attribution theory is concerned with how ordinary people explain social events. The causal explanations people give are treated in terms of being internal to a person (emotions, attitudes, personality traits, or abilities caused the event) or external to him (the people around him, the task he was working on, luck, the weather). Some causes are stable (intelligence, task difficulty); others are unstable (mood, effort, luck).

2. Theorists begin from the assumption that people are strongly motivated to explain the events around them. They do so by looking for *invariance;* that is, which causes are regularly associated with which effects. And they use a *discounting principle;* that is, to the extent that several causes are plausible, they will spread their explanations among them.

3. Kelley's cube theory suggests that people base their attributions upon three kinds of information in particular: consensus (would other people do the same thing in that situation), distinctiveness (is this the only situation in which the person does this), and consistency (does he always do this in this situation).

4. Other people's personality traits and attitudes are normally inferred from their overt behaviors by considering the external forces operating on them at the time. If these forces are strong, attributions are shared between external and internal causes. If these forces are weak, internal attributions are made. A compelling condition for making a *correspondent inference* (the overt behavior accurately reflects the person's internal traits, attitudes, or other states) is that the behavior be low in social desirability.

5. Attribution theory can be applied to self-perception as well as to the perception of others. That is, the same principles may account for how we infer the causes for our own acts and how we infer the causes for others' acts.

6. The internal cues we receive from our own emotional arousal states seem now to be more ambiguous and undifferentiated than has commonly been assumed in the past. Consequently, we infer both the nature and degree of our own emotional arousal by an attributional process that relies on evidence about our own behavior, external indications of our arousal states, and environmental conditions.

7. It is possible to manipulate peoples' perceptions of their own emotions through a process of *misattribution.* When their internal emotional states are ambiguous, they can reattribute their emotions to previously neutral stimuli, such as neutral drugs.

8. Under some conditions, we infer our own attitudes from our own behavior. However, such inferences seem to be most common when we are not especially involved in our attitudes and when they have little consequence for our future lives.

9. In its purest form, attribution theory describes a logical, rationalistic mechanism for arriving at causal explanations. But several systematic biases have been discovered. Most follow from the tendency to attribute too much causality to perceptually prominent causes (that is, to "figure" rather than to "ground"), or to arrive at explanations that are enhancing to one's own ego or to those of one's friends.

10. In general, people ascribe more causality to internal dispositions than they should and less to external forces. This is particularly true for observations of other people's behavior. Self-perceptions may indeed be biased in the opposite direction, and over-attribute causality to external forces.

11. People seem to be quite heavily influenced by the need to give explanations that support or protect their own self-esteem; e.g., externalizing blame or taking credit for success. They also seem to extend this generosity to others, especially those they are close to.

12. People underutilize statistical, abstract information, and often are overly responsive to a few vivid, concrete stimuli. They seem to overestimate the representativeness of occasional concrete instances.

SUGGESTIONS FOR ADDITIONAL READING

BEM, D. J. Self-perception theory. In Leonard Berkowitz (Ed.), *Advances in experimental social psychology*, (Vol. 6), New York: Academic Press, 1972. A straightforward and persuasively argued statement of the self-perception viewpoint. It argues for a reinterpretation of cognitive dissonance phenomena.

HARVEY, J. H., & SMITH, W. P. *Social psychology—An attributional approach.* St. Louis: C. V. Mosby, 1977. A textbook on social psychology written from an attribution theory point of view. Excellent coverage of attribution interpretations across many areas of social psychology.

JONES, E. E., KANOUSE, D. E., KELLEY, H. H., NISBETT, R. E., VALINS, S., & WEINER, B. *Attribution: Perceiving the causes of behavior.* Morristown, N. J.: General Learning Press, 1972. The best and most influential early collection of theoretical statements on attribution theory. Includes excellent papers on the actor-observer effect, self-perception, negativity, and others.

KAHNEMAN, D., & TVERSKY, A. On the psychology of prediction. *Psychological Review,* 1973, *80,* 237–251. An influential and interesting exposition of cognitive biases we all seem to be subject to, yet mostly unaware of.

KELLEY, H. H. Attribution theory in social psychology. In David Levine (Ed.), *Nebraska Symposium on Motivation,* 1967. Lincoln: University of Nebraska Press, 1967. Still the best and most coherent basic statement of attribution theory.

MCARTHUR, L. A. The how and what of why: Some determinants and consequences of causal attribution. *Journal of Personality and Social Psychology,* 1972, *22,* 171–193. A representative early study of Kelley's cube theory of attribution. It uses a role-playing methodology which is typical of much (though not all) research in the area.

ROSS, L. The intuitive psychologist and his shortcomings: Distortions in the attribution process. In Leonard Berkowitz (Ed.), *Advances in experimental social psychology,* 1977, in press. A comprehensive and engaging discussion of the "irrational" biases in attribution. Mostly oriented toward cognitive, nonmotivational explanations for them.

TAYLOR, S. E., & FISKE, S. T. Point of view and perceptions of causality. *Journal of Personality and Social Psychology,* 1975, *32,* 439–445. A clever experimental demonstration of the "point of view" explanation for actor-observer differences in attribution. Its realistic methodology and reasoning are excellent models for attributional research.

5

liking and attraction

proximity

- how proximity operates
- why proximity causes liking
- exceptions to the rule

personal qualities

- warmth
- physical attractiveness

familiarity

rewardingness

- reciprocity
- esteem needs
- the gain-loss phenomenon
- ingratiation

cognitive balance

- forces toward balance
- cognitive origins of the balance model
- unit relations
- exceptions to the balance principle

similarity

- complementarity

intimate relationships

- romantic love
- social penetration
- self-disclosure

racial prejudice

- race and belief
- cooperative interdependence
- contact and prejudice reduction

summary

suggestions for additional reading

In the previous chapters we discussed how people perceive other people. Now we turn to a basic dimension of interpersonal perception and interpersonal relations, that is, how much people like one another. In our discussion of the semantic differential, we saw that the evaluative dimension explains a great deal of the difference in attitudes and perceptions. When we rate anything, whether a book, a house, or the president of the United States, how positive we feel toward the object is a key factor in our rating. This is particularly important when other people are involved, because the extent to which two people like each other is a fundamental determinant of their interaction. It affects practically every phase of their relationship—how much they choose to see each other, how close they stand, what they say to each other, how they treat each other, how much they are influenced by each other, and on and on. Among the first questions we ask ourselves when we meet somebody else are: Will he like me? Will I like him?

Note that we have used the word *like* rather than a more technical or neutral term such as *positively evaluate.* The reason is that we are concerned with something more than a positive evaluation of another person. We may positively evaluate a candidate for the presidency of the United States or a movie actress, but we are not friends with them. The distinction is, of course, not clear, for most of the factors that affect positive evaluation also affect more personal liking. However, we shall use *liking* because we are dealing not only with the question of why someone evaluates another person positively but also with why someone tends to like and become friends with another person.

We shall consider six major determinants of liking—proximity, personal qualities, familiarity, rewardingness, cognitive balance, and similarity. In each case, we shall describe the general effect of the variable but concentrate on trying to explain why it operates as it does and on specifying situations that magnify or minimize its effect. At the end of the chapter, we will apply some of these findings to the development of more intimate relationships, and to race relations.

proximity

Probably the best single predictor of whether two people are friends is how far apart they live. If one of them lives in Brazil and the other in China, it is almost certain they are not friends. If one lives in New York City and the other in Los Angeles, or even if they live on opposite sides of the same city, it is unlikely they are friends. In fact, if two people live only ten blocks apart, it is considerably less likely that they are friends than if they live next door to each other.

how proximity operates

W. H. Whyte (1956) conducted a study of friendship patterns in Park Forest, a suburban residential community. Almost everyone had moved into Park Forest at about the same time. Because all the houses were similar, the residents had chosen their homes and neighborhoods pretty much by chance. There were no "better" areas, no cheap houses—nothing in particular to distinguish the various parts of the town. Thus, the possibility was minimized that people in one area were in some way different from those in another before they moved into the community. It was almost as though a large group had been assigned randomly to houses.

For some time Whyte read the social column in the newspaper and kept a careful check on who gave parties, who was invited by whom, and, in general, who was friendly with whom. The patterns of association he found depended a great deal on proximity. Almost everyone at the baby shower lived within a few blocks of one another, and almost everyone who lived within the area was there. The same was true on the other side of town at the eggnog party. In the whole town there were practically no friends who did not live near one another. Similarly, there was a remarkable occurrence of friendships among people who lived close together.

This same kind of effect occurs in much smaller units than a whole town. A study of Festinger, Schachter, and Back (1950) investigated the patterns of friendships in a large housing development called Westgate West, which consisted of seventeen separate two-story buildings, each containing ten apartments (five on a floor). The layout is shown in Figure 5-1. This housing development was similar to Park Forest in certain respects. For one thing the apartments were almost identical. More im-

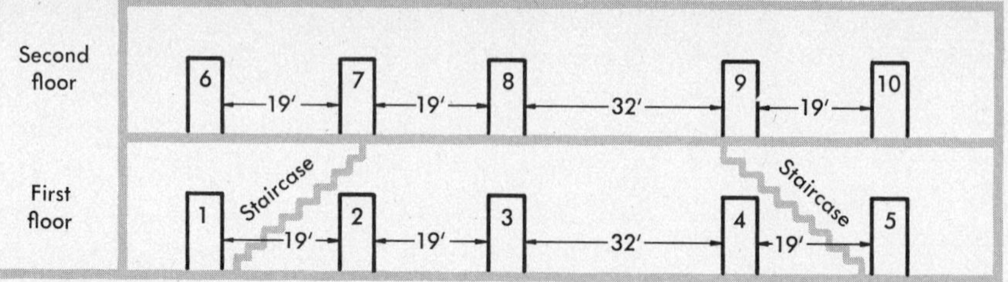

FIGURE 5–1
Floor plan of Westgate West. All the buildings in the housing development had the same layout. In the study, functional distance was defined simply as the number of doors away two people lived—the differences in distance measured by feet were ignored. (Adapted from Festinger, Schachter, and Back, 1950.)

portant, however, residents did not choose where they were to live; they were given apartments as the apartments became vacant. In other words, like Park Forest, Westgate West came close to being a field experiment—the residents were randomly assigned to a condition.

All the residents were asked, "Which three people in Westgate West do you see socially most often?" The results are shown in the graph in Figure 5–2. It is clear that residents were most friendly with those who lived near them. People on the same floor (top line) mentioned their nextdoor neighbor more often than their neighbor two doors away and their neighbor two doors away more often than their neighbor at the other end of the hall. Of nextdoor neighbors, 41 percent were chosen, whereas only 22 percent of those two doors away and 10 percent of those at the end of the hall were. Moreover, it should be noted that the dis-

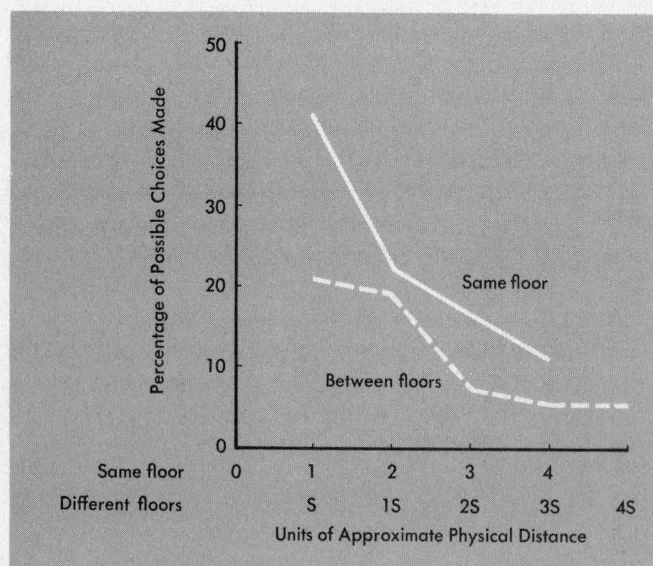

FIGURE 5–2
The relationship between functional distance and liking. The distance between people on the same floor and on different floors was closely related to friendship patterns—the closer two individuals lived, the more likely they were to be friends. Living on different floors (bottom line) reduced the likelihood of friendship because functional distance was increased. (Festinger, Schachter, and Back, 1950.)

and poorly in others (ungrammatical, spelling errors, cliches). A control group got the essays without any picture of the author. As can be seen in Table 5–4, the attractive woman was thought to have written the better essay, regardless of whether it was objectively good or bad.

Other studies have found attractive people treated more leniently when they do something wrong. Dion (1972) found that transgressions committed by attractive children were viewed less negatively by adults than were the same acts committed by unattractive children. Similarly, Landy and Aronson (1969) found that subjects in a mock jury sentenced an unattractive defendant to more years in prison than they did an attractive defendant, given a crime described in exactly the same terms. Moreover, in two different studies they found that killing an attractive victim brought a longer sentence than killing an unattractive victim.

But, as with all things, this attractiveness-based halo effect has its limits. Sigall and Ostrove (1975) hypothesized that jurors would actually be *more* punitive toward a beautiful defendant if her offense were somehow directly related to her attractiveness. So they gave mock jurors the details of a case, along with a picture of the defendant, either an attractive or an unattractive woman. The charge was either one of burglary, which could have almost nothing to do with the defendant's beauty, or swindling, which might be thought to be something a beautiful woman might use her looks to get away with. Verifying this hunch about connecting crime to attractiveness, a control group, not shown the photographs but given the case materials, did in fact rate the swindler as probably more attractive than the burglar. And attractiveness did reduce the burglar's sentence, as in the other studies cited above. But the beautiful swindler was given a somewhat harsher sentence than the unattractive one. The results are shown in Table 5–5. Thus, it helps to be beautiful, as long as it does not *appear* that you are trying to get away with something extra because of it.

TABLE 5–5
mean sentence assigned, in years

OFFENSE	DEFENDANT'S ATTRACTIVENESS		
	Attractive	Unattractive	Control
Swindle	5.45	4.35	4.35
Burglary	2.80	5.20	5.10

Source: Sigall and Ostrove, 1975.

The halo effect conferred by attractiveness may also be weaker when the subjects actually interact with the stimulus person face-to-face, and thus get a more realistic and complete contact with the person. For example, Kleck and Rubenstein (1975) had male subjects interact in an extended interview with a female confederate whose attractiveness was experimentally manipulated through clothes and makeup. They found that the subjects liked the more attractive confederate better but they did not attribute any especially socially desirable personality traits to her.

We cannot understand liking without understanding that some people have likable qualities in greater numbers than do others. As important as these personal qualities are, however, they do not completely account for liking. Much depends upon the type of interaction two people have. And since this is a book about social psychology, and hence about human interaction, we want to emphasize most of those factors that grow out of the interpersonal interaction. Let's turn now to familiarity.

familiarity

Some recent studies have produced results that suggest a particularly fascinating explanation of the effect of proximity on liking. To begin with, when a quality continuum in the English language has both negative and positive poles (e.g., good-bad, right-wrong, tall-short, beautiful-ugly), the word describing the positive pole is almost always used more frequently. Thus, *good* appears in books and newspapers more frequently than *bad*, *right* more frequently than *wrong*, and so on. This finding, by itself, is just a curiosity. Without additional research, there would be no way of knowing whether familiarity made the words positive, or vice versa. But the finding does suggest that familiar things may be or become more positive than unfamiliar things. In some way, familiarity is associated with being good.

As already mentioned, Zajonc conducted several experiments (1968) to demonstrate that familiarity by itself increases liking. His initial demonstrations of this phenomenon involved quite impersonal, nonmeaningful stimuli, such as nonsense syllables or Chinese characters. More directly relevant to our current concern, in another study by Zajonc subjects were shown pictures of faces. Some of the faces were shown as many as twenty-five times, others only one or two times. Afterward, the subjects were asked how much they liked each face and how much they thought they would like the person pictured. The results are shown in Figure 5–4. Familiarity appeared to have the same effect with faces as it had with words. The more often the subjects had seen a face, the more they said they liked it and thought they would like the person pictured. Adding yet another wrinkle to this general finding, Brickman, Meyer, and Fredd (1975) presented subjects with a stimulus person giving word associations. When the stimulus person gave highly familiar associations (such as saying "dog" to "cat"), he was liked better than

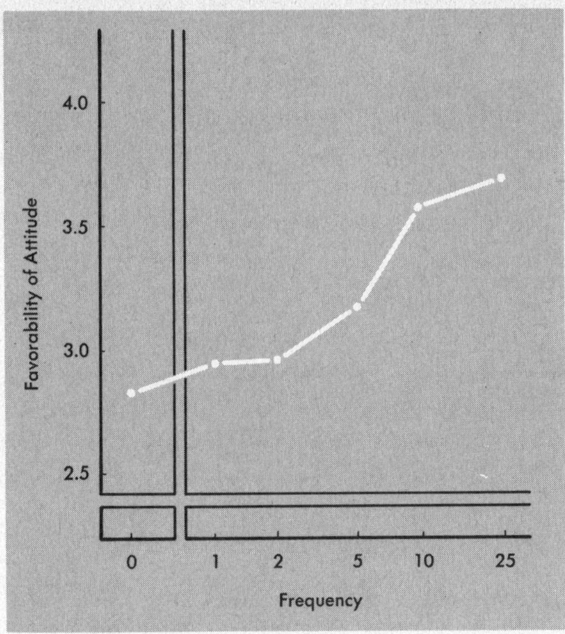

FIGURE 5–4
The relationship between frequency of exposure and liking. Subjects were shown photographs of different faces and the number of times each face was shown was varied. The more often the subjects saw a particular face, the more they said they liked the person pictured. (Zajonc, R. B., "Attitudinal effects of mere exposure," Journal of Personality and Social Psychology, 1968, 8, p. 18. Copyright 1968 by the American Psychological Association, and reproduced by permission.)

when he gave quite unusual, unfamiliar associations (like "blood" to "cat").

We might think this "mere exposure" effect could be limited to pleasant situations. The more times we take our favorite girlfriend out to eat at a restaurant with a pleasant atmosphere, surely the more we will like her. But if all our rendezvous are in a grimy coffee shop, perhaps familiarity would not lead to increased liking. However, it turns out that familiarity seems to increase liking in *either* positive or negative contexts.

Two experiments by Saegert, Swap, and Zajonc (1973) provide strong evidence that the familiarity effect is not dependent on positive situations. In these studies, the amount of exposure to other people was varied as in previous work, and the exposures occurred in either pleasant or unpleasant circumstances. The subjects were all tasting a variety of substances, but for half of them the tastes were pleasant (Kool-Aid), and for half they were quite unpleasant (vinegar, quinine, or citric acid). The results of their first experiment are shown in Figure 5–5. As you can see, for both pleasant and noxious taste conditions, the people liked each other more when they had seen each other more. The second experiment produced almost identical findings. Thus, it seems clear that exposure increases liking regardless of whether the situation is positive or negative.

But there are some limitations on this "familiarity breeds liking" finding. First of all, it may diminish at extreme levels of exposure. That is, overexposure may produce boredom and satiation, and reduce liking. Miller (1976) tested this idea by putting posters up in the commons area of a college dormitory. For the moderate exposure condition, 30 posters were put up (about one every 50 feet of wall) for two days. For the overexposure condition, 170 additional posters were put up for three more days. The dependent variable was the student's attitude toward the message featured in the poster. Miller found that moderate exposure increased liking for the message, but overexposure actually diminished it. However, there has not been enough research for us to know whether or not this is a typical result of high levels of exposure, and if it is, how much exposure is required for liking to start falling off. Most studies are done within relatively short periods of time, so they cannot test very adequately for satiation.

FIGURE 5–5
Liking for another person as a function of the frequency of contact and the pleasantness of taste of the solutions. Even in unpleasant contexts, greater familiarity leads to more liking. (Saegert, Swap, and Zajonc, "Exposure, context, and interpersonal attraction," Journal of Personality and Social Psychology, 1973, 25, p. 237. Copyright 1973 by the American Psychological Association; reproduced by permission.)

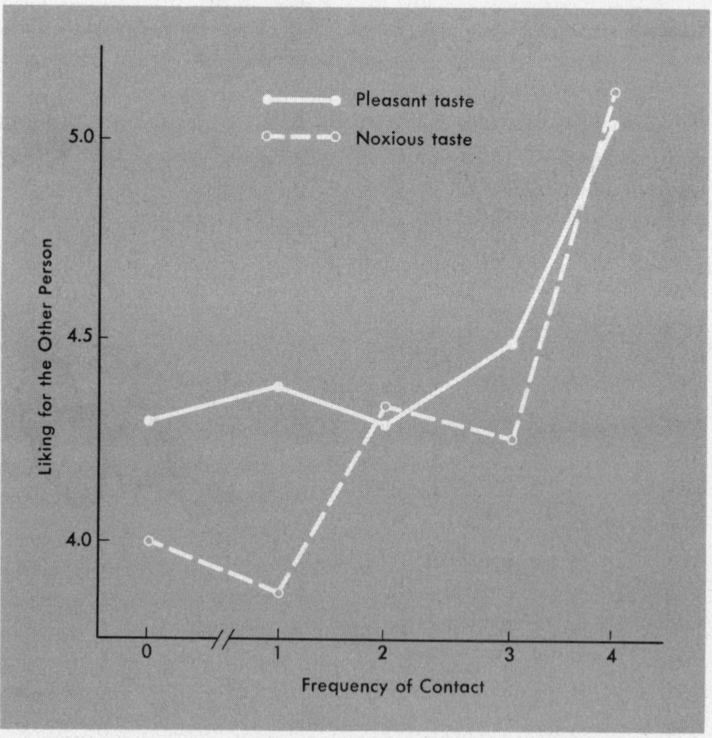

Perhaps more important is that the "mere exposure" effect seems to be limited to stimulus objects that are inherently positive or neutral. That is, greater exposure to *negative* objects does not increase liking for them. Perlman and Oskamp (1971) tested this idea by presenting subjects with pictures of stimulus persons presented positively (as scientists or clergymen), neutrally (dressed in a sports shirt or suit), or negatively (as a janitor or in a police lineup). They found that increased exposure to positive or neutral pictures increased liking, but no such effect occurred for the negative pictures. The results are shown in Figure 5–6. A similar finding emerged from a study by Brockner and Swap (1976). The mere exposure effect held for stimulus persons holding attitudes similar to the subject's, but liking for those with dissimilar attitudes was unaffected by frequency.

The general principle appears to be that exposure enhances liking when the object is intrinsically pleasurable or at least neutral, but not when it is strongly negative. To make this point graphically, Zajonc uses the example of seeing a particular man in handcuffs repeatedly over a period of weeks. After a while we become convinced he really is a criminal, rather than coming to love him. But even if an initial rating is only mildly negative, increased familiarity does have a strong effect. For example, in Zajonc's studies, many of the initial ratings were on the negative side of neutral, and he did get the familiarity effect. Thus, it appears

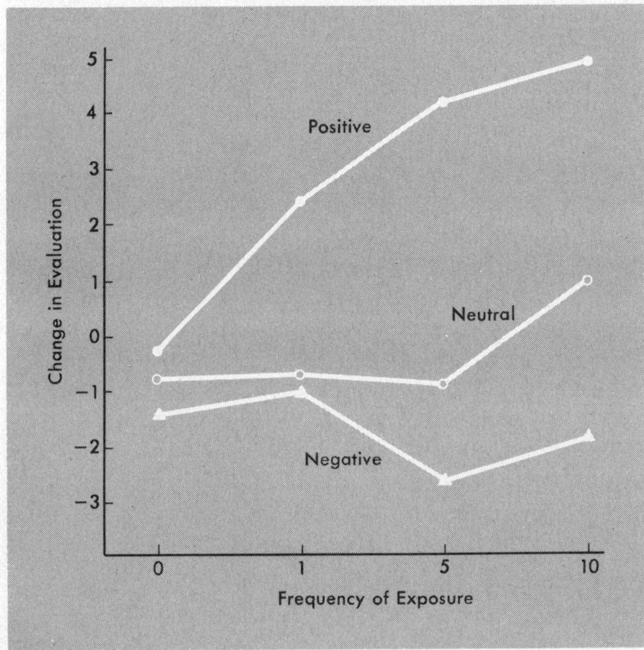

FIGURE 5–6
Mean change in evaluation of stimulus persons, as a function of frequency of exposure and picture content (positive, neutral, or negative). Positive scores indicate a positive shift in evaluations. Source: Perlman and Oskamp, 1971.

that only a strongly negative initial evaluation or perhaps one that is anchored in some actual occurrence is not affected by the familiarity phenomenon.

Another exception to the general tendency of contact leading to liking occurs when people have conflicting interests, needs, or personalities. As long as they see little of each other, the conflicts are minimized. They may not particularly like each other, but they have little reason to dislike each other. When contact is increased, however, the conflicts are exaggerated and aggravated. Under these circumstances, they may sometimes dislike each other more as a result of closer contact.

rewardingness

People like others who reward them or who are associated with pleasant experiences. We like beautiful women or handsome men because we enjoy looking at them. Kind people reward others constantly and are therefore liked more. The same is true of people who are friendly, sincere, trustworthy, warm, and so on. Someone with these qualities is nicer to be with than somebody without them.

The effect of rewardingness can be explained in terms of simple learning principles. If somebody rewards us or we share a rewarding experience with him, the positive aspects of the experience or the reward are linked with the other person. He thus becomes more positive and we like him more.

reciprocity

The *reciprocity principle* is perhaps the most important application of the rewardingness idea. We like people whom we know like us. If the only information we have about someone is that he likes us, we are predisposed to like him also. If he dislikes us, this feeling too will be reciprocated.

This effect has been illustrated in an experiment by Aronson and Linder (1965). They had subjects go through a series of brief interactions with a confederate who was posing as another subject. After each interaction the subject overheard an interview between the confederate and the experimenter in which the confederate gave his impressions of the subject. In one condition, the confederate was quite flattering and said at the beginning that he liked the subject. He continued to make positive statements about the subject after each of the interviews. In another condition, the confederate was critical. He said he was not sure that he liked the subject much and gave fairly negative descriptions of him. He continued being negative throughout the study. Afterward, the subjects were asked how much they liked the confederate. The results are shown in Table 5–6. (The third condition will be discussed later.) As expected, the subjects reciprocated the confederate's evaluation of them, liking him when he liked them and disliking him when he disliked them.

Of course, this does not mean that *all* likes and dislikes are reciprocal. Sometimes we like someone who dislikes us, and vice versa. But other things being equal, there is a strong tendency to like those who like us. Although there are various explanations for this phenomenon, as we shall see below, probably the main reason for it is that the nicest thing anyone can tell us is that he likes us. It is extremely rewarding, and we like those who give us this reward.

TABLE 5–6
liking in response to another's evaluation

CONDITION	LIKING[a]
Positive evaluation throughout	6.42
Negative evaluation throughout	2.52
Negative-positive evaluation	7.67

[a]Figures are ratings on a scale from −10 to +10.
Source: Adapted from Aronson and Linder (1965).

esteem needs

Rewardingness may seem like a simple principle, but actually it has a number of complexities. For one thing, if liking results partly from the rewardingness of the other person, then liking ought to be dependent partly on how needy for those rewards the subject is. For example, a person who needs a lot of praise, affection, and support ought to like someone who gives it to him more than would a less needy, more satisfied person. In general, people with low self-esteem have more need for esteem-boosting rewards than do people with high self-esteem. Therefore they ought to like more those people who give them positive evaluations, and dislike more those people who give them negative evaluations, than would be the case for those with high self-esteem. Put another way, a person with high self-esteem already has most of his esteem needs met, so he will be relatively indifferent to what he gets from others. But a person with low self-esteem is really needy, and so will like or dislike another person very strongly depending on whether the other person gratifies or frustrates his esteem needs.

An early experiment showing this effect was done by Dittes (1959). After his subjects filled out various tests measuring their levels of self-esteem, he had them interact in a small group. At the end of the discussion, each group member rated each of the other members. False ratings were then given to each member, supposedly showing how the others felt about him. Some ratings were quite positive, others more negative. Then everyone was asked how much he liked the group. For low self-esteem subjects, liking for the group was highly dependent on how much the group liked them. This was not so true for the high self-esteem subjects. A similar finding was reported in an experiment by Friedman (1976). He had subjects work with a confederate on a cooperative task. At the end they received a certain number of points, based on their performance. The confederate then took the lead in dividing these points very unequally, to the subject's advantage: 80 percent for the subject and only 20 percent for the confederate. This good deed led low self-esteem subjects to like the confederate more and want more to be her friend than it did the high self-esteem subjects. Jones (1973) has reviewed a large number of such studies and has concluded that such findings are quite typical of realistic experimental situations. The general point is a fairly obvious one: The dependence of liking on rewardingness seems to determine liking most when the subject most needs the rewards the other person can give him. Without those needs, the rewards do not affect liking as much.

the gain-loss phenomenon

Reciprocity is very important in liking, presumably because it controls one of the rewards most central to a human being: another person's affection. But some research indicates a complication in the simplest version of the reciprocity principle. It is not always just the *number* of rewards another person gives you; sometimes it is whether they are increasing or decreasing. Aronson and Linder, in the study described above, suggested that we like best those people who show increasing liking for us, and dislike most those who show decreasing liking. According to this *gain-loss* principle, we do not react as extremely to those who are more steadily positive or negative to us.

In Aronson and Linder's study, subjects heard a confederate making either positive or negative statments about them and the subjects generally reciprocated the confederate's evaluations. But the experiment included one other variation—a condition in which the confederate began by making negative statements about the subjects and became more and more positive in his descriptions throughout the course of the experiment. By the last few interviews, he was making as positive statements about the subjects in this condition as he did when he was positive throughout. In other words, some subjects heard a confederate who liked them at the beginning and continued to like them, whereas other subjects heard a confederate who did not like them at the beginning but ended up liking them. Although in both these conditions the subjects liked the confederate, they liked him even more when he began critically and ended positively than when he was positive throughout (see Table 5–6). Note that this seems to run counter to a simple reinforcement or reward theory, because the confederate delivered more total reinforcements when he was nice all through the experiment than when he was positive only toward the end.

Aronson has suggested an ominous implication of this gain-loss principle, which he calls "Aronson's law of marital infidelity." A wife may come to take for granted, and disregard, her husband's constant compliments. But should a handsome stranger come along and tell her how beautiful she is, she might be "gained" right off her feet into some extramarital escapade. How, Aronson asks, can a long-term relationship remain attractive to a person if newly won affections are more attractive than constant, long-standing ones? There is no definitive answer to this question yet. One thing we can say is that the gain-loss phenomenon is not universal. A number of studies have indeed followed Aronson and Linder in getting such an effect. Clore, Wiggins, and Itkin (1975), for example, presented videotapes in which an actress performed warm behaviors toward a male (facing him, smiling, nodding her head) and/or cold behaviors to him (frowning, looking around the room). The subjects were asked to rate how much the male in the videotape probably liked the woman. When she changed from cold to warm, she was thought more likable than when she was constantly warm; and when she changed from warm to cold, she was thought less likable than when she was constantly cold. This fits the gain-loss theory. But a number of other studies have obtained only the simpler pattern, that the warmer the better and the colder the worse, irrespective of any changes (Berscheid, Brother, and Graziano, 1976). The best we can say now is that the gain-loss phenomenon does occur sometimes, but so far we cannot say exactly when.

There are two general explanations for the gain-loss phenomenon. Aronson and Linder originally suggested that the initial negative statements caused the subjects some anxiety, self-doubt, etc., all of which are painful feelings. When the statements gradually became more positive, they not only were rewarding in themselves but they also reduced these previous negative feelings. Thus, the later positive statements were more rewarding than they would have been without the initial negative evaluations. The negative statements increased the need for positive evaluations, and this made them more rewarding when they finally came.

Another explanation offered by the authors concerned the manner in which the subjects perceived the confederate. When the confederate liked them immediately and continued to like them, there may have been some doubt in the subjects' minds as to how honest or discriminating the confederate was. They may have said to themselves, "This guy likes everybody." On the other hand, when the confederate began in a negative way, he must have impressed the subjects as being the type of person who could say unpleasant things about others and who takes time to make up his mind about them. That is, the critic appeared more discriminating and perhaps more reliable. Then, when he said nice things about the subjects, his opinion carried more weight and was therefore more rewarding. The subjects might have thought, "This guy is pretty careful about making up his mind about people, but he likes me." The determining factor in the subjects' liking the confederate was how much they were rewarded by the nice things he said, and it is more rewarding to be praised by a careful, discriminating person.

This explanation has been supported in two studies by Mettee (1971a, 1971b) in which the discernment of the person making the positive or negative statements was varied. In one case he appeared to be quite discerning, made some negative statements and some positive ones, and generally gave the impression of someone who made careful, deliberate discriminations. When the discerning person made positive statements about the subject, he was liked more than was someone who seemed less discerning.

ingratiation

We can see that saying something nice about someone is almost always rewarding. The more he believes us and values our judgment, the more it is rewarding. To the extent that he distrusts us and does not value our opinion, it is less rewarding. We like people who say or do nice things for us, but the strength of our liking is determined by how much we trust the motivation behind the action and how much we value the action itself. In particular, there is an important distinction between *genuine* reciprocity and ingratiation. If we assume that the other person is being nice to us for ulterior motives, we do not reciprocate the affection as much as if we trust his behavior as being genuine.

E. E. Jones (1964) has conducted a series of studies on this ingratiation phenomenon. In one experiment, female subjects were given a standard interview in which they were asked about their backgrounds, values, and personal opinions. While they were answering these questions, they knew they were being observed by somebody sitting behind a one-way mirror. After the interviews, the observer told the subjects her impression of them. Regardless of the manner in which the subjects had acted, the observer always responded in one of three set ways—she gave neutral responses, responses that were as similar as possible to a subject's own self-concept, or positive evaluations.

In addition, subjects were given two different types of information about the observer. In what was called the accuracy condition, the subjects were told that the purpose of the experiment was to discover how accurately people form impressions of others. The observer in this condition was supposed to be a first-year graduate student in clinical psychology who was participating as part of her training. It was mentioned that clinical psychology students received special training designed to enable them to be objective and to prevent their own feelings from influencing their judgments. Subjects in what was called the ulterior-motive condition were told that the observer was a graduate student who had asked to take the place of the regular assistant just for the day, because she was hoping to use the subjects in her own experiment in exchange for serving as the observer. The experimenter remarked that the observer would be very grateful for the subject's cooperation but that the decision was up to the subject. In this condition no mention was made of the importance of accuracy, nor was anything said about special training in being objective. In other words, in one case the observer was an objective, disinterested judge; in the other case she was someone who wanted a favor and was under no special pressure to be objective. After hearing the observer's judgments of her, each subject was asked to rate the observer. It was made clear that these ratings would be confidential and would not be shown to the observer. The subjects rated the observer on a variety of scales, all designed to indicate how much they liked her.

To begin with, the findings showed a strong effect of reinforcement. The more favorable rating the observer had made of the subject, the more the subject liked the observer. The effect of the different instructions was very interesting. Regardless of the type of remarks the observer had made, the observer who had an ulterior motive was liked less than the one who was trying to be objective and accurate. Most important, the largest difference in liking between the accuracy and ulterior-motive conditions and the only one in which there was an appreciable effect occurred when the observer made consistently positive evaluations of the subject. Under these circumstances, it probably appeared that the observer who had the ulterior motive was not being honest but was making the statements in order to get the subject to agree to take part in her experiment. Therefore, she was rated lower than the objective observer.

Apparently it is nice to receive favorable comments from somebody even if we suspect the person's motives. But we will like the other person less if we have suspicions than if we do not. When a person has something to gain from us, when we are in a superior position, there is a tendency to perceive behavior as ingratiating rather than honest. The nice things he says do not have the same effect. In general, flattery does not make us like others as much as honest compliments do. Under some circumstances it may actually make us dislike them, presumably because we feel they are being dishonest and are trying to take advantage of us. In other words, although there is a general tendency to like someone who says nice things, the effect is not as strong when the compliments are seen as ingratiation.

It will be recalled that a very similar phenomenon was discussed in connection with attribution theory in the last chapter. Mass communicators who were making self-serving statements or who were presenting a position supporting the self-interests of their audience were not trusted very much. Nor were they very persuasive. As indicated by attribution theory, people tend to make causal attributions for others' behavior. When there are strong external forces (such as something to be gained by a particular statement) an observer makes an external attribution for the statement. So whether the insurance salesman says he thinks we need insurance, or tells us how wonderful a personality we have, we tend to discount the statement and attribute it to some opportunistic motive. This, then, is another example of how we regularly make attributions of *intent* about others' behavior, and that partly determines our own reaction to the behavior.

cognitive balance

It has often been observed that people like to be surrounded by those who generally agree with them. As a result, they like best people who agree with them most. In an effort to explain such phenomena, Fritz Heider, Theodore Newcomb, and others have proposed a theory of cognitive balance or, as it is commonly called, the *balance model.* The basic assumption behind this model (and other similar models which are discussed in Chapter 8) is that people tend to prefer consistency. They want things to fit together and to be logical and harmonious, and this holds for their own beliefs, cognitions, thoughts, and feelings. In particular, people want their feelings about other people and objects to be consistent.

forces toward balance

The simplest situation to illustrate consistency in this context is one person's feelings about another person and both their feelings about an object. For example, consider a student's attitude toward a teacher and both their feelings about busing school children for racial integration. If we limit ourselves to simple positive-negative feelings, there is a limited number of combinations of these elements. They are diagrammed in Figure 5–7 with the initials S, T, and B standing for the student, teacher, and busing, respectively. The arrows indicate the direction of the feelings. A plus sign means a positive emotion, and a minus sign means a negative one. Thus, the first diagram shows that the student likes the teacher and they both support busing.

On the left side of the diagram are four possible balanced situations—situations in which the relations among the elements are consistent with each other. When the student likes the teacher and they both support busing, the structure is balanced. It is certainly consistent when two people who like each other like the same things—their relationship is harmonious because they both agree. If the student likes the teacher and they both dislike busing, balance (harmony) also exists—neither

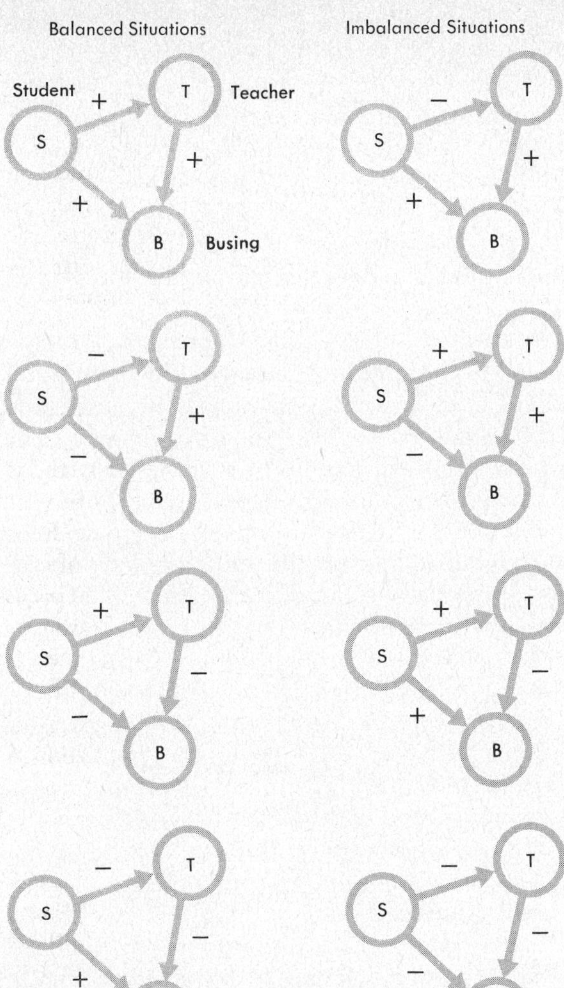

FIGURE 5–7
The balance model of liking. There are eight possible configurations of two people and an object. According to the model, the imbalanced structures tend to become balanced by a change in one or more elements.

likes busing, and they are united in opposition to it. Finally, if the student dislikes the teacher and likes busing while the teacher dislikes it, or if the student dislikes the teacher and dislikes busing while the teacher likes it, balance exists. In either case, they disagree about busing, but the student dislikes and would not want to have much to do with the teacher anyway, so there is no conflict. For convenience, notice that each of the four balanced structures contains an even number of minus signs (negative relations). Whenever there is one negative relation, another is necessary to balance it.

The unbalanced structures have an odd number of negative relations. They occur when the student and the teacher like each other but disagree, or dislike each other and agree, about busing. The imbalance of these situations may be less obvious; the inconsistency lies in the fact that we expect those we like to have similar likes and dislikes to ours and those we dislike to have different likes and dislikes from ours.

The second assumption of the balance model is that imbalanced configurations tend to shift toward balanced ones. It is this assumption that gives the model its importance. Unstable systems produce pressures toward change and continue this pressure until they are balanced; that is, the structures on the right side of the diagram will shift toward those on the left.

The change from imbalance to balance can occur in many ways. Any of the relations may be altered to produce balance. For example, if both the student and the teacher like busing, but the student dislikes the teacher, balance could occur by any one of the following changes. The student could decide that he really does like the teacher or that he actually dislikes busing. Alternatively, he might distort reality by believing that the teacher is antagonistic to busing. Which mechanism is chosen depends on the ease of using it and on the individual doing the changing. We shall discuss this in more detail in Chapter 9. For the moment, the important point is that various possibilities exist.

cognitive origins of the balance model

The notion of balancing forces comes originally from Gestalt theories of perceptual organization. As we indicated in the last two chapters, people try to achieve "good form" in their perceptions of others just as they try to achieve "good form" or "good figures" in their perceptions of inanimate objects. Balanced relations between people "fit"; they "go together"; they make a sensible, coherent, meaningful picture. Thus the main motive pushing people toward balance is trying to achieve a harmonious, simple, coherent, and meaningful view of social relationships. One of the implications of this theory is that people will try to impose or restore such perceptual order on social situations when they are ambiguous, or have become perceptually confused and chaotic. Numerous studies have presented subjects with hypothetical social situations such as "John likes his roommate Harry and Harry voted for Jimmy Carter." The subject is then asked to complete the triad: "How does John feel about Jimmy Carter?" The general finding is that people tend to develop balanced triads when they are initially incomplete or imbalanced.

Such research has shown these balancing forces affecting a number of cognitive operations. People *learn* balanced social situations more readily than they learn imbalanced ones; they *recall* balanced triads more readily than they recall imbalanced ones (Picek, Sherman, and Shiffrin, 1975); they *misrecall* relations as balanced when the triad is in fact imbalanced; they *group and classify* balanced triads together as being similar more than they classify according to dimensions other than balance (Cottrell, 1975). They *expect* balanced triads to occur more often than imbalanced (Crockett, 1974). They *predict* incomplete triads will ultimately *be completed* in a more balanced than imbalanced way (DeSoto and Kuethe, 1959). They expect imbalanced situations to *change over time* toward greater balance (Burnstein, 1967).

unit relations

Heider, the originator of balance theory, makes a distinction between two kinds of relations that can exist in such triads: *sentiment* relations and *unit* relations. Sentiment relations involve feeling—liking or disliking the other person or the attitude object. Unit relations involve the perceived connectedness of objects. Objects which "belong together" comprise a unit. Most people would perceive me as having a unit relation with my dog, with my car, with my sister, with my typewriter, with my fellow Americans, and with the other people attending a lecture with me. In more formal terms, unit relations can be perceived because of the proximity of two objects, contiguity in time, similarity, physical kinship, nationality, ownership or common fate. These are among the standard perceptual conditions inducing a coherent "good figure," as discussed in the last chapter (see Figure 4–2). Heider actually specifies two main classes of unit relations: those which come about as a result of choice, and those which do not. If we see someone choosing an object (dating a

H. Armstrong Roberts

particular person or buying a new red Chevy Nova), we are likely to perceive them as connected. We will wait until Chapter 12 to discuss the effects of choice, since that is most commonly investigated in the context of dissonance theory; here we will be concerned only with the effects of no-choice unit relations upon liking.

Most of the work on balance theory has involved sentiment relations. Forces toward balance move people toward agreeing with people they like, and disagreeing with people they dislike. But Heider also suggested that we balance our sentiments with unit relations. We feel a social relationship "fits" and makes a coherent, reasonable picture when people are connected to those they like, and disconnected from those they dislike. If unit relations are expected to be balanced with sentiment relations, when should this most affect liking? The most obvious case is when we are in a unit relation with someone we dislike. Then our positive unit relation is imbalanced with our negative sentiment relation. Suppose that you hate your older sister. You are connected to her by virtue of being sisters. You certainly didn't *choose* her. But perhaps you feel oppressed and put down and infantilized by her. So what do you do? The prediction from balance theory is that you would try to balance your unit relation with your sentiment relation. This gives you two options: you could break off your relationship with her, claim she is no longer your sister or you don't care about her, never see her or call her, don't give her presents at Christmas, and so on. Or you could reevaluate her, see some of the good in her, try to avoid the unpleasant situations you get into with her, think she is after all your sister and part of your family and someone you love (warts and all), and generally change your sentiment from negative to positive. The issue comes down to which of those relations, unit or sentiment, you are more likely to change.

Often it is nearly impossible to break off the unit relation. It is hard to cut off a relationship with your sister. And when the unit is unlikely to change, but the sentiment is negative, the balance prediction is that liking will increase. Tyler and Sears (1977) conducted two experiments to test this idea. They reasoned that a unit relation occurs between two people when they expect to have to interact together. They presented subjects with stimulus persons that were either positive or negative (to induce positive or negative sentiments), then varied whether the subject would have to interact with the stimulus person or not. They predicted that anticipated interaction with negative stimulus persons would increase liking to restore balance, whereas liking would be unaffected by anticipated interaction with an already likable stimulus person.

In the first experiment, the subject was presented with a short essay supposedly written by a fellow student and with an attitude questionnaire supposedly filled out by the same student. In the critical condition, designed to create a negative, disagreeing person, the essay said this woman did not like most other college women because they were "silly and uninformed" about most issues. Moreover, the attitude questionnaire was carefully tailored to disagree with the subject on most current social and political issues. Then the subject was told either that she would have to have a discussion with this stimulus person, or that she would be having a discussion with someone else. Finally, the subject was asked how much she liked this SP. The results were quite clearly in line with balance theory. As shown in Table 5–7 anticipated interaction substantially boosted liking for this obnoxious SP. And anticipated interaction did not increase liking for the pleasant SP very much.

TABLE 5–7
effect of anticipated interaction on liking for stimulus person

	STIMULUS PERSON	
	Pleasant	Unpleasant
Experiment 1: anticipating future interaction with stranger	+0.72	+3.95
Experiment 2: anticipating further interaction with present discussion partner	−1.56	+3.78

Note: Entry is increased (or decreased) liking for stimulus person, on a 24-point scale.

Adapted from Tyler & Sears, 1977.

The second experiment was designed to be more realistic. In it Tyler and Sears tried to see if the unit relation could swing liking for an obnoxious other person in a more positive direction, even when the subject had already had some direct contact with the SP and thus had quite a clear impression of her. In this experiment they got confederates to act in an obnoxious manner in an initial discussion with the subject. They did this by, among other things, forgetting the subject's name, snapping gum, blowing smoke in her face, saying the subject was saying silly things, and not looking at the subject when she was talking. Then anticipated further interaction was varied: the subject expected to talk for forty more minutes with the SP, or with some other person. Finally, the subject was taken into a separate cubicle to fill out a questionnaire which, among other things, asked for liking ratings of the SP. Again, the results supported balance theory, as shown in Table 5–7. Liking for the obnoxious SP increased with anticipated interaction—although not as much as in the first experiment, presumably because the unit relation's effect had to overcome the strong and clear impression derived from the initial period of interaction. And in both experiments, liking for an initially positive SP was not much affected by anticipated interaction, as balance theory would predict.

Unit relations also have been shown to affect liking in another way. The "halo" of a beautiful woman extends to a man who is seen as being associated with her. Sigall and Landy (1973) manipulated the attractiveness of a female confederate by having her either tastefully dressed and made up, or wearing an unbecoming wig, no makeup, and unflattering clothes. When she met the subject, she was with a male stimulus person. She either described him as her "boyfriend" and held his hand, or she ignored him. The attractiveness of the confederate generalized to greater liking for the male stimulus person when he was described as her boyfriend, but not otherwise. In a later study, Bar-Tel and Saxe (1976) varied the attractiveness of man-woman pairs as presented to subjects in slides. The personality traits of one partner were seen as more positive when the other was more physically attractive—but again one person's attractiveness generalized to his or her partner only when they were described as being married, not when they were described as unrelated.

exceptions to the balance principle

There are two exceptions to the balance principle that ought to be kept in mind. They do not in any way invalidate it, but they do suggest some limits on it. First of all, balancing forces seem to occur mainly with positive relations between the two people involved. These are the top four situations in Figure 5–7. When the person dislikes the other person, balancing forces seem to be relatively weak. Newcomb (1968) has described such situations as being "nonbalanced." He suggests that when we dislike someone, we simply become disengaged from the situation, and do not care much whether we agree or disagree with him. What the other person thinks and how it bears on our own attitudes, is of little concern to us; we simply lose interest in him and he drifts out of our lives. This notion has been supported in several studies, which indeed find subjects simply to be less involved when triads include a negative P-O relation (Crano and Cooper, 1973), and balance not to be preferred very much to imbalance (Crockett, 1974). In other words, it is important for our friends to agree with us, but it does not much matter whether our enemies agree or disagree with us.

Second, the balance principle is not the only one that applies to these simple triads. People also tend to learn better, and like better, triads that embody positive relations between the two people. In Chapter 3 we referred to this tendency, in another context, as the "positivity bias." And there is also some tendency for people to learn more readily, and like better, triads embodying agreement on the attitude issue. Regardless of whether a person likes another or not, agreement is preferred. In these ways, people seem to gravitate toward more pleasant, as well as toward conceptually and perceptually simpler, social relations.

This discussion of the balance model is, of course, greatly simplified. We have considered a system with only two people and one object and have ignored the multitude of other objects that are involved in any such structure, as well as the feelings of the teacher toward the student. But the basic principles work in more complex and realistic systems as well. Instead of only the issue of busing, we could include hundreds of things ranging from books to music, religion, politics, drugs, and law. Each item on which the student and teacher agree tends to make them like each other more; each item on which they disagree has the opposite effect. They may both like music, drugs, and law and dislike religion and books; but one may like the Democrats and the other the Republicans. Thus, they agree on five and disagree on one. Assuming for the moment that the topics are equally important and ignoring the possibility that their strength of liking and disliking for them may differ, this structure of items should tend to make them like each other. If their agreement were split four-two, the effect would be weaker; if they agreed on only one and disagreed on five, they would dislike each other. The more items they agree on, the more they should like each other.

similarity

The major implication for liking of the tendency to seek balance is that people like others who are similar to them. The student who likes busing but dislikes the teacher who also likes busing is faced with a conflict that might cause him to change his opinion and end up liking him. Similarly, if the student likes busing and the teacher dislikes it, the student will tend to dislike the teacher. Thus, if we meet someone about whom we know nothing except that he shares our love of skiing, or busing, or anything else, we will tend to like him.

The influence of similarity on friendship patterns is pervasive and important. In friendships or marriages or even simple likes and dislikes, there is a strong tendency for people to like others who are similar to them. Moreover, society generally assumes this to be true. The current vogue of computer dating is based almost entirely on this idea. In applying for a date, people list their interests and characteristics and the computer matches them with someone of the opposite sex who has similar interests and characteristics. Presumably this would lead to a better date than one chosen at random or one that does not take into account the importance of similarity.

The effect of similarity is seen most clearly with people who share gross cultural and demographic characteristics, attitudes, beliefs, interests, and backgrounds. Frenchmen like Frenchmen and Americans like Americans; elderly people tend to like other elderly people and young people like other young people. Such characteristics as national background, religion, politics, social class, educational level, age, sophistication, and skin color influence friendship patterns. Also influential are profession, intelligence level, talent in a given field, and probably even

Drawing by Charles Barsotti: © 1968.

"Oh dear! I knew *we should have invited another tall person for Mr. Harrelson."*

height, weight, physical agility, and strength. In fact, on practically every dimension except perhaps personality characteristics (which we shall discuss at greater length below), people who are similar tend to like each other more.

Theodore Newcomb conducted an extensive study of friendship (1961) by taking over a large house at the University of Michigan and running it on an experimental basis. Students lived there just as they would have in any other dormitory except that they agreed to take part in the study and were questioned at periodic intervals. Newcomb had control over room assignments, and on the basis of information from tests and questionnaires he assigned some boys who were similar to each other to be roommates and others who were dissimilar to be roommates. He then intervened very little in their affairs. Under these circumstances, the effect of similarity proved to be powerful. Those roommates who were selected as being similar generally liked each other and ended up as friends; those who were chosen to be dissimilar tended to dislike each other and not to be friends. Thus, this study gave evidence that the computer dating services are correct in assuming that putting similar people together usually leads to a more successful, friendlier relationship than putting dissimilar people together.

The same effect has been observed in even more closely controlled situations. In laboratory experiments (Byrne, 1961; Byrne and Nelson, 1964), subjects were given a description of another person and asked how much they thought they would like him. The descriptions included his attitudes, opinions, and other characteristics. The important variation was that some descriptions made the other person seem very similar to the subject (with the same characteristics), whereas others made him seem very different. The results indicate that the similarity of the description determined how much the subjects thought they would like the other person. The more similar he was described, the more they liked him.

Similarity of values and attitudes produces greater liking even under what might seem to be unfavorable conditions. For example, Bleda (1974) gave subjects the usual questionnaire supposedly filled out by another subject. This stimulus person varied in similarity of attitudes to the real subjects. But in the attached sheet presenting other personal information, one stimulus person was described as maladjusted: she had recently had a nervous breakdown, had been hospitalized, and was seeing a psychiatrist. No such information was provided for the other

Monkmeyer/Paul Conklin

Drawing by Gallagher; courtesy Cartoon Features Syndicate.

"You're the kind of man we need around here"

stimulus person. But in both cases, similarity of attitudes was strongly related to liking. So we tend to like people with attitudes similar to our own, even if in other ways they are not very attractive.

For similarity to affect liking, of course, the two people must discover they have similar values and attitudes. Yet in many first-acquaintance situations, those topics of conversation may not come up. When you first meet someone of the opposite sex, it is natural to be influenced most of all by how they look, because that is what you first notice. Then you may learn something about their style of talking—whether they are talkative or more reserved, whether they use good grammar and a wide vocabulary, or slang expressions you are accustomed to using. Often the initial conversation is so dominated by small talk that you never get around to talking about values, or goals, or how you feel about more general issues. But even if you do, other first-impression factors are of overriding importance.

Thus it is not too surprising that other variables—especially physical attractiveness—turn out to be more important than similarity in first-acquaintance situations. Kleck and Rubenstein (1975) had a female confederate and a male subject read off their attitude responses to each other, and then had the confederate interview the subject on a variety of innocuous topics about campus life. Attitude similarity did not affect the subject's rating of the social desirability of the confederate's personality traits, her likability, or her desirability as a work partner. However, her physical attractiveness did affect most of these ratings. Similarly, Curran and Lippold (1975) set up a computer dating service and arranged for dates between college students. After the first date, the students rated each other. In two separate studies, the similarity-liking relationship was assessed, and in neither case was it very strong, for either men or women. Again, physical attractiveness was a stronger influence.

If the manipulation of similarity is extreme enough, and if the two people are explicitly instructed to spend their time talking and exploring each others' ideas, then similarity seems to have a more powerful effect. Byrne, Ervin and Lamberth (1970) matched couples for similar or dissimilar attitudes, and then sent them off for a 30-minute coke date. After the "date" they measured mutual liking, and then contacts between the two during the rest of the semester. After this short acquaintance, similarity was indeed related to liking. Moreover, the "similar" couples sat closer together when they returned from their "date" to be interviewed by the experimenter. But even in this situation, physical attractiveness once again proved to have a strong effect.

A final point in our analysis of the effect of similarity on liking is that we tend to exaggerate the similarity between ourselves and someone similar to us, and the dissimilarity between ourselves and someone different from us. Moreover, if we like someone we tend to exaggerate how similar he is to us, and if we dislike someone we tend to exaggerate how different he is from us. Thus, two tendencies work in the same direction. As well as tending to like someone similar to us, we tend to perceive someone we like as being more similar to us than he is. In addition, we tend to exaggerate the similarity that does exist, which makes us like the person still more. In contrast, those who are dissimilar and whom we dislike are seen as even more dissimilar and are disliked even more. The result is that those we like are eventually seen as extremely similar to us and those we dislike as extremely dissimilar. So, the already strong effect of similarity on liking or disliking is greatly enhanced.

complementarity

We have seen that there are a number of reasons why people like others who are similar to them. Thus far, however, we have omitted discussing one important characteristic—personality. Is it also true that people tend to like others whose personalities are like theirs? This issue has created some controversy in the literature. Many studies of friendship and marriage have indicated that people tend to like and marry those who are similar to them in terms of personality. On the other hand, some studies have shown that there is a tendency for people to seek out those whose personalities complement theirs, that is, those who have opposite qualities. For example, a dominant person may prefer a submissive person. The question of whether similarity or complementarity in personality is the critical factor is quite complicated. The answer seems to be that both are important determinants.

As our discussion has demonstrated, under almost all circumstances similarity is an important consideration in liking and marriage.

This applies to personality characteristics as well. Under most circumstances, a quiet, thoughtful, introverted person likes somebody similar to himself more than he does a loud and flighty extrovert. And the same is probably true of most important personality dimensions—aggressive-nonaggressive, stable-unstable, neurotic-nonneurotic, and so on. There is good reason to believe that friends tend to be similar on these types of dimensions.

But what kind of woman does a man who is extremely assertive, aggressive, and domineering marry? It would seem that if he married a woman who was similar to him, there might be an explosion. Fortunately, there is evidence that marriage partners seem to be complementary rather than similar on these kinds of dimensions. A domineering man tends to marry a passive woman; a talkative woman probably marries a quiet man. In other words, on certain kinds of personality dimensions, opposites do seem to attract.

Although at first glance the effect of complementarity seems to contradict the principle of similarity, the two are sometimes consistent. The domineering male and the dominated female actually are similar in one sense—they share similar attitudes and values as to the role of the man and the woman in marriage. They both agree that the male should be dominant and the female submissive. This is not simply playing with words in order to disguise the contradiction. There is an important similarity in this kind of marriage. If they were both domineering, they might seem to be more similar because they behaved similarly, but their views on their individual roles would necessarily be different. So if we consider basic values and attitudes the most important aspects of personality, the similarity principle continues to hold because the man and woman define their respective roles in the same way.

On the other hand, there are times when real complementarity is important in determining liking. When the needs of one person satisfy the needs of another, the two tend to like each other. A dominant and a submissive person have complementary personalities, for the need of one (to dominate) satisfies the need of the other (to be dominated), and vice versa. Thus, they can form a stable relationship and should tend to like each other. The same is true of a sadist and masochist, a person who likes to talk and one who likes to listen, and so on. In these instances, the complementarity should lead to liking. The situation is probably quite different when complementary attitudes do not satisfy each other. A person who likes to talk would probably not be friendly with a person who dislikes discussions; a person who enjoys activity would probably not like a person who enjoys being quiet; a music lover would probably not like a music hater; and so on. In these cases, complementarity does not lead to mutual reinforcement and to liking.

Our original question—of the relative importance of similarity and complementarity to liking—can be resolved as follows: When two people have similar roles, as in most friendships, the dominant determinant of liking is generally similarity. When two people have different roles, as sometimes occurs in marriage, friendships, and professional relationships in which one is superior to the other, complementarity is important. In these cases, people tend to like others whose behavior fits their role. Since their roles are different, their behaviors tend to be complementary rather than similar. However, even with differing roles, the major determinant of liking in most relationships is similarity on dimensions such as cultural characteristics, socioeconomic class, and so on.

intimate relationships

Most of the material on liking we have been discussing concerns only first-acquaintance relationships, or the beginning stages of more lasting friendships. Although that is an important stage in relationships, and certainly a very common level of relating to people, it is obviously not the only or the most important one. But it turns out that the factors we have

"There's really not much to tell. I just grew up and married the girl next door."

discussed in this chapter play a major role in deeper, longer-term relationships as well. Take proximity, for example. A sociologist named Bossard examined 5,000 marriage license applications in Philadelphia in the 1930s and found one-third of the couples lived within five blocks of each other. Similarity of demographic characteristics is important too. Over 99 percent of the married couples in the United States share the same race; 94 percent share religion, and so on (Rubin, 1973). Similarity of attitudes and values is another important variable; Kerckhoff and Davis (1962) found that couples who shared values moved closer to a permanent relationship over a seven-month span than couples who did not.

romantic love

One factor that clearly differentiates deep attachments from first impressions is romantic love. Unfortunately, it is one of the topics that social psychologists have been particularly negligent about studying. Perhaps they are in awe of its mysteries and do not want to meddle with it, for fear of discovering something mundane or demeaning about a beautiful phenomenon. Or perhaps their methodologies are not appropriate for a highly emotional, changeable phenomenon. About all we can do is point to some beginning efforts to theorize about love and tie it in to the other theories we have been discussing.

Berscheid and Walster (1974) have suggested that romantic love, like any other set of emotional feelings, can be analyzed according to Schachter's (1964) two-factor theory of emotions we discussed in the last chapter. He theorizes that any emotional experience consists of intense physiological arousal, plus the appropriate cognitive labeling. Romantic love, then, would consist of intense arousal, plus such labels as "this must be love," "the real thing," "she's all I can think about," or "he's the one for me." No one would be surprised by the assertion that positive emotional experiences, such as sexual gratification, excitement, and need of satisfaction, increase arousal and thus heighten the feeling of "being in love." But their theory also implies that even unpleasant emotional experiences should be arousing and, if properly labeled as part of "being in love," should enhance the experience of romantic love. So, fear, rejection, frustration, and challenge should all contribute to the feeling of love.

Not much solid research evidence is available to support such a hypothesis, partly due to the fact that so little work has been done on it until recently. One attempt was made by Driscoll, Davis, and Lipitz (1972) who investigated the effects of parental interference on the relationships of married and dating couples. They found couples with high levels of parental interference reported *more* love than did couples with little interference. And increases in such interference over time were associated with even further increases in reported romantic love. They

Popperfoto

describe this finding, consistent with the Berscheid-Walster theory, as the "Romeo and Juliet effect," after that pair of star-crossed lovers seemingly cursed by the violent rivalry between the Capulet and Montague clans.

Another implication of this theory is that the "hard to get" woman, because she is so frustrating, ought to induce more love and be more attractive than one who produces less arousal because she is easier to get. In one series of studies, Walster, Berscheid, and Walster (1973) arranged for a female confederate to respond to calls under the guise of a computer date program. To one set of callers she responded that she would be delighted to go out on a date. To others, she only agreed to go out reluctantly. However, contrary to the theory, attraction to the woman did not differ in the two conditions. In another study, the confederate was a prostitute who suggested to half her prospective clients that she would take on any client; to the other half, she suggested she was quite selective and would only see a limited number. In all cases she then had sexual intercourse with the client. Liking was measured by how much she was paid, whether or not the subject called back for a second appointment, and by her estimate of how much the subject liked her. Again the "hard to get" version was liked no more than the "easy to get" one. The same authors followed these studies with one testing a more refined hypothesis, that what is most attractive is being "selectively hard to get," rather than being hard to get in general. In this case, the same two conditions were used as in the previous studies, in computer date situation. The "generally easy to get" woman said she was very eager to date anyone; the "generally hard to get" woman said she was willing but not eager to date anyone. The crucial condition was "selectively hard to get," a woman who said she was eager to date the subject but not anyone else who had called. And this, as might be expected, yielded the most attraction. But this finding is not very supportive of the original idea: it is not very negative, frustrating, or challenging to have a woman tell you she would be delighted to date you, but is uninterested in any other man. Rather, she seems to have good taste and that is pleasing.

All in all, there is not much hard data for the idea that negative emotional experiences increase the experience of romantic love. It is certainly a popular myth, contrary to the simple rewardingness idea we discussed earlier, that such negative experiences increase romance. But so far we can say little about whether it is true or not.

social penetration

How do people move from the first-impression stage, in which they develop a general feeling of liking based on similarity, attractiveness, seemingly desirable qualities, and so forth, to deeper and more meaningful levels of relationship? Altman and Taylor (1973) have developed a theory about the process by which people gradually attain closeness and intimacy, a process they have called *social penetration*. It describes both the overt interpersonal behaviors that take place, and the accompanying internal subjective feelings. Penetration occurs, in this view, along two different dimensions: breadth and depth. *Breadth* refers to the number of different areas of a person's life and personality that are involved in the relationship, such as work, family, sexual behavior, hopes and fears, financial life, and so on. *Depth* refers to the intimacy, or closeness to the core of the person's being, at which the relationship exists in any given area. For example, a casual acquaintance might be familiar only with a person's approximate frequency of dating, and some idea of with whom; a real intimate might be familiar with some of the individual's more private anxieties, preferences, sexual fantasies, and so on.

The theory of social penetration suggests (1) that social penetration processes proceed from superficial to intimate levels of exchange; (2) that interactions continue and expand to a given level of intimacy, and move to adjacent areas and slightly more intimate levels; and (3) that the pacing of penetration varies over time, and is highly subject to the rewards and costs of intimacy at whatever level, and in whatever area, it has already been established.

Generally, at first (the "orientation" stage) people scout out rather narrow areas of each other, assembling little tidbits of information at a rather superficial level. This is a cocktail-party level of getting acquainted. In this stage there is a strong effort at positive self-presentation, and an avoidance of any criticism of the other person. The second stage ("exploratory affective exchange") involves still relatively peripheral levels of the personality, but expands in richness into new areas and becomes more spontaneous. The flow of interaction becomes more synchronized and smooths out, becoming more friendly, relaxed, and casual. When it touches on even intermediate levels of the person though, exchange is still inhibited and based on stereotyped responses. The third stage, "affective exchange," characterizes close friendships or fairly extensive courtship relationships. The two people interact across many areas of the outer layers of personality, and are fairly free in praise and criticism. Many of the barriers are down in intimate areas, although there are still some elements of caution and restrictiveness. The two tend to be rather tentative and cautious in exploring truly central layers. Finally, the last stage ("stable exchange") embodies facile exchange in intermediate levels of intimacy, and both persons allow access to very private feelings and belongings.

self-disclosure

The disclosure of broader and more intimate aspects of personality is obviously the key to advancing social penetration. If we are willing to allow the other person access only to our most superficial and public selves, penetration cannot go very far. Under some circumstances, self-disclosure and probes into intimate realms of another person can proceed fairly quickly. Altman and Haythorn (1965), for example, tested for intimacy of self-disclosure to three persons: (1) best friend, (2) a peer with whom the subject (all were Navy recruits) was isolated for a period of ten days, and (3) a casual acquaintance. They found that both the breadth and depth of self-disclosure decreased across these three relationships, but significant amounts of self-disclosure occurred both to a best friend and to a casual acquaintance with whom one was isolated for several days. Isolation of two people increased the intimacy both of the breadth and depth of self-disclosure.

The most influential early experimental work on self-disclosure was done by the late Sidney Jourard. His initial hypothesis was that self-disclosure would increase liking, since it is a major mechanism for increasing penetration or intimacy with another person. He reasoned that having the self open to another person is intrinsically more gratifying then being closed up tight, and that this good feeling should generalize to the person to whom one was disclosing. And in turn, we should like a disclosing person more than a nondiscloser. To test this, Daher and Banikiotes (1976) presented subjects with stimulus persons varying in intimacy of self-disclosure, and then measured liking for the SP. They used a long series of items about the self, to which the SP had supposedly responded. These items were graduated in intimacy of self-disclosure, so that they could be experimentally varied. The subjects liked better the SPs who gave more self-disclosure. A number of similar studies have also found that liking for an SP increases as he or she becomes more self-disclosing (Cozby, 1973; Jourard and Friedman, 1970). But it must be remembered that this self-disclosure was still at a rather superficial level: the subject only read the SP's responses to these items, which were in multiple-choice format. And the subject did not have to disclose anything about himself.

The social penetration thesis of Altman and Taylor leads us to expect a more complex relationship between self-disclosure and liking, in two ways. First of all, they argue that self-disclosure will lead to liking only if it is carefully paced. It must be slow enough that it does not become threatening to either person. If it races ahead prematurely into areas of great personal intimacy, it will arouse anxiety and defensiveness. Interpersonal barriers will go up, and it will have the effect of promoting distance between the people, rather than closeness. So someone who "comes on too strong and too fast" will be disliked rather than liked.

One example is a study by Kaplan, Firestone, Degnore, and Moore (1974). They varied both the formality of the interaction setting, and the intimacy of the subject's own self-disclosure. College male subjects were brought into the laboratory to be interviewed in one of three contexts. One was highly formal: the panelled and carpeted room was decorated with management and business journals, and the interviewer was supposed to be a business student. Then there was a medium-formality condition, in which the lab was stocked with psychotherapy literature and the interviewer was supposed to be a clinical psychology student. In the low-formality condition, decoration consisted of marital counseling and sexological literature, and the interviewer was a "human relations" student learning how to do sexual counseling. The questions asked were either highly intimate ("How often do you masturbate?" and "Would you describe any things that you dislike about your mother?") or nonintimate ("What are the kind of movies that you like to see" and "How many hours of sleep do you need to feel your best?"). Ratings of attraction to the interviewer were obtained in an unusual way: After every question, the subject pressed a button indicating liking, ostensibly to give an ongoing measure of the "interviewer's" performance. The results are shown in Figure 5–8. Liking for the interviewer was highest in the informal setting with nonintimate questions—that is, for quite a modest level of so-

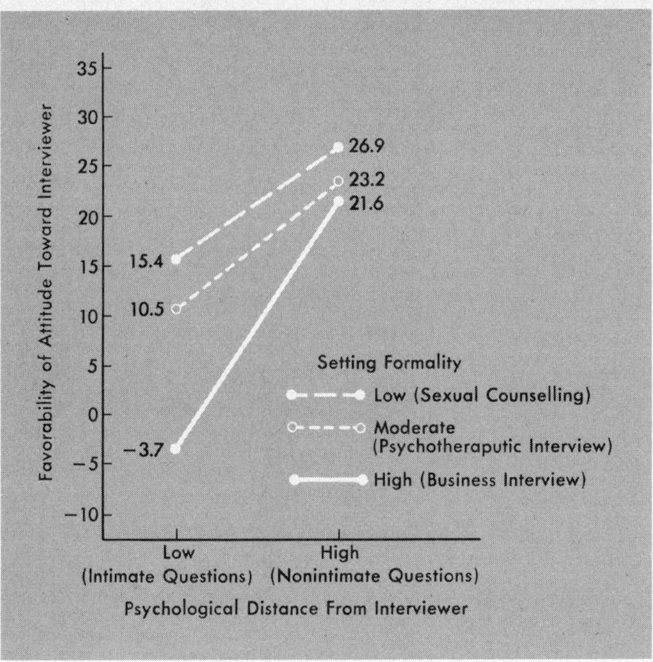

FIGURE 5–8
Interview setting formality and liking. (From Kaplan et al., 1974.)

cial penetration, between two complete strangers. Liking was least for the formal-context interviewer asking intimate questions. Clearly, this person was probing at too deep a level, too fast. His demands for intimate self-disclosure were especially inappropriate given his own formality.

This example leads us to the second modification Altman and Taylor urge for Jourard's original hypothesis. This is that a *reciprocity norm* in self-disclosure determines liking. We like best people who self-disclose at about the same level of intimacy we do. Someone who discloses more intimate detail about himself than we do threatens us with a premature rush into intimate territory, and we want to put on the brakes. But if we are disclosing at a more intimate level than the other person, we are left feeling vulnerable and out on a limb. There is quite a bit of evidence that reciprocity of self-disclosure is a key factor in liking. In the Kaplan et al. study, the formal interviewer was asking for extremely intimate self-disclosure, but was providing none himself (or even promising any implicitly, as the "psychologist" and "human relations" interviewers might have been). And he was not liked.

In the Daher and Banikiotes study cited earlier, subjects tended to like best an SP who matched the subject's own level of self-disclosure as established in an earlier questionnaire. In another study, Davis (1976) set up an acquaintance exercise in which two people took turns disclosing to each other. He found that the average intimacy level increased through the exercise, as might be expected from our discussion of "penetration." More important for the reciprocity norm, he found that both the average level of intimacy and the rate of increase of intimacy were closely matched between partners. As one person became more intimate, or slowed down, so did the other.

But the most direct test of the reciprocity idea would involve experimentally manipulating the intimacy level of both persons' self-disclosures. Chaikin and Derlega (1974) videotaped two actresses' improvisations of a first-acquaintance encounter in a school cafeteria. They each were instructed to do it two ways: at a high and at a low level of self-disclosure. Then the experimenters presented the performances to subjects in each of the four combinations of self-disclosure: both high, both low, and high-low or low-high. In the high self-disclosure case, one woman told immediately of her relationship with her boyfriend "Bill," her first sexual partner, and of her parents' reactions; the other woman's high-intimacy disclosures concerned her mother's nervous breakdown and hospitalization, her fighting with her mother, and the possible divorce of her parents. In the low self-disclosure cases, they talked about the problems of commuting to school, where they went to high school, the courses they were taking, and so on. The main finding is that liking for both women was higher when they were at the same level of intimacy than when they were at different levels. Breaking the reciprocity norm led to less liking, but for different reasons. The woman who disclosed too little (relative to the other) was thought cold, whereas the more intimate normbreaker was thought maladjusted.

Altman and Taylor (1973) conclude their discussion with some speculations about historical changes in intimacy and self-disclosure in American relationships. They suggest that up through the 1950s, the middle-class norm emphasized a great deal of self-restraint, reserve, caution, and self-protectiveness about revealing intimate details. Close, intimate penetration was not allowed very much. Then a reaction set in, which was best characterized by such phenomena as encounter or T groups, in which perfect strangers were supposed to disclose at a very intimate level at their first meeting. Moreover, the "sexual revolution" meant that people climbed in and out of intimate relationships (as well as bed) much more often, freely, and intensively than they had in previous eras. Altman and Taylor offer some cautionary comments about this trend, suggesting that this "instant intimacy" may prove illusory, as people give each other only a superficial, stereotyped version of their innermost feelings. And such people may grow to mistrust intimate relationships, because they prove so transitory. In general, they caution us to remember that true intimacy comes slowly, that it comes only with trust and with experience with the other person, and that it bears risks and costs. We therefore should not take it too lightly or too much for granted, but treat it with respect and with care.

Racial prejudice has been one of the most tenacious social problems in American history. It dates back at least as far as the earliest contact English colonialists had with Africans in the fifteenth century, and was enormously exacerbated by the mass importation of Africans to the United States to serve as slaves. Since the Civil War and the emancipation of the slaves, it has been a long, hard struggle to provide genuine equality for black Americans, and to try to erase the harsh antiblack prejudices held by most, if not virtually all, white Americans. Whites today are much more accepting of formal equality than they were even twenty years ago, strongly supporting black rights to equal public accommodations, equal political rights, fair housing, and so on. But there is still strong resistance to full racial equality in other areas; for example, in cases of school integration and affirmative action (Campbell, 1971; Greeley and Sheatsley, 1971).

The causes of racial prejudice lie principally in the early training of the child. White children simply learn, by being told and by observing the society in which they live, that blacks are socially inferior in a variety of ways. The consequence of this is that prejudice is considerably stronger in some areas of the society than in others. For example, it is stronger in the old South than in other regions, it is stronger in the working class than in middle-class homes, it is stronger among older people (who were brought up in a more segregationist period) than among younger whites, and so on (see Maykovich, 1975; Middleton, 1976). But this does not mean that prejudice cannot be changed somewhat, and particularly it does not mean that white individuals cannot come to like black individuals. Can the various principles of liking we have discussed help us understand the effect of various factors and experiences on liking for members of a minority group?

race and belief

Using the notion that "similarity breeds liking," a series of studies (Byrne and Wong, 1962; Rokeach and Mezei, 1966; Stein et al., 1965) has compared the relative importance of racial and attitudinal similarity. In most of this work, subjects were given a description of another person who was either similar to them in attitudes and dissimilar racially or the reverse. Each subject was then asked how much he thought he would like the other person. The typical, although not unanimous, finding was that similarity of attitudes was more important in determining liking than belonging to the same racial group. These findings have been interpreted as showing that racial differences are relatively unimportant when compared to differences in attitude.

It would be nice to believe that this is true when real contacts are involved, for it would indicate that getting to know someone of another race and discovering that his attitudes are similar to one's own would make one like him regardless of the racial difference. The logical projection would be that a simple program of educating people about other races would reduce racial conflicts. However, these findings held only for relatively nonintimate relationships such as working together. Race was considerably more important than belief when closer relationships, such as dating or marriage, were concerned.

In addition, we think it is a mistake to give too much weight to these particular studies. Most of them involved a role-playing situation, in which subjects are presented with hypothetical stimulus persons or with paper-and-pencil descriptions of perfect strangers. Under these circumstances, there were strong pressures against weighting race very high and toward being rational and objective. In actual situations, there is much less pressure toward the rational, objective approach—biases and prejudices become more important than in the experimental situation. So, as the relationship becomes more realistic and consequential for the individual, race begins to overtake belief similarity as a determinant of liking. Silverman (1974) presented incoming college students with descriptions of various stimulus persons, supposedly also incoming freshmen, and asked for their attraction to them. Through the cooperation of the college housing office, in one condition (high consequences), the person chosen would actually be the subject's roommate for the coming year. In the other condition, the subjects were told to *imagine* the stimulus person would be their roommate. Racial discrimination was much more important in the actual choice of a roommate than in the imagined choice. But belief similarity played a significant role in both cases, and this tends to be a typical finding in many studies of this kind. Therefore, these studies do hold out some hope that under appropriate circumstances people will weigh attitude similarity more heavily than racial similarity and that, in the long run, prejudice can be reduced by learning about members of other races.

cooperative interdependence

A somewhat more elaborate version of the same idea has become popular within social psychology as a prime mechanism for reducing prejudice. This is the "equal status, cooperative interdependence" approach. It suggests that when whites and blacks are in a close relationship, have shared goals, and must interact in a cooperative manner for either of them to attain their goals, prejudice is likely to lessen. The critical point is, according to this notion, that mere interracial contact is not enough. It must be interdependent contact, rather than parallel, independent contact; and it must be cooperative rather than competitive. The interaction must be at equal status, rather than under conditions in which the white is of superior status.

Stuart Cook and his colleagues have developed the most systematic research program to explore this hypothesis. In order to give it the most challenging test, they have picked as subjects young whites from rural southern areas, since that is the background most productive of antiblack feeling. They then put them in small groups to work on a series of management training game activities. These involve the participants' filling various offices on a railroad—communications officer, equipment officer, and shipping officer. They must work together to keep railroad cars maximally used and profits rolling in. The key dependent variable is attraction for a confederate who serves as one of the group members. In some conditions the confederate was white; in others, black.

In three different studies, various aspects of the cooperative interdependence hypothesis were varied: (1) the success or failure of the group's efforts, (2) the subject's level of participation in decision making, (3) the competence level of the minority person's behavior, (4) whether or not the subject is in a position to help the minority person in an active manner, and, of course, (5) the race of the confederate. What they found, in general, was that the most consistent factor in determining attraction for the confederate was the success or failure of the group's efforts (Blanchard, Adelman, and Cook, 1975; Blanchard, Weigel, and Cook, 1975; Blanchard and Cook, 1975). The more successful the group, the more the confederate was liked. This is what we would have expected, knowing that people generally come to like those who are associated with delivery of rewards. Incompetent behavior on the part of the confederate led to less liking—though when the subject was in a position to help the confederate, that led to more liking. The race of the confederate had surprisingly little effect. These variables affected the liking of black and white confederates in about the same way. The implication is that the effects of interpersonal interaction upon liking are about the same for blacks and whites. Racial prejudice may be difficult to overcome, but the same principles seem to hold for changes in interracial liking as for changes in any other kind.

contact and prejudice reduction

Using this theory, what kinds of situations would be likely to reduce prejudice, and what kinds would not? Being teammates on a professional football team would. Being fellow conspirators in a prison break would. Having a black janitor in an office building, or a black maid in a middle-class household, would not. Having both races in a lecture class would not. Having interracial teams set up to solve homework problems in a statistics class would. Put another way, mere desegregation would not be enough; integration would be required. And it would have to be done in such a way as to promote equal-status relationships between the races.

Are the most helpful kinds of situations common in our society? Unfortunately, through most of our history they have not been. Prior to World War II, American society was organized in a way that afforded almost no opportunities for equal-status, cooperative interdependent contact between blacks and whites. Almost all American institutions were segregated. There were white colleges, and there were black colleges. Only whites were permitted to play professional sports in the major leagues. Black athletes had to play on all-black teams in black leagues. Military units were either all-black or all-white. Most blacks lived in the South, and of course in the South segregation was the law in public accommodations, schools, transportation, politics, and every other social institution. At that time there were such gross differences between blacks and whites in income, education, and occupational status that the chance of widespread equal-status contact was minimal.

Since World War II, however, for a variety of reasons, America has gradually become desegregated. The change gave social scientists opportunities to test the effects of contact. In World War II, when black and white soldiers fought together, racial prejudice decreased and so did antagonisms (Stouffer et al., 1949). There were no realistic conflicts between the groups because they were fighting a common enemy and were not competing. With this lack of conflict, unrealistic stereotypes decreased markedly because of the greater knowledge gained by the increased familiarity. Most of the other research on this problem also indicates that increased contact reduces antagonism, prejudice, and stereotypes. Studies on public housing (Deutsch and Collins, 1951; Jahoda and West, 1951; Works, 1961) have found less antagonism in both blacks and whites in integrated areas than in segregated areas. Similar results have been reported in studies that concerned integrated working conditions. When blacks were hired to work in department stores in New York City, white clerks became progressively more accepting of their black co-workers (Harding and Hogrefe, 1952). The white customers had similar positive reactions (Saenger and Gilbert, 1950). Comparable results have been found in the Army (Stouffer et al., 1949) and the Merchant Marines (Brophy, 1946) and among police officers (Kephart, 1957) and government workers (MacKenzie, 1948). Thus, most of the research indicates that greater familiarity, even under trying conditions, leads to less antagonism.

Although we do not yet know enough about the effects of contact on prejudice to draw definite conclusions, it seems likely that the crucial factor is the type of contact. It is overly simple to conclude that more contact is always good. However, it is probably correct that more *appropriate, equal-status contact* reduces both bias and antagonism. Contact of this type generally occurs in the armed forces, where blacks and whites fight together with more or less equal rank (at least among enlisted men), and in factories and stores in which members of the two races hold comparable jobs. But in many businesses, professions, and schools, interracial contact is often between people of different status. Integration frequently occurs by bringing blacks in at the bottom of the ladder, whether as students or apprentices, or in the least desirable jobs. They then have to interact with whites who outrank them; and so on. Under these circumstances, increased contact seems less likely to have a positive effect and may even have a negative effect on relations between blacks and whites. Thus, those who expect that integration of any kind or on only one level will reduce racial tensions may be disappointed, at least in the short run. But integration backed up by programs of equal jobs, education, and housing will have the desired effect. That is why it is important that affirmative action programs be instituted at all levels, rather than just at the bottom. They can promote equal-status contact, and thus long range prejudice reduction even if they have the short-run effect of increasing tensions by increasing job competition between the races.

SUMMARY

1. Simple proximity is one of the most important determinants of liking. Some of the reasons are that people who live or work near us tend to be more available for us to relate to, because anticipated continued interaction produces pressures to like someone, and because familiarity generally breeds liking.

2. Proximity does not tend to increase liking for intrinsically unpleasant, negative people. But most people are evaluated positively, as described by the positivity bias, so proximity increases liking most of the time.

3. Certain personal qualities produce greater liking, especially sincerity, warmth, and physical attractiveness. Each of these produces a halo effect, so that more attractive people are seen also as having a variety of other positive qualities, whether or not they do in fact.

4. Familiarity produces more liking, except in the case of clearly negative stimulus persons or other objects. Then familiarity produces less liking, if anything.

5. Rewardingness increases liking; we like people who provide valuable rewards for us. One of the most potent rewards is liking itself; hence we like those who like us (the reciprocity principle). We especially like those who like us increasingly over time.

6. The value of rewards (such as reciprocated liking) depends partly on our attribution of the other person's intent. If we perceive him as trying to ingratiate us, rather than genuinely liking us, we like him less.

7. The principle of cognitive balance is another important determinant of liking: we like people who agree with us, and dislike those who disagree with us. Therefore, similarity of values and attitudes is a crucial determinant of liking.

8. Moreover, we come to like those with whom we are connected through a unit relation; that is, those we will have a continuing connection with over time.

9. Whether similarity or complementarity in personality traits is more important is still quite a murky issue.

10. More intimate relationships develop through a process of "social penetration", in which the relationship gradually expands in breadth across each person's life, and deepens to more personal levels.

11. Reciprocity of self-disclosure is also a key determinant of liking. If one person discloses at a level of intimacy much greater than the other person does, it makes the latter uncomfortable and promotes distances. But if the first person's self-disclosure is too superficial, it simply perpetuates distance.

12. Belief dissimilarity is one determinant of racial prejudice. Prejudice can be broken down, to some extent, when people of different races work together on tasks involving cooperative, equal-status, interdependence. As America has become more racially integrated, such situations have become more common.

SUGGESTIONS FOR ADDITIONAL READING

ALTMAN, I., & TAYLOR, D. A. *Social penetration: The development of interpersonal relationships.* New York: Holt, Rinehart, & Winston, 1973. A provocative short paperback book on the development of intimate relationships. It embeds a description of experimental research in a larger theoretical framework, and contains thoughtful speculations about how people attain, and maintain, close and enduring relationships with each other.

BYRNE, D. *The attraction paradigm.* New York: Academic Press, 1971. A systematic and dogged effort to show how similarity produces liking in a wide variety of different situations.

DION, K., BERSCHEID, E., & WALSTER, E. What is beautiful is good. *Journal of Personality and Social Psychology,* 1972, *24,* 285–290. A classic study of the "halo effect" induced by beautiful women.

HEIDER, F. *The psychology of interpersonal relations.* New York: Wiley, 1958. One of the most influential books in modern social psychology. It develops the ideas of balance theory and of causal attribution, as they grow out of Gestalt theory. Also full of wise observations.

HUSTON, T. L. *Foundations of interpersonal attraction.* New York: Academic Press, 1974. A valuable collection of recent essays from almost all of the current active researchers on attraction, summarizing and speculating about their research. Ranges from cognitive development, power, cross-cultural studies, similarity, and love, among others.

RUBIN, Z. *Liking and loving—An invitation to social psychology.* New York: Holt, Rinehart, & Winston, 1973. A most literate, readable, chatty paperback covering what social psychologists now think about liking and loving. Students find this one of the most interesting books in social psychology, perhaps because it ties research so closely to relationships between young people.

ZAJONC, R. B. Attitudinal effects of mere exposure. *Journal of Personality and Social Psychology Monograph Supplement,* 1968, *2,* 1–27. An impressive coordinated program of research trying to develop the idea that "mere exposure" increases liking.

aggression

In the previous chapter, we discussed the factors that cause people to like or dislike others. Clearly, liking is one of the most important aspects of interpersonal relationships. A closely related factor is how well we treat others. In a sense this is the behavioral counterpart of our feelings toward them. Treatment of others can range from very negative to very positive, but most of the research and interest have centered on aggression.

Although it might seem that everybody understands what aggression is, there is considerable disagreement as to what behavior should be considered aggressive. The simplest definition and the one favored by those with a behaviorist or learning approach is that aggression is any behavior that hurts or could hurt others. The advantage of this definition is that the behavior itself determines whether or not a particular act is aggressive. We merely have to ascertain whether an act was potentially harmful.

Unfortunately, this definition ignores the intention of the person who does the act—and this factor is critical. As indicated in chapter 4, people normally come to some causal attribution about other people's actions, and aggressive acts are no exception. One of the first attributions they come to regarding aggression is of the person's intent. If a person tries to hurt someone, we ordinarily consider him to be aggressive; if he is not trying to cause harm, he is not being aggressive. Thus, the definition of aggression should be any action that is *intended* to hurt others. This conception is more difficult to apply, because it does not depend solely on observable behavior. Often it is difficult to know someone's intention, and thus we cannot judge whether he is being aggressive. But we must accept this limitation, for only by including intent can we define aggression meaningfully.

If we used the behavioral definition, some actions that most people consider aggressive would not be labeled as such because, for one reason or another, they are actually harmless. Suppose someone fires a gun at someone else, but the gun turns out to be either unloaded or loaded with blanks. The shooter was trying to cause harm, but in fact his act was harmless. It could not have hurt anyone because firing an unloaded gun or one loaded with blanks is not dangerous. Despite the fact that he was enraged and was trying to kill someone, by the behavioral definition, he was not being aggressive.

Ignoring intention also forces us to call some acts aggressive that are not, by the usual meaning of the term. If a golfer's ball accidentally hits a spectator, has the golfer committed an aggressive act? He has certainly done something that could cause harm. A golf ball traveling over 100 miles an hour is a dangerous object. In addition, he has in fact caused somebody a great deal of pain. Thus, the act fits one of the popular definitions of aggression: a response that delivers noxious stimuli to another organism. But surely no one would believe that the golfer was being aggressive. He was playing a game that, of all popular games, involves perhaps the least aggression.

Another category of pain-causing acts that should not be considered aggressive are those in which the ultimate goal is to help another person. Consider a dentist who gives his patient an injection of Novocain. Although an injection is painful, most patients are grateful for it because it prevents them from feeling the pain caused by drilling. Therefore, they would not consider the dentist to be acting aggressively when he provides them with the painkiller. Moreover, if the Novocain did not work for some reason, they would still not consider its administration an aggressive act, because the dentist was trying to ease their pain even though he was unsuccessful. We can see that ignoring intent forces us to call acts aggressive that, by common sense and any reasonable criteria, are not. We must therefore define aggression as behavior that is designed to hurt others.

But there is yet another distinction to be made. Normally we think of aggression as bad. After all, if an aggressive act is one that results from an intent to hurt another person, it must be bad. But some aggressive acts are good. We applaud the police officer who shoots a terrorist who has killed some innocent victims and is holding others hostage. The important distinction here is between *antisocial* and *prosocial* aggression. The question is whether the aggressive act violates commonly accepted social norms, or is in support of them. "Prosocial aggression is aggression used in a socially approved way for purposes that are acceptable to the moral standards of the group" (Sears, 1961, p. 471). Antisocial aggression is not. Unprovoked criminal acts that hurt people, such as assault and battery, murder, and gang beatings are clearly in violation of social norms, so they are described as antisocial. But many aggressive acts are actually dictated by social norms, and therefore are described as prosocial. Acts of law enforcement, appropriate parental discipline, or following the orders of commanders in wartime are regarded as perfectly all right and even necessary. Finally, there is yet another category of aggressive acts, falling somewhere between prosocial and antisocial, which we might term *sanctioned aggression*. This includes aggressive acts that are not required by social norms, but which are well within their bounds. They do not violate accepted moral standards. A coach who disciplines a disobedient player by benching him is usually thought to be well within his rights. So is a person who in self-defense hits someone who is criminally assaulting him, or a woman who strikes back at a man who is trying to rape her. None of these things is required of the person, so none is prosocial. But they fall within the bounds of what is permitted by social norms, so they are not bad either.

The key to understanding the differences among antisocial, sanctioned, and prosocial aggression is in knowing what social norms are relevant to the individual's act. That in turn depends, as will be seen in later chapters, on knowing what his reference groups are. Here it is enough to point out that it is usually easy enough to distinguish antisocial and prosocial aggression except in unusual cases. Most of the time we all agree on what is appropriate and what is inappropriate aggression. Occasionally we do not agree. In the 1960's, blacks rioting in protest of discrimination and inattention often felt quite justified in their aggression, whereas whites generally felt quite the opposite (Sears and McConahay, 1973). Members of youth gangs may feel retaliatory killings are

Barton Silverman/de Wys

justified, whereas most other people would disagree. Members of the Johnson and Nixon administrations felt the mass killings of North Vietnamese were justified because of the threat of communism, whereas antiwar protestors called them war crimes. But such dramatic instances of disagreement should not obscure the consensus all humans share about the vast majority of aggressive acts. Unprovoked aggression against an innocent victim is wrong. Killing is wrong except in certain very clearly specified cases. Aggressive acts in the service of social control, by duly authorized authorities, are permissible within certain boundaries. All over the world, and in all cultures, there is broad agreement on such general principles.

Our basic goal in this chapter is to explain why people are aggressive, and as usual we shall answer the question in terms of the factors that increase or decrease the effect. However, our discussion of aggression is somewhat more complicated than that of other subjects, such as affiliation, because it must consider two distinct phenomena, aggressive feelings and aggressive behavior. Generally when we feel like affiliating with others, we do so if others are available and they do not reject our company. The desire to affiliate usually leads to affiliation. But with aggression, as with certain other behaviors (e.g., sex), internal feelings are not always expressed openly. Whereas society welcomes and encourages affiliation, it discourages and condemns many, if not most, forms of aggression. Society can exist only if people control their aggressive feelings most of the time. We cannot have people hitting other people, breaking windows, or acting violently whenever they feel like it. Society places strong restraints on such expression and most people, even those who feel angry much of the time, rarely act aggressively. Therefore, specifying the factors that increase aggressive feelings does not completely answer the question of what produces aggressive behavior. It provides part of the answer because people rarely act aggressively if they do not feel that way, but it does not tell us when people will or will not turn their aggressive feelings into action. We need to consider both the factors that increase aggressive feelings and the restraints that may prevent them from being translated into aggressive action. We thus have two questions—what produces aggressive feelings and what produces aggressive behavior.

sources of aggressive impulses

An aggressive impulse or feeling is an internal state that cannot be observed directly. We all experience anger, and virtually everyone at one time or another would like to hurt someone else. But these feelings are not necessarily expressed openly, and therefore aggressive impulses must be studied largely by asking individuals how they are feeling or by inferring the existence of their internal state from physiological measures or behavior, neither of which is a reliable indicator. Nevertheless, there has been a considerable amount of research on the factors that arouse anger. In discussing the question we shall consider three major factors—instinct, annoyance or attack, and frustration.

instinct

It has been proposed by Freud, McDougall, Lorenz, and others that humans have an innate drive or instinct to fight. Just as they feel hungry, thirsty, or sexually aroused, so they feel aggressive. Although there are no known physiological mechanisms connected with aggressive feelings, as there are for the other drives, aggression is considered a basic drive.

Freud argued that there were only two basic drives—the *libido*, which is constructive, sexual energy, and *thanatos*, which is destructive, aggressive energy. He suggested that all people have within them strong self-destructive impulses—death wishes, he called them—which sometimes are turned inward and sometimes outward. When these impulses are turned inward, they cause people to restrict their energies, to punish themselves, to become masochistic, and, in the extreme case, to commit suicide. When the impulses are turned outward, they are manifested in aggressive, warlike behavior.

As with other explanations in terms of instinct, the instinctual theory of aggression is difficult to evaluate. The ideal test would be to raise someone in complete isolation, being careful to eliminate all external stimuli that might arouse aggressive feelings. Then, if the individual acted aggressively when given the chance, the indication would be that aggression is, at least in part, instinctive. Since we cannot conduct this type of experiment, we rely heavily on investigations of aggressiveness among nonhumans.

Animals certainly do a great deal of fighting. They fight for food, to protect their territory, to defend their young, and so on. But one of the difficulties in evaluating this evidence is that our definition of aggressiveness may not be appropriate to much of this behavior. A lion that chases and kills a zebra obviously intends to harm the zebra. On the other hand, as far as we know, the killing is not done in response to anger or with intent to cause suffering. The lion must hunt for food and the zebra happens to be its natural prey. Even if we do consider this aggression, it does not indicate the presence of an instinctive aggressive drive. The lion is hungry and kills in order to get food with which to satisfy the hunger. The instinctive drive is hunger, not aggression.

The same argument holds for fighting among members of the same species. They fight for mates, for territory, and for dominance. The first type of fight is motivated by sexual drives; the second, by the need for sufficient food supply. Battles for dominance are more complicated. Sex and hunger may be involved, because the dominant male usually has his choice of mates and the most desirable bits of food. Also, demonstrating dominance avoids unnecessary fights in the future, because the less dominant animals always give way before the more dominant. They fight only once to establish their positions and from then on coexist peacefully. Establishing dominance also facilitates the protection of the group, because it determines which animals will play what roles in defense. Thus, fighting for dominance serves many purposes and cannot be interpreted as evidence of instinctive aggressive impulses.

However, the instinct notion does make one prediction that most other formulations would not—that aggressive impulses build up within the animals regardless of the external environment. If these impulses are not expressed, they continue to build up and the animals feel increasingly aggressive. According to the theory, a tropical fish swimming alone in an aquarium should feel gradually more aggressive, even if all its basic needs are satisfied. After, say, a week, the fish should be more likely to attack than it would have previously. On the other hand, if aggression is aroused only by external factors, the fish should not be especially aggressive, because it has spent a week swimming in a comfortable pool.

Although this ideal experiment has never been performed, Konrad Lorenz (1963) observed tropical fish under a variety of circumstances similar to those just described. He reported that certain male fish normally attack other males of the same species but ignore other fish. If, however, all the males of the same species except one are removed from the aquarium, the one remaining attacks fish of other species he had previously left alone. And if all fish are removed except a female of his own species, he will eventually attack and kill her. Lorenz interpreted this behavior as showing that fish have instinctive needs to be aggressive and that when the ordinary targets are removed, these needs cause them to attack whatever target is available.

Lorenz bases much of his argument for an aggressive instinct on the response to crowding. He claims that animals who are put in small spaces with many other animals of the same species will inevitably become aggressive. This response to a lack of space, often called territoriality, seems to suggest an instinctive aggressive response to a common life situation. However, as we discuss in detail in Chapter 15, the evidence for territoriality and for this aggressive response to crowding is questionable. This phenomenon does seem to occur among some species, but it is almost certain that it does not occur among humans. People do not consistently respond aggressively to a lack of space. Thus, responses to crowding should not be considered evidence for an aggressive instinct in humans.

The work by ethologists such as Lorenz and Tinbergen is fascinating. It indicates that many species respond instinctively to specific cues and have many instinctive drives. It does not, however, provide evidence concerning humans. The research relevant to humans has generally been done under less than ideal conditions, and definitive experiments have not yet been performed. Although some ethologists continue to be convinced that all animals have instinctive aggressive drives, most psychologists would now dispute this. Among animals relatively low on the phylogenetic scale, instinct plays an important role in producing aggression, but as one ascends the ladder, instinct probably becomes less and less important. In particular, there seems litttle reason to believe that humans have any instinctive impulses toward aggressiveness.

annoyance and attack

When we are bothered or assaulted by someone, we tend to feel aggressive toward that person. Imagine the reaction of a driver who is waiting for a traffic light to change from red to green when, before it does, the driver of the car behind him starts blowing his horn. Or that of someone peacefully reading the newspaper when somebody pours a glass of water down his neck. Or, finally, imagine a student's reaction when he expresses an opinion in a class and someone else disagrees with him and says he is stupid to hold such an opinion. In all these cases, someone has done something unpleasant to someone else. Depending on how the injured person takes it, he has been annoyed or attacked. It is extremely likely that he will become angry and feel aggressive toward the source of the attack.

The most common technique for measuring aggression in experiments has involved attack. Since it comes up at a number of points below, we should describe the standard procedure here. Obviously, there are ethical problems when it comes to measuring aggression. We define aggression as the intent to harm another person, but we do not want to set up experiments that really do result in harm. So Buss (1961) had the inspiration to devise a machine which the subject could use and think he was hurting someone else, but which in reality hurt no one. The technique is to tell the subject and a confederate that they are to participate in a learning experiment. They toss for roles, and the toss is rigged so the subject becomes the "teacher" and the confederate becomes the "learner." Then the "teacher" is supposed to punish the "learner" for errors. The punishment is electric shock. The "teacher" has a box with a number of buttons to push, each indicating higher and higher levels of shock. The subject then gives as much shock as he wants after every error made by the "learner." Of course, no shock is ever really administered (the confederate is usually in an adjacent room so the subject does not know that no shock is used). But the measure of aggression is the intensity and/or duration of shock supposedly administered by the subject.

frustration

Frustration is the interference with or blocking of the attainment of a goal. If one wants to go somewhere, perform some act, or obtain something and is prevented, we say he is frustrated. One of the basic tenets in psychology is that frustration tends to arouse aggressive feelings.

The behavioral effects of frustration were demonstrated in a classic study by Barker, Dembo, and Lewin (1941). Children were shown a room full of attractive toys but were not allowed to enter it. They stood outside looking at the toys, wanting to play with them but unable to reach them. After they had waited for some time, they were allowed to play with them. Other children were given the toys without first being prevented from playing with them. The children who had been frustrated smashed the toys on the floor, threw them against the wall, and generally behaved very destructively. The children who had not been frustrated were much quieter and less destructive.

Holmes (1972) produced frustration by causing the subjects to sit around waiting because one subject (actually a confederate) arrived late for the experiment. No explanation for his tardiness was given. In another condition, all of the subjects arrived on time. The participants were subsequently given an opportunity to behave aggressively toward the latecomer or toward an innocent member of the group. Holmes found that subjects who had been frustrated by having to wait were more aggressive toward both the latecomer and the innocent bystander.

Sybil Shelton/Monkmeyer

This effect of frustration may be seen in broader perspective in society at large. Economic depressions produce frustration that affects almost everyone. People cannot get jobs or buy things they need and are greatly restricted in all phases of their lives. The consequence is that all forms of aggression become more common. Evidence of this was presented by Hovland and Sears (1940) and confirmed by Mintz (1946). They found a strong relationship between the price of cotton and the number of lynchings in the South during the years 1882 to 1930. When cotton prices were high, there were few lynchings; when prices were low, the number of lynchings was relatively high. A drop in the price of cotton signified a depressed period economically. This depression produced frustration, which in turn led to more aggression. An extreme manifestation of the increased aggression was the increase in lynchings.

These examples illustrate the typical effect of frustration, but the original statement of the relationship between frustration and aggression was in more absolute terms. Dollard, Doob, and others at Yale were the social psychologists who began the work on this problem. They asserted: "This study takes as its point of departure the assumption that aggression is always a consequence of frustration. More specifically, the proposition is that the occurrence of aggressive behavior always presupposes the existence of frustration and, contrariwise, the existence of frustration always leads to some form of aggression" [Dollard et al., 1939, p. 1]. It appears now that neither *always* in these assumptions is correct. Although frustration usually arouses aggression, there are circumstances when it does not. And, as we shall discuss below, factors other than frustration can also produce aggression.

arbitrariness of frustration

The frustration-aggression hypothesis was originally phrased in a very strong form: all frustrations produce aggression, and all aggression comes from some kind of frustration. Over time, this statement has been qualified somewhat. Not every frustration seems to breed aggression. Arbitrary frustrations produce more anger and aggressive behavior than do nonarbitrary ones. If the frustration is perceived as being unintended, nonarbitrary, justified, mitigated by extenuating circumstances, or accidental, then apparently it does not make people as angry, and they are less likely to be aggressive. A hitchhiker on a cold, windy night feels frustrated when a car whizzes past him, but he feels differently if the car is a large sedan with only one occupant than if it is an ambulance rushing to a hospital. Although he is frustrated in both cases, he is angrier and more aggressive if it is the car that passes him than if it is the ambulance. A teacher who prevents her class from taking a trip to the zoo is frustrating their wishes. If she explains that the trip is a bad idea because rain is expected and because many of the animals are ill and will not be on view, less aggression will be aroused than if she offers no explanation or a poor one. A good reason for frustration minimizes aggressive feelings.

The key is that the victim must perceive the frustration or attack as intended to harm him if it is to instigate anger and aggressive behavior. That is, the victim must arrive at an attribution that his tormentor intended to frustrate or annoy him.

The arbitrariness revision of the original theory suggests that lack of intent to harm can reduce this frustration, and hence reduce the resulting aggression. Consistent with this view, Nickel (1974) suggested that both the received attack *and* intent to harm would increase aggression. The new implication is that the subject will respond aggressively to *intended* harm, even if the *actual* harm done to him was not very great. He tested this using the standard Buss-type sham-learning experiment we described above. This particular study began with the confederate administering shocks to the subject; in some cases they were strong shocks, and in others weak. Lights on the subject's machine showed what level of shock the confederate intended to give him. For half the subjects, low shocks were sent; and for the other half, high shocks. But within each group, partway through the experimenter said he had made a mistake and had reversed the scale. He then changed it. So half the subjects had been receiving lower shocks than they thought the confederate "intended," while half had been receiving higher shocks than "intended." It turned out that the subject himself retaliated more both when he had in fact received higher shocks and when he perceived the confederate to have intended to send high shocks (even though "by mistake" they had turned out in fact to be low shocks). These data are shown in Table 6–1. This, then is a simple demonstration of how the intention to harm can, all by itself, increase aggression.

TABLE 6–1
subject's shocks delivered in retaliation to confederate's shocks

SHOCKS "INTENDED" TO BE SENT BY CONFEDERATE	ACTUAL SHOCK SENT BY CONFEDERATE	
	High	Low
High	4.85	2.96
Low	3.86	2.56

Adapted from Nickel, 1974, p. 487. The entry is the mean level of shocks sent, on a seven-point scale.

Thus, an individual's understanding of a situation influences his reaction to frustrations and attacks. In the last two chapters we discussed how the person's attributions about his environment determine the emotion a person feels when he is physiologically aroused, and how the individual's perception of another's motives is a major factor in how much he likes someone who compliments him. In both these cases, cognitive interpretation of the situation has a major effect on motives and emotions. The interaction between cognitive and emotional factors occurs continually and is an important thread running through much of social psychology.

So one possible interpretation of the effects of intent on aggression is that here too, cognitive factors affect the arousal of emotions. Without perceived intent, the frustration or attack will not make us angry. The other obvious possibility is that when there is no perceived intent to harm, the harmed person experiences angry emotions anyway, but restrains overt aggressive behavior. Perhaps he *feels* angry that the teacher won't take the class to the zoo, but restrains himself from overtly expressing it because he knows it would not be fair: who can go to the zoo when it is pouring cats and dogs? Put most generally, the issue is whether perceived intent increases anger arousal, or whether it increases only aggressive behavior without affecting the underlying emotion of anger.

To test this contrast, Zillmann and Cantor (1976) did an experiment that varied whether the subject was informed of mitigating circumstances before being provoked, right after being provoked, or, in a control condition, not informed at all of mitigating circumstances. The idea is that if intent affects angry feelings (as well as aggressive behavior), then informing the person of mitigating circumstances before provocation should prevent anger from being aroused. But if intent only affects aggressive behavior, then the early-informed victim will get angry anyway, but will not become aggressive himself. The subject came into the laboratory and went through a long, complex series of events, which involved hooking the subject up to physiological recording equipment, showing him slides of magazine advertisements, and showing him videotaped pictures of other students. During this time he interacted with two experimenters. One was rude and one was polite. During the course of the experiment, the rude experimenter constantly scolded both the subject and the polite experimenter: "Haven't you finished yet?" "Apparently you don't listen to instructions very well. You were told you had to sit still. This machine shows that you've been moving." The independent variable, mitigating circumstances for all this unpleasant behavior, was the polite experimenter saying "he's really uptight about a midterm he has tomorrow." In the prior condition, he said this before the rude experimenter insulted the subject. In the after condition, he said it afterward. In the third, control condition, he never said it. The findings very clearly showed that the subjects never got very angry at the rude experimenter if they knew in advance why he was unpleasant. Both physiological measures (such as blood pressure and heart rate) and evaluations of the rude experimenter showed that the prior-to-provocation subjects were much less aroused and less angry than were either the control or the after-provocation subjects. What this means is that the subject's attribution about the cause of his tormentor's attacks affects his experienced emotion, anger, as well as his ultimate aggressive behavior. Being attacked when we know there are mitigating circumstances does not, at least according to this study, produce heightened angry emotions. So it appears that in aggression, as in so many other contexts discussed in Chapter 4, the person's attribution is a key determinant of the response to frustration. If he believes his tormentor intended to harm him, he will respond much more aggressively than if he thinks it was an accident, or unintended. And if he knows from the beginning that there are external reasons for the harm done to him, he will not get as angry or as aggressive as if he finds out only later on.

A lot of annoying things happen to us all the time, of course, and only some of them come attached with "intent-to-annoy" attributions. This is not to say that we *never* feel angry unless there is some intent to annoy. Inanimate objects can create a great deal of anger: flat tires, snowdrifts, leaky faucets, burnt scrambled eggs, and rocks on which one stubs one's toe are not usually ascribed the human property of trying to harm us (though there are exceptions to everything!). What it does suggest is that when no intent to harm is present, many frustrations and annoyances will make us less angry than common sense might suggest. A good example is the effects of heat. Common sense certainly tells us we are more irritable and susceptible to becoming aggressive when it is too hot. Folk wisdom tells us that it is the heat of ghetto summers ("a long hot summer") that is partly responsible for riots and crime. In fact, one study showed that most of the 1967 ghetto riots broke out after several days of above-average temperature (Goranson and King, 1970).

But high heat is normally not something we perceive as resulting from an intent to harm us. And a series of rather careful experiments have shown that heat, by itself, does not increase hostility or aggressive behavior. Nor does it make angry people any more likely to aggress. In fact, the opposite tended to happen: heat (averaging 94° vs. averaging 73°) tended to diminish the aggressive behavior of subjects angered by a confederate, and increase that among nonangered subjects (Baron and Bell, 1975, 1976). In yet another study, both groups showed less aggression when it was hot than when it was cold (Baron, 1972). Why heat has, if anything, a calming effect upon angry persons is not clear. But it certainly is possible that under oppressive heat, an angry person attributes his anger to the environment, rather than to an annoying confederate. And he may attribute the anger-arousing behavior by the confederate to the heat, and for that reason react less angrily to the confederate's apparently justified annoyance.

nonspecific emotional arousal

Another source of aggressive behavior that is generalized or nonspecific emotional arousal, but labeled as "anger." This notion of course follows from Schachter's two-factor theory of emotions discussed in Chapter 4.

The argument is that physiological arousal is fairly undifferentiated, so people have a hard time knowing what emotion they are experiencing simply on the basis of internal cues. When they are physiologically aroused, they look to the external environment for cues regarding which emotion they feel. If the environment gives them reason to think they are angry, they will experience anger, and this in turn will lead to aggressive behavior.

The implication of this view is that arousal stemming from any number of sources might promote aggressive behavior, as long as it is labeled anger. Loud noises (Geen and O'Neal, 1969), competitive behavior (Rocha and Rogers, 1976), or vigorous exercise, seem to increase aggressiveness when they occur in a situation that seems to call for anger. For example, Zillmann and Bryant (1974) did a study which varied both arousal and initial provocation by a confederate, on the supposition that provocation by another person would help the subject label his own feelings as "anger." The high-arousal task was to pedal a bicycle ergometer for one minute. The low-arousal task was to thread nickel-size disks with off-center holes onto a plastic-coated wire. The provocation came in the context of a modified "battleship" game: in the low-provocation condition the confederate said: "How many trials did it take me?" Under high provocation, he said: "Jesus Christ, who needs strategy for him? The dumb ass led me right to it!" The subject was allowed to deliver loud, painful noises to the confederate each time the latter missed. As is shown in Table 6–2, the highest aggression was delivered in the high-arousal, provocation condition. Those subjects who were angry and exercised subsequently behaved more aggressively than when the exercise was not included. But arousal actually led to the *least* amount of aggression when there had been no provocation, when the subject had no basis for labeling his arousal as anger. Thus even arousal that is apparently irrelevant to aggressiveness or anger (like exercising, in this case) produces an increase in aggressive behavior, provided that it occurs in a situation that labels any arousal as "anger."

TABLE 6–2
mean noise intensity

	PROVOCATION	NO PROVOCATION
High arousal	126.5	58.0
Low arousal	90.1	75.0

Source: Adapted from Zillmann and Bryant, 1974, p. 789.

It seems, as we have discussed in previous chapters, that individuals have considerable difficulty labeling the emotions they are feeling, and the relationship between one emotion and behavior is not always specific. Arousing any kind of drive or emotion may increase the performance of a behavior even if it is irrelevant. But in order to produce aggression it is necessary that somehow the person misinterpret the arousal as stemming from anger, rather than from exercise, or the game, or whatever else is in fact arousing him.

aggressive behavior

Frustration, annoyance, and attack all tend to make people feel angry, and these angry feelings constitute one important element producing aggressive behavior. Ordinarily, the more angry a person feels, the more likely it is that he will act aggressively. But people often feel angry and behave peacefully, or at least are not overtly aggressive; and it is also possible for people to *be* aggressive without *feeling* aggressive. Thus, the factors that control the expression of aggression are as important as those that arouse it in the first place. And the main mechanism determining human aggressive behavior is past learning.

learned aggressive responses

To be sure, many animals respond aggressively to certain stimuli whenever they appear and these responses appear to be instinctive. If two male Siamese fighting fish are put in the same tank, they immediately attack each other and fight until one is badly mauled or dead. The presence of another male is sufficient to produce this aggressive behavior in each one. For our purposes, the important point is that it seemed to be triggered automatically by the other's presence and was obviously not learned. There are countless other examples of similar reactions. Many animals have instinctive aggressive responses to particular stimuli—the presence of these stimuli immediately sets off a specific aggressive reaction. When the stimuli are removed, the aggressive behavior ceases. There is, however, little evidence that humans have this kind of instinctive response to external cues.

In contrast humans' aggressiveness is primarily influenced by what they learn. A newborn infant expresses aggressive feelings in an entirely uncontrolled manner. Whenever he is the least bit frustrated, whenever he is denied anything he wants, he cries in outrage, flails his arms, and strikes out at anything within range. In the earliest days of life, an infant does not realize that other people exist and therefore cannot be deliberately trying to harm them. When he does discover the existence of others, he continues to vent his rage and probably directs much of it toward these people.

But by the time he is an adult, this savage, uncontrolled animal has his aggressive impulses under firm control and aggresses only under certain circumstances, if at all. This development is primarily due to learning. Anything which teaches a child that aggression is acceptable will increase his overall level of aggressiveness; anything which teaches him that aggression is wrong will have the opposite effect. However, most learning related to aggression is more specific than this. Individuals learn to aggress in one situation and not in another, against one person and not against another, and in response to one kind of frustration and not another.

This learning defines whether aggression is good or bad, as already indicated. Some aggression is bad; we earlier used the term *antisocial* aggression to describe it. Other kinds of aggression are viewed as actually required in a given situation, acts we called *prosocial* aggression. Then there is a third category of aggressive acts—those which are at least acceptable, and may even be essential to have a decent life, but which are neither forbidden nor required by society's expectations. These we called *sanctioned* aggression. Although these distinctions are sometimes quite subtle, individuals must learn them in order to function effectively in society. Those who never control their aggression will not be allowed to remain free; those who never use aggression are probably worse off than those who use it at appropriate times. Therefore, the critical problem in socialization is not how to teach children never to aggress but how to teach them when aggression is appropriate and when it is inappropriate.

reinforcement

The first mechanism by which this learning occurs is reinforcement. When a particular behavior is rewarded, an individual is more likely to repeat that behavior in the future; when it is punished, he is less likely to repeat it. Just as a child learns not to track mud onto a rug, so he learns not to express aggression. He is punished when he punches his brother, throws stones at the girl next door, or bites his mother, and he learns not to do these things. He is rewarded when he restrains himself despite frustrations, and he learns this also. For example, in one study (Geen and Pigg, 1970) subjects were verbally reinforced ("that's good," "you're doing fine") for shocking a confederate. Other subjects in a control group shocked the confederate but were not rewarded for it. The reinforced subjects gave considerably more intense shocks than did nonreinforced subjects. We could give many other examples making the same point: Aggressive acts are to a major extent learned responses, and reinforcement is a major facilitator of aggression.

imitation

Imitation is another mechanism that plays an important role in shaping a child's behavior. All people, and children in particular, have a strong tendency to imitate others. A child watches people eat with a fork or lis-

Drawing by Charles Schulz; © 1965 United Feature Syndicate, Inc.

tens to them talking and tries to do the same. After a while, he also uses a fork and talks. This imitation extends to virtually every kind of behavior, including aggression. A child observes other people being aggressive and controlling their aggression, and he copies them. He learns to aggress verbally—to shout at people, to curse, and to criticize—and not to resort to violence—not to punch people or throw stones or blow up buildings. He also learns when, if ever, each of these behaviors is permissible. At certain times he should not aggress even verbally (e.g., when he disagrees with his parents), but at others, any kind of aggression is not only allowable but even necessary (e.g., when he is being attacked). Thus his own aggressive behavior is shaped and determined by what he observes others doing.

An experiment by Albert Bandura (Bandura, Ross, and Ross, 1961) illustrated the effect of witnessing aggression. Children watched an adult play with tinker toys and a Bobo doll (a 5-foot, inflated plastic doll). In one condition, the adult began by assembling the tinker toys for about a minute and then turned his attention to the doll. He approached the doll, punched it, sat on it, hit it with a mallet, tossed it in the air, and kicked it about the room, all the while shouting such things as "Sock him in the nose," "Hit him down," "Pow." He continued in this way for nine minutes, with the child watching. In the other condition, the adult worked quietly with the tinker toys and ignored the doll.

Some time later, each child was left alone for twenty minutes with a number of toys, including a 3-foot Bobo doll. The children's behavior was rated as shown in Table 6–3. They tended to imitate many of the actions of the adult. Those who had seen the adult act aggressively were much more aggressive toward the doll than those who had witnessed the adult working quietly on the tinker toys. The first group punched, kicked, and hammered the doll and uttered aggressive comments similar to those expressed by the aggressive adult.

TABLE 6–3
aggression by children witnessing violent or neutral model

	AMOUNT OF AGGRESSION	
Condition	Physical	Verbal
Violent model	12.73	8.18
Neutral model	1.05	0.35

Source: Based on Bandura, Ross, and Ross (1961).

The children in this situation learned to attack a certain type of doll. They might also attack the same kind of doll in a different situation, and perhaps a different kind of doll, as well. Just how far this would extend—whether or not they would also punch their sisters—is not clear; but it is clear that they would be somewhat more likely to attack some things than they were before. Through the process of imitation, these children showed more aggressive behavior.

Two studies (Baron and Kepner, 1970; Baron, 1971) demonstrate that modeling can not only increase but also decrease the amount of aggression. In both studies some subjects observed a model who gave a great many shocks to a confederate while other subjects observed a model who gave very few shocks. There was also a condition in which there was no model. Subjects who observed the aggressive model gave more shocks and those who observed the unaggressive model gave fewer shocks than when there was no model present.

Children do not imitate indiscriminately—they imitate some people more than others. The more important, powerful, successful, and liked the other people are, the more a child will imitate them. Also, the people they see most often are the ones they imitate most. Parents, who fit all these criteria, are the primary models for a child during the early years. Since parents are both the major source of reinforcement and the chief object of imitation, a child's future aggressive behavior depends greatly on how his parents treat him and on how they themselves behave.

This joint dependence on the parents for reinforcement and imitation produces an interesting consequence. Punishing a child for acting aggressively might be considered an effective method of teaching him not to be aggressive, but it often produces the opposite effect. Punishment should make the aggressive behavior less likely in the future. The child learns that he will be punished if he hits his sister, so he avoids the punishment by not hitting her. More generally, he will not be aggressive whenever he expects to suffer for it. He will not ordinarily start a fight with someone who is certain to beat him; he will not start a fight, even if he can win it, if he expects to be severely punished for it afterward. Parents are aware of this simple relationship and employ it to stop children from fighting.

As far as the parents are concerned, this tends to have the desired effect. A child who is punished for fighting does tend to be less aggressive—at home. Home is where the risk of punishment is greatest and therefore where the threat of punishment has the strongest inhibiting effect. Unfortunately, the situation is quite different when this child is out of the home. A child who is punished severely for being aggressive at home tends to be more aggressive outside than does a child who is punished less severely (Sears, Whiting, Nowlis, and Sears, 1953). The punishment inhibits aggression in the home but seems to encourage it outside the home.

The explanation for this effect is that the child imitates his parents'

"This will teach you not to hit people."

aggressive behavior. When he is in a situation in which he has the upper hand, he acts the way his parents do toward him. They are aggressive and so is he. Thus, the punishment teaches him not to be aggressive at home, but it also teaches him that aggression is acceptable if he can get away with it. Regardless of what parents hope, children will continue to do what their parents do as well as what they say.

aggression-eliciting cues

A third variant in this learning approach is that people learn to aggress as a habitual response to certain cues, and such aggression-eliciting cues therefore become necessary conditions for anger to be converted into aggression (Berkowitz, 1965). Any stimuli regularly and repeatedly associated with aggression take on this cue property, by a process of classical conditioning. Guns may do this, as may aggressively toned words ("punish," "hurt,"), or the bully in the schoolroom, or a police officer. So the expression of aggression is to some extent controlled by the presence or absence of such cues. In one study (Berkowitz and LePage, 1967) some subjects were made angry by being shocked by a confederate and some were not angry. They were then all given the opportunity to deliver shocks to the confederate. When the subjects sat down at a table to deliver the shocks, they noticed a gun or a badminton racket lying near by. The measure of aggression was how many shocks the subjects delivered, and the experimenters found that angered subjects gave more shocks when the gun rather than the badminton racket was present.

Although this is a fascinating effect, later research has not confirmed it. Page and Scheidt (1971) found that the effect occurred only when subjects were aware of what the experimenters were trying to demonstrate and were also cooperative. Similarly, Turner and Simons (1974) explicitly induced the subject to be suspicious of the experimenter by having a confederate "leak" information to the subject that the purpose of the experiment was not what it seemed. Given such suspiciousness, subjects with weapons delivered no more shock than subjects without them. Perhaps even more damaging, Buss, Booker, and Buss (1972) repeated the original study almost exactly and did not get more aggression when the gun was present. In four different experiments they tested the effect of having subjects fire a weapon before delivering shocks. They argued that if the presence of a gun should increase aggression, surely actually firing a gun would have an even greater effect. Yet they found that subjects who fired a gun were no more aggressive subsequently than subjects who had not fired a weapon.

But the theoretical idea may still be valid, even if these "weapons experiments" are too artificial to support it. In a much simpler study, Turner and Layton (1976) first had subjects learn, in a standard paired-associate learning paradigm, a series of aggressively toned, highly concrete words (e.g., fist, gun, punch, or smash). Control subjects learned neutral words. Then the subjects were placed in the Buss sham-learning shock procedure. More intense shocks were given by subjects who had learned the aggressive words. In another example, Turner, Layton, and Simons (1975) drove a pickup truck around in a mixed business and residential area of Salt Lake City on a Saturday between 9 am and 5 pm. At stop lights they would wait for 12 seconds after the light turned green before they drove on. They measured how often the car behind them honked, as an indication of aggressive behavior. Again they varied the presence or absence of aggressive cues. The most aggressive had a .303 caliber military rifle in a plainly visible rifle rack in the rear window of the cabin, and a bumper sticker saying "Vengeance." In this condition, 60 percent of the cars honked. The middle condition had the rifle, plus a sticker saying "Friend" and 38 percent honked. The least agressive had no rifle or bumper sticker, though the rifle rack was in plain sight, and only 27 percent honked.

In general, appropriate cues probably increase aggressiveness when they alter the subject's perception of the situation. If they cause the subject to feel that aggressiveness is more appropriate or more expected, this would certainly increase aggression. Also if the cue causes the subject to feel that the other person is a more aggressive person or more deserving of being aggressed against, that too would tend to increase aggression. For example, in the Berkowitz and LePage study the subjects were told that the gun belonged to the confederate, who was using it in another experiment. This may have suggested to the subject that the confederate was a violent person, lowered his estimation of the confederate, and therefore caused him to be more aggressive. In contrast, Buss et al. (1972) described the gun as belonging to the confederate, who was lending it to a friend, not using it himself. This apparently was a crucial difference, probably because it did not make the confederate seem as violent a person. Thus, we would conclude that humans tend to be particularly affected by the presence of aggression-arousing cues in those circumstances in which the cues produced a marked change in the perception of the situation.

reducing aggression

Aggressive behavior has always been a major problem for human societies. Freud viewed aggressive and sexual instincts as constituting the major problems for social control. The human being has the capacity for great anger and for very destructive behavior, so it is as vital to understand what reduces aggressiveness as to know what causes it.

As described above, whether or not somebody aggresses in a particular situation is determined by two variables—the strength of his aggressive impulses and the degree to which he has learned to express aggression in the given situation. The strength of the impulse is determined partly by the degree of frustration or annoyance that produced it and partly by the extent to which the individual, because of learning or personality characteristics, tends to react to this frustration with feelings of aggression. The tendency to express this aggression is determined by what he has learned about aggressiveness in general and the situation in particular. This analysis, by itself, suggests some of the ways in which human aggression can be minimized. One, the potential for frustration can be reduced. The Kerner Commission, for example, recommended a sweeping set of social changes after the riots of the 1960's to improve the treatment of blacks in our society, on the assumption that reducing their frustration would reduce the chance of further rioting. Or, people can learn non-aggressive responses to attack or frustration. A hungry child can learn to deal with his frustration in ways other than fighting or screaming. He can learn to make himself a peanut butter sandwich rather than pummeling his busy mother. These are essentially preventive measures. But there are other approaches to aggression reduction.

catharsis

One ancient idea, following this kind of analysis, is that aggressive drive can be reduced simply by expressing the aggression. Freud called this process the *catharsis* of aggressive feelings. In commonsense language, it involves "letting off steam" or "getting it out of your system." By expressing aggression, we feel less aggression inside. The major implication of the catharsis notion is that if a person feels aggressive, committing an aggressive act should reduce the intensity of his feelings. This, in turn, should make him less likely to act aggressively afterward. The idea is that aggressing is very much like eating. Whether or not someone eats is determined partly by how hungry he is and partly by the situation in which he finds himself. If he eats something when he is hungry, he reduces his hunger and will eat less later. If someone annoys us by honking his horn at us, we feel aggressive. If, at the next traffic light, we find ourselves behind his car and honk at him, this should reduce our aggressive feelings toward him.

The earliest version of the catharsis theory was Freud's, and it presupposed that we all always have a reservoir of instinctual aggressive energy with us. So no matter what the situation is, we have a certain amount of aggressiveness that we need to "get off our chest." The problem with this view is that it predicts reduction in aggressive drive following *any* expression of aggression. There is some empirical evidence that contradicts this: when nonangry people aggress, they often seem thereafter to be even *more* aggressive, rather than "letting off steam" (Doob and Wood, 1972; Doob and Climie, 1972).

Drawing by Jack Tippit; reprinted by permission, Parade Magazine.

"Go ahead, Dad . . . release all that hatred and resentment. It's good to get it out of your system."

With the later rise of the frustration-aggression hypothesis, it became more generally accepted that aggressive drives are not instinctual, but are instigated by situational factors like frustrations, annoyances, and attacks. The implication was that expression of aggression would produce catharsis only for those people who were frustrated or annoyed or angered to start with. This hypothesis suggested research to manipulate frustration and the opportunity to express aggression, and then measure the person's tendency to aggress even further. The prediction would be that angered people, when given the opportunity to express that anger, would show reduced levels of aggression later on. For nonangered people, however, expressing aggression would not reduce the aggression potential, because they would have no built-up reservoir of angry feelings to discharge.

The major competing hypothesis for such situations is a *disinhibition* hypothesis. It assumes that we all control our anger fairly tightly most of the time. But if it is once released, particularly when it seems to be socially approved, we will relax our inhibitions about further hostilities. The disinhibition hypothesis can apply to anyone, or to previously angered persons only, just like the catharsis hypothesis, depending on whether one or not we assume a constant reservoir of aggressive drive even in the nonangered persons (Konecni and Ebbesen, 1976).

RESEARCH FINDINGS One way to test these hypotheses is to look at physiological arousal, as an index of angry feelings. Here most of the research is consistent with the catharsis analysis and predictions. To begin with, two studies (Hokanson, 1961; Hokanson and Burgess, 1962) provide evidence that expressing aggression decreases anger. In these studies, subjects were insulted by a low-status person, with the immediate effect being to increase their systolic blood pressure, indicating that the annoyance had increased physiological tension. We can interpret this as evidence that the subjects were made angry. Some of the subjects were then given an opportunity to deliver shocks to the experimenter who had annoyed them; some were not given this opportunity. Physiological measures showed that being allowed to express aggression resulted in lower systolic blood pressure—evidence that subjects who are originally angry will be less angry if they are allowed to express some aggression toward the source of their annoyance.

More direct evidence comes from behavioral studies of aggression. An influential early study of catharsis was conducted by Seymour Feshbach (1955). First, most of the subjects were angered by being insulted in class by their instructor. Then half the subjects were allowed to express aggression on a fantasy task—responding to four TAT cards (cards showing ambiguous pictures for which the subjects were to make up a story). The other half of this group did not respond to the cards, but all the subjects in an uninsulted group did. Afterward, there was another measure of aggression, the results of which are shown in Table 6–4. The insulted subjects who were given the opportunity to express aggression on the fantasy task were less aggressive on the final measure than were the insulted subjects who did not do the fantasy task.

TABLE 6–4
effect of fantasy expression of aggression on subsequent aggression

CONDITION	AGGRESSION
Angered:	
With fantasy task	21.17
Without fantasy task	23.09
Not angered	14.92

Note: Figures indicate the amount of aggression on a scale from 0 to 36.

The clearest prediction of the catharsis approach is that physical aggression against your frustrator should reduce the tendency to aggress against him or her later on. A study by Doob and Wood (1972) makes this point. Once again, subjects were either angry or not angry. Some of the subjects in each condition then gave electric shocks to the confederate, while other subjects did not. When the subjects were then allowed to give shocks themselves, the results fell into a nice pattern that is shown in Table 6–5. The angry subjects gave fewer shocks when they had shocked the confederate previously. The subjects who were not angry, however, gave more shocks than they did when no shocks had been given in the first place. In other words when the subjects were angered, catharsis resulted from giving shocks to the confederate; when the subjects were not angered, the opposite occurred, with more shocks being given than otherwise.

TABLE 6–5
number of later shocks given by annoyed and not annoyed subjects who first gave shocks themselves, witnessed shocks being given, or saw no shocks

CONDITION	SUBJECT SHOCKS	WITNESSED EXPERIMENTER SHOCKING	NO SHOCKS GIVEN
Subject annoyed	6.80	7.60	10.67
Subject not annoyed	8.07	9.73	6.60

Source: Adapted from Doob and Wood (1972).

Perhaps the best recent experiment on this topic is by Konecni and Ebbesen (1976). First, the subject was insulted. She did an anagram task with the confederate, who finished her own problems quickly and then proceeded to insult the subject, criticize her for being so slow, and express doubts about her intellectual ability. Then some subjects were given the opportunity to aggress against the confederate, while others were not. Using a variant on the standard sham-learning situation, the subjects were required to deliver "loud, but quite safe" blasts of noise to the confederate each time she made an error. Control subjects did not send any noise to the confederate. The dependent variable involved a "creativity test" in which all subjects were given a two-button box, one labeled "good" and the other "noise." The subject could administer either reward or punishment, depending on her feelings. The results clearly showed that delivering blasts of noise at the confederate reduced a subsequent tendency to do so.

This reduction of aggressiveness through catharsis is apparently not limited to direct aggression against one's tormentor. It even helps to aggress against someone else. In an experiment by Konecni and Doob (1972), angry subjects gave fewer shocks to their tormentor when they had been given an opportunity to shock either their tormentor or someone else than when they were not given this opportunity. Apparently, behaving aggressively to anyone reduces aggressive feelings somewhat and thereby reduces subsequent aggressive behavior. Once again, there was no catharsis effect with subjects who were not initially angry.

Witnessing someone else aggressing against one's frustrator seems to relieve our own anger as well. Doob and Wood also had a condition in which the subject simply witnessed the experimenter shocking the tormenting confederate. And as can be seen in Table 6–5, the annoyed subjects also reduced their own aggression after watching the confederate getting shocked.

Whether catharsis occurs when angry people watch *any* kind of aggression (even that against innocent parties) is a much more complicated question. Clearly it is very relevant to the hot political issue of whether violence on television or in the movies affects aggressive behavior. If watching a crime movie actually reduced our aggressiveness, it would be quite an important matter, so we will discuss this issue in some detail later in the chapter.

Finally, aggressive humor also seems to reduce aggression. Leak (1974) had an experimenter insult some subjects and not others. Then the subject rated twenty jokes. Half the subjects read and rated hostile jokes, and the other a series of jokes with little hostility in them. Later, ratings of the experiment and experimenter showed that insulted subjects liked both much better if they had had an opportunity to relieve their aggressiveness by reading hostile rather than nonhostile jokes. So keep some hostile cartoons handy in case you ever get someone really angry.

LIMITATIONS OF THE CATHARSIS HYPOTHESIS What are some of the limitations of the catharsis hypothesis? One which we have mentioned in connection with most of the studies is that the expression of aggression usually *increases* aggressiveness in peaceful, nonangered, nonannoyed persons. The disinhibition hypothesis seems to account for their behavior best. Expression of aggression mainly releases some of their normal inhibitions against further expression.

Secondly, aggression against one's frustrator does not produce catharsis if the original frustration is perceived as not caused by that person. That is, if someone frustrates you but you do not think it is his fault, expressing aggression back at him will not relieve your anger. Suppose you want to deposit a $20 bill in your checking account, but the bank teller, saying it is counterfeit and worthless, won't take it. You certainly feel frustrated, and you may get openly hostile, but you will not be able to reduce your angry feelings by yelling at the teller.

The Konecni-Ebbesen study illustrates this lack of catharsis when the anger is not causally attributed to the apparent frustrator. In one condition, anger was created by having the confederate deliver noise to the subject, but at the experimenter's command rather than out of personal choice. The confederate in fact was perceived as being forced to deliver this annoyance to the subject. Subsequent attacks by the subject upon the confederate did not produce catharsis under these conditions, unlike the catharsis mentioned earlier, produced when the original annoyance had been gratuitous insults by the confederate. In other words, the frustration has to be perceived as intentionally caused by the frustrator, rather than attributed to some other cause, for aggression toward the nominal frustrator to produce catharsis. This result was also obtained in a nearly identical study conducted by Geen, Stonner, and Shope (1975).

In a field study that makes the same point, Ebbesen, Duncan, and Konecni (1975) took advantage of a marvelous opportunity when a large aerospace firm recruited several hundred engineers and technicians to work on a new contract for the Department of Defense. After nearly a year of successful work, the contract was abruptly canceled, and the company had no choice but to lay off about 200 disgruntled workers. To take advantage of the hostility caused by these layoffs, the researchers arranged for separation interviews with many of the workers. These interviews provided an opportunity for expression of aggression. They varied in focus, some concerned with the worker's feelings about the company, others with his supervisor, and still others with his own situation. After the interview, in an apparently unrelated action, the worker was administered a questionnaire on his attitudes toward these objects.

The interview did not seem to reduce these workers' anger. In fact, in general it had the effect of *increasing* aggression toward the supervisor or company, either relative to nondiscussed objects, or relative to the aggression expressed by nonangered workers (those not laid off, but interviewed anyway because they were leaving the company). Presumably no catharsis occurred because the layoffs were caused by a tormentor who was not explicitly discussed: the Department of Defense. The supervisor, company, and employee himself all were pretty much innocent victims. So this study is consistent with the earlier evidence that catharsis works only in response to intended aggression by a responsible agent. When it occurs in response to a frustrator who had no choice about it, there is no catharsis. This provides further evidence of how important causal attributions can be. Catharsis works only when an internal attribution is made to the frustrator or annoyer.

A third limitation is that within any given sequence of behavior, aggression seems to escalate rather than to decline. That is, catharsis only seems to reduce aggression when there is some break in the action, a change in the victim, or some change in the mode of expression of aggression. So if you get into a fight, it is likely that the fighting will increase your aggression toward your opponent rather than decrease it. This has been a common finding with the Buss aggression machine, which has been used in so many aggression experiments. As the experiment goes on, the "teacher" almost always gives increasingly strong shocks to the "learner," no matter what conditions they are in. Goldstein, Davis, and Herman (1975) found the same thing with verbal responses, using the same teacher-learner situation. The subject was given a list of standard verbal responses from which he could choose, depending on whether the "learner" had made an error or not. The subject tended to give more and more intense punishments for errors. So for example, if the subject first responded to an error with "That's no good," he later would escalate with "You're a jerk," through "I never met anyone as dumb as you," to "Stupid son of a bitch." This escalation phenomenon appears to be another case of the disinhibition hypothesis. The authors suggest perhaps the same thing happened with the escalation of the bombing of North Vietnam in the late 1960s and early 1970s, and also in the case of the "battered child" syndrome. In these cases, the same behavior is committed over a period of time against the same victim, and it seems to escalate in intensity. It would seem that either a change in behavior or situation is required for catharsis to occur.

Thus, the research quite consistently demonstrates that angry people who express aggression become less angry and are then less aggressive, whereas people who are not angry to begin with are either unaffected by acting aggressively or actually become more aggressive. Although this provides support for the original notion of catharsis, the situations involved seem to be limited to those in which the individual himself behaves aggressively or observes his tormentor suffering. It seems also to be limited to cases in which the tormentor is perceived as having been responsible for frustrating the person. And it seems to be limited to cases in which there is a "break in the action" that allows the person to feel he has indeed "gotten it out of his system" rather than feeling he is still in the process of getting it out.

fear of punishment and retaliation

It would seem to be obvious that the fear of punishment and/or retaliation would suppress aggressive behavior. For example, Bond and Dutton (1975) and Wilson and Rogers (1975), both using the shock-learning paradigm, found reduced shocking when the subject was told that later in the experiment the roles would be reversed, so he (or she) would be in the position of being shocked. But as a general matter it turns out not to be so simple. As noted earlier, children who are frequently punished for being aggressive turn out themselves to be more aggressive than normal. Perhaps it is because they model themselves upon an aggressive parent. Perhaps it is because frequent punishment generates a lot of anger itself. And sometimes harsh punishment produces disguised aggression that may escape punishment but expresses the anger. In any case, there is clearly no simple inhibition of aggression caused by harsh punishment.

One interesting line of research has considered how aggressive whites are toward blacks when blacks later will have the opportunity to retaliate. The Donnersteins placed white subjects in the sham-learning situation, in which the "learner" was a black confederate. Then they tested how much the subject shocked the confederate, depending on whether their roles would later be reversed or not. Presumably, if the roles would reverse later on, the black might retaliate against the white.

In several such studies, the Donnersteins (1972a, 1972b, 1975) found that potential retaliation markedly reduced the direct aggression performed by whites against blacks. In this teacher-learner situation, direct aggression was indexed by the intensity of the shock delivered by the subject when the confederate made an "error." Expecting to reverse roles increased the amount of reward given by the white subject to the black confederate for "correct responses."

But potential retaliation also had the effect of increasing covert, indirect, substitute forms of aggression against the black confederate. Indirect aggression was measured by setting the shock machine at one particular intensity, so the subject had no control over intensity, and then telling the subject he had to deliver shock for every error, so the subject had no control over whether to shock or not. But the subject did control the duration of shock; he could give either a quick one or a long one. The long one was a relatively disguised form of aggression; after all, the subject was just following instructions by giving the shock! And potential retaliation actually increased such indirect, relatively covert, disguised forms of aggression. So the black potential for retaliation against a white aggressor does indeed seem to reduce the white's direct aggression against him (and increase rewards given to him as well) —but it increases, instead, subtle and indirect forms of aggression.

Finally, it is interesting to note that all these effects occurred for black targets and not for white. Apparently the threat of black retaliation for white aggression is most potent. And it occurred much more toward a dissimilar black confederate (dissimilar in terms of attitudes and values, in the vein discussed in the last chapter) than it did toward a similar one (Donnerstein and Donnerstein, 1975). So the conversion of direct aggression into indirect aggression, because of threatened retaliation, occurred with dissimilar blacks, but not so much with whites or similar blacks.

It is important to repeat that the effects of anticipated punishment or retaliation are not simple. Sometimes they do simply suppress aggression, as the person quite rationally wants to avoid future pain. But sometimes they convert direct aggression into something more covert, which may be just as harmful but harder to catch and punish. And sometimes the threats are simply interpreted as attacks, and inspire even more aggression. So it is wrong to think that punishment alone can control aggression—as indeed we all know, if we think about our own experience for a moment.

learned inhibitions

While punishment, or threat of retaliation, may be temporarily effective in suppressing direct aggression in any given situation, it is expensive. There are too many people in too many places for all to be monitored constantly. As it is, many people who commit serious crimes, such as murder, are never caught and punished. It is simply impossible to depend upon external controls to minimize violence, and anyway we would not want a society with that degree of control of behavior. So instead people must learn to control their own aggressive behavior, whether or not they are in danger of being punished.

AGGRESSION ANXIETY The learned inhibition of aggression can be called *aggression anxiety* (or *aggression guilt*). The person feels anxiety when nearing an aggressive response. Like a burnt child approaching a stove, he then backs off and suppresses the urge to aggress. Not everyone has equal amounts of aggression anxiety, of course. Children reared in middle-class homes tend to have more than children reared in lower-class homes. Middle-class norms are more forbidding of open physical aggression, and probably also urge more suppression of spontaneous outbursts of verbal aggression as well. It also appears that we are especially likely to grow up anxious about aggression if our parents use reasoning and withdrawal of affection as disciplinary techniques. If they use high degrees of physical punishment, we are likely ourselves to be relatively free about our own aggressiveness (Feshbach, 1970).

People who are low in aggression anxiety tend, not surprisingly, to exhibit higher levels of openly aggressive behavior. Knott, Lasater, and Shuman (1974) found subjects low in aggression guilt to be high in a measure of overt aggression that involved shocking another subject. This measure was taken before any variables were manipulated. But then they introduced a conditioning procedure, in which the subject was reinforced with a friendly response from the confederate (who was supposedly being shocked) every time the subject shocked him. Aggression guilt made the conditioning process slower, however; subjects with more aggression guilt did not respond to reinforcement by shocking as much as did those without so much guilt. In short, aggression anxiety not only inhibits the person from expressing aggression openly under ordinary circumstances, but makes him or her less likely to learn to be aggressive, even when reinforced for it.

Aggression anxiety does not come only from early childhood training, though surely that is an important source. It also comes from the internalization of the norms of people important to us. All through our lives we are learning and relearning "the ropes," or the social norms of our immediate associates. Students learn not to curse their professors to their faces, and professors learn not to throw things at their students. We learn that it is all right to yell and scream at our children, but that it is not all right to beat them up. We can kill animals for sport or food, but we cannot kill each other or someone's pet animal. When you think about it, we all possess a great amount of information, with many finely graded built-in distinctions, about what is and what is not permissible aggression. These learned inhibitions represent the most potent controls on human violent behavior we have; no police force could ever be numerous

"No need to apologize. You had a job to do and you did it."

enough, far-sighted enough, or quick enough even to come close to them.

The experience of having been a victim also seems to inhibit aggression. In Bond and Dutton's (1975) experiment, using a shock-learning paradigm, the subject was supposed to be the teacher. But before the actual learning phase of the experiment began, the experimenter put half the subjects through the shock procedure themselves. The other half had no such experience of being shocked. The result was that subjects who themselves had been shocked gave consistently lower-intensity shocks to other subjects than did those with no personal experience.

PAIN CUES What kind of restraints, if any, does the victim's reaction to aggression have on the aggressor's further violence? Signs of the victim's distress might arouse, vicariously, a similar negative emotional state in the aggressor: he might identify with the victim, have empathy for his suffering, and inhibit further attack. On the other hand, since the intent of aggression is to hurt, we might expect that the signs of pain in another person might simply reinforce the aggression, and increase it still further.

To test these possibilities, a number of studies have been done varying the "pain cues" transmitted by victim to aggressor. In addition, the aggressor's anger has usually been varied, on the supposition that inhibition might occur when the aggressor has been only mildly provoked, whereas reinforcement might be more common with higher levels of anger. In one such study, Baron (1971a) used the shock-learning paradigm. The supposed physiological reactions of the shock victim were transmitted to the subject in the form of a "pain meter." This registered either "high" or "mild" levels of pain. The subject was angered in two ways: by having his own initial efforts at solving a problem criticized by the confederate, and by having the confederate shock him.

In this study, pain cues reduced further aggression, whether the subject had been angered or not. Then Baron did another one (1971b), this time varying similarity, following the hunch that pain cues from someone markedly dissimilar would not bring an empathic reaction from angered subjects, and thus would increase aggression. The similar confederate was a fellow student with political attitudes like the subject's; the dissimilar one was supposedly an electrician with discrepant attitudes. But even here pain cues led only to a decrease in aggressive behavior. Baron next (1974) suggested that pain cues might increase aggression if higher levels of anger were used. This time, instead of just giving the confederate instructions to shock the subject to induce anger, the experimenter told him he could either shock the subject or deliver light flashes. The confederate then shocked the subject, totally incensing him, and arousing high levels of anger, as planned. This time pain cues did increase further aggression, at least in the angry condition. In general, then, signs of a victim's suffering inhibit further aggression, except in cases of extreme anger, when they are taken as signs of successful hurting.

DEHUMANIZATION For such reasons, it is often argued that victims become "dehumanized" when they are far away or anonymous to their attackers. For example, it was thought that it was easier to bomb North Vietnamese from the great heights of a B-52, or to order troops into battle from the distance of Washington, D.C., than to attack at closer, more personal range. The idea is that having the victim distant or anonymous makes aggression easier, because the "pain cues" are absent. Conversely, making him more human, so that the attacker can have empathy for his suffering, should reduce aggression.

A neat example of this dehumanization process occurred in the Turner et al. (1975) study involving the pickup truck that waited too long at a green light and got honked at. The experimenters either left a curtain across the rear window open or closed it. In one case the victim (the driver who got honked at) was visible, and in the other case he was not. This produced big differences in honking. The visible driver was honked at 31 percent of the time, the invisible one 52 percent of the time. It is easier to aggress against someone we cannot see or identify in any very personal way. Another example of this same phenomenon will come up in Chapter 11, when we discuss Milgram's obedience experiment. There, it turns out to be much easier to give dangerous shocks to someone in another room whom we can't hear than to shock someone sitting right next to us. Johnson, Sears, and McConahay (1971) have used the same argument with respect to discrimination against blacks. They suggest it is much easier to condone discriminatory practices as long as the minority is "invisible." They present considerable data on the low levels of interracial personal contact and on the low levels of media coverage of blacks to support the argument that up to the time of the ghetto riots in the 1960s, blacks were invisible to most whites. This meant that most whites passively supported institutions and practices that worked against blacks, but never had to confront the human suffering they created. The riots, and the subsequent increases in media attention to blacks (in the news, in advertising, and in entertainment shows), began to reverse this "invisibility," and presumably helped to make whites more aware of the true cost of racial inequities.

ALCOHOL AND DRUGS It is sometimes said that "the conscience is soluble in alcohol." Among the aspects of conscience that can be ignored when drinking, learned inhibitions against expressing aggression would seem to be prime candidates. Barroom brawls and murders by drunken husbands are legendary aspects of the American scene. They raise the question of whether or not alcohol generally has a disinhibiting effect on aggression.

To test the effects of alcohol on inhibitions against aggression, Taylor and Gammon (1975) conducted a study in which the subject engaged in a competitive reaction-time task, opposed by a confederate. He was supposed to select an intensity of shock that would be delivered to the confederate if he (the subject) proved faster than his opponent. Similarly, the confederate could shock the subject if he were faster. Before they began, however, they were given either a high dose of alcohol (1.5 oz. per 40 pounds of body weight, which would be about three or four stiff drinks for the average subject), or a low dose (0.5 oz. per 40 pounds). As can be seen in Figure 6–1, the shock subject delivered more shock if he had drunk more alcohol (regardless of whether it was vodka or bourbon).

Not all studies show this relatively simple disinhibition of aggression resulting from alcohol. Part of the effect here seemed due to the competitive nature of the task, which meant that the opponent could fight back. When the victim is more helpless, alcohol may actually depress aggression. And even in this experiment, the low dose of alcohol actually reduced aggression below the level shown by a no-alcohol control group. There are happy drunks and harmless, hapless drunks as well as obnoxious or angry drunks. Another disinhibiting drug, marijuana, has the reputation of not increasing aggression. No substantial amount of experimental research has yet been done on it which would allow an

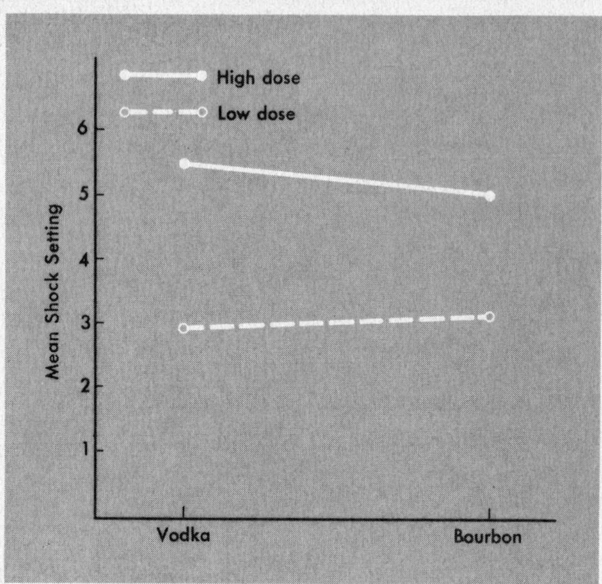

FIGURE 6–1
Mean shock settings as a function of type of alcohol and dose. (Taylor and Gammon, 1975, 171.)

estimate of its effects upon releasing aggressive behavior. However, a careful recent review of the extensive clinical and field research on marijuana concludes that marijuana does not precipitate violence in the majority of those people who use it chronically or periodically. It does leave open the possibility that some people might have such poor impulse control that marijuana would trigger their aggressiveness, but the research evidence on this point is too skimpy to draw a firm conclusion now (Abel, 1977).

displacement

This brings us to a discussion of what happens to aggressive feelings when, for one reason or another, they cannot be expressed against the cause of the feelings. People are often frustrated or annoyed by someone but unable to retaliate against that person—he may be too powerful, not available, or they may be too anxious and inhibited to do it. In such a situation, they can satisfy themselves in several other ways, one of which is called displacement, that is, expressing aggression against a substitute for the original source.

For example, in the experiment by Holmes (1972) which we discussed earlier, some of the frustrated subjects were allowed to behave aggressively toward the person who had caused their frustration by appearing late for the experiment. Other subjects, however, were not given this opportunity but instead were allowed to aggress against someone who had nothing to do with the frustration. It was found that frustration increased aggressiveness toward the innocent person just as it did toward the guilty party.

When a man forbids his son to go to the movies, the boy feels angry and aggressive. He cannot attack his father because his father is too strong and because there are social inhibitions against it. Also, doing so would probably make it less likely that he would be permitted to go to the movies in the future. So he vents his rage on someone else. He has a wide range of people available. There is his mother, his older brother, his older sister, his younger brother, and a boy his own age who lives next door. All these people can be placed on a continuum in terms of their similarity to the boy's original source of frustration—his father. Although this similarity depends primarily on the boy's own view of the situation, let us suppose that he ranks them in the order listed, ranging from his mother to the boy next door. The question is, what determines which of these people he will select and how much aggression he will express?

The basic principle of displacement is that the more similar a person is to the original source of frustration, the stronger will be the individual's aggressive impulses toward him. Thus, as shown by the solid line in Figure 6–2, the boy's aggressive impulse is strongest toward his father and gets weaker as the person toward whom it is directed becomes less similar to his father.

When the only reason for not aggressing against the primary source of frustration is that he is not available, the aggression will be directed toward the next best person. Thus, if the boy cannot express his aggressive feelings toward his father simply because he left town, he would aggress against his mother—the person most similar to his father. Next would come his older brother, then his sister, and so on. The anger he feels toward his father is displaced to these people in the order listed.

The more complicated and probably more common situation is one

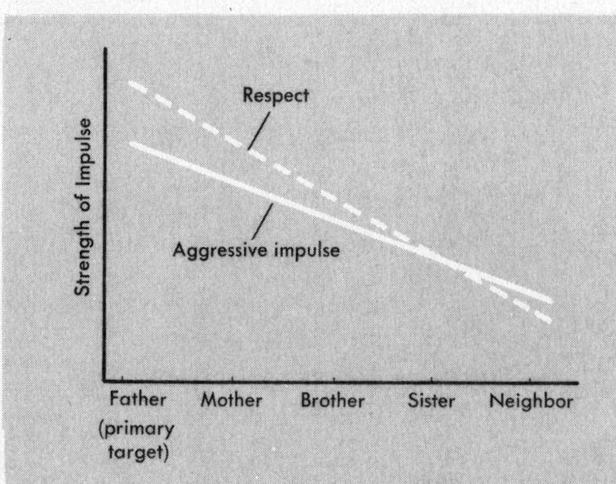

FIGURE 6–2

Feelings of aggression and respect are strongest toward the primary target. The strength of the aggressive impulse and of the respect decreases as the distance from the primary target increases. Since respect declines faster at some point the aggressive impulse is stronger. It is then that the child expresses his anger. The height at which the two emotions cross determines the strength of the aggression expressed.

in which aggression is not expressed because the victim has some reason for restraining himself. If, for example, he feels so much respect for his father that he cannot attack him, his respect operates in much the same way as does his aggressive impulse. Just as his impulse to hurt the source of frustration generalizes to other people, so does his respect for the source. As with the aggression, the more similar the person is to this source, the stronger the respect felt for him. This is shown by the dotted line in Figure 6–2. The boy is most respectful of his father, less respectful of his mother, still less of his sister, and not at all respectful of the boy next door.

An important characteristic of the situation is that the respect declines faster than does the aggressive impulse, which means that eventually the two lines must cross. As long as the respect is stronger than the aggressive impulse, the individual will restrain himself; when the tendency to aggress becomes stronger than the respect, the individual will express his aggression. Thus, in our diagram, the boy would not attack his mother or his older brother because his respect for them is stronger than his aggressive impulse. But his sister is just dissimilar enough to his father that there is relatively little respect for her and similar enough that the aggressive impulse is still quite strong. So because the boy is unwilling to hit his father, he makes a nasty comment to his sister.

Note that the relative strengths of the two tendencies (respect and aggression) determine who will be the target of aggression and how much aggression will be expressed. When the aggressive response is almost as strong as the respect, the two gradients will cross quickly, the target of aggression will be very similar to the primary target, and the amount of aggression will be great. When the respect is much stronger than the aggressive feelings, the target will be quite different from the primary object and there will be relatively little aggression expressed.

It should be pointed out that the dimension along which similarity is determined need not be as simple as the one in our example. Much of the aggression in society may be due to displacement along complex and subtle lines. For example, many adolescents tend to have feelings of anger against their parents. Parents are the source of power in the family, they are the authority, and they must inevitably frustrate their childern's wishes to some extent. Thus they arouse feelings of anger. In some cases, this anger is expressed directly against the parents in adolescent rebellion and breaks with the family. In many cases, however, it is displaced to other people who represent authority. Adolescents need not select those who are related to their parents by family ties or friendship. School administrators, trustees, teachers, the government, and so on fit the criterion and become likely objects for aggression.

Displacement may occur along a dimension of response similarity as well as along a dimension of target similarity. Imagine a president who gets angry at key members of the Washington press corps because he feels they are misinterpreting his actions. He may be quite inhibited from attacking them directly, because he fears they will become even more unsympathetic to him, and make him even more unpopular than he already is. But he can attack them indirectly, by making snide comments about them behind their backs, by refusing to invite them to receptions at the White House, by reducing the number of telephones available to them in the press room, by refusing to call on them at press conferences, and so on. None of these responses is a direct act of aggression in response to the frustration he feels; rather, he displaces his aggression to subtler, more covert forms. In fact, there is a term for persons who habitually resort to such indirect forms of aggression: the passive-aggressive personality.

We have already discussed one series of experiments, by the Donnersteins, illustrating such displaced aggression. White subjects, afraid their black targets might retaliate against them, refrained from increased direct aggression; rather, they turned to indirect aggression that might plausibly be blamed on the experimenter rather than on themselves. Another example of this displacement emerges from a study of Israeli children who had been subjected to frequent artillery shelling from across the border. Ziv, Kruglanski, and Shulman (1974) compared children in settlements that had been shelled with children from settlements never subjected to shelling. These children did not differ in degree of militarism in their attitudes toward war, nor in attitudes of overt aggressiveness against enemy terrorists. But they were more covertly aggressive. Their dream preferences supported victory in war more often, and on a projective test of reactions to frustration, they produced more responses of aggression toward others, rather than aggression toward the self or nonaggressive responses.

SCAPEGOATING Displacement occurs when the source of frustration or annoyance cannot be attacked. There are some occasions, however, when there is no visible, identifiable source of frustration. Lightning hits a man's home, he gets a flat tire on the highway, there is a depression and he loses his job. The man feels angry and aggressive, but there is no obvious person at fault. Under these circumstances, there appears to be a tendency to find someone upon whom to vent aggressive feelings. People look for a scapegoat whom they can blame for their difficulties and whom they accordingly can attack.

The choice of a scapegoat is determined by a number of factors. Children learn that it is more acceptable or safer to be aggressive toward some people than toward others. They probably discover early in life that they should not fight someone who is bigger or stronger than they are—whenever they engage in a fight with such a person, it turns out badly. Thus, they learn that ideal scapegoats should be weak and unable to retaliate. In addition, children learn that certain groups in society are relatively acceptable targets of aggression. These "socially approved" targets depend on which subculture the children are members of. In the white working-class subculture of Cicero, Illinois, or Little Rock, Arkansas, blacks seem to be favorite objects of aggression. In a similar subculture in San Jose, California, it might be Mexicans or Orientals. Elsewhere, Catholics, Jews, Okies, Poles, or Yankees would be targets of aggression. And in some black subcultures, it appears that whites in general are now accepted objects of aggression. It is likely that children learn to express more aggression toward whomever their parents and the rest of the subculture choose for this role than against others.

It is difficult to pick someone at random from the general population to attack—after all, he has done nothing to justify it. If, however, a scapegoat has some distinguishing characteristic that sets him off from the rest of the population, the problem is less acute. He is not like everyone else; he is distinctly different. Then when he, or his entire subgroup, is chosen for attack, people do not feel they are blaming the whole world for their ills—they are blaming one specific, distinguishable group.

Another more important reason why scapegoats typically have a distinguishable characteristic is that people are generally suspicious of and somewhat antagonistic toward those who are different from themselves. As we saw in the last chapter, dissimilarity breeds disliking. The mere fact of the difference, regardless of how they are different, seems to produce a negative reaction. Group members treat other members better than they do nonmembers because they feel closer to the other members, know more about them, feel more loyal to them, and so on. But the suspiciousness and aggressiveness that is displayed toward people who are different seems to be more than a reaction to group loyalty. There seems to be a general tendency to mistreat people who are different.

An experiment by Freedman and Doob (1968) illustrated this phenomenon. Six subjects took a long, complex personality test that was described to them as being an extremely good indicator of their personalities. Afterward, each subject was given a sheet of paper on which the test scores of everyone in the group were indicated as well as the distribution of scores of a large sample of subjects similar to themselves. On these sheets, half the subjects were told that their scores were different from those of the rest of the group, and also from most of the people in the larger sample. Scores were given on five scales, and they received deviant scores on all five. The other half of the subjects received scores at or near the middle of the scale. The purpose was to make some subjects feel deviant and others nondeviant. In addition, all the subjects were led to believe that one of the others was extremely deviant. His scores were consistently extreme. Thus, each subject saw the group as consisting of himself, four nondeviants, and one deviant. The scores were indicated by a code letter and the subjects knew only their own letter; they did not know which score belonged to whom.

The experimenter then explained that the second part of the study consisted of a learning test. One of the subjects would serve as a learner while the rest would act as judges. The learner would try to give good responses to an originality test, and the others would decide whether his responses were good. Whenever they judged a particular response to be not good, the learner would receive a severe electric shock. The experimenter said he did not care which subject served as the learner and that it was customary to let the group decide this. He then asked each subject to rank the others in the order that he wanted each of them to be the learner. In other words, the subjects were given an opportunity to select one of their number for an extremely unpleasant, painful task. The data appear in Table 6–6.

TABLE 6–6
deviant and nondeviant subjects' choice of deviant for shock and reward

SUBJECT CHOOSING	FOR SHOCK	FOR REWARD
Deviant	2.18	3.73
Nondeviant	3.91	2.82

Note: Figures are the mean rankings for the deviant on a scale from 1 to 4; the higher the number, the more the deviant was chosen.
Source: Adapted from Freedman and Doob (1968).

Almost all the nondeviants chose the one deviant subject in the group for the unpleasant task. The deviant subjects showed the opposite tendency; they chose a nondeviant for the painful role. Thus, all the subjects picked someone who was different from themselves—despite the fact that they had no idea how the one they chose differed from them.

It might be noted that this tendency to pick out people who are different is not entirely indiscriminate. When subjects in this same situation were asked to pick somebody for a good role (one in which he would earn money), they tended to pick someone who was similar to themselves rather than someone who was different. Thus, not only did they choose deviants for an unpleasant task, they avoided choosing them for a pleasant one.

We can now see why scapegoating might be one of the bases of prejudice. Ideal scapegoats are weak, different, and easily distinguishable—qualities that seem to be characteristic of the groups that are the major targets of prejudice, at least in the United States. American blacks share all these characteristics. They are in a relatively weak position in society because they are poor and less well educated than whites. They are also noticeably different from the white majority. Catholics and Jews are not distinguishable from the Protestant majority by anything as noticeable as skin color, but they do tend to have different names, different national backgrounds and, most important, different religious practices. We are not stating that scapegoating is the only or even the major cause of prejudice, but it is one of the mechanisms that produces it. As we mentioned above, learning the appropriate targets of aggression from parents or peers is a major factor that keeps prejudice alive from generation to generation. Scapegoating may be one explanation of how it began in the first place.

observed aggression in the laboratory

The catharsis theory suggests that expressing aggression reduces anger, and consequently the chance of further aggressive behavior. We have already discussed the most obvious, direct form of the catharsis hypothesis—namely, that direct aggressive retaliation (physical or verbal) against one's frustrator will reduce the level of future aggressive behavior. But other, more indirect, forms of aggression are also thought to reduce anger. In these cases, anger is supposedly reduced through fantasy aggression. Sometimes the person is directly and actively involved with fantasied aggression. One such case is the Feshbach (1955) study we discussed earlier, in which angered subjects became less aggressive after they wrote out stories about projective test stimuli that involved aggressive scenes. And the same catharsis through fantasy-expression idea was involved in Leak's (1974) finding that hostile subjects became less aggressive after reading hostile cartoons.

But there is still one more version of the catharsis hypothesis. This is that anger is reduced by observing other people's aggression. The idea is that people experience the aggression vicariously and become less

Leo de Wys

angry, just as if they were doing the actual aggressing. Aristotle originated this version of the catharsis idea in his discussion of the purpose and effect of Greek tragedy. Members of an audience experience a variety of emotions while viewing a play. For example, when the hero is insulted, they experience anger themselves even though they are not directly involved. This anger does not affect their behavior directly—they do not assault the insulter. Instead, they express their hostility empathically through the actions of the play's hero. According to Aristotle, this arousal and expression of emotion results in a purging, or catharsis, of the emotion, by which he meant that the viewers are less likely to experience this emotion in the future. If we watch a play depicting an endless string of invective and argument between people, like Albee's *Who's Afraid of Virginia Woolf*, we come out drained of any angry impulses ourselves.

This hypothesis is of great potential social importance. Many social critics have complained in recent years that violence on television or in the movies increases aggression among those who watch it. The catharsis theory makes exactly the opposite prediction; it predicts that watching aggression of violence done by others will actually reduce anger among those who are feeling angry. Which is correct?

The strongest proponent of the catharsis theory in situations involving observed aggression has been Feshbach. He did a pioneering experiment (1961) in which angered and nonangered subjects were shown either a violent boxing film or a neutral film. Measures of aggression taken after the film showed that watching the boxing film lowered the aggressiveness of angered subjects and slightly increased the aggressiveness of the subjects who were not initially angry. So this study appeared to give some support for the catharsis prediction. Observing others involved in aggression, like engaging in fantasy aggression yourself, can be a way of working through your own angry feelings, reducing your anger, and consequently reducing aggressive behavior. But this one demonstration of the anger-reducing capacity of witnessed aggression stands as an exception in the large body of laboratory studies done on the subject. Practically all the other laboratory studies have shown that watching brief, violent films actually increases subsequent aggressive behavior. These studies have typically followed one of two patterns.

imitative aggression

The imitation experiments done by Bandura using a Bobo Doll represents one type. The point of these experiments was to demonstrate how young children learn aggressive behavior by imitating the aggressive behavior of adults. Preschool-age children were mildly frustrated, and then they observed an adult batting a Bobo doll around. When the children themselves were placed in the room with the doll, they repeated many of the aggressive behaviors performed by the adult. The key theoretical notion in these experiments is that children learn specific aggressive responses by observing others perform them. It therefore follows that such vicarious learning should be increased when the adult's behavior is reinforced, and when the situation promotes identification with the adult model. So in these Bandura experiments, there is more imitative aggression (1) when the model is rewarded, (2) with a model of the same sex as the child, and (3) when the child has had a previous nurturant relationship with the model (e.g., when the model is a friend or teacher of the child) than when there has been no relationship between the two.

disinhibition

The other important laboratory pattern used in many studies was originated by Leonard Berkowitz and his students. These typically involved showing a brief film embodying violent physical aggression to college students who have either been angered (typically by insult) or not angered. The dependent variable has usually been shock supposedly administered to a confederate, in a sham-learning situation. Most of these studies used a seven-minute clip from a boxing film starring Kirk Douglas called *The Champion.* Viewing the violent film generally produces greater attack on a confederate whether or not the subject himself had previously been attacked (e.g., Geen and O'Neal, 1969). For example, Hartmann (1969) used subjects who were male adolescents under court commitment to the California Youth Authority (i.e., they were institutionalized). Half the subjects were angered by listening to tape recorded critical comments from a confederate regarding the subject's lack of social competence, sophistication, social judgment, and so forth. Then one of two films was shown, either an aggressive film depicting an argument leading up to a fist fight, or a neutral film depicting two boys shooting baskets. Each film was two minutes long. Then all subjects were placed in a sham-learning situation. As in the Bobo doll experiments, watching the aggressive film increased subsequent aggression. The insulting comments also contributed to greater aggression, consistent with many earlier studies of insult and attack which we have discussed.

In another variant, subjects who were shown verbal aggression, in the form of a short film involving Don Rickles, subsequently showed greater overt aggressiveness themselves (Berkowitz, 1970). As in the Bobo doll studies of preschoolers, aggression was increased by increasing identification with aggressors in the film. For example, when subjects were told to identify with the winner of the boxing match, they displayed more aggression than did subjects who were told to identify with the judge or were not given any instructions about how to watch. Similarly, when the film presented justified aggression, by presenting the loser of the boxing match in an unfavorable light, more aggression was displayed (see Berkowitz and Rawlings, 1963; Berkowitz and Geen, 1967).

Another variant on this approach is based on Berkowitz's classical conditioning theory of aggressive behavior. This predicts that aggressive behavior is a joint function of anger arousal and of situational cues to which aggressive responses have been conditioned. In other words, aggression-linked cues are required if aggressive behavior is to be triggered in an angry person. Berkowitz has done a number of studies showing that aggressive films can present cues that do trigger aggressive responses. For example, in one study the confederate was described either as a boxer or as a speech major. After watching a seven-minute clip from *The Champion,* subjects shocked the "boxer" confederate more than the "speech major" (Berkowitz, 1965). Similarly, a confederate named "Kirk" got more shocks than one named "Bob" after seeing Kirk Douglas being beaten up in the film (Berkowitz and Geen, 1966); and a confederate given the same name as Kirk Douglas's fictitious film name (Mitch Kelly) got more shocks than the confederate named "Kirk." In all these cases the model in the film presented cues that elicited aggressive behavior against the confederate. Naturally these cues can either stimulate aggression, as in these cases, or they can inhibit aggression, as in research discussed earlier showing that pain cues from the victim actually reduced aggression in most conditions, because the response most of us have learned to the cues of another person's pain is inhibition of aggression.

The vast majority of these laboratory experiments have shown that observing aggression provokes greater aggressive behavior, not less. The catharsis effect simply does not occur in these experiments, except in rare instances. Whether one describes the effect as imitating, stimulating, activating, or triggering aggression, the result is the same: observing aggression in these laboratory experiments produces heightened aggressive behavior.

Feshbach concedes that most such experiments do not support the catharsis approach. But he says they are not fair tests of catharsis. For catharsis to occur, there has to be a reasonable opportunity for the person to work his angry impulses through in a fantasy manner. That means having a filmed presentation which is clearly fantasy, and one that is long enough for the discharge of anger to occur. The experiments that have been done generally present very brief film clips, too short for an extended fantasy involvement. And the material has generally been quite realistic. Feshbach admits that under the conditions of most of these experiments (brief, realistic presentations of aggression), the processes described by Bandura and Berkowitz will prove dominant: imitation of rewarded aggression, and elicitation of previously learned aggressive responses. However, Feshbach maintains that a cathartic effect will occur for fantasy aggression when the observed aggression is longer in time and when it is more clearly fantasy, as in cartoons or obviously fictional presentations. Under these conditions, he says, people are able to work through their aggressive impulses in fantasy, and this will reduce their aggression.

A number of studies have been done testing this realistic-fantasy distinction, and generally have supported it. Berkowitz and Alioto (1973) presented subjects with a film of U.S. Marines storming a Japanese-held Pacific island during World War II. In one condition the film was described (accurately) as a documentary; in the other, it was described as a Hollywood-made reenactment. The realistic film produced more aggression than did the fictional version. A similar study done by Feshbach (1972) found the same result. However, contrary evidence was obtained by Meyer (1972). Also, Worchel et al. (1976) compared a documentary on the Attica prison rebellion with the early Brando motorcycle-hoodlum film *The Wild Ones* and found no greater anger expressed following the more realistic film. So there is no conclusive evidence as yet on this fantasy vs. realism question.

media violence

It is an understatement to say that in recent years movies have begun to portray a great deal of violence. Fighting, beating, killing, and murder have always been common in Westerns and gangster movies. But recent movies have escalated the amount of carnage as well as its vividness. It might be said that *Bonnie and Clyde* and *The Wild Bunch* made blood red for the first time in American movies. People did not just die at a distance or clutch their stomachs and fall slowly to the ground. In these movies they actually bled and suffered; the bullet wounds gaped; blood pumped rhythmically from victims' bodies, rather than slowly staining their clothes. Television is also quite dependent upon violence for its

© Punch/Rothco

programming. With the exception of talk, variety, doctor, and comedy shows, virtually all original programming for prime time television, as well as shows designed specifically for children, involve violence in one form or another. Westerns, police, gangsters, and spy shows, and most television movies include a full complement of fighting, shooting, and killing. Although the violence on television is much less explicit and vivid than that in the movies, it is remarkably pervasive. All of which leads to the question of how this constant exposure to violence affects behavior.

politics

The politics of media violence have become very important. As a result of congressional action, an enormous amount of money was made available for research on media violence in the late 1960's. A report was finally prepared for the surgeon general of the United States Public Health Service, which had administered the research grants. This report concluded, rather cautiously, that:

> [There is] a preliminary and tentative indication of a causal relation between viewing violence on television and aggressive behavior; an indication that any such causal relation operates only on some children (who are predisposed to be aggressive); and an indication that it operates only in some environmental contexts (Surgeon General's Scientific Advisory Committee on Television and Social Behavior, 1972, p. 11).

This report immediately came under harsh attack, partly because some of the members of the committee that prepared it had been representatives of the television networks, and it was felt (quite understandably, though possibly inaccurately) that they therefore could not be disinterested scientific observers (Carter and Strickland, 1975). Thereafter other reports were prepared, with widely varying conclusions (contrast especially Comstock, 1975, with Kaplan and Singer, 1977). But most of the criticism held that the commission had underestimated the effects of media violence.

This disagreement is understandable since much of the evidence is contradictory. As we have discussed in some detail, the evidence from laboratory experiments and some of the theoretical explanations suggest that viewing violence would, if anything, make the individual more violent himself. The child who watches someone get beaten up may get aroused somewhat himself and may also learn that this kind of aggression is acceptable and even desirable in society (particularly if it is the hero who wins the fight). Both of these reactions could tend to increase the child's tendency to behave aggressively in the future. On the other hand, viewing violence might possibly decrease aggressiveness if it allowed him to express aggressive feelings vicariously and thus produce a cathartic effect. But all the laboratory evidence suggests that only by behaving aggressively himself or by watching the source of his anger punished will the individual's aggressive feelings be reduced. Since this ordinarily does not happen on television, whatever aggressive feelings the child has should not be reduced and thus his aggressiveness should not decline. Just on the basis of laboratory experiments alone, then, we should expect media violence to increase agressive behavior.

external validity

Conventional wisdom holds that media violence does indeed produce greater interpersonal aggression. This conclusion has for the most part been based upon extrapolation from the laboratory studies we have just reviewed. There can be little question that most laboratory studies do show an increase in aggressive behavior following exposure to observed violence. But there is quite a long step between the typical laboratory study and the real-life situation to which we might want to generalize. This involves judging these laboratory experiments in terms of their external validity. As defined by Campbell and Stanley (1963), "*External validity* asks the question of *generalizability:* to what populations, settings, treatment variables, and measurement variables can this effect be generalized?" (p. 5). Therefore it is important to try to assess their external validity.

One way to approach the question of external validity is to make explicit the situation to which we most want to generalize, and then see how closely it matches the experimental situations we have been studying. The concern about media violence has been expressed most about television, since it is piped free into the home, so exposure is virtually uncontrolled (and nearly uncontrollable). Mostly the concern is that male adolescents (who are responsible for most violent crimes) will watch a great deal of violent television, then go out and commit violent crimes. But laboratory studies of observed violence differ in some very important ways from this real-life situation. Consider the independent variables. The films presented to subjects are normally very brief, unlike television programs and viewing. And they are almost entirely composed of a single violent episode. In contrast, the normal child in real life watches up to four hours of television a night, composed of a number of different programs. And each program contains quite a mixture of romantic stories, humor, altruistic behavior, heroism, ordinary conversation, and all sorts of other human acts having nothing to do with violence. So instead of the brief, concentrated dose of exposure to violent models typical of experiments, television in real life presents children with a varied diet of all manner of possible behaviors to copy. Put another way, the experiments present the subject with a pure aggressive diet; normal television presents a much broader range of human behavior.

But the difference between network television and laboratory experiments is most evident in the dependent variable: aggressive behavior by the viewer. Most important, in all experiments this aggression is fully sanctioned. Never does an experiment measure aggression the subjects knows is wrong, or will be disapproved, or for which he will be punished or suffer any negative consequences at all. In other words, the laboratory experiments always investigate aggression the subject knows is perfectly all right to engage in (indeed, somtimes he is actually encouraged, or instructed, to be aggressive). Children know it is perfectly all right to hit the Bobo doll; nobody will disapprove of them or think they are bad for doing it. The Bobo doll is clearly a plaything. Indeed, experiments that show the model being punished for hitting Bobo show markedly reduced imitative aggression. Most of the other experiments using somewhat older subjects have used a variant of the Buss shock-learning machine. The subject is told he is in a learning experiment and he is supposed to punish the victim for his errors. This is not an instance of socially disapproved, unsanctioned, or antisocial aggression; it is an instance of sanctioned aggression. The subject knows it is perfectly all right to shock the confederate, because the experimenter commanded him to.

In real life, in contrast, we are most concerned about unsanctioned, antisocial aggression. We are worried about unprovoked assaults, armed robbery, assault and battery, rape, and murder. The concern about media violence is not coming from a concern about excessive sanctioned or prosocial aggression. Mostly we are not too concerned about sanctioned aggression in athletics or in dramatic productions, or complaints about unfair treatment by siblings, parents, teachers, shopkeepers, and so on. The anxiety about media violence has solely to do with antisocial, unsanctioned aggression—and that is never measured in laboratory experiments.

Laboratory measures of aggression differ from real-life violence in several other ways. There is normally no possibility of retaliation; indeed, where there is, aggression is reduced. Often the aggressive task is fun, novel, and a game; one writer has described Bobo-beating as "solitary aggressive play." A five-year-old playing with what is obviously a new toy is obviously a far cry from a gang of teenagers holding up a gas station and shooting the manager. Finally, in these experiments the aggression measure is taken immediately after exposure to the film. The reason is that any delay would obviously reduce the effect of the film. In fact, it is hard to imagine a seven-minute film clip having an effect that would last more than a couple of hours. Several studies have shown that the effects wear off very quickly, perhaps within a matter of minutes. But in real life, the boy does not rush out of his living room with a knife and

"I've had enough of it! Nothing but sex and violence!"

attack the first person he sees. Most crime is committed quite a long time after the person has watched television. People who are roaming the streets are not home watching television; in fact, we might all be safer if they were.

So the external validity of these experiments seems rather poor. But more important, these differences between laboratory experiments and real life all work in one direction: promoting more aggressive behavior in the laboratory than in the comparable real-life situation. That is, the conditions of laboratory experiments differ from those of real life in ways we know increase aggression and therefore present an exaggerated portrait of the aggression inspired by violent films. They are done in such a way as to maximize the chances of getting an imitating or activating effect of film violence. They are brief, almost purely aggressive in tone, the subject's aggressive behavior is measured immediately, and his aggression is completely "safe": there is no chance of retaliation. And it is completely sanctioned (indeed, often encouraged or demanded). All these things have been shown to increase aggression, themselves.

field experiments

One solution to these problems is to do experiments that are more realistic; that is, experiments that come closer to matching the real-life conditions to which we want to generalize. To do this, we would want to maintain the experimental variation of exposure to violent, as opposed to neutral or nonviolent, films. But we would want to do it in the context of something more closely resembling the normal television diet of adolescents, and then observe their aggressive behavior in ordinary, day-to-day situations. Such studies are called *field experiments*, because they are done in the individual's natural situation, or in "the field." All told, five major field experiments have been done. Because the issue of media violence is so controversial and because both sides appeal to scientific evidence, we think it is a good idea to present a little information about each of these studies.

The first major study attempting to investigate this problem in a realistic situation was conducted by Feshbach and Singer (1970). Boys in private boarding or state residential schools were randomly assigned to two groups: One group watched largely aggressive television programs such as "Gunsmoke" and "The FBI," while the other group was limited to nonaggressive programs such as the "Ed Sullivan Variety Show" and "Bachelor Father." The boys watched only shows on the designated lists and could watch as much as they wanted as long as they spent at least six hours a week watching television. Various measures of aggressiveness were given before and after the six-week viewing period, and both peers and adults supervisors also rated the boys' aggressiveness.

The results showed that particularly in the state schools boys who watched aggressive programs were actually less aggressive themselves. They engaged in fewer fights and argued less with their peers. The effect was the same but somewhat weaker for the boys in the private schools. This impressive study thus indicates that, at least under some conditions, observing television violence might actually decrease aggressive behavior. The explanation offered for this effect follows from the catharsis notion, that the children identified with both the heroes and the villains in the programs, and thus did vicariously express some of their aggressive feelings through the violence on television. On the other hand, it must be noted that the effect could be due to the fact that boys who were limited to the nonaggressive programs might have been annoyed because they were not allowed to watch their favorite television shows. Despite this possible alternative explanation, the study does attempt to establish how ordinary television affects aggressiveness, and it does suggest that the effect may not be negative.

Wells (1973) attempted to repeat the Feshbach-Singer procedure, using a narrower age range (only junior high school), a broader time span, and ten schools. He found that violent vs. nonviolent television diets made very little difference. Boys watching the nonviolent diet were slightly more verbally aggressive (which he attributes to their frustration over being denied their favorite programs), while those watching the violent diet were slightly more physically aggressive. But neither trend was of very great magnitude. Leyens, Camino, Parke, and Berkowitz (1975) conducted a similar study in a Belgian private school for problem adolescent boys. After a week of observation, the boys in two dormitories were shown a week of five violent movies (e.g., *Iwo Jima, Bonnie and Clyde*), and in two other dorms were shown five neutral films (e.g., *Lily, Daddy's Fiancee*). Then they were observed for an additional week. Boys in one of the two dorms shown the violent films did increase their aggressive behavior immediately after watching the film, though the effect had disappeared by the following noon. There was no effect in the other dorm shown violent films.

Friedrich and Stein (1973) put nursery school children on a diet of twelve violent cartoons *(Batman, Superman),* or prosocial entertainment (*Mister Rogers*) or neutral films (e.g., about nature) for a period of four weeks. They were carefully observed by trained observers. They had three measures of aggression, and five others of good classroom behavior (rule obedience, delay tolerance, task persistence, cooperation, and prosocial behavior). The groups differed significantly on at most two of these eight measures, so the effect of the filmed violence cannot have been very great.

A somewhat different set of studies was done by Milgram and Shotland (1973). They prepared special versions of a prime-time television show—"Medical Center"—that included illegal (but nonviolent) acts. Three different versions of the episode were prepared. In one, the protagonist smashes several charity-drive collection boxes, steals the money, and escapes to Mexico. The second was identical except that he went to jail rather than to Mexico. In the third (a prosocial version), he hovers over the box with a club, but eventually drops a coin in instead. In the first four experiments subjects viewed the program in a theater, and then were offered a free radio if they would show up at a downtown office a week later. At the office, though, there was a sign saying there were no more radios, and there was a charity donation box containing some money, including a $1 bill sticking partway out. Concealed TV cameras coded the subject's behavior. But in none of these experiments did viewers of different versions differ. In a fifth experiment, subjects watched at home, and were informed of the radio offer. Again the differing versions had no effect. In a sixth, they watched at a specially prepared room in a downtown hotel, which included a charity box. This time, all the money was taken from the box more often in the neutral conditions, but single dollars were slipped out more often in the antisocial version. One other experiment portrayed the protagonist haranguing a telethon solicitor. Immediately following the program, charity solicitation was made on the air, with a prominently displayed telephone number. But there were too few calls resulting from any version to allow for reliable analysis.

Each of these studies has its flaws. In the Feshbach-Singer and the Wells studies, the adolescent boys in the nonviolent conditions were deprived of their normal favorite programs. This frustration could by itself have increased their aggressiveness, thus eliminating any possible differences between the violent and nonviolent conditions. The Friedrich-Stein and Leyens et al. studies used statistics that were dubious for technical reasons; if they had used appropriate statistics, the violent and nonviolent groups would not have differed in aggressiveness. The Milgram-Shotland studies were at the mercy of the idiosyncrasies of their specific versions of "Medical Center," and in most cases so little real-life antisocial behavior emerged that it would have been hard for anything at all to influence it much one way or the other.

But all studies in social science are flawed. It is a myth that a perfect study can be devised. The minute we patch up one problem, another emerges (often created by the patch, in fact). The way to come to a conclusion about an important area of research is to stand back a little, and look at the pattern of the data. What pattern seems to emerge here? It seems quite clear that the effects of these violent vs. nonviolent TV field experiments are not very dramatic. Feshbach and Singer get diminished aggression from the violent diet, but only in one social class. Wells gets no strong results. Friedrich and Stein get differences on at most two of eight measures. Leyens et al. get an immediate effect, but it does not last and may be an effect more of group contagion than individual arousal. Milgram and Shotland get no differences in seven experiments. So it is difficult to see a very powerful effect of movie or TV violence on aggressive behavior leaping out at us from these studies. Rather, observed violence in movies or television seems not to affect aggressive behavior much, one way or the other.

conclusion

Laboratory studies seem quite generally to show that observed violence increases aggressive behavior. But these studies have been conducted in such a way that they may not be especially applicable to the real-life instances of antisocial violence that we are concerned with as private citizens. The film clips are not particularly representative of what is shown on television and in the movie houses today; the subjects tend to be preschool children and college students, rather than potentially criminal adolescents; the dependent variable is quite "safe," strongly approved aggression, indeed often playful aggression, instead of genuine harm to others; and the impact is measured immediately after exposure, rather than some hours or days later, as is presumably the case in real life. For all these reasons, we do not have much confidence in generalizing from these laboratory studies to crime in the streets.

The field experiments we have described come much closer to realistic replicas of real life. They have presented the typical movie and tele-

Victor Englebert/de Wys

vision fare of the day to male adolescents living in their normal life situations (though most of these have been in boarding schools, rather than living at home with their parents). They have measured genuine interpersonal aggression in a free, unconstrained atmosphere. However, these studies have generally shown that media violence has little or no systematic effect upon interpersonal aggression. Some show a modest, temporary increase in aggression. Others show a debatable decrease in it. But the majority show no impact at all. Therefore, it seems correct to say that at the moment the field studies show media violence having no impact.

From a policy point of view, the question is whether the evidence is strong enough to urge the suppression of certain kinds of entertainment programs in order to reduce crime and violence. There are social conditions which we all know are terribly important in producing violence, such as unemployment, racial prejudice, poor housing, poor medical care (especially for people with mental health problems), the widespread availability of guns and alcohol, a highly mobile population that does not settle into tight little self-policing communities, and indifference to the welfare of children, among many other things. It seems to us that, at most, television and the movies could contribute only a small amount above and beyond such large social factors.

And we must be very careful about censorship of any kind. Today the government might decide that it is illegal to depict a knifing on television; tomorrow some censor may decide that it is illegal to depict an adulterous act, because people might imitate that; and the next day he may decide that it is illegal to depict protest demonstrations. Once the principle of censorship is accepted, it becomes harder and harder to draw the line. So it is no idle academic matter, this business of the effects of media violence upon interpersonal aggressiveness. We should recognize that no matter how passionately we feel about the issue, we must not take a stand until we have sufficient evidence. It is fair to say that most psychologists today believe that TV violence does increase aggressiveness and crime, but in our opinion the actual empirical evidence is weak and by itself does not justify the imposition of restrictions upon entertainment programs.

SUMMARY

1. Aggression is defined as an action which hurts another person, and which is perceived as intended to do so.

2. Aggressive acts can be antisocial, prosocial, or merely sanctioned, depending on whether they violate or conform with social norms.

3. Aggressive feelings, or anger, need to be distinguished from aggressive behavior.

4. Instinctual bases for either aggressive feelings or behavior in humans, while sometimes urged by ethologists and psychoanalysts, are not widely accepted by social psychologists.

5. The major determinants of aggressive feelings seem to be annoyance and attack, and frustration. Frustrations which are not attributed to intent on the part of the frustrator do not create as much anger. Generalized, nonspecific arousal states can result in experienced anger if they are accompanied with the appropriate cognitive labels.

6. Aggressive behavior has as its major determinant other than angry feelings the learning of aggressive responses. This learning can take place through direct reinforcement of aggressive responses, or through imitation, or the conditioning of aggressive behavior to certain eliciting cues.

7. Direct aggression against an attacker or frustrator can reduce aggressive feelings, through a process of catharsis. However this too depends on perceiving the tormentor as the responsible agent.

8. Fear of punishment or retaliation can reduce aggressive behavior. However it may sometimes result instead in covert aggression, or actually increase aggression over the longer run.

9. Learned inhibitions over aggression represent the most important control over it. Anxiety can be associated with the expression of aggression in general, or with its expression in quite specific contexts. Most people reduce their aggression when they see the signs of pain in others. Such inhibitions can also result in the displacement of aggression to other innocent parties, and to the scapegoating of members of minority groups.

10. Observed aggression generally increases aggression in laboratory studies, whether they are done with small children, adolescents, or adults. It is especially potent in increasing aggression when the model is rewarded or when the observed victim is similar to the target of the subject's own aggression.

11. Field experiments of televised or movie violence, on the other hand, have not generally shown that they increase aggressive behavior in real-life settings. Therefore it is not clear that the laboratory studies of observed aggression should be generalized to real-life situations. There is no good evidence yet that media violence makes an important contribution to violence and crime in our society.

SUGGESTIONS FOR ADDITIONAL READING

BANDURA, A. *Aggression: A social learning analysis*. Englewood Cliffs, N.J.: Prentice-Hall, 1973. The definitive statement by the most influential spokesman for the social learning and imitation approach to aggression.

DOLLARD, J., DOOB, L., MILLER, N. E., MOWRER, O. H., & SEARS, R. R. *Frustration and aggression*. New Haven: Yale University Press, 1939. The original statement of the theory that frustration breeds aggression. As well as discussing their laboratory experiments, it ranges far into the larger social manifestations of aggression, such as criminality, war, and fascism.

FREUD, S. *Civilization and its discontents*. London: Hogarth Press, 1955 (first published, 1930). The classic exposition of how civilization must deal with aggressive instincts. One of Freud's most brilliant and influential critiques of society.

HARTMANN, D. P. Influence of symbolically modelled instrumental aggression and pain cues on aggressive behavior. *Journal of Personality and Social Psychology*, 1969, *11*, 280–288. A typical laboratory study showing the stimulating effects of observed violence. It is one of the best of its kind, both in simplicity of design and in using an interesting subject population (adolescent boys in jail).

KAPLAN, R., & SINGER, R. Violence and viewer aggression: A reexamination of the evidence. *Journal of Social Issues*, 1976, *32*, 35–70. The most recent and most carefully argued review of the media violence research by two social psychologists skeptical of its capacity for inducing aggressive behavior in real life.

KONEČNI, V. J., & EBBESEN, E. G. Disinhibition versus the cathartic effect: Artifact and substance. *Journal of Personality and Social Psychology*, 1976, *34*, 352–365. A most sophisticated recent experiment on catharsis effects, with careful attention to previously overlooked methodological issues.

LORENZ, K. *On aggression* (trans. M. K. Wilson). New York: Bantam Books, 1966. The most influential statement on aggression by an ethologist.

Sears, D. O., & McConahay, J. B. *The politics of violence: The new urban blacks and the Watts riot.* Boston: Houghton-Mifflin, 1973. An application of frustration-aggression theory to the origins of ghetto riots.

Surgeon General's Scientific Advisory Committee on Television and Social Behavior. *Television and growing up: The impact of televised violence* (Report to the Surgeon General, U.S. Public Health Service, U.S. Department of Health Education, and Welfare, Publication N. HSM 72-9090). Rockville, MD: National Institute of Mental Health, 1972.

7

altruism and prosocial behavior

altruism defined

altruism in other animals

altruism and bystander intervention

- effect of other people
- individual interpretation

social justice and equity

- the evidence for equity
- receiving a favor

transgression and guilt

- the effect of confession
- feeling good or bad

summary

suggestions for additional reading

One night several years ago, a young woman named Kitty Genovese was walking along the street in a quiet neighborhood in Kew Gardens, New York. Suddenly, a man came out of the shadows and attacked her. She struggled and screamed for help. After a short fight, during which she was badly injured, she managed to escape from her assailant and ran down the street shouting for someone to help or to call the police. Some minutes later, the man caught her and the struggle began again. It continued for half an hour, during which time she continually screamed and shouted, until finally she was killed. Her screams and the sound of the struggle were heard by at least thirty-eight people living in buildings near the scene. Many of these people came to their windows to see what was happening. Yet, not one person came to Kitty Genovese's aid, nor did anyone even call the police.

A recent newspaper article described a similar event with a somewhat different ending. A woman in Toronto was attacked by a man in an alley in broad daylight. As he attempted to rape her, she screamed for help. A great many people heard her cries and even watched the struggle from their windows, but for many crucial minutes no one offered help. Finally, two men driving by in a car heard the screams, stopped the car, and rushed into the alley. They pulled the attacker off the woman and held him for the police.

There are countless stories of this sort. Sometimes people help, sometimes they do not. We hear of individuals who are beaten, raped, and killed while those who could give assistance stand by; we also hear of amazingly brave acts in which people rush into burning buildings to save children, jump into the water to rescue drowning men, and come to the aid of people who are being attacked. Clearly, human beings are capable of helping or ignoring others in distress. Why do people commit these acts of bravery and altruism, why do they help others in need, and why, sometimes, do they fail to give help when it is needed?

altruism defined

Before trying to explain this kind of behavior, let us be clear about what we mean by altruism and prosocial behavior in general. An altruistic act is one performed to help someone else when there is no expectation of receiving a reward in any form (except perhaps a feeling of having done a good deed). That is, if you give to charity because you expect that charity to help you or because you want to impress the person who is asking or for any other concrete reason of this kind, it is not altruism in the pure sense. It is still, obviously, an act that benefits others, but it is not altruism. Prosocial behavior is a broader category that includes any act which helps or is designed to help others. The distinction may not be important to the person who is helped, but the explanations of the two kinds of behaviors may be quite different.

altruism in other animals

In a book that has attracted a great deal of attention and stirred controversy, E. O. Wilson (1975) proposed that altruistic behavior in humans is genetically determined. In other words, just as Konrad Lorenz has suggested that aggression is built into the human system, Wilson says that altruistic tendencies are inherited. They are a natural part of "human nature," play an important role in our survival, and do not have to be learned. This, like Lorenz's argument, is almost impossible to test and actually has few implications for social psychology. The one consequence of accepting this view would be that we would then think of humans as more controlled by instinctive forces than we usually do, but at least some of those instincts would be positive rather than negative. This would fit in with the ideas of humanistic psychologists such as Carl Rogers and Fritz Perls, who have a highly positive, optimistic view of human nature. In any case, Wilson's suggestion is a valuable addition to the general explanation of human behavior in terms of instinct, since there is no reason to believe that only negative impulses such as aggression can be inherited. For our purposes, the important aspect of Wilson's work is that he points out many instances of behavior by other animals that have much in common with what we think of as altruistic behavior. Remember that any act which benefits another with no expectation of return is considered altruistic in the strict definition of the term. With that in mind, here are some of Wilson's examples.

In termite hives, the soldier termites will defend a nest against an intruder by putting themselves in front of the other termites and thus exposing themselves to danger (Wilson, 1971). Many soldiers will die with the result that others live and the nest survives.

When fire ants are attacked, those who have been injured are more likely to leave the nest than uninjured ants, and the former are also more aggressive in fighting the intruder. The injured ants are thus risking their own lives, and because an injured ant is less useful to the nest than an uninjured one, it looks like a case of self-sacrifice.

Among honeybees, the workers will attack intruders by stinging them. When this occurs, the stinger stays in the intruder, thus killing the worker who did the stinging (Sakagami and Akahira, 1960). Once again, the worker bee dies and in so doing increases the hive's chance of survival.

Chacuma (Hall, 1960) and other varieties of baboon have a characteristic pattern of responding to threats. The dominant males take the outside, most exposed positions and may rush at the intruder. In addition, as the tribe of baboons moves away from the threat, the males will remain behind for a while to protect the rest of the group. Among many animals, parents will sacrifice themselves when their young are threatened. This is most evident among birds, who have a variety of techniques designed to draw off or distract the threat. An impressive example is the female nighthawk, who flies from the nest as if she has a broken wing, flutters around at a low level, and finally lands on the ground right in front of the intruder but away from the nest (Armstrong, 1947; Gramza, 1967). Once again, the individual risks its own life and thereby helps another.

Animals of all kinds therefore often engage in behavior that increases the risk to their own lives while decreasing the risk to that of others. Whether we want to call this altruistic behavior in the same sense as a fireman rushing into a burning building is unclear. Perhaps an important factor is whether we believe the animal "knows" that it is risking its life or is simply acting automatically. The human knows his life is in danger; the nighthawk probably does not. Yet, both are in fact performing an act that helps another with little or no possibility of reward to themselves.

The importance of these examples is that they help to put human altruistic behavior in perspective. We see that other animals also take risks to help others and do not always protect themselves, and that self-preservation is not the overwhelming motive we sometimes think it is. On the contrary, it seems natural for other animals and therefore at least as natural for humans to protect each other from harm and even to take risks to accomplish this. Thus, in explaining altruistic behavior, we should not feel that it is a mystery but rather a reasonable behavior in the context of what we know of biology. The job of the social psychologist is to explain why altruism occurs at some times but not at others and to discover the critical factors that control this important human behavior.

altruism and bystander intervention

Much of the work on altruism has focused on the conditions under which people spontaneously help other people. Interest in this question was stimulated by the kinds of incidents described at the beginning of the chapter, in which people who desperately needed help were not assisted by people who could easily have come to their aid. Latané and Darley, who have done much of the work on this problem, refer to it as bystander intervention.

effect of other people

One of the striking findings is that the presence of other people seems to reduce the likelihood of intervention. In one experiment (Latané and Darley, 1968), subjects were put in a room either alone or with other subjects. Smoke began to pour into the room through a small vent in the wall. The critical measure was whether or not and how soon the subjects reported the presence of the smoke to the experimenter. When a subject was alone in a room, there was a very strong tendency to report the smoke soon after noticing it. Of the subjects in this condition, 75 percent reported the smoke within six minutes of the time they first noticed it and 50 percent reported the smoke within two minutes. In contrast, when other subjects were present, there was a strong tendency not to report the smoke at all. In various other conditions, the number of people reporting the smoke ranged from 38 percent to as low as 10 percent. Simply having other people present reduced the likelihood that the subjects would report the presence of smoke pouring into the room.

In another experiment (Latané and Rodin, 1969), subjects also waited either alone or with others, but they were given the opportunity to

Drawing by Whitney Darrow, Jr., © 1972 The New Yorker Magazine, Inc.

"Hang in there, old man. There's bound to be a Good Samaritan along any time now."

help a lady in distress. When the subjects arrived, they met an attractive young woman who gave them a questionnaire to fill out and said that she would be working for a while in the adjoining room. She went into the room, shuffled papers, opened drawers, and made other noises for a few minutes; then she went into a carefully rehearsed act designed to make it appear that she had fallen off a chair and hurt herself. The subjects heard a chair fall loudly, the woman scream and then yell "Oh, my God, my foot . . . I . . . I . . . can't move. . . . it. Oh . . . my ankle. I . . . can't get this . . . thing . . . off me." The whole thing lasted just over two minutes, and the main dependent variable was whether or not the subjects did anything to help the victim. Of the subjects who were waiting alone, 70 percent offered to help the victim in some way. When two strangers were present, only 40 percent of the groups went to the aid of the victim. When a passive confederate was present, only 7 percent of the subjects intervened. Once again, the presence of other people generally inhibited the tendency to intervene in this emergency.

Subsequent research has tried to pin down the specific reason for this effect. One plausible explanation is that when others are present, the subject feels that they can help and that therefore he doesn't have to. Schwartz and Clausen (1970) had subjects waiting in groups of two, six, or six including a medical student. They then heard a person in distress who obviously needed medical care. The females in the experiment were more likely to help in groups of two than in groups of six and were least likely to help when the group of six included the medical student. For some reason, however, the effect was confined to females—the males were unaffected by the composition of the group. Bickman (1971) and Ross (1971) lend more convincing support to this notion. In Bickman's study, the subjects were in three different conditions—by themselves, with others who were also taking part in the study, or with others who were in the study but in another building. Subjects who were with others helped less than those who were alone, but if the others were in a separate building, it was just as if they were alone. In other words, if the other people were essentially irrelevant because they could not help, their presence did not matter. Ross varied whether subjects were alone, with two other adults, or with two children, As would be expected, the presence of children had much less effect than the presence of other adults, presumably because the children were less able to give help.

We can increase the amount of help by making the individual feel especially responsible. In a study by Moriarty (1975), some subjects were asked to watch a suitcase or radio while someone was away, and other subjects were not asked. When a confederate then came by and attempted to take the item, subjects who were asked to watch it were much more likely than the others to stop the theft (over 90 percent to only 20 percent intervened). In both conditions, many other people were present, but this had little effect on those who felt personally responsible. All this research indicates that at least one factor which affects the amount of help given is whether someone else who could also give help is there. If there is another person, each individual seems to feel less responsible and to have a tendency to wait for the other to give the assistance needed rather than offering it himself.

individual interpretation

Perhaps an even more important factor in these situations is how the individual interprets what is going on. As Latané and Rodin have suggested, it seems likely that our interpretation of the situation depends in large part on how other people are reacting. If someone yells "Fire!" in a theater and you see some people running for the exits, you assume that there must be a fire and you try to get out as quickly as you can. But if everyone remains seated, you will probably assume that the cry was a joke or a false alarm and you too will stay where you are. In other words, as we have discussed in terms of attribution theory, how we interpret the situation affects our behavior, and our interpretation is based in part on the behavior of others.

The same process operates in a bystander intervention situation. Suppose we hear someone crying for help from an adjoining room or outside the window. Although in retrospect it may seem obvious that the person really did need help, at the time it may not be so easy to decide. Perhaps it is a joke, perhaps a psychology experiment, perhaps the per-

Christy Park/Monkmeyer

son is only slightly injured and is exaggerating, and perhaps there is no crisis at all. Even in the Kitty Genovese case, her need for help was probably not so clear to the people who heard her cries. It is quite common under these circumstances, especially when you cannot see exactly what is happening, to assume that it is a lovers' quarrel and that you should not intrude (Shotland and Straw, 1976). Perhaps that is unfortunate, but it means that the lack of help was due to the interpretation of the situation. When there are other people present and they sit calmly, minding their own business, the individual may decide that the situation is less serious than he might otherwise have imagined. When three people in a room ignore cries of distress, perhaps (so the subject may think) there is no emergency. If other people are upset, we get upset; if other people are calm, we remain calm. And in the present context, if other people seem to have decided that a cry for help need not be answered, there is a tendency to draw the same conclusions.

Many studies support this interpretation. When the situation is so unambiguous that the subject must recognize the existence of an emergency, the presence or absence of other individuals has little effect. This has been found by Clark and Word (1971) and by Piliavin, Rodin, and Piliavin (1969). The latter study involved victims who collapsed on a New York subway train. The confederate who posed as the victim either appeared sober and carried a black cane, or pretended to be drunk. In the cane condition the victim received spontaneous help 62 out of 65 trials. The number of people in the subway car and their proximity to him had no effect at all. When someone seems ill and is obviously in distress, people appear to offer help whether or not there are others who could also give assistance. The "drunk" victim received help only 19 of 38 trials (the lower rate presumably due to less concern for a drunk and some fear of getting involved), but even here the amount of help given was unrelated to the number of people present. A second study by Clark and Word (1974) found that help was given between 91 and 100 percent of the time when the situation was totally unambiguous, and the amount of help was unaffected by the size of the group. Only when ambiguity was introduced, in fact a high degree of ambiguity, did individuals who were alone help more than those in groups.

A study by Smith, Smythe, and Lien (1972) also lends support to the notion that a subject's interpretation of the situation is determined in part by how the other people behave. These authors report the typical finding that there was less helping when the subject was alone than when others were present. In addition, they found that the similarity of the other people to the subject was a critical factor. When the others were dissimilar, there was more helping than when the others were similar. This is what would be expected from an explanation in terms of normative behavior. The subject's interpretation should be more influenced by people who are similar than by those who are not. When similar others sit and do nothing, it should reduce the subjects' tendency to help even more than when dissimilar others do not help.

Thus there are a variety of explanations of the reduction of helping when others are present. Other people are available to give help and it is therefore less necessary for the subject to help. Others are not helping and therefore the situation is interpreted as less serious. In addition, there may be some diffusion of responsibility—each person waits for the other to offer help and feels less personally responsible. Finally, the individual may face a higher likelihood of being embarrassed by intervening when other people are present than when he is alone. If it turns out that it was inappropriate to offer help or he finds himself in some other embarrassing situation, he would probably prefer to be alone. Whenever others are present, it increases the possibility of embarrassment and accordingly reduces the likelihood that the individual will take the chance of acting in an ambiguous situation.

social justice and equity

What are some of the underlying factors that affect altruism and other prosocial behavior in general? One of the basic motives that seem to affect social interactions is a sense of justice and equity. People feel that each person should get what he or she deserves based on that person's effort, skill, and whatever other considerations they think are important. Homans (1961) called this a sense of social justice and Adams (1965) called it equity, but the two notions are essentially identical. If two people put the same amount of effort into a task, they should in principle receive the same reward. If one receives more than the other, inequity exists. People will generally try to restore equity by redistributing the rewards. In particular, the person who received more than his share may

American Red Cross

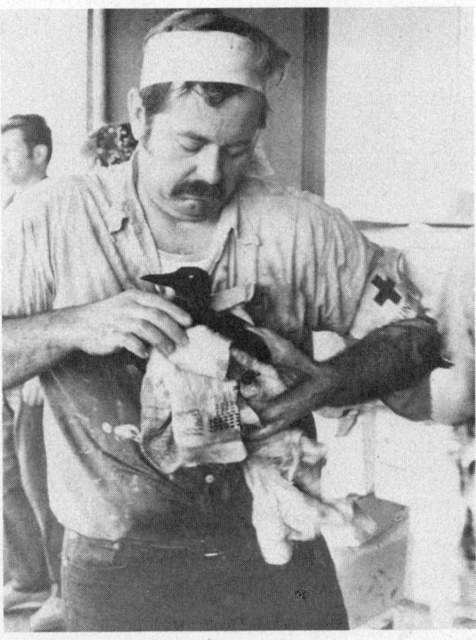

give some to the person who receives too little; or some third person, observing the situation, might be tempted to give to the one who suffered.

Presumably this is one of the motives behind charity, philanthropy, and social welfare programs. People tend to believe that every human being deserves at least a minimal share of the world's resources, and someone who has nothing often is given something to partially restore equity. But we also believe that people who make an effort deserve more than those who do not, and this may explain opposition to public welfare programs that give assistance without regard to whether the individual is trying to get a job, is incapacitated, or has some other special reason for deserving help. In other words, in addition to a general feeling that everyone should be taken care of and given food and shelter, we tend to feel that some are more deserving than others, depending on the amount of effort or contribution they make.

This does not mean that everyone is always fair with everyone else, that greed does not exist in the world, or that people are not pleased when they get more than they deserve. The point is that, to some extent, people do feel pressure toward social justice, and they show some tendency to act to achieve it. One implication of this phenomenon concerns the effect on a person when he has caused someone to lose something, or even observed somebody lose something, and when he himself has not suffered the same loss. If someone has lost $5, someone else at the same time has gained $5, and neither of them had apparently done anything to deserve their particular fate, a state of inequity would exist between them. One gained while the other lost, when they both deserved to be treated equally. The feeling of inequity would probably be most strong if the person who gained $5 had caused the loss to the other person but should hold even if he was simply aware that the other had lost the money. The feeling should exist whenever the one who gained deserved no more than the one who lost. In some sense, it is unjust for one to gain while someone else loses when they both had exerted the same amount of effort; therefore, there is a feeling that injustice has been done. The important point is that there is a tendency to redress this imbalance and produce a state of equity.

the evidence for equity

A number of studies have demonstrated this. In several of them (Berscheid and Walster, 1967; Berscheid et al., 1969), subjects played a game in which one, through no fault of her own, won a lot of money or trading stamps while the other one lost. At the end of the game, the winner (the real subject) was given an opportunity of returning some of the money to the other subject. Under these circumstances, there was a strong tendency to give back some of the winnings, even though they had been won legitimately. In contrast, when the winnings were equal, there was little tendency for the subject to give any winnings to the other player.

Schmitt and Marwell (1972) also found evidence for equity. When one member of a team was given two, three, or five times as much as his partner, he tended to give some of his money to his partner in order to make their rewards more equal. In addition, the overrewarded partner often chose to play a different game when he was assured that this would result in more equal partitioning of the rewards. In other words, not only did he give up some of his own money in order to produce a more equitable division, but he avoided the situation that produced the inequity in the first place.

Leventhal, Michael, and Sanford (1972) found that a subject who was asked to divide money among the members of a team gave higher rewards to better performers. But there was some evidence that, apparently in order to prevent conflict in the group, the worst performer was given somewhat more than he might have deserved and the best performer somewhat less. That is, the difference in rewards was somewhat smaller than performance would have warranted.

Several studies by Lerner show that quite young children sometimes follow rules of equity. At kindergarten age, children who play a game and can divide rewards seem to ignore equity and instead use what Lerner calls parity—that is, everyone gets the same amount regardless of his contribution to the game. But somewhat older children take into account each team member's efforts and give larger rewards to those who were more important members of the team (Lerner, 1974). In addition, those who contributed more seem to expect larger rewards. In another study (Long and Lerner, 1974), children who were overpaid for doing a job subsequently donated more to charity than those who were paid the amount they expected. An interesting feature of this result was that this difference occurred regardless of whether or not the donations were public. Apparently the children were contributing because they wanted to or felt it was the right thing to do, not in order to impress anyone.

Other results of this seeking of equity or social justice are less altruistic. Apparently the individual is also very concerned about receiving just treatment himself. If one member of a team is given all the money to divide, under most circumstances he will divide it equally. But if the amount of money he is given is either less than he expected or considerably more, there is a tendency for the individual to give himself more than he gives his teammates (Lane and Messé, 1972). Presumably, the person doing the dividing wants to make sure that he gets at least what he deserves (in the case where there is less money than there should have been) or that he benefits particularly from the excess when there is more money than he expected. This is not exactly fair or equitable, but it does fit in some odd way with a sense of social justice (at least for himself). Similarly, if the person doing the dividing feels he is better at the task than his teammate, he will tend to take more than half of the available money, whereas if he is worse than his teammate he will actually take somewhat less than half (Leventhal and Lane, 1970; Leventhal and Anderson, 1970). In other words, given the chance, the individual will try to give each person what he deserves in terms of his performance. But when there is either too much or too little money, selfishness seems to be predominant and the divider protects his own interests first.

receiving a favor

Another implication of the notion of equity concerns the effect of doing a favor for someone. If we are working in a hot, stuffy room and someone brings us a cold, refreshing drink, he has done us a favor. We are grateful; we feel pressure to repay him. If he subsequently asks us to do something for him, we are more likely to agree than if he had not done us the favor. Similarly, if we are working on a dull, tedious task and someone comes along and offers to help, we would be more likely to help him in return than if he had not helped us.

When someone does a favor, he has upset the precarious balance of equity. He has done something for us; we have not done anything for him. We owe him something. In order to restore equity, we must do a favor for him. We would be under considerable pressure to help if he made a request. Even if he asked us to do something that involves more effort than he exerted in doing us the favor, we would find it hard to refuse.

Berkowitz investigated this phenomenon in a number of studies (Berkowitz, 1968; Berkowitz and Daniels, 1964; Goranson and Berkowitz, 1966). In his experiments, each subject worked on a task and a confederate offered to help him. Later, the subject had an opportunity to help the confederate on a similar task. A subject was more likely to offer help when he had previously been given help than when he had not been helped. In these experiments, the favor done for the subject was the same as the one he did for the favor-doer. A study by Regan (1968) demonstrated a similar effect when the favors were different. College students were tested in pairs, one of each pair actually being a confederate of the experimenter. The study was described as dealing with perceptual and esthetic judgment. The subjects were put in separate rooms, shown a series of pictures, and asked to rate how much they liked each of them. After they had rated one series of pictures, there was a short break and the subjects were told they could do what they wanted as long as they did not talk about the experiment. At this point, the confederate got up, left the building, and returned several minutes later carrying two bottles of Coke. He handed one to the subject, saying, "I asked him [the experimenter] if I could get myself a Coke and he said it was okay, so I brought one for you, too." The subject took the Coke, and the experimenter then gave them a second series of pictures to rate. In another condition, the experimenter went out, returned with two Cokes, and handed one to the confederate and one to the subject, saying, "I brought you guys a Coke." In the third condition, no Coke was given to the subject.

After the second series of pictures was rated, there was another short break, during which the confederate asked the experimenter (loud enough for the subject to hear) whether he could send a note to the subject. The experimenter said that he could as long as it did not concern the experiment. The confederate then wrote the following note:

> Would you do me a favor? I'm selling raffle tickets for my high school back home to build a new gym. The tickets cost 25 cents each and the prize is a new Corvette. The thing is, if I sell the most tickets I get 50 bucks and I could use it. If you'd buy any, would you just write the number on this note and give it back to me right away so I can make out the tickets? Any would help, the more the better. Thanks [Regan, 1968, p. 19].

The measure of helping was how many tickets the subject agreed to buy. The data are shown in Table 7–1. When the confederate gave the subject a Coke and then asked him to do a favor, there was considerably more helping than when the experimenter gave the subject a Coke or no Coke was given. Helping in the latter two conditions did not differ appreciably. According to this study, it appears that having a favor done for us and then receiving a request from someone other than the person who did the favor does not make us more likely to comply with the request. But the study does show that one way of increasing helping is by doing somebody a favor. The recipient of the favor feels obligated to the favor-doer and is more likely to comply with a subsequent request by him than if no favor had been done.

TABLE 7–1
effect of doing a favor on helping

CONDITION	NUMBER OF TICKETS BOUGHT
Confederate gave Coke	1.73
Experimenter gave Coke	1.08
No Coke	.92

Source: Adapted from Regan (1968).

The tendency to reciprocate a favor seems to be quite strong and universal. It has been shown to operate in many cultures, including the United States, Japan, and Sweden (Gergen et al, 1975). However, it is affected by various factors in the situation. For example, Greenberg and Frisch (1972) found that a larger favor was reciprocated more often than a smaller favor. In addition, when the initial favor was viewed as intentional, reciprocation was higher than when it was seen as somewhat accidental. Similarly, Goranson and Berkowitz (1966) showed that this effect depends in part on the individual's perception of why the other person helped him. In their study, the confederate either offered help voluntarily or was ordered to do so by a supervisor. When the help had been given voluntarily, subjects were more likely to reciprocate by helping the confederate than when the help was compulsory. Apparently, relatively little feeling of obligation is aroused when an offer to help is not made by choice. The study also suggested that the feeling of obligation is felt primarily toward the person who offered the help. Subjects who had been helped by someone tended to repay that person but showed considerably less tendency to offer help to someone else.

In addition to feelings of obligation, another possible explanation of the effect of doing a favor on helping is in terms of liking. Doing a favor is usually perceived as a friendly act. The recipient will tend to like the favor-doer more than he would like someone who did not do him a favor, and this liking may lead to greater compliance. At the moment, however, there is little evidence that liking is an important factor affecting compliance, so this explanation must be considered as speculative. It seems likely that the effect of doing a favor is due primarily to feelings of pressure toward social justice and equity.

transgression and guilt

The idea that a feeling of guilt tends to lead to expiation is probably as old as the concept of guilt itself. Guilt is aroused when someone does something he considers wrong. When one feels guilty, he generally tries to reduce his guilt. This can be accomplished in several ways: the individual can perform a good act to balance the bad one; he can subject himself to some kind of unpleasantness and thereby punish himself for his misbehavior (Wallington, 1973); or he can attempt to minimize the negative aspects of the guilt-arousing action. The first two techniques would make the person more likely to comply with a request for help. If the request involved doing somebody a favor, performing a good act, or subjecting himself to unpleasantness or pain, agreeing would tend to reduce the individual's guilt. Therefore, people who feel guilty should be more likely to give help than people who do not feel guilty. A number of experiments have demonstrated this.

Carlsmith and Gross (1969) conducted a study using a situation involving the giving of electric shocks by subjects. Each subject was told that he was taking part in a learning experiment. One person would be the learner and the other the teacher. In all cases, the subject was the teacher and a confederate played the part of the learner. The subject's job was to press a button whenever the learner made a mistake. For one group of subjects, pressing the button sounded a buzzer and supposedly delivered an electric shock to the learner; for the other group, the button only sounded a buzzer. Thus, half the subjects were doing something quite unpleasant—shocking another subject. The other half were doing something innocuous—simply signaling when the other person made a mistake.

After a series of trials, the experimenter indicated that the study was completed and asked both the subject and the confederate to fill out a short questionnaire. While they were doing this, the confederate turned to the subject and, in a casual way, made the critical request. He asked the subject whether he would be willing to make a series of calls in connection with a campaign to save the California redwood trees. (In all cases, the confederate did not know which condition the subject was in.) The measure of helpfulness was whether or not the subject agreed to make any calls and, if he did, how many he agreed to make.

The results are shown in Table 7–2. Presumably, shocking the confederate made the subjects feel guilty, whereas delivering buzzes did not. If guilt increases compliance, subjects in the shock condition should have agreed to make more calls. This is what occurred. Those subjects who thought they had delivered electric shocks were more likely to comply than were those who delivered only buzzes.

TABLE 7–2
guilt and helpfulness

CONDITION	HELPED	DID NOT HELP
High guilt (delivered shocks)	75	25
Low guilt (delivered buzzes)	25	75

Note: Entries are percentages.
Source: Adapted from Carlsmith and Gross (1969).

Other studies involved other kinds of transgressions. In one study (Freedman, Wallington, and Bless, 1966), the experimenter told the subjects that it was extremely important that they not know anything about the test they were going to take, and the situation was set up so that virtually all the subjects said they knew nothing about it. Some of the subjects, however, had been told about the test by a confederate. Thus, these subjects were lying to the experimenter. Telling a lie and thereby perhaps ruining an experiment is expected to arouse guilt. It did. There was almost twice as much compliance among the "liars."

In another experiment by the same authors, the subjects sat at a table waiting for the experiment to begin. In some conditions, the table was specially prepared so that the slightest touch would tip it over and scatter index cards, which had been described as needed for somebody's thesis, all over the room. When the subjects tipped the table, they presumably felt responsible and guilty for mixing up the cards. In one control condition, the table was tipped by a confederate. In another, the table was stable and the cards were not scattered. Once again, there was more helping in the guilt than in either control condition.

This effect of guilt on voluntary helping was demonstrated in two very nice studies (Konečni, 1972; Regan et al., 1972). In the former, the subject was a pedestrian strolling along a street in Toronto. As he walked along, one of the experimenters suddenly dropped some index cards in front of him and gave the subject an opportunity to help pick them up. The measure of altruism was simply how many cards were picked up. In some instances the experimenter brushed against the subject and made it appear that this encounter caused the cards to fall. This was called a "restitution" condition because the subject had caused the harm but was being given an immediate opportunity to make up for it. In another condition the innocent subject strolling along the street "ran into" one of the experimenters, causing him to drop some books. The experimenter immediately picked up the books and walked off, obviously upset by the encounter. Subsequently a second experimenter dropped the index cards in front of the subject, who then had an opportunity to help him. This was called a "generalized guilt" condition because the subject had caused harm to one person and was given the opportunity of helping another. In a "sympathy" condition the subject watched as someone else bumped into the experimenter, knocking his cards down. The one who supposedly knocked the cards down kept walking, but the subject who had witnessed this sad event could help if he wished to. And finally there was a control condition in which nothing happened except that the cards were accidentally dropped in front of the subject.

The results are shown in Table 7–3. As before, it was found that subjects who had themselves caused the accident or who had caused an accident previously (the restitution and guilt conditions) helped considerably more than those in the control conditions. Unexpectedly, subjects in the sympathy condition who had merely watched someone else knock the cards down helped even more than those in the guilt conditions. Causing harm yourself does tend to increase altruism, but simply witnessing harm done by another sometimes also increases helping.

TABLE 7–3
the effect of guilt, sympathy, and restitution on voluntary helping

	CONDITION			
	Control	Sympathy	Restitution	Guilt
Percentage helping	16	64	39	42

Source: Adapted from Konecni (1972).

The results of these and other experiments involving transgressions have been consistent. Regardless of the type of transgression—whether it consisted of lying, scattering valuable notes, delivering electric shocks, breaking an expensive machine, or taking something valuable from a partner—subjects helped more when they had transgressed than when they had not. The obvious explanation is that the transgression aroused guilt, which in turn led to the increase in helping.

It is important to note that in most cases the effect was not caused simply by sympathy or compassion for someone who had been hurt. In Carlsmith and Gross's study, for example, there was one condition in which subjects did not push the button themselves but watched the confederate receive shocks. There was no difference in compliance between this group and one that merely delivered buzzes. And in the card-mixing study, when the table was tipped by the confederate rather than the subject, there was no more compliance than when the table was not tipped by anyone. Simply watching someone suffer does not usually increase altruistic behavior.

The research also shows that the person making the request need not be the one about whom the subject feels guilty. In some of these studies, the request was made by someone other than the person whom the subject had hurt. Even then, guilty subjects complied more than nonguilty ones. In addition, it appears that the request need not even benefit the victim. Subjects in several of the experiments were asked to do something that had nothing to do with the person they had injured. Once again, guilty subjects complied more than did nonguilty ones. This seems to indicate that the effect of guilt is not entirely specific to the person injured. People can reduce their guilt by doing a good deed for someone else. Thus, someone who feels guilty for any reason is more likely to comply with a request even when that request is not directly related to the cause of his guilt.

Some of the evidence suggests that although the subject would like to help his victim, he also wants to avoid contact with him. Guilty subjects have a tendency to comply less when the request involves associating with the victim than when they need not actually meet the person they injured. A guilty person seems to have two different motivations. On the one hand, he wants to make up for his guilty act by helping the victim or by doing something good for someone; on the other hand, he wants to avoid confronting his victim, probably because he is afraid of discovery or embarrassment. This implies that the effect of guilt is maximized when the guilty person can help without having to come into contact with the person about whom he feels guilty.

the effect of confession

An interesting aspect of the relationship between guilt and helping involves the effect of confession. One of the most common assumptions about confession is that it is good for the soul, by which we presumably mean that it is a form of expiation. This, in turn, implies that confession should reduce feelings of guilt. If confession does reduce guilt, it should also reduce helping. Studies by Carlsmith, Ellsworth, and Whiteside (1968) and by J. Regan (1968) supported this prediction. In the first study, subjects believed they had ruined an experiment because they used information they were not supposed to have. Some of them were allowed to confess what they had done; others were not given this opportunity; and a third group, who did not think they had ruined the study, served as a control. All the subjects were asked to volunteer for further experiments. The results are shown in Table 7–4. It is clear that guilt increased helping—those who used illicit information complied more than those who did not have the information. It is also clear that confessing, which reduced guilt, also reduced helpfulness—those in the guilt condition who confessed complied little more than those in the control group.

TABLE 7–4
guilt, confession, and helping

CONDITION	NUMBER OF HOURS VOLUNTEERED
Guilt	4.33
Confession	2.67
Control	1.92

Source: Carlsmith et al. (1968).

Regan's study, which used a different method for creating guilt, compared guilty subjects who were allowed to talk about what had happened, although not necessarily confess what they had done, with others who were not allowed to talk and with control subjects who had not transgressed. As usual, guilt increased helping, this time in the form of contributing money to an experimental fund. And again, those guilty subjects who talked helped less—they gave less money than did the guilty subjects who were not allowed to talk and the same amount as the controls. Presumably, talking reduced their guilt and they had no more reason to comply than did the controls. This work demonstrated that someone who is made to feel guilty and then confesses his wrongdoing helps less than if he is not given a chance to confess.

A series of studies (Berscheid and Walster, 1967; Lerner and Matthews, 1967) showed that when guilt is aroused specifically by harming another person, its effect on helpfulness depends to some extent on other aspects of the situation. The guilty person wants to make reparations to his victim. If he has the opportunity to do so, he will. If he cannot pay him back fully or if the only available payment is much too great, he reacts in other ways. He tends to decide that the victim deserved the harm inflicted—that the victim is not nice or that he did something wrong himself. He devalues the victim, reduces his liking of him, and in other ways justifies hurting him. He may also minimize the amount of harm he did by deciding that it was not serious, that electric shocks do not hurt much, and so on. Finally, he may seek justification in other ways, such as by deciding that he caused the harm for a good reason, for science, or because he was ordered to. Thus, one response to guilt is to expiate it by doing something good in return; another response is to minimize the guilt in any way available. The former response will increase altruism and helping; the latter might actually decrease it.

feeling good or bad

A possible explanation of the effect of guilt on helping is that the person feels bad and wants to do something in order to feel better. This suggests that anything that makes someone feel bad might increase the tendency to offer help. On the other hand, we also know that when we are feeling really good, we have a more cheerful view of the world and of our fellow humans and may accordingly be more likely to be altruistic. There is some evidence to support both ideas, but the second appears to be more powerful and consistent. In fact, feeling bad may sometimes increase helping, but at other times it may do exactly the opposite.

Probably the most impressive demonstration of the "feel good" effect is provided by Isen and Levin (1972), who arranged to have subjects find a dime in a public telephone. Subjects entered a phone booth to make a call, and some of them had the good fortune to discover a dime that had been placed there by the experimenters. Soon after leaving the booth, all subjects saw someone on the street drop some papers and had

American Red Cross

the opportunity to help pick them up. Whereas almost none of the subjects in the control (no dime) condition helped, virtually all of those who found the dime did help. Obviously it was not the 10 cents that mattered, but the warm glow produced by getting a free phone call. Similar results are produced by having people succeed or fail on tests (Isen, 1970; Isen, Horn, and Rosenhan, 1973). Those who succeed are subsequently more helpful than those who fail. In a similar vein, Aderman (1972) had some subjects read statements describing good moods (elation, euphoria, satisfaction) while others read statements describing bad moods (depression, dissatisfaction). Even reading about good moods increased helping relative to the bad mood condition. Feeling good makes you more helpful.

Another study (Isen and Levin, 1972) indicates that the good mood affects helping specifically and does not make people agree more to any request. Some students sitting in the library were given cookies by someone who walked around distributing them, and other students did not get the cookies. Then all subjects were given one of two requests: helping on a job that involved doing good for people or assisting in a rather mean study that involved disturbing people in the library. The results are shown in Table 7–5, which shows that those receiving cookies were more likely to agree to the nice request but considerably less likely to do the nasty favor. Apparently, when you feel good, you want to do good.

TABLE 7–5
feeling good and helping

	TYPE OF REQUEST	
Condition	Do a Nice Job	Do a Mean Job
Cookies (feel good)	69[a]	31
No Cookies	50	64

[a]Percentage agreeing to request.
Source: From Isen and Levin (1972).

The effect of failure is less clear. In one study (Isen, 1970) people who failed on a test were somewhat less likely to help than control subjects who were not told how they had done. But in another study (Isen, Horn, and Rosenhan, 1973), when subjects who failed a test were given the opportunity to contribute to charity in front of the person who saw them fail, they contributed more than if they received no feedback on the test. In other words, the act of contributing was probably used as a way of reducing the effect of the failure by showing what good people they were. Thus, this research generally does not support the notion that we are altruistic or helpful in order to reduce a bad feeling. Guilt specifically does increase helping, presumably because the helpful act serves as a direct atonement for the act of transgression that produced the guilt. But except for the special case where we want someone to think well of us, a bad mood seems, if anything, to reduce helpfulness, while a good mood increases it.

SUMMARY

1. Altruism is helping someone when there is no expectation of a reward. Other animals often behave so as to put themselves in danger, the result of which is to protect another member of their species or family. It is suggested that altruism of this sort may be instinctive in animals and perhaps in humans as well.

2. Bystander intervention is coming to the aid of someone in distress. Research has shown that people are less likely to intervene when others are present and could help, and that this effect is due mainly to an interpretation of the situation based on what others are doing. If they do not help, it is assumed that help is not really needed or appropriate. There is also some tendency to feel less responsibility because others could help.

3. Social justice and equity lead to helping when someone is seen to suffer unfairly. People tend to act so as to reestablish equity. Doing someone a favor produces a sense of obligation so that the person is then more likely to offer help to the one who did the favor.

4. Transgressing a norm produces guilt which in turn increases helping. If the person who feels guilty is given a chance to confess, and thereby reduce guilt, helping is reduced.

5. Feeling good is also likely to increase helping. There seems to be a "warm glow" that makes people want to share their good fortune. In contrast, feeling bad generally reduces helping unless the bad feeling comes specifically from guilt.

SUGGESTIONS FOR ADDITIONAL READING

MACAULAY, J. R. & BERKOWITZ, L. (EDS.) *Altruism and helping behavior.* New York: Academic Press, 1970. A series of articles for background.

LATANE, B. & DARLEY, J. M. *The Unresponsive Bystander: Why doesn't he help?* New York: Appleton-Century-Crofts, 1970. Discusses research on this issue and presents some possible explanations.

WILSON, E. O. *Sociobiology.* Cambridge, Mass.: Harvard University Press, 1975. A fascinating account by a biologist of how genetic factors may affect behavior. Highly controversial and tough going, but well worth reading.

attitudes: theoretical background

What makes someone a Republican or a Democrat, a conservative or a liberal, a Protestant or an atheist? Why are some people anti-Semitic, others antiblack, and still others not prejudiced at all? Why do people decide that one toothpaste is best or that drugs are horrible? What determines whether or not someone will change his mind about toothpastes or drugs? If someone is a Republican, how can we convince him to vote for a Democrat? Conversely, how can we prepare someone to meet an attack on his opinions so he will be able to resist the attack? These are the kinds of questions that form the basis for the extensive work on attitude formation and change, which in a sense has been the central core of social psychology in the United States for many years.

In 1937, in the first textbook mainly devoted to experimental studies in social psychology, Murphy, Murphy, and Newcomb wrote: "Perhaps no single concept within the whole realm of social psychology occupies a more nearly central position than that of attitudes [p. 889]." Although interest in this problem has probably declined somewhat in recent years, it is safe to say that in the past thirty years or so, social psychologists have devoted more time to the study of attitude formation and change than to any other topic. This is due, in part, to the great interest in interpersonal influence, since attitude change is one of the forms this influence takes. It is also due to an increasing emphasis on cognitive development and cognition in general. The work on attitudes therefore reflects both major concerns of social psychologists. By concentrating on how attitudes are developed and changed, we can gain insight into the process of social influence and cognitive structure and how these two phenomena affect behavior.

definition

Each of the traditional definitions of attitudes contains a slightly different conception of what an attitude is or emphasizes a somewhat different aspect of it. G. W. Allport (1935) proposed that "an attitude is a mental and neural state of readiness, organized through experience, exerting a directive or dynamic influence upon the individual's response to all objects and situations with which it is related (p. 810)." He saw an attitude primarily as a set to respond in a particular way, and his emphasis clearly was on its behavioral implications.

In contrast, Doob (1947) defined an attitude as "an implicit, drive-producing response considered socially significant in the individual's society (p. 138)." He emphasized what an attitude is rather than its implications. His statement did not include overt behavior, although it contained a clear assumption that an attitude would affect how an individual acts. This definition, derived from a learning or stimulus-response tradition, conceptualized an attitude as simply another response, albeit an implicit rather than explicit one.

Today a third definition, is more common. An attitude toward any given object, idea, or person is an enduring system with a *cognitive* component, an *affective* component and a *behavioral* tendency. The cognitive component consists of beliefs about the attitude object; the affective component consists of the emotional feelings connected with the beliefs; and the behavioral tendency is what Allport referred to as the readiness to respond in a particular way. For example, a student's attitude toward Robert Redford might include the knowledge that he is a man, blond and blue-eyed, very handsome, an actor and a good skier; feelings of attraction and liking; and the behavioral tendency to see all his movies. This is the definition that most social psychologists today seem moderately content with and the one we shall use throughout our discussion.

Before considering the definition of attitudes in more detail, it is important to distinguish between attitudes and facts. Although it is difficult to draw a sharp dividing line between the two, the main distinguishing characteristic of attitudes is that they involve an evaluative or emotional component. A scientist believes that it is 250,000 miles to the moon or that human beings have forty-six chromosomes. He also has a complex collection of other facts about the moon and chromosomes. But under most circumstances, he does not have any emotional feelings toward either—he does not think that the moon is good or bad, he does not like or dislike chromosomes. In contrast, he has a collection of facts about Robert Redford or poison gas, but he also *does* have emotional feelings about these. We can distinguish between facts and attitudes, to some extent, in terms of either the presence or absence of an evaluative component.

This distinction is important because facts and attitudes function somewhat differently. The crucial difference between them is that attitudes, once established, tend to be much more resistant to change. The scientist who believes that humans have forty-six chromosomes in most cases has no strong commitment to that belief or strong feelings about it one way or the other. Not so many years ago, scientists were convinced that humans had twenty-four chromosomes. Then somebody discovered that there were forty-six. Those who originally believed we had twenty-four chromosomes probably changed their opinion quite readily when they saw the evidence. Certainly high school and college biology students, who were in no way involved in the controversy, changed their "knowledge" almost instantaneously. Unless someone was involved with the research, he had no reason not to change his mind when the new research results appeared.

This is different from the way people react when their attitudes are concerned. As we shall see, attitudes tend to be highly resistant to change, do not generally respond to a few new facts, and are more complicated in this respect than facts. People do not change their attitudes without putting up a fight and being exposed to a considerable amount of pressure. The presence of the evaluative component seems to change the dynamics considerably; it makes the attitude-change process much more difficult.

cognitive complexity

Thus we conceive of an attitude as a collection of thoughts, beliefs, and knowledge (cognitive component), and as including positive and negative evaluations or feelings (affective component), all relating to and describing a central theme or object—the attitude object. This knowledge and feeling cluster tends to produce certain behavior. Figure 8–1, which is a schematic representation of a hypothetical person's attitude toward smoking cigarettes, is one example.

Around the central object are clustered the *cognitions* related to it in the person's mind. These cognitions describe the object and its relations to other objects. The relations can be many and varied. The surrounding cognitions may be simply descriptions or characteristics of the core object—in our example, cigarettes are smoky, taste of nicotine, and are expensive. Or, they may involve causal links to the core object—cigarettes are likely to cause lung cancer and heart disease, they cut down on your wind, they offend people in elevators, they relax you in a social situation or when studying, your parents don't like them but your roommate does, and so on. In Figure 8–1, the causal links to other objects are indicated with a line, and the sign by the line indicates whether it is a positive or a negative relationship. Cigarettes *are* dangerous (the person thinks), they *help* reduce discomfort, and they *facilitate* studying. These are all positive links. On the other hand, his parents

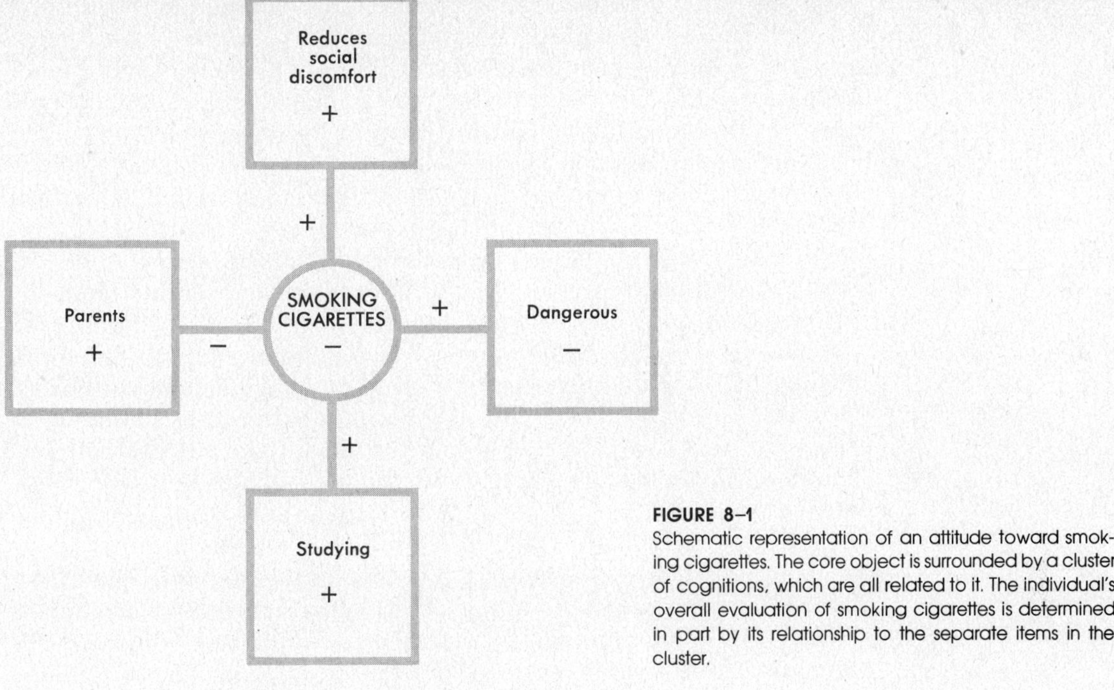

FIGURE 8–1
Schematic representation of an attitude toward smoking cigarettes. The core object is surrounded by a cluster of cognitions, which are all related to it. The individual's overall evaluation of smoking cigarettes is determined in part by its relationship to the separate items in the cluster.

do not approve of them. That is a negative link. For simplicity we have shown only a few of the multitude of cognitions that an individual could have regarding cigarettes, but these should be sufficient to give a picture of the attitude. Remember, however, that the real cluster would contain all the person's thoughts in connection with cigarettes.

evaluative simplicity

Next, there is the *affective* or evaluative component. Many of the separate cognitive elements themselves have positive or negative feelings connected to them, and the central object does too. Positive and negative evaluations of the elements and central object are indicated by plus and minus signs, respectively. The individual in our example has a strong negative evaluation of cigarettes. He dislikes and is afraid of them. This is shown in the diagram by the minus sign in the central circle. The evaluations of the related objects are shown in the boxes. The person likes his parents, likes to have social discomfort reduced, and likes studying to go easier. But he does not like danger.

A number of other factors to be considered are not included in the structure. For example, each of the cognitions can vary in its importance (e.g., the fact that cigarettes are expensive is probably less important than the fact that they are dangerous) and in the strength of its valence (e.g., it may be good or very good to be exciting). As you can see, the picture can get quite complex, potentially including a great many cognitions that vary in the nature of their relationship to the core and in their evaluative component. So this picture is an oversimplification, in some cases, of the way attitudes are in real life. For example, just think of the Pandora's box opened up by the fact that the related cognitions are often related to one another and to many other cognitions, rather than existing in a vacuum. The thought that cigarettes help studying is meaningful only when an attitude toward studying is considered. And then attitudes toward studying can bring in attitudes toward parents, teachers, a future career, and so on.

Nevertheless, for most purposes our diagram is, if anything, overly complex. Most people have rather simple attitudes about most things. When the average citizen is asked about a hot debate going on in Congress, let us say about a foreign economic aid bill, he will say, "Unnnhhh, I don't know, . . . I suppose we have to help out some, but . . . unnnhhh, . . . how much do they want to give again?" The interviewer usually finds that further probing is useless. Even in thinking about Robert Redford, most people most of the time do not consider all the things they know about him—they do not remember many details of his movies or his personal life; rather, they simply have a positive attitude, consisting mainly of feeling attracted to him. Or in thinking about hard core drugs, most police officers do not think of the scientific facts they once were told, or the preaching against drugs in childhood. Rather, the drugs are illegal, and the people they see on drugs are pathetic and abhorrent, so they simply hate drugs. The multitude of cognitions exists in their minds and may have some influence on them, but by and large, their attitude, particularly the evaluative component, is less complex.

There have been many demonstrations of the simplicity of most attitudes. One is provided by the work on the semantic differential, described in Chapter 3. Osgood showed that much of the variance in our conceptions of objects, people, and so on, is accounted for by a simple evaluative factor. Whatever is being considered, a large part of an individual's conception of it or reaction to it consists of liking or disliking. Second, survey research has repeatedly shown that most people have rather little information about political matters and that their political attitudes tend not to be tightly interrelated (Sears, 1969). There are exceptions. On racial issues, for example, white Americans tend to have highly interrelated attitudes. If they are opposed to government action to promote school integration, they are also likely to be opposed to civil rights demonstrations, affirmative action programs, busing of school children for integration, and so on. And there is evidence that Americans' political and social attitudes became somewhat more structured during the late 1960s and early 1970s (Nie, Verba, & Petrocik, 1976). But on most issues most of the time, most people do not show very broadly structured or complex cognitions.

Finally, Anderson and Hubert (1963), among others, have shown that attitude change can persist even after the content that produced it is forgotten, emphasizing that the affective component is more durable and central than the cognitive component. Thus, although the total structure of an attitude is complex, one important part of it, the part consisting of affects or feelings, is often very simple.

The contrast between the cognitive complexity of the attitude and its apparent evaluative simplicity is extremely important. For example, both police officers and drug users know a great deal about drugs, have all sorts of complicated pieces of information, understand a variety of interrelationships between drugs and other aspects of the world. And each of these pieces of information to some extent influences their general feelings toward drugs and has a substantial effect on their behavior. Knowing what drugs look like, how much they cost, where they can be obtained, the difference among various kinds, and so on, affects the activities of both the users and the narcotics squad. Nevertheless, the relatively simple evaluative component of the attitude is the major determinant of behavior. Although the details of users' and police officers' behavior toward drugs is influenced by the knowledge they have, the general direction of their behavior is influenced primarily by their overall evaluation—whether they consider drugs as positive or negative.

Thus, two facets of attitudes must be kept in mind. First is the contrast between the cognitive complexity and the evaluative simplicity. Second is that all elements of the attitude, such as they are, can be interrelated, and that each can therefore have some effect on the total attitude and on the other elements.

theoretical frameworks

Now that we have a general view of an attitude, we can consider the theoretical frameworks within which attitudes have been studied. The major approaches to attitude formation and change have been (1) conditioning and reinforcement, (2) incentives and conflict, (3) functionalism, and (4) cognitive consistency. The conditioning approach sees attitudes as habits, similar to anything else that is learned; principles that apply to other forms of learning also determine the formation of attitudes. The incentive theory is that a person adopts the attitude that maximizes his gains. There are reasons for accepting each side of an issue, and the side for which the reasons are better, from the individual's sometimes selfish point of view, will be adopted. This approach implies a maximization of gains. A variant of this approach considers attitudes in terms of what function or use they serve for the individual. Finally, the cognitive consistency theory asserts that people tend to seek harmonious relations among their cognitions and behavior. It emphasizes acceptance of ideas that are consistent with previous attitudes. Individuals tend to accept attitudes that fit into their overall cognitive structure. The four approaches are not contradictory or inconsistent. They represent different theoretical orientations and differ primarily in the factors they emphasize when explaining attitude formation and change.

conditioning and reinforcement

The conditioning and reinforcement model is most closely associated with Carl Hovland and others at Yale University. The basic assumption behind this approach is that attitudes are learned in much the same way as other habits. Just as people acquire information and facts, they also learn the feelings and values associated with these facts. A child learns that a certain animal is a dog, that dogs are friends, that they are good; finally, he learns to like dogs. And he learns this attitude through the same processes and mechanisms that control other kinds of learning.

This means that the basic processes by which learning occurs should be directly applicable to the formation of attitudes. In developing an attitude, the individual acquires information and feelings by the processes of *association*, *reinforcement*, and *imitation*. Associations are formed when stimuli appear at the same time and in the same place. If a

Michael D. Sullivan

police chief, a parent, or a television reporter shows us a dirty, broken-down, man and says the word *drug*, an association is formed between the image and the word. When the newspapers, television, and magazines talk about drugs being dangerous, when ministers and parents say drugs are evil, when we see people who have taken drugs looking miserable, these images become associated with drugs. Conversely, we may be exposed to positive things that can become associated with drugs: a friend says they are good; we see a movie in which someone on drugs seems to be having a pleasurable time; we take a drug and have a good experience.

Learning the characteristics of an object, a person, or an idea is obviously an important aspect of developing an attitude. Although the studies described in the chapters on person perception and liking were conducted in a somewhat different context, many of them illustrate this effect. For example, Norman Anderson conducted experiments in which he listed a number of attributes of a person and then asked subjects to state their impression of that person. The subjects formed their attitudes on the basis of the listed characteristics (warm, friendly, intelligent, ambitious, courageous, and so on). Having learned the characteristics, the subjects, in a sense, also learned an attitude.

Similarly, Donn Byrne told subjects that someone either agreed or disagreed with them on a variety of issues and values. Presumably, each time the other person agreed with them, it was a positive attribute and each time he disagreed with them, it was a negative attribute. The subjects learned that these were the characteristics of the other person and on the basis of these characteristics, they formed an attitude toward the other person, including a feeling about how much they would like him.

This process works as well for things as for people. Individuals learn the characteristics of a house, a country, an idea, a bill pending before Congress, or anything else. An attitude consists of that knowledge plus some evaluative component based in part on that knowledge and in part on other factors (which we shall discuss later). The simplest factor in the formation of attitudes is thus the development of associations between the object and other words or qualities.

Learning also occurs through reinforcement. If one takes a drug and has a pleasant experience, the act of taking the drug is reinforced—one would be more likely to take the drug in the future. Similarly, if one says "Drugs are great" and someone else applauds, making the statement is reinforced. Then both acts (taking drugs and saying they are good) become part of the cluster that forms an attitude. One element is the knowledge of taking them and another is telling people they are good.

Finally, attitudes can be learned through imitation. As we mentioned before (Chapter 6), people imitate the behavior of others, particularly if the others are strong, important people. Children tend to imitate their parents, and this imitation extends to both behavior and attitudes.

In this way, a child learns and accepts the values and attitudes of his parents even when they are not overtly rewarding the child.

Imitation is not limited to the parent-child relationship. Teachers, friends, public figures, baseball players, actors, and so on, are imitated. Individuals learn many different attitudes by imitating different people. As we shall discuss below, they often find they have learned contradictory values from different people and are under great stress to resolve the conflicts. As you know, many college students find themselves confronted with ideas and values different from those they had previously learned from their parents.

Association, reinforcement, and imitation are the major mechanisms by which the learning of attitudes occurs. As a result, this has been the dominant theoretical approach to the acquisition of attitudes. The learning approach to attitudes is relatively simple: it views the individual as primarily passive. He is exposed to stimuli, he learns through one of the learning processes, and this learning determines his attitude. The final attitude contains all the associations, values, and other bits of information the individual has accumulated. His ultimate evaluation of, say, drugs depends on the number and strength of the positive and negative elements he has learned.

incentives and conflict

The theory based on incentives and conflict is particularly relevant to attitude *change*. Indeed, formulations in terms of learning principles and incentives have pervaded much of the work on attitude change. They

Foto/Dick Swift

view the attitude situation in terms of an approach-avoidance conflict. The individual has certain reasons for accepting one position and other reasons for rejecting it and accepting the opposite position. He thinks drugs are dangerous; he knows they are illegal; and he wants to finish college and get into law school. These considerations produce a negative attitude. However, he believes drugs are exciting, and he knows many of his friends take them. These considerations tend to give him a positive attitude. According to the incentive theory, the relative strengths of these incentives determine his attitude. If his initial attitude was negative, it would become more positive only if there were greater incentive for taking this new position than for maintaining the original one.

This view is similar to the conditioning approach in that the attitude is determined more or less by a sum of positive and negative elements. The difference is that the incentive theory emphasizes what the individual has to gain or lose by taking a particular position. Whether or not his friends would like him, how enjoyable the experience is, etc., are the critical considerations. When there are conflicting goals, the individual adopts the position that maximizes his gains. Unlike the conditioning approach, cognitive elements that do not involve gains or losses are relatively unimportant.

functionalism

In the functionalist approach, the individual selects his initial attitude, or changes to a new attitude, in terms of what psychological function or use it serves for him. In the most detailed forms of this approach—those of Katz (1960) and Smith, Bruner, and White (1956)—a limited set of functions has been identified as most crucial.

An attitude may be adopted because it is *instrumental* to some goal the individual has. It may serve his economic self-interest, as in the case of a businessman voting for a conservative Republican who promises to cut corporate income taxes, or it may serve a social adjustment purpose, as in the case of a bride accommodating herself to the dogmatic political beliefs of her new mate.

A second major function of an attitude is to be *value-expressive*. Part of the individual's self-image is wrapped up with his central values, and he feels gratified when his attitudes express some cherished aspect of these values. If he thinks of himself as a generous, altruistic humanitarian, then it is gratifying to hold attitudes that further those values, such as supporting charities or voting for political candidates who favor aid to the poor, the blind, and the disabled. Another person might value freedom very highly and hold attitudes opposing gun control, affirmative action programs, minimum wage laws, and other measures he imagines would interfere with freedom. He adopts these attitudes because even if none of these measures would particularly interfere with *his* freedom in any instrumental way, they help him express his values, instead.

Attitudes may also serve an *ego-defensive* function. For example, some historians and psychoanalysts hypothesized that white southern men were historically so antiblack and so punitive of even the slightest trace of sexuality between black men and white women (whether rape or gentle seduction), because this attitude served as an ego-defense mechanism. In the past, southern women were said to be on a pedestal, unapproachable, pure and chaste, and white southern men were said to have been inhibited in their sexual approaches to them. This inhibited sexuality was then projected onto black men, and was violently condemned and suppressed. The white man could thus control his own sexuality by suppressing the black man's sexuality. Other attitudes have similarly been analyzed as serving an ego-defensive function; e.g., cynicism for those with intrapsychic conflicts about the expression of love and tenderness, and so on.

The other major category of commonly identified functions is *knowledge* or *object appraisal*. Some attitudes simply help the individual understand his world, and develop readiness to behave with respect to attitude objects he might encounter. Presumably people respond to much of what they see on television or read in the newspaper in this fashion. They adopt attitudes about a great many things that will never have any instrumental value to them, and are of no great help in resolving unconscious conflicts, simply to understand and place things.

The functionalist approach to attitude formation and change has not stimulated much research. A few studies have attempted to measure the individual's needs, or have tried to vary his needs experimentally, and then have tried to determine whether or not he would be especially responsive to need-satisfying attitude positions. However, this line of research has not provided much supporting evidence. More often, the functionalist approach has been used by historians, political scientists, and sociologists as a way of explaining *after the fact* why certain individuals or groups of people have held the attitudes they have.

cognitive consistency

The other major framework within which attitudes have been studied is cognitive consistency theory. Actually, there are a number of somewhat similar theories associated with Lewin, Heider, Abelson, Festinger, Osgood, and others. The theories differ in some important respects, but the basic notion behind them is the same. They begin with the assumption that there is a tendency for people to seek consistency among their cognitions and that this is a major determinant of attitude formation. An individual who has several beliefs or values that are inconsistent with one another strives, according to these theories, to make them more consistent. Similarly, if his cognitions are consistent and he is faced with a new cognition that would produce inconsistency, he strives to minimize

Monkmeyer/Freda Leinwand

the inconsistency. Since this theoretical approach has been developed primarily with reference to attitudes, rather than other psychological phenomena, we shall consider it in some detail.

BALANCE THEORY In Chapter 5 we described a simple cognitive system to which consistency theory may be applied. Such a system consists of two objects (one of which is often another person), the relationship between them, and an individual's evaluations of them. In the system, there are three evaluations—the individual's evaluation of each of the objects and of the relationship of the objects to each other. Assuming that each evaluation is positive or negative, with no differences in strength, there are four possible situations shown in Figure 8–2: all evaluations can be positive, two can be positive and one negative, one can be positive and two negative, or all can be negative. The first and third situations are considered balanced or cognitively consistent. This approach to cognitive consistency, proposed by Fritz Heider (1958) and others, has been called the *balance model.* The major point of the model is that a system in a state of imbalance will move toward a state of balance.

This approach need not be limited to the simple situation just described. Theoretically, it could apply to any number of pairs of objects, although most of the research has used situations involving two persons, an object, and the relationships among them. This is convenient for the study of attitude formation and change, because it can deal with the basic situation of one person receiving information from a second person about some object. However, research has also been conducted on situations in which there are interpersonal relations among three people and on the cognitive structure of one person thinking about two objects.

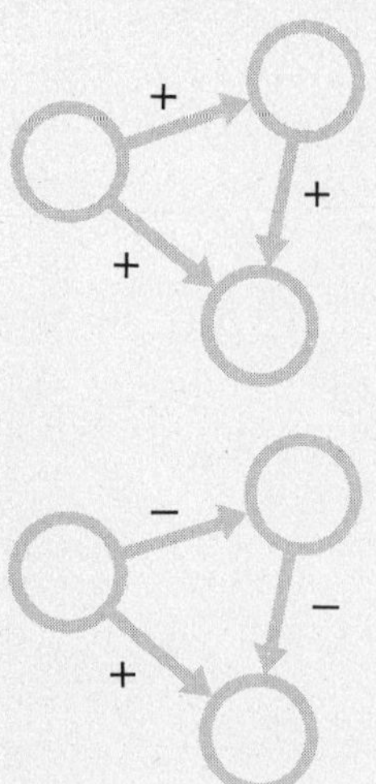

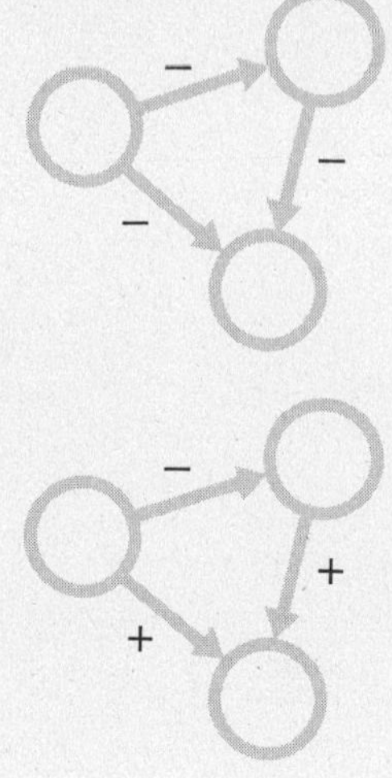

FIGURE 8–2
Balanced and imbalanced cognitive structures. Plus and minus signs indicate positive and negative relationships, respectively; arrows indicate the direction of the relationships. The theory states that imbalanced structures tend to change and become balanced.

From the point of view of balance theory, though, all these situations are the same. They all involve *triads*—that is, three elements. The elements may be two persons and an attitude object, or three persons, or one person and two attitude objects. In each case, the affective relationship between each pair of elements can be described as either positive (good, like, favorable, approve, support, endorse) or negative (bad, dislike, unfavorable, disapprove, oppose). This then yields three affective relationships within the triad. And there is a simple rule for remembering when the triad is balanced, and when it is unbalanced: balance holds when an even number of these three relations (that is, either zero or two) is negative. So if Joe loves Susan, but she likes cigarettes and he does not, the triad is unbalanced (one negative). As long as Nixon, Mitchell, and Haldeman like each other, the triad is balanced. If Mitchell and Haldeman start to fall out, there is trouble. If you like birth control pills and good health too, your attitudes are balanced unless you believe the pill has potential dangers for your health; then the negative relation between the pill and good health is unbalanced with your positive attitudes toward each.

According to balance theory, imbalance leads to pressure to change in order to restore a state of balance. Change can occur in a variety of different ways, which we will discuss more later on. Here it is enough to say that balance theory uses a *least effort* principle to predict the effects of imbalance. The person will change as few affective relations as he can, and still produce a balanced structure. Joe will decide either to put up with cigarettes, perhaps deciding they are not so bad after all; he may diminish his affection for Susan; or he may try to persuade her to give them up. But he will probably not change his mind about cigarettes, persuade her to stop smoking, *and* give her up, even thought that would also produce balance.

The main value of this research is that it describes the notion of cognitive consistency in extremely simple terms and provides a convenient way of thinking about and conceptualizing attitudes. The balance model makes it clear that in a given situation there are many ways to resolve an inconsistency. It focuses our attention on one of the most important aspects of attitude change—the factors that determine which of the various modes of resolution are adopted. We shall return to this in the next chapter.

CONGRUITY THEORY The variant of balance theory most directly applicable to attitude change situations is *congruity* theory, proposed by Osgood and Tannenbaum (1955). It is concerned exclusively with the effect of one person's taking a positive or negative position toward another object or person—perhaps the simplest attitude-change situation. When person P says something good or bad about object X, what effect does it have on our attitude toward both P and X?

Like balance theory, congruity theory conceives of a basic attitude-change situation as having three elements, each of which is connected by an evaluation: the other person (whom we might like or dislike), the attitude position about which he speaks (which we might like or dislike), and his own feeling about that position (he might say he is for it or against it). Congruity, like balance, consists in an even number of negatives among these three evaluations. Incongruity produces pressure to change, and the *direction* of change is again toward consistency. But congruity theory goes further, and takes into consideration the *intensity* of each of these evaluations. We can like the other person a little or a lot. We can be slightly opposed to capital punishment, or strongly opposed to it. This allows a much more specific prediction about which evaluation will change, and how much change will occur. Congruity theory assumes that the amount of change in each element will be inversely proportional to its relative intensity. We will change the most intense evaluation least (though probably we will change each evaluation at least a little). If a fanatical member of the National Rifle Association hears his new, relatively unknown governor come out in favor of gun control, he probably will not change his opinion about gun control much, but he will come to dislike the governor. Suppose, on the other hand, that he goes to the market with instructions to buy an oven cleaner, picks a brand at random because he has never heard of any of them, and on his return is told he picked the least effective brand. He is likely to change his attitude toward the cleaner, and not toward his wife.

The main application of congruity theory is in the prediction of a communicator's effectiveness in producing attitude change: Yet as these examples illustrate, one must not forget that changes in our evaluation of the communicator occur, and the theory is also applicable to this situation. In political life one can observe many instances of politicians attempting to build their reputations by supporting popular and attacking unpopular causes. An unknown conservative running for governor may try to become popular by attacking crime or high property taxes, which the general public tends to oppose. This is known as the "I'm against sin" ploy. The opposite tactic finds an unknown politician taking a stand in favor of safe streets and a strong America. This is the "I'm in favor of motherhood" gambit. Both tactics are effective, and thus most politicians try to find unpopular causes to attack and popular ones to support—not to affect the popularity of the causes, but to increase their own popularity.

AFFECTIVE-COGNITIVE CONSISTENCY Both balance and congruity are theories about how people reconcile their *affects* or feelings toward various objects: How does the NRA member make his feelings about gun control and about the new governor consistent with each other? But one of the important further implications of the consistency approach is that people also try to make their cognitions consistent with their affects. That is, our beliefs, our "knowledge," our convictions about the facts of the matter are determined in part by our affective preferences. Not only does the NRA enthusiast *like* the new governor less because of his position on gun control, but he comes to have different *beliefs* about the man; he may think of him as being gullible, soft, wishy-washy, not very bright, a liberal, a man who doesn't pay much attention to the genuine needs of his constituents, and so on. In other words, he changes his cognitions to make them consistent with his affective preferences.

Rosenberg (1960) provided a striking demonstration of the ramifying cognitive changes created by a change in affect toward the core object. He obtained from subjects a comprehensive description of their attitudes toward blacks, racial integration, and the whole question of relations between blacks and whites. He then hypnotized the subjects and told them that their attitude toward blacks moving into their community was the opposite of what it had previously been. If the subject had previously been strongly against integrated housing, he was told that he now was in favor of it, and vice versa. That is, he changed the subject's affect toward integrated housing. The subjects were then awakened from their hypnotic trance and questioned about their current attitudes about blacks and integration.

Rosenberg found that the change he had produced under hypnosis in this one affect was followed by many dramatic reversals in the subjects' beliefs and other cognitive elements relevant to integration. They came to believe housing integration was necessary to remove racial inequality, that it was necessary to maintain racial harmony, and so on.

Thus, these ramifying cognitive changes tended to reduce the imbalance that had resulted from the induced change. As the theories of cognitive consistency would predict, there were pressures toward reducing inconsistency, which resulted in a variety of cognitive changes.

DISSONANCE THEORY The last of the cognitive consistency theories is cognitive dissonance theory, first proposed by Leon Festinger in 1957. The most distinctive focus of dissonance theory has been upon inconsistencies between beliefs and overt behavior. As originally proposed, dissonance theory focused upon two principal sources of belief-behavior inconsistency: the effects of making decisions, and the effects of engaging in counterattitudinal behavior. Such inconsistencies produce cognitive dissonance, which may be reduced in a number of different ways. We will discuss this theory only briefly here, because Chapter 12 is largely devoted to spelling out its numerous interesting predictions and the ingenious research it has led to.

Festinger proposed that each alternative involved in a decision could be thought of as having positive and negative attributes. When a person makes a decision between two alternatives, the positive attributes of the chosen alternative, and the negative attributes of the rejected alternative, are consistent (or consonant, in the terms of dissonance theory) with the decision. That is, these attitudes about the choice alternatives are consistent with the overt behavior of deciding. However, dissonance arises because these are not the whole story with either alternative: usually the chosen object has some bad attributes, and the rejected object has some good ones. Both represent cognitions that are dissonant with the decision. And most decisions carry with them some dissonance, no matter how deliberate or rational they are. If we decide to buy a Jaguar instead of a Volkswagen, the Jaguar's comfort, speed, and stylishness, and the Volkswagen's crampedness and homeliness, are consonant with the decision. But the Jaguar's price, and its penchant for expensive repairs, and the inexpensiveness and ease of upkeep of the VW, are dissonant with the decision.

There are also cases in which people engage in behavior which is counter to their attitudes. Sometimes they are forced into it, because they have been drafted into the army, or because a hated regime has taken over their country. Sometimes they are simply seduced into it, or charmed into it; sometimes guilt makes them do it. In Chapter 11 we will discuss a number of the reasons why people do things they do not believe in. The point here is that engaging in behavior discrepant from attitudes leads to cognitive dissonance.

Dissonance theory spells out a number of the conditions affecting the magnitude of dissonance, and the mechanism of dissonance reduction most likely to occur. In cases involving attitude-behavior discrepancies, clearly the two major modes of dissonance reduction are revoking the behavior in some way (or claiming it really didn't matter very much), or changing one's attitudes.

SUMMARY We have not described the balance model, the congruity model, or dissonance theory in great detail. Only the main points of the theories have been presented, because they have been influential per se and they give some idea of the basic notions behind the theories of cognitive consistency. They differ mainly in the phenomena they address, rather than in the predictions they make. Balance theory has been used most widely to deal with attraction in interpersonal relationships, and especially with similar attitudes as a basis for attraction between people. It has also been widely applied to consistency among various subparts of an attitude structure. Congruity theory has been applied principally to inconsistencies arising in mass communication situations when a communicator takes a position disagreeing with his listener's opinion. And dissonance theory has been mostly concerned with how an individual resolves inconsistencies between his attitudes and his overt behavior. Nevertheless, all these models agree on two major points: when there is inconsistency, there is a tendency for a system to move toward a more consistent structure; this move can be accomplished in a variety of ways, with the individual generally choosing the easiest mode of resolution.

attribution theory

Attribution theory has also been applied to problems of attitude change, in an interesting way. Conventionally, psychologists have assumed that people determine their own attitudes by reviewing the various cognitions and affects in their consciousness, then expressing the result. As we have already seen, Bem (1965) has made the argument that people know their own attitudes not by inspecting their insides, but by inferring from their own external behavior. In other words, people infer their own attitudes in the same way that they infer other people's attitudes: by inspecting whatever external cues are available, and then making the appropriate attribution. By this theory, attitude change results from behavior change, as long as an internal attribution is made.

Bem does not hold that people never use internal evidence to infer their own true attitudes, but his work does suggest that to a surprising degree people rely upon the external evidence of their overt behavior, and the conditions under which it occurs, as evidence for inferring their own attitudes. We shall discuss research related to this idea in chapter 12. For the moment, the important point is that even attitudes, which are usually considered to be internally determined, may to some extent be affected by attributions based on overt behavior.

attitudes and behavior

At the beginning of the chapter, we distinguished between the affective, cognitive, and behavioral components of an attitude. One of the important controversies in attitude research has concerned the behavioral component of attitudes. Originally it was simply assumed that a person's attitudes determined his behavior. A person who favors a certain politician is likely to vote for him; if you like marijuana you are likely to smoke it; if you are prejudiced against blacks, you are unlikely to send your child to a school in which blacks are in the majority. Virtually all the interest in attitude change has been generated by the assumption that attitudes do affect behavior.

But there has been questioning of this assumption. In a classic study, LaPiere (1934), a white professor, toured the United States with a young Chinese student and his wife. They stopped at 66 hotels or motels, and at 184 restaurants. Although at the time in the United States there was rather strong prejudice against Orientals, all but one of the hotels and motels gave them space, and they were never refused service at a restaurant. Sometime later a letter was sent to the same motels and restaurants asking whether they would accept Chinese as guests. Of the 128 establishments replying, 92 percent said they would not. That is, the Chinese couple received nearly perfect service in person, but nearly universal discrimination in the subsequent letters. LaPiere, and many after him, interpreted these findings as reflecting a major inconsistency between behavior and attitudes. Almost all the proprietors *behaved* in a tolerant fashion, but they expressed an intolerant *attitude* when questioned by letter.

Recently there has been a good bit of controversy about how typical this early study was. Wicker (1969) conducted one widely cited review. He looked at studies testing for consistency between attitudes and behavior in the areas of race relations, job satisfaction, and classroom cheating. Summarizing thirty-one separate investigations, Wicker concluded: "It is considerably more likely that attitudes will be unrelated or only slightly related to overt behavior than that attitudes will be closely related to actions." Yet this conclusion has in turn been widely criticized as underestimating attitude-behavior consistency. Indeed, numerous studies show much higher degrees of consistency than Wicker reports. For example, in one study a large sample of Taiwanese married women was asked "Do you want any more children?" In the subsequent three years, 64 percent who had said "Yes" had a live birth, whereas only 19 percent who had said "No" had a child. Another example is voting behavior. Kelley and Mirer (1974) analyzed large-scale surveys conducted during the four presidential election campaigns from 1952 to 1964. Voters' partisan attitudes, as revealed in preelection interviews, were highly related to their actual voting behavior: 85 percent of the respondents showed a correspondence between attitude and behavior, despite the fact that the interviews took place over a two-month span prior to election day. Moreover, most (84 percent) of the inconsistencies occurred for persons whose attitudes showed only weak preferences for either candidate or party.

Such studies led the most recent careful reviewers to the following conclusion: "Our review has shown that most attitude-behavior studies yield positive results. The correlations that do occur are large enough to indicate that important causal forces are involved, whatever one's model of the underlying causal process may be" (Schuman and Johnson, 1976, p. 199). But everyone acknowledges that there is substantial variation across different situations in just how consistent attitudes and behavior are. So in recent years, the major research effort has gone to trying to determine the conditions that yield greater or lesser degrees of consistency.

strength and clarity of the attitude

Clearly one set of important conditions concerns the attitude itself: it needs to be a *strong* and *clear* one that *does not change* before the behavior measure is taken, and one that is *specifically* and *directly relevant* to the behavior in question. Inconsistencies can come from weak or ambivalent affects. As mentioned, Kelley and Mirer (1974) found that most attitude-vote inconsistencies come from voters with conflicted or weak attitudinal preferences to start with. Or behavior may not be consistent when the affective and cognitive components conflict. Norman (1975) considered both the behavior of volunteering for a psychology experiment and a person's attitude about volunteering. He found attitudes and behavior were closely related when both the cognitive and affective components of their attitudes were consistent, but they were not closely related when the cognitive and affective components conflicted.

When the attitude is made particularly *salient,* then it is more likely to be related to behavior. Snyder and Swann (1976) assigned subjects to a mock jury situation and gave them a sex discrimination case. In one condition their attitudes about affirmative action were made salient by instructing them to take a few minutes before the case to organize their thoughts on affirmative action. In the other, the not salient condition, the subjects were not given any warning that affirmative action was involved. When attitudes were made salient, they were highly related to jurors' verdicts in the case; but attitudes about affirmative action were not closely related to verdicts when they had not been made salient.

The more *specific* the attitude measure is, the more it tends to be correlated with behavior. For example, Heberlein and Black (1976) tested how closely related drivers' attitudes about environmentalism were to their purchasing of lead-free (as opposed to regular) gasoline. Lead-free gasoline is supposed to be good for the environment, so you would think environmentalists would buy it more. To test for specificity, the authors used several attitude dimensions, varying in how specifically relevant the attitudes were to lead-free gasoline. At the least specific level, the attitude dimension concerned general environmentalism; beliefs about air pollution in general were somewhat more relevant; and beliefs about lead-free gasoline were even more relevant. Finally, the most specific attitudes concerned the degree of personal obligation to buy lead-free gasoline felt by the driver. The most general attitudes (about environmentalism) were very weakly related to actual purchase of lead-free gasoline. But the most specifically relevant attitude, that concerning a personal obligation to buy lead-free gasoline, was very strongly related to actual purchase behavior (a correlation of .59).

To underline the importance of using attitudes specifically relevant to behaviors, we could mention a similar study done by Weigel, Vernon, and Tognacci (1974), again on environmentalism. Here the behaviors in question concerned willingness to engage in various actions on behalf of the Sierra Club. They too found that very general environmental attitudes were not particularly related to activist behavior (indeed, here the correlation was not even significant), but attitudes specifically toward the Sierra Club were (a correlation of .68). Weinstein (1972) found much the same thing regarding which attitudes were correlated with signing a protest petition against the quarter system. General attitudes were not, but specific attitudes were.

Similarly, if the behavior chosen is not directly *relevant* to the attitude measured, one would not expect to find a strong relationship. For example, several studies have asked subjects whether they believe in God or consider themselves religious, and then noted whether the subjects attended church. Typically there was only a weak relationship between the answers to those two questions and church attendance. But attending church is not directly related to a belief in God or even to being religious. Many people who believe in God and even consider themselves religious do not think that attending church is meaningful to them. Other people do not believe in God and may not even consider themselves religious, but attend church for a variety of reasons having nothing to do with these particular beliefs. That may be their one convivial, social outing of the week. Thus, it is not surprising that the answers to these two questions do not relate directly to church attendance. On the other hand, if the subjects were asked whether they thought attending church was a good idea, presumably the relationship to actual church attendance would be much stronger.

Finally, a fairly obvious but critical point is that as time elapses between the attitude measurement and the behavior assessment, the attitude may change. One would not expect to find a close relationship between a college girl's attraction to a boy and her dating behavior with him, if her attraction is measured when she is a freshman, and her behavior when she is a senior. Therefore, consistency between attitudes and behavior ought to be maximum when they are measured at about the same time. Kelley and Mirer (1974) found that errors in predicting the vote declined quite rapidly as the preelection interviews got closer to election day.

situational pressures

Whenever a person engages in overt behavior, he can be influenced both by his attitudes and by the situation he is in. In a later chapter we will show just how powerful situational pressures are in determining a person's overt behavior. For now, it is enough to make the obvious observation that when situational pressures are very strong, attitudes are not likely to be as strong a determinant of behavior as when situational pressures are relatively weak. One example is in the Snyder and Swann (1976) study of mock jury deliberations in a sex discrimination case mentioned above. Half the subjects were expected to discuss the case with another subject whose attitudes on sex discrimination generally differed from their own. The other half expected to discuss it with somebody whose attitudes were unknown. Presumably, expecting to be disagreed with is a strong situational pressure. And indeed, expecting disagree-

Monkmeyer/Mimi Forsyth

ment reduced quite sharply the consistency between the subject's own attitudes and his own verdict.

This is also easy to see in the LaPiere study we began with. Well-dressed, respectable-looking people asking for rooms are hard to refuse, despite feelings of prejudice against their ethnic group. The external pressures are even clearer when there is a law requiring rental to anyone. Under these circumstances, even the most prejudiced person must rent to Orientals, blacks, or anyone else unless he wants to close his motel.

methodological improvements

The failure to find an attitude-behavior relationship is sometimes due to poor methodology. The measure of attitudes could be faulty or have low reliability. If the subjects do not give correct answers, if they are unable to answer the question intelligently, if they do not understand the question, or if the question is so vague that it is difficult to answer, the questionnaire is then not measuring the attitude it is supposed to be measuring, and lack of relationship with a relevant behavior would be understandable.

Rather simple and obvious methodological improvements have been made in recent years in attitude-behavior studies, with resulting increases in consistency between the two. For example, it is a fundamental principle of measurement that if we use one item or one response from the individual, we have a less reliable measure of the variable than if we use a number of different items. In the LaPiere example, only one behavioral response was used (either providing or not providing service for the Chinese couple) and only one attitude response collected (either responding positively or negatively in the letter). In later studies, this procedure has been improved upon by increasing the number of different behaviors observed, and increasing the number of different items on which an attitude measure is done. This has improved the attitude-behavior correlation enormously. For example, Weigel and Newman (1976) correlated a generalized environmental concern scale with fourteen different behaviors, including things like signing petitions, recycling, picking up litter, and so on. The mean correlation when these behaviors were taken individually was .29. When they were all added up into one composite behavior scale, the total correlation was .62 with the environmental concern scale.

summary

We believe a great deal of evidence supports the idea that attitudes affect behavior. It seems correct to say that attitudes always produce pressure to behave consistently with them. However, external pressures and extraneous considerations can cause people to behave inconsistently with their attitudes. Any attitude or change in an attitude tends to produce behavior that corresponds with it, but this correspondence often does not appear because of other factors involved in the situation.

conclusions

The formulations that we have called the conditioning-reinforcement, incentive-conflict, and cognitive consistency approaches are the bases for virtually all the work in the area of attitudes. They provide the framework within which most of the research has been conducted and serve as basic principles with which to explain the findings. It should be noted that at times there have been conflicts between the approaches, particularly between consistency and incentive. Researchers have tended to work within one of these two frameworks and have tended to be suspicious of derivations from and results of experiments conducted within the other one. Despite this occasional friction, it seems clear to us that the approaches are not mutually exclusive but, on the contrary, are complementary. In the succeeding three chapters, we shall see that in some areas one approach is more useful, in some the other, and in some the experimental results can be explained only by recourse to a combination of theoretical approaches. Throughout the discussion, we shall refer to one or more of the theoretical positions in an attempt to fit together and explain what is known about attitude formation and change.

SUMMARY

1. Attitudes are generally thought of today as having a cognitive (thought) component, an affective (feeling) component, and a behavioral component.

2. "Facts" or "knowledge" differ from attitudes mainly in that they have no affective component.

3. Most people do not have very complex, broadly structured, or detailed attitudes about most things. Rather, like personality impressions, they are simple, and organized around the affective (or evaluative) dimension.

4. The conditioning and reinforcement approach views attitude formation and change as primarily a learning process. Attitudes are learned by association, reinforcement, and imitation.

5. The functionalist approach views attitudes in terms of the use that the attitude serves for the person.

6. There are several cognitive consistency theories, all of which view a person as attempting to maintain consistency among his various attitudes, between his affects and his cognitions toward a given object, and between his attitudes and behavior.

7. It is usually assumed that a person's behavior stems from his attitudes, but considerable research questions how consistent the two are with each other.

Now it appears that behavior is consistent with attitudes only under certain conditions: strong, clear, specific attitudes, and with no conflicting situational pressures.

SUGGESTIONS FOR ADDITIONAL READING

ABELSON, R. P., ARONSON, E., MCGUIRE, W. J., NEWCOMB, T. M., ROSENBERG, M. J. & TANNENBAUM, P. E. *Theories of Cognitive Consistency: A Sourcebook.* Chicago: Rand McNally, 1968. An extensive compilation of papers on almost every version of consistency theory, by almost everyone who ever wrote about it. Its nickname is TOCCAS.

BEM, D. J. Self-perception theory. In L. BERKOWITZ (ED.), *Advances in Experimental Social Psychology,* Vol. 6. New York: Academic Press, 1972. The clearest and best statement of the attribution approach to attitudes.

FISHBEIN, M. & AJZEN, I. *Belief, Attitude, Intention and Behavior: An Introduction to Theory and Research.* Reading, Mass.: Addison-Wesley, 1975.

KATZ, D. The functional approach to the study of attitudes. *Public Opinion Quarterly,* 1960, 24, 163–204. The classic statement of the functionalist point of view.

KIESLER, C. A., COLLINS, B. E., & MILLER, N. *Attitude change: a critical analysis of theoretical approaches.* New York: John Wiley, 1969. A good overview of the several different approaches to attitude theory covered in this chapter. The most recent comprehensive social-psychological approach to attitudes. It especially emphasizes consistency approaches, and the attitude-behavior problem.

OSGOOD, C. E., & TANNENBAUM, P. H. The principle of congruity in the prediction of attitude change. *Psychological Review,* 1955, 62, 42–55. A highly formal presentation of the consistency theory most appropriate for studying the effects of mass communication.

9

attitude change

In 1959, Carl Hovland and Irving Janis suggested a useful model of attitude change. Figure 9–1 illustrates a model based largely on theirs but simplified and changed to bring it more in line with recent work in this area. It begins with what Hovland called the observable persuasion stimuli. There must be a *communicator* who holds a particular position on some issue and is trying to convince others to hold this position. To do so, he produces a *communication* designed to persuade people that his position is correct and to induce them to change their own positions in the direction of his. This comunication is presented in a given *situation*. These, then, constitute the attack—the source, the communication, and the surroundings.

In the typical attitude-change situation, individuals are confronted with a communication in favor of a position different from the one they hold. They may have a negative attitude toward marijuana and someone tells them that it is really very good; they may be Democrats listening to

FIGURE 9–1
Model of the attitude-change situation, showing examples of important factors at each stage. The amount of attitude change that occurs is determined by variables at each point in the process.

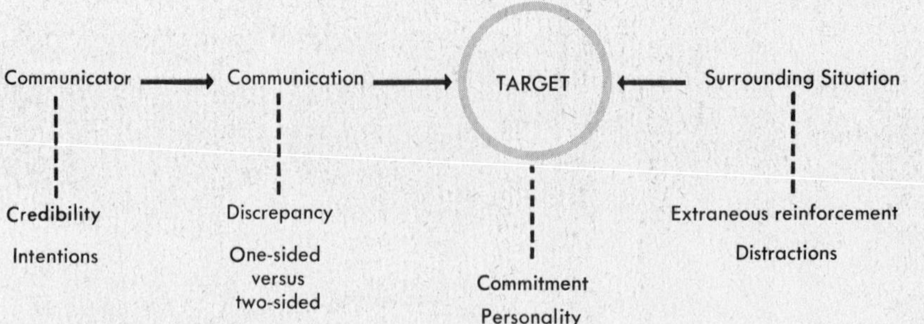

a Republican campaign speech; they may be smokers reading the Surgeon General's report on cigarette smoking and cancer. Under these circumstances, stress is produced by the discrepancy between the individuals' attitude and the attitude expressed in the communication. This stress has been called conflict, incongruity, imbalance, or just inconsistency. Whichever model we choose, there is general agreement that there is pressure on the individual to resolve the discrepancy.

The focus of most research has been on ways of increasing attitude change. If individuals change their attitudes in the direction advocated by the communication, the discrepancy between the two positions is reduced. Since this discrepancy is the source of the stress, reducing the discrepancy reduces the stress. But this is only one alternative. Throughout our discussion of the factors affecting the amount of attitude change in such a situation, it is important to keep in mind that people have open to them a variety of ways of resolving the stress. The emphasis on so-called alternative modes of resolution is one of the important contributions of Carl Hovland's model of attitude change and of the cognitive consistency models.

From the point of view of the communicator, this means that one major problem is to maximize the likelihood that targets will choose attitude change as their mode of resolution and to minimize or eliminate the use of alternative modes of resolution.Therefore, one of the critical factors in any attitude-change situation is whether or not alternative modes of resolution are present and, if they are, the extent to which they are used. Before discussing attitude change in detail, we shall describe briefly the most important alternative mechanisms the individual can use. That is, we need to consider how the person can resist persuasion and still reduce the stress created by a discrepant communication.

how the target resists persuasion

REFUTING THE ARGUMENTS An individual can attempt to refute the arguments contained in the discrepant communication. He can engage in a debate with the content of the communication and attempt to demonstrate to himself that his own position has more merit than the other one. This debate can be implicit or explicit, verbal or nonverbal, perhaps even conscious or unconscious. He can argue against the discrepant communication, produce evidence to support his own position, show how the other side is illogical or inconsistent, and in general do anything he can to weaken the impact of the communication. To the extent that he is able to refute these arguments, the stress should be reduced.

The problem with this mode of resolution is twofold: usually a rather lazy recipient is up against a more expert communicator. Most people, most of the time, are not very motivated to analyze in close detail the pros and cons of complex arguments. Moreover, persuasive messages are usually designed so that it is difficult to reject them on purely logical grounds. The authors of the communication naturally present as strong a case as they can, and the communicator is generally better informed on the topic than the recipient of the communication. Therefore, although arguing against the discrepant communication and attempting to reject it is a rational mode of resolution, it is often difficult to employ.

DEROGATING THE SOURCE Someone who is faced with a discrepant communication can reduce the stress by deciding that the source of the communication is unreliable or negative in some other way. If we look at the balance or congruity models described in Chapter 8, we can see that there is nothing inconsistent about disagreeing with a negative source. In fact, people expect to disagree with a negative source. Thus, by deciding that the source is negative or the information unreliable, they can balance the system and remove all stress.

Such an attack on the source of a communication is common in politics, informal debating, courtroom trials, and partically every kind of adversary proceeding. The defense attorney in a trial tries to discredit the damaging witness when she cannot rebut his evidence. The politician calls his opponent a Communist or a fascist or some other negative term when he finds it difficult to argue on the issues themselves.

This device is extremely effective because it not only eliminates the threat from the current argument, but also makes all future arguments from the opponent much less powerful. When an opponent has been discredited, anything he says carries less weight. Thus, attacking the source of the communication is an effective way of reducing the stress produced by a discrepant communication.

DISTORTING THE MESSAGE Another type of resolution people sometimes employ is distorting or misperceiving the communication so as to reduce the discrepancy between it and their own position. The surgeon general says it is extremely dangerous to smoke because smoking has been shown to be a significant cause of lung cancer. The confirmed smoker reads this message and decides that the surgeon general is recommending a decrease in smoking but that the evidence on lung cancer is not yet conclusive. The smoker may do this by a gross misperception of the article when he reads it, by distorting the article in his memory, or perhaps by reading only part of the article and reconstructing the rest of it in his own mind. However he accomplishes it, the result is the same—the message becomes considerably less discrepant.

Alternatively, he may exaggerate the extremity of the communication so as to make it ridiculous. Many environmentalists want to slow down the development of undeveloped lands, and restrict the building of pollution-causing plants and buildings. Developers and many other businessmen naturally oppose the restrictions environmentalists support. It is fairly common for them to distort the positions taken by environmentalists, claiming they want to prevent the building of any new industrial plants at all and avoid any economic growth at all. This of course is an exaggeration but it is easy to come to in the heat of debate. The distorted position is so unreasonable that if the general public believed it, they would never support the environmentalists' side.

Hovland has suggested that distortion of the message follows certain rules. When a discrepant position is quite close to that of an individual, he perceives it as closer than it actually is. This is called *assimilation.* When it is quite far away, he perceives it as farther away than it is. This process is called, *contrast.*

Both kinds of misperceptions should reduce the stress in an attitude-change situation. Assimilating the discrepant position makes it seem closer than it actually is. This reduces the amount of discrepancy and, accordingly, the amount of stress. The opposite tendency, exaggerating the discrepancy of an already distant communication, makes the communication so extreme that it loses its credibility. When a communication or its source becomes unbelievable, there is no pressure on the individual to change his position in response to it. Thus, both assimilation and contrast are effective means of reducing pressure caused by a discrepant communication.

RATIONALIZATION AND OTHER DEFENSIVE PROCEDURES An interesting article by Abelson (1959) has described a number of ingenious, complicated modes of resolution similar, in some ways, to the defense mechanisms for emotional conflicts described by Anna Freud. The individual intellectualizes, encapsulates, denies, displaces, and, in general, does whatever he can to minimize the stress in a situation. Abelson described how a person can decide there is no discrepancy because he and the other person are talking about different things. A man who thinks he is for civil rights and freedom for everyone but is also against laws that prohibit discrimination in housing would seem to be a prime subject for attitude change. We may say to him that denying blacks fair housing is denying them freedom. But he avoids the issue, and the stress, by saying that we and he mean different things by *freedom.* He wants people to be free to do as they please, and forcing people to rent their houses to blacks abridges freedom. He says he wants blacks to be free to rent any house that both they and the owner agree on, but that we should not force anyone to do anything. As far as he is concerned, by separating the argument into two issues, there is no discrepancy.

There are many ways of shifting or explaining away discrepancies. They probably produce other stresses in an individual's cognitive system, but they often are successful in reducing stress due to discrepant communications. The challenge for the communicator is to block their use and create attitude change instead.

BLANKET REJECTION This is probably the most common mode of resolution. Rather than trying to refute the arguments on logical grounds or weakening them by attacking their source, individuals seem to be able simply to reject arguments for no apparent reason. A typical response by a smoker to a well-reasoned, logical attack on cigarette smoking is to say that the arguments are not good enough to make him stop. He does not answer them; he just does not accept them. When someone who believes in capital-punishment is shown overwhelming evidence that it does not serve as a deterrent to homicide, he tends to be unconvinced. He shrugs off the evidence, says he does not believe it, and continues to maintain his position. It often takes more than a good argument to convince people of something. Much of the time they respond in an illogical, nonrational manner to discrepant communications. They merely say "No, that's not right." We do not understand this mechanism very well because it has not been directly studied, but it seems to be an alternative that is often employed in attitude-change situations.

With this background, we can turn to a consideration of the specific factors that increase or decrease the amount of attitude change produced by a persuasive communication after it has reached its target. Following the model in Figure 9–1, these factors are divided into several classes: factors involving the communicator, factors concerning the communication itself, factors in the surrounding environment that are extraneous to the communication and the participants, and factors that involve characteristics of the individual who is the target of the persuasive attempt.

the source of the communication

One of the most straightforward and reliable findings is that the higher the evaluation of the communicator, the more attitude change is produced. This follows from any of the cognitive-consistency models. If a person thinks that marijuana is terrible but a friend says it is great, the system is imbalanced. One way of reducing the imbalance is to change his attitude toward marijuana and agree with his friend. In contrast, if someone he dislikes has an attitude different from his, there is no imbalance and no pressure to change. Thus, the more favorably people evaluate the source of a discrepant communication, the more likely they would be to change their attitude. But there are a variety of different ways in which a communicator can be evaluated favorably, and not all of them yield exactly the same results.

communicator credibility

The dimension that has been studied most is credibility. By *credibility* we refer primarily to how expert the communicator is perceived to be in the area of concern, and also how much he is trusted by the individual receiving the communication (though we will consider trustworthiness separately). For example, when evaluations of a new medicine are attributed to a noted doctor, they are more persuasive than when they are attributed to a well-known comedian. If T. S. Eliot says that a certain poem is good, he should have more influence than a barber saying it is good.

This effect of credibility was demonstrated in a study by Hovland and Weiss (1952). Subjects heard communications concerned with four issues: the advisability of selling antihistamines without a prescription, whether the steel industry was to blame for the then-current steel shortage, the future of the movie industry in the context of the growing popularity of television, and the practicality of building an atomic-powered submarine. Each communication came from either a high- or low-credibility source. For example, the communication on atomic submarines was supposedly either by J. Robert Oppenheimer, a noted physicist, or from *Pravda*, the Russian newspaper. The results indicated that communications attributed to high-credibility sources produced more change than those from low-credibility sources.

In another study (Aronson, Turner, and Carlsmith, 1963), subjects were told they were in an experiment on esthetics and were asked to evaluate nine stanzas from obscure modern poems. They then read

"Before I begin, I'd like to make a brief statement on American foreign policy."

someone else's evaluation of one of the stanzas they had not liked very much. The communication argued that the poem was better than the subject had indicated. It was described as being somewhat better, much better, or very much better than the subject had thought. The crucial variable was that the communication was supposedly from either T. S. Eliot or Agnes Stearns, who was described as a student at Mississippi State Teachers College. After reading the communication, the subjects reevaluated the poems. Regardless of the level of discrepancy between the communication and the subject's initial position, there was more change with the high-credibility communicator than there was with the low-credibility one.

An interesting question, not yet answered, is whether an expert in one field can transfer the influence of his expertise to another field. If T. S. Eliot, who is highly respected in the field of poetry, had taken a stand on politics or education, would his opinion have carried more weight and produced more attitude change than someone less well known? Although there is little evidence on this question, it seems likely that an expert may be able to transfer some of his influence to *related* fields. For example, T. S. Eliot's comments on the teaching of English or even of music would probably be quite influential. However, as the area of concern became more different from his own area, the fact that he was an expert would matter less and he would be less able to transfer his power of persuasion. His comments on the teaching of music or on contemporary theater would also be quite persuasive; his comments on politics or ethics would be less persuasive; and his comments on space technology or submarine warfare would probably be no more persuasive than anybody else's. However, for the moment this is just speculation. The question of the transferability of prestige is an open one that should be more fully investigated in the future.

trustworthiness

Regardless of the expertise of the communicator, it is extremely important for the listener to trust his intentions. Even though someone may be the world's greatest expert on poetry, we would not be influenced by his writing reviews of his own poetry or of poetry written by a friend of his. We would not be concerned about his inherent ability to write accurately; we would be concerned about his objectivity and, therefore, his trustworthiness. As we saw in our discussions of ingratiation (Chapter 5) and attribution in general (Chapter 4), to the extent that a communicator is not a disinterested observer, his trustworthiness may be in doubt and what he says will have less effect. If he is perceived as having something to gain from the position he is advocating or if he is taking that position for any other personal reasons, he would be less persuasive than someone perceived as advocating the position for entirely objective reasons.

A major problem for a communicator is how to convince an audience that he is a disinterested observer. As we saw in the chapter on attribution, this means convincing the audience that the speaker's position is his or her genuine position (an internal attribution) rather than a position taken for opportunistic reasons, such as the desire to win popularity or votes or money (an external attribution, to something the speaker has to gain by not being honest).

One way to appear trustworthy is for him to argue for a position that appears to be counter to his self-interest. A district attorney, whose main role is supposed to be procuring convictions, would be expected to argue in favor of greater power for law enforcement agencies. But if he does so, his credibility would be lessened, because he clearly has something to gain from this position. On the other hand, if he argues for greater protection of the rights of individuals and against strengthening law enforcement agencies—that is, if he argues against his self-interest—his credibility should be enhanced. We would expect that a district attorney would be more persuasive and produce more attitude change when he takes the latter rather than the former position. A study by Walster, Aronson, and Abrahams (1966) concerned the effect of a communication from a convicted criminal. When the criminal argued in favor of more individual freedom and against greater powers for the police, he produced virtually no attitude change. When he argued in favor of a stronger police force, he produced a great deal of attitude change. This is shown in Figure 9–2. Thus, even a low-prestige and highly doubtful communicator appears to have a considerable amount of influence when he argues in favor of a position that would hurt rather than benefit him.

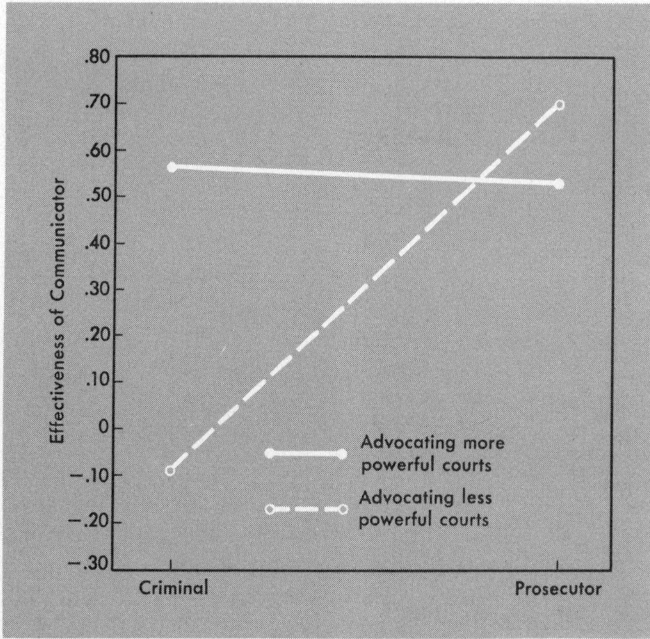

FIGURE 9–2
Effectiveness of communicators when advocating positions for and against one's own self-interest. SOURCE: Walster, Aronson, & Abrahams (1966), p. 333.

A similar effect is produced when the target thinks the communicator does not intend him to hear the communication. People tend to be more influenced when they "accidentally" overhear a persuasive communication than when it is directed at them (Walster and Festinger, 1962; Brock and Becker, 1965). This effect also seems to be due to the perceived credibility of the communicator. If he knows people are listening, he may try to convince them and may not be entirely honest. If he does not know anyone is within earshot, it is less likely that he is being dishonest. People are more likely to believe the message in the latter case and are therefore more likely to be convinced.

Given these findings, it might be thought that perception of intent to influence would have a major impact on attitude change. If the target thinks the communicator is trying to change his opinion, presumably the target should be more suspicious and change his attitude less. But that is not always so. The target's perception of the source's intent to persuade sometimes decreases the effect of the communication and sometimes increases it.

When the communicator has extremely high credibility or is well liked, perceived intent to persuade produces more positive attitude change. Under these circumstances, the individual generally does whatever he can to please the communicator. When he knows exactly what the communicator would like him to do, he is more likely to do it than when the communicator's intent is disguised. For example, Mills and Aronson (1965) showed that men were more influenced by a woman they liked when they knew she was trying to influence them than when her attempt to influence was less obvious. This enhancement of the effect should generally occur whenever the source of the communication is a liked figure whom the target wants to please and has no particular reason to distrust. Thus, although at first glance it seems that intent to persuade would always decrease the effect of the communication, there are times when it has the opposite effect.

liking

As we discussed in detail in the chapter on liking, there is a strong tendency for people to like those who have views similar to theirs. Similarly, as the consistency theories suggest, people change their attitudes so they will agree with the people they like. However, the psychological process by which liking produces attitude change is somewhat different from that by which expertness works. According to a theory proposed by Kelman (1961), liking produces attitude change because people try to identify with a liked communicator and thus tend to adopt that person's attitudes, tastes, modes of behavior, and modes of dress. His reasons or arguments for his attitudes are not very important. On the other hand, expertness produces attitude change because people pay more attention to an expert's arguments and consider them more seriously.

The implication of this theory is that good arguments are critical to an expert's persuasiveness, but should not be terribly important for a liked nonexpert. Norman (1976) tested this idea by using two sources: an unattractive expert and an attractive nonexpert. Since the topic was the number of hours of sleep required per night by the average person, the expert was a professor of physiological psychology who had just coauthored a book on sleep; the nonexpert was a twenty-year-old college student. Their pictures and other personal information were also presented, revealing the student to be an attractive, athletic young man recently elected to the student government, whereas the professor was middle-aged and not very attractive. In each case, half the subjects received extensive arguments on why people should cut down on their sleep, while the other half received the simple statement that they should cut down. Consistent with Kelman's theory, the addition of arguments significantly increased the expert's persuasiveness, but it did not affect the amount of attitude change produced by the attractive nonexpert.

In another test of this theory, Mills and Harvey (1972) varied the timing of information about the communicator: some subjects were told of the communicator's attractiveness (or expertness) before reading the message, and others learned about the communicator only after reading the message. Mills and Harvey reasoned that the attractive source would produce attitude change in either case, because all the subject needed to know was the communicator's opinion in order to identify with him and accept his position. On the other hand, learning after the message that the communicator was an expert would do no good, because the opportunity to scrutinize and consider his arguments more carefully would have been lost by that time. That was how their data came out. The attractive communicator was equally effective in producing attitude change whether he was described before or after the message, but the expert communicator produced attitude change only when he was described before the subjects read the message.

As indicated in Chapter 5, *similarity* is one of the most important bases of liking. Not surprisingly, then, people tend to be influenced more by those who are similar to them than by those who are different. But similarity also increases influence for another reason. Suppose someone is similar to us in terms of national, economic, racial, and religious background, and we also share many ideological values. If he then says that he thinks drugs are bad, we would probably assume that he made this judgment on the same bases that we would. He is not using irrelevant or incorrect (in our eyes) criteria. Accordingly, his judgment tends to carry considerable weight. If he were different from us in terms of background and values, his attitude toward drugs would be less meaningful, because we could assume it was based on criteria different from those we would apply. Thus, in terms of both increased liking and shared perspectives, the greater the similarity between the source and recipient of a discrepant communication, the more attitude change is produced.

In general, any characteristic of the communicator which implies that he knows what he is talking about (is an expert), is being honest (has no ulterior motive), or is likeable increases the effectiveness of the communication. Since derogation of the source of the communication is one of the major ways of avoiding attitude change, these variables relating to the communicator are extremely important. Any disliking of the communicator, or lack of trust in his competence or credibility makes it relatively easy to reject the message by attacking him. In this way, the target frees himself from the pressure of worrying about the complex details of the message itself. Therefore, preventing this particular mode of resolution by emphasizing the honesty and expertise of the source of the communication is a major concern in the attempt to influence. In most cases, it is clear that the communicator is trying to change one's attitude, and he is therefore already somewhat suspect. It is usually quite difficult to convince an audience that he is a disinterested commentator, and thus, at least in politics and advertising, there is great emphasis on the sincerity of the speaker, on his basic integrity and honesty, and on his likability.

reference group

One of the strongest sources of persuasive pressure is a group to which an individual belongs. The group could be as large and inclusive as all American citizens or the middle class or a labor union or college students or all liberals or all blacks. It can also be a much smaller, more specialized group, such as a college fraternity, social psychologists, the Young Republicans, or the Elks Club. And it can be extremely small, such as a group of friends, a bridge club, a discussion group or just five people who happen to be in a room together.

As we will see in the chapter on conformity, there is a strong tendency for individuals to go along with the group, particularly when everyone else in the group holds the same opinion or makes the same response. In these cases, however, there is little actual change in the individual's opinions—he conforms to the group overtly but does not change his internal attitude. Nevertheless, the opinion of the group can also be an extremely persuasive force and can cause the individual to change his internal attitude on an issue. If the Young Republicans endorse a particular candidate, there is a tendency for all the members of the club to feel he is a good candidate. If a group of friends tells us they are in favor of student activism or like a particular movie, we probably are convinced by them. If most of the members of a fraternity think initiations are a good idea, the rest of the members may agree with them.

The reasons why reference groups are so effective at producing attitude change are those we have just discussed: liking and similarity. If people value a group, it is a highly credible, highly esteemed source of communication. When the group says something, each member tends to trust it and believe the message. In addition, because they consider

Drawing by Kraus; © 1964 The New Yorker Magazine, Inc.

"And I thoroughly understand the problems of the caveman, because I'm a caveman myself."

themselves members of the group, they tend to evaluate themselves in comparison with it. In essence, the group serves as the standard for their own behavior and attitudes. They want to be similar to the other members. When the other members express a particular opinion, each members thinks his own opinion wrong if it is different. Only when their opinion is the same as the group's would it be correct or "normal." Therefore, they tend to change their opinion to make it agree.

Attachment to the group can also serve to prevent somebody from being influenced by a communication from an outside source. If the group agrees with the individual's opinion, they provide him with strong support. Consider a fraternity member whose fraternity believes strongly in initiations. He may occasionally be exposed to an attack on initiations from someone outside the fraternity. Whenever he is so exposed, knowledge that his group agrees with him provides strong support and makes it easier for him to resist persuasion.

This dual effect of groups--changing a member's opinion to make it coincide with the rest of the group and supporting a member's opinion so he can resist persuasion from without—depends to some extent on how strong the individual's ties are to the group. The more he wants to be a member of it and the more highly he evaluates it, the more he would be influenced by the group's beliefs. Kelley and Volkart (1952) demonstrated the effect of attachment to the group on members' resistance to outside influence. A communicator attempted to change some Boy Scouts' opinions on various issues that were closely related to their troop's norms. The more the Scouts valued their membership in the troop, the less effect the communicator had on their opinions.

Another way of demonstrating the potent effect of group norms is to show how changes in the group's position can pull people away from their old positions. Kelley and Woodruff (1956) played subjects a tape recording of a speech arguing against their group's norm—they were education students, and the speech argued against "progressive education." The speech was interrupted periodically by applause which the experimenters attributed to faculty members and recent graduates of the college in one experimental condition ("members' applause"), or to an audience of college-trained people in a neighboring city, interested in community problems related to education ("outsiders' applause"). Attitude change toward the speech, away from old group norms, was much greater in the "members' applause" condition. This gives additional evidence of the potency of groups in producing or blocking attitude change; in this case, subjects confronted with an apparent change in their group's norm were likely to change their own attitudes to line up with the group's new position. This study was repeated later with some variations (Landy, 1972) and produced essentially the same results: fellow group members (in this case, fellow students) applauding a communication discrepant from the subject's initial attitude created more attitude change than did the applause of a less attractive group (supposedly members of the American Nazi party and their wives).

Michael D. Sullivan

the communication

Social psychologists tend to concentrate on factors that increase the effectiveness of a message rather than on the content of the message itself. This is because we are looking for general laws that determine the effectiveness of all messages. Naturally it is easier to sell something good than something less good. Crest toothpaste was successful in part because it offered protection against cavities; the automobile became popular because it was a great product; and some political candidates are more qualified than others. A good campaign does better than a poor one, but a really terrible product would be difficult to sell even with great advertising. Given a particular product or opinion to sell, however, a number of variables in the communication itself have important effects on the amount of attitude change that is produced.

discrepancy

As mentioned earlier, the major source of stress in any influence situation comes from the discrepancy between the target's initial position and the position advocated by the communication. The greater the discrepancy, the greater the stress. If smokers are told that smoking may cause their teeth to turn yellow (a mildly negative statement), there is less stress than if they are told that smoking causes cancer (an extremely negative statement). If someone who thinks John Kennedy was a great president hears a communication arguing that he was only moderately successful, the individual's attitude is under pressure; if the communication argues that Kennedy was a terrible president, there is much more pressure. If on a scale there are 2 points of discrepancy, 2 points of attitude change would eliminate it. If there are 5 points of discrepancy, 5 points of change are necessary. An individual who changes his attitude under the pressure of a discrepant message must, accordingly, change it more with greater discrepancy. Therefore, within a wide range, there is more attitude change with greater discrepancy (Fisher and Lubin, 1958; Hovland and Pritzker, 1957).

However, the relationship between discrepancy and amount of change is not always this simple. There is more stress with greater discrepancy, but it does not always produce more change. The complicating factors are that as discrepancy becomes quite great, the individual finds it more difficult to change his attitude enough to eliminate the discrepancy and that extremely discrepant statements tend to make the individual doubt the credibility of their source. Suppose someone thinks Kennedy was a very great president and is faced with a discrepant opinion from a teacher of political science. What happens as the discrepancy between his and the teacher's opinions increases? This is diagrammed in Figure 9–3.

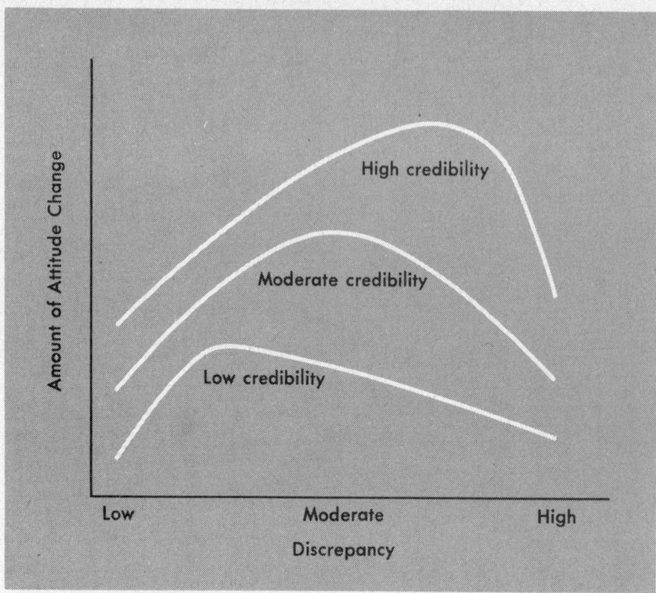

FIGURE 9–3
Discrepancy, credibility of the communicator, and attitude change. Maximum change is always produced by intermediate levels of discrepancy, but the point at which it occurs is determined by credibility. The more the credibility, the greater the discrepancy that produced the maximum change.

We shall consider this situation in terms of two modes of resolution—attitude change and rejection of the communicator—and, for the moment, shall ignore other modes. If we can reject the communicator, we need not change our opinion; if we cannot reject the communicator, we must change our opinion. At low discrepancy, when the teacher says he thinks Kennedy was not a great president but still a pretty good one, the individual is likely to be somewhat influenced. There would be some pressure on him to change his opinion in the direction of the teacher's, and if the teacher presented a fairly persuasive argument, the individual would probably do so. In this situation, it is difficult to reject the moderately credible communicator but easy to change one's opinion the little bit required to reduce the discrepancy. It is fairly easy to decide that Kennedy was not a great president but only a good one; it is considerably more difficult to decide that a teacher in political science is not a valid source of information about politics. Since attitude change is easier than rejection of the communicator, the individual tends to resolve the situation by changing his attitude. He would, however, change his attitude only slightly, because that is all that is necessary to reduce the discrepancy.

With somewhat greater degrees of discrepancy (e.g., the teacher thinks Kennedy was a mediocre president), it becomes harder to reduce the discrepancy by changing our attitude. It is one thing to change from thinking Kennedy was great to thinking he was only good; it is more difficult to change from great to mediocre. Nevertheless, it may still be easier to change our opinion than to reject the communicator, and research results indicate that this is what happens. With moderate discrepancy, subjects still resolve the situation primarily by changing their attitudes rather than by rejecting the communicator. Note that moderate discrepancy results in more attitude change than small discrepancy because greater change is necessary in order to reduce the discrepancy. Thus, as discrepancy increases from slight to moderate, the amount of attitude change also increases.

As the discrepancy becomes extreme, however, it becomes still harder for individuals to reduce the stress by changing their opinions. A greater change in opinion is necessary in order to reduce the discrepancy, and the greater the change that is necessary, the more difficult it is to make it. It is extremely difficult for those who thought Kennedy was great to decide that he was terrible.

As discrepancy increases, something else important happens. Congruity theory points out that a communicator who makes an extremely discrepant statement tends to lose credibility. If we think Kennedy was great and someone says he thinks Kennedy was terrible, there is a tendency to decide that this communicator does not know much about government or men. The extremity of his statement compared to our initial belief tends to cast doubt on his credibility. Thus, as discrepancy becomes quite great, it becomes relatively easy to reject the source of the communication.

There are thus two factors operating as discrepancy increases—attitude change gets more difficult, and rejection of the communicator gets easier. At some point, rejection becomes easier than attitude change as a means of removing the stress. Perhaps it is when the teacher says he thinks Kennedy was a poor president; perhaps it is when he says he thinks Kennedy was a very bad president;. When this degree of discrepancy is passed, people begin to reject the communicator rather than change their attitudes, and the amount of attitude change decreases. This relationship between discrepancy and attitude change has now been well documented (Freedman, 1964; Bochner and Insko, 1966; Rhine and Severance, 1970; Eagly and Telaak, 1972).

discrepancy and credibility

Thus far we have been considering situations in which the communication comes from a person of moderate credibility. Higher credibility makes it more difficult to reject the source. If one's most respected teacher says that Kennedy was a poor president, it is harder to decide that she does not know what she is talking about. Only extreme statements from her could make the individual come to this conclusion. Therefore the greater the credibility of the communicator, the higher the level of discrepancy at which the maximum change occurs. Similarly, a lower-credibility source makes rejection relatively easy and the maximum point occurs at lower levels of discrepancy. The study of Aronson, Turner, and

Carlsmith (1963) described earlier demonstrated this effect. Subjects read opinions about poetry that were slightly, moderately, or greatly discrepant from their own. When the discrepant opinion was attributed to T. S. Eliot, maximum attitude change occurred with the highest discrepancy. When another student was the source, maximum change was produced by the moderately discrepant message. Presumably, even T. S. Eliot's credibility has some limits, and if discrepancy became great enough, attitude change would begin to decline.

This relationship is nicely illustrated in Figure 9–4, which shows the effect of discrepancy and credibility on opinion change. Bochner and Insko (1966) had a Nobel Prize winner (high credibility) and a YMCA instructor (low credibility) give messages regarding the number of hours of sleep the average person requires per night. Each subject received one message from one source. Some subjects received a message saying eight hours were required, others a message saying seven hours were required and so on. Since the great majority of subjects initially thought eight hours was correct, these messages varied in discrepancy accordingly; zero discrepancy for the eight-hour message, one-hour discrepancy for the seven-hour message, and so on. As you can see in Figure 9–4, there was more change at moderate levels of discrepancy than at higher

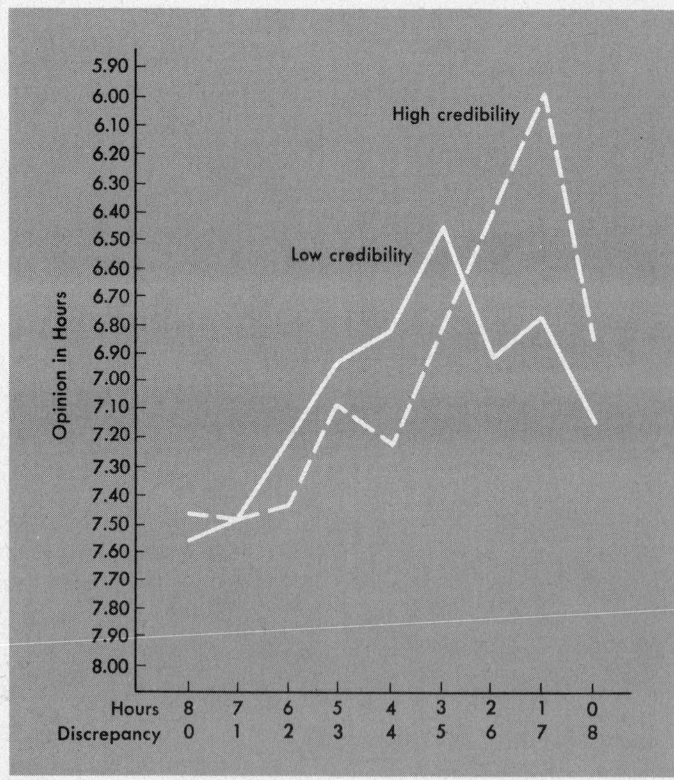

FIGURE 9–4
Opinion change produced by high- and low-credibility communicators at low, moderate, and high discrepancy. (Bochner and Insko, 1966.)

levels. In addition, as expected, the optimal level of discrepancy was greater for the high credibility source.

Thus, the level of credibility does not change the basic relationship between discrepancy and attitude change, but it does change the point at which maximum change occurs. A similar effect is produced by any other factor that affects the difficulty of rejection or the difficulty of changing. The more difficult it is to reject the communicator, the greater the discrepancy at which maximum change occurs; the more difficult it is to change one's attitude, the lower the discrepancy producing maximum change. This example illustrates how an interplay of forces determines which mode of resolution is adopted in a given situation and how the use of one mode implies less use of another.

Usually the effects of discrepancy are analyzed in terms of consistency theory: when a good source argues something very bad, the subjects must change their evaluation of the source or change their attitude in order to restore consistency. But Eagly and Chaiken (1975) have applied an attribution theory analysis to this situation. We noted above that communicators who advocate unexpected positions (one against their own interest, or against the interest of their audience) are regarded as more credible because the subject attributes the communicator's statement to his genuine beliefs about the topic in question, rather than to situational factors such as what will please his audience, or what is the most opportunistic or conformist position about the topic. Eagly and Chaiken further make the assumption that likable people are generally expected to advocate desirable positions, and unlikable people are generally expected to advocate undesirable positions. Following this logic then, Eagly and Chaiken predict that the most effective communicators will be likable people advocating undesirable positions, or unlikable people advocating desirable positions, because these are so unexpected.

Their experiment, on the topics of venereal disease and unemployment sustained their hypotheses. Indeed, likability and desirability of position were expected to go together; the attractive source was more persuasive on the undesirable position; and the unattractive source was more persuasive on the desirable position. This is simply a restatement of the finding shown in Figure 9–3 that high credibility sources can more successfully advocate more discrepant positions than can low credibility sources, but, using attribution theory, it gives a somewhat different theoretical explanation for it.

The effect is heightened by the tendency to assimilate or contrast the position advocated in the discrepant communication. As mentioned earlier, discrepant positions that are close to the individual's are often seen as closer than they actually are, whereas those that are far away are seen as farther away than they are. Exaggerating the closeness of a discrepant position makes it easy to change enough to reduce the small discrepancy, or it may eliminate change by making the two positions essentially identical. Exaggerating the remoteness of a position makes it easier to attack the credibility of the person advocating it.

In order to test this notion. Hovland, Harvey, and Sherif (1957) asked subjects to rate communications designed to be similar to their views, moderately different, or extremely different. The issue chosen was one that the subjects felt strongly about—it was prohibition, and they were living in a "dry" state. Shortly before the study began, the state had voted, by a narrow margin, to retain the existing prohibition laws. The "dry" subjects consisted of members of the Women's Christian Temperance Union, a group of Salvation Army workers, and students in seminaries or in strict denominational colleges. Moderate positions were represented by college students in classes in journalism, speech, education, and chemistry, etc. A group of "wet" subjects was secured on the basis of personal knowledge of their views. (The experimenters did not describe how they obtained that personal knowledge).

All the subjects listened to a taperecorded speech described as having been made by a proponent of the stand advocated. A "wet" (repeal) communication was presented to the extreme "dry" and moderate subjects. The "dry" (prohibition) communication was presented to the extreme "wet" and moderate subjects. And the moderate communication

FIGURE 9–5
Average placements of position of moderately wet communication (F) by Ss holding various positions on the issue plotted against hypothetical assimilation-contrast curve. (Source Hovland, Harvey and Sherif, 1957).

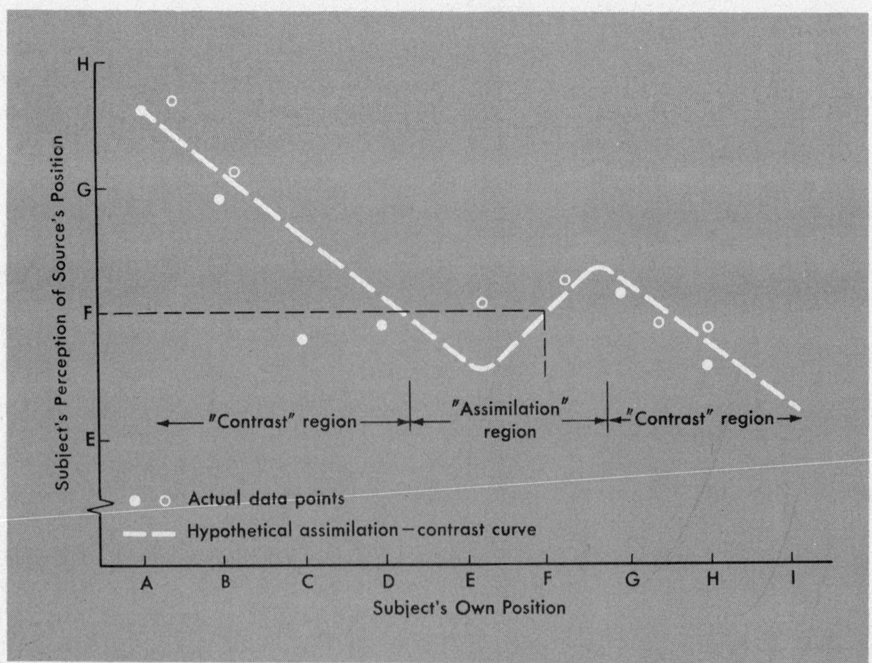

was presented to everyone. After listening to each communication, the subjects indicated where they thought it fell on a scale ranging from extreme dry to extreme wet.

The results supported the expectation that assimilation and contrast would occur. Subjects who held a strong wet position rated the moderate communication as much dryer than did the moderate subjects; subjects who held an extreme dry position rated it much wetter than did the moderates (contrast). The extreme dry subjects judged the moderate communication as much dryer than did the moderate subjects; subjects who held an extreme dry position rated it much wetter than did the moderates. In fact, the extreme dry subjects judged the moderate communication to be a wet communication, despite the fact that it was, by any objective criterion, not at all extreme. This is shown in Figure 9–5.

fear arousal

Arousing fear is one of the most natural ways of trying to convince someone of something. A mother tells her young son that he will be run over if he crosses the street without her. Religious leaders frighten their followers with threats of eternal damnation and suffering. Political philosophers and candidates warn that if their opponents are elected, the country will be ruined, people will starve, and civilization will collapse. Advocates of population control warn of mass starvation; environmentalists warn of mass lung disease, skin cancer, DDT in our vital organs, dying fish in our polluted oceans, lakes, and streams; opponents of environmental improvements warn of rising tides of unemployment; others try to scare us into energy conservation by painting a fearsome picture of imminent energy shortages. Given a particular argument in favor of a position, how does the amount of fear aroused affect the success of the argument?

The original study in this area was conducted by Janis and Feshbach in 1953. They showed high school students a film that emphasized the importance of brushing one's teeth three times a day, after every meal. The film described the dangers of not doing this and explained the advantages of good dental care. High fear was aroused by showing pictures of badly decayed teeth and gums, closeups of diseased teeth, mouths in which the gums had pulled away from the teeth, and so on. In the mild-fear condition, subjects saw less dramatic and less frightening pictures. And in the no-fear, or control, condition, the subjects saw no pictures of diseased teeth. The subjects in the high-fear condition reported being more impressed by the presentation and agreeing with it more. However, a week later it was found that the subjects in the no-fear condition had changed their behavior more than had subjects either of the fear conditions. The authors concluded that the maximum effect was produced by the persuasive arguments without the fear-arousing slides.

This result has generally not been repeated in later experiments. Much of the work done in recent years has produced the opposite result. For example, a series of experiments conducted by Howard Leventhal at Yale University (Leventhal, Jones, and Trembly, 1966; Leventhal and Singer, 1966) have shown that the arousal of fear tends to facilitate both attitude and behavioral change. In one study (Dabbs and Leventhal, 1966), college students were urged to get inoculations for tetanus. The disease was described in detail—it was pointed out how serious it was, that it was often fatal, and that it was easy to catch. In addition, the students were told that the inoculation was extremely effective and that it gave almost complete protection against the disease.

The message was delivered under several different conditions of fear arousal. In the high-fear condition, the descriptions of the disease were extremely vivid, the symptoms were made very explicit, and everything was done to make the situation as frightening as possible. In the second condition, a moderate amount of fear was aroused; and in the third, very little. Students were then asked how important they thought it was to get the inoculation and whether or not they intended to get one. The university health service, which was nearby, recorded how many of the students went for inoculations during the next month.

The findings (Table 9–1) are straightforward and impressive. The greater the fear aroused, the more the subjects intended to get shots. Perhaps more important, higher fear induced more subjects actually to go to the health service and receive inoculations. Thus, fear arousal not only produced more attitude change, but also had a greater effect on the relevant behavior.

TABLE 9–1
effects of fear arousal on attitudes and behavior

CONDITION	INTENTION TO TAKE SHOTS[a]	PERCENTAGE TAKING SHOTS
High fear	5.17	22
Low fear	4.73	13
Control	4.12	6

[a]The figures are ratings on a scale from 1 (lowest) to 7 (highest).
Source: Adapted from Dabbs and Leventhal (1966).

Various other studies have used a wide range of issues, including automotive safety, atom bomb testing, fallout shelters, and dental hygiene, to study the effects of fear. Higbee (1969) has made quite a careful review of these many studies. He concludes that there is a predominant weight of evidence favoring the positive effect of fear. Only five studies clearly showed low fear having more effect (e.g., Janis and Feshbach, 1953; Janis and Terwilliger, 1962), whereas over twenty experiments conducted by a number of different experimenters have shown fear facilitating attitude change (e.g., Berkowitz and Cottingham, 1960;

Haefner, 1964; Insko, Arkoff, and Insko, 1965; Rogers and Thistlewaite, 1970; and the work by Leventhal). Harris and Jellison (1971) even showed that simply making subjects *think* they were more afraid increased persuasion. They used the false physiological feedback technique discussed in Chapter 4, telling some subjects they were very upset and others that they were less upset by a communication. The former

This Space Contributed by the Publisher

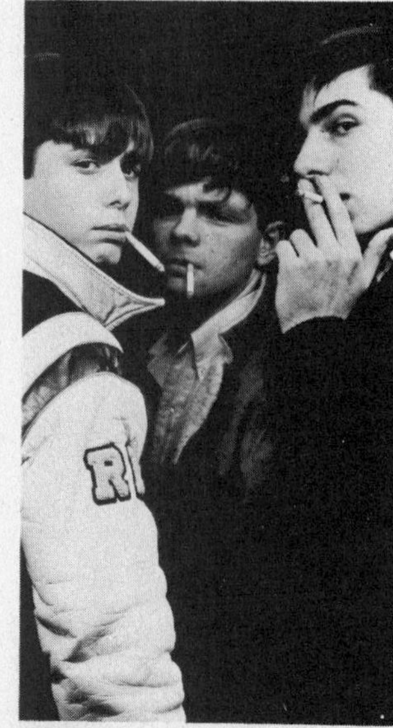

You cats have just one life. Why blow it?

Here's where it's at, baby. Cigarettes can kill you. Smoke enough and, chances are, they will. For real. For good. And forever. You've got just one life, pussycat. Why blow it?

american cancer society

actually changed their opinions more, even though everyone received the same message. Some studies, such as Dabbs and Leventhal (1966) and Evans et al. (1970), also indicated that high fear had a greater effect on relevant action, although the evidence for this is somewhat less consistent. From all of this research, it seems clear that under most circumstances fear arousal increases the effectiveness of a persuasive communication.

There may be some situations, however, in which fear does reduce the effectiveness of a communication. Janis has suggested that the relationship between fear and attitude change depends on the level of fear involved. He argued that at low levels, greater fear produces more attitude change, but that at some point the fear becomes too intense, arouses defensive mechanisms, and thereby produces less change. This would explain the seemingly contradictory results that have been found because the studies have involved different amounts of fear. For example, high fear normally has had its strongest persuasive effects in experiments on tetanus, which is a simply prevented disease and rarely scares people much. However, high fear arousal rarely is more successful than low fear arousal on lung cancer and smoking, probably because lung cancer causes too much fear and is too difficult for a lifelong smoker to prevent. Janis has reanalyzed a number of experiments in these terms, and although not all the data fit this model, most of the results appear to be consistent with it.

To sum up, the evidence indicates that under most circumstances arousing fear increases the effectiveness of persuasive communications. But arousing too much fear may be disruptive. Causing a person to be too frightened can make him either so paralyzed that he is unable to act or so threatened that he tends to deny the danger and reject the persuasive communication. Aside from such cases, however, it appears that fear-arousing arguments are more effective in producing attitude change than are arguments that arouse little or no fear.

the arousal of aggression

One interesting explanation of the effect of motivational arousal on attitude change concerns the appropriateness of the motive aroused. In most of the studies on fear arousal, the persuasive communication contains information about a real danger such as cancer, tetanus, or reckless driving. When fear of cancer is aroused by vivid pictures, the fear is appropriate because it is realistic to be afraid of cancer. Perhaps more important, the messages are urging the subjects to take steps that would reduce the danger and the fear. If one takes a tetanus inoculation, one is, in fact, less liable to get tetanus and should no longer fear the disease. In situations such as these, the arousal of fear is appropriate to the attitude-change situation, and therefore the arousal should increase susceptibility to the message.

A study by Weiss and Fine (1956) on the arousal of aggression is relevant to this explanation of the effect of motivation. Some subjects were put through an annoying, frustrating experience designed to make them feel aggressive. Other subjects had the opposite experience—they went through a pleasant, satisfying experience. Then, both groups were exposed to a persuasive communication that took either a lenient or a punitive attitude toward juvenile delinquency. Thus, the experiment exposed aggressive and nonaggressive subjects to lenient or punitive persuasive communications.

The experimenters hypothesized that the subjects who had been made to feel aggressive would be more likely to accept the punitive communication than the lenient one and that the nonaggressive subjects would be more likely to accept the lenient communication. The rationale was that the punitive message would satisfy the motivational needs of the aggressive subjects by providing them with a way of displacing their aggression. The lenient message would be more likely to satisfy the relatively nonaggressive needs of the other subjects. The results were in line with these expectations—the aggressive subjects were more influenced by the punitive communication, and the nonaggressive subjects were more influenced by the lenient one. We have already seen in Chapter 6 how people displace aggression to new targets when the original

Michael D. Sullivan

source of frustration is too anxiety arousing or unavailable. This experiment suggests that displaced aggression occurs in our attitudes as well as in our behavior, but it requires an appropriate new target, one that is a natural channel for the expression of aggressive impulses.

characteristics of the target

Even after a message from a particular source has reached the target, the problems of attitude change are not over. Various characteristics of individual personality and factors in immediate and past experience are important determinants of reaction to the message. These factors affect primarily the tendency to trust the message or its source, the ability to argue against the message, the motivation not to change an opinion, and the confidence in one's own position.

commitment

Another important aspect of the attitude-change situation is the strength of the target's commitment to an attitude. Two of the many factors that affect the strength of commitment are action taken on the basis of the attitude and public statement of the attitude. If a person has just bought a house, she is more committed to the belief that it is a fine house than if she had not yet bought it. Changing her opinion of the house has broader implications for her if she owns it than if she is only thinking about buying it. Someone who has just stated on television that he thinks smoking is bad for health and is an evil, dirty habit is more committed to this attitude than if he had made these statements only to his wife or had kept them to himself. Changing his attitude is harder if he expressed it on television, because then the change would involve publicly admitting he was wrong. Whenever changing an attitude would cause the individual to give up more, suffer more, or change more of his other attitudes or behaviors, his commitment to his initial attitude increases and makes it more difficult for him to change it.

In addition, it appears that freely choosing a position produces a greater feeling of commitment than being forced. In a study on this problem (Freedman and Steinbruner, 1964), subjects were given information about a candidate for graduate school and asked to rate him, under circumstances of either high or low choice. The subjects were made to feel either that they had made up their own minds and freely selected the particular rating or that they had virtually nothing to do with the decision and had been forced to select the rating. The subjects were then exposed to information that strongly contradicted their initial rating and were allowed to change their rating if they desired. Those who had made the first rating with a feeling of free choice changed less than did those in the low-choice condition.

A fourth factor affecting commitment is the extent to which the attitude is imbedded in other behaviors and attitudes. Someone in favor of fluoridation of drinking water may feel very strongly about it, but this attitude probably stands by itself to a large extent. Most people have taken no action related to fluoridation and have few attitudes related directly to it. Changing their attitude toward it from favorable to unfavorable would involve relatively few other changes in their cognitive systems. This is not so for a dentist who has been fighting tooth decay for years, who has been coating teeth with fluorides, who has donated money to fluoridation campaigns, and who has read extensive literature supporting fluoridation. Changing his opinion about it would involve many contradictions, inconsistencies, and changes in his cognitive and behavioral system. Thus, he is more committed to his attitude and would find it harder to change.

The effect of commitment of this kind is to reduce the amount of attitude change produced by a persuasive communication. Greater commitment makes it harder for the individual to change his attitude and means that he is more likely to use other modes of resolution instead.

The joint effects of commitment and discrepancy on attitude change are similar to those of credibility and discrepancy. As described previously, the credibility of the source does not change the relationship between discrepancy and attitude change but does affect the point at which maximum change occurs—the higher the credibility the greater the discrepancy at which there is maximum attitude change. Commitment to an initial position also shifts the maximum point, but in the opposite direction. The harder it is to change position, the lower the discrepancy at which rejection of the source is easier than change. Therefore, the greater the commitment, the lower the discrepancy at which maximum attitude change occurs (Rhine and Severance, 1970).

inoculation and support

Another source of resistance to change in the target comes from past experience with the issue. William McGuire and his associates conducted a series of experiments on the effects of giving people experiences designed to increase their ability to resist persuasion. McGuire has used a medical analogy to describe the influence situation. He pictured the individual faced with a discrepant communication as being similar to somebody being attacked by a virus or a disease. The stronger the persuasive message (virus), the more damage it would do; the stronger the person's defenses, the better able he is to resist persuasion (disease). There are two different ways of strengthening someone's defense against a disease. We can strengthen his body generally, by giving him vitamins, exercise, and so on; or we can strengthen his defenses against that particular disease by building up antibodies. McGuire argued that these two approaches are also applicable to the influence situation.

To begin with, he identified a number of *cultural truisms*—opinions so universally held in our society that they are almost never subjected to any kind of attack. One example is the belief that it is good to brush one's teeth after every meal. Probably almost everybody in the United States believes that this is basically a good idea in terms of dental health. And most people have never heard anything to the contrary. Thus, someone holding this opinion is analogous to an individual who has never been exposed to the smallpox germ. He has never been forced to defend himself from attack so has never built up any defenses against attack.

One procedure that strengthens resistance is to build up the person's opinion directly, by giving the individual additional arguments supporting his original position. If he believes that it is good to brush his teeth three times a day, he is shown a study by the United States Public Health Service which shows that people who do so have fewer cavities than those who brush their teeth less often or not at all. Giving individuals this kind of support for their position does, in fact, increase their resistance to a subsequent persuasive communication. Thus, one way of increasing somebody's resistance to persuasion is simply to give him more reasons for believing what he already does. This gives him more ammunition to use in the coming argument, and he therefore changes his opinion less.

A different approach is to strengthen the individual's defenses against persuasion rather than to strengthen his opinion. McGuire has argued that, as with diseases, the most effective way of increasing resistance is to build up defenses. If a person is given a mild case of smallpox that he is able to fight off, his body produces antibodies, which in the future provide an effective and strong defense against more powerful attacks of smallpox. Similarly, if a particular opinion has never been attacked, it is extremely vulnerable because no defenses have been built up around it. When such an opinion is suddenly and surprisingly subjected to persuasive pressure, the individual does not have a set of defenses immediately available, and the opinion tends to be relatively easy to change. However, if the opinion has been attacked and the individual has successfully defended himself, he should be better able to resist subsequent attacks because he has built up a relatively strong defensive system around that opinion. In other words, McGuire argued that it is possible to inoculate individuals against persuasive attacks just as we can inoculate them against diseases.

This is accomplished by weakly attacking the individual's attitude. The attack must be weak or it would change his attitude and the battle would be lost. To be certain that this does not occur, the target is helped to defend himself against the mild attack. He is given an argument directed specifically at the attack or is told that the attack is not very good and he should be able to refute it.

One study by McGuire and Papageorgis (1961) used both the supportive and inoculation methods to build up defenses. There were three groups of subjects: one group received support for their position; one group had their position attacked weakly and the attack refuted (the inoculation condition); and the third group received neither of these procedures. Afterward, all groups were subjected to a strong attack on their initial position. Table 9–2 shows how much each group changed as a result of the attack. It is clear that the supportive method helped subjects resist persuasion—the group receiving support changed less than the group that had no preparation. But the inoculation method helped even more; subjects receiving this preparation changed least of all.

TABLE 9–2
support, inoculation, and resistance to persuasion

CONDITION	AMOUNT OF ATTITUDE CHANGE
Support	5.87
Inoculation	2.94
Neither	6.62

Source: Adapted from McGuire and Papageorgis (1961).

Later research has shown that support tends to be particularly effective when the subsequent attack contains arguments similar to the content of the supporting arguments, but it is relatively ineffective when new arguments are used. In contrast, inoculation is effective even when the attack includes new arguments.

The specific mechanism by which inoculation operates is not yet clear. It may be that in refuting the mild attack, the individual uses and therefore exercises all his defenses. He prepares arguments supporting his own position, constructs counterarguments against the opposing position, derogates the possible sources of opposing views, and so on. This would make each of the defensive mechanisms stronger and would provide the individual with a generally more effective position.

Another explanation is that giving the target a counterargument or telling him that the original argument is not good strikes at the reliability and credibility of the source of the discrepant communication. Showing an individual an argument against his position and then telling him that this argument is all wrong is the standard technique of setting up a straw man and then knocking it down. This probably serves to make anyone who takes the other side seem somewhat foolish, misguided, and ignorant. The person is told, in effect, that these are the stupid kinds of arguments that some people have put forth against a commonly held idea. Then, when he comes across another argument against the position, even if he is not capable of refuting it himself, he may assume that it is just as stupid as the first argument and therefore may not be influenced by it. Thus, the refutation serves as an attack on the source of any discrepant message and is effective even when subsequent messages have different content. The opposition has been made to look unreliable; anything they say is suspect and unpersuasive.

personality factors

Some people are generally more persuasible than others, regardless of the issue involved or the type of influence being attempted. Experiments have been conducted (Hovland and Janis, 1959) in which subjects were exposed to persuasive communications on a variety of issues with different types of appeals and arguments and in different attitude-change situations. They indicated that the subjects who were highly persuasible under one set of conditions tended to be highly persuasible under others. The effect is not very strong; it explains only a small percentage of the total variance. But considering the diversity of the situations and issues studied, the consistency found offers convincing support for the existence of the trait of general persuasibility. However, relatively little is known about the specific sources of this trait. Quite a number of personality characteristics have been suggested as affecting persuasibility, but only a few of these suggestions have been supported by the data.

SELF-ESTEEM One fairly consistent finding has been that subjects with low self-esteem tend to be more persuasible than those with high self-esteem. The variable has been defined in various ways by different experimenters. Low self-esteem has been considered to entail feelings of inadequacy, social inhibitions, social anxiety, and test anxiety. Self-esteem has also been defined as the discrepancy between the ideal and the actual self, with greater discrepancies indicating lower self-esteem. Although the actual measures have varied somewhat, the basic notion has been similar. Self-esteem is defined implicitly or explicitly as the worth the person places on himself or how much the person esteems himself.

The traditional explanation of the relationship between self-esteem and persuasibility is that low self-esteem people place a low value on their opinions just as they do on everything else about themselves. Since they do not value their own opinions, they are less reluctant to give them up and are more likely to change them when they are attacked. McGuire (1969) has added one complexity to this theory. Although he grants that low self-esteem should be related to acceptance of a message, he hypothesizes that it will at the same time be negatively related to comprehension of the message. Thus a low self-esteem person may be quite gullible, accept almost anything someone tells him, and thus be likely to show a great deal of attitude change. However, he may at the same time have trouble understanding complex communications, frequently miss the point of their arguments, and, as a result, show reduced attitude change.

This hypothesis has been tested most directly by Zellner (1970). She reasoned that low self-esteem should be strongly related to influence in very simple situations where the subject would have no trouble understanding the point advocated, whereas it would be negatively related to influence in complex situations, where the low self-esteem subject's gullibility would be of little help, since he would have trouble understanding the communication. She tested the effects of self-esteem on influence in three situations ranging from simple to complex. In the simple ("suggestion") situation, the subject was required to write out the message in a sentence repeatedly; in the moderate ("conformity") situation, the message consisted of four "facts" in a list of fifteen "facts" the subject was supposed to learn; in the complex ("persuasion") situation, the messages were complex essays. As expected, the data showed that low self-esteem was positively related to influence in the simple situation, while the reverse held in the complex situation. This provided support for the hypothesis that self-esteem affects persuasibility both by affecting the tendency to accept influence, and by affecting comprehension of the communication.

INTELLIGENCE One factor that has often been said to affect persuasibility is intelligence. It has seemed likely to many people that individuals with high intelligence would be less persuasible than those with lower intelligence. However, research has not supported this assumption; there is no evidence that level of intelligence is consistently related to degree of persuasibility. On the average, people of high intelligence are persuaded just as much as people of low intelligence.

Although intelligence has no overall effect on persuasibility, there is reason to believe that it does have some effect on the kinds of persuasive appeals that are most effective. People of high intelligence are influenced less by inconsistent and illogical arguments than are people of lower intelligence, and the latter may be influenced less by complex, difficult arguments. Some evidence for this was provided in work on the relative effectiveness of stating or not stating a conclusion. The research suggested that stating the conclusion was more effective for relatively uninformed and less intelligent audiences and not stating the conclusion was more effective for relatively informed and intelligent audiences. It is important to note that the lack of an overall correlation between intelligence and persuasibility does not necessarily mean that intelligence is entirely unrelated to the influence process. Rather, it indicates that the relationship is complex and that level of intelligence affects how much the individual is influenced in any given situation.

DEFENSIVE STYLES One of the explanations offered for the effect of self-esteem on persuasibility is in terms of the types of defenses used by different people, specifically, that people of high self-esteem tend to deny or forget unpleasant information, whereas people of lower self-esteem do this to a lesser extent. Whether or not this is a sufficient explanation of the effect of self-esteem, the kind of defensive process an individual uses to protect himself from negative information does determine to some extent how much he is influenced by a particular persuasive attempt.

Some theorists have treated people's defenses against persuasion in the same vein as their defenses against their own unacceptable impulses; i.e., as being similar to the ego defense mechanisms Freud (1936) and others have written about. These defenses do not attempt to attack or weaken the content of the communication but, rather, to protect the individual's opinion in less logical but nevertheless often extremely effective ways. For example, a white person might protect his strong "law and order" attitude by projecting his own unconscious hostilities onto blacks, and then advocating a hard line against criminals to save us from these vicious people.

People differ considerably in the extent to which they rely on such defense mechanisms. Katz, Sarnoff, and McClintock (1956) investigated the effect of defenses on reactions to persuasive communications. They divided the subjects into those who relied heavily and those who relied less heavily on defense mechanisms (high-and low-defense users). They then presented two kinds of persuasive communications dealing with prejudice against blacks. One message, which they called an information appeal, contained a variety of facts about blacks and whites, all of which

De Wys/Bill Grimes

were designed to show that prejudice was not based on sound reasoning. The other message, which they called the insight appeal, described the psychodynamic relationship between defense mechanisms and prejudice. It attempted to communicate the unhealthy personality dynamics underlying racial prejudice.

The results showed that the high- and low-defense users responded quite differently to the two appeals. The highly defensive subjects were hardly affected by the insight appeal and were more influenced by the information appeal; those who used defense mechanisms relatively little were more influenced by the insight appeal. The authors explained these results by saying that the high-defense subjects strongly resisted the attack on their defensive mechanisms, whereas the low-defense subjects were relatively open to this kind of attack.

Other experiments, principally by Sarnoff, have shown that the specific defense mechanism a person tends to use may determine to some extent how much he is influenced by a given appeal. In order to be maximally effective, an appeal should attack a weak defense and should be designed not to arouse defenses that are favored and strong. If someone tends to deny or ignore negative information, the appeal should attempt to introduce the information in a subtle way so that the target is exposed to it before he can put the mechanism of denial into operation. On the other hand, if he does not use denial but tends to argue against persuasive messages, it is important to concentrate on the strength of the attack and not to worry too much about how it is presented. Knowledge of the kinds of defensive mechanisms a person tends to use should enable the communicator to concentrate on avoiding the target's strongest defenses and attacking his weakest.

In summary, relatively little is known about the effect of personality on persuasibility. We know that some people are generally more persuasible than others, and we are fairly sure of a number of personality traits that affect this trait. Other than the evidence for the few factors that have been mentioned, however, there is little to support hypotheses about how other aspects of personality affect persuasibility. There have been many suggestions (e.g., authoritarianism, richness of fantasy), but the evidence for any of these is rather weak at the moment. We are therefore left with few solid findings except consistent evidence that personality does affect persuasibility. A detailed specification of which dimensions of personality are most important is not yet possible.

situational factors

The factors described thus far are concerned solely with the communicator, his message, and the target. Yet mass communications usually are delivered within a broader context in which other things are happening, and these also often prove to have decisive effects upon the success of persuasion attempts. Let us now consider some of the most important situational variables in an attitude change setting.

forewarned is forearmed

If someone is told ahead of time that he is going to be exposed to a discrepant communication on an issue he cares strongly about, he is better able to resist persuasion by that message. In a study by Freedman and Sears (1965), teenagers were told ten minutes beforehand that they were going to hear a talk titled "Why Teenagers Should Not Be Allowed to Drive." Other teenagers were not told about the talk until just before the speaker began. Thus, one group had a ten-minute warning and the other group had no warning at all. Under these circumstances, those who had the warning were less influenced by the talk than were the others. In some way, the warning enabled them to resist this very unpalatable message better. Dean, Austin, and Watts (1971) found a similar though somewhat weaker effect.

This is certainly a plausible finding, and it seems to be believed by many people in the business of persuasion. For example, we often hear an advertisement on radio or television with no warning that this is going

Rothco/Punch

to be an advertisement. Instead, the station sneaks in the ad before we are fully aware of what it is. A similar, although more altruistic example is the dentist who warns us that something is going to hurt. He seems to feel that we will be better able to withstand the pain if we are warned. In fact, there is some experimental evidence that subjects who are warned ahead of time that they are going to receive an electric shock report that it hurts less than subjects who are not warned.

All this sounds plausible and reasonable, but why does it occur? Why does a ten-minute warning help people resist persuasion? It is important to keep in mind that all the subjects know that the speaker disagrees with them—the only difference is that some people know it ten minutes ahead of time and others know it only just before the speech. The greater resistance shown by those with the longer warning is due to some process, some mechanism that goes on during those ten minutes between the warning and the speech. And most likely, as with the inoculation procedure, the individual's defenses are in some way exercised or strengthened.

Although there is little evidence that directly demonstrates how these defenses are strengthened, we can cite those that the individual probably indulges in. In marshalling and strengthening his defenses, he employs all the defensive maneuvers and tactics we discussed previously. He constructs arguments supporting his own position and attempts to refute the arguments that may come from the opponent. In the warning experiment, the teenagers probably say to themselves, "The message is going to present arguments against teenage driving. It will probably say that teenagers don't drive as well as adults. Well, that's not true. I know teenagers drive better, so that's a bad argument." The teenagers would also think about arguments in favor of teenage driving, such as "Old enough to fight, old enough to vote and drive." They would also employ derogation of the discrepant source. As discussed above, the person who has been through the inoculation procedure has ample opportunity to derogate the opponent. Similarly, the forewarned person has ten minutes to convince himself that the communicator is unreliable, prejudiced, and misinformed.

In other words, the individual who is warned (or who, in the inoculation situation, has just experienced a mild attack) is like a fighter who has prepared for a match. He has been through training, so when the fight comes, he is in better shape and better able to meet his opponent. He also spends time convincing himself that his opponent is not very good and that he, himself, is great. This makes him more confident and better able to fight his best.

When the listener is not very committed to his initial position, though, forewarning turns out to have the opposite effect—it actually helps to precipitate attitude change. When the person is unlikely from the start to cling very tightly to his original attitude, the forewarning seems to operate as a cue to propel him along the road he was destined for sooner or later anyhow. For example, Apsler and Sears (1968) hypothesized that forewarning would facilitate attitude change among subjects who were not personally involved in the topic, whereas it would help block it among highly involved subjects. They gave subjects a persuasive communication advocating replacement of professors by teaching assistants in many upper division courses, a change opposed by almost all subjects. Some subjects were told the change would come quickly, in time to affect their own education (high involvement); others were told it was several years off and would not affect them (low involvement). Forewarning helped block change among the highly involved subjects, just as it had among the teenagers who were highly involved in the issue of teenage driving in the Freedman and Sears experiment. However, it facilitated change in the low-involvement condition. This is shown in Table 9–3.

TABLE 9–3
attitude change as a result of warning and low involvement

CONDITION	MEAN ATTITUDE CHANGE		
	High involvement	Low involvement	Total
Warning	1.5	2.4	1.9
No warning	1.8	0.7	1.2
Effects of warning	−0.3	1.7	

Note.—$n = 20$ in each cell. The larger the score, the greater the amount of change in the advocated direction on a 16-point scale.
Source: Apsler & Sears (1968), p. 164.

These two effects of forewarning frequently can be detected even before the subject receives the communication. The highly committed person seems to begin to resist even before he is exposed to the forthcoming communication, while the uncommitted person seems to moderate his stand. In one experiment, subjects highly committed to their initial position became more extreme (and presumably more resistant to change) when forewarned of a forthcoming debate, while weakly committed subjects became more moderate (and presumably more receptive to change) while anticipating the debate (Sears, Freedman, and O'Connor, 1964). Cooper and Jones (1970) have shown that these anticipatory changes are due to the subjects' expectations of exposure to the communications and their likely effects, rather than just to the knowledge of their existence. Weakly committed subjects changed when forewarned of forthcoming exposure to the communication, but not when merely told that such a communication existed without any implication of forthcoming exposure. And Cialdini, Levy, Herman, and Evenbeck (1973) found that forewarning moderated subjects' opinions when they expected to discuss the issue personally with the speaker, but not when they merely expected to listen to him. Presumably those who anticipated discussion wanted to stake out a moderate position until they could see how the other person would feel about them.

The most popular explanations for these effects of forewarning are twofold. In cases where forewarning increases resistance to change, most researchers assume that the subject begins generating counterarguments, or rejecting the forthcoming position, prior to actual exposure. Some of these cases of anticipatory attitude change seem to be accounted for by the assumption that weakly committed subjects have little resistance to change, and if they anticipate powerful arguments, nothing restrains them from granting the point from the start. In other cases it appears that subjects are more motivated to resist change, but are worried about their ability to stand up to counterarguments. They therefore tend to change in advance so they will not have to go through the embarrassment and loss of self-esteem of knuckling under later on. Anticipatory change allows them to maintain a positive self-concept.

We do not mean to give the impression that all these maneuvers are done deliberately. Especially in the forewarned situation, most people probably do not decide to strengthen their defenses. There is no evidence that they worry about the coming attack, feverishly preparing themselves either to defend their positions to the death, or give them up quietly and gracefully. Rather, they tend to think about the issue a little, go over some of the points in their minds, and in this way prepare for exposure. As far as we know, the process is all quite casual and almost accidental. But the effects are clear.

distraction

In parts of our discussion, we have described the individual as actively fighting the persuasive message. Although he may sometimes be quite passive, the person whose opinions are attacked usually tries to resist changing. He counterargues, derogates the communicator, and generally marshals all his forces to defend his own position. One important implication of this is that the ability to resist persuasion is weakened by anything that makes it harder for the individual to fight the discrepant communication. In particular, distracting his attention from the battle may enable the persuasive message to get through without being fought.

A study by Festinger and Maccoby (1964) demonstrated this effect of distraction. Subjects listened to a speech against fraternities while watching a film. For some of the subjects, the film showed the person making the speech. For others, the film was "The Day of the Painter," a funny, somewhat zany satire on modern art. Presumably, those watching the irrelevant film were more distracted from the antifraternity speech than were those watching the person speak. Subjects who initially disagreed with the speech (who were in favor of fraternities) were more influenced in the distraction than the nondistraction condition. Taking the subjects' minds off the speech increased its effectiveness.

There is some debate about how reliable this finding is, and about the mechanism that is responsible for it, if it is reliable. As indicated in a review of several subsequent studies, the results have been quite mixed, with as many failing to find distraction advancing attitude change as those finding it doing so (Osterhouse and Brock, 1970). It seems to occur primarily when the subjects are initially strongly opposed to the position being advocated, when they are quite familiar with the topic, when they attend to the distraction rather than to the message (Zimbardo, Snyder, and Gurwitz, 1970), and when they have the opportunity to develop counterarguments in the absence of the distraction. Consequently, Osterhouse and Brock (1970) have argued that when distraction works, it does so by blocking a subvocal process of developing counterarguments. So far the evidence on this point is mainly inferential, since no one has yet devised a technique for directly measuring subvocal arguing.

In any case, the effect logically must depend on the right amount of distraction. As usual, there is a conflict between getting the message through and getting it accepted. Obviously, too much distraction prevents the persuasive message from being heard at all and reduces its effectiveness to zero. Advertisers may want to distract television viewers from the main point of commercials by having irrelevant pictures and action going on during the speech. They do not, however, want to have the irrelevancies so fascinating or interfering that the message is lost. Having a beautiful girl in the background during a soap commercial may help sell soap; having her in the foreground may even help; but having her in the foreground singing so loud that the commercial can barely be heard would certainly reduce the effectiveness of the ad. Thus, the effect of distraction may work under limited conditions, but is is important that the distraction be not too great or the effect will be reversed.

the effect of reinforcement—"things go better with coke"

Much of our discussion has been influenced by the reinforcement or incentive approach to attitude change. One of the basic ideas of this approach is that an attitude-change situation consists of an interplay of forces—some pushing the individual to change his attitude and some pulling him back to his initial position. All the arguments in the persuasive communication are, in a sense, a motivation for changing his opinion or approaching the new position. On the other hand, all the reasons he initially had for maintaining his own position are reasons for continuing to maintain it and for avoiding the new position. Under these circumstances, anything that associates additional incentive with either position should affect the outcome.

This argument suggests that associating the persuasive message with some reinforcing stimulus increases the effectiveness of the message. A simpler line of reasoning is that the more positive the persuasive message is seen to be, the more effect it has, and reinforcement simply makes the message more positive. Whatever the rationale for the prediction, conceptualizing the situation in terms of approach-avoidance and positive and negative reinforcements does suggest this effect.

The advertising industry and political campaigners have been acting on this assumption for some time. Television commercials are one example. They have recently been referred to as "one-minute movies," because they are so elaborate and so much care goes into making them as attractive and even enjoyable as possible. We are not simply shown a sleek car and told how powerful, quiet, and comfortable it is. Rather, while the message is being delivered, we are shown beautiful women, handsome men, and lovely children, with perhaps a couple of graceful horses or cute dogs cavorting around. The car may be endorsed by a famous athlete or movie star. Presumably, all this beauty, fame, and popularity are reinforcing. The reinforcement becomes associated with the message, which is asking us to buy the car, and with the car itself. The hope is that the reinforcement will increase our positive feelings toward the car and thus increase the likelihood that we will buy it.

Research has provided some support for this widespread idea. Subjects were presented with a persuasive communication in the usual manner, but some subjects were given an extraneous reward whereas others were not given the reward. For example, while reading a persuasive communication on foreign aid, some subjects were given a Pepsi Cola to drink and others were not given anything (Janis et al., 1965). In this study, the reward, or positive stimulus, had nothing to do with the content of the persuasive message or the issue itself. Nevertheless, the subjects receiving a reward tended to be influenced more than those who did not receive a reward.

One possible alternative interpretation of this finding is that the reward acted primarily to make the subjects feel more positive toward the experimenter and the experimental situation as a whole. Or, it may simply have put them in a better mood, which would probably have had the effect of making the subjects feel positive toward everything and therefore less likely to disagree with the persuasive communication—

particularly when the communication came directly or indirectly from the experimenter. In other words, it may have been simply a halo effect. This explanation is considerably less interesting than that involving reinforcement theory, which implies that the subject is actually more influenced, but at the moment it is difficult to choose between the two. We do know that giving a reward increases the amount of agreement with the persuasive communication, but the specific mechanism behind this effect is as yet somewhat unclear.

Thus, many factors affect attitude change primarily by increasing the trust in the communication, by strengthening the persuasive message, and, in general, by determining how much the individual believes what is being said. An attempt to influence someone's opinion need not, however, be done in an entirely logical, unemotional, cognitive situation. The situation may, and often does, involve strong motivations, appeals to deep-seated needs, and a great many factors that are extraneous to the logical arguments contained in the message itself. An entirely rational, cognitive person would be influenced only to the extent that the arguments presented were logically sound. But since there are few, if any entirely rational beings, motivational and emotional factors are also important in determining the effectiveness of a persuasive communication.

SUMMARY

1. A useful model of the attitude-change situation classifies possible influences upon the target in terms of communicator, communication, situational, and target variables.

2. The major mechanisms by which people resist persuasion include refutation of the communicator's arguments, simple blanket rejection of the message, derogating the communicator, and distorting the message.

3. The target's evaluation of the source of the communication is one of the most critical factors in the success of a persuasion attempt. More attitude change is likely if the source is viewed as credible, trustworthy, and/or is generally liked by the target.

4. A reference group with which the target identifies is another potent source of influence.

5. The most important aspect of the communication is how far its position differs from that already held by the target; that is, its discrepancy. The more discrepant the communication is, the more influence it has – up to a point, when it starts to fall off again. The point at which it falls off depends on source credibility and the target's commitment to this initial opinion. With high credibility and/or low commitment, the fall-off point occurs at higher levels of discrepancy.

6. Generally speaking, attitude change increases with greater fear arousal. But at very high levels of fear, when the message becomes too threatening or disruptive for the person, fear-arousing communications may become ineffective.

7. The degree of commitment to an opinion is a critical determinant of persuasion. With higher commitment, there is less persuasion.

8. A person can become inoculated against persuasion by being exposed to weak versions of the forthcoming persuasive arguments, and learning to combat them.

9. Forewarning of the position to be advocated tends to increase resistance to change when the listener is highly committed to a very discrepant position. But with weak commitment, forewarning can help to get the persuasion process started, and attitude change occurs even before the full communication is heard.

10. Distraction can help create persuasion by reducing the listener's defenses against very discrepant messages.

SUGGESTIONS FOR ADDITIONAL READING

ABELSON, R. P. Modes of resolution of belief dilemmas. *Journal of Conflict Resolution*, 1959, 343–352. An imaginative and speculative essay on the dynamics of cognitive reorganization as a response to inconsistency.

BOCHNER, S., & INSKO, C. Communicator discrepancy, source credibility, and opinion change. *Journal of Personality and Social Psychology*, 1966, 4, 614–621. A well-designed experiment showing the effects of varying discrepancy and credibility.

HOVLAND, C. I., HARVEY, O. J., & SHERIF, M. Assimilation and contrast effects in communication and attitude change. *Journal of abnormal and social psychology*, 1957, 55, 242–252. The classic study showing both attitude change and perceptual distortion, given high ego involvement and varying levels of discrepancy.

HOVLAND, C. I., JANIS, I. L. & KELLEY, H. H. *Communication and persuasion*. New Haven, Conn.: Yale University Press, 1953. The original presentation of the best program in experimental studies of attitude change. Much of the rest of the work described in this chapter springs from work originally presented here.

LEVENTHAL, H. & NILES, P. A field experiment on fear arousal with data on the validity of questionnaire responses. *Journal of Personality*, 1964, 32, 459–479. An ingeniously designed, realistic field experiment conducted at the New York City Health Exposition, on the effects of fear arousal regarding smoking and lung cancer.

MCGUIRE, W. J. The nature of attitudes and attitude change. In G. Lindzey & E. Aronson (Eds.), *Handbook of social psychology*, Vol. III., Reading, Mass.: Addison-Wesley, 1969. Pp. 136–314. The most complete review of attitude research and theory that has been written. Although published some years ago, it is still fairly up-to-date.

McGuire, W. J., & Papageorgis, D. The relative efficacy of various types of prior belief-defense in producing immunity against persuasion. *Journal of Abnormal and Social Psychology*, 1961, 62, 327–37. An early "immunization" paper; this research was inspired by reports of "brainwashing" by the Chinese Communists during the Korean War.

Triandis, H. C. *Attitude and attitude change.* New York: John Wiley, 1971. A concise and direct treatment of experimental research on attitude change, reasonably up-to-date.

10 attitude change in the real world

media campaigns in the real world
- the case of television news

obstacles to attitude change
- communication interferences
- resistance to persuasion

the development of attitudes
- selectivity
- parental influence
- peer influence
- cognitive consistency in everyday life

overcoming obstacles to change
- attitude change versus behavior change

summary

suggestions for additional reading

Hovland pointed out (1959) that the success of persuasion depends in part on whether it is attempted in an experimental laboratory or in the real world. In the controlled environment of a psychologist's laboratory, it is generally easy to change attitudes. Even a simple written essay can produce changes in attitudes toward foreign aid, atomic submarines, tuition rates in college, brushing teeth, cancer and cigarettes, the quality of a poem, and so on. A subject reads or hears a communication, is asked to state his own belief, and tends to agree with the communication more after he reads or hears it than he did before (or than does a control group that did not read or hear it). In contrast, attempts to change people's attitudes in the world outside the laboratory tend to be quite unsuccessful. Advertisers, politicians, and other propagandists know this, or at least should know this. This chapter is concerned with these attempts. Most of its examples are from the world of politics, because that is where the best research has been done. But the same principles should hold for any other area of life as well—race relations, religion, health, advertising, education, or wherever people are trying to persuade others.

media campaigns in the real world

In general, campaigns conducted through the mass media are not successful in producing mass changes in attitudes. There are some exceptions. A high-powered, clever advertising campaign built around a grammatical error ("*like* a cigarette should") catapulted Winston cigarettes from a small seller to the most popular cigarette in the United States. Similarly, Crest toothpaste (which did have something substantial to offer in the way of protection from decay) became one of the largest sellers after its introduction. Occasionally, a person who is virtually unknown at the beginning of a political campaign can win the election by virtue of intensive advertising and face-to-face contacts. Remember "Jimmy who?" He became President Carter.

In spite of these exceptions, it is usually extremely difficult in a short period of time to produce any sizable change in people's opinions on any issue they really care about and are involved in. Most Americans know after the nominating conventions how they are going to vote in the presidential election in November, and the tens of millions of dollars spent during the intervening months does not produce much change. The results of surveys of American elections are shown in Table 10–1. The data show that the way a person says he is going to vote early in the campaign is a good predictor of how he actually does vote in November.

TABLE 10–1
changes in party preferences during election campaign

YEAR OF SURVEY	FIRST POLL	LAST POLL	PERCENTAGE OF CHANGE
1940	May	November	8[a]
1948	June	August	8[b]
	August	October	3[b]
1960	August	November	7[c]
1964	August	November	10[c]

Sources:
[a]Lazarsfeld, Berelson, and Gaudet (1948, pp. 65–66).
[b]Berelson, Lazarsfeld, and McPhee (1954, p. 23).
[c]Benham (1965).

Only 7 to 10 percent of those surveyed changed parties during the campaigns. True, those who have not decided in May may be influenced by a campaign, but these people did not yet have an opinion. The campaign, therefore, did not change an opinion—it *produced* one, which is quite a different matter. Of course, because the undecided votes often decide an election, the campaign can be extremely important. The 8 percent who do change their opinion can be decisive if more of them change in one direction than in the other. Nevertheless, the data indicate how difficult it is to change the opinion of those who have already made a decision.

There are other, similar, examples. Among the big media events in recent years have been televised debates between the major presidential candidates. In 1960 there were four televised debates between John F. Kennedy and Richard M. Nixon, each covered live, and whole, by all three major TV networks. Audience studies revealed that 55 percent of the adult population watched all four debates, and 80 percent watched at least one. Journalists widely ascribed Kennedy's narrow victory to his success in these debates. Yet careful survey research revealed that there were no substantial changes in vote preference (Kraus and Davis, 1976).

Other attempts at persuasion have had similarly meager effects. The campaigns to induce people to stop smoking are a case in point, at least in this country. There was a slight decrease in the amount of smoking immediately following each intensive antismoking campaign by the Public Health Service, but the changes evaporated quickly. In recent years the smoking rate has, if anything, been creeping upwards. Again, the National Safety Council's admonitions against unsafe driving and the warning that "The life you save may be your own" does not seem to have made people drive any more safely. The Johnson and Nixon Administrations tried everything they could think of to rally the American public behind the Vietnam War, only to see public support ebb away steadily through the late 1960's and early 1970's. Following the energy crisis of 1973–1974, caused by the Arab oil embargo, the government tried to keep public energy consumption down. But most indices of consumption (e.g., gasoline use) soared right back up again when the crisis was past. And let us not forget Richard Nixon's lack of success in trying to persuade that American public that he was "not a crook," despite his unprecendented access to prime television time to make his pitch.

Similarly, the so-called brainwashing that occurred during the Korean War turns out to be another failure to influence opinions. American prisoners were subjected to an intensive long-term campaign to make them give up their belief in American democracy and adopt the principles of Chinese communism. In this situation, the campaign did not have to fight counterpropaganda and the Chinese could do just about anything they wanted, since the soldiers were held captive. The situation was ideal for changing attitudes.

A great deal has been made of the fact that some Americans were influenced by this campaign and that a small number actually defected to Communist China. But in fact, the campaign was remarkably unsuccessful. A great many prisoners were subjected to this intensive campaign under ideal circumstances, but only a handful were influenced appreciably. Practically all the American soldiers—even the uneducated, unsophisticated, tired, weak, lonely, and perhaps not strongly pro-American ones—were able to resist the attempt to change their opinions.

Social and political commentators often express a good deal of anxiety about the possible incidental persuasive effects of information communicated to the public for ostensibly nonpersuasive reasons. For example, many worry about the effects of communicating the results of political polls to the public. As usual with such anxieties, they are not very specific about their actual predictions: some worry that polls will create a "bandwagon" sentiment that will make someone temporarily pacing the field into an insurmountably strong frontrunner, while others worry that an "underdog" sentiment will give an artificial boost to a candidate running behind. Again there is no evidence that either occurs; polls seem to have remarkably little effect on voter preferences (Mendelsohn and Crespi, 1970). The same kind of anxiety has been expressed about early televised projections of a candidate's victory or defeat on election day; when Walter Cronkite says, at 5 p.m. Pacific Time, that a given candidate is losing, that may inspire depressed apathy (or maybe frantic activity) among his potential supporters. Again it turns out, with careful research, that such broadcasts have remarkably little impact on anyone's voting behavior later in the day (Mendelsohn and Crespi, 1970).

To understand this seemingly consistent lack of persuasive impact in real life, let us start by looking in a little detail at one particular case, that of television news.

the case of television news

To many people, television seems to be a permanent bogeyman, constantly being blamed for every ill of contemporary American society. In recent years television has come under attack for, among other things, becoming the root source for Americans' lost faith and confidence in their government. Supposedly the TV coverage of the major news events of the late 1960s and 1970s—the ghetto and campus riots, the Vietnam war, the growth of the drug culture, the Watergate and sex scandals in Washington—was so critical of conventional American institutions and leaders that it caused the public to become cynical, to think nega-

De Wys

tively about politics and governments, to stop voting, and so on. Spiro Agnew complained about the "nattering nabobs of negativism" whom he imagined infested the network news staffs, and ultimately his complaints became echoed in academic journals under the label of "video-malaise" (M. Robinson, 1976). It was undeniable that Americans had become much more cynical and distrusting of the federal government (Miller, 1974; Citrin, 1974), and that fewer people were voting. But did television, and especially the dreaded nightly news programs, have anything to do with these changes?

First of all, it turned out that the audiences for those three nightly network news programs—Walter Cronkite, Chancellor-Brinkley, and Smith-Reasoner—were a bit smaller than most critics would have you believe. Actually only 23 percent of the adult (age 18 and above) population was watching one of those programs on an average weeknight, and most adults (53 percent) failed to watch even one such program in an average two-week span (J. Robinson, 1971). Even the watchers seem not to have been watching very carefully. In a telephone survey in the San Francisco Bay Area of people who had watched one of the shows earlier in the evening, Neuman (1976) found that people could recall, on the average, only 1.2 of the 19.8 stories covered in the average program. Memory improved when the interviewer ran down the list of headlines: another 4.4 stories were remembered with supporting details, and 4.3 without, but still half the stories were completely forgotten. In another national survey, J. Robinson (1972) found that people who watched TV news frequently were not significantly more familiar with the names of such public personalities as Ralph Nader, Martha Mitchell, and Bob Dylan than were people who never watched TV news at all. So far, scarcely an awesome impact.

A second assumption made by critics of television news was that the content of the programs was negative, critical, and disrespectful toward American leaders and institutions. A number of systematic content analyses were therefore done both of the TV news programs and, for contrast, of frontpage news coverage in the nation's major newspapers and of presidential candidates' TV ads. These content analyses turned up a couple of interesting findings. One is that TV news, at least during presidential campaigns, seems to spend a great deal more time on the hoopla of the campaign than it does on either the issues or the personal qualities of the candidates. Patterson and McClure (1976) found that during the period September 18 to November 6, 1972 (spanning the main campaign period), the three network evening news programs spent an average of 130 minutes on "the contest"—campaign strategy, rallies, motorcades, polls, and so forth; 14 minutes on the candidates' personal and leadership traits, and only 36 minutes on their stands on issues. As a result, regular viewers increased their knowledge of the candidates' policies scarcely more than nonviewers, as shown in Table 10–2.

TABLE 10–2
the impact of network news exposure on people's issue awareness during 1972 general election

	NONREGULAR VIEWERS OF NETWORK NEWS	REGULAR VIEWERS OF NETWORK NEWS
	%	%
Nixon policies:		
Vietnam war	4	11
Government spending	14	3
Military spending	27	36
Busing	35	35
China	38	32
Russia	25	28
Foreign commitments	37	50
Taxes on upper incomes	7	0
Law and order	2	− 6
Jobs for the unemployed	15	16
Amnesty	41	49
Drugs	8	7
McGovern policies:		
Military spending	63	58
Vietnam withdrawal	38	67
Amnesty	38	31
Political corruption	− 4	9
Taxes on upper incomes	14	40
Jobs for the unemployed	45	45
Average on all issues	25	28

Note: Figures represent percent increase or percent decrease (−) in people's issue information during the 1972 general election.
Source: Patterson & McClure, 1976, p. 50.

The other finding is that the TV news programs were, during this period, surprisingly positive about the candidates, and about government in general. Graber (1976) has shown that the commentary about both Nixon and McGovern on the TV news was overwhelmingly positive in the 1972 campaign, despite the fact that McGovern spent a good bit of his own campaign time attacking Nixon. She reports that the newspaper coverage of the campaign was substantially more negative. But Miller, Erbring, and Goldenberg (1976), who did a careful content analysis of frontpage news throughout the country during the 1974 congressional campaign, found that only 31 percent of the stories could be coded as critical of the government, the president, Congress, the parties, or various candidates, despite the fact that the campaign was run in the immediate aftermath of Watergate and Nixon's resignation. These content analyses seem to suggest that the alleged "negativism" of the TV news (and the press more generally) is considerably overstated by critics of the media.

So, if exposure to TV news is rather limited, and attention is somewhat disappointing, and if the content of the news is not so negative and destructive as often alleged, did watching it regularly make people more politically cynical and apathetic? Apparently not. In both 1968 and 1974, frequent exposure to TV news was, if anything, associated with *greater* feelings of political efficacy (the feeling that government is responsive to the individual citizen's needs and desires) and political trust (though in the latter case, the pattern was more complex for people with less-than-average levels of education). The same held true for reading the newspaper regularly (Miller et al, 1976). The only circumstance that seemed to support Agnew's concern about the "nattering nabobs" was that people did become more cynical if they regularly, in 1974, read one of the minority of newspapers that presented predominantly critical news. People who read them sporadically, or who read the majority of papers that had mainly positive content—that is, the majority of the people—did not become more cynical or lose their feelings of efficacy, as a result of exposure to the press.

A simple graphic case of the limited persuasive power possessed by TV news coverage was the public reaction to the 1968 Democratic convention in Chicago. That convention featured violent and bloody confrontations in the streets between antiwar demonstrators and the Chicago police. The TV commentators covering the events were outspokenly shocked and horrified by the brutality of the police. Yet 57 percent of a national sample said that the police had used "not enough" or "the right amount" of force, whereas only 19 percent said they had used "too much force" and the others had not followed the events (Robinson, 1970). The mail to CBS ran 11 to 1 against the news commentators. Apparently TV news is not able to influence the attitudes of the public at its whim.

obstacles to attitude change

To understand in a more general way what happens when someone makes an attempt to change their attitudes, we can go back to the model of the attitude-change situation introduced in the last chapter (Figure 10–1). There, it will be remembered, we said that four conditions were necessary for attitude change to take place: (1) a powerful communication must reach the target from (2) a credible communicator, (3) the target must not be too resistant to change, and (4) situational variables must be favorable. What normally happens in real life?

communication interferences

Although our model of the attitude-change situation begins with a communicator, we shall first discuss the factors that intervene between the source and the target. To paraphrase a familiar expression, "what you don't hear can't change your attitude." If a message does not reach its target, for all intents and purposes there is no attitude-change situation. Thus, these intervening variables are the first hurdle that must be cleared in order to influence someone.

LOW LEVELS OF EXPOSURE People in the business of trying to affect attitudes are generally aware that their most critical and difficult problem is reaching the people they want to influence. Advertisers, politicians, propagandists, and teachers must devote a considerable amount of their efforts to making sure that their messages reach the targets to which they are directed. Teachers have the least trouble in this respect, because they can require attendance in class. This does not guarantee that the students are listening, but at least the vibrations caused by the teachers' speech are striking the students' ears. This is a major advantage. An advertising man has to spend millions of dollars and use great ingenuity to accomplish the same thing. He must select some medium, say, television, find a program that people watch, and then try to keep them from leaving their seats or turning down the sound or switching channels during the ads. And even when all this is achieved, he reaches only a small percentage of his prospective audience—perhaps 30 percent of those owning sets if he selects the most popular program on the air. The average newspaper editorial is only read by 25 percent of the newspaper's readers (Becker, McCombs, and McLeod, 1975). And as mentioned above, only about 23 percent of the adult public watches the network national news on television any given evening.

The propagandist and political campaigner have even more difficult tasks. Very few people watch discussions of public affairs on television. One representative case is a twenty-hour telethon conducted in San Francisco by the Republican candidate for governor in 1958, the weekend before the election. Only 11.5 percent of the adults in the city watched any part of the telethon (Schramm and Carter, 1959). The main problem for most candidates for most offices is not persuasion, or overcoming a negative image, but merely establishing "name recognition"—just getting any exposure at all.

The debates during the 1960 and 1976 presidential campaigns were remarkable and almost unique exceptions. Eighty million people watched at least one of these debates, but other political programs are lucky to get 8 million viewers. If a typical presidential hopeful buys prime television time at perhaps $50,000 for thirty minutes, he cannot expect more than a few million people to tune in. Many would not be watching television at all, and most of those who were would be watching other shows. Most viewers consider a football game, a western, or a good movie more interesting than a political speech.

Some indication of the low level of exposure to political information can be obtained from surveys in which people in the United States are asked various questions relating to politics. The range of knowledge (and ignorance) is indicated in Table 10–3. (The data are from a number of studies conducted over the fifteen-year period from 1947 to 1962.) It is perhaps reassuring that practically everyone knew who the president was. Unfortunately, when we move beyond this level, ignorance was rampant. Only 57 percent could name even one of their senators, 35 percent could name both, and 38 percent were capable of reporting the name of their congressman. The same held for issues. An encouraging 96 percent were familiar with the United Nations and 71 percent were familiar with the Peace Corps, but only 22 percent knew what the Common Market was and only 26 percent had even heard the term "bipartisan foreign policy."

TABLE 10–3
public's information about politics

ITEM	PERCENT CORRECTLY IDENTIFYING PERSON OR ISSUE
Person:	
President	98
Vice President	69
Secretary of State	66
One senator	57
Both senators	35
Congressman	38
Issue:	
United Nations	96
Peace Corps	71
Bipartisan foreign policy	26
Common Market	22

Source: Adapted from Sears (1969).

This lack of knowledge is not surprising, however, when we look at the extent to which people are exposed to this kind of information. In the 1958 congressional campaign, which was more hotly contested than most, only 24 percent of the people had heard something about both candidates in their district and only 54 percent had heard something about either of them. This means that 46 percent of the people had been exposed to *no* information about any candidate. No wonder they could not name their congressman—they had never heard of him.

Thus, getting through to people is exceedingly difficult and chancy. Particularly in the area of politics and public affairs, people tend to be exposed very little to persuasive messages. And regardless of the topic, the percentage of the potential audience that is reached by any message tends to be quite small.

TWO-STEP FLOW OF INFORMATION There is evidence that some of the material does reach its intended audience through the mass media, but only indirectly. As we have said, most people do not watch public affairs programs or read editorials. But some people do, and they tend to be the most influential members of their community or group. Called *opinion leaders* because of their considerable impact on the attitudes of their associates, these people are exposed to the persuasive information through the mass media and, to some extent, pass it on to their friends. By means of this two-step flow of communication, some of the persuasive material does eventually reach the people. Thus, reaching the opinion leaders is critical. If they hear a candidate's speech, many others will be exposed to the material it contained. Since generally the candidate cannot reach many people directly, this is one way of increasing exposure to his message. Overall level of exposure is still low, and the exposure that does exist tends to be through these relatively influential and informed members of society.

The major implication of the low level of exposure is that it is one explanation of the relatively slight effects of most mass campaigns. Obviously, if the messages do not even reach most of the people, there is going to be little general effect. The person who watches a favorite program on TV and misses the candidate's speech on another channel is not going to be influenced by what the candidate says. If the message does reach him, it may still be ineffective, but it must reach him to have a chance.

DE FACTO SELECTIVE EXPOSURE As difficult as the low level of exposure makes life for a propagandist, he has other problems. When a message does get through to someone, it is likely that the person it reaches already agrees with it. This is the phenomenon of *selective exposure.* Persuasive communications tend not to reach the people they are designed to influence. People tend to be exposed relatively less to information that disagrees with what they believe. Democrats mostly hear talks by other Democrats; Republicans hear talks mostly by other Republicans. Religious people hear talks in favor of religion; nonreligious people hear talks against religion; and members of any particular religion obviously hear ministers of that religion rather than ministers of some other religion. Similarly, businesspeople tend to read articles in favor of business, and farmers tend to read articles in favor of farmers.

Almost every attempt to assess exposure to the mass media systematically has come up with the same kind of findings. For example, in the 1958 California gubernatorial campaign mentioned earlier, Senator William Knowland, the Republican candidate, spent twenty hours on television. The survey conducted just after the telethon showed that only 10 percent of the Democrats watched any part of it, whereas more than twice as many Republicans did. And among those who watched, the Republicans watched twice as long. Thus, Senator Knowland spent twenty hours on television and failed to reach 90 percent of the Democrats he was trying to reach. It is clear he was not getting to most of the people whom he wanted to hear him. (He lost the governorship by over a million votes.)

These examples could be multiplied almost indefinitely—people tend to be exposed disproportionately to opinions and information that they already agree with. This simple fact of life has been called *de facto selectivity* (Sears and Freedman, 1967). The same phenomenon seems to occur in every political campaign and in practically every area in which mass media campaigns are used. Thus, in addition to the low level of overall exposure, another explanation of why campaigns in the mass media are less than overwhelmingly effective is that they fail to reach the very people they are trying to reach. But why does this type of selective exposure occur?

MOTIVATED SELECTIVITY Some communications specialists (e.g., Lazarsfeld, Berelson, & Gaudet, 1948) have interpreted this pattern as reflecting a psychological preference for supportive information. That is, they assumed that individuals deliberately seek out supportive information and avoid nonsupportive information as a way of maintaining the consistency of their own attitudes. This added assumption has been called *motivated selectivity.* Cognitive dissonance theory carried the reasoning still another step further, and suggested that people were especially motivated to expose themselves to supportive information under conditions of high dissonance; that is, when new information might be most helpful in restoring a state of consistency.

We have seen that selective exposure partly explains why people resist persuasion by the mass media or in society in general. However, unless we can be certain that selective exposure is produced in part by real preferences for supportive information, it would not be a good explanation of how people resist persuasion in relatively controlled situations in which they are given a choice between positive and negative information. That is, does an individual tend to listen more to a speaker who agrees with him than to one who disagrees with him? Do people deliberately avoid information that disagrees with them and deliberately seek out information that agrees with them?

There has been a great deal of research on selective exposure in controlled situations, but unfortunately, the evidence is somewhat inconsistent. In an early study (Ehrlich et al., 1957), individuals who owned new cars were asked to choose among envelopes that contained advertisements on a variety of cars, including their own. It was found that people preferred to read material about their own car. This seems to indicate that people, at least in this situation, want to expose themselves primarily to information supporting their own decision—information consistent with their own actions.

People who smoke cigarettes are strongly committed to that behavior. Presumably they enjoy smoking, many have smoked for a long time, and most of them would find it exceedingly difficult to stop. An article that argued that cigarettes cause lung cancer would be a nonsupportive communication for these people. On the other hand, such an article would be supportive, or at least neutral, for people who do not smoke. When Feather (1963) gave smokers and nonsmokers a choice of reading either an article that indicated that smoking causes cancer or one that indicated that it does not cause cancer, there was no difference between smokers and nonsmokers in their preferences. There was no indication of selective exposure for either group.

During the great antiwar protests of the spring of 1968, many college students signed an antidraft petition—called the "We won't go" pledge, and many others gave a great deal of thought to the possibility of it. It was an issue of great personal importance to young men who thought they might be drafted, and possibly killed, in a war they regarded as immoral. Janis and Rausch (1970) tested for selective exposure to propledge and antipledge communications among four different kinds of Yale students: those who immediately refused to sign the pledge, those who refused after some deliberation, those who favored the pledge and said they might sign, and those who had already signed it. Each student was given the titles of eight articles on the war, four of which supported the pledge and four opposed it. Each student then rated the articles for his interest in reading them. Selective exposure would have been reflected in a propledge student's greater interest in propledge than antipledge messages, with the reverse holding for antipledge students. In fact, however, Janis and Rausch found selective exposure in only one of the four groups (those who might sign but hadn't yet), while both groups opposed to the pledge were primarily interested in counterattitudinal information. Table 10–4 shows the results. So in this study, if anything, the general trend was for subjects to be interested in messages *opposing* their own position.

Other studies have also shown that people sometimes actually prefer information that *disagrees* with them to information that agrees with

TABLE 10–4
comparison of men who oppose the "we-won't-go" pledge with men who favor the pledge: mean scores on interest in being exposed to pro and anti articles

	OPPOSED TO PLEDGE		IN FAVOR OF PLEDGE	
Articles	Promptly refused to sign ($n = 12$)	Refused after deliberation ($n = 16$)	Might sign ($n = 11$)	Have already signed ($n = 23$)
Propledge	9.83	11.81	11.09	10.38
Antipledge	7.50	9.38	10.09	11.31
Selective exposure	−2.33	−2.43	+1.00	−0.52

Note: The ratings are of four articles, each on a five-point scale, so the total scale is from 4 (no interest) to 20 (great interest).

Source: Janis & Rausch, 1970, p. 50.

them. In a study by Freedman (1965), subjects listened to an interview and were then asked to rate the person who had been interviewed. After they had made their rating, they were given a choice of reading an evaluation of the individual that agreed or one that disagreed with their own rating. There was a strong tendency for the subjects to prefer the evaluation that disagreed with them. All but one subject chose the nonsupportive evaluation.

Overall, the findings of the various studies range from a strong preference for supportive information to a strong preference for nonsupportive information. Of the studies in this area, there are just about as many producing a preference for supportive information as there are producing a preference for nonsupportive information, and a large number show no difference at all (Sears, 1968). The most likely conclusion from the research seems to be that motivated selectivity is just not a very strong force, in most situations. When a person is given a clear choice between negative and positive information, selective exposure does not operate strongly, if it operates at all. In relatively well-controlled situations, in which a person can expose himself easily to either supportive or nonsupportive information, the mechanism of *motivated* selective exposure is not an important explanation how people resist persuasion.

But how can there be a general pattern of de facto selectivity if people are not strongly motivated to ensure that incoming information will support their prior attitudes? It is obvious that thare are many reasons for exposing oneself to a particular communication (or not exposing oneself to it) other than the attitudinal position being advocated. Few people decide to watch a particular program because it is advertising a particular product. They decide to watch it because they like the program or because it is at a convenient hour or for some other reason that is entirely irrelevant to the program's commercial message. Similarly, people choose a newspaper for a variety of reasons, most of which are more important to them than its political persuasion. Businesspeople read the *Wall Street Journal* primarily because it is useful to them—it contains business news, stock-market reports, and so on. Psychologists tend to read the *American Psychologist* because it contains a lot of information they are interested in. The fact that the *American Psychologist* is also biased in favor of psychology is more or less irrelevant for purposes of exposure. The Republican businessman's daughter plays with a Republican stockbroker's daughter because she lives next door, not because they sit around agreeing about politics all day long.

In all these cases, the individual is exposed primarily to information and ideas with which he already agrees. The businessperson who reads the *Wall Street Journal* reads editorials that are favorable to business. The psychologist who reads the *American Psychologist* reads pro-psychology articles. The businessman's and stockbroker's daughter both reflect their parents' conservative Republicanism. In Senator Knowland's case, it is possible that the Republican's were more familiar with

Michael D. Sullivan

him and more interested in seeing him than were the Democrats. The Republicans therefore watched in greater numbers, not necessarily because they supported him for governor, but because they were curious about him.

It is tempting to interpret such phenomena as being caused by a general preference for supportive information. However, de facto selective exposure seems mostly to be caused by factors other than a preference for supportive information (Sears, 1968). Probably the most important factor producing selective exposure is the disproportionate *availability* of supportive information. Most people live in an environment that contains more information supporting than not supporting their attitudes. A Republican tends to live and work near other Republicans, to read a Republican newspaper because his town has only one newspaper and it is Republican, to be sent Republican literature through the mails, and so on. The same would be true of an advocate of black power, opponents of nuclear power, and practically every other attitude.

Communicators also often *bias* their messages to suit the attitudes of their listeners. For example, Newtson and Czerlinsky (1974) had moderates on the Vietnam war communicate their positions to hawks and to doves. The communications were significantly displaced toward the positions they expected the audiences to hold; they communicated a more hawkish position to the hawks, and a more dovish position to the doves, than they actually held.

Other important factors are *utility* and *believability*. People tend to expose themselves to useful, believable, and interesting information more than to information that lacks these qualities. And apparently supportive information has these characteristics more than nonsupportive information. The *Wall Street Journal* illustrates how utility tends to go along with supportiveness. The editors and reporters are interested in and concerned about business and tend to be Republican. The newspaper therefore contains financial news and has Republican editorials. The news is useful to other businesspeople, who tend to agree with the editorials. A liberal Democrat could publish the *Journal* or be a reporter on it, but he would be less likely to be interested in financial news and therefore less likely to be associated with that kind of newspaper. This is even more obvious with specialized journals such as the *American Psychologist*, which is actually edited by a psychologist.

Thus the work on selective exposure indicates that the communicator does not have to worry too much about the target person *deliberately* avoiding nonsupporting information. If the communicator can get his message near the target and give him a clear choice as to whether or not to listen to it, the target will not avoid it simply because he disagrees with it. On the contrary, there is even some evidence that he prefers information that disagrees with him to information that supports his position. Thus, the difficulty of getting a message to someone who disagrees with it is due primarily to the sociology of people's life circumstances rather than to the narrow-minded preferences of the individual.

SELECTIVE ATTENTION AND SELECTIVE LEARNING Much research has also been done on other avoidance mechanisms, especially selective learning and selective retention. Here the idea is that people avoid discrepant information by not learning it, or by forgetting it quickly. Yet a number of careful studies done in recent years show that people do not learn supportive information more quickly than nonsupportive information, nor do they retain it longer or more completely (Smith and Jamieson, 1972). They do learn familiar information more quickly, but apparently not because it agrees with their position; they learn familiar discrepant arguments quite quickly also (Greenwald and Sakumura, 1967).

Seemingly, the major exception to this lack of selectivity in information acquisition is *selective attention*. A number of clever experiments have been done in which the subject is given the opportunity to press a button to eliminate static masking a persuasive communication. Brock and Balloun (1967) found that subjects would be more likely to tune in to a supportive than to a nonsupportive message. And Kleinhesselink and Edwards (1975) took it a step further, finding that people would selectively attend even to dissonant, nonsupportive messages as long as they were easy to refute. But they would let the static block out nonsupportive messages that were hard to refute. They selected students who were strongly pro-marijuana, and another group that was strongly anti-marijuana. Then they exposed all students to two tape-recorded speeches: a neutral speech (on imprinting in domestic chickens), and a speech urging legalization of marijuana. But the strength of arguments in the latter was varied. In one condition, the students heard strong, difficult-to-refute arguments (e.g., prohibitions against popular drugs never work, it is better for you than alcohol, present marijuana laws socialize criminality) or weak, easy-to-refute arguments (it would bring the American family back together and make rock musicians less paranoid). When listening to the neutral speech, and to one of the marijuana speeches, the subject could press a button to eliminate static. As shown in Table 10–5, button-pressing (an index of full attention) went up for the difficult-to-refute supportive arguments, and for the easy-to-refute nonsupportive arguments. In other words, attention was highest for the arguments that would be least threatening to the subject's own position.

TABLE 10–5
attention (button pressing)

CONDITION	NEUTRAL MESSAGE	MARIJUANA MESSAGE	DIFFERENCE
AGREE WITH MESSAGE			
Difficult to refute	11.41	11.93	.52
Easy to refute	10.18	8.24	−1.94
DISAGREE WITH MESSAGE			
Difficult to refute	10.15	7.53	−2.62
Easy to refute	10.56	10.00	−.56

Source: Kleinhesselink & Edwards, 1975, p. 789.

These findings, that people will briefly tune in and out of attending to messages depending on their supportiveness, stand in contrast to the apparent lack of *motivated* selectivity in either exposure or learning.

resistance to persuasion

Assuming that the communicator has been successful in getting his message to the target, he is still a long way from changing the target's opinion, as could be expected from the research presented in the previous chapter. For example, both Democrats and Republicans watched the Kennedy-Nixon TV debates in 1960, but they differed enormously in their evaluation of them. The overwhelming journalistic consensus was that Kennedy had "won" the first debate. To the extent that impartial observers existed, they agreed with this evaluation. Yet, as you can see in Table 10–6, only 17 percent of pro-Nixon viewers thought Kennedy

TABLE 10–6
who did the better job in the first nixon-kennedy debate in 1960 as rated by pro-nixon, pro-kennedy, and undecided viewers

		KENNEDY	NO CHOICE	NIXON	TOTAL PERCENT
Pre-debate Preference	Kennedy	71	26	3	100
	Undecided	26	62	12	100
	Nixon	17	38	45	100

Source: Adapted from Sears and Whitney (1973).

had won the debate. Consistency thus has a major impact. New information is interpreted in terms of existing attitudes as much as it is evaluated on its merits, and sometimes more so. This is even clearer in the case of the first 1976 Carter-Ford debate (Table 10–7). This seems to be a typical response to most such mass communications. New information seems to be incorporated into existing attitudes without changing them very much. Why is this so?

TABLE 10–7
who did the better job in the first carter-ford debate, as rated by pro-carter, pro-ford, and undecided viewers

		CARTER	NO CHOICE	FORD	TOTAL PERCENT
Pre-debate Preference	Carter	62	32	6	100
	Undecided	25	47	28	100
	Ford	5	25	70	100

Source: Adapted from *The Ann Arbor News,* September 24, 1976, p. 1.

MODES OF RESOLUTION A large part of the reason is that people use modes of resolution other than attitude change to restore cognitive consistency when it is upset by a discrepant persuasive communication.

For one thing, people are likely simply to reject outright arguments that are discrepant from their own previous attitude, as we saw in Chapter 10. Pressures toward cognitive consistency cause the beliefs and values that fit into the already existing structure to be more easily accepted than those that do not fit in. For example, if someone had developed a negative attitude toward drugs, he would be more likely to accept negative statements about marijuana than he would be to accept positive ones. Similarly, if both his parents were Democrats and he therefore considered himself a Democrat, he would be extremely selective in what he believed about Democrats and Republicans. He would be more likely to believe positive things about the former and negative things about the latter. He would also be more likely to favor ideas proposed by Democratic politicians than to favor those proposed by Republicans. His attitude toward a bill in Congress would be shaped, to a large extent, by these preexisting attitudes. Given entirely equal information about the two sides of an issue, an individual tends to accept the side that fits better into his already existing cognitive and attitudinal structure.

Source derogation also takes place. When a politician takes a position on the unpopular side of a hotly contested issue, his own reputation suffers. George McGovern, in 1972, was on the "wrong" side of a whole series of issues, at least according to popular perceptions. Most people thought him too sympathetic to abortion, marijuana, reduced defense budgets, amnesty for draft resisters, busing, and campus unrest. As a consequence, voters did not change attitudes on these issues very much; rather, they derogated McGovern (Miller, Miller, Brown, and Raine, 1976). In general, political campaigns seem remarkably unsuccessful in changing the public's policy preferences. Instead, the candidate's evaluations became aligned with the voters' attitudes toward campaign issues and their perceptions of his positions.

Perceptual distortions follow the same pattern. In both 1968 and 1972, voters tended to distort the positions taken by the presidential candidates on issues like Vietnam to make them more consistent with their candidate preferences. Nixon supporters tended to see Nixon as agreeing with them more on Vietnam than he did in fact (an "assimilation" effect), and Humphrey and McGovern supporters also assimilated their positions to their own. Interestingly enough, in neither case was there much evidence of a "contrast" effect. That is, voters did not exaggerate their differences of opinion with the candidates they opposed, even when, in absolute terms, they evaluated such candidates negatively (Granberg and Brent, 1974). It has also been found that "unit relations" of the sort discussed in Chapter 5 contribute to these assimilation effects. Voters tend to assimilate the issue positions of the candidate they expect to win the election (Kinder, 1975), independent of whether they like or dislike him or plan to vote for him or not. It seems that people want to feel they agree with the president, even if they would prefer someone else in that office.

LEARNING WITHOUT ATTITUDE CHANGE As a consequence, one of the most common contrasts that emerges from the study of mass communications in real life is that between the increased factual information they can provide, and their relative impotence in creating attitude change on important attitudes. One of the earliest demonstrations of this was in wartime research done by Hovland, Lumsdaine, and Sheffield (1949). The Army commissioned them to evaluate the effectiveness of orientation films shown to incoming draftees and volunteers. These films were intended to explain the reasons for World War II, make new soldiers more sympathetic to the war effort, and turn them into enthusiastic fighters. The researchers did find markedly increased levels of information about the war. For example, the film clearly communicated factual details about

De Wys/Rocky Weldon

the Battle of Britain such as the relative sizes of the German and British air forces, the focusing of German bombings on ports and ships, and the fact that the Germans would have physically invaded England except for the resistance of the British air force. But opinions about the British and the war—such as whether the British were going all out, whether or not they would have given up with more bombing, or whether they would hold out to the end—along with attitudes toward the Germans and Japanese, were largely unaffected.

Similarly, the televised 1960 presidential debates were quite effective in conveying images of the candidates and their issue stands, but changed few attitudes about the candidates. And the televised spot ads for the candidates in 1972 were strikingly effective in communicating their issue positions (much more than were the TV news programs), but seemed to have rather little persuasive impact, even among undecided voters (Patterson & McClure, 1976).

STRONG COMMITMENTS So much resistance to attitude change suggests that the attitudes in question must reflect fairly strong commitments. And that turns out in fact to be one of the main problems with trying to achieve attitude change in real life situations. The communications that attract enough attention to get past all the exposure barriers happen also to encounter strong, highly committed attitudes in a great many people, and that makes them quite resistant to attitude change. Racial attitudes, attitudes toward the nation and toward the prevailing system of political authority, identification with a political party and sometimes with a social class, certain democratic slogans (e.g., freedom of speech, the right to vote), occasionally very well-known public figures (e.g., Hitler, FDR, the Kennedys, the president), and numerous general social values (e.g., the value of hard work, obedience to constituted authority, physical aggression is mostly bad) are matters on which most adult Americans have strong attitudes already in place (Sears and Whitney, 1973). Thus it is easy to see why some of the propaganda campaigns we mentioned above failed.

But there is more we can say. In the examples here we are dealing with important, deeply held attitudes that generally have been built up over many years, are related to a great many other attitudes and beliefs, are supported by strong emotional feelings, and, accordingly, are highly resistant to change, even though they can sometimes be influenced by long-term, powerful persuasion. But many other attitudes are quite susceptible to influence. People change their attitudes toward politicians, products, ideas, and behavior all the time.

To understand why some attitudes are almost impossible to change whereas others are easy to change, we need to understand the individual's history: why is he more or less committed to his position?

the development of attitudes

As mentioned earlier, attitudes are assumed to be learned in the same way as are any other dispositions. The basic processes of association, reinforcement, and imitation determine this acquisition. Children are exposed to certain things about the world. They are also reinforced for expressing some attitudes or, perhaps, for actually acting on the basis of them; thus they learn them. In addition, imitation or identification is important in the learning process. Children spend a great deal of time with their parents and after a while begin to believe as they do simply by copying them—even when there is no deliberate attempt at influence. The same process works with figures other than parents, such as peer groups, teachers, or any important figures in a child's life.

For example, how have American children traditionally built their attitudes toward their country? Very early in life they were told that they were Americans. They learned the name of their country and heard people say positive things about it. The words great, good, strong, beautiful, free, bountiful, rich became associated with America. When the children made positive statements about America, everyone smiled and rewarded them, when they said negative things, people frowned and punished them. They soon realized that parents, teachers, and friends thought

America was a great country; by a process of imitation, they tended to accept this view. Thus, by the mechanisms of association, reinforcement, and imitation they learned that their country is great.

selectivity

One of the significant aspects of this process is that the children were exposed primarily to one view of their country. Everyone, or almost everyone, they knew had a similar belief. Of course, this varies somewhat for different children and different issues. Not all adults have a purely positive evaluation of their country. Some may even make a occasional negative statement about it in front of their children. And on other issues, there is even more conflict. Children tend to be exposed to both sides of the issue of smoking, particularly if one parent smokes and the other does not.

But, as we discussed in the chapter on liking, by and large children in any culture grow up in an extremely homogeneous environment in terms of attitudes and values. Parents and friends tend to belong to one nation, come from the same ethnic and class origins, prefer the same political party (typically, 90 percent of marriage partners vote for the same party), have similar views on religion and morality, have similar prejudices and tastes, and so on. Thus, the children are exposed to a very biased sample of the available information, even on those issues that, outside the family, are highly controversial. The children's own friends are similarly determined to an important degree by their parents' environment. The daughter of a rich white Republican businessman, living in the suburbs, is very unlikely to be friends with a poor black girl from the central city, or an Arab guerrilla's daughter, or an auto mechanic's daughter. This de facto selective exposure occurs because children are exposed to only a selective, rather than a representative, subsample of the attitudes other people have. The selectivity arises merely out of the fact of the children's life circumstances, rather than from any special motivation in the children, or by law, or any other deliberate choice (Sears & Freedman, 1967).

Historically, racial prejudice has been among the clearest examples of selectivity. Regional differences in antiblack prejudice have overridden any other single predictor of prejudice. The southern states have the largest amount, the border states are next, and the remainder of the United States falls in line behind them. Independent of any other variable, then, a white child who grows up in the Deep South is surrounded by people who are considerably more racially prejudiced than are the people surrounding a child growing up in a comparable area of the North or West (Middleton, 1976; Maykovich, 1975).

parental influence

The effect of this selective exposure is that children tend to adopt the same attitudes as those in their environment. For young children, especially, and on some issues, this means the parents have a great deal of influence. For example, as shown in Table 10–8, a high percentage of high school seniors favored a given political party when both parents agreed on that party, with only about 10 percent having the opposite preference (Jennings and Niemi, 1974). The same national survey of high school seniors and their parents revealed that 83 percent agreed on a presidential candidate (in the 1964 campaign), and that there were similarly high levels of agreement regarding other partisan preferences. However, parent-offspring agreement was much less in many other attitudinal areas.

In general, it would appear that parents have their maximum influence on simple, concrete, recurrent issues like partisan choice, religious denomination, or prejudices against minority groups. They seem to have relatively little influence on more diffuse, subjective, occasional issues, such as broad matters of religious philosophy, political cynicism, interpersonal trust, or civil liberties (Jennings & Niemi, 1974).

A key intervening variable in the parent-to-offspring influence process seems to be the clarity and frequency of communication between

TABLE 10–8
relationship between party preferences of parents and children

PARENT (AS INDEPENDENTLY REPORTED)	HIGH SCHOOL SENIORS (N= 1852)			
	Democratic	Independent	Republican	Total
Democratic	32.6%	13.2%	3.6%	49.4%
Independent	7.0	12.8	4.1	23.9
Republican	3.4	9.7	13.6	26.7
Total	43.0	35.7	21.3	100.0

PARENTS (AS RECALLED BY RESPONDENT)	ADULT RESPONDENTS (N = 1281)			
	Democratic	Independent	Republican	Total
Both Democrats	36.9%	8.2%	6.2%	51.3%
Split, one uncertain, both shifted	7.1	6.1	5.6	18.8
Both Republicans	4.8	6.0	19.0	29.8
Total	48.8	20.3	30.8	99.9

Source: Adapted from Sears, 1969.

them. Obviously a parent is much more likely to communicate clearly and repeatedly his presidential preference in the heat of an election campaign than he is to communicate some subtle, relatively abstract aspect of his philosophy of life. In the same study 92 percent of the students were able to report accurately which candidate their parent favored, but on other issues they were quite strikingly inaccurate—indeed, often it appeared they were simply guessing about their parents' beliefs (Niemi, 1974).

Within the family, this lack of communication leads to some predictable biases and misperceptions about one another's attitudes. One might be called a "generosity" bias. Children tend to attribute a socially desirable characteristic to the parent when they are ignorant of the truth. For example, 16 percent of the children whose parents voted for the losing candidate misperceived their preference, but only 4 percent were wrong about parents who voted for the winner. Similarly, they wrongly claimed their parent had in fact voted 39 percent of the time, but wrongly claimed a voting parent had not voted in only 2 percent of the cases (Niemi, 1974).

Another is the "self-directed" bias, in which a child falsely attributes the same attitude to the parent as he himself holds, a type of perceptual distortion we described earlier as an "assimilation" effect. Such biases are pervasive throughout the family. For example, 69 percent of the errors made by high school students regarding their parents' presidential preferences were in the direction of their own preferences.

Michael D. Sullivan

On more diffuse and obscure issues, children and husbands and wives all seem to exaggerate terribly the extent to which they all agree (Niemi, 1974).

All these biases, and the considerable gaps in communication they attempt to fill, limit the degree of influence parents have over their children's attitudes. Indeed, Tedin (1974) has shown that when the child accurately perceives his parents' attitudes, the parent has a high level of influence across a wide variety of the child's attitudes. But, as we have seen, the child is not very accurate about a lot of what his parent thinks. In those areas, other sources of influence overpower the parents. For example, take the use of marijuana. Adolescent use of marijuana is extremely highly correlated with friends' use, and hardly related at all to whether or not their parents use drugs, as shown in Table 10–9 (Kandel, 1974). The political issue of legalization of marijuana shows higher levels of agreement with parents. But there is a good bit of inaccuracy in adolescents' perceptions of their parents' attitudes. When that is taken into consideration, agreement becomes much more impressive. Among adolescents who are uncertain of their parents' attitudes about marijuana, there is little agreement. But among offspring who are accurate, agreement is extremely high (Tedin, 1974).

TABLE 10–9
adolescent marijuana use related to best-school-friend use and parental psychoactive drug use

	HAS BEST-SCHOOL-FRIEND USED MARIJUANA?	
PARENT USED PSYCHOACTIVE DRUG?	No	Yes
No	13%	56%
Yes	17	67

Note: Entry is % in each category that use marijuana. Use patterns for each group are self-reported.
Source: Kandel (1974).

peer influence

More generally, friends turn out to be the dominant influence over adolescents' attitudes in a large number of areas that do not lend themselves to early, simple, repetitive, accurate communication of parental attitudes. So the parents' influence tends to be more limited than many early observers originally felt (Jennings and Niemi, 1974). We should repeat that the child's friends normally do not communicate attitudes markedly different from his parents'. At this stage, various socioeconomic factors determine what he hears. His neighborhood, newspaper, school, church, friends tend to be more homogeneous than the rest of the world. If he is wealthy, he would live in an expensive house and be relatively conservative politically. His neighbors would also have money and tend to be conservative. If he attended a public school, his classmates would come from his neighborhood and have attitudes similar to his. If he attended a private school, the similarity in financial and religious backgrounds (in parochial schools) would be even greater. His parents might read the *Wall Street Journal* to keep up with the financial news, and he would be exposed to its conservative views. And so on. All these factors would continue to present him with biased information that would be consistent with the attitudes he had already developed.

Thus, attitude formation begins primarily as a learning process. An individual is exposed to information and experiences relating to a particular object and forms an attitude toward that object by processes of reinforcement and imitation. Once the attitude begins to be formed, however, the principle of cognitive consistency becomes increasingly important. The individual is no longer entirely passive; he begins to process new information in terms of what he has previously learned. In particular, he strives to form a consistent attitude. He tends to reject or distort inconsistent information and to accept more readily consistent information. By and large, the information that continues to come to him tends to reinforce his prior attitudes—though frequently there is not much information coming in.

cognitive consistency in everyday life

The discussion so far suggests that we should find high levels of cognitive consistency in everyday life. And that is true, as long as we are dealing with high commitment attitudes. Party identification, which most people do not change during their lifetimes, is strongly related to how people vote (Wolfinger and Page, 1972). Racial attitudes, attitudes toward nation and authority, and the other such attitudes all affect voting, evaluations of public figures that take prominent stands on such matters, evaluations of public events, and so on (Sears, 1969). And as we have mentioned in connection with the Knowland telethon and the Kennedy-Nixon debates, people tend to evaluate media presentations in terms of longstanding attitudes to which they are committed, when relevant (and on most important issues they are relevant).

Second, consistency is more common when people are greatly involved in the issue in question. Members of Congress tend to have much more consistent attitudes on matters of public policy than does the public at large (Converse, 1964); women using birth control techniques tend to have much more consistent attitudes on a wide variety of birth control issues than do women not using birth control (Insko et al., 1970); college students in Montreal have consistent attitudes about French-Canadian separatism (Rothbart, 1970); and blacks living in Watts had highly consistent attitudes about the Watts riot after it had happened (Sears and McConahay, 1973).

Consistency also seems to increase with greater popular attention to the attitude objects in question. During the politically quiet times of the mid- to late 1950s, the consistency of the ordinary citizen's political attitudes was quite low. Attitudes on one domestic issue were not very strongly related to attitudes on another. Foreign policy attitudes were not closely related to one another, nor were domestic issue attitudes closely related to foreign policy attitudes (Converse, 1964). But in the mid-1960s all this changed. Political attitudes of all kinds suddenly began to be quite closely linked up. It became easier and easier to predict how a person would stand on racial issues, let us say, by knowing how he stood on hippies or marijuana. People tended to be liberal or conservative on most issues (Nie, 1974). The most probable explanation for this sharp change was that politics had become much more important to the public than it had been earlier. Many more issues were brought to the public's attention, in more vivid form, than had been the case in the 1950s. And this heavier dose of communication inspired greater consistency.

Finally, people with greater education and higher levels of political information generally have more consistent attitudes than the less educated and informed, and their attitudes generally tend to revolve more around abstract ideological principles. For example, consistency between generalized tolerance for dissent (e.g., "Do you think people should be allowed to hold a peaceful demonstration to ask the government to act on some issue?") and specific applications of it (e.g., allowing black militants to demonstrate) increases quite markedly with higher educational levels. Less educated people often tend to endorse the general principle of the right to dissent but refuse its application to unpopular groups. Better educated people tend to support or oppose the principle in both forms (Lawrence, 1976).

Indeed, one irony is that people with the most simple-minded attitudes—that is, those with the most consistent attitudes, whose attitudes seem to revolve around one underlying dimension rather than being multidimensional and complex—are those with the highest cognitive ability. Stimson (1975) has shown very convincingly that it is the best-informed, best-educated segments of society that show the simplest, most consistent structure of beliefs on political issues. This suggests a caution for college students and for professors as well. Since we circulate primarily among people with some college education (other students and professors), we are likely to overestimate the degree of consistency present in the general public's attitudes. Nevertheless, it is true that consistency is probably the single most important determinant of people's reactions to communications from other people, at least on hotly controversial issues involving strong commitment to attitudes deriving from early socialization.

overcoming obstacles to change

Even if change of high-commitment attitudes is the exception, it must occur sometimes. What are the occasions on which it is most likely to happen? To start with, there are, broadly speaking, two possible reasons for this lack of change. One is that the environments people construct around themselves tend to expose them selectively to information supporting their pet beliefs, so their attitudes are only infrequently challenged. The other possibility is that people are so committed psychologically to their attitudes in these areas that even massive assaults on them are ineffective.

One way of choosing between these explanations is to look at cases in which the wall of selective exposure breaks down. Selectivity is of course never perfect, whether deliberate or accidental. Throughout his life and particularly as he grows older, an individual is exposed to information that disagrees with his attitudes. The extent to which negative, inconsistent information reaches him varies greatly and is more prevalent for some issues than for others. For example, most people develop attitudes in favor of honesty, peace, and motherhood, and they are rarely exposed to information inconsistent with these attitudes. Similarly, a belief that democracy is the best political system is not often attacked in the United States. In contrast, a devout Catholic or an atheist and a conservative Republican or a liberal Democrat would be exposed to information that disagrees with their attitudes on religion or politics. Although they would be exposed to more supporting than nonsupporting information, they would have to face occasional disagreement.

A sudden exposure to conflicting opinions is an almost universal characteristic of the first year of college. Students who have spent most of their years living in their parents' house and surrounded by childhood friends are introduced to an environment containing many different kinds of people with many different beliefs. This seems to be particularly true of students raised in a conservative political household and of students who have strong religious beliefs, but it is also true of students with liberal views on politics or little religious background. Most college students find themselves in a more heterogeneous environment, in terms of attitudes, than they were in previously. They are exposed to ideas, beliefs, facts, and attitudes they may never have heard before. Not surprisingly, this exposure has a profound effect on many of them. They change many attitudes they had held since childhood; they reevaluate other attitudes in the light of the new information; and, in general, much of their belief system may undergo considerable reorganization.

Bennington College is a small, exclusive women's college in Vermont that was started, with a very liberal faculty, in the early 1930s. In a famous study (1943), Newcomb traced the changes in attitudes that some students experienced during their college years. Most of the students came from affluent and conservative homes, yet there were large and marked changes toward liberalism as the women progressed through the school.

Perhaps the most interesting finding of the study concerned the students' attitudes after they left school. Did their new-found liberalism persist or did they regress to their parents' conservatism? Newcomb and his associates (1967) studied the women twenty years later and found that their political views had remained remarkably stable. Those who left college as liberals were still liberals, and the conservatives were still conservatives. More precisely, the women's senior-year attitudes were better predictors of their ultimate attitudes than were their freshman attitudes.

Newcomb attributed this stability to the social environments the women entered after college. He found almost perfect political agreement between the graduates and their husbands; these affluent-but-liberal women had found affluent-but-liberal husbands. Moreover, the oc-

*"They sent her to Bennington to lose her Southern accent, and then she turned her back on **everything**."*

casional attitudinal regressions could be attributed to the fact that some liberal women had married conservative husbands, or husbands in occupations, such as banking or corporation law, in which they could be expected to move in a conservative world.

This study emphasized as an important determinant of individuals' opinions the attitudinal environment in which they live. Social acquaintances, family, spouse, and so on have a major impact on political views. The study also emphasized the malleability of the young, *if* they are placed in a sufficiently closed environment. However, it is a rare college that embodies the political homogeneity of the small, exclusive, isolated, and highly liberal Bennington campus (Newcomb's followup revealed that today even Bennington does not embody the same degree of liberalism). And the college experience is in some sense unique as an opportunity to be exposed to new ideas, because it is specifically designed to be just that. Most of society is not designed for this purpose, and in the past many people were never exposed to views that contradicted some of those they learned in childhood. They continued to be surrounded by people who held views similar to their own and never had an opportunity even to hear the other side of issues. It seems likely that, to some extent, the growth of television changed this. Although people still may not hear both sides of unimportant issues or issues on which only a small minority disagrees, most people in our society probably are now exposed to both sides of any important, controversial issue.

Even college students seem to be immune to anything short of massive assaults on their pet attitudes. The literature on attempts to reduce antiblack prejudice reads like a dirge of smashed hopes. Ashmore (1970) has done the most careful job of summarizing the vast number of studies on prejudice reduction, and concludes that only under a very limited set of circumstances—extensive interracial contact under conditions of equal status, and shared coping to accomplish shared goals—can much headway be made. Stuart Cook (1970) has done research attempting to validate this hypothesis. He tested the racial attitudes of a group of white southern college girls, hidden in a long battery of tests on other subjects. He selected the most prejudiced of these students. Then, in a completely different setting (actually at another college) and with different personnel, he put each student through a one-month experiment that involved about 40 hours of close contact with a black co-worker. Most of this time was spent in coordination with the black woman as a co-worker on a complicated and difficult task that required complete cooperation between them. The rest of the time was spent in casual contact—mostly lunch breaks. A few months later, all the subjects were retested for racial prejudice, again in surroundings completely removed from the experimental procedure.

Cook found that about 40 percent of the subjects became less negative toward blacks, as indicated on measures of attitude toward segregation and attitudes about interracial situations in general. This was considerably greater than the positive change shown by a control group that had not participated in the contact experience. Yet about 20 percent of the experimental subjects changed in a more negative direction, and a large number did not change at all. So even when a massive effort is made, under seemingly ideal circumstances—all the correct social-psychological variables, with relatively young and open-minded college students—rather little change took place. And this is a typical finding of even the most massive efforts to change racial attitudes, or other attitudes of high commitment. Once people reach adulthood, the return is pretty small.

In general, attitudes that have been socialized early in life and to which the person is highly committed do not change very much in adulthood. They are largely unaffected by mass communications, as we have seen earlier, or by such life changes as aging, geographical mobility, or social mobility, which would seem to put considerable pressure upon them (Sears, 1975). Nor do they change very much as the consequence of public events, such as hotly contested election campaigns, the presence of charismatic candidates on the opposite side, and so on (Campbell et al., 1960).

There are some circumstances in which attitude change does occur rather generally. It appears that low-commitment attitudes are fairly easy to change in adults once a communicator can break through the usual barriers of lack of interest, low levels of exposure, and de facto selectivity. High-commitment attitudes tend to be very difficult to change regardless of the circumstances. As indicated in the previous chapter, a high-credibility communicator who makes a fairly low-discrepancy appeal probably can achieve small amounts of attitude change, though nothing very dramatic. And as the Bennington example or Cook experiment illustrate, sometimes young adults can be exposed to strong influence from a dominant social environment, and substantial changes will occur. Finally, of course, the early socialization of children can readily be influenced (though parents and school boards and other supporters of the status quo do strongly resist tampering with children). In short, exposure seems to be the greatest problem for children and adolescents, whereas the resistance born of commitment is most important for adults.

attitude change versus behavior change

We have emphasized the difficulty of changing attitudes in adults in real life. Antiprejudice campaigns, presidential election campaigns, and even the Chinese brainwashing attempts seem to have had only slight impact upon their targets' attitudes. As we will see in the next chapter, however, it is not nearly as difficult to change people's overt behavior. There are tried and true techniques of social influence (or other forms of power) that can produce behavior wholly contradictory to the person's attitudes, or even his perceptions of reality. Subjects freely administer shock to inoffensive people when they are told to, or express beliefs that wholly contradict their sense perceptions. In considering these dramatic cases it is well to contrast the ease of behavior change with the manifest difficulty of attitude change, at least of attitudes that matter.

This is no trivial fact, because attitudes are the important matter in many situations. Attitudes determine who gets elected to public office, and therefore who runs all major government offices, because voting is an expression of attitude. Attitudes determine who gets hired and who gets fired, in large measure, whether it is the arbitrary judgment of a casting director in a large movie studio or the vote of a faculty meeting on a tenure decision, or the decision made by a civil service grievance panel. In court, attitudes determine who goes to jail and who goes free, whether it is from a jury's vote, a judge's decision, or the prosecutor's decision about whether or not to prosecute. Prejudices, when verbally expressed, can have a chilling effect upon members of minority groups who are attempting to exercise their equal rights; however courageous they may be, they are only human, and sometimes want to retreat away from a place where "they are not wanted," as indicated by snide comments, upturned noses, and averted eyes. Public opinion polls have increasingly played a role in policy decisions by government officials, ranging from decisions about whether or not to reinstitute capital punishment, to legalize marijuana smoking, or to continue to pursue an aggressive military policy in Vietnam. In all these cases, people's attitudes have a major impact on others' lives—sometimes even on the lives of thousands or millions of other people—so the question of attitude change is of major social consequence.

SUMMARY

1. It is rare that propaganda campaigns in the real world produce far-ranging attitude changes. Some examples are advertising campaigns, presidential campaigns, presidential debates, and the Chinese "brainwashing."

2. Television news did not seem to have the effect attributed to it during the 1960s and early 1970s, of making the public more politically cynical.

3. One set of obstacles to attitude change in the real world is lack of exposure to discrepant information, because of low absolute levels of exposure (and low information), and selective exposure.

4. De facto selective exposure can occur in the absence of any very general tendency for people to seek out supportive information (motivated selectivity).

5. Real-life propaganda also is often ineffective because it encounters highly committed attitudes, so any new information is selectively interpreted by the person to reinforce his prior attitudes.

6. These strong commitments frequently develop in childhood and adolescence. Although parents have an important part in the development of commitments, they are by no means the only, or even necessarily the most important source of preadult attitude acquisition.

7. Mass attitude change can occur with low commitment attitudes if there is a high level of exposure. Sometimes young adults can be swayed when they live in a social environment dominated by attitudes contrary to their preadult socialization.

SUGGESTIONS FOR ADDITIONAL READING

ASHMORE, R. D. Prejudice: causes and cures. In B. E. COLLINS (ED.), *Social psychology.* Reading, Mass.: Addison-Wesley, 1970. A comprehensive review of the numerous approaches to prejudice formation and reduction taken by social psychologists.

HOVLAND, C. I. Reconciling conflicting results derived from experimental and survey studies of attitude change. *American Psychologist,* 1959, 14, 8–17. An influential early attempt to compare the findings of laboratory and field studies of attitude change.

KRAUS, S. & DAVIS, D. *The effects of mass communication on political behavior.* University Park, Pa.: Pennsylvania State University Press, 1976. The most current summary of all such research.

NEWCOMB, T. M. Persistence and regression of changed attitudes: long-range studies. *Journal of Social Issues,* 1963, 19, 3–14. A brief, readable report of the followup interviews with the Bennington alumnae. One of the real classics of social psychology.

PATTERSON, T. E., & MCCLURE, R. D. *The unseeing eye: the myth of television power in national elections.* New York: Putnam, 1976. An interesting study of television news and political advertising in the 1972 campaign. Describes the political content on television, along with a good assessment of its effects.

SCHEIN, E. H. The Chinese indoctrination program for prisoners of war. *Psychiatry,* 1956, 19, 149–72. A fascinating account of the techniques used by the Chinese during the Korean War, and how they relate to social psychology.

SEARS, D. O. Political behavior. In G. LINDZEY & E. ARONSON (EDS.), *Handbook of social psychology, 2nd ed.,* Vol. 5. Reading, Mass.: Addison-Wesley, 1969. The most complete account of research on public opinion concerning politics in the United States. Relates that research to the social-psychological principles discussed in this chapter.

SEARS, D. O. Political socialization. In F. I. GREENSTEIN & N. W. POLSBY (EDS.), *Handbook of political science,* Vol. 2. Reading, Mass.: Addison-Wesley, 1975. A detailed review of research on preadult attitude acquisition, particularly focusing on political attitudes.

SEARS, D. O., & WHITNEY, R. E. Political persuasion. In I. DES. POOL & W. SCHRAMM (EDS.), *Handbook of Communication.* Chicago: Rand-McNally, 1973. A readable brief review of research on political persuasion. It includes an extensive discussion of the positivity bias.

ZIMBARDO, P. G., EBBESEN, E. B., & MASLACH, C. *Influencing attitudes and changing behavior (2nd. Ed.),* Reading, Mass.: Addison-Wesley, 1977. A provocative and wide-ranging analysis of how attitude change research applies to a wide variety of real life situations.

11

conformity and compliance

Five students arrived to take part in a study on perception. They sat around a table and were told that they would be judging the lengths of lines. They were shown a white card on which three black lines of varying lengths had been drawn and a second card containing one line. Their task was to choose the line on the first card that was most similar in length to the line on the second card. As shown in Figure 11–1, it was an easy task. One of the lines was exactly the same length as the standard, whereas the other two were quite different from it.

When the lines were shown, the subjects answered aloud in the order in which they were seated. The first subject gave his choice and each of the others responded in turn. Since the judgment was so easy, there were no disagreements. When all had responded, a second set of lines was shown, responses were given, and a third set was produced.

At this point, the experiment seems dull and pointless. On the third trial, however, the first subject looked carefully at the lines as before and then gave what was obviously the wrong answer. In the example in Figure 11–1, he might have said A rather than B. The next subject gave the same wrong answer, as did the third and fourth subjects. When it was time for the fifth subject to respond, he was quite disturbed. It was clear to him that the others were giving wrong answers. He knew that B was the line most similar to X. Yet everyone else said it was A.

Under these circumstances many people sitting fifth gave the wrong answer—they agreed with the others even though they knew it was incorrect. In fact, among these college students with good eyesight and presumably sharp minds, the incorrect answer was given about 35 percent of the time. Some subjects never gave the wrong answer, some did all the time; but overall they averaged about one wrong response in three. Of course, in this classic study by Solomon Asch (1951), the situation was staged. The first four "subjects" were confederates of the exper-

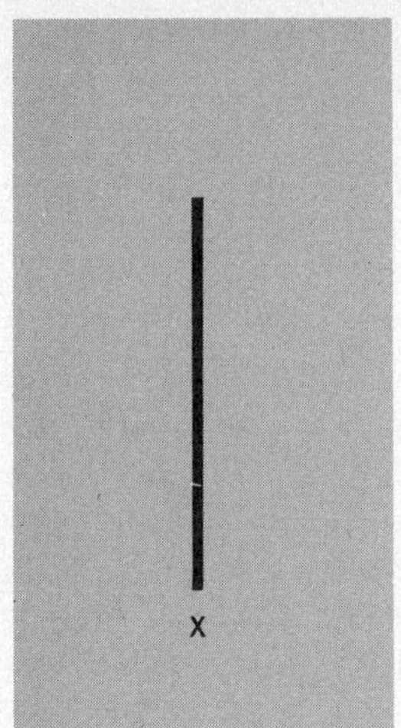

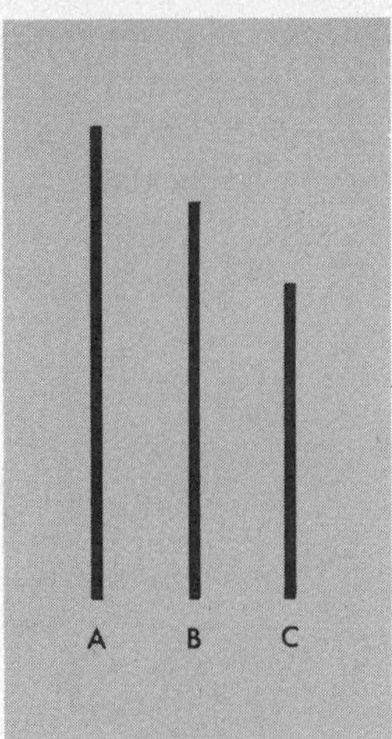

FIGURE 11–1
A representative stimulus in the Asch study. Subjects were shown the four lines simultaneously and asked which line was most similar in length to line X. When a number of confederates unanimously gave the incorrect answer (e.g., C), subjects conformed about 35 percent of the time.

imenter and were responding according to a script. But the real subject did not know this and gave the wrong answer rather than disagree with the others.

Residents of a northeastern city answered a newspaper ad asking for people to participate in a psychology study. They arrived in pairs and were told that the purpose of the study was to investigate the effect of punishment on learning. One of them was selected by chance as the learner and the other as the teacher. The teacher's job was to read aloud pairs of words which the learner was supposed to memorize. Each time the learner made a mistake, the teacher was to administer the punishment. He sat in front of a large, impressive "shock machine" containing a number of levers, each of which was labeled with the amount of shock it would deliver, ranging from 15 volts all the way up to 450 volts. Above the number representing voltage were labels describing the severity of the shock: "slight," "extreme intensity shock," and finally "danger severe shock."

The learner was put in a chair in another room, his arm was strapped down to the chair, and electrodes were taped to his arm. He could not be seen by the teacher or anyone else; they communicated entirely by intercom. Before the testing began, the learner mentioned that he had a slightly weak heart but he was assured by the experimenter that the shocks were not dangerous. Then, the experimenter gave the teacher a sample shock. It was actually fairly severe and hurt considerably, but the teacher was told that it was a mild shock.

During the testing, the learner made a number of errors. The teacher told him he was wrong and delivered a shock. Whenever a shock was given, the learner grunted. As the level of shock increased, the learner's reactions became increasingly dramatic. He yelled, begged the teacher to stop shocking him, pounded the table, and kicked the wall.

Toward the end, he simply stopped answering and made no response at all. Through all this, the experimenter urged the teacher to continue. "The experiment must go on. It is necessary for you to continue. You must continue." He also said that the responsibility was his, not the teacher's.

Under these circumstances, a large number of subjects dutifully delivered supposedly severe electric shocks. More than half of them continued to the end of the scale and administered the shocks labeled 450 volts and marked XXX. They did this even though the person they were shocking screamed for mercy, had a heart condition, and was apparently experiencing great pain. In this dramatic demonstration study by Stanley Milgram (1963), the "learner" was actually a confederate of the experimenter and did not receive any shocks. All of his responses, including errors, grunts, and groans, were carefully rehearsed and then tape-recorded to make them identical for all subjects. The teacher, however, had no way of knowing that the situation was staged.

In both studies, people performed acts they would rather not have performed. In the first case, the pressure on them was subtle. There was no direct command or even request—they were seemingly free to give any response they wanted, and were, in fact, specifically told to give the response they thought was correct. But there was great pressure from the group. Everyone gave the same response and the individual was strongly motivated to agree with the rest of the group. When someone performs an act because everyone else is doing it, we call it *conformity*. In the second example, the pressure to give the shocks was open and direct. The experimenter asked and then demanded that the teacher cooperate. When people do what they are asked to even though they would prefer not to, we call it *compliance* or *obedience*. Conformity might be considered a special case of compliance—giving into group pressure—but it is an especially important phenomenon that we shall consider separately.

The question of how you can induce someone to behave in a particular way, especially against their own inclinations, might at first glance seem of interest primarily to totalitarian governments or manipulative people who are trying to control others. Actually, the question is relevant to practically every phase of social life. We are constantly being urged to act in some way and we often do the same to others. We are asked to do homework, obey laws, pay taxes, drive carefully, save energy, give to charity, be courteous, support political movements and candidates, and get dental checkups. The socialization of children consists in large part of getting them to behave in ways that are consistent with the needs, laws, rules, and demands of society. In every case, some person or organization is trying to get others to perform some action when the others would just as soon not. What factors determine whether the act will be performed? Let us consider conformity in detail first before turning to the more general case of compliance.

conformity in perspective

Human beings are remarkably diverse. Our behavior, attitudes, thoughts, feelings, and values have almost unlimited variations. We speak in hundreds of different languages, believe in hundreds of gods, a Trinity, one God, or no god at all. In some cultures, men take many wives; in some, they take one; and in a few, women take many husbands. In some cultures, pork is forbidden; in others, it is a delicacy. Almost every aspect of behavior—business, courtship, marriage, friendship, bargaining, communication—varies from culture to culture. The diversity is so great that members of one culture find it difficult to exist in another unless they have studied it carefully. They cannot eat the food, their sexual practices are considered unnatural, their manners rude, their every act foreign and wrong. They continually offend people and are offended themselves.

In contrast to this great diversity, however, people the world over have much in common. We are, after all, members of the same species; we have similar physical characteristics, needs, and abilities. Although we speak different languages, we all have language and use it quite similarly; although we have different sexual habits, we all have family structures and prohibitions against incest. The exact forms of behavior may differ, but we do perform many of the same acts, play many of the same games, and have many of the same cares and problems. Thus, the huge differences among people must be seen against the background of basic innate, genetic similarities.

Mimi Forsyth/Monkmeyer

Moreover, within any subculture, the similarities tend to predominate. Just as there is a fantastic diversity among cultures, great similarity exists within any given culture. Almost everyone speaks the same language and has the same values, the same behavior, and the same interests. In the United States, practically everyone likes hamburgers; in Japan, practically everyone likes sushi. The similarity of behavior and values is even greater in subcultures. The smaller the unit of society, the greater the similarity among its members. In the white, middle-class subculture in the American Midwest, almost everyone has similar attitudes toward marriage and courtship, behaves the same in business, and so on. Any outsider entering a different culture is immediately struck by the fact that everyone seems to be behaving similarly. From the outsider's point of view, it looks as though the people are all conformists.

It is true, of course, that people in a culture do behave similarly. But it is important to note that, by and large, this kind of conformity is an adaptive and necessary phenomenon. Members of the society must be able to assume, to some extent, that others will behave in certain ways, will have certain values, will interpret behavior in particular ways, and so on. It makes life much simpler and allows society to operate. People can interact smoothly, interpret correctly what others are doing, and communicate easily. Perhaps the most dramatic instance of this is provided by language. If everyone spoke different languages or had different meanings for the same words, social interaction would be almost impossible.

Language is only one form of behavior that is shared by members of a society. They have an almost unlimited number of conventions and behaviors in common. For example, sexual relations tend to be highly ritualized and specific to a culture. How does one express affection for someone of the opposite sex without being improperly forward? How does one communicate that he wants to be friends but not lovers? How do two people of the same sex express friendship without implying a homosexual attraction? These questions are difficult to answer in any society, but the answers that do exist depend largely on the rituals and customs of that society. An arm around a waist, a light kiss, and holding hands are acceptable approaches in some societies but are improper in others. In some societies, they would show friendship; in others, they would be proposals of marriage. Two men kiss when they meet on the street. In many places, this is quite typical and demonstrates normal affection; in the United States, it is unusual and might be interpreted as a sign of a homosexual relationship. Not knowing these customs, or not following them, makes it difficult to make one's feelings and intentions known. By conforming to the norms of society, however, we can communicate our feelings unambiguously and avoid disastrous or embarrassing misunderstandings.

Similarity among the members of a culture is also due to similar backgrounds, experience, and learning. Children learn to do things in a

particular way, to accept certain beliefs, and to develop certain motivations. To a great extent, all children in a society learn the same things. Then when they are adults, they behave in similar ways—not because they choose to, not because they even think about it, but because this is the way they learned to behave.

Conformity should therefore be considered within this context. Much of the similarity of behavior and beliefs that we see in society and that we call conformity is due to necessity and learning. Thus, although conformity usually has a negative connotation, there are often good reasons for people to be similar.

true conformity

There are times, however, when people behave similarly in the absence of common learning or necessity. Often a person who is free to behave in two different ways and who has no personal preference for either will do what he sees other people doing. If, when driving behind a number of other cars, he sees all the others turn left at a particular intersection, he would probably be strongly tempted to turn left, unless he had additional information about his correct route. When somebody on the street looks up, other people tend to look up also. If someone says that a Campbell's soup can twenty times its normal size is great art, someone else agrees and pays thousands of dollars for the privilege of having it in his living room.

Sherif (1935) provided a forceful demonstration of this kind of conformity. He took advantage of the perceptual effect known as the *autokinetic phenomenon*—a single point of light seen in the dark appears to move even though it is completely stationary. During World War II, pilots who were supposed to follow the lights of the plane ahead of them were bothered by this effect, because the lights seemed to move around in erratic and confusing ways. The pilots sometimes became disoriented and flew off course. Eventually, the problem was eliminated by using lights that blinked, which prevented the autokinetic effect. Two important characteristics of this effect for Sherif's purposes are that it appears to virtually everyone and that it is extremely difficult for the person watching the light to estimate how far it moves. Typically, it seems to move erratically, at varying speeds and in different directions.

In Sherif's experiment, each subject was taken into a totally dark room and shown a single point of light. The subjects were told that the light was moving (since they were unfamiliar with the autokinetic effect, they believed it) and that their task was to estimate how far the light moved. The estimates varied enormously. Several subjects thought the light moved only 1 or 2 inches, whereas one thought it moved as much as 80 feet. (Apparently, this subject thought he was in a gymnasium, although actually he was in a small room.) In other words, the distance the light moved was quite ambiguous. Although the subjects had some idea how far it moved, they were far from certain because they had no guidelines, no background on which to base their estimates.

Into this ambiguous situation, Sherif introduced another subject who was supposedly also judging how far the light moved. This other subject was, in fact, a confederate who had been told to make his estimates consistently lower or higher than those of the subject. The procedure worked as follows: There was a trial during which the light presumably moved, the subject gave his estimate, and the confederate then gave his estimate. The same procedure was repeated for a number of trials. Under these circumstances, the subject soon began to make estimates that were more and more similar to those of the confederate than the ones he had made at the beginning. For example, if the subject began by estimating that the light moved between 10 and 15 feet and the confederate said it moved only 2 feet, on the second trial, the subject would tend to lower his estimate, and on the third trial, he would lower it more. By the end of the series, the subject's estimates were very similar to those of the confederate.

This was a situation in which the subject was not sure of his position. He had some information but it was ambiguous. He encountered somebody else who seemed quite sure of himself, even though they both seemingly had the same information. (Note that the confederate gave consistent estimates over the course of the trials and therefore probably seemed much more sure of himself than the subject felt.) Thus, it was not simply a matter of the subject's conforming because he thought the other had more information. Rather, the subject was influenced because someone said something different from him, because this other person kept saying it, and probably because this other person seemed sure of himself. This happened even though the subject was told by the experimenter that the important thing was to give his own opinions because he was interested in the subject's perception of the situation.

This is quite a strong demonstration of agreement in the absence of a realistic reason, but it could be argued that it does not really show blind conformity. After all, the stimulus that the subject was trying to judge was extremely ambiguous. The subject had no idea how far the light moved, and he was guessing when he gave his estimate. In contrast, the confederate seemed to have definite ideas about how far the light moved. It is true that there are large differences in the perceptual ability of individuals, and the subject might have thought that the other person was better than he at judging how far a light moved in a dark room. Under these circumstances, it would be reasonable for the subject to go along with the other person or at least to use the estimates of the other person as a frame of reference within which to make his own judgments. In other words, although it appeared to be blind conformity, it may have been that the subject had reason to conform.

This is the way Asch reasoned. He thought that once the effect of this frame of reference was removed, there would be little or no conformity. He felt that people are rational enough so that they would trust their own perceptions and beliefs when reality supported them and that they would accordingly remain independent even in the face of a group that unanimously disagreed with them. He constructed the experiment we described earlier and found a great deal of conformity—about 35 percent.

Although his study used line judgments, conformity has been found with other physical stimuli, opinion statements, statements of fact, and logical syllogisms. Subjects have agreed that there is no population problem in the United States, because there is a distance of 6,000 miles between San Francisco and New York; that men are 8 to 9 inches taller than women on the average; and that male babies have a life expectancy of only twenty-five years. In other words, regardless of the type of stimulus and of how clear and unambiguous the correct choice is, when individuals are faced with a unanimous group opinion that differs from the correct one, the pressure exerted by the majority is strong enough to produce an appreciable amount of conformity.

It is important to keep the unambiguousness of the situations in mind if we are to understand the phenomenon. There is a tendency to think that the conforming subjects are uncertain of the correct choice and therefore are swayed by the majority. This is not always the case. In many instances, the subjects are quite certain of the correct choice and, in the absense of group pressure, would choose correctly 100 percent of the time. When they conform, they are conforming despite the fact that they know the correct answer.

These results are very clear. People do conform to other people—even when to do so means they are going against their own perceptions of the world in an unambiguous situation. They do not really accept what the others are saying; in most cases, they believe themselves to be correct. Nevertheless, when asked to respond, they give the same response the others give. This is what we mean by conformity. People have an opinion and all the information necessary to support it, and yet they express an opinion that conforms to the opinion expressed by others.

why do people conform?

An individual in a conformity situation is under pressure from several sources. Most of the factors that affect conformity can be grouped into classes in terms of the kind of pressure they apply. There are those that determine the amount of trust an individual has in the group and in himself. These affect how much information the individual thinks the group's responses convey. Other factors in the situation affect the degree to which an individual wants to be similar to the group or, stated differently, how much he is concerned about being deviant. In addition, various characteristics of the individual himself determine his tendency to conform. Throughout our discussion of the variables that affect conformity, it will be helpful to keep these classes in mind. The operation of the specific variables can be most clearly understood in terms of these more general categories.

information and trust

Other people are an important source of information. They often know something we do not, so by doing what they do, we may gain the benefit of their knowledge. A thirsty traveler at an oasis in the Sahara Desert who sees Arabs drinking from one well and avoiding another would do well to drink from the well they are using. Similarly, someone waiting for his turn at a Coca-Cola machine who sees someone lose a quarter but then have success by using two dimes and a nickel would do well to try the small change before the quarter. And a student who does not know an answer on a test and copies from the person sitting next to him is also indulging in an adaptive bit of conformity. All these people are doing what someone else is doing because the other has or seems to have information they do not.

In a conformity situation, the individual initially holds one view and discovers that the group holds an opposing one. The individual wants to give the correct response. Therefore, the more he trusts the group or thinks it is a good source of information, the more likely he is to conform. At the extreme, if he thinks that the group is infallible, he will always go along with it, even though he might be quite certain of his own opinion. Similarly, if the group has vital information he does not have, conformity would be high. In either case, the individual would decide that he is mistaken and the group correct. The same mechanism operates in less extreme circumstances. The more confidence a person has in the group, the more shaken his own belief will be and the more he will conform. This does not necessarily mean that he is convinced by the group. It means his confidence in his own position is shaken enough so that he does not want to disagree. Therefore, the more the individual trusts the other members' opinions and distrusts his own and the more information he thinks their opinions convey, the more he will conform.

fear of deviance

The fear of being deviant is a basic factor in almost all social situations. We do not want to stand out as different, we want to be like everyone else. An individual faced with a group that disagrees with him is reluctant to be deviant. He wants the group to like him, to treat him well, and to accept him. He is afraid that if he disagrees with them, they might dislike him, mistreat him, and consider him an outcast. He tends to conform in order to avoid these consequences.

This fear of being deviant is justified by the group's response to deviancy. In almost any group, there are strong pressures toward uniformity, and someone who does not conform risks grave consequences. When someone disagrees with the rest of the group, various efforts are made to get him to conform. The most straightforward is trying to convince him that he is wrong and the group right. This was shown in a study by Schachter (1951), in which three confederates were included in a group—one of them consistently took a position deviant from that of the group, one started deviant and changed, and one took the same position as the group. Under these circumstances, the rest of the group spent a great deal of time trying to change the position of the two confederates who held deviant positions. They argued with the deviates, presented reasons to support their own position, cajoled, and did whatever they could to change the deviates' stand to agree with the group's.

Being the object of such an intensive campaign is not pleasant. The deviate feels great pressure to change in order to please everyone and to stop the attacks. If he does change, he is accepted and treated much like any other member of the group. If he maintains his deviant position, eventually the communication to him stops. The group decides that it cannot influence him and begins to ignore him. In the study, the group liked him less than someone who agreed with the group and tended to ostracize and reject him. When the time came to assign jobs, the deviate was never elected to top positions, was never the leader. Instead he was given the worst jobs.

Similar negative consequences of being deviant were found in the study by Freedman and Doob that was discussed in Chapter 6 (Aggression). A group of people who had never met before were brought together and given some information about each other. One of them was described as being different from the others, but just how he was different was not made clear. All the group knew was that his personality was in some way different from theirs. The group was then asked to choose one of their members to take part in a learning study. Whoever was chosen would have the job of responding, and whenever he made an incorrect response, he would receive an electric shock. It was clearly an unpleasant position to be in. The group chose the deviate overwhelmingly for the job of receiving the shocks, of suffering. In another situation, the group had to choose someone to receive a reward of several dollars for taking part in a simple learning study. For this favorable position, the group avoided choosing the deviate and instead picked an average member. In other words, deviates are selected for painful, bad jobs and not for rewarding, good ones.

A group can also apply sanctions directly to a deviate. In a study at the Hawthorne plant of the Western Electric Company, observations were made of the behavior of a number of workers whose wages depended on their productivity. By working harder and accomplishing more, each worker could receive higher pay. However, the employees had developed their own standards as to the right amount of work to do in a day. Every day, after they had accomplished this amount of work, they slacked off. By working just this much, they earned a reasonable sum of money and did not have to work hard. Anyone who did work hard would make the others look bad and might cause management to increase its expectation of output. Thus, the group wanted to maintain its productivity at a fairly low average level.

In order to do this, the group exerted intense pressure on its members to be sure they did not surpass the established level. To begin with, the group set up a code of behavior. A person should not work too much or else he was a "rate buster." Nor should a person work too little—that would make him a "chiseler." In addition, the group devised a unique method of enforcing this code. Anyone who worked too fast or too slow could be "binged." Binging consisted of giving the deviate a sharp blow on the upper arm. Not only did this hurt but it was a symbolic punishment for going against the group's accepted behavior. Any group member could deliver the punishment, and the person who was binged could not fight back. He had to accept the punishment and the disapproval it indicated.

Binging is merely a dramatic example of the kinds of pressure present in all groups that cause members to conform to the accepted opinions, values, and behaviors. By persuasion, threats of ostracism, direct punishment, and offers of rewards, groups put pressure on individuals to conform. If they conform, they are accepted and treated well; if they remain deviant, they must face the consequences.

"I fear we must have misread the invitation."

The strength of the desire not to be deviant varies considerably from person to person and from situation to situation. Some people probably do not feel it at all or even prefer to be deviant; and in some circumstances, most people would probably like to be deviant. But for most people in most situations, there is a tendency to avoid it.

The conformity situation is, of course, perfectly designed to raise the individual's fear of being deviant. Everyone is taking one position and he knows that position is incorrect. He is already deviant in his own mind, but by going along with the group, he can avoid appearing different to the other people. Thus, he is in great conflict: on the one hand, his own senses or intelligence tell him that the group is wrong; on the other hand, the group members all agree and he will stand out if he does not go along with them. The joint effect of fear of being deviant and lack of confidence in his own opinion will often cause someone to conform. The strength of these two motives varies considerably depending on the situation, and each of the factors we shall discuss can be understood in terms of how it affects the two basic considerations.

group unanimity

An extremely important factor in producing conformity is the unanimity of the group opinion. When someone is faced with a unanimous group decision that he disagrees with, he is under great pressure to conform.

Under these circumstances, at least in the Asch situation, there is approximately 35 percent conformity with a majority of three. If, however, a group is not unanimous, there is a striking decrease in the amount of conformity. When there is even one person who does not go along with the rest of the group, conformity drops precipitously to about one-fourth the usual level. This is true when the size of the group is small, and it also appears to hold when the group is quite large, up to fifteen people. One of the most impressive aspects of this phenomenon is that it does not appear to matter who the other nonconforming person is. Regardless of whether he is a high-prestige, expert figure or has low prestige and is not at all expert, if he does not agree with the group, conformity tends to drop about three-fourths (Asch, 1951; Morris and Miller, 1975).

In one study (Malof and Lott, 1962), white southern students were put into the standard Asch situation and faced with unanimous majorities who gave incorrect responses. Then, a black student in the group broke the unanimity by disagreeing with the majority. The amount of conformity—for both prejudiced and nonprejudiced subjects—greatly decreased. In fact, the black student disagreeing with the group caused conformity to decrease as much as did a white student disagreeing. Apparently, the presence of someone else who disagrees with the majority always makes it easier for an individual to express his own opinion, regardless of his feelings about the other person.

Moreover, this effect is found even when the other disagreer gives the wrong answer. If the majority says A, another person says C, and the correct answer is B, the subject is less likely to conform than if everyone agreed on one incorrect answer. Simply having some disagreement with-

"Well heck! If all you smart cookies agree, who am I to dissent?"

in the rest of the group makes it easier for one person to remain independent despite the fact that no one agrees with him.

In a study by Allen and Levine (1971), subjects were presented with either a unanimous majority, a three-man majority and a fourth person who gave the correct answer, or a three-man majority and a fourth person who gave a different answer but one that was even more incorrect than that of the majority. The subjects made three kinds of judgments—perceptual evaluations such as those used by Asch, information such as whether Hawaii was a state, and opinion items for which there was no actual correct answer but for which there were popular ones. The results are shown in Table 11–1. For all three items, the unanimous majority produced more conformity than either of the nonunanimous conditions. The effect was strongest for the perceptual items and weakest for the opinion items.

TABLE 11–1
conformity produced by unanimous majorities, and by majorities with one dissenter who gives either the correct or an even more incorrect choice

	TYPE OF JUDGMENT		
	Perception	Information	Opinion
Unanimous	.97	.78	.89
One correct	.40	.43	.59
One more incorrect than majority	.47	.42	.72

Source: Adapted from Allen and Levine (1969).

The fascinating finding was that for both perceptual and information items, there was practically no difference in amount of conformity when the fourth subject gave the correct answer from when the fourth subject gave an even more incorrect answer than the majority. Even when the dissenter gave an answer further away from the subject's own impression than that given by the majority, conformity was cut approximately in half. The results were somewhat less clear for opinion items. On these, when the dissenter agreed with the subject's opinion, there was a little less conformity than when he gave an even more discrepant answer; but even then there was somewhat less conformity than when the majority was unanimous.

A study by Wilder and Allen (1973) showed that the effect of breaking the unanimity works well on opinion items even if the dissenter is also wrong. In this experiment, one person either gave the correct answer or gave an answer that was at the opposite end of the scale from the incorrect majority. In other words, in the latter case, both the majority and the dissenter were wrong, but the subject's own opinion fell in between them. Under these conditions, any break in unanimity greatly reduced conformity compared to a unanimous majority.

This effect appears to be due to several factors. First, the amount of trust in the majority decreases whenever there is disagreement, even when the person who disagrees is less expert or less reliable than those who make up the majority. Of course, this is in a situation in which the person himself is also disagreeing with the majority. That is, he initially holds an opinion different from theirs, and he discovers that someone else does also. The mere fact that someone else also disagrees with the group indicates that there is room for doubt, that the issue is not perfectly clear, and that the majority might be wrong. This reduces the individual's reliance on the majority opinion as a source of information and accordingly reduces conformity. Second, if another person takes the same position that the individual favors, it serves to strengthen his confidence in his own judgment. As we shall discuss in more detail below, greater confidence reduces conformity. A third consideration involves the individual's reluctance to appear deviant. When he disagrees with everyone else, he stands out and is deviant in both his own and the others' eyes. When someone else also disagrees, neither of them is as deviant as he would be if he were alone. Thus, there is less tendency to conform in order to avoid being deviant and, consequently, less conformity.

This last result should probably be taken as encouragement to speak one's mind even when he disagrees with almost everybody. In the story "The Emperor's New Clothes," for example, the whole crowd watched the naked emperor in his supposedly beautiful new clothes. However, when only one person had the strength to say that the emperor was naked, everyone else found strength to defy the pressures of the majority. After a while the majority had become the minority and perhaps even disappeared. Certainly, this is a strong argument for freedom of speech, because it suggests that even one deviant voice can have a sizable, important effect as long as there are other people who inwardly disagree with the majority but are afraid to speak up. It may also explain why in totalitarian states and some orthodox religions no dissent is allowed. Even one small voice disagreeing with the ruling powers could encourage others to do likewise. Then, after a while, the regime would be in danger of toppling. Perhaps it is dangerous to make too much of this one finding, but it does stand out as one of the most striking aspects of the conformity process.

group size

Suppose there were two people in a room and one of them said that it was very warm. If the room was, in fact, quite cold, the second person would be unlikely to agree with the first. He would feel cold himself and would assume that the other was mistaken or feverish. If forced to make a public statement on the temperature of the room, he would probably say he thought it was rather cold.

If the room contained five people and four of them said it was warm, the situation would change markedly. Even if one person felt cold, he would be likely to doubt his own perceptions. After all, it is somewhat unlikely that all four of the others were feverish or mistaken. If he were asked how he felt, he might be uncertain enough to agree with the rest. He might say that the room was warm and then wonder what was wrong with him. When one person disagrees with you, he is feverish; when four others do, you must be sick yourself. Four people tend to be more trustworthy than one, in terms of both honesty and the reliability of their opinions; it is harder to mistrust a group than one person. Four people saying something offer better information than just one.

A series of experiments has demonstrated that conformity does increase as the size of the unanimous majority increases, at least up to a point. In some of his early experiments, Asch (1951) varied the size of the majority from two to sixteen. As shown in Table 11–2, he found that two people produced more pressure than one, three a lot more than two, and four about the same as three. Somewhat surprisingly, he found that increasing the size of the group past four did not increase the amount of conformity, at least up to sixteen. Thus, he concluded that to produce the most conformity, the optimal group size was three or four and that an additional increase did not have any effect.

TABLE 11–2
group size and conformity

SIZE OF UNANIMOUS MAJORITY	ASCH STUDY (MALES)	GERARD STUDY (MALES)	GERARD STUDY (FEMALES)
1	2.8	12.6	
2	12.8		21.0
3	33.3	25.9	
4	35.0		33.6
5		24.1	
6			34.6
7		30.1	
8	32.0		
16	31.3		

Source: Adapted from Asch (1951) and Gerard, Wilhelmy, and Conolley (1968).

Gerard, Wilhelmy, and Conolley produced somewhat different results in a more recent study (1968). They tested male subjects with unanimous majorities of one, three, five, and seven and female subjects with majorities of two, four, and six. The amount of conformity with each size group is shown in Table 11–2. It can be seen that there was a large increase when the group size was increased from one to three for men and from two to four for women. This is essentially what Asch found—the major effect of group size occurs when the group is increased beyond size two. Unlike Asch's results, however, these new data suggest that additional conformity is produced by still larger groups. Although there is a slight dip for men in groups with a majority of five, both males and females conform most when faced with the largest groups.

Using quite a different procedure and different measures, Milgram et al. (1969) produced similar results. The situation was very simple. On a very crowded street in New York City, a number of people played the old game of looking up in the sky to see whether anyone else would look up also. This time it was done as a deliberate experiment and careful observations were made of the passers-by. The confederates stood and looked up at the sixth-floor window of an office building across the street. Either one, two, three, five, ten, or fifteen confederates stood around looking up at the window. The chief measure is what percentage of those who passed by actually stopped and looked up at the window also. When one person was looking up, only 4 percent of the passers-by conformed to his behavior; with five it went up to 16 percent; with ten it was 22 percent and with fifteen it was 40 percent.

Given these results, it is probably safe to say that, within limits, increasing the size of the group does put more pressure on the individual to conform. In some situations a group of three or four produces a great deal of pressure to conform, and increasing the size of the group does not produce a comparable increase in the amount of conformity. In other situations a group of that size produces relatively little pressure, and therefore the amount of conformity will increase substantially as the size of the group increases. In either case, it may be that a much larger group, say five hundred, would produce a great deal more conformity. Although there is no evidence to support this, it seems plausible that it is harder to resist five hundred people who are, for example, all saluting than it is to resist only five or ten. For the moment, however, this is untested in an experimental situation. We are left with the general statement that a larger group produces more conformity up to some point, and the increase in conformity then levels off.

expertise of the group

Another characteristic of groups that is relevant to conformity is the expertise of the members. How much do they know about the topic under discussion? How qualified are they to give information?

The more expert a group is in relation to an individual, the more he should trust them and consider their opinion valuable information. If, in our example concerning room temperature, the other people in the room were ill with the flu or were Eskimos just off the plane from Alaska, the individual would probably be inclined to discount their opinions and trust his own. He would be less likely to conform than if the others were neighbors who were in good health. On the other hand, suppose the scene was shifted to the wilds of northern Alaska, and the problem was to discover the right way back to camp. If the individual had a strong feeling that the correct route was to the left but the rest of the group disagreed with him, he obviously would be more likely to trust four Eskimos than four neighbors from home. He would conform more to the Eskimos than to his neighbors.

Similarly, when an acknowledged expert agrees with the group, conformity is increased (Crano, 1970; Ettinger et al., 1971). Although the evidence is rather meager, it appears that the more expert a group is in terms of the particular judgments being made, the more conformity will be produced.

individual self-confidence

The other side of the coin, of course, is that anything that increases the individual's confidence in his own ability will decrease conformity. One factor that has a powerful effect on confidence and, consequently, on the amount of conformity is the difficulty of the judgment to be made. The more difficult the judgment, the less confidence the individual tends to have and the more likely he is to conform to others' judgments.

If someone asks us to name the capital of our home state, we know the answer and are sure we know it. Even if four other people gave a different answer, we probably would trust ourselves more than them. We are unlikely to conform, at least not because of lack of confidence in ourselves, although we may still conform for the other reasons cited. However, if we are asked to name the capital of Sierra Leone, the question is more difficult. Even if we have some idea of the correct answer, we are probably less certain. Then, if four people disagree with us, we are more likely to trust them and conform. The same is true with any problem. As difficulty increases, our confidence decreases and we conform more.

Coleman, Blake, and Mouton (1958) presented subjects in a conformity situation with a series of factual questions that varied in difficulty. The correlation between difficulty and conformity was .58 for men and .89 for women. That is, the more difficult the item, the more likely the subject was to conform to an incorrect response.

Additional evidence supports the idea that this effect of difficulty was due to confidence. In a similar situation (Krech and Crutchfield, 1962), subjects were asked to indicate how certain they were of their judgments on several items. On those items the subjects were quite certain of, there was only 15 percent conformity; items that the subjects were fairly certain of produced 24 percent conformity; and when the subjects were somewhat uncertain, there was 36 percent conformity. It seems quite clear that as the subjects' judgments became less ambiguous, as the problems became easier, there was less conformity. Conversely, as the problems became more difficult and the subjects found it harder to make certain judgments, there was more conformity.

A related variable is how competent a person feels to make the responses. Obviously the question about Sierra Leone's capital would be easier for an expert on Africa than for a social psychologist. If a person considers himself a math expert, he would be more confident of his answers to math problems than if he were not an expert; this holds even if the problems are quite difficult for him. Someone with good eyes would be more confident in making visual discriminations than someone with bad eyes.

This means that you should be able to make someone feel more knowledgeable about some subject and thereby decrease conformity. Sure enough, several studies have demonstrated just this (Mausner, 1954; Snyder, Mischel, and Lott, 1960; Croner and Willis, 1961). In Snyder's study some subjects were given a lecture on art just before being asked to make artistic judgments; other subjects did not hear this lecture. As you would expect, those who heard the lecture and supposedly felt more expert than they had before conformed less. Similarly, Croner and Willis showed that people who were successful on a particular task tended to conform less on related items than did others who failed the task.

group cohesiveness

Another important dimension affecting conformity concerns the individual's relationship to the group. Do the members feel close to the group or not? How much do they want to be members of the group? The term *cohesiveness* has been used to include all these considerations. It refers to the total sum of the forces causing people to feel drawn to a group and making them want to remain members of it. The more the members like one another, expect to gain from group membership, feel loyalty, and so on, the more cohesive the group is.

Greater cohesiveness leads to greater conformity. When working for a valuable prize, a group produces more conformity than when there is no prize or a smaller one. A group that considers its task important or values itself highly produces more conformity among its members than one that puts less value on its task or itself. Moreover, group members conform more in a group with a lot of group spirit.

This increased conformity is due to the individuals' reluctance to be deviant. As we saw earlier, being deviant involves the risk of rejection. Someone who is deviant too often or on too important an issue may be mistreated and, in the extreme case, may be ejected from the group. The more one cares about the group, the more serious his fear of rejection is and the less likely he is to disagree. The less he cares about the

Omikron

group, the less serious his fear is and the more he would disagree. If someone is a member of a small group of friends, he has a tendency to avoid being a minority of one on any issue. Fear of rejection or expulsion is at least one reason for this. If, however, he no longer likes the group or feels that it is restricting his social life, this pressure to conform decreases. The worst that could happen if he deviates is that he would be thrown out of the group. When this ceases to be a serious threat, there is less reason for conforming and he feels freer to be deviant.

can only cease though: if the person feels that there is another group that he could join (i.e.: southern city, deviation could mean total soc. ostracization.

commitment

Another factor that influences conformity is the degree of an individual's commitment to his initial judgment or opinion. We can define *commitment* as the total force that makes it difficult to give up a position, that binds the person to his position. Typically, we think of commitment in terms of an individual's feelings of being bound. Does he feel free to change his opinion or does he feel, for some reason, that he cannot or should not change it?

There are many ways of producing commitment to an initial judgment. The subject can write it down, say it aloud in the presence of others, or take any action that establishes his opinion in his own or others' eyes. In the standard Asch situation, the subject feels little commitment to his initial judgment. He has looked at the stimuli and presumably made a judgment. But he has not communicated this judgment to anybody. He has not said it aloud, written it down, or in any way made it a concrete decision. He would not embarrass himself by changing; he would not be admitting that he was wrong or that he was a weak person. There is no reason for him to stick to his initial judgment except a belief that it is correct. Under these circumstances, maximum conformity occurs.

Once the subject expresses his opinion, he becomes more committed to it. If others know his initial opinion, they would know that he has changed. The rest of the group accordingly might feel that he is allowing himself to be influenced by group pressure, that he does not have the courage of his convictions, and so on. The individual himself would feel this way. On the other hand, if he has never made his feelings concrete in any way, he can tell himself that his initial judgment was only a first impression, that he was never sure of it, that he changed because he thought it over more carefully. Thus, once one commits himself to a position, he is more reluctant to give in to group pressure and conforms less.

The degree of the subject's commitment to his first judgment was varied in a study conducted by Deutsch and Gerard (1955). Some subjects (no-commitment condition) saw the stimuli but did not make a public or private statement of their opinion until they had heard the judgments of the rest of the group. Others gave a minimal private commitment by writing their answers down on a magic pad before hearing any other responses. A magic pad is a familiar child's toy which has a piece of cellophane over a layer of graphite. When one writes on the cellophane, it presses into the graphite and the words appear. Lifting the cellophane causes the words to disappear. In this condition (self-commitment, magic pad), the subjects wrote their responses on the magic pad, heard the others' responses, gave their own response, and then erased the pad. In a third condition (strong self-commitment), the subjects wrote their answers on a sheet of paper that they knew was not going to be collected and that they did not sign. Finally, there was a public-commitment condition, in which the subjects wrote their response on a piece of paper, signed the paper, and knew that it was going to be collected at the end of the study. Thus, the four levels of commitment were none; private, magic pad; private, written; and public.

The results are shown in Table 11–3. Clearly commitment reduces conformity. Even the magic-pad condition, in which the subjects knew that no one would ever see what they had written, produced less conformity than the non-commitment condition. The stronger commitments reduced conformity even further. Interestingly, there was no difference between public and strong private commitment, perhaps because the latter produced such strong commitment that conformity was already at a very low level.

A somewhat different type of commitment involves the behavior of

TABLE 11–3
commitment and conformity

COMMITMENT	PERCENTAGE OF CONFORMING RESPONSES
None	24.7
Private, magic pad	16.3
Private, written	5.7
Public	5.7

Source: Adapted from Deutsch and Gerard (1955).

conforming itself. Someone who, for one reason or another, does not conform on the first few trials tends to become committed to this nonconforming behavior. Similarly, someone who does conform at the beginning tends to get committed to that behavior. An individual can be induced to conform from the start by giving him difficult discriminations. When he is subsequently given easier problems, he tends to continue to conform. If, on the other hand, he is given easy problems at the beginning and does not conform to the obviously wrong answers of the other people, he will continue to be independent even when he is later given difficult problems.

This is particularly true when responses are public. When others know a subject's responses, they know whether or not he is conforming. This increases his commitment to a conformist or independent line. Thus, in a face-to-face situation, someone who conforms on early trials continues to conform, and someone who does not conform is generally independent throughout. In a non-face-to-face situation, this effect is less strong, and, in fact, there is a general tendency for most subjects to conform more on later trials. Commitment, therefore, can be to either a particular response (e.g., A is the right answer) or a type of behavior (e.g., conforming).

characteristics of the individual

Thus far, we have been talking about factors that vary with the group or the situation. These tend to operate in much the same way for all individuals. In addition, there are variables that each person brings with him to a situation. There are enormous individual differences in how much people conform, even in the same situation. Some people conform on 100 percent of the trials; others conform on no trials. How do the conformers and nonconformers differ?

To begin with, although there are few controlled experiments on this variable, there appear to be differences in the amount of conformity shown by people of different nationalities. For example, a direct comparison of Norwegians and Frenchmen (Milgram, 1961) found that in a vari-

Vincent Serbin/De Wys

ety of situations and with a variety of different types of subject, the Norwegians conformed more than the French. Exactly why this occurred is not clear, but it seems to be consistent with the traditional emphasis on individuality in French life and the stronge sense of social responsibility and group identification found in Norwegian society.

In another study (Frager, 1970) Japanese students were found to engage in anticonformity more than American students, i.e., they deliberately took a minority position, even when it was wrong. Anticonformity was also related to alienation—to rejection of contemporary Japanese society, and nostalgia for the old days of Japan. Schneider (1970) found that both black and white children conformed more when the majority was white than when the majority was black. However in this study, as in others on the matter, there was no general tendency for black children to be more conforming than white children, despite the common hypothesis that racial prejudice forces blacks to be more submissive than whites. It seems likely that there are considerable differences among other ethnic groups and subgroups, with some tending to conform a lot and others tending to conform relatively little.

There are also great differences in the amount of conformity shown by different individuals within a society. A number of studies have been conducted on this problem, but, unfortunately, the results tend to be somewhat weak and inconsistent. Other than the ethnic and national differences, there are no individual factors that have consistently been shown to affect conformity. We tend to think that intelligence, education, feelings of self-esteem, and so on should make people more independent and reduce conformity. However, the evidence simply does not support these intuitions. There is some hint that these factors lead to less conformity, but the results are contradictory and weak. For the moment, there does not appear to be a conformist type, nor are any particular personality characteristics clearly associated with a high degree of conformity.

sex differences

For many years it seemed as if the one exception to the previous statements was the sex of the person. Studies conducted over many years found that women conformed more than men. Julian et al. (1966) found that women conformed 35 percent of the time in a wide variety of experimental conditions, whereas men conformed only 22 percent of the time. In a later study (Julian et al., 1967), the comparable figures were 28 percent for women and 15 percent for men. These figures are representative of a wide variety of studies conducted during the 1950s and early 1960s which almost invariably found women to be more conforming than men. The finding was widely interpreted as evidence that cultural prescriptions for docility and submissiveness in the female overrode other personality variables.

For years this difference between males and females in amount of conformity was widely accepted as more or less a fact of life. However, the recent women's movement has brought about a heightened awareness of possible forms of subtle discrimination and unfair treatment of women. This in turn has caused experimenters to look more closely at the conformity situation in order to discover whether women are inherently more likely to conform or whether their greater conformity is brought about by other factors. In particular, some investigators have begun to question whether the earlier findings reflected greater docility among women, or whether they were due to the use of male-oriented materials in experiments conducted by men, about which women would naturally not be especially expert or confident in their own judgment.

This suspicion has led to studies in which the sex-relatedness of the materials has been varied, to test the hypothesis that women would be more conformist on male-oriented materials and men would be more conformist on female-oriented materials. Perhaps women are quite conformist about sports and cars and politics, whereas men are more conformist about high fashion, cooking, perfume, child care, and other matters conventionally associated with the female sex role. Sistrunk and McDavid (1971) tested this hypothesis with considerable care. They began with a pool of 100 statements about a variety of everyday opinions and matters of fact; then had 53 subjects judge them for sex relatedness. Those items that at least 80 percent of these subjects judged as of greater interest and sophistication for men than women were used as "masculine" items, and a similar cut-off point was used to select "feminine" items. All these items (along with some neutral filler items) were then

Drawing by Booth; © 1977 The New Yorker Magazine, Inc.

"Thank you for not smoking."

given to 270 new subjects from high schools and colleges in Florida, in four separate experiments. A faked "majority response" was indicated on each item, and the subject's conformity was measured by the extent to which he or she agreed with this "majority response."

The results are shown in Table 11–4. In all four experiments, there was no significant effect of sex by itself. Women were not appreciably more conforming than men. On neutral items the two sexes conformed almost exactly the same amount. However, males conformed more on feminine items, and females conformed more on masculine items. Thus what has generally been accepted as a basic difference between men and women in terms of conformity may turn out to be simply a function of the particular experimental situation. The male experimenters who have done most of the research on conformity probably did not choose the items in order to discriminate against women by showing that they were more conformist. Yet because men were doing the research, they tended to choose items with which they were more familiar and thus unintentionally did produce a biased situation. As of now there has not been enough research using unbiased items to eliminate entirely the possibility that overall sex differences do exist, but this recent research casts considerable doubt on the previous findings to this effect.

TABLE 11–4
amount of conformity by males and females for items considered masculine, feminine, and neutral

	TYPE OF ITEM			
	Masculine	Feminine	Neutral	Total
Males	34.15	43.05	39.65	38.95
Females	42.75	34.55	39.10	38.80

Source: Adapted from Sistrunk and McDavid (1971).

compliance and obedience

Conformity is a limited example of the more general question with which we started this chapter—how to get people to commit an act they would rather not perform. Social pressure in the form of a unanimous majority is one way, and as we have seen, many factors determine the effectiveness of this pressure. But there are many other ways to produce compliance.

rewards, punishments, and threats

One way to produce greater compliance is to increase external pressure on the individual to force him to perform the desired behavior. The use of rewards and punishments is a familiar means of eliciting compliance. A parent who wants her twelve-year-old son not to smoke often uses threats or bribes. She threatens to revoke his allowance, give him a beating, or deprive him of his favorite TV program if he disobeys her. Or she may promise him a bigger allowance or extra TV if he obeys. A third alternative is the use of cajolery, reasoning, and argumentation. She can tell him the medical reason why he should not smoke, or that it is unattractive, or anything else she thinks will convince him. All these methods work. A person with acne who is offered $10,000 for giving a testimonial for a skin cream is more likely to agree to have his scarred face appear on television than is one who is offered only $1. Someone who is told that LSD may cause irreparable brain damage and psychosis is more likely to avoid taking the drug than is someone who is told that it will make him dizzy (assuming they both believe what they are told). Within limits, the more the reward, threat, or justification, the more the compliance.

Compliance can also be affected by modeling and imitation. As with many other behaviors, an individual will tend to do what he sees someone else do. In an aggression situation, if the other person behaves aggressively, he will tend to become more aggressive; if the other person is not aggressive, it will reduce his own aggression. The same kind of effects occur with compliant behavior. If the individual witnesses someone else being highly compliant, he will tend to be more compliant then he might otherwise have been. In contrast, if he witnesses somebody being noncompliant, he will tend to be less compliant than he might have been. This kind of effect has been amply demonstrated by Bryan and Test (1967), Grusec (1970), and others.

At least for compliance, however, the effects of modeling appear to be somewhat limited. White (1972) demonstrated that imitating someone who donated money produced a smaller increment in donations than when the subject actually went through the motions of donating the money himself. And Grusec (1970) showed that to be effective the model must actually engage in the behavior and not just talk about it. The situation was one in which subjects could either share rewards or not share them. There were three conditions—no model, a model who said that she would share her rewards but did not actually do it, and a model who did share her rewards. Those subjects who had witnessed a model sharing were more likely to share themselves than those for whom there was no model. But those who merely heard a model say that she would share did not themselves share any more than if there was no model present. In other words, as with many things in life, it appears to be not what the model says that has the effect, but what she actually does.

As might be expected, direct instruction by telling the subject how to behave also had a considerable effect on degree of compliance. For example, telling a subject that he should donate money and reminding him when he does not causes him to donate more even when he is later left alone (White, 1972). Similarly, telling a subject ahead of time that he must not enter a particular room inhibits him from subsequently going into that room to help someone who is in distress, whereas specifically telling him that he can enter the room naturally increases the likelihood that he will (Staub, 1971). When the experimenter specifically tells someone how to behave, it is to be expected that under most circumstances the subject will be more likely to behave in that way than if he had not been told.

pressure from the situation

The effect of direct instructions and social pressure varies considerably, depending on the circumstances. One way to maximize compliance is to place the individual in a well-controlled situation in which everything is structured to make noncompliance difficult. The individual is asked to do something and is free to refuse. However, refusal is made difficult because everyone expects him to comply. A familiar example of this phenomenon can be seen in a doctor's office. Someone is sitting quietly, enjoying a magazine while he waits to see the doctor. Then the nurse asks him to come into the doctor's office. He knows the doctor is still busy with two other patients and will not be ready to see him for another fifteen minutes. He would be more comfortable staying where he is, and there are no obvious threats for refusing the nurse or rewards for complying. Nevertheless, he walks docilely into the office and waits uncomfortably, this time without his magazine and maybe without his clothes—all because the nurse asked him to do so and the situation is set up so that it is difficult for him not to comply.

The phenomenon is even more clear in psychology experiments. Subjects find it extremely difficult to deny the experimenter anything. They have agreed to take part in a study. By doing so, they have, in effect, put themselves in the experimenter's hands. Unless the experimenter deliberately frees them from this obligation, the subjects tend to agree to virtually any legitimate request. If a group of subjects are brought into a room and asked to eat dry soda crackers, they will do their best to eat as many as they can. After they have eaten several dozen and their mouths are parched and they are extremely uncomfortable, the experimenter can simply go around and say "Would you eat just a few more," and the subjects try to cram a few more soda crackers down their throats. They will do so even though they are given no justification, offered no direct rewards, and threatened with no punishments. Students have been reported to eat huge numbers of crackers in this situation.

The dramatic study by Milgram (1963) described earlier strikingly demonstrated this phenomenon. Many people dutifully delivered supposedly severe electric shocks to a man who screamed for mercy, had a heart condition, and was apparently experiencing great pain. The pressures of the situation, the urging of the experimenter, the lack of perceived choice (although, of course, they could have stopped at any time), and the acceptance of full responsibility by the experimenter made refusal difficult.

Any factors that make the individual feel more responsible for his own behavior or that emphasize the negative aspect of what he is doing will reduce the amount of obedience. In subsequent studies (1965), Milgram has shown that bringing the victim closer to the subject has a substantial effect. In the extreme case, when the victim is placed not in another room but actually right next to the subject, compliance decreases dramatically. Tilker (1970) supported this finding and demonstrated that reminding the subject of his own total responsibility for his actions makes him much less likely to administer the shocks. The results demonstrate that under these circumstances the subject feels enormous pressure from the situation and from the demands of the experimenter. Opposed to his feelings are this pressure of responsibility and concern for the welfare of the victim. As long as he can shift the responsibility to the experimenter and minimize in his own mind the pain the victim is enduring, he will be highly compliant. To the extent that he feels responsible and is aware of the victim's pain, he will tend to be less compliant.

the Hawthorne effect

One of the most effective ways of exerting pressure on an individual to persuade him to do something is to make him happy and to show him that we really care about him and want him to do this thing very much. This is probably implicit in most laboratory situations. The experimenter is sincere, presumably is dedicated to what he is doing, and talks individually to the subject to tell him what he wants him to do. The subject has put himself in the experimenter's hands, feels that the experimenter wants him to perform the acts, is having a lot of attention paid to him, and finds it hard to refuse any request that is even remotely reasonable. He feels obligated to the experimenter and therefore wants to help him.

In a classic study (Homans, 1965), the purpose of which was to investigate the effect of various working conditions on rate of output, six women from a large department at the Western Electric Company's Hawthorne plant were chosen as subjects. The experiment took place over a period of more than a year. The women, whose job consisted of assembling telephone relays, worked in their regular department for the first two weeks (the first period) to provide a measure of their usual rate of output. They were average workers. After this initial period, they were removed from their department and put into a special test room identical to the main assembly room, except that it was provided with a method of measuring how much work each woman did. For the next five weeks (the second period), no change was made in working conditions. During the third period, the method of paying the women was changed. Their salary had previously depended on the amount of work turned out by the entire department (100 workers); now it depended only on the amount of work turned out by the six women. During the fourth experimental period, five-minute rest pauses were introduced into the schedule—one in the morning and one in the afternoon. In the fifth period, the length of the rest pauses was increased to ten minutes. In the sixth period, six rest periods of five minutes each were established. In the seventh, the company provided a light lunch for the workers. During the three subsequent periods, work stopped a half-hour earlier each day. In the eleventh period, a five-day workweek was established, and finally, in the twelfth experimental period all the original conditions of work were reinstituted, so that the circumstances were identical to those with which the women had begun.

From the point of view of the experimenters, this seemed like a good, scientific way of testing the effect of various working conditions. Presumably the rate of work would be influenced by the conditions, so it could be determined which promoted work and which interfered with it. The results, however, were not what the company expected. Regardless of the conditions, whether there were more or fewer rest periods, longer or shorter work days, each experimental period produced a higher rate of work than the one before—the women worked harder and more efficiently.

Although this effect was probably due to several reasons, the most important was that the women felt they were something special, that they were being treated particularly well, that they were in an interesting experiment, and that they were expected to perform exceptionally. They were happy, a lot of attention was paid to them, and they complied with what they thought the experimenter (their boss) wanted. They knew that the main measure of their work was the rate at which they produced, they knew that this was what was being watched, so it did not matter what changes were introduced. They always assumed that the changes were for the good, that they were supposed to increase their work—therefore they worked harder. Each change stimulated their efforts further.

Making someone feel special by manipulating his environment, by setting him apart, by watching his work particularly closely exerts a lot of pressure on him. If he knows what is expected of him, he will do everything he can to go along with it as long as there is no particular reason why he wants to resist. Just as in a typical psychological experiment in a laboratory, the women at the Hawthorne plant knew they were being studied and tried their best to produce the appropriate result, although what the women thought was appropriate was not what the experimenters actually expected.

limits of external pressure

We have described a number of ways of increasing compliance. The most straightforward is to exert pressure on the individual, which can be done with threats, rewards, justification, or social pressure. He can also be exposed to a model who is doing what the experimenter wants, and the individual will usually imitate him. A different approach is to place the person in a highly controlled situation designed to put subtle pressure on him and to make refusal difficult. It is important in this technique to give the impression that the subject is expected to comply, that the possibility of his not complying was never considered, that the experimenter is dependent on him, and that he, in essence, agreed to comply when he entered the situation. Another factor in this technique is the assumption of responsibility by someone other than the subject. The experimenter or someone else relieves the individual of personal responsibility, so he feels freer to do whatever is required. The consequences are not his concern, not his fault.

These procedures tend to increase compliance. However, they are not foolproof. Someone trying to elicit compliance often does not have large rewards, threats, or justifications at his disposal; and it is rare that he has sufficient control over the situation to produce the conditions necessary to make refusal difficult. In less ideal circumstances, people find it fairly easy to refuse even simple requests.

There are also times when the amount of external pressure that it is possible or appropriate to use produces less compliance than desired. The heroic solider refuses to divulge the secret information even when subjected to unbelievable tortures; the typical nonheroic smoker refuses to give up cigarettes despite the tremendous danger of cancer and heart disease; the letter writer refuses to use zip codes despite a variety of threats and cajolements from the Post Office. In these cases, increasing the amount of external pressure would increase compliance, but for one reason or another, it is impractical or undesirable to increase the pressure beyond a certain point.

REACTANCE In addition, increasing the amount of external pressure sometimes actually decreases the amount of compliance. Under certain circumstances, too much pressure causes the person to do the opposite of what he is asked to do. A series of studies conducted at Duke University by Jack Brehm (1966) explored this phenomenon, which Brehm calls *reactance*. The basic notion behind his work is that people attempt to maintain their freedom of action; when this freedom is threatened, they do whatever they can to reinstate it. Whenever increasing the pressure on an individual is perceived by him as a threat to his freedom of action, he protects it by refusing to comply or by doing the opposite of what is requested. We are all familiar with the child who, when told to do something, says "I won't," but when his parents then say, "All right, then, don't," the child goes ahead and does what was requested. This kind of "countercontrol" or reactance also occurs in adults.

The clearest demonstration of reactance is an experiment (Brehm and Sensenig, 1966) in which subjects had a choice of two problems to work on. The problems were essentially identical, but the subjects were told that some people were better at one and some at the other and, therefore, the experimenter was giving them their choice. Into this simple situation was introduced external pressure in the form of a note from another subject who was supposedly making the same choice in another room. In one condition, the note read, "I choose problem A." The other subject was expressing his preference, and this put some pressure on the subject to agree with the choice. In the other condition, the note read, "I think we should both do problem A." With this note, the other subject was not only expressing his preference but also directly trying to influence the subject's choice. Although the external pressure was greater in the second condition, it produced less compliance. In the low-pressure condition over 70 percent of the subjects complied by choosing the problem suggested on the note. In the high-pressure condition only 40 percent of the subjects complied—60 percent of them chose the other problem. Thus, by increasing the pressure on the subjects in such a way that they felt their freedom of choice threatened, reactance was aroused and the amount of compliance actually decreased. This study demonstrated that even when it is possible to exert more external pressure on an individual, it may not always produce the optimal amount of influence. It may sometimes boomerang and result in less influence than would milder pressure.

This effect has been shown in a variety of situations. It seems to work with both behavior and attitudes. Thus, although increasing the amount of external pressure is usually an effective way of increasing compliance, there are many situations in which it is necessary to find other ways of doing so. When the possible amount of external pressure would produce less compliance than desired, when increasing the pressure would arouse reactance and therefore decrease compliance, or when it is important to produce the desired behavior with little or no obvious pressure in order to maximize its subsequent effect (attitude-discrepant behavior, discussed in Chapter 12) it is important to look for factors other than external pressure that affect the amount of compliance. It is these other factors that we shall deal with now.

other factors in compliance

In order to make an individual more likely to comply with a request, it is possible, rather than increasing external pressure on him, to expose him to some experience or situation that would have the same effect. Ordinarily such an experience would occur before the request was made (instead of at the same time), but it would increase subsequent compliance.

the foot in-the-door technique

Sometimes one's goal is to get someone to agree to a large request that people ordinarily would not accept. One way of increasing compliance in such cases is to induce the person to agree first to a much smaller request. Once he has agreed to the small action, he is more likely to agree to the larger one.

This technique is employed explicitly or implicitly by many propaganda and advertising campaigns. Advertisers often concentrate on getting the consumer to do something, anything, connected with their product—even sending back a card saying they do not want it. The advertisers apparently think that any act connected with the product increases the likelihood that the consumer will buy it in the future.

A study by Freedman and Fraser (1966) demonstrated this effect. Experimenters went from door to door and told housewives they were working for the Committee for Safe Driving. They said they wished to enlist the women's support for this campaign and asked them to sign a petition, which was to be sent to the senators from California. The petition requested the senators to work for legislation to encourage safe driving. Almost all the women contacted agreed to sign. Several weeks later, different experimenters contacted these same women and also others who had not been approached before. At this time, all the women were asked to put in their front yards a large, unattractive sign, which said "Drive Carefully." The results were striking. Over 55 percent of the women who had previously agreed to sign the petition (a small request) also agreed to post the sign, whereas less than 17 percent of the other women agreed. Getting the women to agree to the initial small request

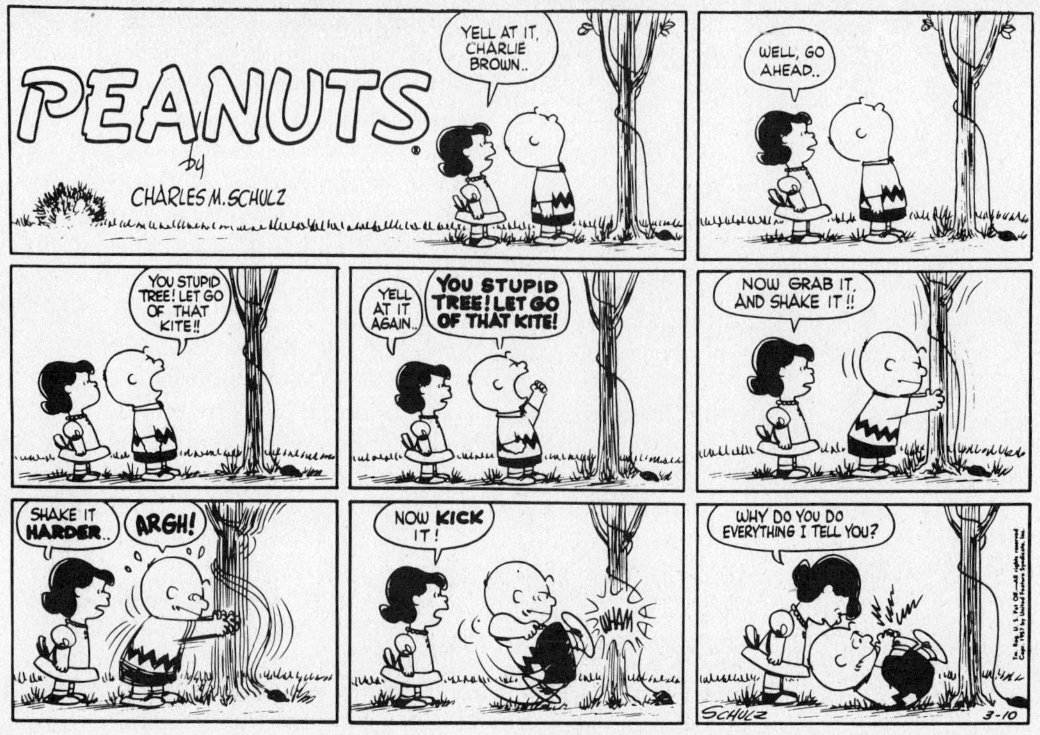

Drawing by Charles Schulz; © 1957 United Feature Syndicate, Inc.

more than tripled the amount of compliance to the large request. This effect was replicated in studies by Pliner, Heather, Kohl, and Saari (1974), and in a somewhat different setting by Snyder and Cunningham (1975).

Why this technique has such a strong effect is not entirely clear. The most likely explanation is that people who agree to a small request get involved and committed to either the issue itself, the behavior they perform, or perhaps simply the idea of taking some kind of action. Any of these involvements would probably make someone more likely to comply with future requests.

Another explanation might be that in some way the individual's self-image changes. In the safe-driving experiment, for example, a woman may have initially thought of herself as the kind of person who does not take social action, who does not sign petitions, who does not post signs, or, perhaps, who does not even agree to things that are asked her by someone at the door. Once she had agreed to the small request, which was actually difficult to refuse, she may have changed her perception of herself slightly. Since she agreed to sign a petition, perhaps, after all, she is the kind of person who does this sort of thing. Then, when the second request was made, she was more likely to comply than she would have been otherwise. Thus, performing the first action changes an individual's attitude toward either himself or the action itself. In either case, this change makes him less resistant to performing a similar act in the future, even when the second request entails a much more extensive commitment.

On the other hand, sometimes the opposite technique also works. Two experiments have demonstrated that asking first for a very large request and then making a smaller one can increase compliance to the small one compared to asking only the small favor. In one study (Cialdini et al., 1975) some subjects were asked to contribute time to a good cause. Some were asked first to give a huge amount of time and when they refused, as almost all did, the experimenter immediately said then perhaps they might agree to something else, a much smaller commitment of time. Other subjects were asked only the smaller request, while a third group was given a choice of the two. Although 16.7 percent in the small-request only condition and 25 percent in the choice condition agreed, 50 percent who heard the large request first agreed to the smaller one.

This effect would be familiar to anyone who engages in a bargaining situation with a used car salesman, a union, or management. The tactic is to ask for the moon and settle for less. The more you ask for at first, the more you expect to end up with eventually. Presumably, the idea is that when you reduce your demands the other person thinks you are compromising and the amount seems smaller. In a compliance situation such as asking for charity the same might apply—a quarter doesn't seem much money when the organization initially asked for a hundred dollars.

Clearly, both the foot-in-the-door and the reverse tactic work at times, but we do not yet know which strategy is better nor when each of them will operate. One difference seems to be that the reverse effect has been shown when the smaller request follows the large one immediately and is obviously connected; the foot-in-the-door works even when the two requests are seemingly unconnected.

labeling

Closely related to the "self-image" explanation of the foot-in-the-door effect is the effect of labeling the individual's behavior. If you reinforce people's image of themselves by providing a verbal name or label, it tends to make them behave consistently with the label you provide. In a study by Kraut (1973), people were asked to contribute to charity and were then labeled either "charitable" or "uncharitable" depending on whether they had contributed. Other subjects were not actually called by the label. Later, they were asked again to contribute. The labels had the effect of making them behave the way they did the first time—those who had given the first time and were labeled charitable gave more than those who were not labeled; and those who had not given and were labeled uncharitable gave less than if they were not labeled.

On the other hand, providing an inappropriate label may make people try to compensate for the label by behaving differently from what would be expected. Steele (1975) called people on the phone and said that it was common knowledge that they were (or were not) involved in the community or said something negative that was irrelevant to the community. He then asked them to help form a food cooperative for the community. As you can see in Figure 11–2, the labels or as he termed it "name calling" increased compliance compared to using no label at all. But the negative labels produced even more compliance than the positive one, presumably because the subjects felt that the label was unfair and they wanted to show that they were community-minded.

In both situations, the label seems to affect the person's image. Sometimes a label can solidify that image and make the person behave consistently with it; other times, the label can make the person worry about his image and try to do something to make it better. When we combine this research with that on the foot-in-the-door, it appears that cognitive elements, and especially what the person thinks of himself, play an important role in compliance.

motive arousal

People comply or are obedient for a variety of reasons. They are afraid of the consequences if they do not comply, they are seeking rewards if they do, they feel internal obligations that cause them to comply, and so on. In any situation, some of these reasons are stronger than others. Whether or not compliance occurs depends to some extent on whether the situation makes relevant the particular concern that at that moment is impor-

FIGURE 11–2
Any kind of label increased compliance, but a negative label, especially an irrelevant one, increased it the most. (Based on Steele, 1975)

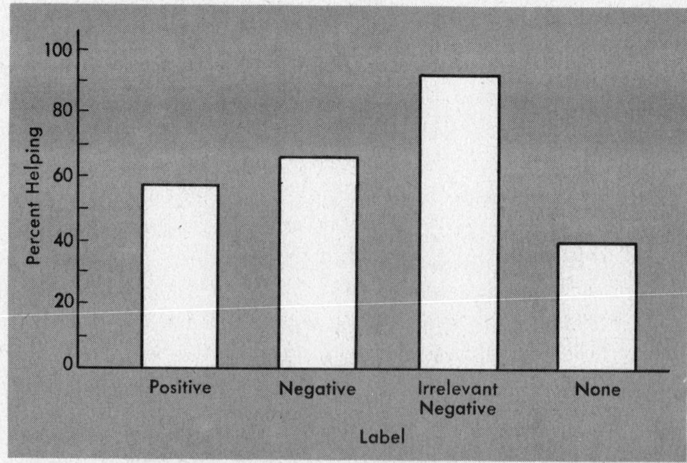

tant to the individual. If the person is primarily worried about being punished, for example, a situation that involves the threat of punishment should be more effective in evoking compliance than a situation involving only rewards. Conversely, someone who is unconcerned about punishment but desirous of rewards would comply most in a potentially rewarding situation. This is analogous to the operation of other drives. If someone is hungry, food is a good incentive; if he is thirsty, water is better than food; and so on.

In a study by Carlsmith, Lepper, and Landauer (1969), some children were asked by a threatening adult to pick up 150 tennis balls. Some children picked up all of them, some picked up 40 or 50, and some picked up only a few. Overall, there was a considerable amount of obedience. Other children were asked to perform the same task by a warm, rewarding adult. Again, some of them picked up a lot of the balls and some picked up a few, but the average number of tennis balls picked up was quite high. Both threats and promises are reasonably successful means of inducing obedience.

The situation changed dramatically when some of the children were frightened and some were not. In the former condition, children had just watched a frightening movie, while the others had watched a happy, lighthearted movie. The frightened group should have been particularly concerned about being punished, about negative things happening to them. These concerns would be especially strong when the adult was someone whom they knew might punish them if they disobeyed him. If he asked them to pick up the tennis balls, they should obey him more (from fear of being punished) than they would someone whom they knew was a nice, rewarding person. In contrast, the children who had watched the happy movie should be relatively unconcerned about negative outcomes and more concerned about positive ones. The threatening adults should not impress them because they were not frightened. Instead, they would respond more to the nice adult because he would give them what they want—rewards. As may be seen in Table 11–5 this is what happened. The frightened children obeyed the stern, punishing adult more than the warm, rewarding adult, whereas the children who were not frightened obeyed the warm adult. This result was repeated by Lepper (1970) using a somewhat different situation. He

TABLE 11–5
motive arousal and compliance

MOVIE	STERN	WARM
Scary	108.5	62.4
Happy	69.9	99.8

Note: Entries are the number of tennis balls picked up.
Source: Adapted from Carlsmith, Lepper, and Landauer (1969).

found that subjects who were made anxious responded more strongly to punishment than to positive reinforcements while less anxious subjects showed the opposite preference, responding more strongly to positive reinforcements than to punishment.

deviance

Finally, deviance seems to play a role in compliance just as it does in conformity. Filter and Gross (1975) have shown that people who think they are deviants are more likely to comply to a request than nondeviants. Moreover, this effect held whether or not other people knew about the individual's deviancy. And Apsler (1975) demonstrated that making people embarrassed or anxious increased compliance. He had subjects engage in silly tasks in front of an observer and then they were asked to do something by either that observer or someone who had not watched them. Those who performed the silly tasks and were presumably more worried about being embarrassed complied more than others who had not done the tasks. And, as in the previous study, the amount of compliance was the same to the observer and the other person. Apparently, the fear of exposure or the desire to relieve their discomfort produces the increased compliance, rather than any specific concern about making themselves look better in front of others.

SUMMARY

1. Performing an act because everyone else performs it is called conformity. Performing an act when someone asks you to even though you would rather not perform it is called compliance.

2. Conformity is often adaptive because it is necessary to get along with others and also because other people's actions may give you information about the best way to act in a particular circumstance.

3. In controlled situations, when neither of the above considerations were relevant, there was still a great deal of conformity—about 35% in the Asch judgment experiments.

4. People conform because they use the information they get from others, because they trust others, because they are afraid of being deviant.

5. When the rest of the group is not unanimous, conformity drops sharply.

6. Other factors producing greater conformity are larger groups, expertise of the group, and a lack of confidence by the individual. Greater commitment to an initial position reduces conformity. Males and females appear to conform at about the same rate when the situations are made comparable.

7. Compliance and obedience can be increased by the use of rewards, punishments, threats, and pressures from the situation. However, too much external pressure can backfire and produce reactance, a tendency to resist limitations on one's freedom of action that causes the individual to do the opposite of what is requested.

8. Compliance can be increased by first asking a small request and then a larger one—the foot-in-the-door effect. Under some conditions, the reverse also increases compliance—a very large request followed by a small one.

SUGGESTIONS FOR ADDITIONAL READING

ASCH, S. E. Effects of group pressure upon the modification and distortion of judgments. In H. Guetskow (Ed.) *Groups, Leadership and Men.* Pittsburgh: Carnegie Press, 1951. The classic study, still well worth reading.

FREEDMAN, J. L. & DOOB, A. N. *Deviancy.* New York: Academic Press, 1968. An experimental study of the effects of feeling and seeming deviant.

MILGRAM, S. Behavioral study of obedience. *Journal of Abnormal and Social Psychology,* 1963, 67, 371–78. Provocative experiment though just what it means is certainly in question.

12

cognitive dissonance

theory of cognitive dissonance

- magnitude of dissonance
- dissonance reduction

postdecisional dissonance

- disconfirmed expectations
- lasting commitment
- choice
- certainty of consequences
- responsibility for consequences

attitude-discrepant behavior

- threats
- positive incentives
- incentive theory
- self-perception theory

summary

suggestions for additional reading

The preceding chapters have dealt with situations in which the target of influence is a more or less passive listener. This, of course, is the way much influence in our society takes place. Mass communications, such as TV commercials or PTA meetings, have that character. Even person-to-person exchanges or influence exerted in small groups frequently represent one-way communication. But in many other situations, the target of influence is very much involved in the process, as an active participant. So we turn now to research that builds in the target's own behavior as an ingredient in predicting attitude change.

The theory that has led to most of this research is that of cognitive dissonance. Although it nominally can be applied to inconsistencies between any cognitions, in fact the most creative of the research it has generated has dealt with inconsistencies between behavior and attitudes. The most important work has dealt with the effects of making a decision or committing oneself to something, and with the effects of engaging in counterattitudinal behavior. Reducing dissonance in these situations has been studied as a predictor of attitude change.

theory of cognitive dissonance

Like several other theories we have discussed, cognitive dissonance theory assumes that there is a tendency toward cognitive consistency. According to the theory, inconsistency, which it calls *dissonance,* exists between two cognitions when the opposite of one follows from the other. Or more technically, if there are two cognitions *X* and *Y* and if not-*X* follows from *Y*, dissonance exists. For example, if the two cognitions are "All marijuana smokers are filthy and degenerate" and "This well-dressed, respectable lawyer smokes marijuana," dissonance exists between them. It follows from the first cognition that all marijuana smokers, and therefore the lawyer, must *not* be respectable. Similarly, if one has the cognitions, "I detest violence," and "I am committing violence," dissonance exists, because if the individual detests violence, it follows that he should not be committing it.

The definition of dissonance includes two somewhat difficult interpretations—of the terms *cognition* and *follows from. Cognitions* are defined in much the same way as *elements* in the cognitive system. They are anything a person is aware of or has knowledge of. They may be facts, beliefs, opinions, or anything else and may be stated in terms of the person's knowledge or awareness. He knows that he smokes cigarettes, that he believes in God, that the earth is round. But if the person is not aware of it, it does not fit into the system. For example, if he is diabetic but does not know it, he does not have the cognition "I am diabetic" and this is not part of the system. Any two cognitions are either *consonant,* that is, one follows from the other; *dissonant,* the opposite of one follows from the other; or *irrelevant,* the existence of one implies nothing about the other.

Now we get to the difficult problem of the meaning of *follows from,* an extremely important aspect of the theory. The consistency or inconsistency that exists between two cognitions is defined entirely in terms of the psychological implications for the individual. Two cognitions are dissonant if, from the individual's point of view, the opposite of one follows from the other. They can be logically inconsistent but are not dissonant unless the individual notices and accepts the inconsistencies. If he has an unusual logical system or is unaware of the rules of logic, dissonance may not exist between the two cognitions, because as far as he is concerned, the opposite of one does not follow from the other. Dissonance exists only when, for a particular individual taking two cognitions alone, the opposite of one follows from the other.

This can be made clearer by considering the ways in which two cognitions can be dissonant. The first and simplest is logical inconsistency. If all lions are yellow, any particular lion must be yellow. If if is black, inconsistency exists. The two statements "All lions are yellow" and "This lion is black" cannot both be correct. Most individuals are usually aware of simple logical fallacies of this sort, and therefore these fallacies produce dissonance.

A second important source of dissonance is inconsistency between an attitude and a behavior or between two behaviors of the same individual. If someone hates war, it follows psychologically (although not necessarily logically) that he would not engage in war. If he has the cognition that he is engaging in war, it is dissonant with the cognition that he hates war. If someone believes smoking causes cancer and still smokes, it causes dissonance. The same is true of two inconsistent acts. If someone contributes money to a pacifist movement but also enlists in the Marines, the two acts are probably seen as dissonant.

In other words, dissonance can arise because of inconsistencies

Michael D. Sullivan

between beliefs, between beliefs and behaviors, or between behaviors. Some of these will be logical inconsistencies and some will not be. In all cases, however, the crucial and necessary condition for the production of dissonance is that psychologically the two elements are inconsistent in the sense that the opposite of one follows from the other.

This then is the definition of dissonance. Note that it is described flexibly. Unlike some of the other theories we have discussed, it does not deal only with certain kinds of cognitions nor does it require certain structures in order to be balanced. Rather, it relies on the individual's own psychological structure and simply says that when inconsistency exists for the individual, dissonance is aroused. This phenomenological definition makes it difficult at times to be certain that dissonance exists in a given situation, and the theory is sometimes criticized as being too vague. Nevertheless, the theory is provocative and useful—particularly when it is applied to situations that unequivocally arouse dissonance.

magnitude of dissonance

Dissonance varies in magnitude: individuals can experience a little dissonance or a lot; a cognitive structure can have little dissonance or a great deal. Two factors determine how much dissonance is produced—

the number of dissonant elements that exist relative to the number of consonant ones and the importance of these elements.

All the examples we have given involve only two cognitions, because in determining whether or not any dissonance exists, only the relationship between two cognitions is considered. They either are or are not dissonant. In determining how much dissonance exists, however, the total cognitive system must be considered. Enlisting in the Marines is dissonant with a belief in pacifism. On the other hand, the enlistment may be consonant with other elements. The individual may think he is doing a great service for his country, he may have enlisted because he was afraid of being drafted, and so on. The enlistment may also be dissonant with a number of other elements. He may be giving up a good job, he may be taking a cut in salary, he may find the living conditions in the Marines unpleasant and bleak. Each consonant relationship decreases the amount of dissonance; each dissonant relationship increases it. Thus, if everything about the Marine Corps is consonant with joining it except for the fact that it uses violence and the individual is a pacifist, there is less dissonance than if he is also giving up a good job in order to join. And there is still more dissonance if he not only is giving up a good job and going against his pacifist principles, but also dislikes the living conditions. The total amount of dissonance is determined in part by the number of dissonant elements relative to the total number of elements in the situation.

The other factor affecting the amount of dissonance is the importance of the elements involved. Joining the Marines is a fairly major behavior and one's knowledge that he has done so is therefore an important element in the cognitive system. If he is a life-long pacifist and holds these principles strongly, that too is an important element. When dissonance exists between important elements, its magnitude is greater than when it exists between less important elements. If, instead of joining the Marines, the pacifist punched someone during an argument, there would probably be less dissonance, because throwing one punch is less important than joining the Marines. Similarly, if someone dislikes uniforms but joins the Marines, some dissonance is produced because the behavior is inconsistent with his attitude. However, since his attitude about uniforms is probably less important than a belief in pacifism, less dissonance would be produced in this case than in the earlier example. And finally, if somebody does not like mashed potatoes but eats them anyway, some dissonance would be produced, but very little, because neither a dislike of mashed potatoes nor eating them is a particularly important part of the cognitive system.

dissonance reduction

We now know when dissonance is produced and what determines its magnitude. The next question concerns the effect dissonance has on the individual. The basic assumption is that when dissonance exists, there is a tendency to reduce or remove it. And the greater the dissonance, the more pressure there is to reduce it. In other words, dissonance operates much like any other drive: if we are hungry, we do something to reduce the hunger; if we are afraid, we do something to reduce the fear; and if we feel dissonance, we do something to reduce it also.

There are three major ways to reduce dissonance: by reducing the importance of the dissonant elements, by adding consonant elements, or by changing one of the dissonant elements so that it is no longer inconsistent with the other. Since the magnitude of the dissonance is dependent on the importance of the elements and the number of consonant and dissonant elements, any of these methods should reduce the amount of dissonance.

If someone thinks a task is extremely dull and tells someone else that it is very interesting, dissonance is produced. He can reduce it by deciding that telling this kind of lie is not important or that how he feels about the task is not important. This method of reducing dissonance is typical of someone who makes a decision and then discovers that certain aspects of his decision were not good. Someone who buys an expensive car and then discovers that it is not comfortable on long drives experi-

Drawing by Jack Tippit; © 1957 Look.

"The service here is slow, but the food is so bad you don't mind waiting for it."

ences dissonance. The knowledge that some aspect of the chosen car is poor is dissonant with the fact that he chose that car. A convenient and effective way of reducing the dissonance is to reduce the importance of the negative characteristic. He could decide that it does not matter how uncomfortable the car is on long drives since he only uses it for commuting two miles to work. Although dissonance still exists between the two cognitions, there is less dissonance because one of them is less important.

It is also possible to reduce dissonance by adding consonant elements to the system. This reduces the relative number of dissonant elements, which reduces the magnitude of the dissonance. The pacifist who joins the Marines probably finds it difficult to convince himself that either his pacifist attitudes or his act of joining the Marines is unimportant. But he can think of other consonant elements in the situation. He may decide that joining the Marines is a way of defending his country and the free world. This belief is consonant with the act of joining and would reduce the total amount of dissonance in the situation. If he has been offered a bonus of $10,000, special training in electronics, and a high rank, these also are good reasons for joining and are consonant with the behavior. His act is still inconsistent—dissonant—with his belief in pacifism, but the total amount of dissonance he feels is reduced. The car buyer might use this same mode of dissonance reduction when he discovers that his car is uncomfortable. If the car handles extremely well, is economical, and attractive, these consonant elements reduce the amount of dissonance he feels. The more consonant elements in the system, the less dissonance is produced by a single dissonant element.

The final means of reducing dissonance is to eliminate or minimize the dissonant elements themselves. One possible method is simply to ignore or try to forget a dissonant element. Unfortunately, this is not easy for most of us in most situations. The dissonant element does exist, and although we can try not to think about it, it is probably hard to forget entirely. What we can do, however, is change one of the elements so as to make it no longer dissonant with the other one. The car buyer may convince himself that the car really is comfortable on long trips. The pacifist who joins the Marines may decide that he does not believe in pacifism any more. The person who lies about the task he found dull can change his evaluation of the task. He can decide that after all it was not so dull, and therefore there is nothing dissonant about telling another person that the task was interesting.

To summarize the major ideas of the theory of cognitive dissonance: (1) when a person holds two cognitions, of which the opposite of one follows from the other, dissonance exists; (2) the more important the cognitions and the greater the proportion of dissonant to consonant cognitions, the more dissonance is aroused; and (3) the dissonance is unpleasant and the individual tends to reduce it.

Since people often encounter inconsistencies in the world—in particular, within their own cognitive world—dissonance theory is applicable to many common situations. Most of the research has focused on an individual's reactions following a decision, and those resulting from attitude-discrepant behavior. Reducing the dissonance aroused in these situations often has an important effect on his attitudes and behavior.

postdecisional dissonance

One particular class of behavior that almost always arouses dissonance is decision making. Whenever we must decide between two or more alternatives, whatever choice we make is to some extent inconsistent with some of our beliefs. After we decide, all the good aspects of the unchosen alternative and all the bad aspects of the chosen alternative are dissonant with the decision. Suppose a person buying a car is trying to decide between a Chevrolet and a Ford. As far as he is concerned, the most important factors are that the Ford handles better and is better built, whereas the Chevrolet is more attractive and comfortable. Under these circumstances, some dissonance will be aroused whichever car he chooses. If he decides to buy a Ford, his decision is dissonant with the knowledge that it is less comfortable and less attractive than the Chevrolet. Taken alone, the cognition "The Chevrolet is more comfortable" is dissonant with the cognition "I bought a Ford." Alternatively, if he buys a Chevrolet, his decision is dissonant with the knowledge that the Ford handles better and is better built. Whenever we have to make a decision in which both alternatives have something in their favor, dissonance is aroused once we have chosen.

This dissonance can be reduced by changing our evaluations of the chosen and unchosen alternatives. Increasing the attractiveness and value of the chosen alternative reduces dissonance, because everything positive about it is consonant with the decision. Dissonance can also be reduced by lowering the evaluation of the unchosen alternative. The less attractive it is, the less dissonance should be aroused by choosing the other. Therefore, after someone has made a decision, there is a tendency for him to increase his liking for what he chose and to decrease his liking for what he did not choose. After choosing a Ford over a Chevrolet, we tend to rate the Ford even higher than we did before and the Chevrolet even lower.

A study by Brehm (1956) demonstrated this effect. College women were shown eight products, such as a toaster, a stopwatch, and a radio, and were asked to indicate how much they would like to have each of them. They were then shown two of the eight products and told they would be given whichever they chose. After the objects were chosen and the subjects received the one they selected, they were asked to rate all the objects again. As shown in Table 12–1, on the second rating there was a strong tendency for the women to increase their evaluation of the item they had picked and to decrease their evaluation of the other item.

TABLE 12–1
dissonance reduction following a decision

CONDITION	RATING OF CHOSEN OBJECT	RATING OF UNCHOSEN OBJECT	TOTAL REDUCTION[a]
High dissonance (objects initially rated close)	+.32	−.53	.85
Low dissonance (objects initially rated far apart)	+.25	−.12	.37
No dissonance (gift—no choice)	.00	–	.00

[a]Figures are the increased evaluation of the chosen object plus the decrease in evaluation of the unchosen object.

Source: From Brehm (1956).

A control group (shown on the bottom line in the table) indicated that the effect was due primarily to dissonance reduction. These women made the first rating but, instead of next choosing between two items and receiving their preference, they were simply given one of the products they had rated high. When they rerated all the products, they showed no tendency to increase the evaluation of the object they owned. This demonstrated that the reevaluation was not simply due to pride of ownership—making the decision was the critical factor.

The tendency toward reevaluation is particularly strong when the two alternatives are initially rated close. If, before making a decision about which car to buy, we much prefer the Ford to the Chevrolet, we have little difficulty deciding and there is relatively little dissonance afterward. There are few reasons why we should have made the opposite choice and therefore few dissonant elements. Since there is little dissonance, there is relatively little change in our evaluations of the two alternatives. On the other hand, if the Ford and the Chevrolet were close in our estimation before we made the decision, it should arouse a great deal of dissonance. The more reason we had for choosing the Chevrolet, the more dissonance is aroused by picking the Ford. Thus, when two alternatives are close, a great deal of dissonance is aroused. After the decision is made, there are greater reevaluations of the two alternatives.

Brehm tested this notion also. He gave some women a choice between a product they had ranked high and one they had ranked only one point below it. Other women were given a choice between a high-ranked product and one that was, on the average, two and one-half points below it. Thus, some had to choose between two products they liked approximately equally, and others had the easier choice between products that were quite different in their evaluation. As shown in Table 12–1, the two conditions differed considerably in the amount of dissonance reduction they produced after the choice. When the products were far apart initially (the low-dissonance condition), there was a total of .37 scale points of dissonance reduction; when the products were quite close (the high-dissonance condition), there was a total of .85 scale points of dissonance reduction. As the theory predicts, the closer the alternatives to begin with, the more dissonance aroused by the decision and the more attitude change after the decision is made.

disconfirmed expectations

Dissonance is especially likely to be aroused when a person puts a great deal of energy into a commitment or decision, and then finds that his expectations about its effects are not fulfilled. Knowing that he is strongly committed to his course of action is dissonant with his disappointment about its effects. Someone sells all his worldly goods because he expects the world to end, but it does not; he goes through a severe initiation to join a group and the group turns out to be terrible; he works hard in high school, fills out a five-page application form, and pays a huge tuition in order to go to a particular college and then the college turns out to be not very good.

When such strongly held expectations are disappointed, the magnitude of the dissonance aroused is a direct function of the amount of work, effort, or expenditure of any kind that the individual has undergone. The cognition "I paid $100 to enter this college" is somewhat dissonant with

the knowledge that the college is no good; the knowledge that I paid $4,000 to enter it is more dissonant. Thus, the greater the initial investment, the more the dissonance that is aroused and the more the dissonance reduction that occurs. If the dissonance reduction is accomplished by reevaluating the outcome (e.g., deciding that the college is really quite good), the more the initial investment, the greater the reevaluation.

When the results of such commitments fall short of expectations, dissonance can be reduced in a variety of ways. One alternative is for the individual to convince himself that things did not really work out too badly. For example, after paying $4,000 to get into college, he tends to convince himself that it really is a good college. Another possibility is for him to decide that his expectation was somewhat incorrect but that the basic idea was correct. This was the reaction of a group who predicted the end of the world (Festinger et al., 1956). They thought that the world was going to end on a particular day but that they would be saved by a spaceship from outer space. The group kept to itself, avoided publicity, and in general was quiet about its beliefs. When the fateful day arrived and passed without the world being destroyed, they were initially greatly shaken. Their response, however, was not to give up their beliefs and return to normal life. This would not have reduced the dissonance caused by all the effort they had put into their plans. Instead, they decided that the day was put off but that the end of the world was coming soon. In addition, they changed their style considerably. Instead of being quiet and avoiding publicity, they suddenly began to proselytize quite actively. They argued that their efforts had postponed the end of the world. In this way, they demonstrated their great faith in their beliefs and also tried to attract others to support them. Presumably, this would reduce the dissonance by showing that their original beliefs were basically correct and that, in fact, more and more people were accepting them.

lasting commitment

A variety of different factors determine the magnitude of postdecision dissonance. One key to attitude change as a dissonance-reducing mechanism is maintaining the person's commitment to the decision. As long as the person feels irreversibly committed to that course of action, dissonance promotes attitude change. But if the person feels that he can get out of the decision if it works out badly, or that he may not have to go through with it at all, dissonance will not be present, and no attitude change may occur. Little dissonance will be created by paying $4,000 tuition if you know you can transfer to the state university after the first quarter and get most of it refunded.

Wilhelmy (1974) conducted a simple demonstration of how dissonance does not occur when the person no longer feels committed to a decision. In this experiment, subjects had to taste a series of very bitter solutions (quinine sulfate). Then they were asked to commit themselves to taking part in a further experiment that would involve the same kind of unpleasant tastes, and for which they would be paid a small amount of money (either $1 or $3). All the subjects agreed. Then their treatment diverged. The *commitment* subjects simply proceeded with the original experiment. But before the *decommitment* subjects did, the experimenter said the experiment might well not take place because of a lack of funds, so the subject need not promise to take part. In other words, he told the subject not to feel too committed to his promise. The subjects all then rated the pleasantness of the solutions they had been tasting. The commitment subjects rated them as much more pleasant than did the decommitment subjects. Presumably, when the latter no longer felt committed to further tasting, no more dissonance needed to be reduced, and they did not need to change their attitudes about the solutions to justify the decision to taste.

choice

A crucial prerequisite to the arousal of dissonance is the feeling of choice about the decision. If you feel you freely and of sound mind chose the Chevrolet, you will have dissonance to reduce afterward. But many times we do not feel much sense of choice about what we do. Maybe the salesperson talked us into signing a contract and writing a check before we knew what was happening. Or maybe our old car had been wrecked and this was the only new one available. Without the feeling of choice, there is no dissonance.

The importance of a sense of choice has been illustrated in some experiments on communicator credibility. The basic idea is that if we choose to listen to a communicator with low credibility, or whom we dislike, that choice creates dissonance. One way to reduce that dissonance is to change our attitudes about the communicator and his message: if we freely chose to listen to him, he must know what he's talking about. So for no-choice situations, the dissonance theory prediction is like that discussed earlier: attractive sources should be more persuasive than unattractive sources. But when the listener must actively choose to expose himself to the communication, dissonance becomes involved, and the prediction changes. Choosing to listen to a negative communicator arouses dissonance that can be reduced by changing one's attitudes to agree with the source's position. Choosing to listen to a positive communicator does not arouse dissonance, so there should be less pressure to change attitudes.

A number of experiments have been done to test this idea. Jones and Brehm (1967) had a communicator, ostensibly the head of the public relations department for the NCAA, either lauding his experience with undergraduates (positive source) or berating them for their irresponsibility, laziness, and so on (negative source). Then the subject's choice was varied about listening to the communication (an argument for doing away with intercollegiate sports). In a no-choice condition the subject was just whisked through the experiment. In the high-choice condition, the experimenter carefully stopped twice and told the subject he did not have to listen to the message if he did not want to, and each time got the subject explicitly to agree to do so. The results showed, as predicted, that choice produced higher agreement with the negative communicator and no choice produced higher agreement with the positive communicator.

This basic study was extended to more realistic situations in later studies. Himmelfarb and Arazi (1974) had the communicator, supposedly a government official, propose tuition increases at Tel-Aviv and Haifa universities. Source likability was varied by having the communicator either attack or praise students. Again it was found that with high choice, the negative communicator was the more persuasive, whereas the reverse held with no choice. Finally, Cooper, Darley, and Henderson (1974) had political campaigners go door to door advocating a change in the tax laws. Some appeared to be "hippies" (the negative sources); others were dressed more conventionally. Respondents who had chosen to listen to the hippie campaigners were more persuaded than those who had chosen to listen to the more conventionally dressed. It seems unlikely to us that in general negative communicators are the most persuasive, even when high choice about exposure is present. But these findings do illustrate that such phenomena do occur sometimes; they also show the rather broad applicability of dissonance theory.

certainty of consequences

An interesting aspect of the effect of decisions is that the reevaluation appears only when the result of the decision is certain. If a person chooses between two alternatives but thinks he may still get both of them, apparently no dissonance is aroused and no reevaluation occurs (Allen, 1964; Jecker, 1964). Students were asked to choose between two popular records and were told they would definitely get the one they chose. In some cases, they were told there was a good chance they would also get the unchosen record; other students were told there was a small chance, and a third group was told there was no chance.

They had previously rated all the records, and after making the choice, they rated them again. Only when they were certain not to get the unchosen record did reevaluation occur. When there was even a small chance that they would get both records, there was little change in their ratings. Apparently, only when we definitely give up one alternative for another is dissonance aroused and the typical postdecisional effect occurs.

A related point is that a person must feel he could have anticipated the negative consequences of a decision, or no dissonance is produced. In a theoretical paper on this topic, Carlsmith and Freedman (1968) argued that there should be nothing dissonant about making a choice or performing an act that turned out badly as long as there was no way for the individual to have anticipated this negative outcome. As the authors said, "nobody's perfect" and nobody therefore expects to make the right decision every time. If, on the basis of all the available information, he makes a choice or performs an act, and then an entirely new and surprising negative event follows, the individual should not experience dissonance. If someone decides to walk to class on the left side of the street rather than the right side, and as he walks along a brick suddenly falls off a roof and hits him on the head, this is a terrible misfortune. But (if he lives) he should not experience dissonance. The cognition "I chose to walk on the left side of the street" is not dissonant with the cognition "a brick hit me on the head." For all intents and purposes, the two cognitions are not relevant to each other. On the other hand, if he knew that there was some chance that he would get hit on the head, perhaps because in the last week three other people had been hit on the head by bricks, then dissonance probably would be aroused. The person must *feel* responsible in order to feel dissonance. If he firmly believes, correctly or otherwise, that he could not possibly have foreseen the negative consequences, there is nothing dissonant about negative consequences. On the other hand, if he thinks that he might have been able to foresee the negative consequences (again whether or not this is rational), he should feel dissonance.

This, then, suggests that dissonance arising from negative consequences of a choice only occurs when the negative consequences could have been foreseen. This theoretical analysis has been supported in a series of very nice studies. In the first, Brehm and Jones (1970) had subjects choose one of two records, just as in the choice studies described earlier. But there were additional positive or negative consequences to the choice: if the subject chose the correct record, she would also get free tickets to the local movie house, but if she chose the wrong one, she would get no tickets. The critical variation was whether these additional consequences of the choice were foreseen or not. So in the "foreseen" condition, the experimenter told the subject about the possibility of the tickets before she made her choice, and said she could probably figure out which was the right record (i.e., the one with the free tickets attached to it) if she thought about it. In the "unforeseen" condition, they were told about the tickets only after making their choice. Then all subjects rated the original records. The dissonance prediction was that dissonance would be maximum when the person's choice had foreseen negative consequences, and much less with foreseen positive consequences, or unforeseen negative consequences. And this is how the data turned out, as shown in Table 12–2. Later studies by Cooper (1971) and Cooper and Brehm (1971) produced similar results.

TABLE 12–2
mean dissonance reduction, as a function of consequences of choice

	FORESEEN	UNFORESEEN
Negative Consequences (got no tickets)	+1.73	+0.25
Positive Consequences (received tickets)	+0.38	+1.07

Entry is sum of increased rating of chosen object and decreased rating of rejected object, following choice

Adapted from Brehm and Jones, 1970, p. 427.

responsibility for consequences

It turns out, however, that even unforeseen negative consequences provoke dissonance, as long as the decision-maker feels responsible for the consequences. If he feels no responsibility for the outcome, there is no dissonance regardless of how disastrous the result. If he does feel responsible, then dissonance occurs whether the consequence could reasonably have been foreseen or not.

The importance of perceived choice is that it brings with it perceived responsibility for all consequences—whether or not it is "logical" to feel responsible for them. As we saw earlier in connection with attribution theory, people tend to make internal attributions whenever behavior is committed under free choice, and assign responsibility to whatever act is internally caused. This is the importance of post-mortems on political disasters, whether large ones, like the Nazi mass murders of Jews, or relatively small ones, like Watergate. The issue is whether the culprits were just "following orders" or not; that is, did they have free choice, and thus responsibility for the consequences? The importance of the dissonance approach to such problems is that when people feel they have no choice, they do not feel responsible for the consequences, so they do not have to defend them. People who felt they were "just following orders" find it easier to criticize their own acts. But people who made the original decisions, and felt free to do so, have to defend their actions more strenuously.

Pallak and his colleagues have designed a series of studies to illustrate this point. In the first one (Pallak, Sogin, and Van Zante, 1974) a boring task was reevaluated in a more favorable direction, consistent with dissonance reduction, even when the negative consequences (learning that the task was just wasted time) were not known until after the task was completed—as long as the subject completed it under high perceived choice. In a second experiment, they found that perceived choice inspired more favorable evaluations of the task only when given unforeseen negative consequences, again consistent with a dissonance analysis. As they say, "initial volition may imply responsibility for unforeseen consequences."

In later work (Sogin & Pallak, 1976), they pinpointed the effect as depending on an internal attribution. If the negative consequences came about because of something the subject felt responsible for, a dissonance reevaluation would take place whether the effects were foreseen or unforeseen. The subjects had to complete a very boring task copying out random numbers; the negative consequences were that the subject's work could not be used. But some subjects were under internal attribution conditions: whether their work could be used or not depended on whether the subject really was doing his job correctly (writing random numbers). In the external attribution condition, it depended on chance. What they found was that choice produced a dissonance effect (i.e., a reevaluation of the task in a more favorable direction) only under the internal attribution condition, and independent of whether the consequences were foreseeable or not. This can be seen in Table 12–3. Notice that nothing much matters when there is low choice; no dissonance is created. And with external attributions, the consequences do not matter much. In all these cases, the subjects feel external forces determined their behavior, and no dissonance is created. But with *both* high choice *and* an internal attribution, the task is evaluated much more favorably. That is the effect of dissonance.

TABLE 12–3
effects of initial choice, foreseeable or unforeseeable negative consequences, and internal or external attribution of causality for negative consequences on task evaluation

NEGATIVE CONSEQUENCES	HIGH CHOICE	LOW CHOICE
Foreseeable		
Internal attribution	46.42	33.50
External attribution	31.50	33.42
Unforeseeable		
Internal attribution	46.00	32.53
External attribution	30.27	37.67

Note. The higher the mean, the more favorable is the task evaluation.
Source: Sogin & Pallak, 1976, p. 305.

So the critical question regarding unforeseen negative consequences is whether or not the individual *feels* his own prior behavior was responsible for them. That is why perceived choice is so important. When a person chooses something that works out badly, he feels responsible for the outcome, and it creates dissonance for him.

attitude-discrepant behavior

The other situation to which the theory of cognitive dissonance has been most often applied is that of attitude-discrepant behavior. Although this is probably the most interesting application of the theory, it is also the most controversial, because dissonance theory comes into the most direct conflict with the incentive and attribution approaches to attitudes. We shall describe first the dissonance analysis and some of the work that has stemmed from it and then some conflicting interpretations of this situation.

The analysis in terms of dissonance is quite straightforward. When an individual holds a belief and performs an act that is inconsistent with it, dissonance is produced, because it follows from the fact that he holds that attitude that he would not perform that particular behavior. If someone is a pacifist, he would not join the Marines. If he does so, he feels dissonance. This dissonance acts like a drive, and he has a tendency to reduce it. He can do so by changing his attitude on pacifism. Someone who believes a task is dull and is then induced to tell someone else that the task is really enjoyable experiences dissonance. He can reduce this dissonance by evaluating the task more positively—if the task were enjoyable, his description is accurate and no dissonance is experienced.

Whenever someone performs an attitude-discrepant behavior, he

Michael D. Sullivan

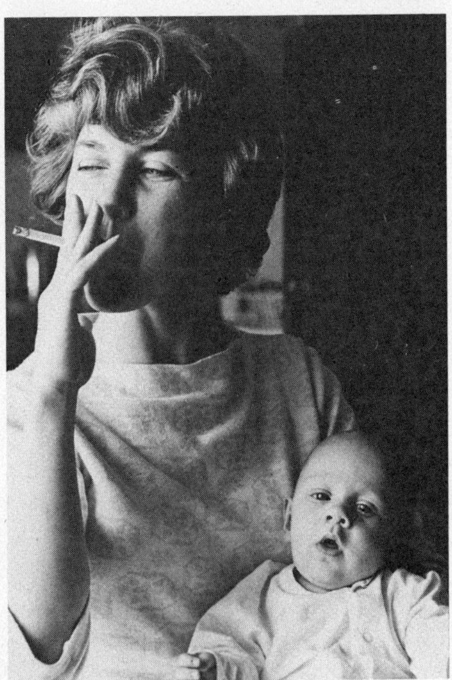

should experience some dissonance and there should be a tendency for his attitude to change. Note that the other element in the situation (his knowledge that he performed the behavior) does not change readily. He has, in fact, performed the act and would find it difficult to convince himself that he did not. Accordingly, most of the pressure must be relieved by changing the attitude. This analysis provides an explanation of why engaging in attitude-discrepant behavior tends to produce changes in the relevant attitude. The discrepant act arouses dissonance that can be reduced most easily by changing the attitude to make it less discrepant from the behavior.

The next question is what determines how much attitude change will occur as a result of such behavior. The more dissonance aroused, the more attitude change will be necessary to reduce it. As discussed previously, the amount of dissonance aroused depends on the importance of the cognitive elements involved and the relative number of dissonant and consonant elements. In particular, anything in the situation that puts pressure on the individual to perform the discrepant act or provides a reason for performing it is a consonant element and should reduce the amount of dissonance.

On the other hand, there has to be enough pressure on the person to

Monkmeyer/Falk

make him commit the counterattitudinal act. A person normally does not act in a way contrary to his attitudes unless there is some reason to do so. So imagine the person as being subjected to a certain level of pressure to perform the attitude-discrepant act. The pressure has to be sufficient to produce the act. Yet beyond that level, the more pressure is exerted, the less the dissonance, and thus the less the attitude change. The optimal level of pressure is thus a *barely sufficient* amount; enough to produce the behavior, but not enough to remove the dissonance. This assumption has led to interesting and provocative predictions regarding the effect of various factors on the amount of attitude change resulting from attitude-discrepant behavior in quite a number of different situations.

threats

Among the most direct and forceful pressures are threats. One way to try to get the individual to perform a particular act is to threaten him with punishment. If he does not pay his income taxes, do his homework, wash behind his ears, or allow himself to be drafted into the army, he is penalized. Threats are also used to prevent people from doing things. If someone drives too fast, steals cookies from the cookie jar, plays with a forbidden toy, smokes marijuana, he may be punished. The severity of the possible punishments naturally varies enormously. He may get a mild reprimand, miss his dessert, be fined $100, spend five years in jail, or even face execution. Assuming the threat of punishment is strong enough to produce the desired behavior or prevent the behavior it is supposed to prevent, greater threat should produce less attitude change.

In experiments by Aronson and Carlsmith (1963) and Freedman (1965), children were shown a group of toys and forbidden to play with one of them. They were threatened with either mild or severe punishment if they played with that particular toy. Under these circumstances, if they obeyed and did not play with the toy, dissonance was aroused. The cognition "I would like to play with that toy" is dissonant with the cognition "I am not playing with it." If there were no other relevant cognitions, it would follow from liking the toy that they would play with it. In this situation, the threat served as a consonant element: "I will be punished if I play with it." The key point is that the more severe threat was a stronger consonant element, and should have resulted in less total dissonance.

If the children did not play with the toy, we would expect the dissonance aroused to produce some change in their attitude toward it. A convenient way to reduce the dissonance would be to decide that the toy was not attractive or to accept the belief that it was wrong to play with it. Either change would make their attitude less dissonant with their behavior. The greater the dissonance aroused, the more changes of this sort should occur. And because the greater the threat, the less the dissonance, there should be more attitude change with lower threats. Thus, the children would experience more attitude change when the mild threat was used to prevent them from playing with the toy than when the severe threat was used.

In these experiments, none of the children played with the toy, regardless of whether they were threatened with mild or severe punishment, because both threats were strong enough to prevent them. In the Aronson and Carlsmith study, the children rerated the toys at this point. In Freedman's study, several weeks after the first session another experimenter came and gave the children an opportunity to play with some toys if they wanted to. The previously forbidden toy was one of the toys and nothing was said about not playing with it; the children were free to play with it if they desired. In this second session, the only thing that would have prevented the children from playing with the toy was some feeling that it was wrong to play with it or that the toy was no longer desirable. The results of the two experiments are shown in Table 12–4. It can be seen that in the Aronson and Carlsmith study, the children reduced their evaluation of the forbidden toy more under mild threat than under severe threat. Similarly, in Freedman's study, fewer children in the mild-threat condition than in the severe-threat condition played with the toy when they were actually given the opportunity to do so. The greater threat presumably served as a consonant element in the situation and reduced the amount of dissonance produced by not playing with the toy in the first session. The greater dissonance in the mild-threat condition was reduced by either devaluing the toy or deciding it was wrong to play with it.

TABLE 12–4
effect of severity of threat on forbidden behavior

CONDITION	PERCENTAGE DEVALUING FORBIDDEN TOY[a]	PERCENTAGE NOT PLAYING WITH FORBIDDEN TOY[b]
Mild threat	36	71
Severe threat	0	33

Sources:
[a]Aronson and Carlsmith (1963).
[b]Freedman (1965).

The implications of this relationship are very interesting. It strongly suggests that severe threats should be avoided whenever possible. The smaller the threat used, the more attitude change is to be expected. For example, if a parent wants to teach his child to be honest, he should try to do so without using strong threats. If he is successful when using only mild threats, the child is more likely to accept the *value* that honesty is good and stealing bad. If, instead, the parent uses strong threats, even if they seem to be successful in making the child behave honestly, it is less likely that the child will accept the value that honesty is inherently good. He may decide that honesty is the best policy if there is a chance of getting caught and therefore act honestly when his parent is present. When the threat (parent) is removed, he will have experienced little internal attitude change to make him sustain honest behavior.

The same is true for the entire legal system. If the goal is to convince people that hard drugs are dangerous and should not be used, the best way to do so would be by threatening them with the mildest possible punishment. If someone does not use drugs because he is afraid of being sent to jail for twenty years, he experiences little attitude change toward the drug. If he is ever in a situation in which he feels safe from prosecution, he is likely to use it, because he has no internal feelings against it. On the other hand, if he refrains from using drugs because of the threat of a $10 fine, he is more likely to change his attitude toward the drug. Then, even if he is in a situation in which he does not fear prosecution, he is unlikely to use it because his own opinion about it has changed. Of course, if the $10 fine does not prevent him from using drugs, no change occurs because there is no discrepant behavior. Thus, the ideal threat is one that is just strong enough to prevent the behavior.

positive incentives

Just as threats serve as negative reasons to prevent people from doing what they want to, so promised rewards and other positive incentives can induce people to do things they otherwise would not want to. Either way, we simply are putting pressure on people to perform acts contrary to their wishes, attitudes, values, or whatever. Any increases in incentive beyond the point that is barely sufficient to induce the behavior serve only to decrease the dissonance.

A number of different positive incentives have been studied. One is the amount of justification for performing a boring task. If someone voluntarily engages in an extremely dull activity, he generally feels dissonance, because knowledge that the task is dull is dissonant with the knowledge that he is performing it. Any reason he has for performing the task reduces this dissonance—if he thinks it is scientifically useful or will help somebody else, he would feel less dissonance than if he believes it is useless. To test this, Freedman (1963) told subjects that his study concerned concepts of numbers and that the experimental method involved their writing a large number of random numbers. The amount of justification they received for doing the task was manipulated by telling some subjects that the work they did would be extremely useful, while others (the low-justification subjects) were told that all the necessary sessions had been conducted the previous week and the data were already being analyzed. These tests would be run because they had already been scheduled, but the data from their performance would not be included in the analysis of the results.

Then all the subjects performed the task, which was to write random numbers in the small squares on graph paper for twelve minutes. (This is an exceedingly dull, tedious task, and twelve minutes is about the limit of most people's endurance.) When the task was completed, the subjects were asked to indicate how much they had enjoyed it. Those who had been given low justification said they enjoyed it considerably more than those who had been given high justification. As found in the other work on this problem, the more reason one has for doing something, the less dissonance is aroused and the less need there is to reduce the dissonance by changing his evaluation of the task.

Another factor that affects the amount of justification one has for engaging in a discrepant act is how much the individual likes the person who is trying to get him to do it. If your best friend asks you to do something—lend him a dollar, drive him to the airport, help him cheat on an exam—there is a considerable amount of pressure to agree. If someone

Drawing by Frascino; © 1975 The New Yorker Magazine, Inc.

"I suppose I shouldn't admit this, but I liked it better at three-fifty."

you dislike asks you, you are under considerably less pressure. Under most circumstances, it is more difficult to refuse a friend. Thus, if you do something for someone, there should be more dissonance aroused if you dislike the other person than if you like him. The more you like the other person, the more justification you have for agreeing (for performing the discrepant act) and the less dissonance there would be. This, in turn, means that agreeing to perform a discrepant act for somebody you dislike produces more attitude change than performing the same act for someone you like.

This effect was demonstrated in a study (Zimbardo et al., 1965) in which subjects were persuaded by two different kinds of experimenters to eat grasshoppers. In one condition, the experimenter was pleasant, casual, relaxed, and friendly. He presented his arguments in an offhand manner and did his best to be as attractive as possible. In the other condition, the experimenter was cold, formal, somewhat aggressive, and rather forbidding. In general, he did everything he could to be unpleasant. After the subjects who had chosen to eat the grasshoppers had done so, they indicated how much they liked them.

The analysis in terms of dissonance is straightforward. If a subject chose to eat the grasshoppers, dissonance existed if he disliked them. This dissonance could be reduced by making his evaluation of the grasshoppers more positive. To the extent that he liked the experimenter and was eating the grasshoppers as a favor to him, he had additional justification for performing the discrepant behavior. Therefore, the more he liked the experimenter, the less dissonance would exist and the less need he would have to decide that he really liked the grasshoppers.

The results were consistent with this analysis. Subjects who ate the grasshoppers when there was a nasty experimenter liked the grasshoppers more than those who ate the grasshoppers when there was a pleasant experimenter. The pleasant experimenter provided justification, which reduced the dissonance and therefore made it less necessary to reevaluate the grasshoppers.

Similarly, the more money someone is paid for performing an attitude-discrepant act, the less dissonance should be produced if he performs it. In a study by Festinger and Carlsmith (1959), volunteers for an experiment worked on an exceedingly dull task. After they had completed the task, the experimenter said he needed their help because his usual assistant was unable to be there that day. He said that he was studying the effect of preconceptions on people's performance on a task. He was studying several groups of subjects who were told good things about the task ahead of time, bad things, or nothing. The next subject was supposed to receive favorable information about the task before performing it. The experimenter then asked the subject whether he would be willing to do this for him. All he would have to do is stop the next subject as he was coming into the room, talk to him briefly about the experiment, and tell him that the task was an exceedingly enjoyable one. In other words, he was supposed to pretend to be a regular subject who was just completing the experiment and to lie to the next subject about the dull task by saying that he had found it enjoyable.

At this point, the key experimental manipulation was introduced. Some subjects were told that the experimenter would pay them $1 for helping, and other subjects were told they would be paid $20. Virtually all the subjects agreed to the arrangement and proceeded to describe the task to the next subject as very enjoyable. There was also a control group, the members of which were not asked to tell the lie. Soon afterward, the experimenter had all the subjects indicate how much they had actually enjoyed the task. Deciding that the task was quite enjoyable would reduce any dissonance the subject might have felt. As expected, all the experimental subjects increased their ratings of how enjoyable the task was more than did the controls.

The interesting finding, however, was the comparison between the $1 and $20 conditions (Table 12–5). Those who were paid $1 rated the task more positively than those who were paid $20. This is what dissonance theory would predict. The larger amount of money served as an additional reason for performing the task; therefore it was a consonant element in the situation and reduced the overall amount of dissonance. The less dissonance, the less attitude change. Thus the more the subjects were paid for performing the discrepant behavior, the less attitude change they experienced.

TABLE 12–5
amount of reward and attitude change

CONDITION	ENJOYED TASK	WILLING TO PARTICIPATE IN SIMILAR EXPERIMENTS
$1 reward	+1.35	+1.20
$20 reward	− .05	− .25
Control	− .45	− .62

Source: Adapted from Festinger and Carlsmith (1959).

Two experiments by Linder, Cooper, and Jones (1967), in which the perception of choice was the crucial factor determining the arousal of dissonance, produced similar results. Subjects wrote an essay that disagreed with their opinion on an issue. Some subjects were made to feel that they had free choice about whether or not they wrote the essay, whereas others were given no choice. Half the subjects in each condition were paid $2.50, and half were paid $0.50. The amount of attitude change in the four conditions for the two experiments is shown in Table 12–6.

TABLE 12–6
reward, choice, and attitude change

CONDITION	FREE CHOICE	NO CHOICE
Experiment 1:		
$0.50 reward	2.96	1.66
$2.50 reward	1.64	2.34
Experiment 2:		
$0.50 reward	3.64	2.68
$2.50 reward	2.72	3.46

Note: The figures are ratings on a scale from 1 to 7. The higher the figure, the greater the attitude change.
Source: Adapted from Linder, Cooper, and Jones (1967).

With free choice, the typical dissonance effect appeared – there was more change with less reward. With no choice, the dissonance effect did not obtain – indeed there was more change with greater reward. As we suggested earlier, perception of choice is necessary for the arousal of dissonance. When there is no choice, dissonance is not produced and the dissonance analysis does not apply.

Additional research has helped to pin down the exact conditions under which dissonance can be aroused and produce attitude change following attitude-discrepant behavior. It does not occur all the time, only under some quite definite conditions. Using the same reasoning we presented earlier regarding post-decisional dissonance, Collins and Hoyt (1972) have suggested that low incentives work best to produce attitude change when (1) the person feels a strong sense of personal responsibility for the consequences of his act and when (2) it has important negative consequences. To test this, they approached student subjects in their dormitories and asked them to write essays against open visitation rights for the opposite sex (virtually all the subjects were in favor of open visitation rights). The design of the experiment was similar to many of the others discussed in this section on dissonance theory, so we can just focus on the particular set of conditions that seem to have produced dissonance, and consequent attitude change. These involved low incentive (50 cents paid to write the essay, rather than $2.50), high negative consequences (university administrators would use the essay in determining university policy, rather than filing it as a document of mere historical interest), and personal responsibility (the subject signed a form taking responsibility for the contents of the essay, rather than stating he was just following an assigned topic and was not responsible for the contents). Under these conditions, the subjects did change their attitudes toward the position consistent with their attitude-discrepant act. That is, they became more opposed to open visitation rights.

These, then, seem to be the conditions under which research most commonly turns up dissonance-induced attitude change following attitude-discrepant behavior: minimum incentive, negative consequences, and personal responsibility. The person must be aware of these conditions when he commits himself to the behavior (Cooper & Goethals, 1974, Gerald, Conolley, and Wilhelmy, 1974). And free choice is a prime cause of the feeling of responsibility. These, of course, are essentially the same conditions that must hold for postdecisional dissonance and the attitude change that it creates. To dissonance theorists, this is a somewhat narrower set of conditions than they originally proposed. Both postdecisional dissonance and dissonance inspired by attitude-discrepant behavior seem not to be as common as had been held in the earliest, most grandiose versions of dissonance theory. But they do seem to occur fairly reliably, given this restricted set of circumstances.

incentive theory

Thus far, we have described the effect of attitude-discrepant behavior entirely in terms of the theory of cognitive dissonance. An alternative conceptualization of the situation has been made in terms of learning or incentive. Someone who engages in attitude-discrepant behavior tends to be exposed to information and experiences he otherwise would not be. A child who is induced to taste spinach, which he thinks he hates, will discover what spinach tastes like; a pacifist who joins the Marines will discover a lot more about the Marines than he knew before; and a police officer who is somehow induced to argue in favor of legalizing marijuana may think of some arguments he would not otherwise have heard or listened to. Exposure to this information may, in itself, change the individual's attitude. He may discover that spinach tastes good or that the Marines are a great group. Moreover, someone who argues against his own position may convince himself. If he tries to come up with the best possible arguments, he will be exposed to very persuasive communications. Thus, rather than dissonance reduction causing the attitude change, it may be due to the usual process of persuasion.

An impressive illustration of the learning effect of engaging in discrepant behavior was provided by Irving Janis. In his work on convincing people not to smoke (Janis and Mann, 1965), cigarette smokers playacted the role of someone who has lung cancer. The subjects became extremely involved in their roles—they looked at X-rays, pretended they were talking to the doctor, playacted their response to the news that they had cancer, imagined themselves waiting for the operation and finally undergoing it, and so on. It was an intense, emotionally arousing experience for them. Janis reported that subjects who went through this experience were more likely to be successful in giving up cigarette smoking than were people who did not participate in this kind of emotional role playing. In a follow-up survey six months later (Mann and Janis, 1968), a large percentage of the people in this condition were still not smoking cigarettes. The subjects who went through less involving experiences, who engaged in less intensive playacting, were considerably less successful in giving up smoking. Apparently, the intensive role playing was an unusually effective persuasive device.

Although the two explanations of the effect of attitude-discrepant behavior are quite different, they are not completely inconsistent. Both cognitive dissonance and learning play a role in the effect of discrepant behavior on attitude change and, under most circumstances, reinforce each other. Each explains a portion of the effect. Individuals do change their attitudes in order to make them consistent with the discrepant behavior; and people are to some extent influenced by their experiences while engaging in the discrepant behavior. Both processes usually work in the same direction. Operating together, they make the effect of discrepant behavior even stronger than it would be if one of them operated alone.

The one apparent contradiction involves the effect of incentives. Dissonance theory predicts that there is more change with less incentive. The learning explanation predicts that, under some circumstances, greater incentive for performing the discrepant act produces more attitude change than less incentive. This occurs when the added incentive in some way exposes the individual to more convincing information. For example, if someone is induced to make a speech defending a position opposite from his own, it might be expected that the more he is paid for doing so, the harder he would work and the better job he would do. Doing a better job means constructing better arguments and presenting them more forcefully. The better the arguments, the more convincing they are. This holds for the individual making the speech as well as for those listening to it. Therefore, if the larger sum of money caused the individual to make a better speech, he would convince himself more and we would expect more attitude change.

The same argument could hold for other kinds of discrepant tasks. Someone who is paid more or given better reasons for engaging in a particular act may perform the act better, become more involved in it, pay more attention to it, and, in general, perform the act more thoroughly and completely. His greater involvement would tend to expose him to more information, might cause him to appreciate the act more, and would tend to convince him of the worth of the act. Anytime that greater incentive causes an individual to perform a discrepant act more fully, there should be some tendency for him to be more persuaded by the act itself and there would be more attitude change.

Another consideration in terms of learning theory is that, as discussed previously, reinforcement can increase the effectiveness of a persuasive communication. Extraneous reinforcement increases attitude change, and the learning approach predicts that related reinforcement would also. If giving someone a Pepsi while he is reading an essay makes him agree more with the essay, paying him $20 for writing an attitude-discrepant essay should make him agree more with the essay he writes. Moreover, this should hold even if the additional reward does not make him write a better essay—the reinforcement alone should increase persuasion.

Thus, there are several reasons from the learning or incentive point of view why greater rewards for performing a discrepant act should produce more (not less) attitude change. Since dissonance theory makes the opposite prediction, there is a clear conflict between the two approaches. As might be expected, there has been a considerable amount of research attempting to determine which prediction is correct, and a clear assessment of the results is difficult. Greater rewards have been shown to increase change, to decrease change, and to have no effect on change. Although it is difficult to weigh this kind of inconsistent evidence, more and somewhat stronger studies have supported the prediction of dissonance theory than that of learning theory. In addition, all the work on other forms of justification, particularly threats, is in line with the dissonance predictions. Since learning theory treats threats in much the same way as it does rewards, data that show greater change with small threats provide strong support for the dissonance interpretation. Thus, it seems that, in general, the dissonance analysis of discrepant behavior has been shown to fit many situations, though not all of them.

This does not mean, however, that one should discard the learning analysis. As we stated earlier, both approaches are relevant, and together give a fuller understanding of the effect of discrepant behavior on attitudes. The apparent contradiction between the two explanations can be resolved by noting that the dissonance effect is dominant under some circumstances, whereas the learning effect is dominant under others. The critical factor is whether or not dissonance was aroused in the first place. If a considerable amount of dissonance has been aroused, most of the effect would be due to dissonance reduction and there would be more change with less incentive; if relatively little dissonance has been aroused, most of the effect would be due to learning and there would be more change with more incentive.

An experiment by Carlsmith, Collins, and Helmreich (1966) demonstrates both these effects and supports this way of resolving the conflict. Individuals were induced to take a stand discrepant from their own opinion by having them take part in a dull task and then say that it was really fun, interesting, and exciting. The assumption was that telling this lie would produce dissonance, primarily when it was told directly to another person. Under these circumstances, the subjects were clearly misleading the other person, making a statement they did not believe, and doing all this in public.

Some subjects, as in the Festinger-Carlsmith study described previously, told the lie in a face-to-face situation to someone who was supposedly another experimental subject. This condition was expected to arouse a considerable amount of dissonance. Other subjects were told to write an essay describing the task as enjoyable. However, these essays were to be anonymous, would never be shown to other subjects, and would be used only as sources of phrases and ideas for an essay the experimenter himself would eventually write. This condition was expected to arouse little or no dissonance, because the subject was simply performing an exercise and was in no way committing himself publicly to the discrepant message. Some subjects in each condition were paid $5 for performing the task; some were paid $1.50; and some were paid $0.50. After performing the discrepant behavior, all the subjects were asked to rerate how enjoyable the original task had been.

The results are shown in Figure 12–1. It is apparent that they are consistent with the explanation above. When the task was designed to arouse dissonance, there was more attitude change with less incentive. The most change occurred in the $0.50 condition, the least in the $5 condition. When the task was designed not to arouse dissonance, the opposite was found—there was more change with $5 than with $1.50, which, in turn, produced more change than $0.50.

Other studies have also demonstrated that the effect of rewards and other forms of justification depend on the particular conditions as already specified in some detail. In general, greater incentives for performing a discrepant act result in less attitude change if dissonance is aroused and that is most likely when the person feels a strong sense of responsibility for negative consequences of his act.

Note that we are referring only to change produced by attitude-discrepant behavior. In these circumstances the dissonance effect is usually the dominant one. Most of the research discussed in Chapters 8, 9, and 10 did not refer to attitude change produced by attitude-discrepant behavior. When change is produced by a persuasive communication or in-

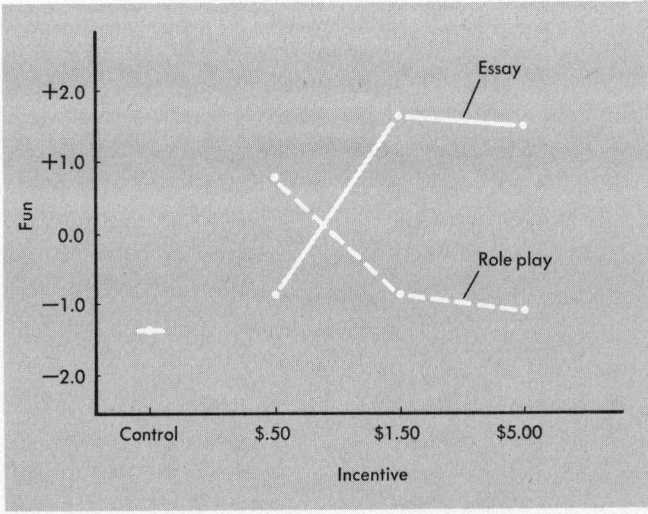

Figure 12–1
Forced compliance, incentive, and attitude change. When dissonance was aroused (the roleplay condition), greater incentive produced less attitude change; when dissonance was not aroused (essay condition), greater incentive produced more change. (Carlsmith, Collins, and Helmreich, "Studies in forced compliance," Journal of Personality and Social Psychology, 1966, 4, p. 9. Copyright 1966 by the American Psychological Association, and reproduced by permission.)

formation of any kind, the learning effect is dominant; then, the more incentive there is in the situation, the more attitude change we expect. Thus, the dissonance explanation is particularly relevant to the effect of discrepant behavior on attitudes, and the learning explanation is more relevant and powerful in the attitude-change paradigm involving discrepant communications from someone else.

self-perception theory

Several alternative explanations of the dissonance phenomena have been offered in terms of one form or another of attribution theory which is discussed in detail in Chapter 4. The most interesting reinterpretation was offered by Daryl Bem (1967) who described the attitude-discrepant behavior situation in terms of what he called self-perception. He argued that all of our attitudes are based on our perceptions of our own behavior. If we eat oranges and somebody asks us how we feel about oranges, we say to ourselves, "I eat oranges; therefore I must like oranges." Accordingly we tell the person that we like oranges. Similarly if we vote for a Republican, we assume that we have Republican attitudes; if we go to church, we assume that we are religious; and so on.

It is easy to see how this might apply to attitude-discrepant behavior. A subject is induced to tell someone that a particular task was very enjoyable. When the subject is subsequently asked how enjoyable he thought the task was, he says to himself, "I said that the task was enjoyable and I must think that it is." Therefore after he had said that the task was enjoyable he will be more likely to rate it as enjoyable. But there is more to the situation than that. If he has been paid one dollar to say that the task was enjoyable, he says to himself, "I said that the task was enjoyable and I was paid only one dollar. One dollar is not enough to make me lie, so I must really think that the task is enjoyable." On the other hand if he is paid twenty dollars, that is a sufficient amount to tell a lie, and he is therefore less likely to believe that he thinks that the task is enjoyable. Thus this explanation makes the same predictions as dissonance theory—the more the subject is paid to make the discrepant statement the less he will believe it. Similar explanations can be offered for virtually all of the dissonance phenomena. The major difference is that instead of the subject reducing cognitive inconsistency by changing his attitudes (as in dissonance theory), the subject simply bases his response to an attitude questionnaire on his perception of his behavior in the situation.

DISSONANCE AS AN AROUSED DRIVE It is always difficult to design an experiment that will test between two plausible theories like dissonance and self-perception. There are, however, two crucial differences between these theoretical positions. One involves the dissonance theory contention that the existence of inconsistency is uncomfortable, that it acts as a drive much like hunger, and that the subject does what he can to reduce this discomfort. Bem's analysis is entirely cognitive and certainly would not expect these situations to arouse any kind of discomfort or drive. Fortunately this difference between theories is directly testable. Waterman (1969), Pallak (1970), and Pallak and Pittman (1972) provide such a test and seem to show clearly that a drive is aroused. In the latter study subjects first performed a dull task with high or low choice. According to dissonance theory, voluntarily performing such a task should be dissonance arousing and the subject should experience some increase in drive level. According to Bem, of course, there should be no change in the level of drive. Subjects then tried to perform a task that involved either high or low levels of competing responses. It has been demonstrated in the experimental literature that tasks with high competition (i.e., there are several competing responses rather than one obvious correct response) are more difficult under high drive than under low drive; while tasks with low competition are easier under high drive than under low drive. The results appear in Table 12–7.

TABLE 12–7
the effect of choice on drive arousal as measured by errors on high and low competition tasks

	TYPE OF TASK	
	Low Competition	High Competition
High Choice (High dissonance)	–.39	+1.61
Low Choice (Low dissonance)	+.41	+ .62

Note: A positive score means an increase in errors
Source: Adapted from Pallak and Pittman (1972).

As expected by dissonance theory, under high choice and therefore high dissonance or high drive, performance on the high competitive task was made worse while performance on low competitive lists was improved. In a second experiment, only the high competitive task was used and subjects performed a dull task under high or low choice and with high or low justification. According to dissonance theory only the high choice low justification condition is high dissonance and accordingly only this condition should have high drive. Sure enough this one condition did worse on the high competitive task than any of the others. Thus, as dissonance theory predicted, a dissonant situation produced exactly the results that would be expected if drive were aroused.

There is another way to get at this drive basis for dissonance. One implication of the misattribution studies discussed in chapter 4 is that subjective arousal states can be reduced to the extent that the person attributes them to other stimuli, such as a pill. This observation can help us determine whether dissonance depends on arousal or not. The theoretical reasoning is this. Dissonance is supposed to occur when one writes an attitude-discrepant essay under high choice conditions. But if dissonance is really an aroused internal drive, then it can be reduced by reattributing the drive to a pill, as well as by changing attitudes to restore consistency. In two studies Pittman (1975) and Zanna and Cooper (1974) have tested whether dissonance effects occur when arousal is attributed to something other than inconsistency. Zanna and Cooper gave subjects a pill, which they were told in one condition was supposed to make them feel tense, and in another, that it would make them feel relaxed. Subjects were then induced to write counterattitudinal essays under either high or low choice conditions.

When they were supposed to feel tense because of the pill, there was no dissonance effect. However when the pill was only supposed to make them feel relaxed, the high choice condition produced more attitude change in the direction of the essay than did the low choice condition, in line with the usual dissonance effect. In other words, when the subject could attribute his arousal to the pill, there was no dissonance effect, and presumably no dissonance. When the subject could not attribute his arousal to the pill, the dissonance effect occured, presumably because he still felt aroused. So this gives additional evidence for supposing that dissonance effects do depend on some kind of physiological arousal mechanism, which can be eliminated or reduced if the subject can attribute his arousal to some extraneous stimulus such as a pill.

SALIENCE OF INTERNAL CUES The other crucial difference between the positions revolves around the fact that dissonance is supposed to result from inconsistency between internal cognitions, while self-perception theory assumes that people are essentially insensitive to any internal cues. Bem (1972, p. 5) says "Individuals come to 'know' their own . . . internal states partially by inferring them from observations of their own overt behavior and/or the circumstances in which this behavior occurs . . . to the extent that internal cues are weak, ambiguous, or uninterpretable, the individual is functionally in the same position as an outside observer, an observer who must necessarily rely upon those same external cues to infer the individual's inner states." Following from this reasoning, then, self-perception phenomena should not occur when the individual's attitude is highly salient to him.

The dissonance expectation is quite different. If a person performs a counterattitudinal act in the presence of highly salient cues as to his original attitude, dissonance should be just as great, because the inconsistency is the key to dissonance arousal. So several investigators have offered this as a critical test between self-perception theory and cognitive dissonance theory. That is, according to dissonance theory making the subject's initial attitude highly salient should not diminish attitude change at all, because dissonance would be as great if not greater. On the other hand, self-perception theory would predict less attitude change, on the grounds that the person would now infer his attitude less from his counterattitudinal behavior than from his now-salient initial attitude.

Several studies of this phenomenon have been conducted (Snyder & Ebbesen, 1972; Ross & Shulman, 1973; Wixon & Laird, 1976; see also Greenwald, 1975). They all followed the same general paradigm, of varying the salience of the subject's initial attitude (on the issue of how much control students should have over university curriculum), inducing the subject to write a counterattitudinal essay under conditions of high or low choice (to manipulate dissonance), and then getting a post-measure of attitude change. But the method of varying the salience of initial attitude itself differed quite sharply across these studies, with predictable consequences for their results.

de Wys/Dorka Raynor

Snyder and Ebbesen did not get an initial measure of attitude at all, but before the essay was written, the student was instructed to "take a few minutes to think about it and organize your thoughts and views on the issue of control over the kinds of courses offered by the university" (p. 506). That is, they made the *issue* salient, but did not say anything about the subject's own personal attitude on the issue. So at the time of filling out the post-measure, the Snyder and Ebbesen subjects had only a vague memory of their general thoughts about the issue, from before writing the essay. This should yield only a diffuse, unspecific set of thoughts about the issue, just the kind of vague internal cues that Bem suggests that would lead to a self-perception effect. As can be seen in Table 12–8, this yielded the self-perception pattern. The predicted dissonance effect (more attitude change with choice than with no choice) occurs when the subjects' initial thoughts are not made salient, as is usual in such experiments. But the dissonance effect is completely erased (and even reversed, though not significantly) when their "thoughts" are made salient. This pattern of results is just what self-perception theory would predict. Presumably these subjects were basing their statements of their own final attitude less on the overt attitude-discrepant behavior, and more on their mulling over their original "thoughts."

TABLE 12–8
mean attitude change (self-perception pattern)

CONDITION	CHOICE	NO CHOICE
Salience	23.0	24.2
No Salience	30.3	19.7

Note: Higher means represent greater attitude change.
Source: Snyder & Ebbesen, 1972, p. 507.

In contrast, Ross and Shulman got the subjects to fill out a questionnaire giving their exact attitudes in a first session. In a second session, subjects were divided into a reinstatement condition (in which these initial attitudes were made salient) and a nonreinstatement condition, in which they were not made salient. In the reinstatement condition, each subject wrote the counterattitudinal essay, then looked at his original questionnaire and recorded his original attitude answer on a separate piece of paper which was put in a separate envelope. Then each gave his final attitude. So the reinstatement subjects had vividly and recently in mind their exact stance on the issue of student control, yielding a very direct confrontation between the position taken in the essay, and the subject's vivid reminder of his contrary original opinion. However, in the nonreinstatement condition, the subject was not allowed to look at his original questionnaire after writing the essay. As shown in Table 12–9, the choice subjects showed more attitude change than the no choice subjects, no matter whether their initial attitudes were reinstated or not. That is, the dissonance pattern (more attitude change with choice than no choice) emerged with salient initial attitudes just as clearly as with nonsalient ones. Contrary to the self-perception hypothesis, then, attitude change depended on the inconsistency of behavior with attitudes under conditions of free choice, rather than simply on perceiving oneself as enacting a particular behavior.

TABLE 12–9
mean attitude change (dissonance pattern)

CONDITION	CHOICE	NO CHOICE
Reinstatement	16.3	3.5
Nonreinstatement	13.0	4.5

Note: Higher means represent greater attitude change.
Source: Ross & Shulman, 1973, p. 143.

Probably the lesson to be learned from these studies is that to some extent people probably do use attribution processes to infer their own attitudes from their own behavior and from their perception of the environment controlling it. But they probably do so only under circumstances in which their own attitudes are, as Bem says, vague and ambiguous. As we have seen in the previous chapters, most of the important and controversial issues that arise in the public domain are not of this kind. Everybody knows how he or she feels about busing, intervention in wars like Vietnam or the Second World War, about abortion, and so on. Under these circumstances self-perception theory seems unlikely to be very helpful. Self-perception theory, on the other hand, is very relevant to the kind of esoteric, uninvolving issues that are very common in laboratory experiments. So we would suggest that the two processes probably work best in these two different arenas: dissonance theory with more controversial, involving, salient issues, and self-perception theory on more amorphous, vague, diffuse, uninvolving, minor issues.

SUMMARY

1. Dissonance exists when the opposite of one cognition follows from another. The magnitude of dissonance is dependent on the number and importance of inconsistent cognitions. Dissonance motivates behavior designed to reduce dissonance.

2. The most important situations producing dissonance involve dissonance created by the individual's behavior. Dissonance arises following decisions, and following behavioral acts contrary to the individual's attitudes.

3. Dissonance can be reduced in a variety of ways. If the behavior itself cannot be revoked, the most important alternative is attitude change to reduce attitude-behavior discrepancies.

4. Postdecisional dissonance is greatest when the person remains committed to his decision for a long time, if he had free choice in his decision, if the consequences of the decision were known in advance and were certain, and if the individual feels responsible for the consequences of his decision.

5. Dissonance following attitude-discrepant behavior depends upon barely sufficient incentives to commit the behavior. These incentives can be either minimal threat, or minimal promised reward.

6. The maximum dissonance following attitude-discrepant behavior occurs with minimum incentive, negative consequences of the act, and clear personal responsibility for the consequences.

7. Alternative explanations for these dissonance effects have been generated by learning and attribution theorists. Research has generally supported dissonance theory explanations, except when the individual has rather vague, undefined attitudes. Under those circumstances the behavioral act may lead to a fresh self-perception by the individual of his own attitude, thus leading to attitude-behavior consistency through an attribution rather than a dissonance-reduction process.

SUGGESTIONS FOR ADDITIONAL READING

BEM, D. Self-perception: an alternative interpretation of cognitive dissonance phenomena. *Psychological Review,* 1967, 74, 183–200. A most provocative reinterpretation of the phenomena of forced compliance discovered by dissonance theorists.

BREHM, J. W., & COHEN, A. R. *Explorations in cognitive dissonance.* New York: John Wiley, 1962. A far-ranging restatement of dissonance theory after a few years' research. It shows how a theory develops as empirical research starts to get done on it.

FESTINGER, L. *A theory of cognitive dissonance.* Stanford, Calif.: Stanford University Press, 1957. The original statement of cognitive dissonance theory. It is elegant in its simplicity, and offers plausible speculations about a broad number of psychological phenomena.

FESTINGER, L., RIECKEN, H. W., & SCHACHTER, S. *When prophecy fails.* Minneapolis: University of Minnesota Press, 1956. A fascinating participant-observer study of a group that thought the world was coming to an end, and the social psychologists who joined the group hoping it would not.

FREEDMAN, J. L. Long-term behavioral effects of cognitive dissonance. *Journal of Experimental Social Psychology,* 1965, 1, 145–55. An impressive demonstration of the lasting impact of attitude change in the "forbidden toy" experiments.

GERARD, H. B., CONOLLEY, E. S. & WILHELMY, R. A. Compliance, justification, and cognitive change. In L. BERKOWITZ (ED.), *Advances in Experimental Social Psychology, Vol. 7*. New York: Academic, 1974. A useful recent synopsis of research on forced compliance, and reinterpretation of it.

LINDER, D. E., COOPER, J., & JONES, E. E. Decision freedom as a determinant of the role of incentive magnitude in attitude change. *Journal of Personality and Social Psychology*, 1967, *6*, 245–54.

WIXON, D. R., & LAIRD, J. D. Awareness and attitude change in the forced-compliance paradigm: the importance of when. *Journal of Personality and Social Psychology*, 1976, *34*, 376–84. An experiment that attempts to resolve differences in previous experiments on the dissonance vs. self-perception controversy.

13

group structure and leadership

aspects of structure
- communication patterns
- leadership

leadership: external factors
- appointed leaders and legitimacy
- amount of communication
- type of communication
- communication networks

leadership: personal characteristics
- verbal activity level
- status
- relation to the rest of the group

effects of structure on group performance
- communication and performance
- communication networks and performance
- type of leader and performance

summary

suggestions for additional reading

Thus far we have been focusing on the individual in social situations. But individuals typically do not live, work, or play alone. We are members of groups that have enormous influence on our lives. In a complex society, most people belong to many groups—a family, a circle of friends, clubs, organizations, and political parties. These groups can be as small as two or three members such as a family or as large as millions, such as all Democrats or Protestants. Social psychologists are interested in two related aspects of groups: how being in a group affects the individual, and how the group as a whole functions. In this chapter we shall discuss the structure of groups and the one most important characteristic of structure—leadership. In the next chapter, we shall consider group dynamics, the processes of group action.

aspects of structure

When a number of people are brought together in a group, they do not remain entirely undifferentiated. They develop patterns of behavior, divide tasks, adopt different roles, and so on; these structural aspects of the group have a profound effect on how it functions. Therefore, we shall begin our discussion of groups with two questions: What kinds of organization and structure appear in groups? How does a structure that is imposed on a group affect other aspects of its organization?

communication patterns

A characteristic of almost all groups is that some people talk a great deal and others say very little. The circumstances of the situation seem to have little effect on this pattern. It does not matter if the group is structured or unstructured, the problem they are discussing specific or general, the members friends or strangers. In a seminar with a permissive instructor, for example, there always seems to be one or two people who monopolize the discussion, regardless of the topic. They do most of the talking, and the rest say only an occasional word or two.

Probably the most striking aspect of this phenomenon is that it occurs despite the size of the group. Regardless of how many members there are, communication follows a fairly regular pattern that can be represented approximately by a logarithmic function. Figure 13–1 illustrates this pattern for groups of four, six, and eight. Note that in all cases one person does a great deal of talking, the next most talkative person does considerably less, and so on—the amount of talking done by each person drops at a logarithmic rate. In an eight-member group, two people contribute 60 percent of the conversation, one other contributes 14 percent, and the other five contribute only 26 percent among them. Clearly, the exact percentage done by each person will vary from group to group. There must even be some groups in which all members make equal contributions. But by and large, a pattern roughly similar to the one illustrated will appear in almost all groups.

Groups also develop other patterns of behavior even before a formal structure emerges. They seem to adopt a wide variety of specific habits and traditions. Merei (1949) noted that after three or more meetings, groups of young children formed traditions such as where each child would sit in the room, who would play with which toy, what sequence of activities would be followed, and so on. Strong patterns of this type have also been observed in mental hospitals. Particular patients sit in particular chairs and follow certain sequences of action. For example, someone sitting in one spot might always have his cigarette lighted by another patient standing near him but might also lend cigarettes to someone else. Or the whole group might shift places at a particular time and

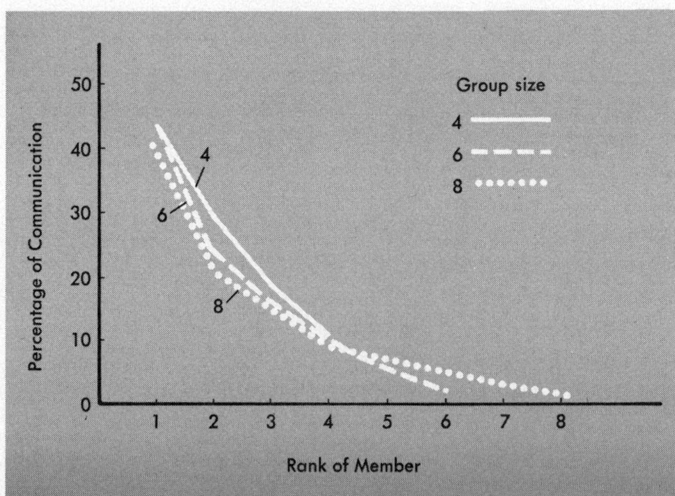

FIGURE 13–1
The amount of communication by members of a group follows a logarithmic or exponential curve. Regardless of the size of the group, the most talkative member does about 40 percent of the communicating and the amount of the other members' communication drops off sharply. The difference between the amount of communication drops off sharply. The difference between the amount of communication of the first and second most talkative people increases as the size of the group increases. (Based on Stephan and Mishler, 1952.)

in a set pattern. These examples are probably more extreme than those occurring in most situations, but one can also notice that college students tend to take the same seat at each meeting of a class—even if they selected a poor one at the beginning of the term. This kind of organization of activity appears in all groups, although few members are consciously aware of it and most might be surprised if it were pointed out. Moreover, although the patterns are informal and unverbalized, they are generally firmly held and highly resistant to change.

The differentiation of communication and development of habits are the beginnings of structure. Each member has a somewhat separate function, some participate more than others, some perform acts that others do not, etc. It is a minimal type of structure but is important as the forerunner of a more explicit type. The communication pattern is particularly crucial, because it is one of the key elements in the formation and identification of leadership in the group.

leadership

The most important feature of group structure is that there are leaders and followers. Almost all groups, both human and nonhuman, seem to have leaders. Groups of sled dogs, baboons, lions, elephants, and chickens all have leaders. Usually the strongest male asserts his dominance and then has the rights and responsibilities of leadership. He gets his pick of mates, food, and position but also must make decisions—such as where to find food—and must lead the defense of the group when necessary. Examples from nonhuman societies could be multiplied indefinitely—virtually all animals that live in groups appear to have leaders.

This is also true of human groups, though, of course, the leader need not be male and physical strength generally is not the main consideration. Teenagers standing on a street corner, men in a foxhole, a work gang, the United States Senate, and subjects gathered in a room to discuss a problem all tend to have leaders. Despite the fact that the purposes, structure, and memberships of these groups are entirely different, they cannot truly function as groups unless they have some kind of leadership.

Although the terms *leader* and *leadership* are so commonly used that everyone probably has similar notions as to their meaning, there are two different ways of identifying the leader of a group. A straightforward approach, and in many ways the most reasonable one, is to ask the group members. If everyone agrees that a particular person is the leader (and they usually do in a group that has existed for any length of time), they must believe it and must look to that person when they want leadership. Thus, in a sense, he or she is the leader. This method avoids the tricky problem of constructing a formal definition, with which not everyone would agree entirely. True, the members of the group may disagree among themselves as to what they mean by leader, but as long as they agree on who the leader is, this is no problem. In fact, it is an advantage, because the person chosen fits all the implicit definitions that the different group members hold.

Although this makes good sense, to some extent it avoids the issue. We really want to say what we think makes a person a leader; we want to be able to tell someone how to identify the leader of a group. If we watch a juvenile gang, the United States Senate, or any other group, we want to be able to identify the leader ourselves without asking for a poll. This is partly because it is often quite an undertaking to ask a group who their leader is. A more basic problem, however, is that we want to be certain we know what we are talking about when we say someone is a leader.

The central attribute of leadership is influence—the leader is generally the person in the group who has the most influence on its activities and beliefs. He is the one who initiates action, gives orders, makes decisions, settles disputes between members, and makes judgments. He is also the one who dispenses approval and disapproval, offers encouragement, serves as inspiration, and is in the forefront of any activity. These functions are merely examples of the general influence the leader exerts over the group. Any particular leader may not perform all of them, but to be a leader, he must perform many. The members do, think, and feel what he wants them to and what he tells them to a greater extent than is true for any other member of the group.

In summary, there are two ways of defining the leader. He or she is the person whom the group says is the leader and/or the person who has the most influence on the group. Both definitions are workable and will usually result in the same person being selected. In fact, some research has shown that the members of a group agree quite closely with outside observers as to who is the leader. In one study (Stein, Geis, and Damarin, 1973) actual groups were videotaped. Later, people were shown the tapes and asked to rate each of the group members on leadership and to select the real leader of the group. Previously, the group had done the same thing while they were meeting. The two sets of ratings were very similar ($r = .82$). Thus, leadership tends to be seen in the same way by group members and objective observers—it may be difficult to define, but not to recognize or measure.

The rules governing dominance in animals are apparently quite simple compared to those in human groups. In virtually all animal groups, the males who have aspirations toward leadership fight, and the winner—the strongest—becomes dominant. There is also some evidence that occasionally leadership or dominance can be achieved by two animals cooperating so that they are stronger than any other single animal. Two male baboons might cooperate to achieve dominance even though neither of them is as big and strong as a single other male. According to Konrad Lorenz (1952), somewhat similar cooperation occurs among jackdaws (birds resembling crows), so presumably this behavior is not limited to primates. But even in these circumstances, leadership depends to a large extent on strength, which is determined in more or less open competition. Determinants of human leadership are considerably more complex.

Why do particular people become leaders? There are two facets to the question. The first deals with the kinds of situations, procedures, or other factors that make a person a leader; the second deals with the kinds of people who become leaders. That is, we can answer the question in terms of properties external to the individual or in terms of personality or other characteristics of the individual.

leadership: external factors

appointed leaders and legitimacy

One way to become the leader is to be appointed by someone outside the group. An army lieutenant is the official leader of his company, and in some courts the person who happens to be selected as the first juror is the foreman. Simply being in a position of authority or being the person who is *supposed* to be the leader tends to make one the leader. This is obvious in the case of the army lieutenant, because he can give orders to the others and no one can give orders to him. Almost automatically he is the leader. It is less obvious and more interesting in the case of the jury foreman, who has no more authority than any other juror, yet tends to lead the discussion and act as the leader of the group. In general, regardless of qualifications, someone who has the formal position of leader performs the functions of the leader.

It should be pointed out, however, that there are often important

Pat Vine/De Wys

differences between leaders who have been appointed and those who have earned their position. In many cases, a group will not agree that an appointed leader deserves that position; they will not think he or she is the legitimate leader. This notion of *legitimacy* can be extremely important. In a study by Raven and French (1958), leaders were either appointed by an outside agency or elected by the group. The elected leaders had considerably more influence and power than the appointed ones. Presumably, this was due to the fact that the elected leaders were seen as more legitimate and their power to lead was therefore recognized by the rest of the group.

In recent years, the question of legitimacy of leadership has been continually raised in American universities and colleges. Even though the trustees and administrators have the legal right to run a school, students and faculty have begun to question the legitimacy of that right. The basis of the argument is that the trustees generally are not elected by the people at the institution. They are either self-perpetuating (electing their own successors) or elected by alumni, who are no longer intimately involved with the school. Similarly, presidents of colleges are usually appointed by the trustees with little or no consultation with faculty and even less with students. The students and faculty do not feel involved in the choices of trustees and administrators and, consequently, accord them little legitimacy. This problem is even more severe in public universities, which tend to be governed by boards of regents whose appointment is usually political and is almost always out of the control of the school concerned. The regents are seen as being imposed on the school by outside forces, and therefore have even less legitimacy than trustees of private schools.

There is no easy solution to this problem, but many schools are moving in a direction that is likely to increase the legitimacy of their governing bodies by giving those who are intimately involved with a school more voice in electing its leaders. In particular, schools that have had self-elected boards of trustees are moving toward more open elections. They are also setting up nominating committees with student and faculty members, consulting with elected representatives of both groups before appointing administrators, and generally trying to get the support of the whole school for new appointments. Similar changes are being made throughout the university structure, with students serving on more committees and many schools having powerful committees composed of equal numbers of administrators, faculty, and students. Of course, increasing the legitimacy of college presidents and trustees does not guarantee that their decisions will always be popular, but it does increase the likelihood that even unpopular decisions will be accepted.

It is clear that being appointed leader does not guarantee that a person has the power that normally accrues to a leader. It does give him the nominal position, but only by legitimizing that position in some way can he guarantee that the group will follow his lead and that he will be effective. An appointed leader should do what he can to gain the support of

Drawing by Handelsman; © 1927 The New Yorker Magazine, Inc.

"This daily metamorphosis never fails to amaze me. Around the house, I'm a perfect idiot. I come to court, put on a black robe and, by God, I'm **it!***"*

the group—by demonstrating his ability, by becoming popular, or by using any other means at his disposal to convince the members that he deserves to be their leader.

amount of communication

One of the critical factors that determines leadership is amount of communication. Generally, the most active member in terms of communication is also the leader of the group. At the simplest level this is because the most active person will have the most influence on the group. He determines the course of conversation (most of what is said comes from him), he initiates interactions by asking questions, he receives the most replies, he makes the most suggestions and gives the most orders. Whatever the group is doing, he plays a central role. An outside observer would consider him the group leader, and the group concurs in this opinion.

This suggests that one way of influencing leadership is to influence communication. To make someone a leader, perhaps all that is necessary is to make him talk more. An experiment by Bavelas, Hastorf, Gross, and Kite (1965) demonstrated this effect. Subjects from industrial engineering classes, who did not know each other well, were recruited to participate in group discussions. They were divided into four-man groups, given a problem to discuss for ten minutes, and told that their discussions would be observed through a one-way mirror. An observer recorded the amount of time each subject talked and the number of times he talked. After the discussion session, all subjects filled out questionnaires in which they were asked to rank the other subjects on general leadership ability and a few other dimensions. Three such sessions were held.

Each subject had in front of him a small box containing a red and a green light, and only he could see his own lights. Before the second discussion session, some subjects were told they would receive feedback on their performance. If the red light went on, it would indicate that they had been hindering or interfering with the discussion; if the green light went on, it would indicate that their contribution was helpful. In other words, they would be negatively or positively reinforced for what they said.

One subject who was at or near the bottom on both verbal output and others' rankings of his leadership potential was selected from each group. During the succeeding discussion period, he was positively reinforced (his green light was flashed) whenever he spoke, whereas the rest of the group was punished (with red lights) for most of their speeches. In control groups, members did not receive reinforcements of either kind. When the discussion period was over, all subjects filled out the rating forms again. Finally, a third discussion session was held without reinforcement and a third rating form was filled out.

Thus, after one session in which the subjects' normal behavior was observed, one subject was encouraged to talk while the others were discouraged. This was followed by a third session, in which no reinforcements were given. In this way, the experimenters could see how positive reinforcement affected the performance of the chosen subject and whether or not the effect lasted. The results are shown in Table 13–1.

TABLE 13–1
effect of reinforcement on verbal output and reading as leader

DISCUSSION PERIOD	VERBAL OUTPUT[a]	RANKING AS LEADER[b]
First (no lights)	15.7	1.77
Second (reinforcement)	37.0	3.30
Third (no light)	26.9	2.70

[a]Figures are percentages of total group output.
[b]Figures are rankings on a scale from 1 (lowest) to 4 (highest).
Source: Based on Bavelas, Hastorf, Gross, and Kite (1965).

During the second session, as one might expect, the positively reinforced subject began to talk more; conversely, the others talked less. After a while, the chosen subject was doing a much greater percentage of the talking than he had to begin with. Moreover, this effect persisted during the third (nonreinforced) session, even though he was receiving no special encouragement.

At one level, it would be easy to say that the reinforced subject was more of a leader than he was before simply because he talked more. Impartial observers would see that he was taking an active, even dominant, role in the group and would rate him more of a leader than he was at the beginning. Another and perhaps more important test was the group's opinion of him. The striking result was that the group also rated him much higher on the leadership scale. In fact, he went from very low to very high.

For our purposes, the main point is that simple verbal activity appears to be a critical factor in determining leadership. The more active a part a person takes, the more likely he is to be the leader.

It should be noted that this research was done in discussion groups, in which one might expect verbal activity to be particularly important. It may be that other kinds of activity are equally or more important in other kinds of groups. For example, the strong, silent athlete may be the captain of this team. We do know, however, that verbal behavior is extremely important in many situations and that a person who talks a lot is for that reason alone perceived as a leader by the group.

But surely you would think that what people say should be more important than how much they talk. Although this sounds plausible, all the research on this issue indicates the opposite—quantity not quality is what counts in terms of leadership. Several studies (Regula and Julian, 1973; Sorrentino and Boutillier, 1975) compared these two characteristics of people's contributions to a group. They found that the perception of leadership was dependent almost entirely on quantity. The more

Nancy Hays/Monkmeyer

someone talked, the more likely that person was to be seen as the leader regardless of how much of a contribution he actually made to the discussion. Quality does have an impact, but on other perceptions. For example, a group member who made high-quality statements was seen as more competent, more useful, and even more influential—all characteristics that would seem to be related to leadership. Yet, high quality did not relate directly to leadership. One study (Stang, 1973) did find that someone who talks a lot and says little may be heartily disliked, but that person is nevertheless considered high in leadership.

These surprising findings must be considered tentative in at least one respect. We know that quantity is very important; that seems clear. But no research has yet investigated the effect of quality over a long period. It may be that in ongoing groups eventually quality will begin to count more than it seems to in the relatively short-term groups that have been studied. However, for the moment, all the work indicates that the more you talk, the more you will be considered the leader, and that what you say (perhaps within some broad range) has relatively little effect.

Of course, as you would expect, groups do take factors other than talkativeness into account when choosing a leader. A study by Gintner and Lindskold (1975) indicates that amount of talking is important chiefly when there is no other good reason for selecting a leader. In this situation, a confederate of the experimenter deliberately talked either a great deal or a moderate amount and also posed either as an expert in the particular area with which the group was involved or as a nonexpert. As you can see in Table 13–2, the expert was chosen as the leader regardless of whether he talked a lot. His rate of participation had no effect on how likely he was to be made leader. Apparently, if you really have something to offer, the group will want you to lead. On the other hand, as in the previous studies, for the nonexpert, talking made a big difference and greatly increased the chance of being picked as leader.

TABLE 13–2
talking, expertise, and leadership choice

	TALKS A LOT	TALKS LITTLE
expert	2.67	2.67
nonexpert	1.67	0.17

The higher the number, the more choices for leader.
Source: Based on Gintner and Lindskold (1975).

type of communication

Although the amount of an individual's communication is one determinant of leadership, the type of his communication is also important. Members of a group differ not only in the amount of talking they do, but also in the kinds of things they say. Analyzing the content of communications in a group is obviously much more complicated than measuring the quantity. The latter can be done by simply recording how often and how long each person talks. The communications themselves can be recorded on tape or witnessed by trained observers. But separating communications into categories is more difficult. Fortunately, Robert Bales has devised a system that makes it possible to analyze a complex communication in terms of a relatively small number of categories, and thereby to describe the interaction with a manageable number of measures.

Every communication—indeed, every interaction whether or not it is verbal—is placed into one of twelve broad categories: showing disagreement or agreement, tension or tension release, solidarity or antagonism; and giving or asking for suggestions, opinions, information. Note that the first six categories are emotional or reactive, whereas the latter six are cognitive. Each communication is broken down into distinct parts, and each part is scored separately. For example, consider the following interaction of a group trying to build a model airplane and its scoring. Member A: Where is the scotch tape? (Asks for information.) I think we need it. (Gives opinion.) Member B: Right. (Shows agreement.) Put it on the tail. (Gives suggestion.) Member C: Clumsy oaf. (Shows antagonism.) Member A laughs nervously (shows tension), and member B then tells a joke (shows tension release). Of course, this interaction is simple and most of the scoring is straightforward. But even in complex interactions, trained observers can use the Bales system with a high degree of reliability.

One point that should be made clear is that the system is designed to score only overt behavior. No attempt is made to deduce an individual's inner feelings during interaction. If someone says, "I agree with you," it is scored *shows agreement*, even if the individual appears to be angry at the other person. Although emotions are important elements in group interaction, they could not be scored accurately simply by observing the interaction. Therefore, the system deals with them only insofar as they are expressed openly. Despite this limitation, the system does allow a specification of the kinds of interactions taking place and the role each member is playing in the group.

Analyses of this kind indicate a marked difference in the communications of the two people who do the most talking in a group. One of these people tends to make supportive, encouraging, conciliatory, friendly statements. He says such things as "This is a great group," "We're doing fine," "How do you think we should do this?" He is also the one who would tell a joke in order to release tension or amuse the group. In Bales' terms, this person initiates more interactions that fall into the categories of showing solidarity, tension release, and agreement than anyone else. He also asks more questions than the others—seeking information, opinions, or suggestions. The other talkative person comes to the fore when a task is being carried out. His communications fall into the categories of giving suggestions, opinions, and information; and he is somewhat high on disagreements. He says such things as "Do it this way," "You work on that," "Let's get going," "That's the wrong way to do it." In general, one person concentrates more on the social aspects of the situation, keeping the group running smoothly and happily, whereas the other concentrates on getting the work done. Accordingly, the two have been labeled the *social,* or *socioemotional,* and *task* leaders, respectively.

The difference in function is most apparent when the group is working on a specific task or toward some goal, but it appears in other circumstances as well. One distinction is that the same person tends to be the social leader throughout the existence of the group, whereas the task leader can change according to the requirements of a particular task. When special skills are needed, someone who has them may assume this role temporarily. Generally, however, one person retains the role of task leader in most situations.

The emergence of the task leader during task-oriented activity and the difference in the types of communications made by the two active people make it seem as if groups actually have two different leaders. The social leader fulfills most of the roles we have described as being the job of the leader—he is the true leader, the one about whom the group revolves. But he may not have the particular skills necessary for a given task and may lack the general organizing skills necessary for carrying it out. If these skills reside in someone else, this person will take over certain aspects of leadership when the group is working. However, this task leader usually has a limited role—he controls, shapes, directs, and organizes the group in carrying out a specific task. Although he may have more influence than the social leader during the activity, his influence is limited to the particular job being done.

The qualities necessary for the two types of leaders are to some extent opposite. The social leader must be agreeable, conciliatory, concerned about the members' well-being and personal feelings, and generally socially oriented. The task leader must be firm, directive, efficient, and generally concerned about getting the job done. It is not probable for one person to have all these qualities; someone who is conciliatory and agreeable ordinarily would not be firm and directive. One who has the characteristics necessary to be a social leader usually would not make a good task leader, and vice versa. The task leader would have to be particularly good in the area the group was working on; he would need special talents and abilities that the social leader would not. Thus, one personal attribute that often produces leadership is outstanding ability in the area of primary concern to the group. But the major effect of this special talent is the determination of the task leader only. He may sometimes be the social leader also, but that would be determined by other factors.

Therefore, most groups do have two leaders, with their relative importance depending on the kind of group, its goals, its degree of task orientation, and the degree to which specific skills are necessary for completion of its task. A group might be extremely task oriented, but if the task does not require special skills and needs a leader merely as a guide and decision-maker, the social leader probably would be dominant. For example, the task might be agreeing on a beauty contest winner, deciding on a movie to see, or simply choosing a topic and holding a meaningful and interesting discussion on it. On the other hand, if the task were to build a clubhouse or defeat a filibuster in the Senate, the person who had the necessary skills for the job would emerge as leader until the task was completed. In an extremely task-oriented group, the task leader might be quite dominant; his skills might be so important that he essentially would become the true leader. But the usual situation is for both leaders to coexist and cooperate with each other. The skills of one complement those of the other, with the relative dominance of the two depending on the group's situation at any particular time.

communication networks

We have been discussing groups as though every member were free to communicate with everyone else. Although this is true in a discussion group, there are many groups in which communications are limited, and this limitation constitutes another important aspect of group structure that is intimately related to leadership. A series of experiments have studied groups having a variety of so-called communication networks. The basic idea is that communication is essential for leadership and that the person who can communicate most freely tends to be the leader.

The importance of communication has not escaped the notice of the revolutionaries of the world. One of the highest priority targets of any coup d'etat is a nation's radio stations. It is not uncommon to read that the rebellious forces of some general are fighting the premier's loyal troops for control of a country's radio stations or that the stations have been occupied and are broadcasting the news that the coup is successful despite the fact that well-informed sources report that fighting continues. The aim is to take over the stations, tell everybody the coup has succeeded, and prevent the other side from saying it has won and from getting in touch with its troops. If one side can hold the stations long enough and assert its victory often enough, perhaps everyone will believe it and then it becomes true. The side that controls communication is not only in a strong position tactically but also has the evidence that it is the victor—the one who can communicate is, or is seen as, the leader. This is what strategists believe, and the research results indicate that, at least in small groups, it is true.

The typical study in this area consists of forming a group to work on some problem and imposing limits on the communication permitted among the members. This is accomplished by putting the subjects in

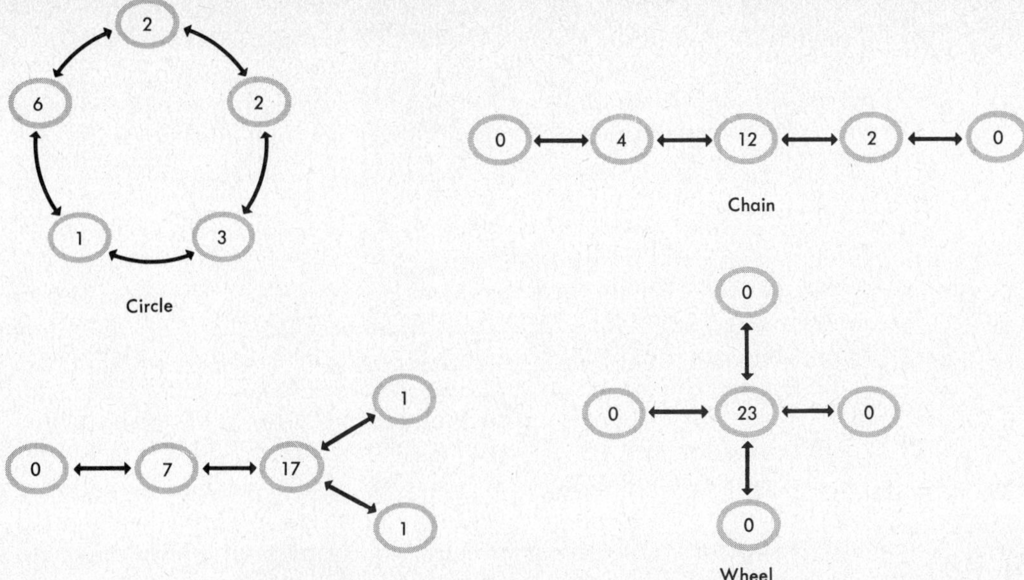

FIGURE 13–2
Communication networks and choice of leaders. The positions connected by a line can communicate directly to each other. The networks range in centrality of communication from the circle (least central, least restricted) to the wheel. The number at each position indicates the number of times the member at that position was considered the leader of the group. (Leavitt, 1951.)

separate rooms or booths and allowing them to communicate with each other only by written messages or an intercom system. In this way, the experimenters are able to control who can talk with whom, and a large number of different communication patterns can be imposed. By examining Figure 13–2, in which some of these patterns are represented for groups of five people, we can see that the structures determine freedom of communication. In the circle, all the members are equal—each of them can talk to his two neighbors and to no one else. In the chain, two of the members can each talk to only one person— obviously, in terms of communication, it is not advantageous to be at the end of a chain. The three other members are equal in terms of the number of persons they can talk to, but the person in the middle is only one away from everyone. The two intermediate people are somewhat isolated from the opposite end. This progression is carried a step further in the Y-shaped structure. With three end members, only one of the others is able to talk to two people and the fifth member is able to talk to three. Finally, in the wheel, one member can talk to everyone else, but all the other members can talk only to the central one.

A study by Leavitt (1951) provides information on what happens when these types of groups are given a problem to work on—a problem that requires communication in order for a solution to be reached. The more freedom the members had to talk, the more satisfied they were.

The person who could talk to everyone was the most content, whereas those on the end of the chain, who could talk to only one other person, were the least content. The networks also played a crucial role in producing a leader. When the members of all the groups were asked if there was a group leader and to name him if there was one, the various groups differed markedly in their responses. There was a clear progression from circle to wheel in terms of the number of times a leader was named and in the agreement among members as to whom the leader was. The number shown at each position in Figure 13–2 is the number of times the person at that position was named leader. Only half the members of circles named any leader at all and there was little agreement among them, whereas virtually all the wheel members named the central person as the leader. The other two structures fell in between on both counts. It appears that simply being in a position to control communication makes a person a leader.

An interesting sidelight on this type of analysis can be seen by examining the structures in Figure 13–3. As Alex Bavelas has pointed out, type B looks to many people to be an autocratic setup, whereas type A appears to be a typical business or hierarchical structure. A second look, however, reveals that the structures are identical, with one person able to talk to everyone else and the rest able to talk only to him.

The initial (mistaken) impression is caused by the assumption that the person who is on top in type A communicates down much easier than the others communicate up. The leader communicates primarily through a subordinate, and this seems to make it easy to communicate to the others and relatively difficult for them to communicate to him. Thus, he seems to be in a stonger position in terms of communications than they are.

Actually, the intermediary, the top figure in type B, is the freest of all in terms of communication because he can talk to everyone, including the leader. He controls who sees the leader and, to some extent, whom the leader sees. Every communication must be relayed through him; not only does he pass on the leader's orders, he also controls communication up to the leader. A General Motors vice-president who wants

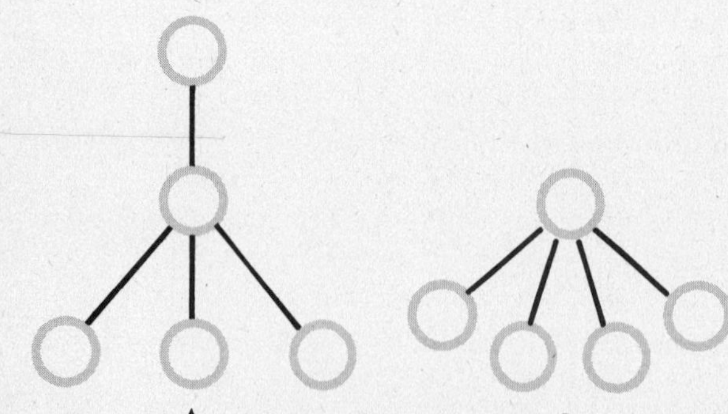

FIGURE 13–3
Hierarchical and autocratic communication networks. These structures are identical in terms of who can communicate to whom, as long as the direction of communication is ignored. The pattern on the left looks like a hierarchical structure, because we assume the man on top can communicate down easier than the others can communicate up.

to talk to the president has to ask the president's secretary. And, although theoretically the leader can communicate with anyone, he too must usually use the intermediary. This description immediately brings to mind the secretary who seems to run every department. Everyone fears him but is careful to remain on his good side, because he dispenses everything from paper clips to new typewriters. He is a very important and powerful person around an office.

What can happen under these circumstances is that the leader relinquishes some authority to the assistant. The latter knows the subordinates better, communicates with them more often, and finds it easier to give the orders. The leader will often let an able assistant make the routine decisions. After a while, the assistant knows more about what is going on and is considered by many of the subordinates to be the one in charge. Once this happens, of course, the "assistant" does have considerable power. Unless the leader is able to reassert his own authority, the

Drawing by Robt. Day; © 1942 The New Yorker Magazine, Inc.

"Oh, I don't know—I just feel sort of out of things."

assistant will emerge as the real leader. In extreme cases, the "boss" may actually lose power completely.

Of course, this picture is somewhat exaggerated. Most of the time the top person retains leadership. Although formally his communications are restricted, actually he can communicate with anyone whenever he wants to. The intermediary merely saves him the trouble by relaying his messages. If the president of General Motors wanted to talk to anyone in the organization, he would pick up the nearest phone and tell whomever answered to connect him with the person he wanted. It is difficult to imagine the president's assistant saying that he could not reach this person. As long as a leader remains the duly constituted authority, he can ordinarily exercise that authority whenever he desires.

However, the situation discussed above, in which the leader's assistant gradually takes over the leadership, is not merely a theoretical possibility; it happens even in important positions. For example, observers have suggested that for many months after President Eisenhower had his heart attack while in office, his assistant Sherman Adams was making most of the decisions in the White House. And at times it seemed as if Kissinger, who talked to the press and met with many other political figures, had more power than Nixon, who often kept himself isolated. One cannot lead unless he can communicate with his followers and they can communicate with him. Thus, one who can communicate freely, particularly when others cannot, is in a strong position to become the leader—and often does.

leadership: personal characteristics

Thus far in our discussion of the determination of leaders, we have been dealing with factors more or less external to the leader. What can we say about the personal characteristics of people who become leaders?

verbal activity level

We have seen that people who talk freely and easily tend to be leaders. If we think of this ability as a personality factor, we could say that this is one of the most important qualities of a leader. At least in small groups, extraversion, garrulousness (perhaps even glibness), high activity level, and assertiveness tend to characterize the leader.

status

Some people are by nature more active than others in any circumstance. However, there are factors other than personality that tend to make someone more or less active and talkative. There is strong evidence, for example, that people of higher status talk more and have more influence than those of lower status. Strodtbeck, Simon, and Hawkins (1958) demonstrated this in a study in which people were selected from regular jury pools and asked to take part in mock trials. The participants listened to a recorded trial, debated, and returned a verdict—very much as in a real trial. After hearing the case, each jury chose a foreman. The members were given no criteria on which to base this choice, they were completely free to pick whomever they pleased.

For our purposes, the major results are the effects of the members' occupational status on the selection of the jury foremen and the amount of participation in the deliberations of high- and low-status people. As shown in Table 13–3, there was a strong tendency to select as foremen people of relatively high status. Proprietors (i.e., professionals, managers, officials, engineers) were chosen almost twice as often as would be expected by chance, whereas laborers (i.e., semiskilled workers, servants, nonfarm laborers) were chosen half as often as would be expected by chance. In addition, high-status jurors participated considerably more than low-status jurors. Proprietors had a participation score of 11.8, laborers of only 6.4, and the other groups fell in between. This finding also holds when the amount of participation by the foremen is eliminated—proprietors still score highest and laborers lowest. Even in a democratic situation such as a jury, socioeconomic status is an almost perfect predictor of participation in discussions.

TABLE 13–3
occupational status, participation, and leadership

		PARTICIPATION[b]	
Occupation	Elected Foreman[a]	Including Foreman	Omitting Foreman
Proprietor	185	11.8	8.9
Clerical	100	9.2	7.0
Skilled	84	7.1	6.3
Labor	54	6.4	5.9

[a]Figures are the percentage of the expected value. A number greater than 100 indicates that members with that occupation were elected more than would be expected by chance.

[b]Figures are percentages of the total group participation. The figure expected by chance was 8.3.

Source: Adapted from Strodtbeck et al. (1958).

Although it is somewhat difficult to separate the effects of status and personality because a person's personality may affect his choice of job, and vice versa, it appears that status is an important determinant of leadership. A high-status person is likely to become a leader even though his status derives from factors entirely extraneous to the group.

relation to the rest of the group

There is good reason to believe that to be chosen leader, someone must not be too different from the rest of the group. Particularly in small groups, members prefer their leader to be one of them—but the best of them. In street gangs, for example, the leaders apparently must share most of the values of the rest of the group. They must not take too independent a stand on anything; they must not be deviates. When they make decisions they must make the choices that most of the group would have made. They can have somewhat different ideas from the rest and can lead the members into new activities and attitudes, but the ideas must not be too different nor the new activities too sudden. If they cease to be "one of the gang," they risk losing their leadership and may, in fact, cease to be a member of the group.

As we mentioned previously, deviancy is rarely accepted, especially in a position of leadership. Research indicates that a group avoids choosing a leader who holds deviant views. In a study by Schachter (1951), groups were set up to discuss a variety of problems. Several confederates were included in each group. One of the confederates (deviate) took a position on the first issue different from that taken by the rest of the group; another confederate (deviate-agreer) also took a deviant position but eventually changed so that he agreed with the group; and a third (agreer) agreed throughout. After the discussion, each group nominated members for the executive, steering, and correspondence committees, which varied in importance in that order. The executive committee was, in essence, the leadership branch of the government. The nominations for the deviate, deviate-agreer, and agreer are shown in Table 13–4. The confederate who took a consistently deviant position was nominated less often for the executive committee than anyone else. The confederate who began deviant and ended by agreeing was treated the same as the one who agreed all along. Thus, the group avoided making the deviate its leader but was willing to accept someone whom it could convince. Other research (Michener and Burt, 1975) shows that the leader is also very sensitive to deviancy in others. Members of the group who appeared deviant were punished by the leader, presumably to bring them into line and also because they were liked less. Thus, the group does not want their leader to be too different from them, but neither do they want him to be an average group member.

The study conducted by Merei mentioned earlier provides some interesting insights into the relationship between the leader and the group. Merei formed groups of young boys and girls and let each group meet for thirty or forty minutes on several successive days. At the end of this time, all the groups had adopted various habits and traditions. At this point, a somewhat older child who had previously shown evidence of being quite dominant, of having initiative, and of tending to be a leader was introduced into each group. The question was whether he would

TABLE 13–4
liking and treatment of deviate, changer, and nondeviate

CONFEDERATE	LIKING[a]	ELECTION TO EXECUTIVE COMMITTEE (GOOD)[b]	ELECTION TO CORRESPONDENCE COMMITTEE (BAD)[b]
Deviate	3.89	−9.46	14.43
Changer	5.24	1.70	1.30
Nondeviate	5.53	−2.69	−6.92

[a]Figures are rankings of the confederate by the group members on a scale from 1 (lowest) to 9 (highest).
[b]Figures are percentages above and below those expected by chance.
Source: Adapted from Schachter (1951).

assume leadership of the already established group and, if so, how he would accomplish it.

The first finding was that, by and large, the new members were unable to change the traditions of the groups. Many tried, but eventually they had to accept these traditions themselves. In this sense, the new member proved weaker than the group. This does not mean that no one can ever enter a group and change it to fit his own values—this does occur sometimes with strong leaders and relatively weak groups. But in most cases, once a group has established some norms, these norms are resistant to change; someone who wishes to become the leader of such a group must, to some extent, accept the established system.

Despite this, most of the new members did manage to become the

Dick Swift

leaders of their respective groups. They were, after all, older and stronger than any of the individual members and therefore would be expected to play somewhat central roles in the groups. Although they were not able to change existing patterns or initiate many new activities, they were looked to as leaders, did make some decisions, and were more influential than any other single member. One way they attained their positions was to give orders that were in line with the traditions of the group. Instead of telling the members to do something new or different, the new leaders ordered them to do what they would have done anyway. If they knew at some point that the groups would begin playing with blocks, they said, "Okay, let's play with blocks now." Then, when the groups were about to stop, they said, "Let's stop now." And so on. Since these orders were consistent with what the groups wanted to do, they obeyed them. After a while, they looked to the new leader to see what they should do. He became their spokesman. He still continued to give orders consistent with group traditions in order to maintain his position, but in a sense he had become the leader.

Many leaders operate this way. Certainly successful politicians often attempt to discover what the people want and then come out in favor of it. In one sense, this seems dishonest, since the politician is saying what he thinks the people want to hear rather than what he believes. In another sense, leaders are supposed to represent their constituency and this is one way to do it. The key point is that any leader must agree with his followers on most issues if he is to have any lasting power. Once he has achieved support he can express some deviant views and perhaps then influence the opinions of the others. Ideally, of course, the leader's attitudes should generally agree with the group's so that he can be honest and still be an effective leader.

Other than these relatively few pieces of information, we know little about the personality of leaders. There is some suggestion that leaders are more intelligent, more flexible, better adjusted, and perhaps more interpersonally sensitive than other members of groups. These variables, however, have relatively small effects. Someone who had them all would be somewhat more likely to be a leader than someone who had none of them, but they do not make a big difference. Some other factors we have mentioned seem to be more important. Leaders usually are more active, more talkative, more assertive, and not too different from the groups they lead.

Psychologists are still puzzled about the quality that is often described in the literature and elsewhere as "the ability to lead" or, more forcefully, as "charisma." Just what, if anything, this consists of is yet to be detailed by controlled research. It does seem that some people make outstanding, forceful leaders and that the few qualities we have mentioned do not fully account for their ability. It may be that they simply have all the right qualities in large amounts, or it may be something additional. At the moment, we do not know.

effects of structure on group performance

Let us now consider how various aspects of a group's organization and structure affect its functioning. As discussed above, many groups are so structured that there are certain limitations on communication. These limitations can take the form of poor communication (members are free to talk to each other but what they say may not get through) or actual restrictions (certain members are unable to talk to others). Both types of limitation affect a group's performance. In addition, there are different types of leaders. The style of leadership in a particular group is a major determinant of its performance.

communication and performance

As might be expected, the ability to communicate plays an important role in determining the performance of a group. To begin with, it seems clear that anything that interferes with communication among group members would hurt group performance. As we shall see below, it is not always necessary or even desirable for all group members to be able to communicate directly with one another. But if communication between two members is permitted, any ambiguities or restrictions in that communication—irrelevant noises, static—have serious interfering effects. Obviously, if two members are trying to talk to each other and have trouble understanding each other's messages, they are unable to operate effectively.

Furthermore, if there is static in the system, it is crucial for the member who is sending a message to be able to get feedback from the recipient. Without feedback, member A can never be sure his message got through—he can only hope that B received it intact. Thus, A does not know whether he should repeat the message or go on to others. If the first message did get through, repeating it might confuse the situation. But if it did not get through and A does not repeat it, that piece of information is not available to B. If B can respond to A, this ambiguity is immediately removed; A can repeat the message until he is sure B understands it. When the lines of communication are freer, feedback is considerably less important, because A can be quite confident his message was received even without it. Thus, both clarity of message and the possibility of feedback are important, and feedback is particularly crucial when the messages themselves are not clear.

Knowledge that the other person has heard and understood is sometimes called *secondary information,* because it is data about the transmission of other data. An example of the importance of secondary information is provided by the "hot line" between Washington and Moscow, by which the president of the United States and the premier of the Soviet Union can call each other directly. One of the primary purposes of these calls is for each to make clear to the other what he is planning to do. For example, during the June 1967 war between Israel and the Arabs, many such calls were supposedly made, with both men making it clear that they were not planning to intervene. At one point, the United States scrambled some planes to protect an American ship, and the president immediately called the Russian premier to explain why the planes were in the air and to assure him that they were not engaged in the war.

Thus, the "hot line" is a fast, efficient means of communication that enables each side to know what the other is doing. But one of the problems in setting it up was that the president and the premier speak different languages and must communicate through interpreters. This introduced difficulty in ascertaining that the messages got through as intended. Clear feedback was needed. It was provided by allowing the two interpreters to hear each other's translations. If the president said, for example, "Our planes are not attacking Cairo," the American translator would listen to the Russian translation so that he would know exactly what the premier heard. If the American thought the translation was incorrect, he could ask the president to clarify his statement to avoid the wrong meaning, innuendo, or connotation. The critical aspect of the "hot line" is that each man knows when the other has misunderstood him or heard the wrong message and is free to correct the communication until it is understood. In this way, possibly fatal misunderstandings can be avoided, or at least minimized.

The importance of secondary information can also be seen in confrontations between groups in our society, such as school administrators and students, or blacks and whites. In a typical situation, black students might ask administrators of a university to admit more minority group students. What the blacks are really asking for, however, is more complicated. They want a minority group member to be involved in admissions and they want to have a part in running the university. But the white administrators think that all the students want is to have more blacks admitted. Both the blacks and the administrators think the administrators have understood. Then, when a program for admitting more black students through the normal admissions procedure is inaugurated, the administrators are surprised and upset that the black students feel they have been tricked because the old admissions procedures were used. Actually, neither side fully understood the other and did not know that they misunderstood. If either side had known, they could have asked for clarification and avoided unnecessary conflicts.

communication networks and performance

Various kinds of communication patterns produce corresponding patterns of power and decision-making ability. The person at the center of the wheel, for example, is generally considered to be the leader of the group, and he is obviously in the best position to make decisions and see that the rest of the group agrees with them. Conversely, the circle structure, in which each person can talk only to his two neighbors, has decentralized communication and leadership. Thus, a highly centralized communication network produces a group with strong centralized leadership and power.

The evidence on how these different kinds of networks affect group performance is not entirely consistent, but most of the data suggest that centralized groups are more effective when the group is working on simple problems, whereas decentralized groups are effective with more complex problems. In some studies, each member of a group was given a card with a number of geometric symbols written on it and the task was to discover which symbol was on all the cards. The solution was trivial—the problem was to get all the information in one place as quickly as possible. This problem is ideally suited to groups with highly centralized communication networks, in which all the information can be quickly given to one person. And as might be expected, they did better than decentralized groups on this type of problem. The leader simply collected the messages from the group members and discovered which symbol they all had.

In other studies, groups were given problems requiring a series of fairly complicated arithmetic manipulations. In order to solve this kind of problem efficiently, each group member should work on part of the problem by himself, at least one other member should check his solution, and all the information should be combined. The evidence suggests that decentralized groups are more effective on this kind of problem than are centralized groups.

The findings can be seen to be due to several different effects of decentralization. On one hand, the more decentralized a group is, the less efficient it is in distributing information. The centralized group can quickly transmit all the information to the leader, who can then, if necessary, redistribute it to the members, also quite efficiently. The decentralized group must expend more effort and almost always must send more messages than the centralized group. Thus, because the centralized group provides more efficient, faster, and clearer communications, to the extent that transmission of information is necessary to arrive at a solution, the centralized group should be superior.

The centralized group also has fewer distractions. As we shall see in Chapter 14, one of the characteristics of almost all groups is that they tend to be distracting. Since ordinarily not everyone need know everything in order for a group to solve a problem, many of the communications in decentralized groups are unnecessary distractions. The less free the communications, the fewer there are; and the fewer the people involved in decisions, the less distractions there are. The centralized group has less total communication and fewer members participating in decisions. Thus, it has the additional advantage of being less distracting. To the extent that concentration is important, then, it should be superior to a decentralized group.

On the other hand, the motivation of the group members is also critical. Members of decentralized groups tend to be happier and more satisfied with their positions and to like the group more. Satisfaction and morale are directly related to an individual's freedom of communication and his sense of participating actively in group decisions. Members who can communicate freely are more satisfied; those who can communicate least tend to be least happy in the group. Therefore, the structure of the wheel produces the least overall satisfaction and the decentralized structure of the circle produces the most. The lower morale in the centralized groups tends to result in less production because the members work less hard. Thus, from this point of view, the decentralized group should be more effective.

The relative effectiveness of the various types of groups depends, therefore, on how important each of these factors is in a particular context. When a group is faced with a simple problem that primarily involves passing information from one member to another and performing easy operations on it, efficiency of communication and lack of distractions are normally the most important factors. In such cases, the centralized group is superior. When the problem is more complex and involves difficult operations or requires more intimate cooperation among group members, the morale of the individuals and their ability to communicate freely are more important, so the decentralized group performs better.

A somewhat different interpretation of the data is that the critical factor underlying the performance differences among groups with the various kinds of communication networks is the relative difficulty of organization. A group that is disorganized and has not yet worked out an efficient operating procedure obviously would do less well than one that is organized. And the simpler the group's communication structure, the simpler it is to organize. For example, the wheel is an exceedingly simple structure that allows only one reasonable organization. A group with this structure should find its organization easy to determine. In contrast, the circle and a group with no restrictions on communication (usually called an all-channel structure) are more complex and allow a variety of organizations. These groups have greater difficulties in setting up organizations. The effect of organization is most marked with simple problems for which a solution depends almost exclusively on the efficient passing of information. Group organization is relatively unimportant in solving complex problems for which a solution depends on considerable individual effort and a more creative combination of information.

Evidence for the organizational interpretation of the effect of communication networks on group performance comes from a study by Guetzkow and Simon (1955). The first and most important finding is that differences in performance on simple tasks tend to disappear with time. After twenty trials the all-channel and wheel groups no longer differed;

United Nations/M. Grant

and although the circle groups continued to be somewhat less productive, the difference declined. Detailed analysis of the group organizations showed that by twenty trials, the all-channel groups had worked out an organization but the circle groups had not yet settled on one.

Another piece of relevant evidence is that the degree of organization was highly correlated with group performance. The groups that had organized satisfactorily did not differ in performance, regardless of their original structure. Well-organized wheel groups were no faster than well-organized all-channel or circle groups. The only difference was that most of the all-channel groups had not become well organized until after at least ten trials and very few of the circle groups had produced a good organization even after twenty trials. Presumably, with more time, all the groups would settle on a good organization and then none would differ in performance. Nevertheless, the circle groups were harder to organize than the wheel groups; under many circumstances, circles might never achieve good centralized organization. Thus, although the structure of the groups did not fully determine their final organization, it did have an important effect. The more centralized the communication network, the more centralized the final organization. A group can overcome a particular structure, but there will still be some tendency for groups with less centralized structures to remain less centralized. Although the effect of communication networks is most apparent at the beginning of a group's meetings, to some extent it continues throughout the life of a group, unless for some reason the group overcomes the initial structure and imposes a different organization on itself.

Although most of the research on communication networks has been conducted in the laboratory, the kinds of networks studied there often play an important role in real groups in our society. For example, university communities vary greatly in their freedom of communication. Some have highly restricted communication networks, which might be called wheel-within-wheel strucures. The top members of the administration talk only to one another and to their immediate subordinates. They in turn talk only to one another and their subordinates, and so on. In addition, the administration talks only to the most senior faculty members, who talk to the junior faculty, who talk to the students. Thus, the junior faculty forms the only link with the students. The students, in turn, are free to talk only to one another and to the junior faculty, but not to senior faculty or administrators. This structure is probably quite efficient in certain respects, but morale is low and dissatisfaction high. At present, many universities are moving toward less centralized structures, in which everyone is relatively free to talk to everyone else. This seems to lead to higher morale and to the feeling that everyone is participating in running the university, but it produces more distractions and is probably less efficient in handling straightforward problems. When everyone can take part in making simple decisions, it is difficult to make them quickly. Thus, this change to a more open communication structure has resulted in somewhat slower action on minor problems but increased satisfaction and more creative solutions to complex, important problems.

type of leader and performance

There has been a considerable amount of discussion in the literature about the relative effectiveness of different types of leadership. In particular, psychologists have tried to compare the so-called democratic and authoritarian types of leadership. A democratic leader allows the group as a whole to make decisions, to choose the jobs they want to do; he generally issues few orders and serves primarily as a guide or chairman. In contrast, the authoritarian leader makes most of the decisions himself, issues a great many orders, and is generally a commander of the group. Part of the interest in the effectiveness of these two types of leaders stems from their correspondence to democratic and nondemocratic political organizations and societies. Of course, the effectiveness of leaders is also important in maximizing the efficiency of any group—in business, in government, and so on.

In a well known study, Lippitt and White (1943) assigned adult leaders, who behaved in either a democratic or an authoritarian manner, to groups of ten-years-old boys. The authoritarian leaders determined all policy, dictated the techniques and activities of the groups in such a way that future steps were uncertain, often assigned the particular work task and work companion of each member, tended to be personal in their praise and criticism of the work of each member, and remained aloof from active group participation. With democratic leadership, all policies were discussed by the group, the complete plan of action was detailed in advance, members were free to work with whomever they chose and on the task they desired, and the leaders were objective in their praise and criticism and tried to be regular group members in spirit. In a third condition, there were laissez-faire leaders, who allowed the group complete freedom and did not really act as leaders at all.

The findings of this study are somewhat mixed. There was some tendency for the quantity of work to be greatest in the autocratic groups and least in the laissez-faire groups. The motivation to work, however, seemed to be stronger in the democratic groups than in either of the other types. There was more aggression as well as more discontent expressed in the autocratic groups, and the members of the democratic groups seemed to be happier and more self-reliant than those in the autocratic groups.

It should be noted that this study has many important limitations. The leaders were imposed on the groups rather than elected by them and, perhaps more important, were adults whereas the group members were children. The groups were informal and not designed primarily to work on specific problems. In addition, the leaders were not free to provide the best possible kind of authoritarian or democratic leadership. They had to follow fairly strict patterns, which may or may not have been the most efficient for the given kind of leadership. For these and other reasons, the results are interesting but can be considered only suggestive.

Other research, however, has produced quite similar results (Lewin et al., 1939; Shaw, 1955). In these studies group members were generally happier and more satisfied with relatively democratic leadership, but often performed better with authoritarian leaders. And a number of authors (Gibb, 1969; Mulder and Stemerding, 1963) have suggested that even satisfaction may depend on the particular situation. When the group is under stress (as in wartime) or the situation is greatly disorganized (as in developing countries), groups seem to prefer strong, autocratic leadership, perhaps because it brings the order that is necessary. In contrast, the leader of an informal, socially oriented group such as an encounter group functions best when he becomes involved with the group members, interacts with them closely, and does not behave in an authoritarian manner.

An extensive series of studies by Fred Fiedler (1958, 1971) demonstrates how leader effectiveness is dependent on many factors in the situation. Fiedler began by distinguishing between two types of leaders on the basis of a personality test in which the key element was the person's feelings about the other group members. According to this test, the most important factor was how much esteem the leader felt for the group member he liked least. Stated somewhat differently, the test measured the minimum amount of esteem he felt for anyone in the group. Thus, the test was called the least preferred co-worker, or LPC, scale.

Someone high on this scale tends, in Fiedler's words, "to see even a poorer co-worker in a relatively favorable manner." A low LPC leader, on the other hand, perceives "his least preferred co-worker in a highly unfavorable, rejecting manner." More generally, high LPC leaders are permissive, passive, and considerate; they are more relaxed, friendlier, more compliant, less directive, and tend to reduce the group members' anxiety. Low LPC leaders are controlling, active, and structuring; they are less tolerant of irrelevant comments, produce less pleasant relationships within the group, are highly directive, and tend to induce anxiety. It can be seen that high and low LPC leaders tend to correspond to certain aspects of democratic and authoritarian leadership, respectively.

A concerted attempt has been made to specify in detail the kinds of situations in which each type of leader is most effective. Although the research has not yet produced definitive answers, there are some findings in which we can have considerable confidence. Under most circumstances, a low LPC leader is more effective when the task is highly structured. With such a task, it is important to assign roles to individual members, to divide the work, and, in general, to organize efficiently. Interactions among the members, discussions, and interchange of ideas are relatively unimportant because the problem is straightforward. The low LPC leader is successful because he knows what has to be done and the main problem is getting it done. Moreover, the rest of the group tends not to resent this kind of leader in this case, because his instructions increase efficiency and make the task easier for everyone. The one instance in which the situation does not hold is when the prior relationship between the leader and the group members is poor. Then, the group seems to react negatively to being ordered around and tends to be less efficient than it would be with the relatively warm, high LPC leader.

With unstructured tasks, the relationship is somewhat less clear. The strong, assertive, low LPC leaders also seem to do well in many unstructured situations. The exception is when the initial relations between the group and the leader are good but the leader's position is weak. This could be caused by a variety of factors, such as rotating leadership or the fact that the appointed leader was of lower status than the rest of the members, Under these conditions, a low LPC leader does quite poorly, for although the group likes him, they are unwilling to accept strong leadership from someone in a weak position.

Fiedler's research indicates that the effectiveness of leadership style depends on a variety of conditions. A study by Wilson, Aronoff, and Messe (1975) suggests that the critical factor is whether a particular kind of leadership and group structure is compatible with the goals of the group. They compared groups with hierarchical structures (a leader with power over the lower-ranked members) to egalitarian groups in which everyone was equal. When the goal of the group was to increase safety—a clear goal that required organization and cooperation—the hierarchical group was more successful. When the goal was to increase the members' self-esteem and their esteem for the group—a social goal that depends primarily on interpersonal factors—the egalitarian groups were better.

Presumably, this would apply to almost any goal that was selected. Certain combinations of leadership style and group structure are best for any given purpose, and no broad generalization can be made about one kind of leadership being better than another.

SUMMARY

1. The typical pattern of communication in a small group is that one or two people do most of the talking, regardless of the size of the group.

2. Almost all groups have leaders, people who are thought by the other members and by outside observers to have the most influence on the group.

3. A problem with leadership is legitimacy—does the leader deserve his or her position. If the leader is appointed, he will often be seen as not legitimate and will have less influence and power.

4. Communication plays an important role in determining leadership. Someone who talks a lot is more likely to be the leader, regardless of the content of what he says. However, often two kinds of leaders emerge from within a group—a socioemotional leader who handles social aspects of the group, and a task leader who focuses on the job.

5. If communication is restricted, the person with the least restricted communication tends to be the leader and is also more satisfied.

6. Personal characteristics that produce leadership include verbal activity level, status, and lack of deviance from the group.

7. When communication is restricted, centralized structures (one person is allowed to talk to everyone, but the other people can talk only to the central person) are efficient for simple problem solving, but decentralized structures produce higher motivation and are probably superior for solving complex problems.

8. Authoritarian leaders seem to produce good performance, but lower member satisfaction when compared with democratic leaders. The effect of leadership style is complex, depending on the type of task and the strength of the leader's position.

SUGGESTIONS FOR ADDITIONAL READING

FIEDLER, F. E. A *Theory of Leadership Effectiveness.* New York: McGraw-Hill, 1967. The clearest, most complete presentation of Fiedler's work. Difficult going nevertheless, but useful for those who are especially interested in leadership.

MACCOBY, M. *The Gamesman.* New York: Simon & Schuster, 1977. One view by psychoanalytically-oriented researcher of who is successful in the business world.

WHYTE, W. H., JR. *The Organization Man.* New York: Simon and Schuster, 1956. A sociological discussion of how people operate in large organizations.

14

group dynamics

social facilitation

- one interpretation: drive arousal
- competition and evaluation
- distraction
- social behaviors

competition versus cooperation

- the trucking game
- prisoner's dilemma

factors affecting competition

- incentive
- motivation
- threats
- communication
- maximizing cooperation
- applicability of the research findings

problem solving by groups

- research results
- limitations of the research
- cohesiveness

groups as mobs

- deindividuation
- other factors

extremity shifts (the "risky shift")

- riskier people are more persuasive
- diffusion of responsibility
- cultural value
- persuasive arguments

summary

suggestions for additional reading

Someone is sitting alone in a room working on simple mathematical problems. He works steadily and makes a reasonable amount of progress. Then someone else comes into the room and begins to work on similar problems. The two people do not know each other; they do not talk to each other; they have little or nothing in common. Yet the presence of the second person has a profound effect on the first one—he begins to work harder, to solve the problems more quickly, and, in general, to be more productive. Merely having someone else in the room has increased the effectiveness of his work.

Three hundred people are having dinner in a restaurant. Suddenly there are cries of fire, and smoke begins pouring out of the kitchen. The crowd rushes for the exits and the first lucky few escape. But there are too many people trying to get through the narrow doorways. They block one another's progress so that no one can get through. The bodies pile up at the doorways within easy reach of safety.

In 1931, a young black man is in a southern jail accused of raping a white girl. There is no evidence against him except that he was in the general vicinity of the crime. A crowd gathers outside the jail, builds up, and gets more and more excited and enraged. Members of the crowd start talk of lynching and before long the crowd has turned into an angry mob. It rushes the jail, breaks down the doors, and drags the prisoner from his cell. He is tortured and killed in a sadistic orgy of violence.

A large advertising company is trying to devise a new campaign for selling soap. The eight executives working on the account have been thinking about the problem separately for several weeks. They they decide to have a brainstorming session. They all get together in a big, comfortable office to discuss their ideas. No one criticizes anyone, everyone is urged to say anything that could be helpful. They all talk freely and accumulate a large number of ideas. Afterward they feel they have accomplished a great deal they could not have done alone.

These examples are representative of the kinds of effects groups have on their members. People are stimulated and distracted by being in a group. They respond to a wide variety of group norms and pressures. Being in a group or just in the presence of other people causes an individual to behave and think differently from when he is alone. This chapter concerns the effects of groups and the processes by which they are produced.

social facilitation

For some time it was reported that people perform tasks better when they are in the presence of others than when they are alone. Although, as we shall see, not every kind of performance is improved, this effect—so-called social facilitation—occurs on a wide variety of tasks. A number of studies conducted at Harvard by Allport (1920, 1924) used five different tasks ranging from simple and trivial (crossing out all the vowels in a newspaper column) to somewhat more difficult (performing easy multiplications) and finally to fairly complex (writing refutations of a logical argument). On all of these, performance was better when there were five people in the room than when there was only one, even though in all cases the participants worked individually. Dashiell (1930) replicated these results; Travis (1925) found facilitation on a pursuit-rotor task; and many recent experiments (e.g., Zajonc and Sales, 1966; Martens, 1969) have demonstrated the social facilitation effect.

The phenomenon is not limited to humans. Chen (1937) compared the amount of sand dug by ants when they were alone or in pairs or in groups of three. He found that groups of two and three did not differ appreciably, but in both conditions the ants dug more than three times as much sand per ant as they did when the animals were alone. It is also worth noting that pairs of rats copulated less when there was a single pair in the cage than when there were three pairs (Larsson, 1956). Thus, for many different species and a number of different behaviors, the presence of another member of the species has been shown to improve performance over that which occurs when an individual is alone.

Despite these impressive findings, it has become clear that under some circumstances the social facilitation effect does not occur. In fact, the presence of others can interfere with performance. In Allport's study (1924), subjects in the group condition wrote more refutations of the logical argument, but the quality of these refutations was lower than when the individuals were alone. Pessin (1933) found that the presence of a spectator reduced performance on a memory task, and Dashiell (1930) showed that there were more errors made in simple multiplications when there was an audience. Recent research has also found that subjects in groups perform less well on certain kinds of tasks (which we will discuss in a moment) than they do when they are alone (e.g., Cottrell, Rittle, and Wack, 1967). This same inconsistent pattern holds for other animals. Cockroaches (Gates and Allee, 1933), parakeets (Allee and Masure, 1936), and green finches (Klopfer, 1958) all performed less well in groups than when alone. Thus, although the majority of the findings do demonstrate a social facilitation effect, there is a substantial body of evidence indicating that under some circumstances the presence of others can actually interfere with performance. How can these diverse results be explained?

one interpretation: drive arousal

Zajonc (1965, 1966) made a very interesting proposal that accounted for virtually all these diverse results. He suggested that being in the presence of another individual causes a person's drive or motivation to be increased, and this increased drive should sometimes facilitate performance and sometimes interfere with it. It is well established that high drive tends to improve performance on simple tasks in which the correct response is well known and dominant, but tends to hurt performance on more complex tasks for which the correct response is not dominant, or on learning tasks. Canceling the vowels in a newspaper, doing simple arithmetic, learning a simple list of words, or performing any other easy, repetitive tasks should be facilitated by an increase in drive level. In contrast, difficult arithmetic problems, complex logical deductions, memorizing a difficult list of words, or performing any other complicated tasks should be inhibited by increased drive. Although it is sometimes difficult to determine which group a particular task falls into, most of the findings seem to fit this formulation quite well. Allport's tasks were relatively simple, and he found a social facilitation effect. The one exception was the quality of the logical refutations, which is presumably a very complex task and should be performed less well with an audience. Digging sand and copulating are both fairly simple tasks for ants and rats, respectively, and are also highly dominant behaviors. Both were facilitated by the presence of other members of the species. Learning a maze is a difficult task for cockroaches and parakeets, and they did less well in the presence of others.

More recent research has been designed specifically to test this explanation. In an experiment by Cottrell, Rittle, and Wack (1967), subjects learned a list of word pairs either alone or in the presence of two other students. Some of the lists were designed to be easy and others to be quite difficult. The easy lists were composed of words that have the same meaning or tend to be associated with each other, for example, adept–skillful and barren–fruitless. The other list contained items that had no meaning in common and accordingly had weak associations—for example, arid–grouchy and dessert–leading.

Of course, the difficult list would be harder to learn under any circumstances, but we are primarily interested in the effect of the social situation on learning. The results show that the easy list was learned somewhat better when there was an audience than when the subject worked alone, whereas the difficult list was learned much more slowly when an

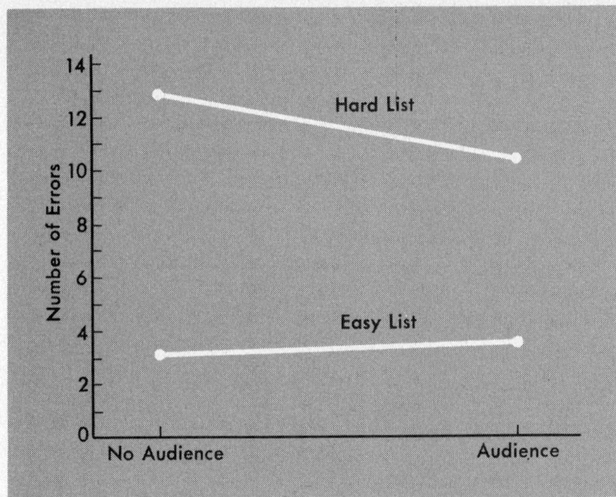

FIGURE 14–1
The Effect of an Audience on Learning.
The audience improves performance on an easy list but interferes with performance on a difficult list. (Based on Cottrell, Rittle and Wack, 1967).

audience was present. The presence of other people improved performance on the simple task where the correct responses were dominant, and inhibited performance on the difficult task where the correct responses were not strong to begin with.

Another study (Zajonc et al., 1969) tested this interpretation using cockroaches as subjects. High drive is expected to improve performance when the correct behavior is the dominant response, but interfere with performance when correct behavior is not dominant. In this study, cockroaches either alone or in pairs had to escape from a light by running down a straight alley or by learning a simple maze. In the alley, the dominant response would help the animals escape, but in the maze it would interfere. As shown in Table 14–1, the roaches did worse in the maze when they were in pairs, but did better in the runway. Apparently being with another animal did increase drive and therefore strengthen the dominant response. A second study by the same authors demonstrated this effect even when the roach was alone in the runway or maze but was being observed by other roaches nearby.

Hunt and Hillery conducted a study similar to Zajonc's but used humans as subjects. Once again the task was to learn a maze that was easy or difficult either alone or in company. The results of the experiment are also presented in Table 14–1. They are almost identical to previous results obtained from the experiments with roaches. People learn the easy maze faster when other people are present, but the difficult maze is learned faster alone.

competition and evaluation

The research thus offers strong support for Zajonc's hypothesis that the presence of others arouses drive. There is some question, however, as to exactly what kind of drive it is and the specific conditions that are neces-

TABLE 14–1
effect of an audience and task difficulty on performance of cockroaches and humans

	EASY TASK		HARD TASK	
	Alone	Audience	Alone	Audience
Cockroaches[a]	40.48	32.96	110.45	129.46
Humans[b]	44.67	36.19	184.91	220.33

[a]Data on cockroaches adapted from Zajonc et al. (1969).
[b]Data on humans adapted from Hunt and Hillery (1973).

sary to produce the effect. It seems likely that at least for humans the presence of other people tends to arouse feelings of competition and also concerns about being evaluated. People tend to interpret virtually every social situation as competitive. As we shall see below, they compete with each other in a simple game even though they know they would win more by cooperating. When two people are in a room, each may feel competitive with the other even when there is no explicit reason to feel so. They may think that there is an implied competition, that someone is comparing their performances, or that the other person is competing with them. Even ruling out these possibilities, the individual may compare his performance with the other person and want to do better, thus providing some sort of internal competition that does not depend on what the other person does.

Another and perhaps more important motive that tends to be aroused by the presence of others is concern about being evaluated. We have already discussed the fact that in any social situation we tend to be worried about being rejected and want to be liked and accepted. Obviously, these motives are stronger when we are actually with another person. When someone else is in the room, there is always the possibility that he is judging you. He may be looking at your appearance, your behavior, or your performance on a particular task. The other person may actually be totally unconcerned with you, but there is a tendency to assume that he is to some extent evaluating you. This concern about evaluation raises the drive level of the individual and produces the kinds of effects we have reported.

Two studies provide direct support for this idea. Henschy and Glass (1968) compared situations in which subjects thought they were being evaluated with others in which nothing was said about evaluation. Whenever subjects expected to be evaluated, the typical facilitation of dominant responses was observed. When no evaluation was expected, there was a much smaller difference between an alone condition and one in which nonevaluating spectators were present. Paulus and Murdoch (1971) conducted a similar study and found the facilitation effect only when evaluation was expected, with no difference between the alone and the spectator conditions.

Leo de Wys

At the moment it seems safe to say that the presence of others under most circumstances increases drive, which produces facilitation on simple tasks and interference on certain complex tasks. It seems likely that concern about evaluation is the dominant drive aroused, but there is some reason to think that feelings of competition are also aroused under certain conditions.

distraction

Although the arousal of drive is probably the most important mechanism activated by the presence of other people, another aspect of the minimal situation is that other people are usually somewhat distracting. When an individual works alone in a room, it is quiet (or perhaps some music is playing), and there is little to attend to except the work. Another person working in the same room may shift around in his chair, chew on a pencil, breathe heavily, and so on. Suddenly, there is much more going on in the room and more to attend to; it becomes difficult to devote full attention to the work. A good example of this is a college library. At certain times, it is an almost ideal place to study. There are empty tables to work on and little noise or activity. But just before an exam period, it is very crowded. The other people talk, move around, sit close together, bump against chairs. Under these circumstances, the presence of others is so distracting that performance is less efficient than if one were alone.

Evidence indicates that distractions caused by others are most annoying when one is trying to learn something new. Learning new material requires concentration on external stimuli (e.g., contents of a book), and extraneous external stimuli interfere with that concentration. When taking an exam instead of studying for one, external distractions are less bothersome—the material is already known and the ability to recall it is relatively unaffected.

Thus distraction should produce the same kinds of effects we would expect from the arousal of competitive or evaluation concerns. Some research indicates that distraction is a considerably less important factor in the situation, but under some circumstances it probably does contribute to the effects that are produced by the presence of other people. The effect depends largely on the task. If the task is familiar and reasonably simple, the increased motivation is generally more important than the distraction, so performance improves. If the task is unfamiliar and difficult, both motivation and distraction have adverse effects, so performance decreases. And if the task entails learning something new, the distraction is particularly harmful.

social behaviors

One final point about the social facilitation caused by being with other people is that certain behaviors may be increased primarily because they are almost entirely social in nature. These behaviors and responses depend on other people and rarely if ever occur when we are alone. Thus, being with other people will make these responses more likely. One example would be blushing, with the accompanying internal feelings of

Michael D. Sullivan

shame and embarrassment. We are almost never embarrassed when we are totally alone because this particular reaction depends on someone knowing what we have done. It is, of course, possible to blush when you are by yourself, but it is much more likely to happen in the presence of others. Similarly, though perhaps less clearly, we laugh more easily when other people are around. Again, we sometimes laugh by ourselves in response to something funny that we read or see on television, but being in an audience greatly increases laughter. This is true for children as young as seven (Chapman, 1973) and certainly holds for adults. Indeed, television producers know this well and therefore usually have shows performed in front of real audiences even if they are taped and shown later. The laughter of the real audience (or canned laughter if necessary) helps takes the place of other people for the TV viewer.

Laughing, blushing, feeling embarrassed, and probably other behaviors occur mainly in social situations. They happen not because of any of the factors discussed in connection with social faciliation—dominant responses being strengthened, distraction, the arousal of competition or evaluation fears. Some actions are direct consequences of being with other people. When we are alone, the action does not occur (or is less likely to) because it is inherently connected to other people and needs their presence to be elicited.

competition versus cooperation

In our discussion of social facilitation in a minimal social situation we have been assuming that the people involved are not interacting directly but are merely in the same place at the same time. When they are not members of the same group but do interact, people often have the choice of cooperating or competing. In most card and board games, one person's gain is another's loss. If you win a pot in poker, the other players lose. In Monopoly, if you land on Boardwalk with a hotel, you lose $2000 and someone else is that much richer. These are called zero-sum games because all the wins and losses add to zero. But in many real life situations, one side's gains need not be offset by the other's losses. They can both win or both lose. Whenever this is true, it is referred to as a non-zero-sum game (the total of gains and losses do not add to zero). In such a game, whether it involves interpersonal relationships, a business deal, or conflicts between nations, the players can cooperate to maximize their total gains or can compete. What determines their actions?

It might be thought that people would behave in all cases so as to maximize their rewards. If getting the most out of a situation meant cooperating, they would cooperate; if it meant competing, they would compete. As we shall see, this is not the case. Regardless of the complications in any situation, deal, or game, it is generally possible to specify the strategy that will produce the most profit. Mathematicians have developed what is called *game theory*—a mathematical analysis of games—which can be applied to complicated as well as simple games and which, in many cases, can tell individuals what to do at each step in order to maximize winnings. Game theory is an interesting and, in some contexts, useful exercise, but it is not applicable to our problem because people do not always follow ideal strategies. Even when it is obvious that cooperation is the best strategy, many—if not most—people compete rather than cooperate. The question, then, is not what is the best strategy, but what factors increase or decrease the tendency to compete.

the trucking game

Deutsch and Krauss (1960) conducted a classic experiment on this problem. Pairs of subjects engaged in a simple game. Each subject was asked to imagine that she was running a trucking company (either the Acme or the Bold Company) and had to get a truck from one point to another as quickly as possible. The two trucks were not in competition; they had different starting points and different destinations. There was, however, one hitch—the fastest route for both converged at one point to a one-lane road, and they had to go in opposite directions. This is shown in Figure

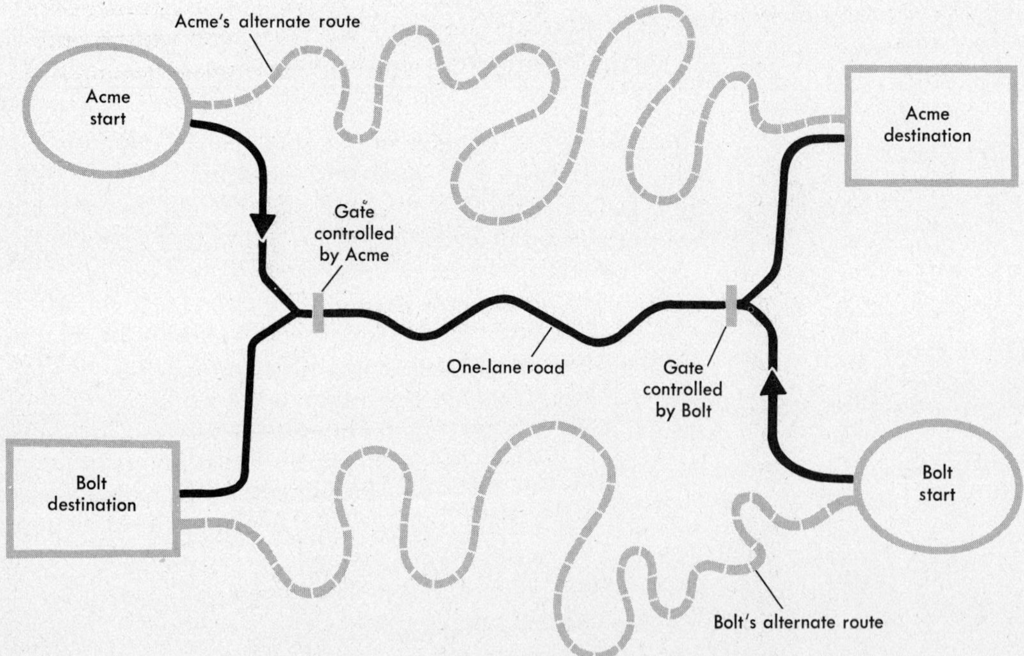

FIGURE 14–2
Road map of the trucking game. The players must get their truck to its destination as quickly as possible. Although they can do this efficiently only by cooperating and sharing the one-lane road, they often compete, particularly when gates are provided. (Deutsch, M., and Krauss, R. M., "The effect of threat on interpersonal bargaining," Journal of Abnormal and Social Psychology, 1960, 61, p. 183. Copyright 1960 by the American Psychological Association, and reproduced by permission.)

factors affecting competition

incentive

The competitive tendency changes somewhat when the incentive for doing well is increased. In most of the studies, subjects were playing simply for points, for imaginary money, or perhaps for small stakes. They earned no more by doing well than by doing poorly. In an occasional study, they could earn a few extra cents by scoring a lot of points, but the subjects—not only those who were fairly affluent college students but even the not so affluent high school students and working women—were not impressed by the chance to earn an extra 15 or 20 cents. Therefore, their natural tendency to compete was predominant over their desire to earn the money. When the stakes are raised, however, and the subjects can earn as much as a few dollars, the desire to earn the money is relatively more important. Under these circumstances, there is a conflict between the competitive urge and the desire to maximize winnings. Yet the effect of incentive on competition is far from clear.

An experiment by Gallo (1966) demonstrated one effect of the size of rewards. Subjects played the trucking game, but for half the pairs the payoffs were in real money, whereas the other pairs played just for points. With real money there was considerably more cooperation. Gallo and Sheposh (1971) obtained similar results when subjects who were given $10 to play with were compared to others who had only points. Once again, those with real money earned more. And a study involving negotiation (Kelly et al., 1970) compared money with points in several different countries. They found that there were more agreements and they were reached more quickly when money was involved.

Other studies, however, have produced conflicting evidence on the role of monetary incentive. Gumpert, Deutsch, and Epstein (1969) found even more competition with real than with imaginary money in a prisoner's dilemma game. Oskamp and Kleinke (1970) conducted two experiments on this problem. In the first, each trial involved a range of payoffs from $.30 to $3, but the total earnings were based on a selection of trials and ranged only from $1.50 to $3. The second study had trials that were either no money (just points), pennies, or dimes with maximum earnings ranging from zero to $9. Although the effects of incentive were not strong, there was a consistent tendency for cooperation to be *greater* with lower payoff. Increasing the incentive actually decreased the amount of cooperative choices.

Finally, another study suggests that the absolute amount of money is not especially important but that people are sensitive to changes in their rewards (Friedland, Arnold, and Thibaut, 1974). As in the other work on this problem, subjects played a game with varying stakes. The amount of competition was unaffected by the amount of money involved.

However, in other conditions the size of the reward changed during the course of the game, getting either larger or smaller. An increase made little difference, but decreasing the stakes reduced cooperation. Presumably, every player has two motives: winning money and beating the other person. When the stakes are suddenly decreased, the money motive becomes less important and subjects concentrate on seeking victory.

This research indicates that incentive does not have a simple effect on the amount of cooperation in these games. Sometimes it seems to increase cooperation, sometimes it decreases it, and sometimes it has little effect. A possible resolution of this seeming inconsistency is that people care more about winning when the stakes are greater, but that does not necessarily make them cooperate more. The temptation to pick a competitive choice and possibly win a big bonus exists both when points are involved and when there is a chance of winning money. Increasing the incentive may simply cause some subjects to concentrate on winning at least some money, but cause other subjects to maximize their winnings by competing. Knox and Douglas (1971) produced results that support this explanation. They compared subjects who were playing for pennies to those playing for dollars. The amount of cooperation was virtually identical for the two conditions, but there was three times as much variance when dollars were involved. Some players cooperated a great deal, others hardly at all. This suggests that the higher incentive caused some subjects to play more competitively and others more cooperatively. When you care more about winning, you choose a more consistent and more extreme strategy, but there is no evidence that you are necessarily more cooperative.

It is important to note that even when the stakes are quite high, subjects tend to make a large number of competitive responses. Apparently, the competitive urges are strong enough to cause people to compete despite the fact that it is to their disadvantage in terms of their total winnings. As we noted in our discussion of social facilitation, the presence of another person seems to arouse competitive feelings even when there is no realistic reason for assuming that any competition is involved. Our present findings reinforce this. Taken together, they seem to suggest that, at least in our society, one of the powerful, dominating factors in most interpersonal situations is the arousal of competitive feelings. This does not mean that people always compete nor that they feel competitive in all situations. But it does suggest that competition is a strong component in many interpersonal relationships even when the situation is structured to favor cooperation.

On the other hand, caution seems appropriate in interpreting this research. We must remember that the participants knew they were taking part in psychological experiments and were playing games. Moreover, even in the highest stakes games, the amounts involved were pretty small for college students. Admittedly, it is nice to be able to win $9. But it is still not much money by most people's standards. Therefore, we

should be careful about generalizing these results on incentive to situations involving substantial amounts of money or other rewards. We can legitimately question whether people would continue to compete if instead of playing for money they were playing to avoid severe electric shocks. Under these circumstances, would most people continue to concentrate on beating the other player (i.e., getting fewer shocks), or would they do anything possible to get the minimum number of shocks themselves? We do not know. For now, we do know that under the conditions of the studies we have described, many people are more concerned about doing better than the other person than they are about winning as much as possible.

motivation

The evidence indicates that most people view the prisoner's dilemma game, at least in part, as a competitive situation. However, this competitive feeling can be influenced to some extent by what the subjects are told about the purpose of the game. The particular motive that is aroused helps determine the amount of cooperation. In a study by Deutsch (1960), subjects were given one of three different instructions: Cooperative instructions stressed concern for the other player's welfare; competitive instructions urged each player to win as much money as he could for himself and, in particular, to win more than the other player; and individualistic instructions stated that the only purpose was to win as much as possible and that the other player's outcome should be ignored.

The different instructions had a major impact on the amount of cooperation. The results are shown in the right-hand column of Table 14–2. Those subjects who were told to cooperate did so on over 90 percent of their choices. In contrast, the individualistic instructions resulted in about 50 percent cooperation, and the competitive instructions produced only about 20 percent cooperation. Clearly, the tendency to view the game as competitive can be altered to a large extent by appropriate instructions.

It should be noted that instructing subjects to compete or to cooper-

TABLE 14–2
communication and effects of motivation on cooperation

	PERCENTAGE OF COOPERATIVE CHOICES		
Motivation Instructions	No Communication	Communication	Average
Cooperative	89.1	96.9	93.0
Individualistic	35.0	70.6	52.8
Competitive	12.5	29.2	20.9

Source: Adapted from Deutsch (1960).

ate affects their behavior in situations other than the kinds of games we have been discussing. In several studies, groups that were working on problems were told either to maximize their individual efforts or to maximize the performance of the group as a whole. When they were urged to compete, there was less communication among the members of the group, they had less influence on one another and accepted one another less, and there was less division of labor and poorer productivity. When they were supposed to cooperate, there was more trust in one another, and the productivity of the group as a whole went up. Thus, in many, if not all, kinds of social interactions, having a cooperative goal produces more cooperation than seeing the situation as competitive.

threats

In some social situations, the people involved have no particular power over each other. If they are bargaining or playing some other social game, they compete or cooperate as equals and have no additional weapons at their disposal. In buying a car, you are trying to get it for the lowest possible price; the salesperson is trying to get the highest price. That's the whole story. If you agree on a price, the deal is closed; if you don't agree, the car stays in the showroom. Now imagine that you work for the local newspaper and threaten to write an unfavorable story about the dealer if he does not give you a good price. That threat may give you a big advantage. Or consider international negotiations on the price of oil. The United States and Saudi Arabia are trying to agree on a price. Each has certain bargaining cards, but they are playing the game by the usual rules. Now suppose the Americans say that if the Saudis do not agree on a reasonable price, their country will be invaded. This unilateral (one-sided) threat would obviously play an important role in subsequent bargaining. Knowing this,the Saudis reply that if there is no agreement, the oil fields will be blown up and no one will get any oil. This is hardly farfetched; a situation much like this occurred in the early days of the OPEC oil cartel. What effect do threats have on cooperation?

In variations of the trucking game, one, both, or neither players were provided with threats in the form of barriers that could be placed across the one-lane road. When only one player had a barrier to use, the condition was called unilateral threat; when both players had them, the condition was called bilateral threat. Note that the barriers in no way prevented cooperation. The players did not have to use them; they could take turns using the road and forget about the barriers.

The existence of the barriers made a sizable difference in the amount of cooperation between the players. When neither one had a barrier to use, there was the most cooperation. When one had a barrier, there was less cooperation and the holder of the threat tended to do better than the other. On a typical trial, the two trucks met in the middle of the road and the question was which would back up first. If the holder of the barrier backed up, she could erect the barrier and prevent the other

from benefiting from the direct route. They both lost, but the one without the threat probably lost more. On the other hand, if the other backed up, there was no barrier to be erected and the first truck could roll through and gain a lot of points. Thus, the few cooperative choices there were tended to favor the one with the threat, and she therefore got a better score. Finally, when both sides had a threat, there was the least amount of cooperation. The typical result was for both sides to erect their barriers and immediately take the long route. This was guaranteed to lose money but avoided the greater loss due to a stalemate at the narrow road.

Although threats can sometimes interfere with maximal performance, a person who has a threat does seem to have a distinct advantage over someone who does not. In the trucking game, when only one person has a gate, he does earn more points (or lose fewer) than the person who does not have a gate. In prisoner's dilemma and other bargaining games, a player who has a threat of any kind is in a strong position. This is particularly true if he seems likely to carry out the threat (Guyer and Rapoport, 1970). Under these circumstances, he will usually get the better of the bargaining—win more points or money or whatever is involved. On the other hand, someone who has power and does not use it may be considered weak and be taken advantage of. Swingle (1970) showed that subjects who have a threat and fail to use it are exploited more than subjects who do not have the threat in the first place. Apparently power is useful only when the other person is convinced that it may be used. Otherwise it may actually reduce the strength of a person's position by making him seem weak and ineffectual.

Black and Higbee (1973), however, found the situation even more complex, because male and female subjects differed in their response to threats. Females were especially cooperative when their partners had threats and did not use them, whereas males behaved differently depending on whether they perceived the other to be a powerful person. If the other was powerful, cooperative, and did not have threats, males exploited him or her more than if the other was seen as weak. But if the other had threats, the males cooperated more with the powerful than with the weak. It would seem that the specific pattern of responses to threats and power is less important than the finding that the relationship is complicated. There is good reason to believe that the particular situation and subjects involved could change the pattern, but it seems clear that threats play an important role and generally improve the outcome of the side that has them.

communication

Throughout our discussion of groups we have repeatedly stressed the importance of communication. The ability to talk to one's partner also plays a major role in determining the amount of cooperation between the two. In the study by Deutsch described above, some subjects with each kind of motivation were allowed to communicate with their partner before playing. The effect of this communication was that cooperation increased markedly, regardless of the kind of motivation that had been aroused (see Table 14–2). However, the effect of communication was most dramatic in the individualistic condition. When subjects were trying to maximize their own winnings and were supposed to ignore those of the other player, being able to communicate increased their percentage of cooperative choices from 35 to over 70.

The Deutsch and Krauss trucking study included three different types of communication conditions. Some subjects were not allowed to communicate; others were given the opportunity to talk if they wanted to; and a third group was required to communicate. The effect was similar to that in the prisoner's dilemma game—there was more cooperation when communication was allowed than when it was not allowed and still more when it was forced. The effect was particularly strong in the unilateral threat condition. When one player was provided with a barrier and not allowed to communicate, there was little cooperation, but when the players were forced to talk, the amount of cooperation increased dramatically.

This effect of communication was demonstrated even more convincingly by Wichman (1970). In a prisoner's dilemma game, some subjects were isolated from their partners; others could see their partners but could not talk to them; others could talk to their partners but could not see them; and still others could both see and hear each other. The amount of cooperation increased in that order. When there was no communication or only nonverbal communication, about 40 percent of the responses were cooperative. When verbal communication or both verbal and visual communication were allowed, cooperation occurred on more than 70 percent of the trials.

Assuming there is any tendency to cooperate, knowledge of the other person and particularly of what he is planning to do should facilitate it. Since the optimal strategy in these games depends almost entirely on the degree of trust in the other person, the ability to communicate is especially helpful. There may, however, be other games in which trust is less important or in which the tendency to cooperate is weaker, in which case being able to communicate might have relatively little effect.

One of the obvious reasons that communication should increase the amount of cooperation is that the players in these games often misperceive the others' intentions. Kelly and Stahelski (1970) showed that it was difficult for individuals in a prisoner's dilemma game to know what the other person was planning to do. More important, someone who was intending to make a cooperative choice was misjudged more often than someone who was planning to be competitive. Apparently there was a general tendency to assume that the other person would make a competitive choice. One of the reasons for this misperception was that the player who was planning to make a cooperative choice was often unable to follow through on this intention. If his opponent consistently made competitive choices, the player who wanted to play cooperatively was eventually forced to protect himself by making the competitive choice also. Thus the misperception of the cooperative player's intentions turned out often to be consistent with what the player actually did. This is another case of the self-fulfilling prophecy, in which one player assumes the other player will be competitive. He accordingly chooses a competitive response, eventually forcing the other person to be competitive also. The net result is that his initial perception that the other person is competitive will turn out to be correct only because he has in fact forced the other person to behave that way. As usual, once you assume the other person is a dangerous character and start treating him as an enemy, he will start acting like one.

The possibility of misjudging the other player is greatly decreased when communication is possible. Accordingly, allowing or forcing players to communicate makes it considerably easier for them to cooperate. They can discuss their plans, urge each other to cooperate, make promises, convince each other they are trustworthy, learn something about each other, and so on. Assuming there is any tendency to cooperate, knowledge of the other should facilitate it.

On the other hand, a study by Smith and Anderson (1975) found that communication can sometimes have negative effects. Playing a game similar to the trucking game, subjects either had free communication or did not, and also either both had threats or neither did. In the no-threat condition, free communication led to more cooperation. In the bilateral threat condition, free communication actually led to somewhat less cooperation than when no communication was allowed. Apparently, these subjects used the opportunity to communicate to make threats and increase confrontation rather than resolve their mutual problem. Taking this finding along with the Deutsch and Krauss results suggests that communication is helpful chiefly when the players are equal, with neither having a threat, or when the communication can make it clear that one has the upper hand (unilateral threat) and allow the weaker player to compromise.

maximizing cooperation

We have seen that many factors, including motivation, threats, communication, the stakes, and perhaps also individual characteristics of the players, determine the outcome. Given a particular situation with particular people playing, are there any procedures or strategies that seem to increase cooperativeness consistently?

One strategy that seems to work quite well is reciprocal concessions—the players take turns giving up a little. I'll go to the movie you want if you go to my favorite restaurant; I'll do the dishes if you cook. This is the traditional compromise solution to most conflicts. Each side starts with an extreme position and then retreats gradually until a common meeting ground is found. If one player makes a small concession and then waits for the other to do the same, there is indeed greater eventual cooperation (Esser and Komorita, 1975). However, a crucial element of this strategy is timing. If one person gives in too much, he may appear weak and the other will not reciprocate. The concessions must be gradual and sequential. In addition, obviously this does not work unless both sides are willing to cooperate to some extent. If one of them is totally competitive, the one who tries cooperating will only be taken advantage of and end up with a weaker position than before.

Perhaps a more general instance of this strategy is rewarding someone for cooperating in order to teach him to cooperate more in the future. There is evidence that, as you might expect, this does work (McNeel, 1973). Unfortunately, it works only for subjects who are initially trying to win as much as possible for themselves, not for those who are trying to "beat" the other player. Rewarding the latter for cooperating is ineffective because they are not interested in getting more points when the other person also gets the same number of points. Since in most games cooperating guarantees that both players earn the same amount, rewarding cooperativeness does not help. On the other hand, it would be possible to design a game so that cooperation of a certain kind helped one player even more than it helped the other, and then perhaps even the competitive player could be taught to cooperate.

applicability of the research findings

Many psychologists have attempted to relate the findings of studies on non-zero-sum games to the world situation and relationships between countries. Countries, too, cooperate or compete. In many cases, they could maximize their gains if they would cooperate, and yet there seems to be a tendency for them to compete. It was hoped that the research on games would reveal some of the basic factors determining relationships between countries. Our feeling is that the findings are more readily generalized to dealings between individuals. Friends, lovers, marriage partners, teachers and students, salesperson and buyer all engage in dealings that often involve the possibility of either competition or cooperation. Unlike some games, these interpersonal relationships typically do not require that one person's gain is another's loss. On the contrary, as in the games we have discussed in this chapter, it is possible for people to cooperate to maximize gains for both parties.

In this context, the most significant research finding is that people are motivated to maximize their profits from several points of view. As we would expect, in any bargaining or game situation, one of the strong considerations, and perhaps the dominant one, is to get as much as we can for as little as we can. But participants also want to maximize their gains in relation to other people. They want to "win" the exchange. Thus they might be willing to accept a slightly less advantageous deal if they felt it meant they were surpassing the other person. Some people refuse to accept a profitable arrangement merely because it means they would not win the exchange. Although they would be getting good value for their payment, the other person would receive equal value. Both accumulation of goods and competition motives are probably present in almost all bargaining situations.

One implication of this is well known to salespeople. Customers want to feel that they are getting a good deal, that they are somehow winning the exchange. Someone selling a used car tries to make us feel he has been talked into a deal he never wanted to agree to, that we are very good bargainers. In that way, we feel we have won the exchange, he feels (probably rightly) that he has won, and everyone is happy. In countries such as Mexico, where bargaining is a common mode of selling, this can be seen more clearly. If a vendor offers a rug for 200 pesos, the customer is not supposed to accept that price. It is deliberately high and the salesperson would be surprised if it were accepted. Part of the selling is the bargaining itself, and both parties enter into it determined to win the deal. Most of the time they settle on roughly the price the vendor had in mind to begin with, but by this bargaining process, both people enjoy the sale more. They feel they have not only gotten good value, but have also managed to beat the other person.

The same is true in relationships between friends and lovers. People do not always agree perfectly. Often they have different values and goals, and these differences give rise to conflicts. To the extent that each person is merely trying to get what he or she wants, the resolution of these conflicts simply requires compromise. As we mentioned earlier, each gives in on some points as long as the other gives in on others. And if the people care for each other, they will both want to find a resultion that gives both of them as much as possible.

Unfortunately, as we all know, the situation is not quite that simple. Many times people are not only trying to get something for themselves, they are also trying to "win" a dispute or "beat" the other person. Sadly, this occurs even between people who have warm and friendly feelings for each other. As the research has shown, competition is an important element in many conflicts. Thus, one reason why personal conflicts are not easily resolved is that each person wants to come out ahead of the other rather than settle for a solution that maximizes both their gains. If both want to win, obviously the resolution is difficult and will usually involve some hard feelings. One possible lesson from the research is that communication can often help. Talking about the conflict may make it easier to find a reasonable resolution and may even lead to cooperation rather than competition. Thus, the current popular emphasis on openness, honesty, and communication in relationships may lead to a more favorable resolution of the conflicts that inevitably arise.

Extending the work to relationships between countries seems to be even more speculative and should be done with great caution. If we wanted to draw conclusions, perhaps the clearest is that in any conflict both sides do want to look good and even like to think that they have won the exchange. Accordingly, the ideal treaty between countries is one that leaves each side thinking it has won the conference. Perhaps the hope that countries will cooperate is unrealistic; it seems more likely that they will always compete, as people do. The hope, then, should be for them to compete in selling cars, playing ping-pong, or in building more impressive dams rather than in armaments.

problem solving by groups

How do groups compare with individuals in solving problems? We have seen that having another person present stimulates performance under some conditions but interferes with it under others. Stimulation and distraction also occur when a group is working on a problem together; and in this more complex situation, additional factors operate. We described above a common practice in business and government—the so-called brainstorming session, an unstructured, free type of group problem solving in which people get together and say anything that they think might be helpful. The idea is that they will stimulate one another into producing better ideas than each would produce alone. People also work together in more restricted types of groups. They can build a spaceship, design an experiment, solve a math problem, even write a novel in groups. In contrast, Thomas Edison invented the phonograph in virtual isolation; Albert Einstein devised the theory of relativity without discussing it with anyone; most novelists and artists work alone. Perhaps Edison would have been more effective in a work group at General Electric. Perhaps an advertising executive would think of a better slogan working alone than in a brainstorming group.

Although the question may seem to be straightforward and one that can be easily investigated, there is some difficulty in knowing just what to compare groups to. In some early studies, the same problem was given to groups of two, three, four, and five people and also to a number of individuals. The experimenters then compared the performance of the groups with the performance of each of the individuals. Examined in this way, the results are very clear: there is strength in numbers. By whatever criteria we choose, a group does better than a person working alone.

It quickly becomes apparent, however, that this is not the basic question. We really want to know whether four people working in a group would do better than the *same* people working separately. To use the people we have most effectively, should we have them work in groups or alone?

research results

In a classic study on brainstorming, (Taylor, Berry, and Block, 1958), subjects were assigned at random to either five-person groups or the individual condition. (Those in the groups had met together several times before.) The people in both conditions were then given five problems and twelve minutes to work on each one. One problem, for example, was stated as follows: "Each year a great many American tourists go to visit Europe, but now suppose that our country wished to get many more European tourists to come to visit America during their vacations. What steps can you suggest that would get more European tourists to come to this country?" The subjects were told that their task was to consider the problems and to offer as many and as creative solutions as they could. There were obviously no "correct" solutions. The following rules, taken from Osborne (1957, p. 84), were outlined to the groups:

1. Criticism is ruled out. Adverse judgment of ideas must be withheld until later.
2. Freewheeling is welcomed. The wilder an idea, the better. It is easier to tame down than to perk up.
3. Quantity is wanted. The greater the number of ideas, the more likelihood of winners.
4. Combination and improvement are sought. In addition to contributing ideas of your own, you should suggest how ideas of others can be turned into better ideas or how two or more ideas can be joined into still another one.

Subjects in the alone condition were divided at random into five-person nominal groups. That is, although each of these subjects worked alone, for purposes of the analysis they were considered a group and their total production was compared to the production of the actual groups. In this way, Taylor compared five hours of work done by a five-person group with five hours done by five individuals working alone. This is the only meaningful way to compare the efficiency of the two procedures.

The results (presented in Table 14–3) can be considered in terms of the quantity of ideas produced and also in terms of their originality. Quantity consisted of the number of *different* ideas produced by the real and the nominal groups. If two members of a nominal group produced the same idea, it was counted as only one idea. As can be seen from the table, the nominal groups (individuals working alone) scored higher than the actual groups. The individuals produced an average of 68.1 ideas, whereas the groups produced only 37.5. Similarly, the nominal groups produced more unique, creative ideas (19.8 versus 10.8). In other words, five individuals working alone produced almost twice as many solutions and unique ideas as five comparable people did working together. Someone working alone can concentrate better than he can in a group and also does not have to worry about competing with other people in order to express his ideas. If the group did provide any mutual stimulation, it was apparently more than offset by the interfering and distracting effects of other people.

TABLE 14–3
performance by real and nominal groups

CONDITION	DIFFERENT IDEAS	UNIQUE IDEAS
Real groups	37.5	10.8
Nominal groups (five individuals working alone)	68.1	19.8

Note: Figures are number of ideas.
Source: Taylor et al. (1958).

limitations of the research

Although the results of the study by Taylor et al. showed that groups are inferior to individuals working alone, this study has several limitations. The most important is that the groups had worked together for a relatively short time. It may be that people have to get to know each other and learn to work together before a group can become an effective unit. At least one study (Cohen et al., 1960) suggested that brainstorming in groups is quite productive when the individuals involved were specially selected to be compatible and were trained to work together.

Another question concerns the effect of dissimilarity of the group members on the quality of the solutions they produce. It appears that relatively heterogeneous groups, in which the personalities of the various members differ considerably, produce better solutions to most problems than do homogeneous groups. In a study by Hoffman and Maier (1961), the two kinds of groups were given problems to work on that varied considerably in terms of whether or not there was an objective solution, the kinds of issues involved, and so on. For example, one problem required the group to think of a way for people to cross a heavily mined road, whereas another involved settling a simulated argument between two of the group's members. The results showed that on several problems, there was a large difference—favoring the heterogeneous groups—in the quality of the solutions offered. With other problems, the difference was considerably smaller. Overall, the results indicated that heterogeneous groups are superior to homogeneous groups on a wide variety of problems.

Another variable in this study was sex. Some groups were composed only of men, whereas others had both men and women. There was some indication that the groups containing both sexes produced higher-quality solutions than did the all-male groups. Thus, heterogeneity, in terms of both personality and sex, seems to improve the performance of groups.

A further limitation concerns the type of problem tackled. How to use foreign aid or what slogan to adopt for a new polka-dot toothpaste, questions that were discussed in the brainstorming research, cannot be resolved by a logical process—these questions have no "correct" or unique solution. It would seem that any stimulating effect a group might have on its members would be most beneficial and any distracting effect would be least harmful when such problems are considered. On the other hand, with problems that can be solved logically and that have unique, correct solutions (solving a math problem, building a spaceship, inventing the electric light, or solving a brainteaser), the stimulating effect of the group might be less important and the distraction more harmful. Groups do provide two important advantages—members can check one another's work and, collectively, they provide a variety of abilities that one individual would be unlikely to possess. However, because these characteristics of groups are helpful only with certain types of problems, the relative effectiveness of groups and individuals depends on the characteristics of the problem.

Groups are quite effective in working on problems that involve a large number of separate operations, such as complex arithmetic problems. In such cases, the ability of members to catch one another's mistakes is particularly important. A group provides a system of checks that is lacking when an individual works alone. On the other hand, with these problems, the group is not really working together—the individual

Everett C. Johnson/de Wys

members are working separately and then checking one another's work. This is quite different from brainstorming, but it does indicate that under some circumstances, groups perform better than individuals working alone.

It is obvious that problems requiring a number of separate skills tend to favor groups. If, in order to solve a problem, it is essential to know calculus, cellular biology, and organic chemistry, only an individual possessing all this knowledge would be able to find the solution. Even among individuals on a college faculty, it is unlikely that any one person would have all these skills. If, however, we form such a faculty into five-person groups, it is considerably more likely that a group of five professors would have, among them, the three necessary abilities. Thus in this admittedly somewhat specialized situation, groups would be better than individuals. It should be noted that many problems that require a number of skills can be worked on in stages. For example, the first stage may require a knowledge only of cellular biology; the second stage, a knowledge only of calculus; and the third, only of organic chemistry. With this kind of problem, it is not clear that groups are superior to individuals so long as we allow the individuals to work on the problem in stages and to distribute their findings at the end of each stage. Thus, the experiments in which groups have tended to be less effective than individuals may be somewhat misleading. We may conclude that groups set up at random and working together for a relatively short time almost certainly will be less effective than would the same individuals working alone. However, the possibility remains that properly constructed and well-trained groups may sometimes be more creative and efficient than individuals.

One final point should be made about group problem solving. Particular characteristics of any of the individuals may have an inhibiting or even a destructive effect on the rest of the group. One person may talk so much that no one else is able to say anything. Or someone may be so critical of everyone else's ideas that the rest of the group becomes reluctant to contribute. Another common phenomenon, discussed in detail in Chapter 13, is that persons of higher status in the group tend to have more influence than those of lower status.

In a study by Torrance (1955), airplane crews consisting of a pilot, navigator, and gunner worked on a series of problems together. A careful recording was kept of the solutions suggested by each group member and of the final solution agreed on by the whole group. It was found that the group almost always unanimously approved the solutions suggested by the pilot, whereas it was rarely influenced by the contributions of the gunner (the lowest-status person). This is not surprising and by itself need not have had an adverse effect on the group's performance. The striking finding concerned the group's reaction when either the pilot or the gunner had the correct answer. Torrance found that when the pilot had the correct answer, the group went along with him 100 percent of the time. However, when the gunner had the correct answer, the group

© Punch-ROTHCO

"J. B. has just had this marvellous brainwave—we'll use your idea!"

accepted it only about 40 percent of the time. This means that if the three men had been working separately, at least the gunner would have been correct the other 60 percent of the time that he knew the answer; but when they worked as a group, all three memebers were incorrect on those occasions when the pilot disagreed with the gunner. The same effect has been found (Riecken, 1958) when a clue is given to various members of a group. When it is given to someone who talks a lot and is a leader, the group solves the problem; when the clue is given to a relatively silent member, the group often fails to use it. This research demonstrates that groups introduce all sorts of complex interactions, conflicts, and pressures that are not present when individuals work alone and that these characteristics of the group are often disruptive.

To sum up, it seems that under most circumstances, groups are less efficient than individuals working alone. Group members distract, inhibit, and generally tend to interfere with one another. Groups do provide a means of catching errors, and on certain types of problems, this might overcome their relative inefficiency. Also, when differing skills are needed for a solution, groups have a big advantage. Finally, as in minimal social situations, group members tend to motivate each other to work harder, and they probably do this to an even greater extent than in the minimal situations. If other incentives have not already produced a sufficiently high motivational level, this would be an advantage of working in groups.

cohesiveness

Interactions and feelings among the group members play an important role in the group's performance. It seems obvious that groups in which there is a lot of internal fighting, disagreement, and lack of cooperation will do poorly on tasks, whereas groups in which people generally agree and cooperate should do very well. In addition, groups in which all the members like each other and are strongly attracted to the group itself should do well. A group of this kind would have high morale, strong motivation, and strong pressures against conflicts that could interfere with performance. This quality of the group is called its *cohesiveness*. The more the members are attracted to one another and to the group and the more they share the group's goals, the greater the group's cohesiveness.

These considerations suggest that highly cohesive groups are more effective than those with less cohesiveness, and research has generally shown this effect (Husband, 1940; Berkowitz, 1956). However, it is important to take into account a group's norms and goals. The more cohesive a group, the more its members follow its goals. Thus, if the group's goal is to work hard and accomplish as much as possible, a cohesive group will be more productive than a less cohesive group. On the other hand, if for some reason the group's goals are to limit the amount of work, a highly cohesive group will be less productive than a less cohesive group (Schachter et al., 1951; Berkowitz, 1954). In other words, whatever the group as a whole decides to do, a cohesive group will do better.

Although it might seem that most groups would want to maximize their productivity, many groups deliberately limit production. A typical example is a union that places restrictions, formal or informal, on the amount of work each person is supposed to accomplish in a given period of time. The workers are expected to do that much and no more, and anyone who does more is considered a deviant and treated accordingly. Of course, in this situation the goal is set by an outside agency (the company management), and the group does not benefit directly from increased output. However, restricting productivity also occurs in more informal groups such as college fraternities and other living units. The members think that a certain amount of studying, for example, is appropriate, but anything more than that amount is "bad form." Someone who wants to study more than the accepted amount may be subjected to kidding, abuse, deliberate distractions, or even rejection. Thus, cohesive groups maintain performance at a set level better than do less cohesive groups, but the level of performance is not necessarily higher with greater cohesiveness.

groups as mobs

Thus far we have been talking about groups in which the members work together to solve a problem. We have focused on the end result of this activity—the quantity and quality of the work accomplished. But groups do many other things and have many effects on individual members other than making them better or worse at problem solving.

The restaurant fire described at the beginning of this chapter is one example of a group acting as a mob. All the individuals wanted to escape.

If they had cooperated and taken turns, they might all have escaped—or at least many more than actually did. Instead, they were disorganized, ignored one another, acted singly, and died.

With clouds of smoke billowing behind the diners, perhaps it was not surprising that they became frantic and disorganized. But this kind of phenomenon is not limited to such extreme circumstances. In the relatively placid setting of an experimental laboratory, each of a group of subjects was given one end of a string, the other end of which was attached to a small wooden spool (Mintz, 1951). The spools were placed in a large bottle, the neck of which was wide enough for only one spool to pass through at a time. The bottle then began to fill with water, and everyone was told to get his spool out before the water reached it. (The analogy to the restaurant fire is obvious.) The water rose slowly enough so that everyone could have gotten his spool out safely as long as only one person at a time tried. The bottle was in plain sight, there was no bonus for getting one's spool out early, and, presumably, there was little or no actual fear of the water. Yet traffic jams almost always developed. Two or more people tried to get their spools through the bottle's neck at once, the spools got caught, and all those that were not already free were covered with water.

Harold Kelley and his associates (1965) repeated this study in a more controlled situation and, as shown in Table 14–4, got the same results. In addition, however, Kelley showed that increasing the actual level of fear (e.g., by threatening the subjects with electric shocks if they did not escape) produced more disorganization and more traffic jams. The main point of this research for our present purpose is that under even mild stress, a group somtimes acts in a disorganized, self-destructive manner and that this tendency increases with higher stress.

TABLE 14–4
effect of threat on escape in a situation requiring cooperation

THREAT	PERCENTAGE ESCAPING
Low	69
Medium	56
High	36

Source: Adapted from Kelley et al. (1965).

deindividuation

One of the most impressive aspects of groups is that people sometimes do things when together that they would not do if they were alone. This is most striking—and frightening—when the action involves immoral or violent acts: lynchings in the South, the killing of referees at soccer matches in South America, urban riots, and so on. Interviews with some of the people involved in riots indicate that they would never have considered performing the acts of violence had they been alone and that, when the riots were over, they were actually shocked at what they had done.

The explanation usually given for this phenomenon is that to some extent individuals lose their personal sense of responsibility when they are in a group. Instead of feeling, as they usually do, that they personally are morally accountable for their actions, group members somehow share the responsibility with one another, and none of them feels it as strongly as he would if he were alone. This is sometimes called responsibility diffusion or *deindividuation*, because the people are responding and being responded to not as separate individuals, but as part of the group. It has been shown that groups differ considerably in the extent to which they produce deindividuation. In addition, there is some evidence that the greater the deindividuation of any group, the more free and uninhibited the behavior of its members.

One implication of deindividuation is that anything which makes the members of a group less identifiable increases the effect. The more anonymous the group members are, the less identifiable they are as individuals, the less they feel they have an identity of their own, and the more irresponsibly they may behave. In a mob, most of the people do not stand out as individuals. They blend together and, in a sense, do not have an identity of their own. Conversely, to the extent that they are identifiable and feel that they are, they retain their feeling of individuality and are less likely to act irresponsibly.

In an experiment by Singer, Brush, and Lublin (1965) to test this notion, some subjects were made easily identifiable and others were made difficult to identify. In the former condition, everyone dressed in his normal clothes, which meant that each was dressed differently from the others. In addition, the subjects were called by name and everything was done to make each one stand out as an individual. In the latter condition, all the subjects put on identical, bulky lab coats. The experimenter avoided using their names and, in general, tried to give the impression that their individual identities did not matter much. The group then discussed a variety of topics, including one that required the use of obscene language.

Groups in the low-identifiable condition showed much more freedom in all the discussions and, in particular, in the one involving obscene words. There were fewer pauses in the conversation, more lively discussions, and, most strongly, a greater willingness to use the obscene language that was necessary for a good discussion of the topic. Subjects who were more easily identified were much more constrained and appeared quite reluctant to use the taboo words.

A more dramatic effect of identifiability was provided in an experiment by Zimbardo (1969). Groups of four girls were recruited to take part in a study supposedly involving empathic responses to strangers. In one condition, the girls were greeted by name, wore name tags, and were easily identifiable. In another condition, the girls wore oversized white lab coats and hoods over their heads, were never called by name, and were difficult if not impossible to identify. All the groups were given an opportunity to deliver electric shocks to a girl not in the gorup. The subjects who were not identifiable gave almost twice as many shocks as the others. Apparently being less identifiable produced a marked increase in aggression, supporting the idea that loss of individuality is one cause of the violent, antisocial behavior sometimes exhibited by groups.

other factors

Although responsibility diffusion is one part of the explanation of mob behavior, it seems likely that other factors are also operating. In a group, one extremely dominant, persuasive person can convince others to do something they would not do if he were not present. Moreover, this effect can snowball, because when the dominant one has convinced a few, they will convince others, until everybody is convinced. As we saw in Chapter 11, when a large part of a group has taken a position, it can exert great pressure on the rest of the group to go along.

Another consideration is the protection afforded by a group. A crowd provides a certain amount of anonymity and, perhaps more important, makes it difficult for legal sanctions to be applied. An individual rarely could perform the acts a group can; but even if he could and did, it is more likely that he would be punished if he were alone than if he did the same things in a group. If one or even five people started breaking the windows of department stores, they would almost certainly be arrested and prosecuted. However, if five thousand people broke windows, only a small percentage would be caught and punished. Thus, from a purely practical point of view, people must be aware that they are more likely to get away with something when they are in a crowd than when they are alone.

It should be pointed out that the phenomenon of a group acting differently from an individual is not limited to immoral, violent acts. Groups sometimes perform socially valued acts that individuals would not perform alone. There are many anecdotal examples of people who band together to help survivors of disasters, rebuild a house destroyed by fire, collect money for a sick child, and on on. These deeds cannot be explained in terms of loss of moral inhibitions or fear of getting caught, since these considerations are not relevant to such positive actions. It appears that at times individuals are swept up in a positive group goal that, in essence, forces them to be better than they would otherwise be. The important point is that, despite our tendency to focus on the negative effect of groups, they have both negative and positive effects on their members causing them to behave better or worse than they would alone.

extremity shifts (the "risky shift")

One interesting effect that groups seem to have on individuals' behavior concerns risk taking. People are often faced with a choice between a course of action that has only a small chance of working but the possibility of a large payoff and one that is more likely to work but would result in a much smaller payoff. For example, in roulette, betting $1 on red results in winning half the time (actually, slightly less than half the time because of the zeros, which are neither red nor black, but for this example we shall ignore them), with a payoff of $1. Betting $1 on a number results in winning about once in thirty-six times, with a payoff of $35. Thus, over many trials, the results would be equal. If either bet were made many times, the losses would be equivalent. The bets are, however, quite different in terms of expected gains and losses on any one trial. The first bet might be called conservative, because half the time the player wins a small amount. The second bet is risky, because the player loses over 95 percent of the time, but when he does win, he wins a lot. A more practical example, perhaps, would be the case of a college senior considering graduate work. She might have to choose between entering a university that has such rigorous standards that only a fraction of the degree candidates actually receive degrees and entering one that has less of a reputation but where almost everyone admitted receives degrees. Here again, there is a risky strategy (entering the more difficult university). The question is whether individuals and groups favor different strategies.

In a series of studies (Dion et al., 1970; Marquis, 1962; Stoner, 1961; Wallach and Kogan, 1965; Zajonc et al., 1972), a number of complex situations were described to the subjects. In each situation, a variety of choices, ranging from very high risk to very low risk, was available. The subjects were asked to consider the situations carefully and decide what recommendations they would make or which alternative they would prefer. One situation was described as follows:

> Mr. E. is president of a metals corporation in the United States. The corporation is quite prosperous and Mr. E. has considered the possibility of expansion by building an additional plant in a new location. His choice is between building another plant in the United States, where there would be a moderate return on the initial investment, or building a plant in a foreign country, where lower labor costs and easy access to raw materials would mean a much higher return on the initial investment. However, there is a history of political instability and revolution in the foreign country under consideration. In fact, the leader of a small minority party is committed to nationalizing, that is, taking over all foreign investments.
>
> Imagine that you are advising Mr. E. Listed below are several probabilities of continued political stability in the foreign country under consideration. Please check the *lowest* probability that you would consider acceptable in order for Mr. E.'s corporation to build in that country.
>
> The chances are 1 in 10 that the foreign country will remain politically stable.

The chances are 3 in 10 that the foreign country will remain politically stable.

The chances are 5 in 10 that the foreign country will remain politically stable.

The chances are 7 in 10 that the foreign country will remain politically stable.

The chances are 9 in 10 that the foreign country will remain politically stable.

Place a check here if you think Mr. E.'s corporation should not build a plant in the foreign country, no matter what the probabilities [Kogan and Wallach, 1967, pp. 234–35].

After listening to this problem, the subjects made individual decisions. They did not discuss the issue; they did not know that they were going to discuss it later. When they had made their decisions, they were brought into a group and asked to discuss the problem to reach a unanimous decision. Under these circumstances, there was a strong tendency for the group decision to involve higher risk than the average of the decisions made by the individuals. For example, in one group, two individuals were for 9 in 10, two for 7 in 10, and two for 5 in 10 when they made their decisions individually. After the group discussion, the unanimous decision was to endorse 5 in 10—a clear shift toward a risky strategy. Moreover, the strong overall tendency to favor riskier choices in groups held for both males and females.

This phenomenon has been referred to as the *risky shift*. It has been demonstrated with a wide variety of decisions involving quite different kinds of materials and with many different subject populations. The risky shift occurs with real life situations such as those just described. It also occurs when subjects have a selection of problems to work on that vary in difficulty and in the number of points they will get for solving them. This is the kind of choice a champion diver makes when he selects either very difficult dives which, if he does them well, will earn him many points, or somewhat simpler dives which are easier to do but will earn him fewer points even if he does them perfectly. And risky shifts also occur (although somewhat less consistently) in gambling situations where there is a choice between low-probability, high-payoff alternatives, and higher probability but lower payoff possibilities. Most of the research has involved subjects (usually students) in the United States and Canada, but the risky shift has also been demonstrated in England (Bateson, 1966), France (Kogan and Doise, 1969), Israel (Rim, 1963), and Germany (Lamm and Cogan, 1970). It is a stable, consistent finding that has attracted a great deal of research in recent years.

Although most of the work on group decisions indicated a shift toward riskier choices, careful analysis of some of the results and some additional findings (e.g. Fraser, Gouge, and Billig, 1971) indicate that sometimes the shift is in the conservative direction. Moreover, the direction of the shift is consistent for a particular decision; some cause most groups to become riskier than individuals, some produce conservative

Leo de Wys

shifts. Thus, the term "risky shift" is not as appropriate as it first seemed. *Extremity shift* or *polarization* (a term favored by Moscovici and Zavalloni, 1969, and by Fraser et al., 1971) are more accurate.

We know that being involved in a group discussion of a decision causes people to shift their preferences, usually in a riskier direction, sometimes in a conservative direction. We also know that this occurs even when group members make their actual decisions individually and in private. How can we explain this effect of being in a group? A number of explanations have been offered and the testing and changing of these various explanations is an interesting case history of research on an intriguing problem in social psychology. Therefore let us consider some of the most plausible explanations in detail.

riskier people are more persuasive

One type of explanation is based on presumed differences between people who ordinarily favor risky choices and those who favor more conservative choices. If riskier people tend to be leaders of groups, participate more, play larger roles in group decisions, or be more persuasive for any reason, it would explain the risky shift. Obviously, if the group is more influenced by riskier people, the group as a whole will end up favoring riskier decisions after a discussion.

Although this is a plausible explanation, the evidence collected so far does not provide much support for it. There is some indication (Rim, 1964) that high-risk people value leadership more and are generally *per-*

ceived as more persuasive by the other members of the group (Flanders and Thistlewaite, 1967; Wallach et al., 1962; Wallach, Kogan, and Burt, 1965). On the other hand, two studies (Nordhoy, 1962; Rabow et al., 1966) have shown that in situations where conservative shifts occur, high-risk people are seen as less persuasive. This indicates that the perception of how persuasive they are is probably not due to any inherent ability on their part, but rather to what happens in the group discussion. If the group is persuaded to be more risky, obviously those who initially favored high risk are seen as causing that shift; if the group ends up less risky, the conservative members of the group are seen as having caused the shift. Since there is no direct evidence that high-risk people are more persuasive, we are forced to conclude that the risky shift is not caused by any inherent differences in ability or persuasiveness among members of the group.

This conclusion is reinforced by the fact that several studies (Blank, 1968; Teger and Pruitt, 1967) have shown that the risky shift occurs without an actual discussion, but with only an exchange of preferences. When no discussion occurs, differences in persuasiveness cannot account for the results. The available evidence thus does not support this explanation of the risky shift, but the possibility remains that differences in persuasiveness may be a contributing factor in some situations even though not the major reason for the effect.

diffusion of responsibility

Individuals in a group may sometimes feel less personal responsibility for their own acts than they would if they were alone. To some extent the decision is made by the whole group and the burden of responsibility is accordingly shared. Even if the person makes the decision on his own following a group discussion, he may feel he is less responsible for it because he is in a group. A second assumption is that most people would like to make risky decisions, but avoid them for fear of failure or other negative consequences. Being in a group reduces the feeling or responsibility, reduces the fear of negative consequences, and therefore allows people to pick riskier choices.

This is an interesting explanation of the risky shift because it conceives of it as a true group phenomenon. Being in the group would be a necessary condition for the effect because group feelings and the accompanying diffusion of responsibility are the crucial elements producing the risky shift. The test of this explanation depends on whether group membership is, in fact, a necessary condition for a risky shift. If the shift occurs without a discussion or even without the individual feeling that he is a member of a group, obviously it cannot be due to diffusion of responsibility. On the other hand, if giving the individual all the necessary information without actually having a group meeting does not produce a shift, it would suggest that diffusion of responsibility or some similar group phenomenon was the explanation. Unfortunately, the evidence on this point is somewhat inconsistent.

One study (Bem et al., 1965) demonstrated that having a discussion produced the effect, whereas merely anticipating a discussion but not having it did not. Similarly, Wallach and Kogan (1965) produced a risky shift when the group had a discussion with a group consensus, when there was a discussion without a group consensus, but not when there was consensus without an actual discussion. On the other hand, watching others discuss the issue seems to be able to produce the effect (Kogan and Wallach, 1967), and, more damaging, some experimenters (Blank, 1968; Teger and Pruitt, 1967) have found the effect when the group knew one another's preferences but did not have a discussion. And making the group more cohesive, which might be expected to increase diffusion of responsibility, actually decreased the size of the risky shift (Dion et al., 1970).

None of these studies entirely rules out the diffusion of responsibility explanation. The crucial question—whether the effect occurs when the individual does not feel he is a member of a group—has never been fully tested. Even those studies that produced the effect without a group discussion did have groups, and perhaps simply being in a group is sufficient to reduce one's feeling of responsibility. Although we cannot confidently reject the explanation, the evidence in favor of it is somewhat questionable. No one has yet produced a study that directly demonstrates the feeling of reduced responsibility nor even that fear of failure is a basic reason for making conservative choices. Thus, although we cannot entirely rule out this explanation, at the moment the evidence in favor of it is not very convincing.

cultural value

An explanation that seems more consistent with the evidence is based on the assumption that under most circumstances risky decisions are valued more highly than conservative ones. In many situations and many cultures, people admire, respect, and value the tendency to take chances. Discussing a decision with other people or even knowing other people's choices makes this cultural norm more important and therefore causes the individual to select a riskier decision than he would if he were alone. In other situations, the culture may value caution. When this is so, the opposite effect should occur—following a group discussion, the choices should be more conservative than before. This explanation says in effect that the risky shift is not truly a group phenomenon, but rather that being in a group is one way in which these culture values can be made important and relevant. There would be other ways also, and they too would produce the risky shift. Thus, group discussion or even group membership is not absolutely crucial, but is merely one effective procedure for producing the phenomenon.

Most of the evidence bearing on this explanation is indirect. To begin with, it is clear that the research on the necessity of group discussion is consistent with this explanation. As we have said, some studies (e.g., Wallach and Kogan, 1965) demonstrated that discussion was necessary in order to produce the effect; others (e.g., Teger and Pruitt, 1967) found risky shift without discussion. In terms of the value hypothesis, we would expect that a discussion would be more likely to produce the effect and would produce a stronger effect, because it would make the cultural norms particularly salient. On the other hand, if the information given to subjects about others' preferences is detailed enough and is presented in such a way as to make these preferences important, the effect should occur even without a discussion. Unfortunately, in several studies information about others' preferences was given to subjects in apparently considerable detail and yet no risky shift was found (e.g., Kogan and Carlson, 1969; Zajonc et al., 1970). If the effect is due entirely to the salience of cultural norms, this kind of information should produce a risky shift, and these studies in which it did not are somewhat damaging.

On the other hand, there is a considerable amount of supporting evidence from individuals' stated preferences. People tend to say they admire high-risk choices in situations that have in fact produced the risky-shift effect (Levenger and Schneider, 1969; Pilkonis and Zanna, 1969) and to rate fictitious risk-takers higher than more cautious people (Madaras and Bem, 1968). In situations that have produced shifts toward caution, people say they admire cautious responses (Levenger and Schneider, 1969; Pruitt and Teger, 1967). In addition, people perceive themselves as riskier than their peers in situations that produce risky shifts (Baron et al., 1970) but see themselves as more cautious on items that produce a conservative shift (Levenger and Schneider, 1969). Thus, just as would be expected from the value explanation, when people value risk, the risky shift occurs; when they value caution, a conservative shift occurs. This is strong evidence that the effect is produced by evaluation of the situation rather than by differences in individual persuasiveness or the diffusion of responsibility.

persuasive arguments

Finally, there is an explanation in terms of the number of persuasive arguments offered in the group discussion. According to this view, proposed most forcefully by Burnstein and Vinokur (1975), the group discussion is an attitude change or persuasion situation. Each individual hears arguments presented by others. His own opinion is influenced by the quality and especially the quantity of those arguments. If there are more arguments in favor of a risky decision, the group members will shift in that direction; if there are more conservative arguments, there will be conservative shift. This explanation requires no assumptions about some people being more persuasive, no deindividuation or cultural values. It relies entirely on the arguments that are proposed.

The key research finding supporting this explanation is the relationship between the number of arguments and the shift that occurs. Several studies (Ebbesen and Bowers, 1974; Burnstein and Vinokur, 1973) have shown that the proportion of risky and conservative arguments agrees quite closely with the shift that the discussion produces. More risky arguments lead to risky-shifts, and vice versa. Obviously, being in a group and hearing its discussion exposes the individual to new arguments. He is influenced by them just as he might be if he heard them in another context.

This explanation can also deal with the finding that simply hearing other people's preferences, without a discussion, can produce shifts. Apparently, knowing that a group has considered the matter and then hearing its choices, sometimes stimulates the individual to make up arguments concerning the decision. When he does this, he tends to make up arguments favoring more extreme positions than he initially held and he then shifts in that direction (Burnstein and Vinokur, 1975). So far so good.

However, we can still ask why the group discussions or merely hearing others' choices tends to produce extreme arguments (Vinokur, Trope, and Burnstein, 1975). If everyone simply argued for his own position, the arguments would be no more extreme than the average of each individual's choice and no shifts should occur. Thus, the crucial question is why these extreme arguments are produced.

One possibility is that each person wants to think up really good arguments to impress the others, or when alone, perhaps to impress himself. As someone searches for new and better arguments, there may be a tendency to construct extreme ones. Certainly, extreme positions tend to be more exciting and impressive than more moderate ones. It is also possible to combine the persuasive arguments explanation with the one in terms of cultural values. Perhaps people make up more extreme arguments because they are more highly valued, or they think they are. Then they change their position in response to the new arguments, some of which they have proposed themselves. Taken together, the two explanations would then account nicely for the extremity shifts. Cultural value explains why certain types of arguments tend to be produced, and the persuasive arguments explanation describes the process by which the shift occurs.

SUMMARY

1. Being with other people produces different reactions from being alone. The simplest effect, without any interaction, is social faciliation. Performance on simple tasks improves, on complex tasks gets worse. This is because the presence of others raises motivation, probably due to concerns about being evaluated. A second possibility is that the presence of others makes the individual feel competitive.

2. People have a tendency to compete even when they would improve their own performance and win more money or points by cooperating. Increasing incentive by raising the stakes does not have a consistent effect on the amount of competition.

3. Threats tend to reduce cooperation when two opposing sides are threatened, but if only one side is threatened, their outcome tends to improve.

4. Communication usually increases cooperation by allowing the participants to make known their intentions.

5. Although a group can usually solve a problem faster and better than an individual, groups are not generally as good as the same number of individuals (i.e., a group of five versus five individuals working alone). However, this depends on many factors, including the number of different skills necessary to solve the problem and probably on how well the people know each other and can work together.

6. Groups sometimes behave like mobs, committing acts that none of the individual members would commit if they were alone. This may be due in part to deindividuation—each person to some extent losing his personality and sense of responsibility. The more identifiable the members of the group the less likely mob behavior will occur.

7. Groups typically make more extreme decisions than individuals where risks are involved—sometimes being more conservative and sometimes more risky. This has been called the risky shift, but would more appropriately be called the extremity shift because it occurs in both directions.

8. Several explanations of the risky shift effect have been offered. (a) Risky people are more persuasive; (b) responsibility is diffused in the group; (c) there is a cultural value to being risky (or for some choices conservative) and the group brings out this value; and (d) the number of arguments that are produced in a group tend to favor the extreme (either riskiness or conservatism), and the sheer number of these arguments persuades the group to change its opinion. The first two possibilities have generally been disproved. On the other hand, the cultural value and persuasive argument explanations are now generally accepted. Perhaps a combination of the two provides a full explanation.

SUGGESTIONS FOR ADDITIONAL READING

LEBON, G. *The Crowd.* London: Benn, 1898. Available in many modern editions. Despite the title, this is really a book on group dynamics, though admittedly it deals with large groups rather than small ones.

RAVEN, B. & RUBIN, J. *Social Psychology: People in Groups.* New York: John Wiley, 1976. This book provides thorough coverage of work on groups. It is rather slow going, but all the information is there.

ZAJONC, R. B. Social facilitation. *Science,* 1955, *149,* 269–274. A clear presentation of his theory of how the presence of others affects us.

15

environmental and urban psychology

noise

- adaptation to short-term noise
- the importance of individual control
- long-term constant noise

personal space: proxemics

- ethnic differences
- sex differences
- the meaning of distance
- territoriality

crowding

- definition
- crowding and animals

crowding and people

- crowding in the real world
- experimental research: short-term crowding
- performance
- physiological effects
- social effects
- sex differences

theories of crowding

- sensory overload and stimulation level
- density-intensity

architectural design

- dormitory design
- high-rise vs. low-rise housing

life in the city

summary

suggestions for additional reading

People are affected by their surroundings. Many people, large buildings, busy streets, much noise, and a great variety of facilities produce a mood and behavior different from the relative quiet and solitude of the country. Living in a thirty-story building with hundreds of other families is quite different from living in your own home. And the specific design of the building as well as particular characteristics of the community will influence you. The rather new field of environmental psychology is concerned with just how all these factors affect people.

In a sense, of course, we could consider everything in the world part of our environment. Every topic we have discussed in this book is to some extent involved in aspects of the environment, broadly defined. Environmental psychologists, however, have made an arbitrary distinction by deciding to focus mainly on the physical rather than the social or personal characteristics of the situation. In particular, this field deals with the effects of noise, our use of space, crowding, the design of buildings, and cities in general. We shall consider each of these in turn, but as you will see, many of these factors are closely interrelated.

noise

Environments differ greatly in terms of how noisy they are. This is an especially important variable because so much of industrial life involves the production of noise. The modern city, with its traffic, construction, machinery of all kinds, and people, is extremely noisy. Perhaps the most striking difference between rural, suburban, and urban communities is the almost constant noise that surrounds us in the city. Naturally, the world is never silent. There are noises of all kinds wherever you are. But country noises, natural noises, are quite different and usually less loud than the noises of the city. Someone who moves from the city to the country or vice versa is immediately aware of the change in noise level, and both shifts often are disturbing. This is certainly true for those who move to the city, but it is also true for city dwellers who find themselves in the country. Just as it is difficult to get used to the sound of cars and trucks in the city, it is usually hard to sleep in the country either because it is too quiet or because the racket caused by crickets and birds is disturbing when you are not used to it. Thus, we know that we notice noises and are often quite sensitive to them. But what effect does noise have on us? The answer is that it has less effect than we might think.

adaptation to short-term noise

The most important finding from research on noise is that people adapt very quickly. When we are exposed to bursts of very loud noise, our initial reaction is strong. Everyone is familiar with one typical response—the so-called startle reflex. An unexpected loud noise causes us to jump, flex our stomach muscles, blink, and generally react physically. Even if we are expecting the noise, we respond physiologically with increased blood pressure, sweating, and other signs of arousal. In addition, loud noise interferes with our ability to perform tasks. We do less well on both simple and complex tasks when we are exposed to loud noise. Clearly, loud noise is somewhat upsetting, causes physiological arousal, and prevents us from functioning at our usual level.

However, these disruptive effects generally last only a short while.

EPA Documerica/Michael Philip Manheim

We quickly get used to (adapt to) even extremely loud noises. It takes only a few minutes for physiological reactions to disappear and for performance to return to normal. After ten minutes or less, people who are subjected to short bursts of extremely loud noise are virtually identical to people who hear moderate or low noise. This is true even for noise levels over 100 decibels, which is roughly equivalent to a big jet coming in low over your house or a huge truck rumbling by right next to you. As long as the noise is not so loud that it actually produces pain or physical damage, people adapt to it very quickly and show few if any deficits (Broadbent, 1971; Glass and Singer, 1972).

You can see this effect in a study by David Glass and Jerome Singer in which people hear no noise, or noise at 108 decibels in short bursts for twenty-three minutes. As shown in Figure 15–1, the loud noise did cause physiological arousal, but the arousal lasted only a few minutes. Moreover, after four minutes, all subjects did equally well on a variety of tasks including simple arithmetic, matching sets of numbers (i.e., deciding whether 68134 and 68243 are identical), anagrams, and higher level mathematics. Once they have gotten used to the noise, people perform almost any task as well with loud noise as they do in quieter environments.

There are a few important exceptions to this finding. Donald Broadbent (1968) and other researchers have shown that certain kinds of monitoring tasks are more difficult to do with loud noise. For example, if someone is required to watch three dials to be sure none of them goes over a certain point, high levels of noise interfere with performance. Similarly, it is apparently harder to do two tasks at the same time in a noisy environment. In one study (Finkelman and Glass, 1970), subjects had to repeat digits they heard over headphones while turning a steering

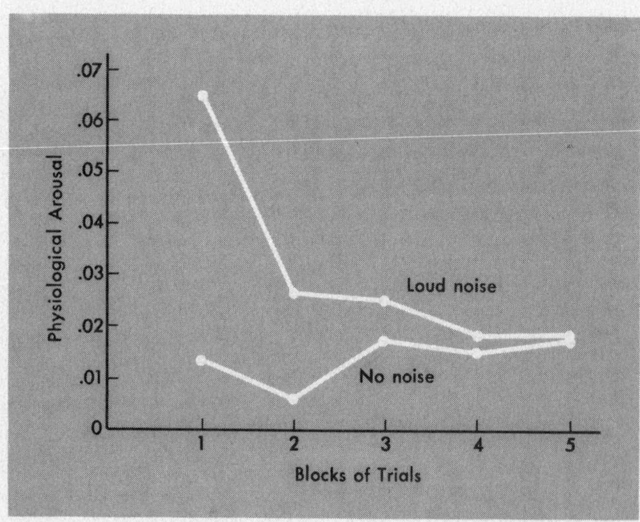

FIGURE 15–1
Physiological (GSR) response to loud noise. After a strong initial response, subjects adapt quickly. Based on Glass & Singer, 1972.

wheel to track a moving line. Noise level did not affect the primary task, which was the tracking, but it made the subjects less accurate at repeating the digits. Presumably, the noise is somewhat distracting and interferes when a person is trying to perform tasks that already strain his capacity to concentrate.

Most of the time we are only doing one thing at a time, so the effects of noise are probably quite limited. On the other hand, it is well to remember that some sensitive jobs do involve exactly the kinds of monitoring tasks that seem to be affected by loud noise. The pilot of a plane must watch many different dials while operating a variety of instruments; flight controllers have similar problems; and even the typical driver of a car has many things to attend to at once. (It is a little frightening to realize that all these jobs, especially those of pilot and flight controller, are performed under conditions of considerable noise.) With this potentially important exception, short-term exposure to loud noise appears to have little detrimental effect.

the importance of individual control

However, this is not the whole story. A series of experiments by Glass and Singer (1972) demonstrate that the adaptation to loud noise may take considerable effort that shows up later, after the noise is no longer present. In particular, this research indicates that these negative aftereffects occur when the noise is not under the control of the individual. If the noise is predictable (occuring every thirty seconds or only when there is warning) or if the person can turn off the noise, there are no bad effects. But if the noise seems to be totally out of the control of the person, certain kinds of performance suffer once the noise ceases.

The experiments are straightforward but quite ingenious. Subjects hear bursts of noise for a set period of time while they are performing tasks. Then they perform other tasks with no noise. The crucial variation is that the circumstances under which the noise occurs either give the person a sense of control or do not. In one study, loud or soft noise occurred in bursts exactly one minute apart or at random intervals. Even though subjects heard just as much noise in the two conditions, the effects were entirely different. During the noise section of the study, all groups performed equally well regardless of how loud the noise was or whether it was predictable. But afterwards, as shown in Table 15–1, those who had heard the predictable noise performed better than those who had heard random noise. In fact, unpredictable soft noise caused more errors then predictable loud noise. This was true despite the fact that subjects reported finding the predictable and unpredictable noise equally annoying. In other studies, subjects were given a feeling of control by telling them they could stop the noise whenever they wanted to by pressing a button or by signaling their partner, who would then stop it. Even though subjects never did actually stop the noise, this feeling of control was apparently enough to eliminate the negative effects. There was no decline in performance either during or after the noise.

TABLE 15–1
after-effects of predictable and unpredictable noise on proofreading

CONDITION	NUMBER OF ERRORS
No noise	26.40
Soft Predictable	27.40
Soft Unpredictable	36.70
Loud Predictable	31.78
Loud Unpredictable	40.11

Based on Glass and Singer, 1972.

We do not know exactly why control is so important, but this finding may help us understand the effects of noise in the real world. Most of the noise in a city is fairly constant or predictable. There is the continuous noise of cars and trucks on the streets, periodic noise of trains in some communities, and the general din caused by many people. On the other hand, some noise is both unpredictable and uncontrollable. Jackhammers, backfiring cars, planes, and sudden loud music from radios fill the air with noise at random intervals and are therefore probably much more annoying than the usual background noise. It seems likely that the absolute level of the noise is less important than this unpredictability, and indeed, it is these kinds of noises that most people complain about.

long-term constant noise

One study suggests that long-term exposure to loud noise can have detrimental effects of a very specific nature. A large apartment house in New York City is built over a highway, and because of the design of the building, the noise levels inside are quite high. Of course, the lower floors are noiser than the higher ones, and this situation provides a natural experiment on the effects of long-term noise. Cohen, Glass, and Singer (1973) measured the reading achievement and ability to make auditory discriminations of children who had lived in the building for at least four years. As you can see in Figure 15–2, those who lived on lower floors did worse on both measures. The louder the noise on their floor, the less well they read and the poorer their auditory discriminations. Although there is as yet no evidence that city children in general are less good at reading or hearing, this study raises the possibility that the high levels of noise in the city (or elsewhere) might have serious long-term negative effects.

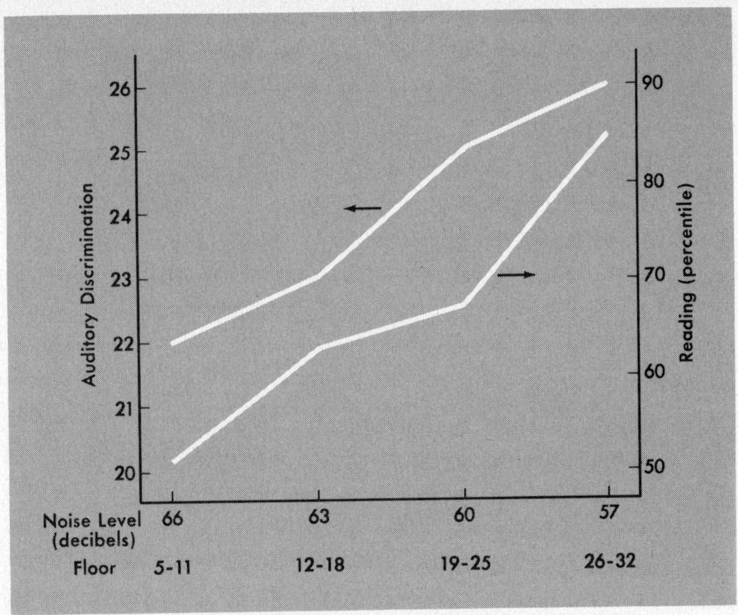

FIGURE 15–2
Noise level in apartment and reading and auditory skills. (From Cohen, Glass & Singer, 1973.)

personal space: proxemics

One of the basic aspects of interpersonal behavior is our use of the space immediately around us. How close do we stand to other people? What does it mean when we stand very close or farther away? Do people differ in their use of interpersonal distance? These questions involve *proxemics,* a term that refers to the personal use of space (Hall, 1959; Sommer, 1969). Since Hall's work in 1959, there has been a great deal of research in this area. In general, it shows that people are quite consistent in their use of personal space; that national, ethnic, and sex differences exist; and that how close we stand does often communicate something about our feelings and intentions.

ethnic differences

People from different cultures have different perferences for how close to stand. White Americans, Englishmen, and Swedes stand the farthest apart; Southern Europeans (Italians, Greeks) stand closer; and South Americans, Pakistanis, and Arabs stand the closest (Watson and Graves, 1966; Hall, 1966; Little, 1968; Sommer, 1968). This work has so far been done only in a small number of countries, but it is clear that the differences exist and are quite consistent.

There are also differences among ethnic groups within the United States. In general, blacks and whites do not differ much in the distances they choose. In early grades, black children seem to stand somewhat closer to each other than do white children, but the differences largely disappear by the fifth grade (Jones and Aiello, 1973). Blacks and whites of the same social class prefer the same distances (Scherer, 1974), but middle class people stand farther apart than lower-class people (Aiello and Jones, 1971). In contrast, Chicanos and other people from Latin America do stand closer than either whites or blacks (Baxter, 1970).

These ethnic differences might be considered a piece of interesting but trivial information if it were not for the fact that preferences in personal distance can sometimes have important consequences. The difficulty is that people from cultures with different preferences may misinterpret one another's actions. For example, an American and a Pakistani have a problem when they stand next to each other to talk. The American likes to stand about three or four feet away, whereas the Pakistani would ordinarily stand much closer. Obviously, they cannot both have their way. If they are unaware of the cultural difference, they may execute a little dance around the room. The Pakistani feels uncomfortably far away and moves closer. The American feels uncomfortable and retreats, which in turn causes the Pakistani to move closer again. This continues until the American is either backed into a corner or flees. Moreover, as this is going on, the Pakistani may feel that the American is being cold and unfriendly, while the American thinks the other is being overly intimate and pushy. This is due to the fact that how close you stand does usually depend in part on your relationship to the other person.

sex differences

As you might have guessed, pairs of women stand closer than pairs of men (Horowitz et al., 1970; Sommer, 1959), although this difference seems to appear only when people are about twelve years old (Aiello and Aiello, 1974). In fact, women always tend to stand closer to whomever they are with (Hartnett et al., 1970; Leibman, 1970). On the other hand, mixed-sex pairs stand closer than same-sex pairs (Kuethe and Wingartner, 1964). This last finding, however, has not been demonstrated in a wide enough range of situations to be certain. As we shall see in a moment, the relationship between the people is extremely important and certainly affects how close the two people will stand.

In addition to these sex differences in interpersonal distance, males and females react somewhat differently to spatial arrangements. For example, when sitting at a table with someone they know and like, women tend to sit next to the person, whereas men choose seats opposite that person (Byrne et al., 1971). Jeffrey Fisher and Donn Byrne (1975) observed the reactions of people sitting alone at a table in a library when a stranger sat down across from them, one seat away, or right next to them. Regardless of the sex of the stranger, females appeared most bothered when the seat taken was next to them, but males disliked most having the opposite seat taken. Men also tried to protect themselves from intrusions by putting books in front of them, whereas women put their books and other possessions next to them. This is, of course, a special situation and may not hold in other contexts, but the sex differences seem quite consistent. As we shall see in the next section, sex differences also appear in responses to crowding.

the meaning of distance

In addition to ethnic and sex differences in the use of personal space, there are substantial differences that depend on the relationship of the people involved. In general, the more intimate the relationship and the more friendly the people are, the closer they stand. Friends stand closer than strangers (Aiello and Cooper, 1972); people who want to seem friendly choose smaller distances (Lott and Sommer, 1967; Patterson and Sechrest, 1970); and people who are sexually attracted to each other stand close (Allgeier and Byrne, 1973). Although most people do not think much about personal space, we are all aware that standing close is usually a sign of friendship or interest. It may be one of the most important and easiest ways of telling someone you have just met that you like him or her. The other person is immediately aware of your interest, and if he is not interested, he will generally move away to make that clear.

Spatial orientation rather than just distance is also affected by the relationship. When you go into a restaurant with a friend, do you sit side by side, across the table, or at a corner? Each has its advantages in terms of talking and seeing each other, but there are consistent preferences. Robert Sommer (1969) found that same-sex friends tend to sit at corners but intimate friends, especially of the opposite sex, like to sit next to each other. In other words, the use of personal space is an important means of nonverbal communication, much like the others such as eye gaze that we discussed in Chapter 3.

territoriality

The research on people's use of space and observations of animals in their natural habitat indicate that space is very important to us. It seems that we actually *need* a certain amount of space and that when less space is available than that required or when this minimum amount is invaded, the individual will become aggressive and defend his space. This need for space and the defense of it is sometimes called *territoriality*. Robert Ardrey (1966), one of the popularizers of the notion, claims that territoriality is instinctive in both animals and humans—that they are born with the need for space and the automatic aggressive response when there is too little. Although some animals may have such an instinct, most psychologists believe that humans do not. We do not require a fixed amount of space, and we do not always or automatically become aggressive even if we have very little space.

On the other hand, people do sometimes consider certain space or property their own and under some circumstances will defend that space from intrusions. As we discussed previously, various studies show that people respond negatively when others invade their space. Certainly, if you are alone in the library trying to study, it is usually annoying to have somebody sit down right next to you. This annoyance may be expressed as defensiveness, anger, or even outright aggression (Felipe and Sommer, 1966; Fisher and Byrne, 1975). We also often react negatively if a stranger stands closer to us than we consider comfortable or appropriate. In this case we would probably retreat if we were able, and if we could not retreat, we might become aggressive. We do have standards for interpersonal distance, we do claim possession of certain areas either temporarily or permanently, and any violations of these spaces produce defensive responses.

However, our need for space is by no means absolute. The amount we need and our reactions to incursions on it depend on the particular situation. In the library example, our response to someone joining us at a table would be quite different if it were the only remaining seat in the library. We might have preferred to have the table to ourselves, but we would see that it was perfectly legitimate for the other person to take the seat if it was the only one free. He too is entitled to sit down. In contrast, if other seats are free, then the person is deliberately choosing to sit next to us and the act has more meaning. The "invader" might be interested in getting to know us, be planning to steal our books, or conceivably be taking his favorite chair in the library. But we would assume that his behavior was motivated—that he chose this seat rather than all the other free ones; and we are therefore more likely to respond to the invasion.

Even then, our reactions depend on other factors in the situation. For example, if you are bored by what you are reading, you might be pleased by the distraction. More to the point, if the other person is an attractive member of the opposite sex, under some circumstances you may be flattered by the attention and perhaps interested in getting to know your new neighbor. True, it is still an invasion, but it may be a welcome one. How we respond also depends on what is appropriate for a given situation. A study by Konečni (1975) involved having someone stand very close to a person who was waiting on a corner to cross the street. In this situation, with lots of space on the sidewalk, it is clearly inappropriate to stand very close. Sure enough, people responded to this invasion by crossing the street much faster than usual in order to escape. Yet the same kind of close contact may be entirely appropriate or even desirable in other circumstances. At a large party people are expected to talk with one another, to meet strangers, and generally to interact in a friendly way. In such a gathering standing quite close to someone would be considered perfectly normal and friendly. If the person approached is not interested in being friendly, he or she is certainly free to move away. But approaching closely would not ordinarily be considered an aggressive act, nor would it produce an aggressive response.

In other words, people do use personal space and are sensitive to territory, but being close is neither always negative nor aggressive as the notions of territoriality suggest. On the contrary, close contact can be either friendly and intimate or aggressive and intrusive. It may be annoying if done by one person but pleasant if done by someone else. Indeed, as most of us know, standing very close to someone has two opposite meanings. Either it is a friendly act or an aggressive one. If the individual has no choice of where to sit or stand, as in a subway in rush hour, being close has little or no meaning and is largely neutral.

crowding

One hundred million people every year; one billion people every ten years—that is the rate at which the population of the world is increasing, and the rate of increase is getting faster and faster. As you can see in Figure 15–3, it took tens of thousands of years for the world population to reach half a billion. Two hundred years passed before the population

FIGURE 15–3
Growth of World Human Population

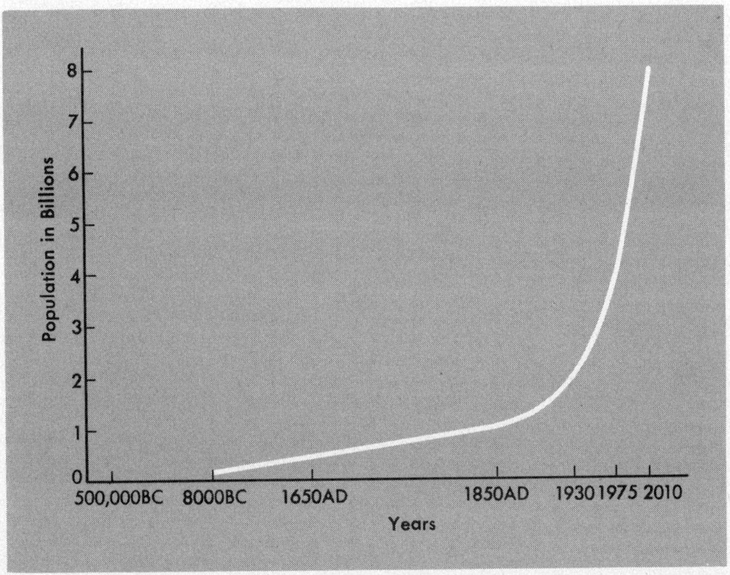

doubled and reached 1 billion. But the next doubling to 2 billion took only eighty years, and it doubled to 4 billion in only forty-five years. At the present rate of growth, the number of people on earth will double again and reach 8 billion in only thirty-five years.

This population explosion obviously has serious consequences for practically every aspect of our lives. It strains the economic resources of the world; exhausts our natural resources; pushes up the cost of fuel, food, and every other necessary item; and leads to pollution. As populations increase, resources must be shared by more and more people. There is just so much good land, so much oil, so much wood for houses, and so on. In the United States, for example, the national parks are so crowded that it is practically standing room only in the more popular ones. They are still beautiful, but they are no longer a place to enjoy in solitude.

One of the consequences of the population explosion is that the concentration of people in and around cities is increasing steadily. Although the central cities have actually lost population over the past twenty or thirty years, the larger metropolitan areas have gained enormously. Most of the populations of the United States, Canada, and the other industrialized countries are concentrated in and around urban centers. Therefore, the question of how this might affect us is of more and more concern. Psychologists have become increasingly interested in this problem, to the point that in the past five years more research has been done on the effects of crowding on people than had been done in the previous fifty. Let us see what has been discovered.

definition

It might not seem that we need to define what we mean by crowding, but it turns out to be quite important because the term has been used in two quite different ways. One is a feeling or an emotion of being cramped and not having enough space. Obviously this feeling is unpleasant and is always negative. When we say that we are "crowded," we are almost always complaining. Moreover, this feeling of being crowded can occur more or less regardless of the amount of space we actually have available. It is more likely to be aroused when we are cramped, but we sometimes feel crowded even though there is plenty of space around us. If you want to be entirely alone, the presence of even one other person would make you feel crowded. There are times when three is a crowd no matter how much space is available. If you like to swim at deserted beaches, the presence of a few other people may make you feel that the beach is overcrowded, whereas you would not feel crowded at a party even if there were fifty other people in a fairly small room. In other words, crowding sometimes refers to the psychological state of discomfort associated with wanting more space than is available regardless of the actual amount of space.

The other meaning of the term is simply the amount of space available per person. This is a purely physical, objective definition and is often referred to as *density* to distinguish it from the psychological state of feeling crowded. As Daniel Stokols (1972) and others have pointed out, it is essential to distinguish between crowding as a psychological feeling of being cramped and crowding as a measure of the amount of space per person. Obviously, the former is an internal psychological state and is almost by definition negative. It is a dependent variable and it is unnecessary to do any research to find out that it is unpleasant to feel crowded. In contrast, the physical situation is neutral, and it is an open question what effect density (crowding) has on people. So keep in mind that throughout this discussion, *crowding* means the amount of space that is available.

crowding and animals

There is a considerable amount of research on other animals which suggests that living under conditions of high population density may have severe negative effects. In a classic study, Calhoun (1962) put a number of rats in an enclosed area, gave them all the food and water they needed, kept the cage clean, and simply let the rats do what they would. Rats are prolific breeders, and that is one of the things they did with great success. The population of the colony grew rapidly under these more or less ideal conditions. However, at a certain point the situation changed dramatically—the population declined sharply. This pattern—a gradual increase in population and then a sharp drop—is consistent under these circumstances. It has been demonstrated in the laboratory with rats, mice, voles, and various other creatures (Christian, 1963; Southwick, 1955; Snyder, 1968; etc.). The same phenomenon has been observed in natural settings when a large group of animals is confined to a small area. A group of deer stranded on an island was seen to go through the same population fluctuations (Christian, Flyger, and Davis, 1960). The most famous example of this phenomenon is the march of the lemmings in Norway. These mouselike creatures live on the frozen tundra, and their population goes through this kind of cycle with considerable regularity. The colony thrives for a while, growing steadily until there is a vast number of lemmings. Then population declines sharply, with some of the remaining lemmings actually ending up falling into the sea.

Observations of the rats in Calhoun's experiment and the mice in Snyder's work tell us something of what goes on when the cages get very crowded. Ordinarily these animals manage to live together fairly peacefully. Each male builds a nest, and finds one or more females to mate with. The females give birth, the young are raised, and so on. As long as there is enough food and water, relatively little fighting goes on. The nests are considered private property, and the females build comfortable quarters for their young, who are well taken care of. Under conditions of very high density, there is a great deal of fighting, nests are invaded, females do not build adequate nests, and the young are not given sufficient care.

The immediate cause of the sharp decline in population is an increase in infant mortality. The number of pregnancies is about normal, there are somewhat fewer live births than usual, but the major change is that very few of the young survive to adulthood. Apparently the reason is that the nests and the care are simply inadequate to keep the young alive. They cannot nurse, they are trampled under foot, they are exposed too young, and occasionally they are even eaten. At the same time, many of the males in the colony become unusually aggressive, fight a lot, mate indiscriminately, and in general suffer a breakdown in their normal behavior.

These dramatic effects of living under high-density conditions have sometimes been interpreted as evidence for the territorial instinct we mentioned earlier. According to this notion, animals require a certain amount of space around them. When this territory is invaded by other animals of their species, it triggers an instinctive aggressive response—the animal automatically fights to defend its territory by driving off the intruder. When a great many animals are crowded together, presumably all their territorial instincts are triggered, everyone fights everyone else, and the colony breaks down.

It seems clear that this is an oversimplification, even for lower animals. Anyone who has ever seen a cage of ten rats or mice knows that these animals do not require a certain amount of space around them. The animals do not space themselves evenly around the cage. On the contrary, all ten rats will probably sleep in a big pile at one end of the cage. There may be an occasional fight during the day, but rats obviously do not avoid close physical contact nor do they drive off another animal that comes too close to them. Under some special circumstances there may be a territorial or self-protective instinct triggered by having too many animals too close to them, but the animals do not have a simple need for a given amount of space.

Another explanation of the effects of high-density living is that the presence of the other animal is extremely stressful and causes a hormonal change (Christian, 1950). According to this theory, the animals in high-density conditions are under great tension, which causes increased adrenal activity. When the adrenal gland is overactive, there is a tendency for the reproductive glands to become underactive. At the extreme, this would cause reduced fertility in the animals, result in fewer births, and obviously cause a decrease in population. Even though there seems to be little evidence that fewer than normal pregnancies occur, it might be that the animals who are born are less healthy because of some hormonal imbalance. Although there is no question that the presence of a great many other animals does cause stress, it seems unlikely that the mere increase in adrenal activity is enough to account for the dramatic increase in infant mortality and social breakdown.

Whatever the explanation of these phenomena turns out to be, the observations do suggest that living under high-density conditions may have negative effects. Yet generalizing from the results of work on other animals to humans is always both difficult and questionable. This is particularly true when complicated social factors and interpersonal relations are involved. As the noted biologist René Dubos has said:

> The readiness with which man adapts to potentially dangerous situations makes it unwise to apply directly to human life the results of experiments designed to test the acute effects of crowding on animals (1970, p. 207).

Thus, although this work on other animals is suggestive, we must look at research on humans to discover how they respond to crowding.

crowding and people

Although this is a relatively new area of research, there has been quite a lot of work done during the past five or ten years. Some of the research has been controlled experiments in the laboratory, some field observations, some experiments in natural settings such as classrooms, some individual interviews of people who live or work in crowded conditions, and some large-scale survey studies of cities and other communities in order to assess the relationship between population density and other measures such as crime and mental disturbance. Thus, even though the amount of research is still rather small compared to most of the topics discussed in this book, we do have a fairly large body of evidence to look at.

By far the most important finding thus far has been that crowding does not generally seem to be harmful to people. Most of the studies have failed to find overall negative effects or relationships. Unlike other animals, people do not usually respond badly to high density. The second major finding is that crowding does have substantial effects on people and those effects are determined by particular characteristics of the situation and the people themselves. Let us consider some of the research and then turn to a discussion of the various theories that have been proposed to explain the complex results.

crowding in the real world

Sociologists and social psychologists have investigated the relationships between living conditions and pathology in natural settings. The standard procedure is to obtain some measure of crowding, either the number of people per square mile or the amount of space available per person in the home, then get measures of various pathologies for the same communities or neighborhoods and see if high density is associated with high levels of pathology.

One series of studies concentrated on the largest metropolitan areas of the United States. The measure of density was simply the number of people per square mile. In other words, this type of study was concerned simply with how many people lived within the boundaries of the city relative to the size of the city. These measures of density were then correlated with measures of the amount of crime committed in the cities. It was found (Freedman, Heshka, and Levy, 1973; Pressman and Carol, 1971) that there was a small but significant correlation between density and crime when only those two factors were considered ($r =$ about .35). Of course density tends to be highly correlated with other factors such as income, and it in turn is also highly correlated with crime rate. It is therefore impossible to tell from the simple correlation whether density causes crime or whether some other factor, such as income, leads to both higher density and higher crime rates. In order to assess this it is necessary to control for income and other social factors and then look at the remaining relationship between density and crime. When this is done by the use of partial correlations or multiple regressions, the relationship between density and crime disappears. Across the major metropolitan areas in the country, once income is controlled there seems to be little relationship between density and crime rate. For example, Los Angeles has one of the lowest densities but has the highest crime rate.

In addition, there have been studies of individual cities along much the same lines. Honolulu, Chicago, and New York have all been investigated to see whether density is associated with juvenile delinquency, mental illness, or any other kind of pathology. Although the results are not perfectly consistent, by and large they show the same patterns found across the metropolitan areas . In Honolulu (Schmitt, 1955, 1961), Chicago (Winsborough, 1965; Galle et al., 1972), and New York (Freedman, Heshka, and Levy, 1975), there were strong simple correlations between population density and various measures of pathology. In these studies density was measured not only by population per acre but also by the number of rooms per person in their dwellings. Thus they were measuring not only the number of people that lived in a particular area, but also how much space people had in their own homes. However, no matter how density was measured, once income and other social factors were controlled, the relationships between density and pathology tended to disappear. The one exception was in Honolulu, where they remained substantial; but in all the other studies the partial correlations were essentially zero.

These studies all dealt with grouped data—they looked at large numbers of people at once. This is an efficient procedure, but there is always the chance that crowding is having serious effects on some people and not on others. Fortunately, in two studies a great many people were individually interviewed. Probably the most impressive research of this type was conducted by Mitchell (1971), who went into a vast number of homes in Hong Kong, one of the most crowded communities in the world. He measured the exact size of each family's living space, computed the density of the home, and took measures of anxiety, nervousness, and various other kinds of mental strain. He found no appreciable relationship between density and pathology. In a similar though less ambitious study, Booth and his associates (1974) focused primarily on physical measures but also obtained some indications of mental and social adjustment. Again, there were no appreciable consistent negative (or positive) effects of crowding. Thus, according to both survey and individual data, people who live in high-density communities or neighborhoods or who have little space in their homes are no worse off in terms of mental, social, or physical pathology than people who live under conditions of lower density.

This may seem surprising, but remember that a great many people, indeed most of the population of the industrialized world, does live under quite high density. New York, Chicago, Toronto and other great North American cities have high population densities, and yet most of the people in these cities seem to function well. The incidence of mental disturbance is no higher in cities than in smaller communities (Srole, 1972; Schwab et al., 1972). People in cities are no more likely to commit suicide than people in smaller communities (Gibbs, 1971). In fact, urban people say that they are just as happy as people who live in suburbs, small towns, or rural areas (Shaver and Freedman, 1976). In a recent

De Wys

book on the urban experience, Claude Fischer writes that he found ". . . little evidence that urbanites are more stressed, disordered, alienated, or unhappy than ruralites" (1976, p. 177). As we shall see, there is reason to believe that some people do well in crowded conditions while others do poorly, and that under some circumstances, crowding can be harmful just as it can sometimes be beneficial. But crowding is not the generally harmful factor it is often thought to be.

However, it still seems to most people that being in a crowded environment is different from being in an uncrowded one. Psychologists have therefore attempted to discover how this difference affects behavior and reactions of all kinds. To do this, investigators have turned to more controlled experiments in laboratories or other settings.

experimental research: short-term crowding

Although some cities are densely populated, very few people actually spend their whole lives under crowded conditions. They may live or work with many other people in a small area, but they also spend time on the street, in parks, and in other situations of relatively low density. Thus, even for people who live in the most crowded cities, such as New York or Hong Kong, exposure to really high levels of density occurs sporadically and for short periods. For example, a New Yorker may find himself in a crowded elevator or subway for a brief period, on a crowded sidewalk while going to work, or in a packed department store. These encounters are due to the high level of population density in the city. Yet, this high level makes itself felt primarily through these short incidents rather than through constant exposure to crowding. Therefore, experiments dealing with short-term crowding may be helpful in telling us how crowding in the real world affects us. In any case, this experimental approach is the only way at the moment to investigate the problem in detail.

The standard procedure for almost all the experimental work is to put some people in a small room, others in a large room, and look for any differences on a wide variety of measures. The one clear finding from this research is consistent with the results from survey studies described above—crowding is not generally harmful to people. Although the research has produced a complex pattern of results, virtually all the experiments show no overall negative effect of crowding. People in small rooms respond just as positively as people in larger rooms. Increasing the density does not lead to a decrement in any measure that has been taken. As we shall see, this does not mean that crowding is good for people, nor that it never has bad effects. What it means is that the effects are complicated and depend on the circumstances.

performance

A number of studies have observed task performance under crowded and uncrowded conditions. Freedman, Klevansy, and Erlich (1971) had hundreds of subjects of various ages and backgrounds work on many different tasks. Some subjects worked under very crowded conditions (as high as 3 to 4 square feet per person), whereas others had lots of space. There were no consistent differences of any kind. This finding has been repeated by many other experimenters (e.g., Griffitt and Veitch, 1971). Moreover, people who are totally isolated from the world under very high density for periods as long as twenty days also perform tasks perfectly well. Isolation studies of this sort have been conducted in connection with air raid shelters, submarine warfare, and the space program. Although not everyone who participates enjoys the experience, and some cannot last the full time, most people do just fine and perform at a high level (Smith and Haythorn, 1972). This is hardly surprising, since we have dramatic proof of people's ability to function under these conditions from both submarines and the space program. The astronauts are obviously highly motivated and well trained. Nevertheless, it is worth noting that at least some members of our species can perform complex and tedious tasks while cooped up in a tiny capsule for many weeks.

This research strongly suggests that crowding is not a stressor in the usual sense of the word. We know from experimental work on learning and motivation that stress such as fear, pain, or hunger leads to a change in performance. Since crowding does not generally produce such change, it seems likely that crowding does not usually produce stress.

physiological effects

Although crowding is not usually a stressor, it can sometimes produce physiological arousal. Several experiments have taken physiological measures of people who are in high and low density situations. At least some of these studies have found that people are more aroused when they are crowded (Aiello et al., 1975). And these same experimenters have found, at least once, that performance is affected by crowding.

How can we reconcile this with the lack of effect on performance in most studies? The answer seems to be that crowding may not usually be arousing, but can be under the right circumstances. In particular, in these studies the degree of crowding is extremely high—6 people in a room only 4 feet by 4 feet. In addition, the subjects were told that the study concerned their responses to the room and were given no explanation for being in such a tiny room. With their attention drawn to the room, with no reason for being in it, and with no social interaction among the subjects, the physical fact of being crowded becomes more important than it usually would be and the people are annoyed or aroused by it. In other words, crowding can sometimes be unpleasant, and these experiments have managed to make it extreme enough to bring about this reaction. It is important to realize that crowding does not ordinarily produce arousal but that it can. Once again, the crucial question is when it has this effect and when it does not.

social effects

As with performance on tasks, crowding has no consistent overall effects on social behavior. People in crowded conditions are not in general more aggressive or more unfriendly than people under less crowded conditions (Freedman et al., 1972; Freedman, 1975). Children who are given half as much space to play in as they are used to are no more aggressive than usual (Price, 1972). As careful observations of children have shown, if they have the same facilities and toys, the amount of space has little or no effect on their aggressiveness (Rabe and Patterson, 1974). And in the isolation study mentioned above (Smith and Haythorn, 1972), some of the subjects had more room than others. Those with less room were actually less hostile than the others. Thus, all this research indicates that crowding does not lead to an overall increase in aggressiveness or any other social behavior.

sex differences

Several experiments have demonstrated that responses to high density may depend on the sex of the subjects. In two experiments (Freedman et al., 1972), all-male or all-female groups were put in high- or low-density conditions and various measures were taken of their competitiveness

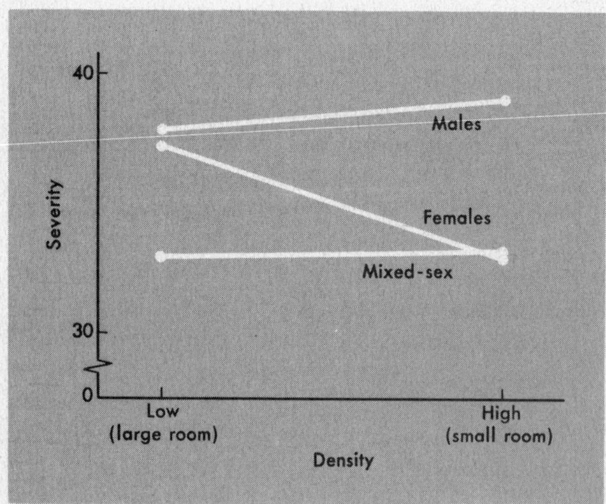

FIGURE 15–4
The effect of density on severity of sentences given by all-male, all-female and mixed-sex groups. Females give less severe sentences, males more severe in high density situations. The effect in this study is much stronger for females than for males. (Based on Freedman et al, 1972.)

and the severity of sentencing they gave in a mock jury situation. It was found that men tended to respond more competitively and to give more severe sentences in the high-density condition than they did in the low-density condition. Women were actually less competitive and gave milder sentences under conditions of high density. Figure 15–4 shows the results of the jury study. In addition, the men in the group liked each other less under conditions of high than low density, and the women liked each other more under conditions of high density. In mixed-sex groups, there were no effects of density.

Other research has also found sex differences in response to crowding, but the effects are not entirely consistent. Most of the studies find that males are more sensitive to density than females, and that males tend to respond more negatively (Ross et al., 1973; Stokols et al., 1973; Paulus, 1976). However, at least one study showed that males reacted more positively (Loo, 1972). In this experiment, groups of young children were put in same-sex groups in either large or small rooms and their behavior was observed. Girls were unaffected by the size of the room, whereas boys became less aggressive in the smaller room. Finally, Marshall and Heslin (1975) found a very complex relationship between sex of the subjects, whether or not the sexes were mixed, and density. The effects are so confusing that the main point of the study is that these effects are not consistent. Thus, although there is a tendency for males to be somewhat more sensitive to density and to respond negatively whereas females respond positively to high density, there is considerable inconsistency. Accordingly, it seems likely that the effects are due not to some basic difference between the sexes in their response to density, but to some more general explanation.

theories of crowding

A number of explanations of the crowding effects have been proposed. It is probably inaccurate to call them theories because they are tentative hypotheses rather than well-formulated explanations. But whatever they are called, they are attempts to come to grips with the findings we have described above.

sensory overload and stimulation level

Stanley Milgram (1970) has discussed crowding in terms of what he calls *sensory overload*. The idea is that whenever people are exposed to too much stimulation, they experience sensory overload and can no longer deal with all the stimulation. Sensory overload is unpleasant and obviously would interfere with a person's ability to function properly. Therefore, people deal with overload by screening out some stimulation and attending only to what is most important. According to this notion, crowding is one source of stimulation and can sometimes produce overload. When it does, people are upset, under stress, and will "turn off" their attention.

Although Milgram has made no attempt to relate this idea to the results of crowding research, it might explain some of these findings. For example, men may be less able to deal with large amounts of stimulation than women. As density increases, the men are overloaded sooner and therefore respond more negatively. Similarly, high density may sometimes not reach the level where overload occurs and therefore may produce no negative effects. Unfortunately, this does not explain why high density sometimes produces positive effects nor why women generally respond positively. In addition, it says nothing about when overload will occur and when it will not. Perhaps additional research will relate this idea more closely to crowding effects. For the moment, it is a provocative notion with little or no research to support it.

On the other hand, a closely related idea does explain many of the crowding results. Assume that everyone has some level of stimulation that he or she finds pleasant and agreeable. Some people like high levels of stimulation—they like the radio blaring all the time, studying in busy rooms, and watching television while carrying on a conversation or doing the crossword puzzle. Others like low levels of stimulation. When they work it has to be quiet; if they watch television they do not want any other distractions; and their idea of a perfect environment is a quiet spot somewhere. The high-stimulation people find high density pleasant and exciting; the low-stimulation people find it unpleasant and disruptive, simply because high density is the right level of stimulation for the former and too high for the latter.

This explanation may help us understand the diverse findings on the effects of crowding. Men and women may differ in the level of stimulation they prefer; different groups may have different preferences; and the preferences themselves may vary somewhat depending on the particular situation (e.g., someone hates distractions when working on a task but does not mind them if he is only engaging in social conversation). Once again, this idea does not specify when high density will have positive, negative, or neutral effects, but it does provide a framework in which to consider individual differences in response to crowding. It would also explain why some people like cities; and others dislike them. Presumably, those who like high levels of stimulation will find cities exciting whereas those who like low levels will be bothered by the variety and the number of activities.

density-intensity

A different explanation of the various effects of crowding is that high density intensifies the usual reactions to a social situation. The idea (Freedman, 1975) is that the presence of other people is one stimulus in the situation and that increasing the density increases its importance. Just as turning up the volume on a hi-fi set magnifies our reaction to music, so increasing density magnifies our reaction to other people. If we are listening to music at a low volume, making it louder will intensify our reactions. If we dislike the music, we will dislike it more when it is loud than when it is soft; if we like it, we will like it more when it is loud. Similarly, whatever our response to the other people who are near us, increasing density intensifies that response. If we like them, we will like them more; if we dislike them, we will dislike them more. If we are afraid, nervous, angry, aggressive, friendly, or anything else under low density, we will feel more of it under high density.

According to this view, the sex differences would be due to different initial reactions to the situation. All-male groups tend to be somewhat suspicious and competitive, so increasing density makes them more competitive and aggressive; all-female groups respond to each other with more friendliness and intimacy, and increasing density makes them friendlier and more cooperative. The inconsistent results are caused by differences in the specific situations. Some elicit negative responses by one sex or the other, and some produce no sex differences under low density. When density is increased, the usual reactions are magnified. But since the typical reactions vary, the effect of density also varies. Some direct support for this view is provided by a series of studies by Freedman, Heshka, Levy, and Staff (Freedman, 1975). In this work, situations are made deliberately either pleasant or unpleasant for both sexes. Increasing density should intensify the responses of both sexes, making the pleasant situation more pleasant and the unpleasant more unpleasant, regardless of sex of subject or whether the groups are mixed. That is what these studies show.

This explanation of the effect of crowding seems to fit quite nicely into our everyday experience. Sometimes crowding is unpleasant and sometimes it is pleasant, but generally it does appear to intensify the social situation. Riding a bus is not especially pleasant. If the bus is crowded, it usually becomes more unpleasant. More to the point, if there are six people in a bus, it does not matter too much who the other people are. They may be frightening or interesting, but scattered around a bus, they have little effect. Now imagine the same six people are in a car. Their characteristics become much more important and our reactions are greatly magnified. If they are frightening, it is much more frightening to be in a car with them; if they are interesting, it is much nicer to be in the car. Or consider a party. If there are only twenty people in a huge room, the party tends to be flat, unexciting, and dull. In fact, under these circumstances people will usually collect in the kitchen or at one end of the room. The same twenty people in a small room will make a much better party, assuming of course that they are pleasant people. If they are unpleasant, the small room will produce a less pleasant experience than the large room. In other words, basically positive situations usually become more positive when density is increased; negative ones become more negative.

This density-intensity notion is consistent with most of the findings and seems to provide a plausible explanation. However, it is still in the speculative stage and much more work is necessary in order to test it. Also, the various theories we have described are by no means contradictory. It seems likely that crowding does sometimes cause overload or at least discomfort due to an inability to deal with the situation; that people do have different preferences for levels of stimulation and those who like high levels will respond more positively to high density; and that high density increases the importance of the other people and therefore intensifies our reactions to them. As with personal space, our reactions to crowding depend on the situation and our interpretation of it.

architectural design

One of the fascinating questions of environmental psychology is how the design of buildings and spaces affects us. Architects are naturally deeply concerned with this issue, but until recently there was no systematic research. In the past few years, psychologists and sociologists have begun to study certain aspects of the problem. Although the work is at a very preliminary stage and nothing can be stated with any certainty, we are beginning to understand some of the ways in which design influences people and in particular to see that the influence is often subtle and complex. The two areas in which most of the research has been done are the structure of dormitories (suites versus corridor) and high-rise versus low-rise housing.

dormitory design

College dormitories generally have two quite different kinds of design. The more traditional type has single or double rooms located along a corridor, with social areas and bathrooms shared by all the residents on the corridor. Some newer dormitories have suites of rooms consisting of several bedrooms located around a common living room, usually with the residents of just these bedrooms sharing bathroom facilities. The amount of space available to each resident and therefore the density is approximately the same for the two designs. Yet the two kinds of buildings seem to have different effects on the residents.

A series of studies by Baum and Valins (1976) compared the corridor and suite arrangements. The research indicates that students who live in suite-type dormitories are more sociable and friendlier. At first glance, this seems obvious. Clearly, if you share a living room with, say, nine other people (five bedrooms with two people each), you will get to know these nine other students. In a sense, you have a family living situation and the rest of the people are part of your "family." If you share a room with only one person, it takes greater effort to get to know other people on the floor and they are not part of your family to the same extent. As we discussed in Chapter 5, proximity is one of the major factors in liking and friendship. The suite arrangement puts more people in close proximity and therefore should lead to more friendships. Thus far, this follows directly from our knowledge of the effects of proximity and certainly would be expected. The striking aspect of Baum's and Valins' work is that these sociability differences seem to carry over into the world outside the dormitory. When the students are observed in the psychology laboratory, the suite residents are friendlier there than the corridor residents. For example, in one study a student arrived at the laboratory and was shown into a room in which another student (actually a confederate) was sitting. There were several chairs in the room and the question was how close to the other student the subject would sit. Suite residents tended to sit closer than corridor residents, and to initiate more conversations.

One of the difficulties with this kind of research (and the work on high-rise housing to be discussed next) is that the people in the two types of dormitories may be somewhat different even before they move in. Although assignment to dormitories at the college is supposed to be entirely random, it is hard to be certain of this. If, for any reason, more sociable people are placed in suite-type dormitories, obviously the differences Baum and Valins found would be due to the initial difference, not to the effect of the dormitory design. Although the authors have tried to eliminate this possibility, the one control study that deals with the problem is not entirely convincing. Thus, the possibility remains that the dormitories are not having the reported effects. Despite this problem, the research is exactly the kind we need to discover how architectural design affects people. Presumably, additional studies will provide more evidence so that we can be certain what effects are due to design and what are due to other factors.

high-rise vs. low-rise housing

Although students are naturally quite concerned about dormitory design, a much more serious problem for our society is the general one of how high-rise housing affects people. During the 1950s and 1960s, a vast number of high-rise buildings were constructed for our rapidly expanding population. Some of these buildings are huge: thirty or forty stories with hundreds or even thousands of individual apartments; others are smaller. But all of them contrast sharply with one- or two-story private homes or four- or five-story apartment houses. It has become a matter of great social importance to determine whether high-rise housing of this sort is a good environment in which to live.

The question is raised because we know that some of these buildings have been failures. They have gotten run down, the halls have been defaced, the apartments have been allowed to deteriorate, crime and vandalism have made the buildings unsafe, and people have moved out whenever they were able. The most dramatic example of this kind of failure is the Pruitt Igoe project in St. Louis, which was eventually demolished by the city because no one was willing to live in it any more. This huge, multimillion dollar housing project was a total loss. Other buildings may not reach quite this point, but clearly some of them have not worked well. On the other hand, we know also that most of the buildings, both public and private, have been successful at least to the extent that people continue to live in them and apparently to function reasonably well. The issue is whether high- or low-rise buildings have different effects on the residents, and in particular whether high-rise housing is harmful.

Almost all the work on this question has been done by urban sociologists, but social psychologists are now beginning to become involved as well. The research results indicate that high-rise housing does not generally have any harmful effects. As Barry Wellman (1974), one of the experts on this issue, notes: "There is no convincing evidence that the experience of living in high-rise buildings is pathological. The residents of such dwellings are similar to other urbanites in their ability to form networks of social relationships, their involvement in urban institutions, and in their mental health." Similar findings are reported by Michelson (1977) and others who have done large-scale studies of urban housing. Perhaps the one exception is the work of Oscar Newman (1973), who

Everett C. Johnson/De Wys

claims that there is more crime in high-rise housing. But most people in the field reject this research because of methodological errors and unsupported conclusions. It is fair to say that at the moment no one has found any good evidence that high-rise housing is bad for us.

On the other hand, it is important to keep in mind that high-rise housing or for that matter any kind of housing may not be suitable for everyone. Although none of the research produced consistent differences between high- and low-rise housing, there is no question that some people prefer one or the other. In particular, parents with young children often complain that high-rise housing presents great difficulties in supervising the children (Michelson, 1970). Someone who lives on the twentieth floor cannot watch a child in the playground on the street floor. Many parents are reluctant to let their young children ride elevators alone, so that even if they can play on the street, it is inconvenient to get them there. Perhaps because of this, residents of high-rise housing generally are less satisfied with their housing than are people who live in their own homes. Moreover, high-rise residents do not value the friendliness of their neighborhood as much (Wellman, 1974). None of these differences is large or related to any noticeable differences in the health or general satisfaction of the residents, but the differences do exist. In other words, people complain more about high-rise housing even though the research has not shown any actual negative effects.

As with the dormitory design studies, work on high-rise housing faces enormous difficulty in equating the residents of the various kinds of buildings. People are not randomly assigned to housing in our society, so that residents of different kinds of buildings almost always differ in a variety of potentially important ways. For example, in Wellman's study high-rise residents were of a somewhat higher socioeconomic class than low rise; in Michelson's study, people in high rises were generally younger than those who lived in their own homes. In cities like New York that have many high-rise apartments, upper, middle, and working class families live in high-rise buildings. It is worth noting that many people who can afford to live anywhere choose to live in a high-rise building in the middle of New York City. In other words, high-rise buildings are not only for low-income families. On the other hand, the middle and upper classes do generally have a choice, whereas the poorer families often are forced to live in a high rise because it is the only housing available. This lack of choice may itself cause problems and it should therefore probably be a matter of public policy to provide choice for all people. That is, if we continue to build high-rise apartments for low-income people, we should also provide the alternative of low-rise buildings for these same people. Although high-rise buildings may not have any negative effect, being forced to live in one (or to live anywhere with no choice) may be harmful. And it is probably no accident that most of the difficulty with high-rise housing has occurred in buildings that are entirely or primarily for low-income families.

To sum up, none of the research shows negative effects of high-rise housing. However, people do complain more about high-rise buildings, and clearly some high-rise apartments have been failures. At the moment we are still uncertain of the specific effects of these two types of structures, but it seems desirable to provide everyone with a choice between high- and low-rise housing whenever that is possible.

life in the city

As we said earlier, the United States and Canada are largely urban societies, with more than 70 percent of the population living in or around cities. It is therefore both relevant and important to ask how living in a city differs from living under other conditions. This question is especially appropriate now. In addition to financial problems, our cities are beset by high crime rates, rundown schools, heavy welfare rolls, unemployment, and generally low morale. Moreover, there appears to be, at least in the United States, a pervasive anticity feeling among many people. When I mention that I live in New York City, people often look at me with either sympathy or horror. They wonder how I can stand it and why I have not ended up in a mental hospital or the morgue. Yet, most of our population is urban and somehow most of us survive. In fact, as we shall see, living in a city has no negative psychological or physical effects on people. The life may at times be dangerous, it may not be to everyone's liking, but it is not harmful to mind or body.

The first point to make is to repeat what we said in the sections on crowding and noise. These two factors, so typical of cities, are the ones

Hugh Rogers/Monkmeyer

most often thought to be harmful, but they have few if any negative effects on people. High density, either in a neighborhood or a crowded apartment, has no overall harmful consequences (Freedman, 1975). It is not associated with higher rates of crime, mental illness, infant mortality, or any kind of disease. People who live in crowded conditions are just as healthy, physically, mentally, and socially, as people who live under less crowded conditions. Similarly, noise has much less negative effect than most of us would have thought (Glass and Singer, 1972). Very loud noise does produce an immediate minor decrement in performance, but this soon disappears. Long-term exposure to loud noise may have some bad effects, but people are marvelously adaptable and they generally adapt to loud noise quite easily.

On the other hand, we have noted that unpredictable and uncontrollable noise seems to be more irritating and might have long-term negative effects. This kind of noise occurs in some cities. If they are drilling the street outside your apartment, you are exposed to occasional bursts of very loud noise. The same is true if there is construction going on nearby, if you live on a quiet street that has a few trucks passing by, and so on. People who live in cities get used to a much higher level of noise than people who live in smaller communities, but it is probably the sudden changes from the usual level that are disturbing. However, we have no idea just how harmful this kind of noise can be, and there is little reason to believe that it has major effects.

The next point to make is that people who live in the city do not have any higher rates of mental disturbance than those who live in small towns, or even in rural communities (Srole, 1972). It might seem that there would be more stress in the city, but whether or not there is, it does not produce more disturbance. The rates of psychosis are about the same everywhere, including primitive societies; and there are no substantial differences in neurosis. Furthermore, city people do not feel any more anxious or unhappy than other people. In a survey of a large number of Americans (Shaver and Freedman, 1976), those who lived in cities said that they were just as happy and calm as those who lived in small towns or rural areas. The study found that the particular type of community, urban, suburban, town, or rural, mattered very little in terms of health, psychological well-being, or anything else.

On the other hand, we all know that some people hate being in a city. They find the noise unpleasant, the crowds of people upsetting, the pace too fast, and the general atmosphere obnoxious. Many people prefer the quieter, more peaceful, slower life in the suburbs or better still in a small town or rural area. If they dislike cities so much, how can we say that cities are not harmful?

The answer is that reactions to the city depend on characteristics of the individual. Just as some people like high levels of stimulation while others do not, so some people like cities and some hate them. In fact, the critical factor may be the level of stimulation you prefer. Obviously, if you like a high level, cities are more likely to produce positive feelings than if you like lower levels. Similarly, if you like a high level of stimulation, you may dislike small towns. In the survey mentioned above (Shaver and Freedman, 1976), many people were not happy with their community. This was true of all kinds of communities. Some people who lived in rural areas were dissatisfied, as were people who lived in urban areas. The amount of dissatisfaction was about the same for all areas (actually slightly lower for the biggest cities than for any other type of community). But the important point is that people who did not like their community tended to be the least happy and healthy. Although the type of community in which people lived did not affect happiness, their satisfaction with their community did. Thus, as we have all observed, some people do dislike cities and are unhappy in them, while others like cities and enjoy living there. Every type of community has some advantages and some disadvantages. Cities are exciting, have a lot of services and opportunities, many different kinds of people, and a high level of stimulation. But they are noisy, crowded, and certainly not peaceful. In contrast, small towns have what big cities lack—peacefulness, a sense of belonging to a family or neighborhood, and ease; and they lack what the city has, excitement and opportunity. It is all a question of what you want, and that is an individual decision.

SUMMARY

1. Environmental psychology deals with how various factors in the environment affect people. Although practically anything could be considered part of the environment, the field has concentrated on the effects of noise, the use of space, crowding, the design of buildings, and cities in general.

2. Noise affects us less than we might think. As long as noise is not so loud that it causes physical damage, people adapt to it very quickly and with no harmful effects. Loud noise does interfere with the performance of certain tasks—those that involve doing several things at once—such as monitoring many different dials.

3. Adaptation to noise does seem to take effort. If a noise is uncontrollable or unpredictable, effects show up after the noise has ceased. In this noise situation people do less well on tasks that require high motivation for good performance. There is also some suggestion that prolonged exposure to loud noise may have negative effects on hearing and reading comprehension.

4. Proxemics is a term used to refer to how we use the space immediately surrounding us—sometimes called personal space. The distance we stand from other people depends on our ethnic background, our sex, and on our relationship to the people. White Americans and Northern Europeans prefer the greatest distance, Southern Europeans stand closer, and South Americans, Pakistanis, and Arabs stand still closer. Blacks and Whites in the United States have similar preferences. Women stand closer than men, and mixed-pairs closer than same sex pairs.

5. Standing close has two quite different meanings. We stand closer to people we like, have closer relationships with, or are sexually attracted to. But standing close can also be an aggressive act when it involves invading someone's space—e.g., he is reading in the library and you deliberately sit next to him. On the other hand, there is no evidence that we have an innate need for a particular amount of territory—it depends on the situation.

6. Crowding and high density have negative effects on non-humans. It produces a breakdown in normal social behavior, but it does not generally have negative effects on people. Crowding does not cause crime, pathological problems or negative consequences either in the real world, or in the laboratory.

7. Under many circumstances, all male groups respond badly to high density while all female groups respond positively. However, it is suggested that crowding acts to intensify the usual reaction to the situation—making positive responses more positive, and negative ones more negative.

8. Another explanation of crowding effects is that some people like high levels of stimulation and others like low levels. Since high density involves higher stimulation, those who like high levels will respond positively while the others will respond negatively.

9. Architectural design seems to have some effects on people's behavior. Suite arrangements in dormitories appear to promote social interactions better than corridor designs. However, high-rise housing is not necessarily worse than low-rise housing.

10. Urban living is not generally less healthy than living in other kinds of communities. It is likely that the effect of type of community depends on the preferences and characteristics of each individual.

SUGGESTIONS FOR ADDITIONAL READING

FREEDMAN, J. L. *Crowding and Behavior.* San Francisco: W. H. Freeman, 1975. Presents all of the research on crowding up to that date as well as the author's theory.

GLASS, D. C. & SINGER, J. E. *Urban Stress.* New York: Academic Press, 1972. Mostly their work on the effects of noise. Lots of research as well as interesting theoretical discussion.

SOMMER, R. *Personal Space: The Behavioral Basis of Design.* Englewood Cliffs, N.J.: Prentice-Hall, 1969. Somewhat out of date, but still the best book on this subject.

glossary

Activity Basic rating dimension on the semantic differential: the activeness or passivity of another person, object, or concept.

Additive model Theoretical position according to which information used in forming impressions is added up or gathered. For example, a positive impression of another person would become more positive with the addition of new, positive information.

Affective component Emotional feelings associated with beliefs about an attitude object; consists mainly of the evaluation of the object (like-dislike, pro-con).

Affective exchange Altman and Taylor's third stage of the social penetration process; the stage in which many of the barriers are down, and criticism and praise are permissible—for example, close friendships.

Affiliation Tendency for people to be gregarious; to be in contact with others; to join with others.

Aggression Any action intended to hurt others; may also refer to internal state of wanting to hurt others (aggressive feelings).

All-channel Type of communication network in which each member can communicate with each other member.

Altruism Performing acts intended to help another even though there is no expectation of reward.

Antisocial aggression Aggressive acts such as murder that violate commonly accepted social norms.

Anxiety Worry based on the arousal of unconscious desires (Freud); being afraid when there is no real danger.

Applied research Research designed to answer questions about specific, real-world issues, usually without concern for any general theoretical or scientific issues.

Archive study Research technique based on the analysis of data already available in published records.

Assimilation Tendency to see discrepant or opposing positions on matters close to an individual as being closer than they actually are.

Association Linking different stimuli that occur together in place and time. Through pairing, evaluations of one stimulus become associated with those of the other; one of the basic processes by which learning occurs.

Assumed similarity Tendency for people to believe that others are similar to them, particularly when they share demographic characteristics such as ethnic background, age, and education.

Attitude Enduring response disposition with a cognitive component, an affective component, and a behavioral tendency; we develop and hold attitudes toward persons, objects, and ideas.

Attitude-discrepant behavior Acts inconsistent with a person's attitudes. When an individual behaves in a way inconsistent with a belief, dissonance is produced and there is a tendency for the attitude to change.

Attribution Process by which people make inferences about the causes of attitudes or behavior. Attribution theory attempts to describe the principles by which these attributions are determined, and the effect they have.

Authoritarian leader Leader who dictates group policies and activities, and who regulates members' work and selection of partners. This leadership style leads to highly productive groups with discontented members.

Autokinetic phenomenon Visual illusion in which a single point of light seen in the dark appears to move even though it is stationary; used in Sherif's conformity experiments.

Averaging model Theoretical position according to which information used in forming impressions is averaged together. For example, a positive impression of another person would not be changed by new information that is also positive.

Balance theory Heider's theoretical model, in which unbalanced relationships (those with an odd number of negative relationships) between two persons and an object tend to change toward balanced ones.

Basic research Research designed to examine general relationships among phenomena rather than specific questions about particular issues.

Bilateral threat Trucking game condition in which both players have the option of blocking their opponent's path. Cooperation is very low under this condition.

Birth order Factor associated with the tendency to affiliate. First-born and only children, when afraid, affiliate more than later-born children, regardless of the size of the family.

Brainstorming Unstructured group problem-solving technique in which the individual participants say anything they think might be helpful to stimulate the group to produce better ideas than any one person would produce alone.

Bystander intervention The act of coming to the aid of a stranger in distress. Research indicates that a person is more likely to intervene when he or she is alone in the situation than when others are present.

Catharsis Freud's idea that the aggressive drive can be reduced by expressing and thus releasing aggression.

Centrality Extent to which a trait is central to an impression through being associated with the stimulus person's other characteristics. Traits such as warm or cold are considered central because they are important in determining impressions.

Centralized communication network Type of network in which only one person receives information from all the other members. These networks are effective for simple tasks and transmit information efficiently, but members tend to dislike the group.

Chain Type of communication network in which any two persons can communicate with only one specified other, and each of the remaining persons can communicate with two others.

Circle Type of communication network in which all members are equal—that is, each member can communicate only with his or her two neighbors.

Cognitive component Part of an attitude; the collection of thoughts, beliefs, and knowledge about an attitude object.

Cognitive consistency Tendency for people to seek consistency among their beliefs; regarded as a major determinant of attitude formation and change.

Cognitive dissonance Theory developed by Festinger according to which inconsistency (dissonance) between two cognitive elements produces pressure to make these elements consonant. It has been applied to a wide range of phenomena including decisions and attitude-discrepant behavior.

Commitment Extent to which a person is tied to, involved in, or for any reason finds it difficult to give up an attitude, judgment, or other kind of position. Higher commitment reduces conformity and attitude change.

Communication network Structure pattern of routes through which a group of people exchange information.

Communication pattern Array of factors that affect interaction in groups.

Complementarity Tendency for people to be attracted to one another because they possess opposite qualities. For example, a dominant person may be attracted to a submissive person and vice versa.

Compliance Performance of an act at another's request.

Conditioning A basic learning process; an approach to the development of attitudes which assumes that attitudes are learned by the same processes and mechanisms that control other kinds of learning.

Conformity Voluntary performance of an act because others also do it.

Congruity theory Variant of the balance theory developed by Osgood and Tannenbaum which has been applied to the prediction of a communicator's effectiveness in producing attitude change.

Consensus Extent to which there is agreement among other persons in their response to a situation. According to Kelley, this is one kind of information used in arriving at causal attributions in his cube theory.

Consistency According to Kelley, one kind of information used in arriving at causal attributions. Extent to which a particular person acts in the same manner at other times and in other situations.

Context Information about another person which affects the impact of new information on later impressions.

Contrast Tendency to perceive attitudinal positions that are far from an individual's own position as being farther away than they actually are.

Cooperative interdependence Idea that blacks and whites who interact in equal-status relationships are likely to weaken prejudiced attitudes.

Correlational bias Assumptions about the interrelationship between various traits and characteristics that tend to bias perceptions of others' behavior.

Credibility How expert a communicator is perceived to be in an area of concern, and how much he or she is trusted by the individual receiving the communication.

Cube theory Kelley's model, according to which people base attributions on three independent kinds of information: distinctiveness, consistency, and consensus.

Correlational research Observing the relationship between two or more variables, without experimental control. This is an efficient approach for collecting large amounts of data, but does not show the cause-effect relationship between the variables.

Correspondent inferences Judgments made that a person's behavior reflects his or her unique stable internal dispositions. These inferences are most common when the behavior is low in social desirability.

Crowding Psychological state of discomfort associated with wanting more space than is available; also, the physical state of being in a situation with little space (often called high density).

Cultural value Explanation for the extremity shift according to which the norm of risk (or caution) is valued by group members, causing them to make decisions which are at least as risky (or cautious) as those of other members.

Decentralized communication network Network in which all members have equal access to one another. Decentralized networks are best for complex tasks, transmit information slowly, and have many distractions, but members tend to like the group.

Decommitment Feeling that a person can change his or her decision if it works out badly, or that a certain course of action does not have to be followed through. Under these circumstances, dissonance will not be present, and attitude change is unlikely to occur.

De facto selectivity Tendency for people generally to be exposed more to attitude positions with which they agree than to attitude positions with which they disagree.

Defensive attribution Tendency to make attributions that enhance the ego or defend self-esteem; for example, attributing success to our own talents and failure to outside forces.

Deindividuation Loss of a sense of personal responsibility when in a group that leads people to do things they would normally not do when alone.

Democratic leader Leader who discussed policies with the group, and allows members to work with whomever they choose. This style has been shown to produce groups that are not necessarily very productive but that have strong motivation to work and happier, more self-reliant members.

Density Physical measure of the amount of space available to each organism in an environment. High density is often called crowding.

Density-intensity Freedman's idea that high density intensifies people's usual reactions to social situations.

Dependent variable The behaviors or attitudes that are measured in an experiment; responses to levels of the independent variable being manipulated.

Deviance Being seen as or actually being different from others.

Diffusion of responsibility Explanation for the extremity shift according to which members of a group advocate extreme courses of action because they can share the consequences of the decision. Evidence in support of this explanation is questionable.

Discounting principle Kelley's idea that people tend to discount the possibility of any given cause in producing an effect if there are other likely causes.

Discrepancy Difference of opinion between a member of an audience and the position advocated in a message. The greater the discrepancy, the greater the stress, and the greater the pressure to change the attitude.

Disinhibition Loosening of the tight control over anger in general by once releasing it under socially approved conditions; that is, once a person has committed a socially approved aggression, he or she has fewer inhibitions about aggressing under other conditions.

Displacement Expression of aggression toward a target other than the source of frustration or annoyance. Typically, it occurs because the original source is not available or because the reasons for restraining aggression against this other target are weaker.

Dissonance Inconsistency between two cognitions which produces tension.

Distinctiveness Extent to which a person's response to a particular stimulus (entity) is unique to that stimulus and not made in response to other stimuli; one of the kinds of information used in arriving at causal attributions in Kelley's cube theory.

Distraction Stimulus that draws attention away from a persuasive message. It sometimes increases attitude change by making it harder for people to defend a position against the arguments in the message.

Empirical research Research designed to gather information about a phenomenon, without regard to a particular theory or hypothesis. Often employs many measures at once.

Evaluation Most important basic dimension underlying impression formation; the goodness or badness of another person, object, or concept.

Experimental research Research in which specific conditions or combinations of conditions are systematically introduced to subjects randomly assigned to conditions in order to see how they respond to them.

Experimenter bias Result of the experimenter's intentional or unintentional communication of expectations and desires to subjects, or treating subjects differently in accordance with these expectations. In either case, it can invalidate the experiment by affecting the responses of the subjects.

Expertise Sum total of a person's knowledge and ability regarding a specific task or judgment. A person is more likely to conform to group judgments when he believes that the expertise of the others is greater than his.

External forces Factors outside the individual, such as task difficulty, luck, social pressure or any other kind of environmental pressure, which cause or influence behavior.

External validity Extent to which the results of an experiment are generalizable to other populations and settings.

Extremity shift Move toward conservative or risky extremes when decisions are made by groups rather than individuals.

Fantasy aggression Imagined act of aggression that tends to reduce direct aggression.

Fear Feeling of dread associated with realistic danger; found to be associated with increases in affiliative behavior in Schachter's experiments.

"Feel good" effect People experiencing pleasant emotional states are more likely to be helpful to others than persons experiencing less positive states.

Field experiment Study in which variables are systematically manipulated and measured in real-life, nonlaboratory settings.

Foot-in-the-door technique Method of increasing compliance with a large request by first getting the person to comply with a smaller request.

Forewarning Telling individuals ahead of time that they will be exposed to a discrepant communication on an issue they care about. Forewarning helps them resist the message better than if they are not warned.

Frustration Interference with or blocking of the attainment of a goal. Frustration usually leads to aggressive feelings.

Functionalism Approach to the development of attitudes which proposes that attitudes are adopted because they are instrumental in the attainment of goals. For example, a businessman may hold positive attitudes toward a certain political ideology if he believes these views help his business.

Gain-loss phenomenon Tendency for people to like best those who show increasing liking for them, and to dislike most those who show decreasing liking. Aronson and Linder have explained this phenomenon in terms of changes in self-esteem that result from changes in others' evaluations.

Game theory Mathematical analysis of games that makes it possible to determine which alternatives would maximize chances of winning.

Gestalt The view that people form coherent and meaningful perceptions based on the entire perceptual field, so that the whole is different from the sum of its parts. In social perception, the implication is that the meaning of a trait is affected by its context.

Group cohesiveness Sum of the forces causing people to feel drawn to a group and making them want to remain a member of the group. The more the members of a group like one another, expect to gain from group membership, and feel loyalty to the group, the greater the cohesiveness and the more members are likely to conform to the group.

Group structure Differentiation among the activities of group members. Stricture includes leadership, amount and direction of communication, division of labor, and so on.

Group unanimity Agreement among members of a group. Unanimity leads to great pressure on any given member to conform; less than total unanimity leads to considerably less pressure.

Guilt Feelings aroused by having done something wrong; reduced by engaging in helping behavior or by self-punishment.

Halo effect Tendency to attribute positive characteristics to others when we perceive them as possessing one positive characteristic or when we perceive them positively in general.

Hawthorne effect Tendency for people to do what is expected of them when they are made to feel special by being studied in an experiment. The performance of workers in the Hawthorne studies improved whenever any change was made in working conditions because the subjects assumed the changes were for their good.

Imitation Learning by watching what others do and doing the same; also applies to forming attitudes by modeling those of others, such as parents or teachers.

Implicit personality theory A person's belief about what traits and personal characteristics tend to go together. This belief helps determine that person's impressions of other people.

Incentive Size or value of the outcomes in a payoff matrix in a prisoner's dilemma game. The effect of incentive in cooperation is mixed; sometimes it increases, sometimes it decreases, and sometimes it has little effect on cooperation. Also, what individuals have to gain or lose by embracing a particular position. When there are conflicting goals, individuals tend to adopt positions that maximize their gains.

Independent variable Factor systematically manipulated by the experimenter in order to determine its effects on some behavior (the dependent variable).

Ingratiation Increasing others' liking for us by making positive responses such as expressing agreement with them, telling them we like them, and so on. Liking will not result when persons are perceived to have ulterior motives for these statements.

Innate characteristic Any trait or quality determined genetically; the organism has it at birth or develops it regardless of the environment. One example is the human infant's inborn dependence on others for food and protection which makes humans necessarily affiliative so that infants can survive.

Inoculation McGuire's notion that people are more resistant to the effects of persuasive communications when they are exposed to weak counterarguments.

Instinct Any behavior or response built into the organism at birth. For example, early social psychologists felt that human affiliative behavior is instinctive.

Instrumental Helping in the attainment of a goal. One view is that attitudes are adopted because they are instrumental.

Internal force Cause of behavior attributable to factors within the individual, such as ability, effort, personality, or attitudes.

Interpersonal distance The distance people keep between themselves while interacting; personal space.

Invariance Tendency to look for the association between a particular effect and a particular cause across a number of different conditions. An effect will be attributed to a particular cause when the cause and effect are frequently associated in many different situations, and if the effect does not occur in the absence of that cause.

Labeling Attaching a verbal name to a person or an action. There is a tendency for people to behave consistently with a label that describes their self-image. For example, people labeled charitable are more generous than those who are not so labeled.

Leader Person in a group who has the greatest influence on its activities and the beliefs of members. Also, the person recognized by the group as its leader.

Legitimacy Extent to which leadership authority is recognized by members. Leaders who are elected tend to be seen as more legitimate than appointed leaders. Greater legitimacy usually results in more influence and authority.

Libido Freud's concept of sexual, creative energy.

Logical error Tendency for people to infer that an individual who has one trait also has various other traits.

LPC scale Least preferred co-worker scale. A measure of leadership personality style developed by Fiedler based on how much a leader likes the person he likes least or, in other terms, how critical he is of the members of his group. High LPC leaders tend to be friendly, relaxed, and considerate; low LPC leaders tend to be strict, controlling, and directive.

Matrix Combination of outcomes available to players for each combination of responses in a prisoner's dilemma game.

Mere exposure Tendency for stimuli to be liked more or perceived as being more positive the more often they are seen (or heard). Familiarity leads to liking.

Misattribution Assigning the cause of a particular behavior or emotional state to a stimulus other than the actual cause, such as thinking a lecture is exciting when actually you are excited by ten cups of coffee.

Modeling Tendency to imitate another's behavior.

Modes of resolution Ways of reducing conflict caused by a discrepant persuasive communication including changing attitudes, source derogation, or perceptual distortion.

Motivated selectivity Idea that people deliberately seek supportive information and avoid nonsupportive information as a way of maintaining the consistency of their own attitudes. The evidence indicates that this generally does not occur.

Natural selection Process by which characteristics that increase an animal's chances of surviving become dominant over many generations.

Negativity effect Tendency for impressions to be more

influenced by negative traits than by positive traits. Hence positive impressions are more vulnerable to change than negative impressions.

Non-zero-sum games Game in which the total of wins and losses does not necessarily equal zero; that is, both sides can win or lose. The trucking game and the prisoner's dilemma game are examples of non-zero-sum games.

Obedience Performing an action because of an order or request.

Person perception Process of forming impressions of others, making judgments about their personalities, and adopting hypotheses about the kind of persons they are.

Personal space The space immediately surrounding a person, especially during social interaction. The amount of personal space we demand or require is affected by characteristics of the person (sex, ethnic group), and the situation (setting, relation to others). *See* proxemics.

Phenomenal causality Heider's notion that people try to discern the causes underlying behavior in order to predict how people are going to behave.

Positivity bias General tendency to express positive evaluations of people more often than negative evaluations. Also called the leniency effect.

Potency Basic rating dimension on the semantic differential: the strength or weakness of another person, object, or concept.

Predictable noise Bursts of sound that occur at fixed or in any way predictable intervals. Glass and Singer found that subjects exposed to predictable noise performed no better than subjects exposed to random noise during the noise phase of the experiment, but performed better afterward.

Prisoner's dilemma Laboratory game designed to study the conditions under which people cooperate or compete. Despite the fact that the game is usually set up so that players can maximize their rewards by cooperating, they tend to compete in order to "beat" their opponent.

Prosocial aggression Aggressive acts that support commonly accepted social norms, such as a parent spanking a disobedient child.

Prosocial behavior Any act that helps or is designed to help others.

Proxemics Term used by Hall to describe persons' use of space and the kinds of social interaction that are appropriate at different interpersonal distances; the study of these phenomena.

Random assignment Placement of subjects into experimental conditions in a manner which guarantees that the choice is made entirely by chance, such as by using a random number table; essential characteristic of an experiment.

Random noise Sounds that occur at irregular, unpredictable intervals. Glass and Singer found that subjects exposed to random noise performed as well as subjects exposed to predictable noise during the noise phase of the experiment, but performed worse afterward.

Reactance Brehm's concept that people attempt to maintain their freedom of action; when this freedom is threatened, they do whatever they can to restore it: reactance is aroused, and compliance decreases.

Reciprocity Predisposition toward liking others who are believed to like us.

Reference Group Group to which an individual belongs, compares himself, and to whose behavior and attitudes he may conform.

Reinforcement The group's norm can act as a persuasive force leading to attitude change, or prevent change by supporting the individual's position when it is attacked.

Basic principle of learning The process by which the probability of engaging in any behavior is altered through the administration of rewards or punishments.

Risky shift Name given to the extremity shift when it was believed that groups made riskier decisions than individuals.

Role playing Research technique in which the investigator describes a situation to subjects, and asks them what they or some other person would do under those circumstances.

Scapegoat Person who, because he or she is weak, different, and easily distinguishable tends to be selected as a target of displaced aggression.

Selective attention Tendency for people to pay more attention to a supportive message.

Selective exposure Tendency for persuasive communications not to reach the intended audience because audience members tend to come into contact mostly with sources they agree with. Sometimes refers to a pressured psychological tendency to avoid nonsupportive information, but the evidence does not indicate such a tendency.

Self-disclosure Process of telling others about ourselves. More intimate revelations are made in more advanced stages of relationships.

Self-esteem Discrepancy between the ideal and the actual self; greater discrepancy indicates lower self-esteem, and is associated with feelings of inadequacy and anxiety. People with low self-esteem tend to be more persuasible than those with high self-esteem.

Self-perception Process through which people arrive at perceptions of their own internal states.

Semantic differential Way of measuring attitudes by analyzing responses to an object on a series of bipolar (opposite) rating dimensions. Osgood has shown that much of the variance in attitudes (especially those involving people) is accounted for by a simple evaluative factor. The other two major factors are potency and activity.

Sensory overload The notion that persons exposed to very high levels of stimulation cannot process all this information. The overloaded state is unpleasant, leading people to reduce overload by screening out less crucial sensory inputs. Milgram has suggested that this occurs during crowding or in urban environments, but no evidence has yet supported this idea.

Sentiment relations Affective reactions, liking or disliking of an attitude object.

Shift-of-meaning Tendency for the connotations of a trait to change when placed in a different context.

Short-term crowding Type of experiment in which subjects are put in rooms of varying degrees of density for brief periods of time. These studies have found that experiencing short-term density does not generally have adverse effects on behavior or mood.

Social comparison Festinger's theory that we have a drive to evaluate ourselves, and in the absence of nonsocial means we seek out others for comparison in order to judge the suitability of our responses.

Social facilitation Tendency for people (and some kinds of animals) to perform better on simple tasks when others are present than when they are alone.

Social penetration Altman and Taylor's theory about the process by which people gradually attain closeness and intimacy with one another.

Socioemotional leader Person who concentrates on keeping the group running smoothly and happily; typically, the same person tends to promote group solidarity.

Spatial orientation Angle of orientation between persons. Sommer found that at a table same-sex friends tend to sit corner to corner, whereas opposite-sex intimate friends tend to sit side by side.

Stable cause Relatively permanent features of an external object (task difficulty), or of the internal dispositions of the actor (ability) that lead to certain behaviors.

Stimulation level Assumption that there are stable individual differences in people's preferences for varying degrees of sensory stimulation. For example, some people like to study with the radio on; others prefer silence.

Task leader Person who controls, shapes, directs, and organizes the group in carrying out a specific task; his or her influence is limited to the particular job being done.

Territoriality The idea that animals consider certain geographic places or areas as their own and defend them from intrusions. The evidence shows that territoriality occurs only for some animals and under some circumstances.

Thanatos Freud's concept of destructive, agressive energy. These self-destructive forces or death wishes, can be turned inward, resulting in self-punishment, masochism, or suicide, or outward, resulting in aggression.

Theoretical research Research designed to test hypotheses derived from a theory.

Triad Group of three persons or objects.

Trucking game Simple laboratory game developed by Deutsch and Krauss to determine how conditions such as threats and communication affect cooperation and competition. Even though the game is set up so that it is to each player's advantage to cooperate, players tend to compete when they have the option of threatening one another.

Two-step flow of information Passage of information from the media to opinion leaders who pass on the information to others.

Unilateral threat Condition in the trucking game in which one player has the option of blocking his opponent's path.

Unit relations Beliefs about the perceived connectedness of objects.

Unstable causes Transitory features, either external (luck), or internal (effort), that cause certain behaviors.

Value-expression Major function of attitudes; gratification associated with the expression of attitudes that express some aspect of a person's central values.

Zero-sum game Game in which the total of gains and losses equals zero. That is, one person's gain is another's loss. Monopoly and poker are examples of zero-sum games.

bibliography

ABEL, E. L. 1977. The relationship between cannabis and violence: A review. *Psychological Bulletin, 84,* 193–211.

ABELSON, R. P. 1959. Modes of resolution of belief dilemmas. *Conflict Resolution, 3,* 343–352.

ADAMS, J. S. 1966. Injustice in social exchange. In L. Berkowitz (ed.), *Advances in experimental social psychology.* Vol. 2. New York: Academic Press.

ADERMAN, D. Elation, depression, and helping behavior. 1972. *Journal of Personality and Social Psychology, 24,* 91–101.

AIELLO, J. R. AND AIELLO, T. 1974. The development of personal space: proxemic behavior of children 6 through 16. *Human Ecology, 2,* 177–189.

AIELLO, J. R., & COOPER, R. E. 1972. The use of personal space as a function of social affect. *Proceedings of the 80th Annual Convention of the American Psychology Association, 7,* 207–208.

AIELLO, J. R., & JONES, S. E. 1971. Field study of the proxemic behavior of young children in three subcultural groups. *Journal of Social Psychology, 19,* 351–356.

ALLEE, W. C., & MASURE, R. H. 1963. A comparison of maze behavior in paired and isolated shelf-parakeets (Melopsittacus undulatus Shaw) in a two-alley problem box. *Journal of Comparative Psychology, 22,* 131–155.

ALLEN, V. L. 1964. Uncertainty of outcome and post-decision dissonance reduction. In L. Festinger (ed.), *Conflict, decision, and dissonance.* Stanford, Calif.: Stanford.

ALLEN, V. L., & LEVIN, J. M. 1971. Social support and conformity: The role of independent assessment of reality. *Journal of Experimental Social Psychology, 7,* 48–58.

ALLGEIER, A. R., & BYRNE, D. 1973. Attraction toward the opposite sex as a determinant of physical proximity. *Journal of Social Psychology, 90,* 213–219.

ALLPORT, F. H. 1920. The influence of the group upon association and thought. *Journal of Experimental Psychology, 3,* 159–182.

ALLPORT, F. H. 1924. *Social psychology.* Boston: Riverside Editions, Houghton Mifflin.

ALTMAN, I., & HAYTHORN, W. W. 1965. Interpersonal exchange in isolation. *Sociometry, 28,* 411–426.

ALTMAN, I., & TAYLOR, D. A. 1973. *Social penetration: The development of interpersonal relationships.* New York: Holt, Rinehart & Winston.

ANDERSON, N. H. 1965. Averaging vs. adding as a stimulus-combination rule in impression formation. *Journal of Experimental Psychology, 70,* 394–400.

ANDERSON, N. H. 1966. Component ratings in impression formation. *Psychonomic Science, 6,* 279–280.

ANDERSON, N. H. 1965. Primacy effects in personality impression formation using a generalized order effect paradigm. *Journal of Personality and Social Psychology, 2,* 1–9.

ANDERSON, N. H. 1968. Application of a linear-serial model to a personality-impression task using special presentation. *Journal of Personality and Social Psychology, 10,* 354–362.

ANDERSON, N. H. 1968. Likableness ratings of 555 personality-trait words. *Journal of Personality and Social Psychology, 9,* 272–279.

ANDERSON, N. H. 1959. Test of a model for opinion change. *Journal of abnormal and social psychology, 59,* 371–381.

ANDERSON, N. H., & HUBERT, S. 1963. Effects of concomitant verbal recall on order effects in personality impression formation. *Journal of Verbal Learning and Verbal Behavior, 2,* 379–391.

APSLER, R. 1975. Effects of embarrassment on behavior toward other. *Journal of Personality and Social Psychology, 32,* 145–153.

APSLER, R., & SEARS, D. O. 1968. Warning, personal involvement, and attitude change. *Journal of Personality and Social Psychology, 9,* 162–166.

ARDREY, R. 1966. *The territorial imperative.* New York: Atheneum.

ARMSTRONG, E. A. 1965. *Bird display and behaviour: An introduction to the study of bird psychology,* 2nd ed. New York: Dover.

ARONSON, E., & CARLSMITH, J. M. 1963. The effect of the severity of threat on the devaluation of forbidden behavior. *Journal of Abnormal and Social Psychology, 66,* 584–588.

ARKIN, R. M., & DUVAL, S. 1975. Focus of attention and causal attributions of actors and observers. *Journal of Experimental Social Psychology, 11,* 427–438.

ARONSON, E. 1972. *The Social Animal.* San Francisco: W. H. Freeman.

ARONSON, E., & LINDER, D. 1965. Gain and loss of esteem as determinants of interpersonal attractiveness. *Journal of Experimental Social Psychology, 1,* 156–171.

ARONSON, E., TURNER, J., & CARLSMITH, J. M. 1963. Communicator credibility and communication discrepancy. *Journal of Abnormal and Social Psychology, 67,* 31–36.

ASCH, S. E. 1946. Forming impressions of personality. *Journal of Abnormal and Social Psychology, 41,* 258–290.

Asch, S. E. 1951. Effects of group pressure upon the modification and distortion of judgments. In H. Guetzkow (ed.), *Groups, leadership and men.* Pittsburgh, Pa.: Carnegie Press.

Ashmore, R. D. 1970. Prejudice: Causes and cures. In B. E. Collins (ed.), *Social psychology.* Reading, Mass.: Addison-Wesley.

Bandler, R. J., Madaras, G. R., & Bem, D. J. 1968. Self-observation as a source of pain perception. *Journal of Personality and Social psychology, 9,* 205–209.

Bandura, A., Ross, D., & Ross, S. 1961. Transmission of aggression through imitation of aggressive models. *Journal of Abnormal and Social Psychology, 63,* 575–582.

Bandura, A., Ross, D., & Ross, S. 1963a. Imitation of film-mediated aggressive models. *Journal of Abnormal and Social Psychology, 66,* 3–11.

Barefoot, J., & Straub, R. 1971. Opportunity for information search and the effect of false heart rate feedback. *Journal of Personality and Social Psychology, 17,* 154–157.

Barker, R. G., Dembo, T., & Lewis, K. 1941. Frustration and regression: An experiment with young children. *University of Iowa Studies in Child Welfare, 18,* No. 1.

Baron, R. A. 1971a. Aggression as a function of magnitude of victim's pain cues, level of prior anger arousal, and aggressor-victim similarity. *Journal of Personality and Social Psychology, 18*(1), 48–54.

Baron, R. A. 1974a. Aggression as a function of victim's pain cues, level of prior anger arousal, and exposure to an aggressive model. *Journal of Personality and Social Psychology, 29,* 117–124.

Baron, R. A. 1971b. Magnitude of victim's pain cues and level of prior anger arousal as determinants of adult aggressive behavior. *Journal of Personality and Social Psychology, 17,* 236–243.

Baron, R. A. 1971. Reducing the influence of an aggressive model: The restraining effects of discrepant modeling cues. *Journal of Personality and Social Psychology, 20,* 240–245.

Baron, R. A. 1972. Reducing the influence of an aggressive model: The restraining effects of peer censure. *Journal of Experimental Social Psychology, 8,* 266–275.

Baron, R. A., & Bell, P. A. 1975. Aggression and heat: Mediating effects of prior provocation and exposure to an aggressive model. *Journal of Personality and Social Psychology, 31,* 825–832.

Baron, R. A., & Bell, P. A. 1976. Aggression and heat: The influence of ambient temperature, negative affect, and a cooling drink on physical aggression. *Journal of Personality and Social Psychology, 33,* 245–255.

Baron, R. A., & Kepner, C. R. 1970. Model's behavior and attraction toward the model as determinants of adult aggressive behavior. *Journal of Personality and Social Psychology, 14,* 335–344.

Baron, R. S., Dion, K. L., Baron, P., & Miller, N. 1970. Group norms, elicited values and risk-taking. Unpublished manuscript. University of Minnesota.

BAR-TAL, D., & SAXE, L. 1976. Perceptions of similarly and dissimilarly attractive couples and individuals. *Journal of Personality and Social Psychology, 33*(6), 772–781.

BASSILI, J. N. 1976. Temporal and spatial contingencies in the perception of social events. *Journal of Personality and Social Psychology, 33*(6), 680–685.

BATESON, N. 1966. Familiarization, group discussion, and risk-taking. *Journal of Experimental Social Psychology, 2,* 119–129.

BAUM, A., & VALINS, S. 1977. *Architecture and social behavior: Psychological studies of social density.* Hillsdale, N. J.: Lawrence Erlbaum.

BAVELAS, A., HASTORF, A. H., GROSS, A. E., & KITE, W. R. 1965. Experiments on the alteration of group structure. *Journal of Experimental Social Psychology, 1,* 55–70.

BAXTER, J. C. 1970. Interpersonal spacing in natural settings. *Sociometry, 33,* 444–456.

BECKER, L. B., MCCOMBS, M. E., MCLEOD, M. M. 1975. The development of political cognitions. In S. H. Chaffee (ed.), *Political communication: Issues and strategies for research.* Beverly Hills: Stage.

BECKMAN, L. 1970. Effects of students' performance on teachers' and observers' attributions of causality. *Journal of Educational Psychology, 61,* 76–82.

BEM, D. J. 1965. An experimental analysis of self-persuasion. *Journal of Experimental Psychology, 1,* 199–218.

BEM, D. J. 1967. Self-perception: An alternative interpretation of cognitive dissonance phenomena. *Psychological Review, 74,* 183–200.

BEM, D. J. 1972. Self-perception theory. In L. Berkowitz, (ed.), *Advances in experimental social psychology,* (vol. 6). New York: Academic Press.

BEM, D. J., WALLACH, M. A., & KOGAN, N. 1965. Group decision making under risk of aversive consequences. *Journal of Personality and Social Psychology, 1,* 453–460.

BENHAM, T. W. 1965. Polling for a presidential candidate: Some observation of the 1964 campaign. *Public Opinion Quarterly, 29,* 185–199.

BERELSON, B. R., LAZARSFELD, P. F., AND MCPHEE, W. N. 1954. *Voting: A study of opinion formation in a presidential election.* Chicago: University of Chicago Press.

BERKEVIC, T., AND GLASGOW, R. 1973. Boundary conditions of false heartrate feedback effects on avoidance behavior: a resultion of discrepant results. *Behavior research and therapy, 11,* 171–177.

BERKOWITZ, L. 1954. Group standards, cohesiveness, and productivity. *Human Relations, 7,* 509–519.

BERKOWITZ, L. 1968. Responsibility, reciprocity, and social distance in help-giving: An experimental investigation of English social class differences. *Journal of Experimental Social Psychology, 4,* 46–63.

BERKOWITZ, L. 1965. Some aspects of observed aggression. *Journal of Personality and Social Psychology,* 2(3), 359–369.

BERKOWITZ, L. 1970. The contagion of violence. In W. J. Arnold and M. M.

Page (eds.), *Nebraska symposium on motivation.* Lincoln: University of Nebraska Press.

BERKOWITZ, L., & ALIOTO, J. T. 1973. The meaning of an observed event as a determinant of its aggressive consequences. *Journal of Personality and Social Psychology, 28,* 206–217.

BERKOWITZ, L., & COTTINGHAM, D. R. 1960. The interest value and relevance of fear-arousing communications. *Journal of Abnormal and Social Psychology, 60,* 37–43.

BERKOWITZ, L., & DANIELS, L. R. 1964. Responsibility and dependency. *Journal of abnormal and Social Psychology, 66,* 427–436.

BERKOWITZ, L., & GEEN, R. G. 1966. Film violence and the cue properties of available targets. *Journal of Personality and Social Psychology, 3*(5), 525–530.

BERKOWITZ, L., & GEEN, R. G. 1967. Stimulus qualities of the target of aggression. A further study. *Journal of Personality and Social Psychology, 5,* 364–368.

BERKOWITZ, L., & LEPAGE, A. 1967. Weapons as aggression-eliciting stimuli. *Journal of Personality and Social Psychology, 7,* 202–207.

BERKOWITZ, L., & RAWLINGS, E. 1963. Effects of film violence on inhibitions against subsequent aggression. *Journal of Abnormal and Social Psychology, 66*(5), 405–412.

BERMAN, J. S., & KENNY, D. A. 1976. Correlational bias in observer ratings. *Journal of Personality and Social Psychology, 34*(2), 263–273.

BERSCHEID, E., BROTHEN, T., & GRAZIANO, W. 1976. Gain-loss theory and the "Law of Infidelity": Mr. Doting versus the admiring stranger. *Journal of Personality and Social Psychology, 33*(6), 709–718.

BERSCHEID, E., DION, K., WALSTER, E., & WALSTER, G. W. 1971. Physical attractiveness and dating choice: A test of the matching hypothesis. *Journal of Experimental Social Psychology, 7,* 173–189.

BERSCHEID, E., & WALSTER, E. 1974. A little bit about love. In T. L. Huston (ed.), *Foundations of interpersonal attractive.* New York: Academic Press.

BERSCHEID, E., & WALSTER, E. 1967. When does a harm-doer compensate a victim? *Journal of Personality and Social Psychology, 6,* 435–441.

BICKMAN, L. 1971. The effect of another bystander's ability to help on bystander intervention in an emergency. *Journal of Experimental Social Psychology, 7,* 367–379.

BLACK, T. E., & HIGBEE, K. L. 1973. Effects of power, threat, and sex on exploitation. *Journal of Personality and Social Psychology, 27,* 382–388.

BLANCHARD, F. A., ADELMAN, L., & COOK, S. W. 1975. Effect of group success and failure upon interpersonal attraction in cooperating interracial groups. *Journal of Personality and Social Psychology, 31*(6), 1020–1030.

BLANCHARD, F. A., & COOK, S. W. 1976. Effects of helping a less competent member of a cooperating interracial group on the development of interpersonal attraction. *Journal of Personality and Social Psychology, 34*(6), 1245–1255.

BLANCHARD, F. A., WEIGEL, R. H., & COOK, S. W. 1975. The effect of relative competence of group members upon interpersonal attraction in cooperating interracial groups. *Journal of Personality and Social Psychology, 32*(3), 519–530.

BLANK, A. 1968. Effects of group and individual condition on choice behavior. *Journal of Personality and Social Psychology, 8,* 294–298.

BLEDA, P. R. 1974. Toward a clarification of the role of cognitive and affective processes in the similarity-attraction relationship. *Journal of Personality and Social Psychology, 29*(3), 368–373.

BOCHNER, S., INSKO, C. A. 1966. Communicator discrepancy, source credibility, and opinion change. *Journal of Personality and Social Psychology, 4,* 614–621.

BOND, M. H., & DUTTON, D. G. 1975. The effect of interaction anticipation and experience as a victim on aggressive behavior. *Journal of Personality, 43*(3).

BOOTH, A., & COWELL, J. 1974. The effects of crowding upon health. Paper presented at the American Population Association Meetings, New York.

BORING, E. G., & TITCHENER, E. B. 1923. A model for the demonstration of facial expression. *American Journal of Psychology, 34,* 471–485.

BREHM, J. W. 1966. *A theory of psychological reactance.* New York: Academic Press.

BREHM, J. W. 1956. Post-decision changes in desirability of alternatives. *Journal of Abnormal and Social Psychology, 52,* 348–389.

BREHM, J. W., & JONES, R. A. 1970. The effect on dissonance of surprise consequences. *Journal of Experimental Social Psychology, 6,* 420–431.

BREHM, J. W., & SENSENIG, J. 1966. Social influence as a function of attempted and implied usurpation of a choice. *Journal of Personality and Social Psychology, 4,* 703–707.

BRICKMAN, P., MEYER, P., & FREDD, S. 1975. Effects of varying exposure to another person with familiar or unfamiliar thought processes. *Journal of Experimental Social Psychology, 11,* 261–270.

BROADBENT, D. E. 1957. Effects of noise on behavior. In. C. M. Harris (ed.), *Handbook of noise control.* New York: McGraw-Hill.

BROCK, T. C., & BALLOUN, J. L. 1967. Behavioral receptivity to dissonant information. *Journal of Personality and Social Psychology, 6,* 413–428.

BROCK, T. C., & BECKER, L. A. 1965. Ineffectiveness of "overheard" counterpropaganda. *Journal of Personality and Social Psychology, 2,* 654–660.

BROCKNER, J., & SWAP, W. C. 1976. Effects of repeated exposure and attitudinal similarity on self-disclosure and interpersonal attraction. *Journal of Personality and Social Psychology, 33*(5), 531–540.

BROPHY, I. N. 1946. The luxury of anti-Negro prejudice. *Public Opinion Quarterly, 9,* 456–466.

BRUNER, J. S., SHAPIRO, D., & TAGIURI, R. 1958. The meaning of traits in isolation and in combination. In R. Tagiuri and L. Petrullo (eds.), *Person perception and interpersonal behavior.* Stanford, Calif.: Stanford.

BRUNER, J. S., & TAGIURI, R. 1954. The perception of people. In G. Lindzey (ed.), *Handbook of social psychology,* Vol. 2. Reading, Mass.: Addison-Wesley.

BRYAN, J. H., & TEXT, N. A. 1967. Models and helping: Naturalistic studies in aiding behavior. *Journal of Personality and Social Psychology, 6,* 400–407.

BURNSTEIN, E. 1967. Sources of cognitive bias in the representation of simple social structures: Balance, minimal change, positivity, reciprocity, and the respondent's own attitude. *Journal of Personality and Social Psychology, 7,* 36–48.

BURNSTEIN, E., & VINOKUR, A. 1973. Testing two classes of theories about group induced shifts in individual choice. *Journal of Experimental Social Psychology, 9,* 123–137.

BURNSTEIN, E., & VINOKUR, A. 1975. What a person thinks upon learning he has chosen differently from others: Nice evidence for the persuasive-arguments explanation of choice shifts. *Journal of Experimental Social Psychology, 11,* 412–426.

BUSS, A. H. 1961. *The psychology of aggression.* New York: John Wiley & Sons.

BUSS, A. H., BOOKER, A., & BUSS, E. 1972. Firing a weapon and aggression. *Journal of Personality and Social Psychology, 22,* 296–302.

BYRNE, D. 1961. Interpersonal attraction and attitude similarity. *Journal of Abnormal and Social Psychology, 62,* 713–715.

BYRNE, D., ERVIN, C. R., & LAMBERTH, J. 1970. Continuity between the experimental study attraction and real-life computer dating. *Journal of Personality and Social Psychology, 16*(1), 157–165.

BYRNE, E., & NELSON, D. 1964. Attraction as a function of attitude similarity-dissimilarity: The effect of topic importance. *Psychonomic Science, 1,* 93–94.

BYRNE, D., & WOND, T. J. 1962. Racial prejudice, interpersonal attraction and assumed dissimilarity of attitudes. *Journal of Abnormal and Social Psychology, 65,* 246–253.

CALHOUN, J. B. 1962. Population density and social pathology. *Scientific American, 206,* 139–148.

CAMPBELL, ANGUS. 1971. *White attitudes toward black people.* Ann Arbor: Institute for Social Research.

CAMPBELL, A., CONVERSE, P. E., MILLER, W. E., & STOKES, D. E. 1960. *The American voter.* New York: John Wiley & Sons.

CAMPBELL, D. T., & STANLEY, J. C. 1963. *Experimental and quasi-experimental designs for research.* Chicago: Rand McNally.

CARLSMITH, J. M., COLLINS, B. E., & HELMREICH, R. L. 1966. Studies in foreced compliance: I. The effect of pressure for compliance on attitude change produced by face-to-face role-playing and anonymous essay writing. *Journal of Personality and Social Psychology, 4,* 1–13.

CARLSMITH, J. M., ELLSWORTH, P., & WHITESIDE, J. 1969. Guilt, confession and compliance. Unpublished manuscript, Stanford University.

CARLSMITH, J. M., & FREEDMAN, J. L. 1968. Bad decisions and dissonance:

Nobody's perfect. In R. Abelson et al. (eds.), *Theories of cognitive consistency.* Chicago: Rand McNally.

CARLSMITH, J. M., & GROSS, A. E. 1969. Some effects of guilt on compliance. *Journal of Personality and Social Psychology, 11,* 232–239.

CARLSMITH, J. M., LEPPER, M., & LANDAUER, T. K. 1969. Two processes in children's obedience to adult requests. Unpublished manuscript, Stanford University.

CARVER, C. S. 1974. Facilitation of physical aggression through objective self-awareness. *Journal of Experimental Social Psychology, 10,* 365–370.

CARTER, D., & STRICKLAND, D. 1975. *TV violence and the child.* New York: Russell Sage.

CHAIKIN, A. L., & DARLEY, J. M. 1973. Victim or perpetrator?: Defensive attribution of responsibility and the need for order and justice. *Journal of Personality and Social Psychology, 25*(2), 268–275.

CHAIKIN, A. L., & DERLEGA, V. J. 1974. Liking for the norm-breaker in self-disclosure. *Journal of Personality, 42*(1), 112–129.

CHAPMAN, A. J. 1973. Social facilitation of laughter in children. *Journal of Experimental Social Psychology, 9,* 528–541.

CHEN, S. C. 1937. Social modification of the activity of ants in nest-building. *Physiological Zoology, 10,* 420–436.

CHRISTIAN, J. J. 1968. Endocrine adaptive mechanisms and the physiologic regulation of population growth. In Mayer and Van Gelder (eds.), *Physiological mammology.* New York: Academic Press.

CHRISTIAN, J. J. 1950. The adreno-pituitary system and population cycles in mammals. *Journal of Mammology, 31,* 247–259.

CHRISTIAN, J. J., GLYGER, V., & DAVIS, D. 1960. Factors in the mass mortality of a herd of sika deer *carvus nippon. Chesapeake Science, 1,* 79–95.

CIALDINI, R. B., BRAVER, S. L., & LEWIS, S. K. 1974. Attributional bias and the easily persuaded other. *Journal of Personality and Social Psychology, 30*(5), 631–637.

CIALDINI, R. B., LEVY, A., HERMAN, P., & EVENBECK, S. 1973. Attitudinal politics: The strategy of moderation. *Journal of Personality and Social Psychology, 25,* 100–108.

CIALDINI, R. B., VINCENT, J. E., LEWIS, S. K., CATALAN, J., WHEELER, D., & DARBY, B. L. 1975. Reciprocal concessions procedure for inducing compliance: The door-in-the-face technique. *Journal of Personality and Social Psychology, 31,* 206–215.

CITRIN, J. 1974. Comment: The political relevance of trust in government. *The American Political Science Review, 68*(3), 973–988.

CLARK, R. D., III, & WORD, L. E. 1971. A case where the bystander did help. Paper presented at the meeting of the Eastern Psychological Association, New York.

CLARK, R. D., III, & WORD, L. E. 1974. Where is the apathetic bystander?

Situational characteristics of the emergency. *Journal of Personality and Social Psychology, 29*, 279–287.

CLINE, V. B. 1964. Interpersonal perception. In B. A. Maher (ed.), *Progress in experimental personality research.* Vol. 1. New York: Academic Press.

CLORE, G. L., WIGGINS, N., & ITKIN, S. 1975. Gain and loss in attraction: Attributions from nonverbal behavior. *Journal of Personality and Social Psychology, 31*(4), 706–712.

COHEN, S., GLASS, D. C., & SINGER, J. E. 1973. Apartment noise, auditory discrimination, and reading ability in children. *Journal of Experimental Social Psychology, 9*, 407–422.

COHEN, D., WHITMYRE, J. W., & FUNK, W. H. 1960. Effect of group cohesiveness and training upon creative thinking. *Journal of Applied Psychology, 44*, 319–322.

COLEMAN, J. F., BLAKE, R. R., & MOUTON, J. S. 1958. Task difficulty and conformity pressures. *Journal of Abnormal and Social Psychology, 57*, 120–122.

COLLINS, B. E., & HOYT, M. F. 1972. Personal responsibility-for-consequences: An integration and extension of the "forced compliance" literature. *Journal of Experimental Social Psychology, 8*, 558–593.

COMSTOCK, G., CHRISTEN, F. G., FISHER, M. L., QUARLES, R. C., & RICHARDS, W. D. 1975. *Television and human behavior: The key studies.* Santa Monica: Rand Corporation.

CONVERSE, P. E. 1964. The nature of belief systems in mass publics. In D. E. Apter (ed.), *Ideology and Discontent.* New York: Free Press of Glencoe.

COOK, S. W. 1970. Motives in a conceptual analysis of attitude-related behavior. *Nebraska Symposium on Motivation, 18*, 179–231.

COOPER, J. 1971. Personal responsibility and dissonance: The role of foreseen consequences. *Journal of Personality and Social Psychology, 18*, 354–363.

COOPER, J., & BREHM, J. W. 1971. Prechoise awareness of relative deprivation as a determinant of cognitive dissonance. *Journal of Experimental Social Psychology, 7*, 571–581.

COOPER, J., DARLEY, J. M., & HENDERSON, J. E. 1974. On the effectiveness of deviant- and conventional-appearing communicators: A field experiment. *Journal of Personality and Social Psychology, 29*(6), 752–757.

COOPER, J., & GOETHALS, G. R. 1974. Unforeseen events and the elimination of cognitive dissonance. *Journal of personality and social psychology. 29*, 441–445.

COOPER, J., & JONES, R. A. 1970. Self-esteem and consistency as determinants of anticipatory opinion change. *Journal of Personality and Social Psychology, 14*, 312–320.

COTTRELL, N. B. 1975. Heider's structural balance principle as a conceptual rule. *Journal of Personality and Social Psychology, 31*(4), 713–720.

COTTRELL, N. B., RITTLE, R. H., & WACK, D. L. 1967. Presence of an audience and list type (competitional or noncompetitional) as joint determinants of performance in paired-associates learning. *Journal of Personality, 35*, 425–434.

COXBY, P. C. 1973. Self-disclosure: A literature review. *Psychological Bulletin, 79*(2), 73–91.

CRANO, W. D. 1970. Effects of sex, response order and expertise in conformity: A dispositional approach. *Sociometry, 33,* 239–252.

CRANO, W. D., & COOPER, R. E. 1973. Examination of Newcomb's extension of structural balance theory. *Journal of Personality and Social Psychology, 27*(3), 344–353.

CROCKETT, W. H. 1974. Balance, agreement, and subjective evaluations of the P-O-X triads. *Journal of Personality and Social Psychology, 29*(1), 102–110.

CRONER, M.D., & WILLIS, R. H. 1961. Perceived differences in task competence and symmetry of dyadic influence. *Journal of Abnormal and Social Psychology, 62,* 705–708.

CURRAN, J. P., & LIPPOLD, S. 1975. The effects of physical attraction and attitude similarity on attraction in dating dyads. *Journal of Personality, 44*(3), 528–539.

DABBS, J. M., JR., & LEVENTHAL, H. 1966. Effects of varying the recommendations in a fear-arousing communication. *Journal of Personality and Social Psychology, 4*(5), 525–531.

DAHER, D. M., & BANIKIOTES, P. G. 1976. Interpersonal attraction and rewarding aspects of disclosure content and level. *Journal of Personality and Social Psychology, 33*(4), 492–496.

DASHIELL, J. F. 1930. An experimental analysis of some group effects. *Journal of Abnormal and Social Psychology, 25,* 190–199.

DAVIS, J. D. 1976. Self-disclosure in an acquaintance exercise: Responsibility for level of intimacy. *Journal of Personality and Social Psychology, 33*(6), 787–792.

DAVITZ, J. R., (ED.) 1964. *The communication of emotional meaning.* New York: McGraw-Hill.

DEAN, R. B., AUSTIN, J. A., & WATTS, W. A. 1971. Forewarning effects in persuasion: Field and classroom experiments. *Journal of Personality and Social Psychology, 18,* 210–221.

DESOTO, C. B., & KEUTHE, J. L. 1959. Subjective probabilities of interpersonal relationships. *Journal of Abnormal and Social Psychology, 95*(2).

DEUTSCH, M. 1960. The effect of motivational orientation upon trust and suspicion. *Human Relations, 13,* 122–139.

DEUTSCH, M., & COLLINS, M. E. 1951. *Interracial housing: A psychological evaluation of a social experiment.* Minneapolis: University of Minnesota Press.

DEUTSCH, M., & GERARD, H. B. 1955. A study of normative and informational social influences upon individual judgment. *Journal of Abnormal and Social Psychology, 51,* 629–636.

DEUTSCH, M., & KRAUSS, R. M. 1960. The effect of threat on interpersonal bargaining. *Journal of Abnormal and Social Psychology, 61,* 181–189.

DIENSTBIER, R. A., & MUNTER, P. O. 1971. Cheating as a function of labeling of natural arousal. *Journal of Personality and Social Psychology, 17,* 208–213.

DION, K. K. 1972. Physical attractiveness and evaluations of children's transgressions. *Journal of Personality and Social Psychology, 24,* 285–290.

DION, K., BARON, R. S., & MILLER, N. 1970. Why do groups make riskier decisions than individuals? In L. Berkowitz (ed.), *Advances in experimental social psychology,* Vol. 5. New York: Academic Press.

DION, K., BERSCHEID, E., & WALTER, E. 1972. What is beautiful is good. *Journal of Personality and Social Psychology, 24*(3), 285–290.

DITTES, J. E. 1959. Effect of changes in self-esteem upon impulsiveness and deliberation in making judgements. *Journal of Abnormal and Social Psychology, 58,* 348–356.

DOHRENWEND, B. P., & DOHRENWEND, B. S. 1974. Social and cultural influences on psychopathology. *Annual Review of Psychology, 25,* 417–452.

DOLLARD, J., DOOB, J., MILLER, N., MOWRER, O., & SEARS, R. 1939. *Frustration and aggression.* New Haven, Conn.: Yale University Press.

DONNERSTEIN, E., & DONNERSTEIN, M. 1975. The effect of attitudinal similarity on interracial aggression. *Journal of Personality, 43*(3), 485–502.

DONNERSTEIN, E., & DONNERSTEIN, M. 1973. Variables in interracial aggression: Potential ingroup censure. *Journal of Personality and Social Psychology, 27,* 143–150.

DONNERSTEIN, E., & DONNERSTEIN, M. 1972b. White rewarding behavior as a function of the potential for black retaliation. *Journal of Personality and Social Psychology, 24*(3), 327–333.

DONNERSTEIN, E., DONNERSTEIN, M., SIMMONS, S., & DITRICHS, R. 1972a. Variables in interracial aggression: Anonymity, expected retaliation, and a riot. *Journal of Personality and Social Psychology, 22,* 236–245.

DOOB, A. N., & CLIMIE, R. J. 1972. Delay of measurement and the effects of film violence. *Journal of Experimental Social Psychology, 8,* 136–142.

DOOB, A. N., & WOOD, L. 1972. Catharsis and aggression: The effects of annoyance and retaliation on aggressive behavior. *Journal of Personality and Social Psychology, 22,* 156–162.

DOOB, L. 1947. The behavior of attitudes. *Psychological Review, 54,* 135–156.

DORFMAN, D. D., KEEVE, S., & SASLOW, C. 1971. Ethnic identification: A signal detection analysis. *Journal of Personality and Social Psychology, 18,* 373–379.

DORNBUSCH, S. M., HASTORF, A. H., RICHARDSON, S. A., MUZZY, R. E., & VREELAND, R. S. 1965. The perceiver and the perceived: Their relative influence on the categories of interpersonal cognition. *Journal of Personality and Social Psychology, 1,* 434–440.

DRISCOLL, R., DAVIS, K. E., & LIPETZ, M. E. 1972. Parental interference and romatic love: The Romeo & Juliet effect. *Journal of Personality and Social Psychology, 24,* 1–10.

DUVAL, S., & WICKLUND, R. A. 1972. *A theory of objective self-awareness.* New York Academic Press.

EAGLY, A. H., & CHAIKEN, S. 1975. An attribution analysis of the effect of communicator characteristics on opinion change: The case of communicator attractiveness. *Journal of Personality and Social Psychology, 32*(1), 136–144.

EAGLY, A. H., & TELAAK, K. 1972. Width of the latitude of acceptance as a determinant of attitude change. *Journal of Personality and Social Psychology, 23,* 388–397.

EBBESEN, E. B., & BOWERS, R. J. 1974. Proportion of risky to conservative arguments in a group discussion and choice shift. *Journal of Personality and Social Psychology, 29,* 316–327.

EBBESEN, E. B., DUNCAN, B., & KONECNI, V. J. 1975. Effects of content of verbal aggression on future verbal aggression: a field experiment. *Journal of experimental social psychology, 11,* 192–204.

EHRLICH, D., GUTTMAN, I., SCHONBACH, P., & MILLS, J. 1957. Post-decision exposure to relevant information. *Journal of Abnormal and Social Psychology, 54,* 98–102.

EKMAN, P., & FRIESEN, W. V. 1971. Constants across cultures in the face and emotion. *Journal of Personality and Social Psychology, 17,* 124–129.

EKMAN, P., & FRIESEN, W. V. 1974. Detecting deception from body or face. *Journal of Personality and Social Psychology, 29,* 288–298.

EKMAN, P., FRIESEN, W. V., & SCHERER, K. *(in press.)* Body movements and voice pitch in deceptive interaction. *Semiotica.*

EKMAN, P., SORENSON, E. R., & FRIESEN, W. V. 1969. Pan-cultural elements in facial displays of emotions. *Science, 164,* 86–88.

ELLSWORTH, P., & CARLSMITH, J. M. 1973. Eye contact and gaze aversion in an aggressive encounter. *Journal of Personality and Social Psychology, 28,* 280–292.

ELLSWORTH, P., CARLSMITH, J. M., & HENSON, A. 1972. The stare as a stimulus to flight in human subjects: A series of field experiments. *Journal of Personality and Social Psychology, 21,* 302–311.

ESSER, J. K., & KOMORITA, S. S. 1975. Reciprocity and concession making in bargaining. *Journal of Personality and Social Psychology, 31,* 864–872.

ETTINGER, R. F., MARINO, C. J., ENDLER, N. S., GELLER, S. H., & NATZIUK, T. 1971. Effects of agreement and correctness on relative competence and conformity. *Journal of Personality and Social Psychology, 19,* 204–212.

EVANS, R. I., ROZELLE, R. M., LASATER, T. M., DEMBROSKI, T. M., & ALLEN, B. P. 1970. Fear arousal, persuasion, and actual versus implied behavioral change: New perspective utilizing a real-life dental hygiene program. *Journal of personality and Social Psychology, 16,* 220–227.

FELDMAN, N. S., HIGGINS, E. T., KARLOVAC, M., & RUBLE, D. N. 1976. Use of consensus information in causal attributions as a function of temporal presentation and availability of direct information. *Journal of Personality and Social Psychology, 34*(4), 694–698.

FELIPE, N. J., & SOMMER, R. 1966. Invasions of personal space. *Social Problems, 14,* 206–214.

FESHBACH, S. 1970. Aggression. In Musser (ed.), *Carmichael's manual of child psychology,* Vol. 2. New York: John Wiley & Sons.

FESHBACH, S. 1972. Reality and fantasy in filmed violence. In. J. P. Murray, E. A. Rubinstein, and G. A. Comstock (eds.), *Television and social behavior,* Vol. 2. Washington, D.C.: Government Printing Office.

FESHBACH, S. 1955. The drive-reducing function of fantasy behavior. *Journal of Abnormal and Social Psychology, 50,* 3–12.

FESHBACH, S. 1961. The stimulating versus cathartic effects of a vicarious aggressive activity. *Journal of Abnormal and Social Psychology, 63,* 381–385.

FESHBACH, S., & SINGER, R. D. 1970. *Television and aggression.* San Francisco: Jossey-Bass.

FESTINGER, L. 1954. A theory of social comparison processes. *Human Relations,* 7, 117–140.

FESTINGER, L., & CARLSMITH, J. 1959. Cognitive consequences of forced compliance. *Journal of Abnormal and Social Psychology, 58,* 203–210.

FESTINGER, L., & MACCOBY, N. 1964. On resistance to persuasive communications. *Journal of Abnormal and Social Psychology, 68,* 359–366.

FESTINGER, L., RIECKEN, H. W., & SCHACHTER, S. 1956. *When prophecy fails.* Minneapolis: University of Minnesota Press.

FESTINGER, L., SCHACTER, S., & BACK, K. 1950. *Social pressures in informal groups: A study of human factors in housing.* New York: Harper & Row.

FIEDLER, F. 1958. *Leader attributes and group effectiveness.* Urbana: University of Illinois Press.

FIEDLER, F. 1971. *Leadership.* New York: General Learning Press.

FILTER, T. A., & GROSS, A. E. 1975. Effects of public and private deviancy on compliance with a request. *Journal of Experimental Social Psychology, 11,* 553–559.

FINKELMAN, J. M., & GLASS, D. C. 1970. Reappraisal of the relationship between noise and human performance by means of a subsidiary task measure. *Journal of Applied Psychology, 54,* 211–213.

FIRESTONE, I. J., KALMAN, J. K., & RUSSEL, J C. 1973. Anxiety, read, and affiliation with similar-state versus dissimilar-state others: Misery sometimes loves nonmiserable company. *Journal of Personality and Social Psychology, 26,* 409–414.

FISCHER, C. S. 1976. *The urban experience.* New York: Harcourt Brace.

FISHBEIN, M., & HUNTER, R. 1964. Summation versus balance in attitude organization and change. *Journal of Abnormal and Social Psychology, 69,* 505–510.

FISHER, J. D., & BYRNE, D. 1975. Too close for comfort: Sex differences in response to invasions of personal space. *Journal of Personality and Social Psychology, 32,* 15–21.

FISHER, S., & LUBIN, A. 1958. Distance as a determinant of influence in a two-person serial interaction situation. *Journal of Abnormal and Social Psychology, 56,* 230–238.

FLANDERS, J. P., & THISTLEWAITE, D. L. 1967. Effects of familiarization and group discussion upon risk-taking. *Journal of Personality and Social Psychology,* 5, 91–97.

FOLKES, V. S., & SEARS, D. O. 1977. Are likers liked best? *Journal of Experimental Social Psychology,* 13.

FONTAINE, G. 1975. Causal attribution in simulated versus real situations: When are people logical, when are they not? *Journal of Personality and Social Psychology, 32*(6), 1021–1029.

FRAGER, R. 1970. Conformity and anticonformity in Japan. *Journal of Personality and Social Psychology, 15,* 203–210.

FRASER, C., GOUGE, C., & BILLIG, M. 1971. Risky shifts, cautious shifts, and group polarization. *European Journal of Social Psychology, 1,* 7–30.

FREEDMAN, J. L. 1963. Attitudinal effects of inadequate justification. *Journal of Personality, 31,* 371–385.

FREEDMAN, J. L. 1975. *Crowding and behavior.* New York: Viking Press.

FREEDMAN, J. L. 1964. Involvement, discrepancy, and change. *Journal of Abnormal and Social Psychology, 64,* 290–295.

FREEDMAN, J. L. 1965. Lone-term behavioral effects of cognitive dissonance. *Journal of Experimental Social Psychology, 1,* 145–155.

FREEDMAN, J. L. 1965. Preference for dissonance information. *Journal of Personality and Social Psychology, 2,* 287–289.

FREEDMAN, J. L., & DOOB, A. N. 1968. *Deviancy.* New York: Academic Press.

FREEDMAN, J. L., & FRASER, S. C. 1966. Compliance without pressure: The foot-in-the-door technique. *Journal of Personality and Social Psychology, 4,* 195–202.

FREEDMAN, J. L., HESHKA, S., & LEVY, A. 1975. Population density and pathology: Is there a relationship? *Journal of Experimental Social Psychology, 11,* 539–552.

FREEDMAN, J. L., KLEVANSKY, S., & EHRLICH, P. 1971. The effect of crowding on human task performance. *Journal of Applied Social Psychology, 1,* 7–25.

FREEDMAN, J. L., LEVY, A. S., BUCHANAN, R. W., & PRICE, J. 1972. Crowding and human aggressiveness. *Journal of Experimental Social Psychology, 8,* 528–548.

FREEDMAN, J. L., & SEARS, D. O. 1965. Warning, distraction and resistance to influence. *Journal of Personality and Social Psychology, 1,* 262–265.

FREEDMAN, J. L., & STEINBRUNER, J. D. 1964. Perceived choice and resistance to persuasion. *Journal of Abnormal and Social Psychology,* 68, 678–68.

FREEDMAN, J. L., WALLINGTON, S., & BLESS, E. 1967. Compliance without pressure: The effect of guilt. *Journal of Pesonality and Social Psychology, 7*, 117–124.

FRENCH, J. R. P., JR. 1944. Organized and unorganized groups under fear and frustration. *University of Iowa studies: Studies in child welfare.* Iowa City: University of Iowa.

FRIEDLAND, N., ARNOLD, S. E., & THIBAUT, J. 1974. Motivational bases in mixed-motive interactions: The effects of comparison levels. *Journal of Experimental Social Psychology, 10*, 188–199.

FRIEDMAN, H. 1976. Effects of self-esteem and expected duration of interaction on liking for a highly rewarding partner. *Journal of Personality and Social Psychology, 33*(6), 686–690.

FRIEDRICH, L. K., & STEIN, A. H. 1973. Aggressive and prosocial television programs and the natural behavior of preschool children. *Monographs of the Society for Research in Child Development, 38*(4, Serial No. 151).

FRIEZE, I., & WEINER, B. 1973. Cue utilization and attributional judgments for success and failure. *Journal of Personality.*

GAGE, N. L. 1952. Judging interests from expressive behavior. *Psychology Monographs, 66* (18, Whole No. 350).

GALLE, O. R., GOVE, W. R., & MCPHERSON, J. M. 1972. Population density and pathology: What are the relations for man. *Science, 176*, 23–30.

GALLO, P. S. 1966. Effects of increased incentives upon the use of threat in bargaining. *Journal of Personality and Social Psychology, 4*, 14–20.

GALLO, P. S., & SHEPOSH, J. 1971. Effects of incentive magnitude on cooperation in the prisoner's dilemma game: A reply to Gumpert, Deutsch, and Epstein. *Journal of Personality and Social Psychology, 19*, 42–46.

GATES, M. F., & ALLEE, W. C. 1933. Conditioned behavior of isolated and grouped cockroaches on a simple maze. *Journal of Comparative Psychology, 15*, 331–358.

GEEN, R. G., & O'NEAL, E. C. 1969. Activation of cue-elicited aggression by general arousal. *Journal of Personality and Social Psychology, 11*, 289–292.

GEEN, R. G., & PIGG, R. 1970. Acquisition of an aggressive response and its generalization to verbal behavior. *Journal of Personality and Social Psychology, 15*, 165–170.

GEEN, R. G., STONNER, D., & SHOPE, G. L. 1975. The facilitation of aggression by aggression: Evidence against the catharsis hypothesis. *Journal of Personality and Social Psychology, 31*, 721–726.

GERARD, H. B. 1963. Emotional uncertainty and social comparison. *Journal of Abnormal and Social Psychology, 66*, 568–573.

GERARD, H. B., CONOLLEY, E. S., & WILHELMY, R. A. Compliance, justification, and cognitive change. In L. Berkowitz (ed.), *Advances in experimental social psychology.* New York: Academic Press.

GERARD, H. B., & RABBIE, J. M. 1961. Fear and social comparison. *Journal of Abnormal and Social Psychology, 62*, 586–592.

GERARD, H. B., WILHELMY, R. A., & CONNOLLEY, E. S. 1968. Conformity and group size. *Journal of Personality and Social Psychology, 8,* 79–82.

GERGEN, K. J., ELLSWORTH, P., MUSLACH, C. & SEIPEL, M. 1975. Obligation, donor resources, and reactions to aid in three cultures. *Journal of Personality and Social Psychology, 31,* 390–400.

GIBB, C. 1969. Leadership. In G. Lindzay and E. Aronson (eds.), *Handbook of social psychology,* 2nd edition, Vol. 4. Reading, Mass.: Addison-Wesley.

GINTER, G., & LINDSKOLD, S. 1975. Rate of participation and expertise as factors influencing leader choice. *Journal of Personality and Social Psychology, 32,* 1085–1089.

GLASS, D. C., & SINGER, J. E. 1972. *Urban stress.* New York: Academic Press.

GOLDSTEIN, J. H., DAVIS, R. W., & HERMAN, D. 1975. Escalation of aggression: Experimental studies. *Journal of Personality and Social Psychology, 31*(1), 162–170.

GORANSON, R. E., & BERKOWITZ, L. 1966. Reciprocity and responsibility reactions to prior help. *Journal of Personality and Social Psychology, 3,* 227–232.

GORANSON, R. E., & KING, D. 1977. Rioting and daily temperature: Analysis of the U.S. riots in 1967. Unpublished manuscript, York University, Toronto, 1970. Cited in R. A. Bacon and D. Byrne, *Social psychology,* 2nd edition. Boston: Allyn-Bacon.

GRABER, D. A. 1976. Press and TV as opinion resources in presidential campaigns. *Public Opinion Quarterly, 40* (Fall), 285–303.

GRAMZA, A. F. 1967. Responses of brooding nighthawks to a disturbance stimulus. *Auk, 84*(1), 72–86.

GRANBERG, D., & BRENT, E. E., JR. 1974. Dove-Hawk placements in the 1968 election: Application of social judgment and balance theories. *Journal of Personality and Social Psychology, 29*(5), 687–695.

GREELEY, A. M., & SHEATSLEY, P. B. 1971. Attitudes toward racial integration. *Scientific American, 223,* 13–19.

GREENBERG, M. S., & FRISCH, D. M. 1972. Effect of intentionality on willingness to reciprocate a favor. *Journal of Experimental Social Psychology, 8,* 99–111.

GREENWALD, A. G. 1975. On the inconclusiveness of "crucial" cognitive tests of dissonance versus self-perception theories. *Journal of Experimental Social Psychology. 11,* 490–499.

GREENWALD, A. G., & SAKUMURA, J. S. 1967. Attitude and selective learning: Where are the phenomena of yesteryear? *Journal of Personality and Social Psychology, 7,* 387–397.

GRIFFIT, W., & VEITCH, R. 1971. Hot and crowded: Influences of population density and temperature on interpersonal affective behavior. *Journal of Personality and Social Psychology, 17,* 92–98.

GRUSEC, J. E., & SKUBISKI, S. 1970. Model nurturance, demand characteristics of the modeling experiment and altruism. *Journal of Personality and Social Psychology, 14,* 353–359.

GUETZKOW, H., & SIMON, H. A. 1955. The impact of certain communication nets upon organization and performance in task-oriented groups. *Management Science, 1,* 233–250.

GUILFORD, J. P. 1929. An experiment in learning to read facial expression. *Journal of Abnormal and Social Psychology, 24,* 191–202.

GUMPERT, P., DEUTSCH, M., & EPSTEIN, Y. 1969. Effect of incentive magnitude on cooperation in the prisoner's dilemma game. *Journal of Personality and Social Psychology, 11,* 66–69.

GURWITZ, S. B., PANCIERA, L. 1975. Attributions of freedom by actors and observers. *Journal of Personality and Social Psychology, 32*(3), 531–539.

GUYER, M., & RAPOPORT, A. 1970. Threat in a two-person game. *Journal of Experimental Social Psychology, 6,* 11–25.

HAEFNER, D. P. October 7, 1964. The use of fear arousal in dental health education. Paper presented at the meeting of the American Public Health Association.

HALL, E. T. 1966. *The hidden dimension.* Garden City, N.Y.: Doubleday.

HALL, E. T. 1959. *The silent language.* Garden City, N.Y.: Doubleday.

HALL, K. R. L. 1960. Social vigilance behaviour of the chacma baboon. Papio ursinus. *Behaviour, 16*(3, 4), 261–294.

HAMILTON, D. L., & FALLOT, R. D. 1974. Information salience as a weighting factor in impression formation. *Journal of Personality and Social Psychology, 30*(4), 444–448.

HAMILTON, D. L., & HUFFMAN, L. J. 1971. Generality of impression-formation processes for evaluation and nonevaluation judgments. *Journal of Personality and Social Psychology, 20,* 200–207.

HAMILTON, D. L., ZANNA, M. P. 1974. Context effects in impression formation: Changes in connotative meaning. *Journal of Personality and Social Psychology, 29*(5), 649–654.

HAMILTON, D. L., & ZANNA, M. P. 1972. Differential weighting favorable and unfavorable attributes in impressions of personality. *Journal of Experimental Research in Personality, 6,* 204–212.

HANSEN, R. D., & DONOGHUE, J. M. 1977. The power of consensus: information derived from one's own and others' behavior. *Journal of Personality and Social Psychology, 35,* 294–302.

HARDING, J., & HOGREFE, R. 1952. Attitudes of white department store employees toward Negro co-workers. *Journal of Social Issues, 8,* 18–28.

HARRIS, V. A., & JELLISON, J. M.1971. Fear-arousing communications, false physiological feedback, and the acceptance of recommendations. *Journal of Experimental Social Psychology, 7,* 269–279.

HARTMAN, D. P. 1969. Influence of symbolically modeled instrumental aggression and pain cues on aggressive behavior. *Journal of Personality and Social Psychology, 11*(3), 280–288.

HARTNETT, J. J., BAILEY, K. G., & GIBSON, F. W., JR. 1970. Personal space as influenced by sex and type of movement. *Journal of Psychology, 76,* 139–144.

HARVEY, J. H., & SMITH, W. P. 1977. *Social psychology—An attributional approach.* St. Louis: C. V. Mosby.

HEBERLEIN, T. A., & BLACK, J. S. 1976. Attitudinal specificty and the prediction of behavior in a field setting. *Journal of Personality and Social Psychology, 33*(4), 474–479.

HEIDER, F. 1958. *The psychology of interpersonal relations.* New York: Wiley.

HEIDER, F., & SIMMEL, M. 1944. An experimental study of apparent behavior. *American Journal of Psychology, 57,* 243–259.

HENCHY, T., & GLASS, D. C. 1968. Evaluation apprehension and the social facilitation of dominant and subordinate responses. *Journal of Personality and Social Psychology, 10,* 446–454.

HIGBEE, K. L. 1969. Fifteen years of fear arousal: Research on threat appeals 1953–1968. *Psychological Bulletin, 72,* 426–444.

HIMMELFARB, S., & ARAZI, D. 1974. Choice and source attractiveness in exposure to discrepant messages. *Journal of Experimental Social Psychology, 10,* 516–527.

HODGES, B.H. 1974. Effect of valence on relative weighting in impression formation. *Journal of Personality and Social Psychology, 39*(3), 378–381.

HOFFMAN, L. R., & MAIER, N. R. F. 1961. Quality and acceptance of problem solutions by members of homogeneous and heterogeneous groups. *Journal of Abnormal and Social Psychology, 62,* 401–407.

HOKANSON, J. E. 1961. Vascular and psychogalvanic effects of experimentally aroused anger. *Journal of Personality, 29,* 30–39.

HOKANSON, J. E., & BURGESS, M. 1962. The effects of three types of aggression on vascular processes. *Journal of Abnormal and Social Psychology, 64,* 446–449.

HOLMES, D. S. 1972. Aggression, displacement and guilt. *Journal of Personality and Social Psychology, 21,* 296–301.

HOMANS, G.C. 1965. Group factors in worker productivity. In H. Proshansky and L. Seidenberg (eds.), *Basic studies in social psychology.* New York: Holt.

HOMANS, G. C. 1961. *Social behavior: Its elementary forms.* New York: Harcourt Brace.

HOPKINS, J. R. Sexual behavior in adolescence. *Journal of Social Issues,* 1977, *33*(2).

HOROWITZ, M. J., DUFF, D. F., & STRATTON, L. O. 1970. Personal space and the body buffer zone. In H. Proshansky, W. Ittelson, & L. Rivlin (eds.), *Environmental psychology: Man and his physical setting.* New York: Holt, Rinehart & Winston.

HOVLAND, C. I. 1959. Reconciling conflicting results derived from experimental and survey studies of attitude change. *American Psychologist, 14,* 8–17.

HOVLAND, C. I., HARVEY, O. J., & SHERIF, M. 1957. Assimilation and contrast effects in reactions to communication and attitude change. *Journal of Abnormal and Social Psychology, 55,* 224–252.

Hovland, C. I. & Janis, I. L. (eds.) 1953. *Personality and persuasibility.* New Haven: Yale University Press.

Hovland, C. I., Lumsdaine, A. A., & Sheffield, F. D. 1949. *Experiments on mass communication.* Princeton: Princeton University Press.

Hovland, C. I., & Pritzker, H. A. 1957. Extent of opinion change as a function of amount of change advocated. *Journal of Abnormal and Social Psychology, 54,* 257–261.

Hovland, C. I., & Sears, R. R. 1940. Minor studies in aggression: VI. Correlation of lynchings with econommic indices. *Journal of Personality, 9,* 301–310.

Hovland, C. I., & Weiss, W. 1952. The influence of course credibility on communication effectiveness. *Public Opinion Quarterly, 15,* 635–650.

Hunt, P. J., & Hillery, J. M. 1972. Social facilitation at different stages in learning. Paper read at the Midwestern Psychological Association Meetings, Cleveland, Ohio.

Husband, R. W. 1940. Cooperative versus solitary problem solution. *Journal of Social Psychology, 11,* 405–409.

Isen, A. M. 1970. Success, failure, attention, and reaction to others: The warm glow of success. *Journal of Personality and Social Psychology, 15,* 294–301.

Isen, A. M., Horn, N., & Rosenhan, D. L. 1973. Effects of success and failure on children's generosity. *Journal of Personality and Social Psychology, 27,* 239–247.

Isen, A. M., & Levin, P. F. 1972. Effect of feeling good on helping: Cookies and kindness. *Journal of Personality and Social Psychology, 21,* 384–388.

Insko, C. A., Arkoff, A., & Insko, V. M. 1965. Effects of high and low fear arousing communications upon opinions toward smoking. *Journal of Experimental Social Psychology, 1,* 256–266.

Insko, C. A., Blake, R. R., & Cialdini, R. B. 1970. Attitude toward birth control and cognitive consistency: Theoretical and practical implications of survey data. *Journal of Personality and Social Psychology, 16,* 228–237.

Jacobs, J. 1962. *Death and life of great American cities.* London: Cape.

Jahoda, M., & West, P. 1951. Race relations in public housing. *Journal of Social Issues, 7,* 132–139.

Janis, I. L., & Feshbach, S. 1953. Effects of fear-arousing communications. *Journal of Abnormal and Social Psychology, 48,* 78–92.

Janis, I. L., Kaye, D., & Kirschner, P. 1965. Facilitating effects of "eating-while-reading" on responsiveness to persuasive communications. *Journal of Personality and Social Psychology, 1,* 181–186.

Janis, I. L., & Mann, L. 1965. Effectiveness of emotional role-playing in modifying smoking habits and attitudes. *Journal of Experimental Research in Personality, 1,* 84–90.

Janis, I. L., & Rausch, C. N. 1970. Selective interest in communications that could arouse decisional conflict: A field study of participants in the draft-resistance movement. *Journal of Personality and Social Psychology, 14,* 46–54.

JANIS, I. L., & TERWILLIGER, R. F. 1962. An experimental study of psychological resistances to fear-arousing communications. *Journal of Abnormal and Social Psychology, 65,* 403–410.

JECKER, J. D. 1964. The cognitive effects of conflict and dissonance. In L. Festinger (ed.), *Conflict, decision and dissonance.* Stanford, Calif.: Stanford.

JENNINGS, M. K., & NIEMI, R. G. 1974. *The political character of adolescence.* Princeton: Princeton University Press.

JOHNSON, P. B., SEARS, D. O., & MCCONAHAY, J. B. 1971. Black invisibility, the press, and the Los Angeles riot. *American Journal of Sociology, 76*(4), 698–721.

JOHNSON, T. J., FEIGENBAUM, R., & WEIBY M. 1964. Some determinants and consequences of the teacher's perception of causation. *Journal of Educational Psychology, 55,* 237–246.

JONES, E. E. 1964. *Ingratiation.* New York: Appleton-Century-Crofts.

JONES, E. E., & DAVIS, K. E. 1965. From acts to dispositions. In L. Berkowitz (ed.), *Advances in experimental sociopsychology* (Vol. 2), New York: Academic Press.

JONES, E. E., & HARRIS, V. A. 1967. The attribution of attitudes. *Journal of Experimental Social Psychology, 3,* 1–24.

JONES, E. E., & NISBETT, R. E. 1972. The actor and the observer: Divergent perceptions of the causes of behavior. *Attribution: Perceiving the causes of behavior.* Morristown, N. J.: General Learning Press.

JONES, E. E., WORCHEL, S., GOETHALS, G. R., & GRUMET, J. F. 1971. Prior expectancy and behavioral extremity as determinants of attitude attribution. *Journal of Experimental Social Psychology, 7,* 59–80.

JONES, R. A., & BREHM, J. W. 1967. Attitudinal effects of communicator attractiveness when one chooses to listen. *Journal of Personality and Social Psychology, 6,* 64–70.

JONES, S. C. 1973. Self and interpersonal evaluations: Esteem theories versus consistency theories. *Psychological Bulletin, 79,* 185–199.

JONES, S. E., & AIELLO, J. R. 1973. Proxemic behavior of black and white first-, third-, and fifth-grade children. *Journal of Personality and Social Psychology, 25,* 21–27.

JOURARD, S. M., & FRIEDMAN, R. 1970. Experimenter-subject "distance" and self-disclosure. *Journal of Personality and Social Psychology, 15*(3), 278–282.

JULIAN, J. W., REGULA, C. R., & HOLLANDER, E. P. 1967. *Effects of prior agreement from others on task confidence and conformity.* Technical Report 9, ONR Contract 4679. Buffalo, N. Y.: State University of New York.

JULIAN, J. W., RYCKMAN, R. M., AND HOLLANDER, E. P. 1966. *Effects of prior group support on conformity: An extension.* Technical Report 4, ONR Contract 4679. Buffalo, N.Y.: State University of New York.

KAHNEMAN, D., & TVERSKY, A. 1973. On the psychology of prediction. *Psychological Review, 80,* 237–251.

KANDEL, D. 1974. Inter- and intragenerational influences on adolescent marijuana use. *Journal of Social Issues, 30*(2), 107–135.

KAPLAN, K. J., FIRESTONE, I. J., DEGNORE, R., & MORRE, M. 1974. Gradients of attraction as a function of disclosure probe intimacy and setting formality: On distinguishing attitude oscillation from attitude change—Study One. *Journal of Personality and Social Psychology, 30*(5), 638–646.

KAPLAN, M. F. 1971. Context effects in impression formation: The weighted average versus the meaning-change formulation. *Journal of Personality and Social Psychology, 19,* 92–99.

KAPLAN, R., & SINGER, J. E. 1976. Violence and viewer aggression: A reexamination of the evidence. *Journal of Social Issues, 32*(4), 35–70.

KARAZ, V., & PERLMAN, D. 1975. Attribution at the wire: Consistency and outcome finish strong. *Journal of Experimental Social Psychology, 11,* 470–477.

KATZ, D. 1960. The functional approach to the study of attitudes. *Public Opinion Quarterly, 24,* 163–204.

KATZ, D., SARNOFF, I., & MCCLINTOCK, C. G. 1956. Ego-defense and attitude change. *Human Relations, 9,* 27–46.

KELLEY, H. H. 1972. Attribution in social interaction. *Attribution: Perceiving the causes of behavior.* Morristown, N.J.: General Learning Press.

KELLEY, H. H. 1967. Attribution theory in social psychology. In D. Levine (ed.), *Nebraska Symposium on Motivation.* Lincoln: University of Nebraska Press.

KELLEY, H. H. 1950. The warm-cold variable in the first impressions of persons. *Journal of Personality, 18,* 431–439.

KELLEY, H. H., CONDRY, J. C., DAHLKE, A. E., & HILL, A. H. 1965. Collective behavior in stimulated panic situation. *Journal of Experimental Social Psychology, 1,* 20–54.

KELLEY, H. H. SHURE, G. H., DEUTSCH, M., FAUCHEUZ, C., LANZETTA, J. T., MOSCOVICI, S., NUTTIN, J. M., RABBIE, J. M., & THIBAUT, J. W. 1970. A comparative experimental study of negotiation behavior. *Journal of Personality and Social Psychology, 16,* 411–438.

KELLEY, H. H., & STAHELSKI, A. J. 1970. Errors in perception of intentions in a mixed-motive game. *Journal of Experimental Social Psychology, 6,* 379–400.

KELLEY, H. H., & VOLKART, E. H. 1952. The resistance to change of group-anchored attitudes. *American Sociological Review, 17,* 453–456.

KELLEY, H.H., & WOODRUFF, C. 1956. Members' reactions to apparent group approval of a counter-norm communication. *Journal of Abnormal and Social Psychology, 52,* 67–74.

KELLEY, S., JR., & MIRER, T. W. 1974. The simple act of voting. *The American Political Science Review, 68*(2), 572–591.

KELLOGG, R. & BARON, R. S. 1975. Attribution theory, insomnia, and the reverse placebo effect: a reversal of Storms and Nisbett's finding. *Journal of Personality and Social Psychology, 32,* 231–236.

KELMAN, H. C. 1961. Process of opinion change. *Public Opinion Quarterly*, *25*, 57–78.

KENDON, A. 1967. Some functions of gaze-direction in social interaction. *Acta Psychologica*, *26*, 22–63.

KEPHART, W. M. 1957. *Racial factors and urban law enforcement*. Philadelphia: University of Pennsylvania Press.

KERCKHOFF, A. C., & DAVIS, K. E. 1962. Value consensus and need complementarity in mate selection. *American Sociological Review*, *26*, 295–303.

KINDER, D. R. 1975. Balance theory and political person perception: asymmetry in beliefs about political leaders. Unpublished doctoral dissertation, University of California, Los Angeles.

KINGDON, J. W. 1967. Politicians' beliefs about voters. *The American Political Science Review*, *61*(1), 137–145.

KLECK, R. E., & RUBENSTEIN, C. 1975. Physical attractiveness, perceived attitude similarity, and interpersonal attraction in an opposite-sex encounter. *Journal of Personality and Social Psychology*, *31*(1), 107–114.

KLEINHESSELINK, R. R., & EDWARDS, R. E. 1975. Seeking and avoiding belief-discrepant information as a function of its perceived refutability. *Journal of Personality and Social Psychology*, *31*(5), 787–790.

KLOPFER, P. H. 1958. Influence of social interaction on learning rates in birds. *Science*, *128*, 903–904.

KNOX, P. D., LASATER, L., & SHUMAN, R. 1974. Aggression-guilt and conditionability for aggressiveness. *Journal of Personality*, *42*(2), 332–344.

KNOZ, R. E., & DOUGLAS, R. L. 1971. Trivial incentives, marginal comprehension, and dubious generalization from prisoner's dilemma studies. *Journal of Personality and Social Psychology*, *20*, 160–165.

KOENIG, K. 1973. False emotional feedback and the modification of anxiety. *Behavior Therapy*, *4*, 193–202.

KOFFKA, K. 1935. *Principles of gestalt psychology*. New York: Harcourt Brace Jovanovich.

KOGAN, N., & CARLSON, J. 1968. Group risk-taking under competitive and noncompetitive conditions in adults and children. *Journal of Education Psychology*, *60*, 158–167.

KOGAN, N., & DOISE, W. 1969. Effects of anticipated delegate status on level of risk-taking in small decision-making groups. *Acta Psychologica*, *29*, 228–243.

KOGAN, N., & WALLACH, M. A. 1967. Risk taking as a function of the situation, the person, and the group. In G. Mandler (ed.), *New directions in psychology*, Vol. III. New York: Holt.

KONECNI, V. J.. 1972. Some effects of guilt on compliance: A field replication. *Journal of Personality and Social Psychology*, *23*, 30–32.

KONECNI, V. J., & DOOB, A. N. 1972. Catharsis through displacement of aggression. *Journal of Personality and Social Psychology*, *23*, 379–387.

KONECNI, V. J., & EBBESEN, E. B. 1976. Disinhibition versus the cathartic effect: Artifact and substance. *Journal of Personality and Social Psychology, 34,* 352–365.

KONECNI, V. J., LIBUSER, L., MORTON, H., & EBBESEN, E. B. 1975. Effects of a violation of personal space on escape and helping responses. *Journal of Experimental Social Psychology, 11,* 288–299.

KRAUSS, R. M., GELLER, V., & OLSON, C. September, 1976. Modalities and cues in the detection of deception. Paper presented at American Psychology Association meetings.

KRAUS, S., & DAVIS, D. 1976. *The effects of mass communication on political behavior.* University Park, Penn.: Pennsylvania State University Press.

KRAUT, R. E. 1973. Effects of social labelling on giving to charity. *Journal of Experimental Social Psychology, 9,* 551–562.

KREBS, D., & ADINOLFI, A. A. 1975. Physical attractiveness, social relations, and personality style. *Journal of Personality and Social Psychology, 31*(2), 245–253.

KRECH, D., CRUTCHFIELD, R. S., & BALLACHEY, E. L. 1962. *Individual in society.* New York: McGraw-Hill.

KEUTHE, J. L. & WEINGARTNER, N. 1964. Male-female schemata of homosexual and nonhomosexual penitentiary inmates. *Journal of Personality, 32,* 23–31.

LAMM, H., & KOGAN, N. 1970. Risk-taking in the context of intergroup negotiation. *Journal of Experimental Social Psychology, 6,* 351–363.

LANDY, D. 1972. The effects of an overheard audience's reaction and attractiveness on opinion change. *Journal of Experimental Social Psychology, 8,* 276–288.

LANDY D., & ARONSON, E. 1969. The influence of the character of the criminal and his victim on the decisions of simulated jurors. *Journal of Experimental Social Psychology, 5,* 141–152.

LANDY, D., & SIGALL, H. 1974. Beauty is talent: Task evaluation as a function of the performer's physical attractiveness. *Journal of Personality and Social Psychology, 29*(3), 299–304.

LANE, I. M., & MESSÉ, L. A. 1972. Distribution of insufficient, sufficient, and over-sufficient rewards: A clarification of equity theory. *Journal of Personality and Social Psychology, 21,* 228–233.

LANGFIELD, H. S. 1918. The judgment of emotions from facial expressions. *Journal of Abnormal and Social Psychology, 13,* 162–184.

LAPIERE, R. T. 1934. Attitudes versus actions. *Social Forces, 13,* 230–237.

LARSSON, R. 1956. *Conditioning and sexual behavior in the male albino rat.* Stockholm: Almqvist & Wiksell.

LATANÉ, B., & DARLEY, J. M. 1968. Group inhibition of bystander intervention in emergencies. *Journal of Personality and Social Psychology, 10,* 215–221.

LATANÉ, B., & RODIN, J. 1969. A lady in distress: Inhibiting effects of friends and strangers on bystander intervention. *Journal of Experimental and Social Psychology, 5,* 189–202.

LAWRENCE, D. G. 1976. Procedural norms and tolerance: A reassessment. *The American Political Science Review, 70*(1), 80–100.

LAZARSFELD, P. F., BERELSON, B., & GAUDET, H. 1948. *The People's Choice,* 2nd ed. New York: Columbia University Press.

LEAK, G. K. 1974. Effects of hostility arousal and aggressive humor on catharsis and humor preference. *Journal of Personality and Social Psychology, 30,* 736–740.

LEAVITT, H. J. 1951. Some effects of certain communication patterns on group performance. *Journal of Abnormal and Social Psychology, 46,* 38–50.

LEPPER, M. R. 1970. Anxiety and experimenter valence as determinants of social reinforcer effectiveness. *Journal of Personality and Social Psychology, 16,* 704–709.

LERNER, M. J. 1965a. The effect of responsibility and choice on a partner's attractiveness following failure. *Journal of Personality, 33,* 178–187.

LERNER, M. J. 1974. The justice motive; "equity" and "parity" among children. *Journal of Personality and Social Psychology, 29,* 539–550.

LERNER, M. J., & MATTHEWS, G. 1967. Reactions to the suffering of others under conditions of indirect responsibility. *Journal of Personality and Social Psychology, 5,* 319–325.

LEVENTHAL, G. S., & ANDERSON, D. 1970. Self-interest and the maintenance of equity. *Journal of Personality and Social Psychology, 15,* 57–62.

LEVENTHAL, G. S., & LANE, D. W. 1970. Sex, age and equity behavior. *Journal of Personality and Social Psychology, 15,* 312–316.

LEVENTHAL, G. S., MICHAELS, J. W., & SRANFORD, G. 1972. Inequity and interpersonal conflict: Reward allocation and secrecy about reward as methods of preventing conflict, *Journal of Personality and Social Psychology, 23,* 88–102.

LEVENTHAL, H., JONES, S., & TREMBLY, G. 1966. Sex differences in attitude and behavior change under conditions of fear and specific instructions. *Journal of Experimental and Social Psychology, 2*(4), 387–399.

LEVENTHAL, H., & SINGER, R. P. 1966. Affect arousal and positioning of recommendations in persuasive communication. *Journal of Personality and Social Psychology, 4,* 137–146.

LEVINGER, G., & SCHNEIDER, D. J. 1969. Test of the "Risk is a value" hypothesis. *Journal of Personality and Social Psychology, 11,* 165–170.

LEWIN, K., LIPPITT, R., & WHITE, R. K. 1939. Patterns of aggressive behavior in experimentally created social climates. *Journal of Social Psychology, 10,* 271–299.

LEYENS, J. P., CAMINO, L., PARKE, R. D., & BERKOWITZ, L. 1975. Effects of movie violence on aggression in a field setting as a function of group dominance and cohesion. *Journal of Personality and Social Psychology.*

LIEBMAN, M. 1970. The effects of sex and race norms on personal space. *Environment and Behavior, 2,* 208–246.

LINDER, D. E., COOPER, J., & JONES, E. E. 1967. Decision freedom as a determinant of the role of incentive magnitude in attitude change. *Journal of Personality and Social Psychology, 6*(3), 245–254.

LIPPIT, R., & WHITE, R. K. 1943. The "social climate" of children's groups. In. R. G. Barker, J. S. Kounin, and H. F. Wright (eds.), *Child behavior and development.* New York: McGraw-Hill.

LITTLE, K. B. 1968. Cultural variations in social schemata. *Journal of Personality and Social Psychology, 10,* 1–7.

LONG, G. T., & LERNER, M. J. 1974. Deserving, the "personal contract", and altruistic behavior by children. *Journal of Personality and Social Psychology, 29,* 551–556.

LOO, C. M. 1972. The effects of spatial density on the social behavior of children. *Journal of Applied Social Psychology, 2,* 372–381.

LORENZ, K. Z. 1952. *King Solomon's Ring.* London: Methuen.

LOTT, D. F., & SOMMER, R. 1967. Seating arrangements and status. *Journal of Personality and Social Psychology, 7,* 90–95.

LUGINBUHL, J. E. R., & CROWE, D. H. 1975. Causal attributions for success and failure. *Journal of Personality and Social Psychology, 31*(1), 86–93.

MCARTHUR, L. A. 1972. The how and what of why: Some determinants and consequences of causal attribution. *Journal of Personality and Social Psychology, 22,* 171–193.

MCARTHUR, L. A. 1976. The lesser influence of consensus than distinctiveness information on causal attributions: A test of the person-thing hypothesis. *Journal of Personality and Social Psychology, 33*(6), 733–742.

MACDONALD, R. A. P., JR. 1970. Anxiety, affiliation and social isolation. *Developmental Psychology, 3,* 242–254.

MCGUIRE, W. J. & PAPGEORGIS, D. 1961. The relative efficacy of various types of prior belief-defense in producing immunity against persuasion. *Journal of Abnormal and Social Psychology, 62,* 327–337.

MACKENZIE, B. K. 1948. The importance of contact in determining attitudes toward Negroes. *Journal of Abnormal and Social Psychology, 43,* 417–441.

MCNEEL, S. P. 1973. Training cooperation in the prisoner's dilemma. *Journal of Experimental Social Psychology, 9,* 335–348.

MADARAS, G. R., & BEN, D. J. 1968. Risk and conservatism in group decision making. *Journal of Experimental Social Psychology, 4,* 350–366.

MALOF, M., & LOTT, A. J. 1962. Ethnocentrism and the acceptance of Negro support in a group pressure situation. *Journal of Abnormal and Social Psychology, 65,* 254–258.

MANN, L., & JANIS, I. L. 1968. A follow-up study on the longterm effects of emotional role-playing, *Journal of Personality and Social Psychology, 8,* 339–342.

MARQUIS, D. G. 1962. Individual responsibility and group decisions involving risk. *Industrial Management Review, 3,* 8–23.

MARSHALL, J. E., & HESLIN, R. 1975. Boys and girls together: Sexual group composition and the effect of density and group size on cohesiveness. *Journal of Personality and Social Psychology, 3,* 952–961.

MARTENS, R. 1969. Effect of an audience on learning and performance of a complex motor skill. *Journal of Personality and Social Psychology, 12,* 252–260.

MAUSNER, B. 1954. The effect of prior reinforcement on the interaction of observer pairs. *Journal of Abnormal Social Psychology, 49,* 65–68.

MAUSNER, B. 1954. The effect of one's partner success in a relevant task on the interaction of observer's pairs. *Journal of Abnormal and Social Psychology, 49,* 557–560.

MAYKOVICH, M. K. 1975. Correlates of racial prejudice. *Journal of Personality and Social Psychology, 32*(6), 1014–1020.

MENDELSOHN, H., & CRESPI, I. 1970. *Polls, television, and the new politics.* Scranton, Penn: Chandler Publications.

MEREI, F. 1949. Group leadership and institutionalization. *Human Relations, 2,* 23–29.

METTEE, D. R. 1971. Changes in liking as a function of the magnitude and effect of sequential evaluations. *Journal of Experimental Social Psychology, 7,* 157–172.

METTE, D. R. 1971. The true discerner as a potent source of positive affect. *Journal of Experimental Social Psychology,* 7, 292–303.

MEYER, T. P. 1972. The effects of sexually arousing and violent films on aggressive behavior. *Journal of Sex Research, 8,* 324–333.

MICHAELSON, W. 1977. *Environmental Choice, Human Behavior, and Residential Satisfaction.* New York: Oxford University Press.

MICHENER, H. A., & BURT, M. R. 1975. Use of social influence under varying conditions of legitimacy. *Journal of Personality and Social Psychology, 32,* 398–407.

MIDDLETON, R. 1976. Regional differences in prejudice. *American Sociological Review, 41,* 94–117.

MILGRAM, S. 1963. Behavioral study of obedience. *Journal of Abnormal and Social Psychology, 67,* 371–378.

MILGRAM, S. 1961. Nationality and conformity. *Scientific American, 205*(5) , 45–51.

MILGRAM, S. 1965. Some conditions of obedience and disobedience to authority. *Human Relations, 18,* 57–76.

MILGRAM, S. 1970. The experience of living in cities. *Science, 167,* 1461–1468.

MILGRAM, S., BICKMAN, L., & BERKOWITZ, L. 1969. Note on the drawing power of crowds of different size. *Journal of Personality and Social Psychology, 13,* 79–82.

MILGRAM, S., & SHOTLAND, R. L. 1973. *Television and antisocial behavior: Field experiments.* New York: Academic Press.

MILLER, A. G. 1975. Actor and observer perceptions of the learning of a task. *Journal of Experimental Social Psychology, 11*, 95–111.

MILLER, A. G. 1976. Constraint and target effects in the attribution of attitudes. *Journal of Experimental Social Psychology, 12*(4), 325–339.

MILLER, A. H. 1974. Political issues and trust in government: 1964–1970. *The American Political Science Review, 68*(3), 951–972.

MILLER, A. H., ERBRING, L., & GOLDENBERG. 1976. *Type-set politics: Impact of newspapers on issue salience and public confidence.* Prepared for delivery at the 1976 Annual Meeting of the American Political Science Association, Chicago, Illinois, September.

MILLER, A. H., MILLER, W. E. BROWN, T. A. & RAINE, A. S., 1976. A majority party in disarray: Policy polarization in the 1972 election. *The Amercian Political Science Review, 70*(3), 753–778.

MILLER, D. T., & ROSS, M. 1975. Self-serving biases in the attribution of causality: Fact or fiction? *Psychological Bulletin, 82*(2), 213–225.

MILLER, R. L. 1976. Mere exposure, psychological reactance and attitude change. *Public Opinion Quarterly, 40*(2), 229–233.

MILLS, J., & ARONSON, E. 1965. Opinion change as a function of communicator's attractiveness and desire to influence. *Journal of Personality and Social Psychology, 1*, 173–177.

MILLS, J., & HARVEY, J. 1972. Opinion change as a function of when information about the communicator is received and whether he is attractive or expert. *Journal of Personality and Social Psychology, 21*, 52–55.

MILLS, J., & JELLISON, J. M. 1967. Effect on opinion change of how desirable the communication is to the audience the communicator addressed. *Journal of Personality and Social Psychology, 6*, 98–101.

MILLS, J., & MINTZ, P. M. 1972. Effect of unexplained arousal on affiliation. *Journal of Personality and Social Psychology, 24*, 11–13.

MINAS, J. S., SCODEL, A., MARLOWE, D., & RAWSON, H. 1960. Some descriptive aspects of two-person non-zero-sum games, II. *Journal of Conflict Resolution, 4*, 193–197.

MINTZ, A. 1946. A re-examination of correlations between lynchings and economic indices. *Journal of Abnormal and Social Psychology, 41*, 154–160.

MINTZ, A. 1951. Non-adaptive group behavior. *Journal of Abnormal and Social Psychology, 46*, 150–159.

MITCHELL, R. E. 1971. Some social implications of high density housing. *American Sociological Review, 36*, 18–29.

MORIARTY, T. 1975. Crime, commitment, and the responsive bystander: Two field experiments. *Journal of Personality and Social Psychology, 31*, 370–376.

MORRIS, W. N. & MILLER, R. S. 1975. The effects of consensus-breaking and consensus-preempting partners on reduction in conformity. *Journal of Experimental Social Psychology, 11*, 215–223.

MORSE, S. J., GRUZEN, J., & REIS, H. 1976. The "eye of the beholder": A neglected variable in the study of physical attractiveness? *Journal of Personality, 44*(2), 209–225.

MOSCOVICI, S., & ZAVALLONI, M. 1969. The group as a polarizer of attitudes. *Journal of Personality and Social Psychology, 12,* 125–135.

MULDER, M., & STEMERDING, A. 1963. Threat, attraction to group and need for strong leadership. *Human Relations, 16,* 317–334.

MUNN, N. L. 1940. The effect of knowledge of the situation upon judgment of emotion from facial expressions. *Journal of Abnormal and Social Psychology, 35,* 324–338.

MURRAY, H. A. 1933. The effect of fear upon estimates of the maliciousness of other personalities. *Journal of Social Psychology, 4,* 310–329.

MURSTEIN, B. I. 1972. Physical attractiveness and marital choice. *Journal of Personality and Social Psychology, 22*(1), 8–12.

NEUMAN, W. R. 1976. Patterns of recall among television news viewers. *Public Opinion Quarterly,* Spring, 115–123.

NEWCOMB, T. M. 1968. Interpersonal Balance. In Abelson, R. P. et. al. (eds.), *Theories of Cognitive Consistency: A Sourcebook,* Chicago: Rand, McNally.

NEWCOMB, T. M. 1943. *Personality and social change.* New York: Holt.

NEWCOMB, T. M. 1961. *The acquaintance process.* New York: Holt.

NEWCOMB, T. M., KOENIG, K. E., FLACKS, R., & WARWICK, D. P. 1967. *Persistence and change: Bennington College and its students after 25 years.* New York: John Wiley & Sons.

NEWMAN, O. 1973. *Defensible space.* New York: Macmillan.

NEWTSON, D., & CZERLINSKY, T. 1974. Adjustment of attitude communications for contrasts by extreme audiences. *Journal of Personality and Social Psychology, 30*(6), 829–837.

NICHOLLS, J. G. 1975. Causal attributions and other achievement-related cognitions: Effects of task outcome attainment value, and sex. *Journal of Personality and Social Psychology, 31*(3), 379–389.

NICKEL, T. W. 1974. The attribution of intention as a critical factor in the relation between frustration and aggression. *Journal of Personality, 42*(3), 482–492.

NIE, N. H., & ANDERSEN, K. 1974. Mass belief systems revisited: Political change and attitude structure. *Journal of Politics, 36,* 540–587.

NIE, N. H., VERBA, S., & PETROCIK. 1976. *The changing American voter.* Cambridge: Harvard University Press.

NIEMI, RICHARD, G. 1974. *The Politics of Future Citizens.* San Francisco: Jossey-Bass.

NISBETT, R. E. 1973. Behavior as seen by the actor and as seen by the observer. *Journal of Personality and Social Psychology, 27*(2), 154–164.

NISBETT, R. E., & BORGIDA, E. 1975. Attribution and the psychology of prediction. *Journal of Personality and social psychology, 32,* 932–943.

NISBETT, R. E., BORGIDA, E., CRANDALL, R., & REED, H. 1976. Popular induction: Information is not necessarily informative. In J. S. Carroll and J. W. Payne (eds.), *Cognition and social behavior*, Hillsdale, N. J.: Lawrence Erlbaum.

NISBETT, R. E., CAPUTO, C., LEGANT, P., & MARECEK, J. 1973. Behavior as seen by the actor and as seen by the observer. *Journal of Personality and Social Psychology, 27*, 154–164.

NISBETT, R. E., & SCHACHTER, S. 1966. Cognitive manipulation of pain. *Journal of Experimental Social Psychology, 2*, 227–236.

NISBETT, R. E., & VALIN, S. 1972. Perceiving the causes of one's own behavior. *Attribution: Perceiving the causes of behavior*. Morristown, N. J.: General Learning Press.

NORDHOY, F. 1962. Group interaction in decision-making under risk. Unpublished master's thesis, School of Industrial Management, Massachusetts Institute of Technology.

NORMAN, R. 1975. Affective-cognitive consistency, attitudes, conformity, and behavior. *Journal of Personality and Social Psychology, 32*(1), 83–91.

NORMAN, R. 1976. When what is said is important: A comparison of expert and attractive sources. *Journal of Experimental Social Psychology, 12*(3), 294–300.

OSBORN, A. F. 1957. *Applied imagination*. New York: Scribner.

OSGOOD, C. E., SUCI, G. J., & TANNENBAUM, P. S. 1957. *The measurement of meaning*. Urbana: University of Illinois Press.

OSGOOD, C. E., & TANNENBAUM, P. H. 1955. The principle of congruity in the prediction of attitude change. *Psychology Review, 62*, 42–55.

OSKAMP, S., & KLEINKE, C. 1970. Amount of reward as a variable in the prisoner's dilemma game. *Journal of Personality and Social Psychology, 16*, 133–140.

OSTERHOUSE, R. A., BROCK, T. C. 1970. Distraction increases yielding to propaganda in inhibiting counterarguing. *Journal of Personality and Social Psychology, 15*, 344–358.

OSTROM, T. M. 1967. Meaning shift in the judgment of compound stimuli. Unpublished manuscript, Ohio State University.

PAGE, B. I., & WOLFINGER, R. E. 1970. Party identification. In R. E. Wolfinger, (Ed.), *Readings in American political behavior, 2nd Edition*. Englewood Cliffs: Prentice-Hall.

PAGE, M. M., & SCHEIDT, R. J. 1971. The elusive weapon effect: Demand awareness, evaluation apprehension, and slightly sophisticated subjects. *Journal of Personality and Social Psychology, 20*, 304–318.

PALLAK, M. S. 1970. Effects of expected shock and relevant or irrelevant dissonance on incidental retention. *Journal of Personality and social Psychology, 14*, 271–280.

PALLAK, M. S., & PITTMAN, T. S. 1972. General motivational effects of dissonance arousal. *Journal of Personality and Social Psychology, 21*, 349–358.

PALLAK, M. S., SOGIN, S. R., & VAN ZANTE, A. 1974. Bad decisions: Effect of volition, locus of causality, and negative consequences on attitude change. *Journal of Personality and Social Psychology, 30*(2), 217–227.

PATTERSON, M. L., & SECHREST, L. B. 1970. Interpersonal distance and impression formation. *Journal of Personality, 38,* 161–166.

PATTERSON, T. E., & MCCLURE, R. D. 1976. *The unseeing eye.* New York: G. P. Putnam's Sons.

PAULUS, P. B., ANNIS, A. B., SETA, J. J., SCHKADE, J. K., & MATTHEWS, R. W. 1976. Density does affect task performance. *Journal of Personality and Social Psychology, 34,* 248–253.

PAULUS, P. B., & MURDOCH, P. 1971. Anticipated evaluation and audience presence in the enhancement of dominant responses. *Journal of Experimental Social Psychology, 7,* 280–291.

PERLMAN, D., & OSKAMP, S. 1971. The effects of picture content and exposure frequency on evaluations of negroes and whites. *Journal of Experimental Social Psychology, 7,* 503–514.

PESSIN, J. 1933. The comparative effects of social and mechanical stimulation on memorizing. *American Journal of Psychology, 45,* 263–270.

PICEK, J. S., SHERMAN, S. J., & SHIFFRIN, R. M. 1975. Cognitive organization and coding of social structures. *Journal of Personality and Social Psychology, 31,* 758–768.

PILIAVIN, I. M., ROBIN, J., & PILIAVAN, J. A. 1959. Good Samaritanism: An underground phenomenon? *Journal of Personality and Social Psychology, 13,* 289–299.

PILKONIS, P. A., & ZANNA, M. P. 1969. The choice-shift phenomenon in groups. Replication and extension. Unpublished manuscript, Yale University.

PITTMAN, T. S. 1975. Attribution of arousal as a mediator in dissonance reduction. *Journal of experimental social psychology, 11,* 53–63.

PLINER, P., HEATHER, H., KOHL, J., & SAARI, D. 1974. Compliance without pressure: Some further data on the foot-in-the-door technique. *Journal of Experimental Social Psychology, 10,* 17–22.

PRESSMAN, I., & CAROL, A. 1969. Crime as a diseconomy of scale. Talk delivered at the Operations Research Society of America Convention.

PRICE, J. 1971. The effects of crowding on the social behavior of children. Unpublished dissertation, Columbia University.

RABOW, J., FOWLER, F. J., JR., BRADFORD, D. L., HOFELLER, M. A., & SHIBUYA, Y. 1966. The role of social norms and leadership in risk-taking. *Sociometry, 29,* 16027.

RAVEN, B. H., & FRENCH, J. R. P., JR. 1958. Group support, legitimate power, and social influence. *Journal of Personality, 26,* 400–409.

REGAN, D. T. 1971. Effects of a favor and liking on compliance. *Journal of Experimental Social Psychology, 7,* 627–639.

REGAN, D. T., & TOTTEN, J. 1975. Empathy and attribution: Turning observers into actors. *Journal of Personality and Social Psychology, 32*(5), 850–856.

REGAN, D. T., WILLIAMS, M., & SPARLING, S. 1972. Voluntary expiation of guilt: A field experiment. *Journal of Personality and Social Psychology, 24,* 42–45.

REGULA, R. C., & JULIAN, J. W. 1973. The impact of quality and frequency of task contributions on perceived ability. *Journal of Social Psychology, 89,* 115–122.

RHINE, R. J., & SEVERANCE, L. J. 1970. Ego-involvement, discrepancy, source credibility, and attitude change. *Journal of Personality and Social Psychology, 16,* 175–190.

RIECKEN, H. W. 1958. The effect of talkativeness on ability to influence group solutions of problems. *Sociometry, 21,* 309–321.

RIEMER, B. S. 1974. Influence of causal beliefs on affect and expectancy. *Journal of Personality and Social Psychology, 31*(6), 1163–1167.

RIM, Y. 1964. Interpersonal values and risk-taking. Paper presented at the First International Congress of Psychiatry, London.

RIM, Y. 1963. Risk-taking and need for achievement. *Acta Psychologica, 21,* 108–115.

ROBINSON, J. P. 1970. Public reaction to political protest: Chicago, 1968. *Public Opinion Quarterly, 34*(1), 1–9.

ROBINSON, J. P. 1972. Mass communication and information diffusion. In F. Gerald Kline and Phillip J. Tichenor (Eds.), *Current Perspectives in Mass Communication Research,* Beverly Hills: Sage.

ROBINSON, J. P. 1971. The audience for national TV news programs. *Public Opinion Quarterly, 35*(3), 403–405.

ROBINSON, M. J. 1976. Public affairs television and the growth of political malaise: The case of "the selling of the pentagon." *The American Political Science Review, 70*(2), 409–432.

ROCHA, R. F., & ROGERS, R. W. 1976. Ares and Babbitt in the classroom: Effects of competition and reward on children's aggression. *Journal of Personality and Social Psychology, 33*(5), 588–593.

ROGERS, R. W., & THISTLEWAITE, D. L. 1970. Effects of fear arousal and reassurance on attitude change. *Journal of Personality and Social Psychology, 15,* 227–233.

ROHE, W. AND PATTERSON, A. 1974, The effects of varied levels of resources and density on behavior in a day care center. In D. Carson (ed.) *EDRA V,* 161–171.

ROKEACH, M., & MEZEI, L. 1966. Race and shared belief as factors in social choice. *Science, 151,* 167–172.

ROSENBERG, M. J. 1960. Cognitive reorganization in response to the hypnotic reversal of attitudinal affect. *Journal of Personality, 28,* 39–63.

ROSENBERG, S., NELSON, C., & VIVEKANANTHAN, P. S. 1968. A multidimensional approach to the structure of personality impressions. *Journal of Personality and Social Psychology, 9*(4), 283–294.

ROSENTHAL, R. 1966. *Experimenter effects in behavioral research.* New York: Appleton-Century-Crofts.

ROSS, A. S. 1971. Effect of increased responsibility on bystander intervention: The presence of children. *Journal of Personality and Social Psychology, 19,* 306–310.

ROSS, L. 1977. The intuitive psychologist and his shortcomings: Distortions in the attribution process. In L. Berkowitz (ed.), *Advances in Experimental Social Psychology,* in press.

ROSS, L., BIERBRAUER, & POLLY, S. 1974. Atribution of educational outcomes by professional and nonprofessional instructors. *Journal of Personality and Social Psychology, 29*(5), 609–618.

ROSS, M., LAYTON, B., ERICKSON, B., & SCHOPLER, J. 1973. Affect, facial regard, and reactions to crowding. *Journal of Personality and Social Psychology, 28,* 69–76.

ROSS, M., & SHULMAN, R. F. 1973. Increasing the salience of initial attitudes: dissonance versus self-perception theory. *Journal of Personality and social psychology, 28,* 138–144.

ROTHBART, M. 1970. Assessing the likelihood of a threatening event: English Canadians' evaluation of the Quebec separatist movement. *Journal of Personality and Social Psychology, 15,* 109–117.

RUBIN, Z. 1973. *Liking and Loving—An Invitation to Social Psychology.* New York: Holt, Rinehart, Winston.

RUBLE, D. N., & FELDMAN, N. S. 1976. Order of consensus, distinctiveness, and consistency information and causal attributions. *Journal of Personality and Social Psychology, 34*(5), 930–937.

RUCKMICK, C. A. 1921. A preliminary study of the emotions. *Psychological Monographs, 12*(3, Whole No. 136), 30–35.

SAEGERT, S., SWAP, W., & ZAJONC, R. B. 1973. Exposure, context, and interpersonal attraction. *Journal of Personality and Social Psychology, 25,* 234–242.

SAENGER, G., & GILBERT, E. 1950. Customer reactions to the integration of Negro sales personnel. *International Journal of Opinion and Attitude Research, 4,* 57–76.

SAKAGAMI, S. F., & AKAHIRA, Y. 1960. Studies on the Japanese honeybee, Apis cerana, cerana Fabricius: 8, two opposing adaptations in the post-stinging behavior of honeybees. *Evolution, 14*(1), 29–40.

SALANCIK, G. R., & CONWAY, M. 1975. Attitude inferences from salient and relevant cognitive content about behavior. *Journal of personality and social psychology, 32,* 829–840.

SARNOFF, I., & ZIMBARDO, P. G. 1961. Anxiety, fear, and social affiliation. *Journal of Abnormal and Social Psychology, 62,* 356–363.

SCHACHTER, S. 1951. Deviation, rejection and communication. *Journal of Abnormal and Social Psychology, 46,* 190–208.

SCHACHTER, S. 1964. The interaction of cognitive and physiological determinants of emotional state. In L. Berkowitz (ed.), *Advances in experimental social psychology.* New York: Academic Press.

SCHACHTER, S. 1959. *The psychology of affiliation.* Stanford, Calif.: Stanford.

SCHACHTER, S., ELLERTSON, N., MCBRIDE, D., & GREGORY, D. 1951. An experimental study of cohesiveness and productivity. *Human Relations, 4,* 229–238.

SCHACHTER, S., & SINGER, J. E. 1962. Cognitive, social and physiological determinants of emotional state. *Psychological Review, 69,* 379–399.

SCHEIER, M. F., FENIGSTEIN, A., & BUSS, A. H. 1974. Self-awareness and physical aggression. *Journal of Experimental Social Psychology, 10,* 264–273.

SCHERER, S. E. 1974. Proxemic behavior of primary school children as a function of their socioeconomic class and subculture. *Journal of Personality and Social Psychology, 29,* 800–805.

SCHIFFENBAUER, A. 1974. Effect of observer's emotional state on judgments of the emotional state of others. *Journal of Personality and Social Psychology, 30*(1), 31–35.

SCHIFFENBAUER, A., & SCHIAVO, R. S. 1976. Physical distance and attraction: An intensification effect. *Journal of Experimental Social Psychology, 12*(3), 274–282.

SCHMITT, D. R., & MARWELL, G. 1972. Withdrawal and regard reallocation as responses to inequity. *Journal of Experimental Social Psychology, 8,* 207–221.

SCHMITT, R. C. 1957. Density, delinquency and crime in Honolulu. *Sociology and Social Research, 41,* 274–276.

SCHMITT, R. C. 1966. Density, health, and social disorganization. *Journal of American Institute of Planners, 32,* 38–40.

SCHNEIDER, D. J. 1973. Implicit personality theory: a review. *Psychological Bulletin, 79,* 294–309.

SCHNEIDER, D. J., & MILLER, R. S. 1975. The effects of enthusiasm and quality of arguments on attitude attribution. *Journal of Personality, 43*(4), 693–708.

SCHNEIDER, F. W. 1970. Conforming behavior of black and white children. *Journal of Personality and Social Psychology, 16,* 466–471.

SCHRAMM, W., & CARTER, R. F. 1959. Effectiveness of a political telethon. *Public Opinion Quarterly, 23,* 121–126.

SCHUMAN, H., & JOHNSON, M. P. 1976. Attitudes and behavior. *Annual Review of Sociology, 2,* 161–207.

SCHWAB, J. J., MCGINNIS, N. H., & WARHEIT, G. J. 1973. Social psychiatric impairment: Racial Comparisons. *American Journal of Psychiatry, 130,* 183–187.

SCHWARTZ, S. H., & CLAUSEN, G. T. 1970. Responsibility, norms, and helping in an emergency. *Journal of Personality and Social Psychology, 16,* 299–310.

SEARS, D. O. 1976. *Positivity biases in evaluations of public figures.* Paper presented at annual meeting of American Psychological Association, Washington, D. C.

SEARS, D. O. 1975. Political Socialization. In F. I. Greenstein & N. W. Polsby (eds.) *Handbook of Political Science,* Vol. II, Reading, Mass.: Addison-Wesley.

SEARS, D. O. 1969. Political behavior. In. G. Lindzey and E. Aronson (eds.). *Handbook of Social Psychology.* Vol. V. Reading, Mass.: Addison-Wesley.

SEARS, D. O. 1968. The paradox of de facto selective exposure without preferences for supportive information. In R. P. Abelson, et al (eds.) *Theories of Cognitive Consistency: A Sourcebook.* Chicago: Rand-McNally.

SEARS, D. O., & FREEDMAN, J. L. 1967. Selective exposure to information: a critical review. *Public Opinion Quarterly, 31,* 194–213.

SEARS, D. O., FREEDMAN, J. L., & O'CONNOR, E. F., JR. 1964. The effects of anticipated debate and commitment on the polarization of audience opinion. *Public Opinion Quarterly, 28,* 615–627.

SEARS, D. O., & MCCONAHAY, J. B. 1973. *The politics of violence: The new urban blacks and the Watts riot.* Boston: Houghton Mifflin.

SEARS, D. O., & WHITNEY, R. E. 1973. Political persuasion. Morristown, N. J.: General Learning Press.

SEARS, R. R. 1961. Relations of early socialization experiences to aggression in middle childhood. *Journal of Abnormal and Social Psychology, 63,* 466–493.

SEARS, R. R., WHITING, J. W. M., NOWLIS, V., & SEARS, P. S. 1953. Some child-rearing antecedents of aggression and dependency in young children. *Genetic Psychological Monographs, 47,* 135–236.

SEGAL, M. W. 1974. Alphabet and attraction: An unobstrusive measure of the effect of propinquity in a field setting. *Journal of Personality and Social Psychology, 30*(5), 654–657.

SHAVER, K. G. 1970. Defensive attribution: Effects of severity and relevance on the responsibility assigned for an accident. *Journal of Personality and Social Psychology, 14*(2), 101–113.

SHAVER, P., & FREEDMAN, J. L. Happiness. *Psychology Today,* August 1976.

SHAW, M. E. 1955. A comparison of two types of leadership in various communication nets. *Journal of Abnormal and Social Psychology, 50,* 127–134.

SHERIF, M. 1935. A study of some social factors in perception. *Archives of Psychology,* No. 187.

SHERMAN, M. 1927. The differentiation of emotional responses from motion picture views and from actual observations. *Journal of Comparative Psychology, 7,* 265–284.

SHOTLAND, R. L. & STRAW, M. K. 1976. Bystander response to an assault: when a man attacks a woman. *Journal of Personality and Social Psychology, 34,* 990–999.

SIGALL, H., & LANDY, D. 1973. Radiating beauty: the effects of having a physically attractive partner on person perception. *Journal of personality and social psychology, 28,* 218–224.

SIGALL, H., & OSTROVE, N. 1975. Beautiful but dangerous: Effects of offender attractiveness and nature of the crime on juridic judgment. *Journal of Personality and Social Psychology, 31*(3), 410–414.

SILVERMAN, B. I. 1974. Consequences, racial discrimination, and the principle of belief congruence. *Journal of Personality and Social Psychology, 29*(4), 497–508.

SILVERMAN, I. 1971. Physical attractiveness and courtship. *Sexual Behavior, 22*–25.

SINGER, J. E., BRUSH, C., & LUBLIN, S. D. 1965. Some aspects of deindividuation: Identification and conformity. *Journal of Experimental Social Psychology, 1,* 356–378.

SISTRUNK, F., & MCDAVID, J. W. 1971. Sex variable in conforming behavior. *Journal of Personality and Social Psychology, 17,* 200–207.

SMITH, M. B., BRUNER, J. S., & WHITE, R. W. 1956. *Opinions and Personality.* New York: John Wiley & Sons.

SMITH, R. E., SMYTHE, L., & LIEN, D. 1972. Inhibition of helping behavior by a similar or dissimilar nonreactive fellow bystander. *Journal of Personality and Social Psychology, 23,* 414–419.

SMITH, S., & HAYTHORN, W. H. 1972. Effects of compatibility, crowding, group size, and leadership seniority on stress, anxiety, hostility, and annoyance in isolated groups. *Journal of Personality and Social Psychology, 22,* 67–79.

SMITH, W. P., & ANDERSON, A. J. 1975. Threats, communication and bargaining. *Journal of Personality and Social Psychology, 32,* 76–82.

SNYDER, A., MISCHEL, W., & LOTT, B. 1960. Value, information, and conformity behavior. *Journal of Personality, 28,* 333–342.

SNYDER, M., & CUNNINGHAM, M. R. 1975. To comply or Not Comply: Testing the Self-Perception Explanation of the "Foot-in-the-Door" phenomenon. *Journal of Personality and Social Psychology, 31,* 64–67.

SNYDER, M., & EBBESEN, E. B. 1972. Dissonance awareness: a test of dissonance theory versus self-perception theory. *Journal of experimental social psychology, 8,* 502–517.

SNYDER, M., & JONES, E. E. 1974. Attitude attribution when behavior is constrained. *Journal of Experimental Social Psychology, 10*(6), 585–600.

SNYDER, M. L., STEPHAN, W. G., & ROSENFELD, D. 1976. Egotism and attribution. *Journal of Personality and Social Psychology, 33*(4), 435–441.

SNYDER, M., & SWANN, W. B., JR., 1976. When actions reflect attitudes: The politics of impression management. *Journal of Personality and Social Psychology, 34*(5), 1034–1042.

SNYDER, R. L. 1968. Reproduction and population pressures. In. E. Steller and J. M. Sprague (eds.), *Progress in Physiological Psychology.* New York: Academic Press.

SOGIN, S. R. & PALLAK, M. S. 1976. Bad decisions, responsibility, and attitude change. Effects of volition, foresee-ability, and locus of causality of negative consequences. *Journal of Personality and Social Psychology, 33*(3), 300–306.

SOMMER, R. 1959. Studies in personal space. *Sociometry, 22,* 247–260.

SOMMER, R. 1969. *Personal space: the behavioral basis of design.* Englewood Cliffs, Prentice-Hall.

SORRENTINO, R. M., & BOUTILLER, R. G. 1975. The effect of quantity and quality of verbal interaction on ratings of leadership ability. *Journal of Experimental Social Psychology, 11,* 403–411.

SOUTHWICK, C. H. 1955. The population dynamics of confined house mice supplied with unlimited food. *Ecology, 36,* 212–215.

SROLE, L. 1972. Urbanization and mental health: some reformulations. *American Scientist, 60,* 576–583.

STANG, D. J. 1973. Effect of interaction rate on ratings of leadership and liking. *Journal of Personality and Social Psychology, 27,* 405–408.

STARKWEATHER, J. A. 1956. The communication value of content-free speech. *American Journal of Psychology, 69,* 121–123.

STAUB, E. 1971. Helping a person in distress: The influence of implicit and explicit "rules" of conduct on children and adults. *Journal of Personality and Social Psychology, 17,* 137–144.

STEELE, C. M. 1975. Name-calling and compliance. *Journal of Personality and Social Psychology, 31,* 361–369.

STEIN, D. D., HARDYCK, J. A., & SMITH, M. B. 1965. Race and belief: An open and shut case. *Journal of Personality and Social Psychology, 1,* 281–289.

STEIN, R. T., GEIS, F. L., & DAMARIN, F. 1973. Perception of emergent leadership hierarchies in task groups. *Journal of Personality and Social Psychology, 28,* 77–87.

STEPHAN, W. G. 1975. Actor versus observer: Attributions to behavior with positive or negative outcomes and empathy for the other role. *Journal of Experimental Social Psychology, 11,* 205–214.

STEVENS, L., & JONES, E. E. 1976. Defensive attribution and the Kelley Cube. *Journal of Personality and Social Psychology, 34*(5), 809–820.

STIMSON, J. A. 1975. Belief systems: Constraint, complexity, and the 1972 election. *American Journal of Poltiical Science, 19,* 393–417.

STOKOLS, D. 1972. On the distinction between density and crowding: some implications for future research. *Psychological Review, 79,* 275–277.

STOKOLS, D., RALL, M., PINNER, B. & SCHOPLER, J. 1973. Physical, social, and personal determinants of the perception of crowding. *Environment and Behavior, 5,* 87–115.

STONER, J. A. F. 1961. A comparison of individual and group decisions involving risk. Unpublished master's thesis, School of Industrial Management.

STORMS, M. D. 1973. Videotape and the attribution process: Reversing actors' and observers' points of view. *Journal of Personality and Social Psychology, 27*(2), 165–175.

STORMS, M. D., & NISBETT, R. E. 1970. Insomnia and the attribution process. *Journal of Personality and Social Psychology, 16,* 319–328.

STOUFFER, S. A., LUMSDAINE, A. A., LUMSDAINE, M. H., WILLIAMS, R. M., JR., SMITH, M. B., JANIS, I. L., STAR, S. A., & COTTRELL, L. S., JR. 1949. Combat and its aftermath. In *Studies in social psychology in World War II.* Vol. 1, The American soldier. Princeton, N.J.: Princeton.

STOUFFER, S. A., SUCHMAN, E. A., DEVINNEY, L. C., STAR, S. A., & WILLIAMS, R. M., JR. Adjustment during army life. In *Studies in social psychology in World War II.* Vol. 1, The American soldier. Princeton, N.J.: Princeton.

STREETER, L. A., KRAUSS, R. M., GELLER, V., OLSON, D., & APPLE, W. Pitch changes during attempted deception. *Journal of Personality and Social Psychology,* in press.

STRODTBECK, F. L., JAMES, R. M., & HAWKINS, C. 1958. Social status in jury deliberations. In E. Maccoby, T. Newcomb, & E. Hartley (eds.), *Readings in social psychology.* New York: Holt.

STROEBE, W., INSKO, C. A., THOMPSON, V. D., & LAYTON, B. D. 1971. Effects of physical attractiveness, attitude similarity, and sex on various aspects of interpersonal attraction. *Journal of Personality and Social Psychology, 18,* 79–91.

SURGEON GENERAL'S SCIENTIFIC ADVISORY COMMITTEE. 1972. *Television and growing up: The impact of televised violence.* (Report to the Surgeon General, U. S. Public Health Service, Department of Health, Education, and Welfare Publication N. HSM 72-9090). Rockville, Md: National Institute of Mental Health.

SWINGLE, P. G. 1970. Exploitative behavior in non-zero sum games. *Journal of Personality and Social Psychology, 16,* 121–132.

TAYLOR, D. W., BERRY, P. C., & BLOCK, C. H. 1958. Does group participation when using brainstorming facilitate or inhibit creative thinking? *Administrative Science Quarterly, 2,* 23–47.

TAYLOR, D. W., & FAUST, W. L. 1958. Twenty questions: Efficiency in problem solving as a function of size of group. *Journal of Experimental Psychology, 44,* 360–368.

TAYLOR, S. E. 1975. On inferring one's attitudes from one's behavior: Some delimiting conditions. *Journal of Personality and Social Psychology, 31*(1), 126–131.

TAYLOR, S. E., & FISKE, S. T. 1975. Point of view and perceptions of causality. *Journal of Personality and Social Psychology,* 32(3), 439–445.

TAYLOR, S. E., & KOIVUMAKI, J. H. 1976. The perception of self and others: Acquaintanceship, affect, and actor-observer differences. *Journal of Personality and Social Psychology,* 33(4), 403–408.

TAYLOR, S. P., & GAMMON, C. B. 1975. Effects of type and dose of alcohol on human physical aggression. *Journal of Personality and Social Psychology, 32,* 169–175.

TEDIN, K. L. 1974. The influence of parents on the political attitudes of adolescents. *The American Political Science Review,* 68(4), 1579–1592.

Tegin, A. I., & Pruitt, D. G. 1967. Components of group risk-taking. *Journal of Experimental Social Psychology, 3,* 189–205.

Teichman, Y. 1973. Emotional arousal and affiliation. *Journal of Experimental Social Psychology, 9,* 591–605.

Thibaut, J. W., & Riecken, H. W. 1955. Some determinants and consequences of the perception of social causality. *Journal of Personality, 24,* 113–133.

Thompson, D. F., & Meltzer, L. 1964. Communication of emotional intent by facial expression. *Journal of Abnormal and Social Psychology, 68,* 129–135.

Tilker, H. A. 1970. Socially responsible behavior as a function of observer responsibility and victim feedback. *Journal of Personality and Social Psychology, 14,* 95–100.

Torrance, E. P. 1955. Some consequences of power differences on decision making in permanent and temporary three-man groups. In A. P. Hare, E. F. Bogatta, and R. F. Bales (eds.), *Small groups: Studies in social interaction.* New York: Knopf.

Travis, L. E. 1925. The effect of a small audience upon eye-hand coordination. *Journal of Abnormal and Social Pxychology, 20,* 142–146.

Turner, C. W., & Layton, J. F. 1976. Verbal imagery and connotation as memory-induced mediators of aggressive behavior. *Journal of Personality and Social Psychology, 33*(6), 755–763.

Turner, C. W., Layton, J. F., & Simons, L. S. 1975. Naturalistic studies of aggressive behavior: Aggressive stimuli, victim visibility, and horn honking. *Journal of Personality and Social Psychology, 31,* 1098–1107.

Turner, C. W., & Simons, L. S. 1974. Effects of subject sophistication and evaluation apprehension on aggressive responses to weapons. *Journal of Personality and Social Psychology, 30,* 341–348.

Tyler, Tom, R., & Sears, David O. 1977. Coming to like obnoxious people when we must live with them. *Journal of Personality and Social Psychology,* 35, 200–211.

Valins, S. 1974. Persistent effects of information about internal reactions: Ineffectiveness of debriefing. In H. London, and R. E. Nisbett (eds.), *Thought and feeling,* Chicago: Aldine Publishing.

Valins, S., & Ray, A. A. 1967. Effects of cognitive desensitization on avoidance behavior. *Journal of Personality and Social Psychology, 7,* 345–350.

Valle, V. A., & Frieze, I. H. 1976. Stability of causal attributions as a mediator in changing expectations for success. *Journal of Personality and Social Psychology, 33*(5), 579–587.

Vinokur, A., Trope, Y., & Burnstein, E. 1975. A decision-making analysis of persuasive argumentation and the choice-shift effect. *Journal of Experimental Social Psychology, 11,* 127–148.

Wallach, M. A., & Kogan, N. 1965. The roles of information, discussion, and consensus in group risk taking. *Journal of Experimental Social Psychology, 1,* 1–19.

WALLACH, M. A., KOGAN, N., & BEM, D. J. 1962. Group influence on individual risk taking. *Journal of Abnormal and Social Psychology, 65,* 75–87.

WALLACH, M. A., KOGAN, N., & BURT, R. B. 1965. Can group members recognize the effects of group discussion upon risk taking? *Journal of Experimental Social Psychology, 1,* 379–395.

WALLINGTON, S. A. 1973. Consequences of transgression: self-punishment and depression. *Journal of Personality and Social Psychology, 28,* 1–7.

WALSTER, E., ARONSON, E., & ABRAHAMS, D. 1966. On increasing the persuasiveness of a low prestige communicator. *Journal of experimental Social Psychology, 2,* 325–342.

WALSTER, E., ARONSON, V., ABRAHAMS, D., & ROTTMANN, L. 1966. Importance of physical attractiveness in dating behavior. *Journal of Personality and Social Psychology, 4,* 508–516.

WALSTER, E., BERSCHEID, E., & WALSTER, G. W. 1973. New directions in equity research. *Journal of Personality and Social Psychology, 25*(2), 151–176.

WALSTER, E., & FESTINGER, L. 1962. The effectiveness of "overheard" persuasive communications. *Journal of Abnormal and Social Psychology, 65,* 395–402.

WARR, P. 1974. Inference magnitude, range and evaluative direction as factors affecting relative importance of cues in impression formation. *Journal of Personality and Social Psychology, 30*(2), 192–197.

WATERMAN, C. K. 1969. The facilitating and interfering effects of cognitive dissonance on simple and complex paired-associate learning tasks. *Journal of Experimental Social Psychology, 5,* 31–42.

WATSON, O. M. & GRAVES, T. 1966. Quantitative research in proxemic behavior. *American Anthropologist, 68,* 971–985.

WEIGEL, R. H., & NEWMAN, L. S. 1976. Increasing attitude-behavior correspondence by broadening the scope of the behavioral measure. *Journal of Personality and Social Psychology, 33*(6), 793–802.

WEIGEL, R. H., VERNON, D. T. A., & TOGNACCI, L. N. 1974. Specificity of the attitude as a determinant of attitude-behavior congruence. *Journal of Personality and Social Psychology, 30*(6), 724–728.

WEINER, B. 1974. *Achievement motivation and attribution theory.* Morristown, N. J.: General Learning Press.

WEINSTEIN, A. G. 1972. Predicting behavior from attitudes. *Public Opinion Quarterly, 36*(3), 355–360.

WEISBROD, R. A. Looking behavior in a discussion group. Unpublished term paper Cornell University, 1965.

WEISS, W. A., & FINE, B. J. 1956. The effect of induced aggressiveness on opinion change. *Journal of Abnormal and Social Psychology, 52,* 109–114.

WELLMAN, B., & WHITAKER, M. 1974. High-rise, low-rise: the effects of high density living. *Ministry of State, Urban Affairs Canada*, B. 74.29.

WELLS, G. L., & HAVEY, J. H. 1977. Do people use consensus information in making causal attributions? *Journal of Personality and social psychology, 35*, 279–293.

WELLS, W. D. 1970. *Television and aggression: Replication of an experimental field study*. Unpublished manuscript, Graduate School of Business, University of Chicago.

WEST, S. G., GUNN, S. P., & CHERNICKY, P. 1975. Ubiquitous Watergate: An attributional analysis. *Journal of Personality and Social Psychology, 32*(1), 55–65.

WHITE, G. M. 1972. Immediate and deferred effects of model observation and guided and unguided rehersal on donating and stealing. *Journal of Personality and Social Psychology, 21*, 139–148.

WHYTE, W. H., JR. 1956. *The organization man*. New York: Simon and Schuster.

WICHMAN, H. 1970. Effects of isolation and communication on cooperation in a two-person game. *Journal of Personality and Social Psychology, 16*, 114–120.

WICKER, A. W. 1969. Attitudes versus action: The relationship of verbal and overt behavioral responses to attitude objects. *Journal of Social Issues, 25*(4), 41–78.

WILDER, D. A., & ALLEN, V. L. 1973. Veridical dissent, erroneous dissent, and conformity. Unpublished master's thesis.

WILHELMY, R. A. 1974. The role of commitment in cognitive reversibility. *Journal of Personality and Social Psychology, 30*(5), 695–698.

WILSON, E. O. 1971a. *The insect societies*. Cambridge, Mass.: Belknap Press of Harvard University Press.

WILSON, E. O. 1975. *Sociobiology, the new synthesis*. Cambridge, Mass.: Harvard University Press.

WILSON, J. P., ARONOFF, J. & MESSE, L. A. 1975. Social structure, member motivation, and group productivity. *Journal of Personality and Social Pxychology, 32*, 1094–1098.

WILSON, L., & ROGERS, R. W. 1975. The fire this time: Effects of race of target, insult, and potential retaliation on black aggression. *Journal of Personality and Social Psychology, 32*, 857–864.

WINSBOROUGH, H. H. 1965. The social consequences of high population density. *Law and Contemporary Problems, 30*, 120–126.

WIXON, D. R., & LAIRD, J. D. 1976. Awareness and attitude change in the forced-compliance paradigm: The importance of when. *Journal of Personality and Social Psychology, 34*, 376–384.

WOODWORTH, R. D. 1938. *Experimental psychology*. New York: Holt.

WORCHEL, S., HARDY, T. W., & HURLEY, R. 1976. The effects of commercial interruption of violent and nonviolent films on viewers' subsequent aggression. *Journal of experimental Social Psychology, 12,* 220–232.

WORKS, E. 1961. The prejudice-interaction hypothesis from the point of view of the Negro minority group. *American Journal of Sociology, 67,* 47–52.

WRIGHTSMAN, L. S. 1960. Effects of waiting with others on changes in level of felt anxiety. *Journal of Abnormal and Social Psychology, 61,* 216–222.

WYER, R. S., JR. 1974. Changes in meaning and halo effects in personality impression formation. *Journal of Personality and Social Psychology,* 29(6), 829–835.

ZAJONC, R. B. 1968. Attitudinal effects of mere exposure. *Journal of Personality and Social Psychology,* Monograph supplement, Part 2, 1–29.

ZAJONC, R. B. 1968. Cognitive theories in social psychology. In G. Lindzey and E. Aronson (eds.), *Handbook of social psychology,* 2nd ed., Vol. 1. Reading, Mass.: Addision-Wesley.

ZAJONC, R. B. 1965. Social facilitation. *Science, 149,* 269–274.

ZAJONC, R. B., HEINGERTNER, A., & HERMAN, E. M. 1969. Social enhancement and impairment of performance in the cockroach. *Journal of Personality and Social Psychology, 13,* 83–92.

ZAJONC, R. B., & SALES, S. M. 1966. Social facilitation of dominant and subordinate responses. *Journal of Experimental Social Psychology, 2,* 160–168.

ZAJONC, R. B., WOLOSIN, R. J., & WOLOSIN, M. A. 1972. Group risk-taking under various group decision schemes. *Journal of Experimental Social Psychology, 8,* 16–30.

ZAJONC, R. B., WOLOSIN, R. J., WOLOSIN, M. A., & LOH, W. D. 1970. Social facilitation and imitation in group risk-taking. *Journal of Experimental Social Psychology, 6,* 26–46.

ZANNA, M. P. & COOPER, J. 1974. Dissonance and the pill: an attribution approach to studying the arousal properties of dissonance. *Journal of Personality and social psychology, 29,* 703–709.

ZELLNER, M. 1970. Self-esteem, reception, and influenceability. *Journal of Personality and Social Psychology, 15,* 87–93.

ZILLMANN, D., & BRYANT, J. 1974. Effect of residual excitation on the emotional response to provocation and delayed aggressive behavior. *Journal of Personality and Social Psychology, 30,* 782–791.

ZILLMANN, D., & CANTOR, J. R. 1976. Effects of timing of information about mitigating circumstances on emotional responses to provocation and retaliatory behavior. *Journal of Experimental Social Psychology, 12,* 38–55.

ZIMBARDO, P. G. 1970. The human choice: Individuation, reason and order versus deindividuation, impulse and chaos. In N. J. Arnold and D. Levine (eds.), *Nebraska Symposium on Motivation, 1969.* Lincoln: University of Nebraska Press.

ZIMBARDO, P. G., & FORMICA, R. 1963. Emotional comparison and self-esteem as determinants of affiliation. *Journal of Personality, 31,* 141–162.

ZIMBARDO, P. G., SNYDER, M., THOMAS, J., GOLD, A., & GURWITZ, S. 1970. Modifying the impact of persuasive communications with external distraction. *Journal of Personality and Social Psychology, 16*, 669–680.

ZIMBARDO, P. G., WEISENBERG, M., FIRESTONE, I., & LEVY, B. 1965. Communicator effectiveness in producing public conformity and private attitude change. *Journal of Personality, 33*, 233–256.

ZIV, A., KRUGLANSKI, A. W., & SHULMAN, 1974. Children's psychological reactions to wartime stress. *Journal of Personality and Social Psychology, 30*(1), 24–30.

indexes

author index

a

b

c

d

e

f

g

h

i

j

k

s

t

subject index

d

e

f

g

h

i

l

m

n

o

p